TIME-SAVER DETAILS FOR ROOF DESIGN

Time-Saver Details for Roof Design

STEVE HARDY

McGRAW-HILL

NEW YORK SAN FRANCISCO WASHINGTON, D.C. AUCKLAND BOGOTÁ
CARACAS LISBON LONDON MADRID MEXICO CITY MILAN
MONTREAL NEW DELHI SAN JUAN SINGAPORE
SYDNEY TOKYO TORONTO

Library of Congress Cataloging-in-Publication Data

Hardy, Steve.
Time-saver details for roof design / Steve Hardy.
p. cm.
Includes index.
ISBN 0-07-026368-X
1. Roofing. I. Title.
TH2431.H37 1997
690'.15—dc21

97-15253
CIP

McGraw-Hill

A Division of The **McGraw-Hill** *Companies*

1 2 3 4 5 6 7 8 9 0 KGP/KGP 9 0 2 1 0 9 8 7

ISBN 0-07-026368-X

The sponsoring editor for this book was Wendy Lochner, the editing supervisor was Virginia Carroll, and the production supervisor was Clare Stanley. It was set in Garamond by North Market Street Graphics.

Printed and bound by Quebecor/Kingsport.

This book is printed on acid-free paper.

Dedication

This work is dedicated to the old roofers who have gone before us, the pioneers of this industry who, through practical experience and with blistered hands, hurt backs, and wind- and sunburned skin, helped the technicians, manufacturers, engineers, and architectural designers determine what would work best on a rooftop. And to the modern-day roof workers, material researchers and developers, manufacturers, and designers, who dedicated their time, efforts, and talents—often without praise from their peers, gratitude expressed from the industry, or adequate compensation—to help us all be better at our profession. And especially to the person who has taken the time and effort to review and use this manual—you are the true innovator and leader of the roof design community, proving that you strive not to be merely adequate at design, but, instead, choose to be the best you can.

Contents

Preface

THE WHO, WHAT, WHEN, WHERE, AND WHY OF THIS MANUAL

Who Created This Manual

The author of this manual has a diversified background in the roofing industry. At the age of 19 he began as a laborer on a commercial roofing crew and proceeded through the United Roofing and Waterproofing Union Apprenticeship Program, Houston, Texas, Local #116. In the years following he became a foreman and then superintendent of roofing companies, both large and small, union and nonunion, traveling through the southern United States. These travels provided an opportunity to learn and experience different means and methods of roofing according to local trade practices.

Returning to Texas, the author became a roofing contractor, learning the business end of the industry. The markets in which this company prospered were commercial, industrial, and historical restoration.

In 1985 the contracting business was phased out to allow more time for a consulting/design/inspection firm. As a roofing consultant, the author has worked closely with numerous architectural design firms as well as commercial and institutional entities.

Practical experience gained on construction sites has been tempered with and complemented by technical knowledge acquired over the years. However, as the saying goes, "You can take the boy out of the country, but you can't take the country out of the boy." Therefore, much of the writing style and context of the manual is in plain and descriptive terms, yet the technical content still threads through the text. We hope this makes the manual easy to use, yet accurate and all-encompassing.

The manual is based upon experience verified through technical research as follows. The author assembled information from countless sources and, after organizing the information into chapters and sections, went to outside experts and sources within a particular field. The text was reviewed for technical accuracy and the resulting edits were then incorporated into the text. On an average, at least two technical reviews per section have been performed, sometimes as many as four.

Many material manufacturers, industry and trade organizations, consultants, designers, chemists, scientists, research and development organizations, and technicians, as well as contractors and private individuals, contributed greatly to the manual. Too many are involved to list, but thanks to all these contributors, our hope is that a designers' practice and the design profession as a whole will benefit as a result of their help, knowledge, and assistance.

What the Manual Is

This manual is a design tool and could be correctly considered as a reference manual. However, the manual is one of a kind in that it can also function as an additional member of the design team. During building design, when the roof system is considered, the manual will guide the architectural team in the proper selection of roof materials and types. The manual covers most of the major components used today to construct and maintain a commercial roof system. (See "Using the Manual.")

When a problem is encountered, either during the roof system design phase or with the roof system as built, this manual will help by providing detailed information on materials and systems. The chapters discuss the characteristics, composition, and properties of particular and specific materials and systems.

In addition to technical information on materials, theoretical discussion is provided. Roof theory explains why materials and systems work together in unison or fail due to incompatibility. This theoretical understanding suggests design combinations of proper roof materials, leading to complete and correct designs. The manual is created and formatted for the design professional who must be proficient at all crafts and trade design, but who is not concerned with becoming a roof systems expert.

The manual addresses most of the major roof systems designed today. The manual does not address composition shingle roofing due to the simplicity of this type of system, although metal flashings as used with this type of water-shedding system are discussed in detail. Single-ply polymeric roof systems are not discussed due to the complexity, magnitude, and specialization of that particular industry. However, many specialty roof materials and systems are discussed, such as clay tile, slate, and copper roofing.

When the Manual Was Created

This manual was created during the mid-1990s. During this time many roof materials and systems, considered new during the 1980s, became standard design options. Also, many of the old-time systems, such as coal tar pitch built-up roofing, were once again becoming more widely used. In addition, we saw metal emerging as a popular roof selection by architects and building owners.

The manual also considers the environment, with *green design* becoming a common term in today's design community. Recyclability of materials, hazardous materials, life-cycle expectancy, solutions, and design options as they relate to the environment are considered.

The manual took two years to create and during this time some of the information became dated and was revised. This is inevitable since roofing is a fluid and ever-changing industry. However, regardless of changes, the solid information contained herein can provide the designer with enough basic as well as technical information to better evaluate any new materials or systems. This knowledge is readily available in the various chapters.

Where the Manual Is Applicable

Information within the manual is applicable to all major climatic regions within the United States. As such, design options for the cold northern climates to the warm humid southern regions are addressed. Information pertaining to freeze/thaw cycles, to earthquake resistance design, and to salt atmosphere subtropic climates is included herein.

Why the Manual Was Created

Roof system design is an intricate and complicated process, probably more so now than in the past. A review of construction drawings from the early 1900s often shows a squiggly line atop a wood roof deck with a dashed notation stating "4-ply built-up roof." Few other detail drawings are included. The specifications are more a listing of materials required than a prescriptive or performance specification.

In the past, there were far fewer roof materials to select from than there are today. For example, roof insulation was very unusual. Surfacing was almost always gravel, covering what was often a coal tar pitch or asphalt built-up roof. Today over 1000 different roof systems can be designed by combinations of different materials.

Some people believe that the overall quality of workmanship and dedication to a craft was more prevalent during this past era than now. Often, verbal contracts were satisfactory. Lawsuits were limited. Today, much construction litigation involves roofing or waterproofing systems. If design is inadequate due to ignorance on the part of the designer, this manual will help. If the designer wishes to create more effective roof systems, either from an energy conservation viewpoint or in regard to life-cycle costs, this manual will help. If the designer must delegate design to others, this manual will help ensure that the delegated team considers the situations and demands required for an effective and correct roof system.

Most architectural building designers have little formal training about roof systems. Normally, experience is gained on the job. However, a good, strong experience base is getting harder and harder to obtain. There are just too many different types of systems, over too many different roof decks, having to comply with too many different codes and standards, further complicated by the necessity of deciding between modified bitumen membranes, metal roofing, built-up systems of either coal tar pitch or asphalt, with gravel surfacings, coatings, or cap sheets as options.

Perhaps this is why we find many design firms of today selecting one type of roof system and consistently specifying it. If the design firm is consistently designing the same type of building, for the same use, in the same climate, built by the same type of worker, this process is acceptable. However, this is seldom the case and may be why roof problems are a major concern within today's design and construction community.

This manual can be used as an information reference source, but is intended more for use as a design aid. We believe that such a tool can be of assistance in today's design marketplace, providing the designer with the flexibility required for a more correct roof design.

USING THE MANUAL

The manual is composed of 15 chapters. Each chapter is specific to a topic, system, group of similar materials, or process which the designer may or must use during roof system design.

Within each chapter are sections. Each section focuses on a particular topic which is relevant to the chapter. Each section, in turn, contains headings and possibly subheadings, depending upon the complexity of the topic. All chapters and sections are numbered, and frequent cross-references to related topics are provided. Figures are numerous throughout this manual and are numbered for easy reference, as well.

Acknowledgments

I have been advised that, instead of trying to name all the people who helped with the creation of this manual, it would be better to just thank everyone born since Adam and Eve.

Instead, I will compromise and not list names, but offer my extreme gratitude to the numerous professionals who helped make this a complete and accurate work. You know who you are—and sometimes that's all we get.

During the process of making my numerous requests to recognized industry leaders for technical edits and review, for assistance with gathering current information, or merely for a brief interview and discussion over the phone, I was often reminded of an old saying, "If you want something done . . . ask a busy person to do it." Many times I received information, time, and help from top-level management executives within large corporations, and from principals in very successful and busy design firms, and from technical people who were hard-pressed for time between flights, correspondence, and phone calls. For these people, time is truly valuable; yet they stopped, listened, and then freely gave of their time to provide maximum assistance.

Too numerous to list, I acknowledge each of you for your valuable contributions of time, experience, and knowledge, and in many instances for going that extra step, without which this manual would not have been possible.

CHAPTER 1

History

1.1 DEVELOPMENT OF ROOF SYSTEMS AND TYPES

PAST

The question of which is the oldest profession may be up for some debate, but roofing surely has to be in the top ten. One of the first things Homo sapiens had to do was find shelter, the key element of which was a roof. Consider this primordial instinct and requirement even as it exists today. How often have parents been known to say to their children, "So long as you are living under my roof . . ."?

It can be speculated that the first manufactured roof systems were water shedders, such as overlapped tree boughs, or thatch, or animal skins stretched over wood frames. As a water-shedding system, these roof materials are not water barriers as is a waterproof built-up roof (BUR) system. A water-shedding system relies on the gravity-induced flow of water. One of the first rules of roofing is that water runs downhill.

For instance, thatch layers shed the flow of water from a top-layer row to a subsequent lower layer until the water is directed off the roof structure. So do composition shingles on most residential houses (see Fig. 1.1). As such, water-shedding systems must be installed on steeper slopes than are water-barrier systems.

The advent of the industrial revolution introduced coal tar pitch and distilled asphalt. Until that time roof coverings were created from naturally occurring pitch and laminate materials, or slate, tile, copper, thatch, sod, wood, and probably many other material types.

In some geographic locations and environments, the roof as a waterproof system was not required. As an example, in arid desert areas where rainfall is minimal, flat roofs evolved as a "fifth wall" with the rooftop serving as an additional, semiopen living area. The rooftop/floor was protected from any periodic rains by awnings and tarps.

As time passed and civilization advanced and expanded, different forms of shelter were needed and desired. The building structure began to take on numerous other aspects than that of mere shelter from the elements. Buildings were required for security, prestige, aesthetics, gatherings, storage, and so on.

As society's needs grew and diversified, so did building structures. As larger and larger spaces had to be spanned, sloped roofs, capable of effectively shedding water and snow, became impractical. Another reason for low-sloped roof systems may be the overall appearance of the building structure and the visual effect of a flat roofline versus that of a sloped roofline. The technology of flat and low-sloped roof systems developed.

In other areas of the world, rigid roof materials or water-shedding materials installed to sloped roof structures were the predominant roof style. Slate roof material applied to a steep slope proved effective for cold regions where snow load is a consideration. In the South Pacific, bamboo and palm tree boughs were the main types of materials used for roof construction.

1.2 BITUMINOUS FLAT ROOF MATERIALS

GENERAL

Bituminous is derived from the word *bitumen,* which is used in this manual to generically describe roof products or materials which are derived from either petroleum or coal. The roofing bitumens made from

Figure 1.1 Thatch roof.

these products are used as interply moppings in built-up roof systems, roof sealants, and adhesives, as well as for the surfacing pour placed on top of a built-up roof into which gravel is embedded. Also, roof bitumen products are the base materials which are further modified with polymer additives to create modified bitumen roof products.

An asphalt, bitumen material will have characteristics that are much different from coal tar pitch bitumen or modified bitumen. Chapters 4, 5, and 9 thoroughly explain the differences.

Bituminous materials from asphalt or coal tar are often applied at high temperatures, 350 to 500°F. They are black and, at application temperatures, they are hot and sticky. They are heated at the job site in a melting kettle (see Fig. 1.2) or can be delivered to the job site in a large tanker truck.

Roof mastics and adhesives are also bituminous materials. These materials are applied cold, in that heating to high temperatures is not required. They come in containers and are spread onto or into the roof system by hand trowel, brush, or airless spray equipment. Once the cold-process adhesives have set and cured they are similar to hot-applied bituminous materials.

Plastic roof cement, normally packaged in a 5-gal pail, is a very common material used with bituminous roof membranes. The roof cement is thick, black, and sticky, requiring hand-troweling of the material to the roof. The material is used at flashing locations and at any place where extra durability and longevity is required. (See Secs. 4.1.5 and 6.1.3.)

In early history, cold-applied bitumen material was the main waterproofing material available, occurring naturally from the ground or sedimentary deposits. Today, bitumen materials are manufactured for specific needs and situations.

In olden times, when someone was tarred and feathered, it was with cold-applied bitumen adhesives. If the substance was from coal tar material, if not fatal, the discomfort was extreme. Coal tar materials are skin irritants and will burn, even removing layers of skin if contact is severe enough. For example, creosotes are from coal tar base–materials. Do not ever hug a creosote-coated telephone pole in the summer when the creosote is hot and runny!

Mankind's ability and ingenuity in finding a use for and development of these materials is extraordinary. Without bituminous materials, the roof industry as we know it today could not exist. From simple and rudimentary origins thousands of years ago, the bitumen industry (asphalt and coal tar pitch) has developed into a scientific, precise, and complicated entity.

1.2.1 Naturally Occurring Asphalt Pitch

GENERAL

Throughout history, naturally occurring asphalt (referred to as *pitch* since as early as the time of Noah, according

Figure 1.2 Roofing kettle.

to the Bible) has been used to create water barriers. In the area once known as Mesopotamia and in ancient Egypt we find evidence that asphalt pitch was used in building walls and baths and even in mummification.

Naturally occurring asphalt has always been in limited supply and is not a predominant material in today's market. Today, when the word *pitch* is used, it normally refers to coal tar pitch, a product quite different from asphalt.

Even though natural asphalt pitch was a waterproofing element, by itself it was not effective as a roof system. The material, being naturally soft with a low melt point, would move from where it was placed to the lowest point available, leaving behind unprotected areas. In other cases the material would stay in place due to natural fillers contained within the matrix, but it would crack soon after placement.

Natural asphalt pitch was gathered from many sources, such as the Dead Sea (known in ancient times as *Lacus Asphaltites*) or, much later, from Lake Trinidad. In these areas the pitch was expelled from the seabed and floated to the top. The asphalt pitch from different areas had different characteristics due to natural minerals and fillers that were contained within the pitch.

In 1595, Sir Walter Raleigh, upon discovering Lake Trinidad, recorded in *History of the Discovery of Guinea:*

> From thence I rowed to another part, called by the naturals "Piche." . . . we made trial of it in trimming our ships to be most excellent good, and melts not with the Sun as the pitch of Norway, and therefore for ships trading the South parts very profitable.

The natural environment has always played a key role in building systems development. Man has learned to take the materials at hand and use them to protect himself from the elements. Sometimes total protection from the elements was compromised as a result of the materials that were available.

For example, during the settlement of the western and midwestern United States, pioneers on the prairies did not have lumber or natural pitch readily available in abundance. The houses they constructed were often built of sod panels stacked one on top of the other for the walls, with sod also used as the low-sloped roof covering. Sod placed atop wood-plank or pole-support decking does not provide complete waterproofing.

DEVELOPMENT

Flat Roofing Design and Good Practice, by the British Flat Roofing Council, reports that true commercial development of asphaltic materials began in 1712 with Eyrinus d'Eyrinus. He discovered "rock asphalt" near Neuchâtel, and created a hot melt mixture that was used as floor covering. Rock asphalt was available throughout Europe, mainly in the form of limestone impregnated throughout with asphalt pitch. In 1797 Count de Sassenay discovered a deposit of rock asphalt near Seyssel in France and developed a much better material from it. In the mid-1880s an Englishman named Richard Claridge took out a British patent for "a Mastic Cement or Composition applicable to Paving and Road making, covering buildings and the various purposes to which Cement, Mastic, Lead, Zinc, or Composition are employed."

However, mastic asphalt, as referred to here, is not an effective roof covering by itself. Reinforcing layers of materials must be incorporated within the asphalt bitumen system to bind and hold the asphalt material in place and to restrict cracking.

It is reported that in the late 1800s roof felts were developed from mixtures of animal and vegetable matter. These organic sheet materials were impregnated with the asphaltic material and used as the reinforcing roof plies within the roof system.

THE PRESENT

Today, with commercial low-sloped asphalt roof systems, we install a layer of asphalt. Into the hot, liquid asphalt a layer of reinforcing felt material is laid. The felt is coated with another application of asphalt and another felt is installed. This building-up process is continued until a built-up roof is the result. (See Fig. 1.3.)

The hot asphalt bitumen is thermoplastic by nature. Once it has cooled to ambient temperatures, the hot-process built-up roof system is hard and solid. Asphalt built-up roof systems can also be created from cold-applied asphalt bitumen products. The technology available today allows the thermoplastic asphalt roof bitumen to be further refined at the manufacturing facility to create these cold-process materials. Petroleum distillates are blended with the asphalt, resulting in a cutback asphalt product.

In warm weather the cold-process material can be applied at ambient temperatures, normally from 5- or 55-gal containers. The materials are brush-applied or spray-applied with industrial equipment to the roof surface. Again, reinforcing felt membrane layers are used in between asphalt application layers to create a cold-process built-up roof system.

As our technical abilities grew, so did our industries. Crude oil was pulled from the ground and refined to make a multitude of materials. The advent of the automobile and gasoline engine was probably the main contributing factor in creating the large petrochemical industry we have today. Along with gasoline, which is created from the distillation of crude oil, we also get asphalt materials from the distillation column. (See Sec. 4.1.1.)

1.2.2 Coal Tar Pitch

GENERAL

Coal tar pitch has a completely different material base than does asphalt. Although up to this point we have been referring to natural asphalt pitch, when the word

Figure 1.3 Built-up roof application.

pitch is used today, it refers to coal tar pitch. Natural asphalt is a pitch material but, as stated earlier, it is of very limited use (in its pure form) on the rooftop.

Tar is a residue product given off or excreted from a material or organism. Coal tar is a residual product created during the manufacture of coke, which is created by the distillation of coal, hence the term *coal tar.* This tar is taken and further refined to create coal tar roof pitch. (See Sec. 5.1.1.)

HISTORY

The first built-up roof systems used in the United States were from a composition of materials we would find strange today, including clay, horsehair, manure, and sand. Contemporary built-up roof systems evolved from what was termed *composition roofing,* developed in the early 1800s.

The materials used in the composition system were varied, as previously described, but a main and usual ingredient was pine-tree tar and/or pine pitch. These materials were used to coat and seal sheets of heavy paper together. The sheets originated from the marine shipping industry, where they were used as a component in waterproofing systems for ships.

The methods and processes from the marine industry were copied for use on roofs. This normally involved installing the heavy paper sheets into pine tar and coating with pine tar. The roof surfacing material installed into the top coating of pine tar was sand, shell, clay, etc.

In the mid-1800s Samuel Warren was a roofer in Cincinnati, Ohio. The Cincinnati Gas Light and Coke Company provided gas for streetlights and coke and coal for heating. A waste product created by the company was coal tar, disposed of in the Ohio River, which acted as the industrial sewer for all the local industries.

Warren decided to create a composition roof using the coal tar and was allowed sole rights to the waste for no charge. He involved his brother, Cyrus Warren, in the new business and together they developed a roof felt material to be used in lieu of the paper sheathing normally used. The rest is history, and the commercial CTP industry as we know it today began to evolve. (See Fig. 1.4.)

DEVELOPMENT

In 1868 Michael Ehret was issued a U.S. patent for the distillation and manufacture of coal tar products. Today over 200,000 products are derived from the distillation of coal tars, including:

- Naphthalene
- Creosote

Figure 1.4 Roof crew of the 1800s. (*Courtesy of United Union Roofers, Waterproofers & Allied Workers, Washington, D.C.*)

- Urethanes
- Sulfonamides
- Aspirin

In 1887 the H. W. Jayne Company was a leader in further developing and marketing coal tar roofing pitch. This company later became the Barrett Company, which was sold to the Jim Walters Company, which also owned Celotex, and so on.

In the 1970s the Koppers Company, a major U.S. supplier of tar roofing pitch, developed a roofing pitch, called Type III, that was less harsh on the workers. Up to that time there had been only Type I pitch used for creating built-up roofs. Overexposure to the fumes given off by the coal tar roof pitch material when heated to 300 to 400°F causes most people discomfort. Type III pitch is manufactured to be what is termed "low-fuming." By reducing the caustic fumes it is hoped that subsequent worker discomfort will be reduced.

At the beginning of the twentieth century, coal tar pitch was the predominant material used for built-up roofing. The roof felts used were created from organic materials—mainly rag and wood-pulp products. The surfacing was normally gravel aggregates.

THE PRESENT

Today coal tar pitch is still widely used. Type III roof pitch is more commonly specified than is Type I. Organic roof felts have been replaced by fiberglass roof felts as the predominant felt material. (See Sec. 7.1.2.)

Other changes are also happening. Coal tar pitch is being modified, resulting in another class of modified bitumen roof membrane. It is hoped that the long-lasting characteristics of tar pitch will be inherent in this relatively new material.

Coal tar roof pitch has been determined to be a carcinogen and is classified as such by the Occupational Safety and Health Association (OSHA). Labeling on each container of roof pitch advises worker caution relating to prolonged contact with the material and inhalation of the fumes, dust, and vapors.

In the early 1990s many of the major built-up roofing material manufacturers discontinued coal tar pitch roof systems from their product lines. Perhaps this was due to the classification as a carcinogen by OSHA or perhaps it was due to some problems reported with fiberglass felt and Type III coal tar pitch roof systems. Mathematical modeling has demonstrated that, in hot climates and conditions, fiberglass felt layers could be displaced within the membrane construction. This is an uncommon problem and will possibly occur only in hot geographical locations. (See Sec. 5.1.4.)

Since the 1800s we have seen the advent of other types of roof systems and the selection of such by designers in lieu of the old tried-and-true coal tar pitch roof system. Modern systems, such as metal roof assemblies and modified bitumen or polymeric single-ply materials, have taken a market share from the pitch roof system as compared to 50 years ago.

However, coal tar pitch roof systems have been documented to last as long as 75 years. This creates very favorable life-cycle cost factors. Being resistant to chemical and pollutant fallout and ponding water, as well as having some self-healing characteristics (see Sec. 5.1.3), coal tar pitch roof systems will be successfully utilized by the knowledgeable designer. (See Fig. 1.5.)

1.2.3 Modified Bitumens

INTRODUCTION

The European community can be credited with developing the procedures for modifying asphalt bitumen, resulting in what we now term *modified bitumens*. This process mixes hot asphalt with synthetic polymers, thereby modifying the asphalt bitumen. This modification gives the asphalt added flexibility and/or resistance to environmental impact, such as ultraviolet sunlight rays, thermal shock, and deck deflections and movements.

This technology was developed in the mid-1900s in Europe and was introduced into the United States in the early 1970s. As with many new products, problems plagued the introduction of modified bitumen membranes and some trial and error and reformulating was required by U.S. manufacturers before we could enjoy the product we take for granted today.

It was learned that an interply membrane located within the approximately ⅛-in-thick sheet was crucial in its field performance. During the early stages of development it was not uncommon to find a modified bitumen membrane (MBM) with strands of inorganic material extending longitudinally through the sheet instead of a complete inner membrane scrim or carrier as we now use. (See Fig. 1.6.)

Even with the use of a membrane material located within the sheet (referred to as a *carrier* or *scrim*), problems with performance still continued if the carrier membrane was excessively stretched during manufacture of the MBM. The stretching during manufacture resulted in the installed MBM roof system pulling away from flashing locations, delaminating at seams, and in general shrinking as the inner scrim membrane tried to relax back to its original size and dimension before the stretching which occurred during manufacture. (See Sec. 9.1.2.)

Figure 1.5 Washington School, Middlesex County, N.J.—erected in 1910, and in 1990 still protected by the original coal tar pitch roof system. (*Courtesy of Koppers Industries, Pittsburgh, Pa.*)

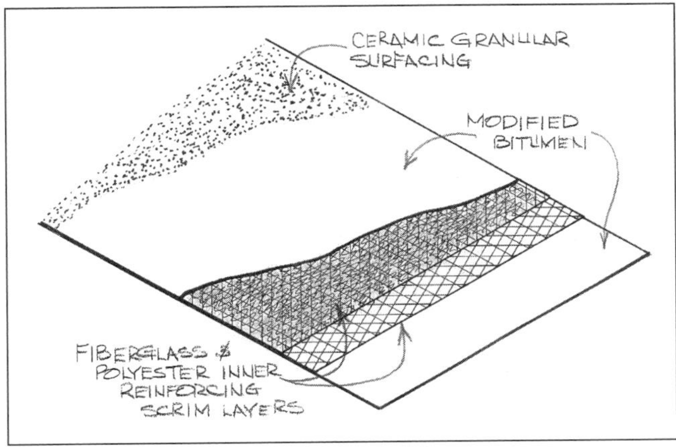

Figure 1.6 Cross-section of MBM membrane.

DEVELOPMENT

Today the manufacturing equipment has been better developed to greatly reduce this stretching. The use of fiberglass carriers instead of polyester, or the use of both a polyester and a fiberglass membrane as the inner carrier, also greatly restricts this problem.

Other processes and procedures have been implemented over the years and are now standard practice used in eliminating problems of the past. For example, the raw polymer modifiers used in one form of MBM, being atactic polypropylene (APP), are a waste material generated during the manufacture of plastics. As waste, this material was discarded to vacant fields, landfills, and so on.

When a use was discovered and the demand for the APP grew, some MBM manufacturers used the waste APP, retrieving it from the disposal sites. The contaminated and unpure APP resulted in poor-quality MBMs. Today APP materials are of much better quality.

Today asphalt is specially created for use in APP modified bitumen membranes. The asphalt used, in many cases, cannot be oxidized via the refining process which is used to make most roofing asphalt. (See Sec. 4.1.1.) The asphalt used for a quality atactic polypropylene–based MBM must be nonoxidized or "unblown" asphalt. When standard roofing asphalt was used, the MBM became brittle, with low elongation and tensile strength properties.

Although an MBM is mainly asphalt which has been modified with a polymer, fillers are also required in the mixture. The fillers used today are mainly limestone-based talc material but in the past have been other materials which proved to be incompatible and produced totally undesirable results. If improper amounts of filler are used, or if the wrong type of fillers are used, a weak roof membrane will be the result.

THE PRESENT

Today manufacturers have dedicated equipment which eliminates problems of the past as discussed here. Field performance experience has taught us how to blend, create, and install MBM roof materials that perform effectively as a system.

Modified bitumen membranes have proven to be excellent materials for use at base flashing locations. They are tough and durable, resisting damage inflicted by rooftop equipment service personnel, and their flexibility allows minor movement between the base flashing and roof assembly without damage. Many of the major built-up roof manufacturers now include a modified bitumen membrane line, if not for use as a total roof system, then for use as bituminous roof flashing materials.

Modified bitumen membranes were once exclusively made of asphalt bitumen base products. Today coal tar pitch bitumen is being used to create a modified bitumen membrane. Additionally, some of the polymer modifiers are being enhanced, creating a new derivative which lends additional characteristics to the modified bitumen membrane system.

It has been learned that the surfacing on a modified bitumen membrane is critical to its long-term performance life. Coatings have been studied and their longevity and performance evaluated. The curing time required before application of a coating is being studied. Types of coatings and their effectiveness on a rooftop where applied to a modified bitumen are constantly being evaluated. (See Fig. 1.7.)

Figure 1.7 Parabolic dome with MBM roof.

1.3 STEEP-SLOPE ROOF MATERIALS

GENERAL

In the previous section we discussed bituminous flat-roof materials. These material types and roof systems are water barriers, capable of waterproofing a structure even though water will gather and stand on the roof surface. Other materials can be classified as steep-slope roofing materials. These materials are water shedders and not water barriers and cannot waterproof a structure where water can gather and stand on the roof surface.

Steep-slope roof materials must be installed on a slope, relying on the gravity created by the slope to move the water in an expedient manner from the roof surface. These roof materials cannot function in situations where water can gather on the roof surface.

Slates, tiles, asphalt shingles, thatch, wood shingles, and metal roofing are included in this category. Some could argue that the exception to this rule may be some forms of structural standing seam metal roof systems which can function on roof slopes as low as ¼-in fall per linear foot. Some of these types of systems can function leak-free in many cases, even if water accumulates on the roof surface. However, the metal panels cannot tolerate ponding water for 48- to 72-h time periods, as can bituminous flat-roof systems. The coating on the panels will be damaged. Material manufacturers' warranties will be voided. Metal roof materials require all water to be immediately drained from the roof surface.

Another factor which can define steep-sloped roof materials is the roof flashings used with the system. For steep-sloped systems the flashings are designed and installed to shed water away from locations where water could enter the building. If the roof slope was low, and water could rise instead of being shed, the flashings would leak and allow water into the building. The flashing systems, like the roof materials, are water shedders and not water barriers.

Again, some structural standing-seam metal roof systems have flashings that supposedly withstand water-level build-up. According to some, this is not proper design, and such situations often lead to roof maintenance and repair of such flashing areas. Therefore, due to the rigid characteristics of the metal systems and their need for water-shedding design, we most definitely classify them as steep-slope roof materials.

1.3.1 Slate Roof Panels

In certain areas and cultures, sloped roofs with water-shedding materials have always been the predominant roof systems. An example is structures within the Bavarian regions of Northern Europe. Large amounts of snow require a roof steep enough to limit the excessive weight of the snow on the roof structure. Ice damming and consistently cold wintertime temperatures require a roof system that can support heavy loads of snow. Slate roof systems have proven effective for this environment.

In the United States we are used to installing natural slate roofing panels in the neighborhood of 10 in × 16 in × ¼ in thick, weighing 800 to 1000 lb per 100 ft^2. In Bavaria, slate roof panels can be about 1 to 2 in thick × 3 ft × 6 ft. Each 100 ft^2 of roof slate installed could weigh as much as 6500 to 8000 lb! (See Fig. 1.8.)

These types of exceptionally large and heavy slates are wired or hung on structural support beams or rafters, with the slates becoming the roof deck. The thickness provides structural and tensile strengths to survive superimposed snow loading and strong wind gusts. Also, slate surfaces are relatively smooth, and on a steep slope, snow will slide off easily.

Slate roofing tiles have been successfully used for centuries—some installed in the eighth century in England are still in existence today. Slate is a metamorphic rock that begins as sediment deposit under a body of water. Tremendous heat and pressure turn the deposit into the hard, fine-grained rock we recognize. (See Sec. 11.4.)

In the United States most slate roofing shingles come from the eastern and New England states. The slate is quarried, hand-split into slabs, and then saw-cut to size. Slates come in many different colors, the most common being a dull gray and the most rare being red, with variegated colors also occurring. Slate roofing is very durable and is often referred to as a "lifetime roof." However, it can be cost-prohibitive and the installation requires specialized craftsmen.

Today we most often see slate roofing on prestigious structures, such as churches, monuments, and government buildings. Slate roofing is most common in areas local to the slate quarries and in areas where there are seaports. Before the twentieth century it was not feasible to ship cross-continent the tons of slate roofing required for one house or building. However, at the seaport towns, ships sometimes arrived with the heavy and dense, non-water-absorbing slate in the holds as ballast.

Slate roofing is fireproof and had another advantage for early settlers: it provided clean drinking water. During rains, dust and debris were first washed from the slate roof surface. Valves were then closed and the water from the roof gutter system was directed into holding tanks called *cisterns,* where it was used by the residents in daily life. This strategy is still used today,

Figure 1.8 Switzerland heavy roof slates. (*Courtesy of Clifford Tile Agency, Dallas, Tx.*)

often with clay tile and metal roof systems, in areas such as the Caribbean Islands.

1.3.2 Cementitious Roof Materials

CEMENTITIOUS SHINGLES

In the early to mid-1900s a material often used in place of slate was introduced. This material was a cement-based roof panel, varying in size and appearance, and often using asbestos fibers as a binding agent within the cement-based matrix. Commonly known at that time as *asbestos shingles* (see Fig. 1.9), the material is now unavailable because of the detrimental health effects caused by asbestos fibers.

Today non-asbestos-fibered cementitious-based roof panels have been substituted for the asbestos shingle. Based upon style of shingle selected and application layout used, the appearance can be similar to that of a slate roof.

Referred to as *cement shake* or *imitation slate,* the roof systems can be expected to provide up to 50 years of service life. Service life with these types of systems is often dependent upon the waterproofing underlayment (see Secs. 7.1.1 and 11.4.1) and metal flashing system (Sec. 11.1). Also of extreme importance is the service record of the particular material as manufactured for the region in which it will be installed. Some cement-based shingles have experienced massive failures in the field due to cracking and splitting.

CEMENT TILES

Developed in the nineteenth century, cement roof tiles are still a common form of upper-scale roof systems. Similar in appearance to a clay roof tile system, but usually less expensive, cement roof tiles are installed much the same way as clay tile. The cement used is light in weight (600 to 900 lbs per 100 ft^2) and the tile as manufactured today can be color-pigmented throughout with a water-resistant additive.

In the early to mid-1900s many roofing contractors manufactured their own cement tiles from molds they owned. A water-resistant paint was either contained within the wet cementitious mix or painted onto the tiles as they dried. The main market for these tiles was the local residential structures, but as building structures became more light in weight and less capable of supporting the heavy load of the cement tile, the market vanished.

Today cement tile systems are installed across the United States but are most common in the western and

Figure 1.9 Asbestos shingle system.

southern United States. Cold climates can adversely affect some concrete tile, particularly if a glaze finish on the tile cannot withstand thermal changes during the annual cycle.

These systems can be considered lifetime roof systems, but in areas where torrential rains and strong winds are common, the continued waterproof integrity of the system is dependent upon the waterproofing felt-layer underlayment installed prior to the cement shingles. In these areas it is suggested that the tile shingles be installed to a batten system and, where budget permits, a batten-counter-batten system is the most effective way of restricting water from the building interior. (See Sec. 11.2.1.)

1.3.3 Clay Tile Roofing

Ever since clay was used to create pottery, there have been clay roofing tiles. Little has changed with the basic manufacturing process, in that a dense clay-base material is mixed to proper consistency and then kiln-fired to a stable, hard state. Kiln-firing allows a colored glaze surfacing to be incorporated onto the tile surface. This provides an extended life to the clay tile and gives the designer more architectural freedom.

Today clay tile roofing is most common in the southern United States, with Florida and California being the states where it predominates. Clay tile was introduced from Europe by the first American settlers.

In some areas clay roof tile was made on site by a very simple process. The clay mixture was created and formed into flat, even squares. Each square was then formed into a curve by placing the flat square of soft clay over the thigh or over a curved, tapered, and smooth log. After drying, the tiles were installed to the roof, overlapping one to the other. This style, called *mission tile,* is effective, although none of the tiles were of exactly the same-size radius. Also, sun drying does not hard-set the clay as will the high temperatures within the kiln during the firing process.

The other basic style of clay roof tile is *Spanish tile* or *S-tile.* It is normally made in a mold to achieve the desired pattern. Functioning on the same water-shedding principals as mission tile, the layout and installation are somewhat more difficult than with mission tile. (See Fig. 1.10.)

Clay tiles are also available in two other basic styles: *flat tile shingle* and *interlocking tile shingle.* Under each of the four categories there can be many sub-styles, varying from manufacturer to manufacturer. This range of styles gives designers the ability to create ornate roof facades which accommodate the prestigious structures on which we most often see clay tile systems.

Clay tiles must be installed much the same way as cement roof tiles. Solid decking is usually required, with a waterproofing membrane covering the deck surface. Battens are normally recommended. Only recently have

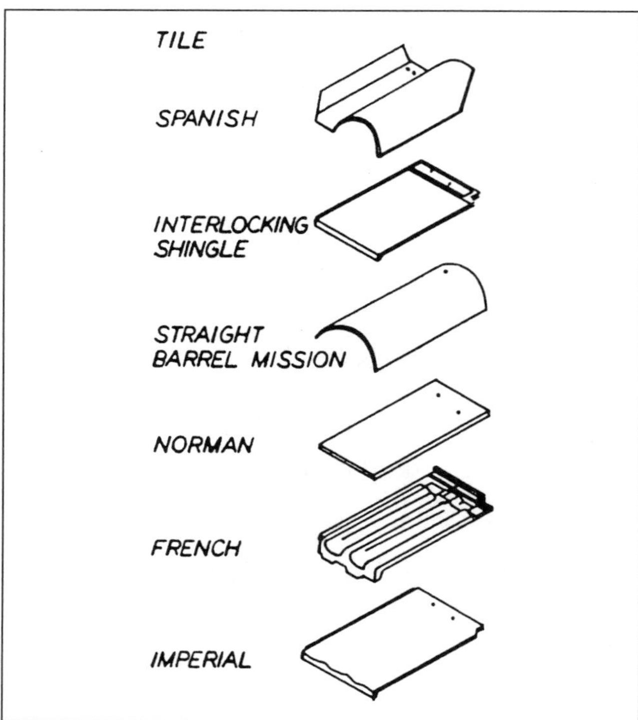

Figure 1.10 Clay roof tile styles. (*Courtesy of Ludowici-Celadon, New Lexington, Ohio.*)

standards been adopted for attachment of tile roof systems to resist wind blow-off.

1.3.4 Copper Roofing

Copper is a very ancient form of roofing. A mosque in Istanbul, Turkey, has a functioning copper roof reported to have been installed in 795 A.D. According to *Modern Applications of Sheet Copper* by the Copper and Brass Research Association, "So far as is known the copper longest in continuous service is the cornice around the central opening of the dome of the Pantheon in Rome, which was placed during the reign of the Emperor Hadrian in 130 A.D., and was still in service up to World War II, a period of 1,812 years."

Dating from possibly as early as 5000 B.C., copper has always been a form of metal that people have found easy and accessible for mining, smelting, and forming. Copper roofing is normally used on structures of importance or prestige, such as cathedrals, monuments, schools, and hospitals.

Copper roofing became a predominant roof system in the sixteenth century, and many of these roof systems are still in existence today, such as:

- St. James Palace, London, England (1520)
- St. Peters, Rome, Italy (1550)
- Holy Ghost Church, Denmark (1582)
- Kronberg Castle, Denmark (1585)

Copper was mined, refined, and produced into flat sheets, approximately 1/16 to 1/8 in thick. The panels were cut as required and further formed at the job site into what is called a *double-lock seam* (see Fig. 1.11). This method of forming and sealing the lap joints of the copper panels was the only method used up until the mid- to late 1800s when batten seam style was introduced. As time went on, other styles have been introduced, with some working fine and others requiring additional refinement.

The theory of copper application to building structures, although developed over centuries, basically has not changed much. We still join panels to each other and to the structure much the same way it was done 1000 years ago.

New advances are roll-forming machines that can produce the panel with all sides bent and formed, ready for application to the roof. Other changes have occurred, such as solder and pop rivets, which are now used extensively, whereas before the twentieth century, white lead paste was normally used in lieu of solder. Today we have automatic seaming machines, sometimes referred to as *robots,* which take the place of the wood block, hammer, and tongs used in the past to form and lock the seam.

Items and procedures such as the making and installation of white lead solder seem to be lost arts today. White lead solder is the only component the author has found that works effectively and permanently in situations where the lap joints of the copper panels are subjected to standing water and thermal movements, but very few craftsmen today know how to make it.

Ornate cornices of copper, cupola ornaments, conductor heads, soffits, moldings, and straps were much more available at the turn of the century than they are now (see Fig. 1.12). These ornate components were usually hand-formed and manufactured, showing off the artisans' abilities. Again, much of the art of fitting and erecting these items has also been lost.

In the twentieth century, the science of metallurgy, and the physics and dynamics of copper (and other forms of metal roofing), became more widely under-

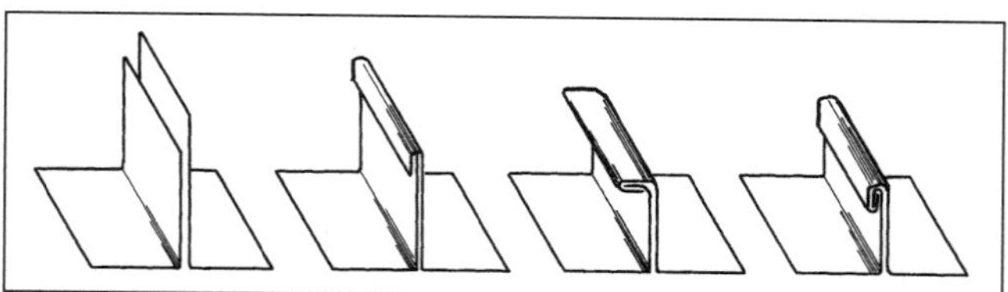

Figure 1.11 Double-lock standing seam.

Figure 1.12 Ornamental copper flashing. (*Courtesy of Coppercraft, Dallas, Tx.*)

stood as a result of advancing technology and science. Today we can calculate to 1/16 in the amount of movement that will occur in a copper roof panel as the result of temperature changes. (See Fig. 11.12.)

The biggest problem experienced with copper and metal roofing is expansion and contraction, and how to join and permanently seal components to each other at the points where this force occurs. As a steep-slope roofing material, the copper flashings should be designed and installed as water shedders. In many situations with copper roofing, this is accomplished by hemmed lips joining each other, without the use of caulks or solder (see Fig. 1.13). Today we see far too much of caulks and solder seams, which will result in leaks if and when the caulk or solder fails to keep the joint watertight.

If you ever have a chance to investigate a copper roof system that is 100 or more years old, you will find very few solder seams and absolutely no caulk. The only solder will be in a hemmed seam that, without the solder, would probably still be watertight. The solder, being white lead solder paste, is merely there as a waterproofing and binding agent to help hold and maintain the waterproof integrity of the lap seam.

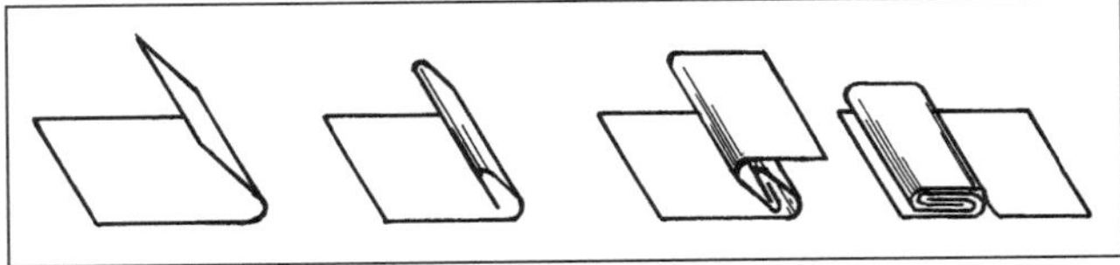

Figure 1.13 Hemmed lip at flashing detail.

1.3.5 Metal Roofing

Metal roofing, being steel, lead, zinc, or aluminum, has played only a minor part in the roofing industry through the ages. Lead roofing is most prevalent in Europe, and is still in use there today, much in the same way as copper roofing. In the United States, steel roofing historically was factory extruded steel panels, corrugated or crimped, used in rural or agricultural settings.

However, in the 1950s and 1960s, premanufactured metal building kits were developed and marketed successfully. Like a giant Tinker Toy set, the entire building unit was delivered to the job site, from one manufacturer, with instructions (blueprints) enclosed. The structural steel components had holes prepunched for the bolts and fasteners, and all essential components were from one source, the metal building manufacturer or distributor.

The metal panels were normally made of economical steel with a painted surface as the protective coating. The erection crew needed limited equipment for the construction and was able to erect the walls, windows, doors, roof, and insulations. The repetition of the contractor's duties from one building to the next allowed for very efficient building labor costs.

As time passed, more manufacturers entered this lucrative market—not only metal building manufacturers but metal building component companies as well. Knowledge increased about the forming of metal panels, and expensive and complicated equipment was developed and purchased for this and other reasons. Space-age technology provided polymers and resins that were unavailable a decade before, resulting in more effective and long-lived coating finishes on the metal panels.

With large capital expenditures by manufacturers for equipment, factories, distribution networks, and R&D departments, the commercial roofing industry, which generates hundreds of millions of dollars per year, was a favorable and untapped market for metal roofing.

In the early 1970s, standing rib panels with exposed fasteners were mainly used as roof panels, commonly called *R-panels.* These R-panels, in truth, were of the same configuration style and material as the wall panels used on the commercial metal buildings. (See Fig. 1.14.) However, being a structural component, the panels could be attached directly to underlying purlins/subpurlins spaced on 4- to 5-ft centers. This eliminated the cost of roof decking, with insulation blanket installed directly under the panels in a time-efficient manner.

As more and more metal buildings were erected, and more and more nonmetal buildings were covered with metal roof systems, the metal roofing industry began to take off. The advent of the structural standing seam with concealed clip fasteners was a major item in promoting

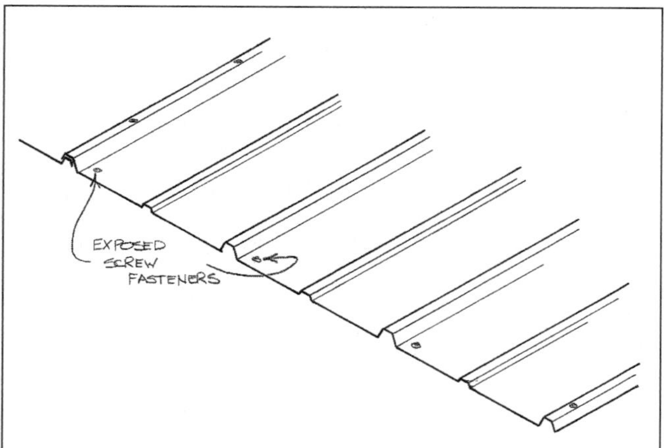

Figure 1.14 R-panel with exposed fasteners.

the use of the metal roof systems (see Fig. 1.15). The concealed clip allows the roof panels to be secured to the roof structure without penetration of the panel by screws, greatly reducing the chance of leaks. Also, the roof panels can slide on the clips, allowing the panels to move with the forces of expansion and contraction. Metal roof systems expand and contract at rates greater than many people realize. The exposed screw fasteners used in the standard R-panel had tendencies to leak once exposed to the annual thermal cycles and stresses thereof.

Today metal roof systems are becoming a predominant system within the building industry. Retrofitting of flat-roof systems is becoming a popular way to reroof a building. With retrofitting over a built-up roof system, for example, the existing system is left in place, with perhaps the loose gravel surfacing removed to reduce the overall dead load to the roof structure (see Fig. 1.16). Upright bracing is installed to support subsequent purlins. To the purlins a metal roof system is installed.

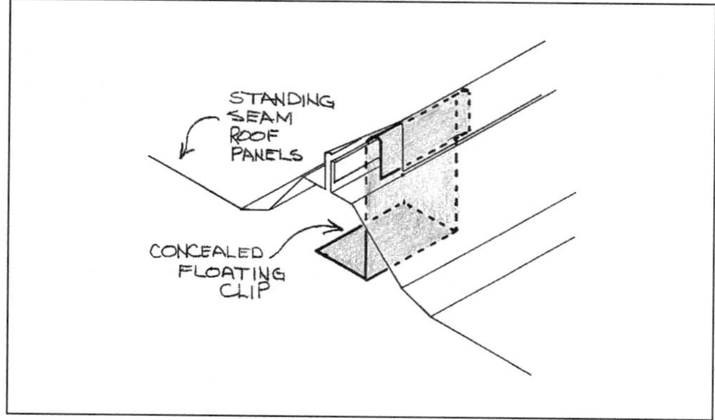

Figure 1.15 Concealed clip on a structural standing seam panel.

Problems have arisen with metal roofing, not as a function of the metal panels themselves, but as a function of improper installation, lack of understanding, and negligence in contemplating all the elements that are factors with a metal roof system. Many environmental and dynamic forces act and react with a metal roof assembly, such as vapor drive which can result in condensation on the bottom side of the metal panels, leaks at improperly designed roof flashings, acoustics, as well as forces of expansion and contraction. See Sec. 2.1 for consideration under a total building design concept.

At present, metal roofing systems are often used on building structures which are not inherently metal building assemblies, in that they are high-occupancy, sealed areas as opposed to warehouse and high-open-ceiling areas with exceptional ventilation. The metal roof assembly often has numerous flashing penetrations and roof-mounted equipment. The roof applicator is often from a metal-building-erection background and may not fully comprehend the complexities required for intricate or complex roof assembly.

In the recent past, relative to the publication date of this manual, we have seen these problems realized, addressed, and corrected. Metal roofing panels have evolved into a sophisticated product offering a large variety of profiles, from nearly flat ribs to high, bold ribs, and everything in between. Interesting shadow lines and aesthetics provide the designer with a full arsenal to select from. In addition, metal panels are available in a variety of widths, paint systems, colors, and gauges.

In the author's opinion, like many of the other roof system types successfully used today, metal roofing systems are evolving into a major force within the roofing industry but will take a few licks along the way.

1.4 POLYMERIC SINGLE-PLY ROOF MATERIALS

GENERAL

Technically, roof systems classified as single-ply systems could include metal roofs, which are composed of a single layer of metal attached to structural support members. However, the only polymers used in the metal roof system would be contained within the paint coating finish.

Some people group modified bitumen membranes under the single-ply category. Modified bitumen membranes, normally composed mainly of asphalt bitumen, use polymers to modify asphalt or coal tar pitch bitumen. The resulting membranes have many of the same characteristics and installation requirements as built-up roofs. Additionally, modified bitumen roof systems are

Figure 1.16 Roof retrofit. (*Courtesy of MBCI, Houston, Tx.*)

normally installed over underlying roof-felt layer(s), making them more than single-ply membranes.

The main types of single-ply roof membranes in popular use at the present time are:

- Chlorinated polyethylene (CPE)
- Chlorosulfonated polyethylene (CSPE)
- Copolymer alloys (CPA)
- Ethylene interpolymers (EIP)
- Ethylene propylene diene monomer (EPDM)
- Polyvinyl chloride (PVC)
- Polyisobutylene (PIB)
- Polyisobutylene/isoprene (neoprene)

Most synthetic polymer single-ply materials were developed for U.S. roof system use in the 1960s. The materials were used prior to this time as tarps for such things as the trucking/shipping industry and pond liners for containment of materials which could not be allowed to leach into the ground and water table.

Single-ply membranes are normally 30 to 60 mil thick. They are made from synthetic polymeric materials with high molecular weights. They are further enhanced by molecular cross-linking of the inherent molecular matrix or by the addition of synthetic additives, oils, fillers, and/or plasticizers.

The roof membrane sheet usually incorporates a reinforcement membrane layer, normally of polyester or fiberglass material. This reinforcement layer is usually within the sheet or can be placed on the back side of the finished single-ply sheet.

During the oil embargo crisis of 1974, asphalt products suddenly underwent great price increases and supply shortages. Many material manufacturers within the up-and-coming single-ply industry took advantage of the moment to mount an aggressive and strong marketing campaign.

An increased market share was garnered from the substantial built-up roof market. This niche was further opened to new materials due to what many felt was the poor performance of asphalt built-up roof systems.

Single-ply membranes can be supplied to the job site in sheet widths from 5 to 50 ft, with the length of the sheet being whatever load the roof deck will support when the roll is placed on it prior to unrolling and installation. The larger the sheets, the fewer side and end laps the roofer has to seal, thereby theoretically reducing the chance of leaks and reducing costs of installation.

Procedures used for flashing details at roof penetrations and parapet walls are entirely different from those used in conventional low-slope built-up roofing. Since this is where many problems develop with built-up roofs, these different approaches were very well accepted by architects and designers.

However, some problems began to arise within the single-ply roof market. The forces encountered daily on a rooftop were not fully understood by some material manufacturers. Also, some contractors did not have enough experienced and trained personnel to properly install the membranes in the many diverse and unusual situations encountered on a rooftop.

The single-ply industry had to make some adjustments. A dedicated effort by the material manufacturers resulted in better and more complete understanding of rooftop situations and forces. Material function, action, and reaction to and with other roof components, on a day-to-day basis, in often adverse situations, is now much better understood. Materials are now formulated, specified, and installed to accommodate these situations, with a single-ply roof being installed as a total system, not just a covering over other components.

Not all single-ply roof membranes had problems. In fact, the majority survived to function effectively. However, when the oil crisis subsided and asphalt prices and materials returned to a more normal level, contractors and manufacturers who had not entered into the single-ply market were quick to point out any problems that had developed or were developing with single-ply systems. Often these problems were overemphasized by people who had their own agendas to serve.

Explanations were hard to understand for lay people. For example, if the single-ply flashing sheet became brittle as a weathered piece of plastic and broke, fractured, and delaminated from the roof, it was difficult for the manufacturer's representative to explain that the problem had been corrected with the "new and improved" roof membrane.

Polymers, copolymers, vulcanized and *nonvulcanized, molecular bonding,* and *cross-linking* are but the basic terminology and processes that need to be understood before real explanations can be provided. Many designers and contractors became skeptical of the systems. Today, single-ply membranes are better understood and have successfully proven their ability to function as long-lived roof systems.

The membrane usually weighs less than 1 lb/ft^2. A single layer of high-performance roof insulation can be used under the single-ply membrane, usually mechanically attached to the roof deck. This saves installation time and material costs as compared with the multilayered roof insulation systems normally required under many other types of low-sloped roof systems.

Single-ply membranes resist a wide range of chemical contaminants and deck and component movements; they are easily inspectable and easy to install—with properly trained and experienced applicators.

The multitude of different polymeric single-ply roof membranes available (and those which are yet to come) are composed of complicated molecular chains and are often installed with chemicals in a two- or three-step process creating a chemical bond, which is, at best, difficult to explain and understand. Adding to the complexity are different requirements of design and installation among material manufacturers, even though they may offer the same type of membrane.

In the author's opinion, this field is too complicated to explain within the constraints of this manual. Accurate and complete information can be obtained from:

The Single Ply Roofing Institute (SPRI)
20 Walnut Street
Wellesley Hills, MA 02181
(617) 237-7879

CHAPTER 2

Design Theory

2.1 TOTAL BUILDING SYSTEM DESIGN CONCEPT

TOTAL BUILDING SYSTEM CONCEPT

There are many systems and materials which, upon completion of installation, form the total roof system. Consider an average modified bitumen roof installed with hot asphalt mopping. For simplicity, let us use as an example a standard one-story commercial office/warehouse building located in Arkansas.

The building has a low-sloped roof system and, for architectural purposes, will have a parapet wall across the front and partway down both sides. The air-conditioning equipment will be located on the rooftop. A gutter and downspout system will feed the water from the rooftop to the ground. A metal roof deck was selected, to which two layers of roof insulation will be installed. To the top of the roof insulation a modified bitumen roof membrane system will be installed with hot asphalt mopping. (See Fig. 2.1.)

COMPONENTS CREATING A SIMPLE ROOF SYSTEM

Following is a list of the materials and steps or processes needed to create this roof system. A simple roof system now seems a little more complicated. Fully realize that if only one of these materials or components fails, the total roof system could be in serious jeopardy.

Materials	***Steps***
Lay out 22-gauge steel roof deck and fasten to structure	1
Wood nailers	1
Lay out roof insulation layer and mechanically attach to deck	1
Attach roof insulation to bottom layer of mechanically attached insulation with hot asphalt moppings	1
Prime interior of parapet walls	1
Install cant strips in hot mopping	1
Install base sheet in asphalt mopping	1
Install modified bitumen cap sheet in asphalt moppings	1
Attach metal edge flashing and prime	1
Install membrane flashings at roof equipment, parapet walls, metal flashings	1
Install bituminous parapet wall flashing	1
Install gutter and downspout system	1
Install coping system to parapets	1
Number of basic procedures	21

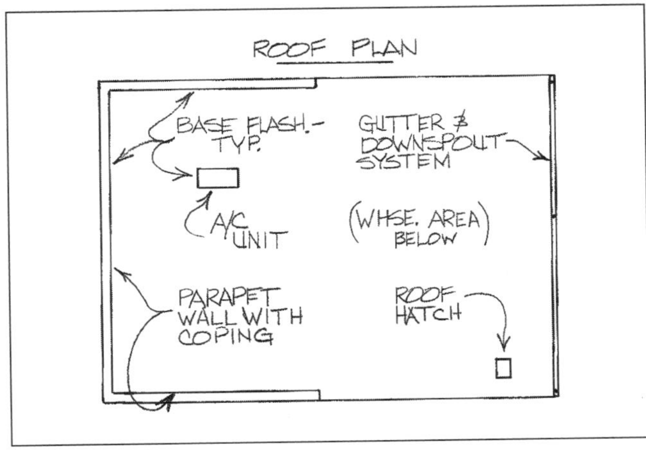

Figure 2.1 Roof plan.

A warehouse/office complex: the design did not take into account such factors as vapor drive into the roof system, which may occur due to outside winter temperatures over the office space. (See Sec. 2.3.3.) Another consideration is whether the overhead door assemblies with the roller-track system suspended in the rear of the warehouse area from the open-web bar joists will cause considerable live loading to the roof deck when they are opened and closed.

What will happen in the winter when the warehouse workers close the overhead doors and heat the space with propane or oil-heated portable space heaters? A gallon of water vapor will be produced for each gallon of heating oil burned, with propane producing 3 gal of water vapor for each 20 gal burned. Vapor drive into the roof can once again become a problem. (See Sec. 2.3.3.)

EFFECT OF BUILDING COMPONENTS AND MATERIALS ON THE ROOF SYSTEM

It is important to recognize all of the dynamic forces acting and reacting with the total building system. In the preceding example, the warehouse door assembly is now an active part of the roof assembly, as is any temporary heating in the warehouse area.

Every component or system:

- upon which the roof assembly rests (building walls, etc.), or
- which is attached to the roof assembly (electrical conduit lines to bottom side of deck, metal coping on parapet walls, etc.), or
- which is installed into the roof system (insulation panels, etc.), or
- which is installed through the roof system (HVAC systems, pipes, structural supports, etc.), or
- which can produce loading on a roof assembly (rooftop foot and equipment traffic, wind, rain, snow, solar radiation, etc.)

must be considered in its variable and overall relation to the roof assembly.

Vibration, movement, deterioration, chemical and galvanic reaction, and expansion and contraction are forces and characteristics that all building materials exhibit, to one degree or another. The type, extent, and assembly of the total building components have an effect on a roof system. They govern what components can be used on and in the roof assembly to blend the roof system harmoniously into the rest of the building.

As an example, consider once again the warehouse/office complex in Arkansas. Let's put the warehouse next to a railroad track off an interstate highway. Railcars passing by the building will most certainly cause building movement—probably to a significant degree—unless extraordinary foundation and wall design is utilized.

If the roof deck support system (bar joists) is placed on top of and supported by the building walls, the roof deck and all roof components attached thereto will experience the transferred building wall movement. However, the metal roof deck will experience additional vertical movement as a diaphragm.

In this example, the roof deck is wall-supported and roof deck movement need not be isolated. (See Sec. 3.1.) However, the vertical movement of the deck as a diaphragm must be allowed for. The cold winter months in Arkansas will require a roof membrane assembly that will remain flexible at cold temperatures.

The styrene butadiene styrene (SBS) modified bitumen membrane selected for the building has the appropriate cold-weather flexural characteristics, whereas a coal tar pitch built-up roof may not. An alternative could be a single-ply membrane.

However, another element must be considered in the roof design: the traffic passing by in close proximity to the building, both on the interstate highway and the railway. The traffic—locomotives, automobiles, and tractor-trailer trucks—emit engine fumes. The fumes and pollution fallout will be minor but continual throughout the life of the building. Before the roof membrane selection is finalized, the manufacturer of the materials needs to be questioned regarding compatibility of the membrane with petroleum-based fumes and fallout.

The climatic conditions at the time of construction must be considered. Extremes of cold as well as hot temperatures affect most materials and processes used to install roof systems.

2.1.1 Total Roof System Concept

Few items within the roof assembly act independently of the others, and for every action of one component or material there is usually a reaction of an associated material or component. The ability of one material or component to function normally (within expected behavioral parameters) has a direct effect on another material's or component's abilities to properly perform. The information included elsewhere within this manual explains and illustrates particular and specific behavioral patterns of materials and components. However, without an understanding of the total system concept, it may not be possible to anticipate material characteristics that will change from one assembly design to the next.

CATEGORIES USED IN DESIGN

There are main categories of function within which roof systems fit. It could be said that a roof's main function is to keep water out of the building. However, a roof has other important functions that it must meet to be considered effective.

- It must control heating and cooling costs, with more energy being lost (or saved) by the roof area than by any other face of the building envelope. (See Sec. 8.1.)
- It has a function in the total noise levels of a structure and sometimes plays the major role in acoustic design (such as for gymnasiums, churches, or industrial site buildings; see Sec. 2.3.2).
- It can either restrict or aid the movement of moisture vapor through the building. (See Sec. 2.3.3.)
- It must resist unusual and extraordinary acts of nature (high winds, hail, earthquakes, etc.).
- It must accomplish these goals within acceptable and normal budget costs, for a reasonable and anticipated amount of time.

All too often, designers select a particular type or category of roof system that they think accomplishes most of the major goals required. This type of roof becomes their system of choice, be it a coal tar built-up roof, a torch-applied modified bitumen, or a metal roof. Each roof assembly has special characteristics which allow it to blend with the overall building design. ***Categories of roofs should not be used as criteria for selection!***

For example, if an existing 10,000-ft^2 building is to be reroofed, and the existing roof is a modified bitumen membrane with an aluminum coating as the weathering surface, a built-up roof with a gravel surface may not be the best solution. The existing roof deck and structural support system may be adequately designed to support the new built-up roof with a gravel surface (which will weigh approximately 5 to 6 lb/ft^2), but for the last 15 to 20 years the building has existed with a modified bitumen roof system weighing approximately 1 lb/ft^2. The dead load of the roof assembly above the roof deck will increase from approximately 10,000 lb to 60,000 lb within a very short time frame. Although the building was originally designed structurally to support these new loads, existing building components will now be adjusted by the new loads. You can hope that the adjustments will stay localized to the roof deck surface and not affect interior finishes, etc.

RADIANT BARRIERS AND THE EFFECT ON THE ASSEMBLY

Other phenomena that must be considered and designed for are items such as insulation factors and the effect the heat-retarding layers have on the surface membrane. The better and more efficient the roof insulation layers are, the hotter (and colder) the roof surface. (See Secs. 2.3.1 and 2.3.4.)

As an example, consider a built-up roof installed to a sloped roof deck having a pitch of 2 in per 12-in horizontal run (2:12). A high-R-value roof insulation system was installed to the roof deck of this building located in the southern United States. Daytime temperature extremes during the summer months can be anticipated to be 90 to 95°F.

Type III asphalt is used as the interply mopping and the flood coat surface into which gravel is embedded. Type III has a softening point between 185 and 205°F and is recommended and accepted for slopes up to 3:12. (See Sec. 4.1.4.) However, after the first summer the asphalt began slipping over the edge of the roof. This resulted from temperature extremes which approached the softening-point range of the asphalt. The temperatures entered this range because of thermal loading accentuated by the high-R-value roof insulation located directly under the roof membrane. In such cases it is not unusual for roof-membrane temperatures to approach 175°F. If the roof had been installed to an uninsulated roof deck, temperature extremes would have been lower and slippage probably would not have occurred.

Thermal Bridging of Insulation Fasteners: Back-out. Temperature changes also lead to other problems, one of which is fastener back-out. The head of a fastener located directly under a roof membrane will become much hotter than the opposite end of the threaded or shank shaft. As the roof membrane temperatures heat the head and top portion of the fastener, that portion expands. The opposite end of the fastener, not reaching the same temperatures, does not expand equally. The fastener has a tendency to "walk out" of the hole in the roof deck. This problem is accentuated if the fastener is place through roof insulation, which will cause greater thermal differences between the top and the bottom of the fastener. (See Fig. 2.2 and Sec. 8.1.)

Thermal Bridging of Insulation Fasteners: Corrosion. Thermal bridging along fastener shafts can also cause other serious problems. In cold weather, dew point can be reached at some location along the fastener shaft, from the part extending below the roof deck into the plenum/attic cavity or to the portion of the fastener directly under the membrane. If dew point is reached somewhere along the fastener shaft, condensation is a strong possibility, often resulting in rusting and deteriorated fasteners and an unsecured roof assembly. Multilayered roof insulation assemblies help prevent this problem. (See Sec. 8.1.)

When a fastener assembly is installed directly under the roof membrane, cold outside temperatures can be transferred by conductance down the fastener shaft.

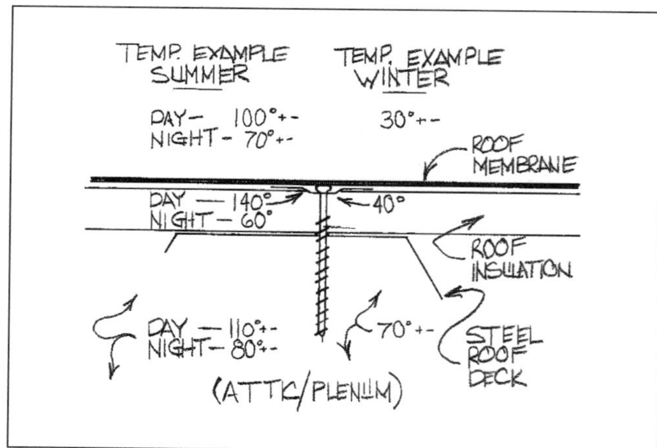

Figure 2.2 Fastener showing thermal bridging.

Warmer temperatures can be reasonably expected toward the lower end of the fastener shank since it exists on the underside of the roof deck in the warmer attic/plenum spaces.

If warm, moist air comes into contact with a portion of the fastener which is at or below dew-point temperature, condensation on the fastener will occur. It perhaps will only occur on the fasteners because they have introduced (by conductance) cold temperature extremes not experienced at the same level and location within the insulation assembly.

Again, multilayered roof insulation systems isolate the fastener assembly from temperature extremes. The layer of roof insulation covering the fastener head prevents the fastener assembly from getting cold enough to reach dew point within a warm and humid attic/plenum cavity. (See Fig. 2.16.) Such extreme conditions usually require a vapor retardant, installed to the top of the insulation layer, which is mechanically attached.

Different types of corrosion-resistance coatings are available on most screw fasteners to resist detrimental actions and reactions. However, even if the screw fastener is rust-resistant, water condensate on a fastener shaft can corrode and compromise the surrounding metal roof decking at the penetration, possibly resulting in an unsecured roof system.

VAPOR DRIVE

Heat flow through the assembly and subsequent moisture vapor drive can be either allowed or restricted by certain material usage and placement within the roof assembly. In the southern United States, where summers are hot and the air humid, vapor retardants are not recommended. In the colder regions of the United States, vapor barriers may be a necessity. (See Sec. 2.3.3.)

Self-Drying Roof Concept. In the southern United States, a self-drying roof concept is normally used in the design. In the cold (30 to 40°F) and less humid winter months, moisture-laden air is driven from the heated building interior toward the cooler and less humid exterior environment.

The upward vapor drive is stopped at the roof membrane, which also acts as a vapor barrier during that season. When the warm and moist air contacts the cooler roof membrane, condensation may occur on the bottom side of the roof membrane. The materials within the roof assembly will have to absorb this moisture.

However, in several months the cycle reverses, with air-conditioning cooling and dehumidifying the interior air spaces. The moisture turns to a vapor and is then driven from the hot and moist roof assembly to the plenum/attic cavity and down into the building interior, where it is displaced to the exterior by the air-conditioning equipment.

Vapor Retarders. In the colder climates, where temperatures are lower for longer periods of time, moisture vapor must be restricted from entering the roof assembly. For example, when the outside air temperature approaches 10°F with 20 percent humidity, and the building interior air spaces are at 70°F with 50 percent humidity, the moisture-laden air will drive toward the colder and dryer air spaces.

If the moisture vapor is allowed to pass upward into the roof insulation and assembly, the roof membrane will stop it. The colder temperatures at the roof membrane will cause the moisture to condense from the moisture-laden air to a liquid, and unlike in the southern climates, the moisture will remain for extended periods of time. Unacceptable saturation is often the result. In such cases a vapor retardant is placed at a strategic location within the roof insulation assembly. Since the insulation layers control temperature ranges, the dew point cannot be reached and no condensation occurs. (See Fig. 2.16.)

Ventilation. Another way to address this problem is to ventilate the plenum/attic space with outside air. Today this is considered by many to be mandatory with metal roof systems, since bottom-side condensation on metal roof panels is a significant problem if vapor drive is not correctly addressed.

By continuously removing air from below the roof deck, unacceptable levels of moisture cannot be entrapped within the attic/plenum cavity, effectively preventing dew point from being reached. (See Sec. 10.2.) This air movement not only controls moisture within the attic/plenum cavity during winter, it also can significantly reduce cooling costs to the building interior during summer months. The disadvantage to this design process is the need to properly incorporate the appropriate number of ventilation openings to the building structure in the correct locations. (See Sec. 10.2.2.)

MOVEMENTS AND LOADS

Another major item which must be considered is loads that are imposed on the roof membranes, roof substrata, and roof supports. Loads can be dynamic (or live), in the form of foot and mechanical traffic traversing the roof surface, snow loads that change in weight with wind and temperature, rainfall, wind loads, earthquakes that cause both vertical and horizontal stress loads, and mechanized equipment, which, when running, causes a live load and, when not running, is a dead load.

Static (or dead) loads can also include the entire weight of the roof assembly, rooftop structures, or debris left on the rooftop. Another type of load—not as obvious but just as important—is thermal loading of the roof assembly.

Deck Deflection. Deck deflection and ensuing ponding water areas can cause serious problems for most roof membranes. A positive slope must be maintained at all locations across the roof plane and is normally achieved today by designing roof decks with a minimum slope of ¼-in fall on a 12-in run.

However, for reroof design, existing slopes and supports must be carefully analyzed. (See Sec. 13.1.3.) The slope of the roof deck was frequently minimal during the original design, and now that age and structural material fatigue have taken a toll, the minimal slope originally designed may no longer exist. In such a case, a tapered roof insulation system can be installed to create proper slopes for roof deck deflected areas. (See Sec. 8.1.4.) Tapered insulation is also used in many cases to create cricket systems which direct water to gutter and downspouts.

Ponding Water. Ponding water on a roof can create serious roof load concerns, with 1 in of water by 1 ft^2 weighing approximately 5 lb. (See Fig. 2.3.) A 10-ft by 10-ft pond of water of 1-in average depth will weigh as much as 500 lb. This weight increases and decreases as rainfall and sunlight add to or take away from the ponded area.

A cycle can be set up in which the pond of water, when at its maximum size, remains long enough to structurally affect the underlying roof support system, which many times is not correct or adequate at that location to accommodate the load. The pond can continue to grow due to its self-imposed weight, which therefore keeps increasing.

Another serious problem caused by ponding water areas on a rooftop is temperature variations within the ponded area. A temperature difference will exist at the roof membrane surface covered by ponding water, as opposed to the membrane surface outside of the ponding water area. (See Fig. 2.4.)

Temperature extremes are equalized within a very short distance between the cooler area within the pond and the hotter dry roof membrane surface. Many roof membrane systems will be adversely affected by this extreme temperature difference within the very short distance.

Figure 2.3 Water ponding. (*Courtesy of Centrum Engineering, Winston-Salem, N.C.*)

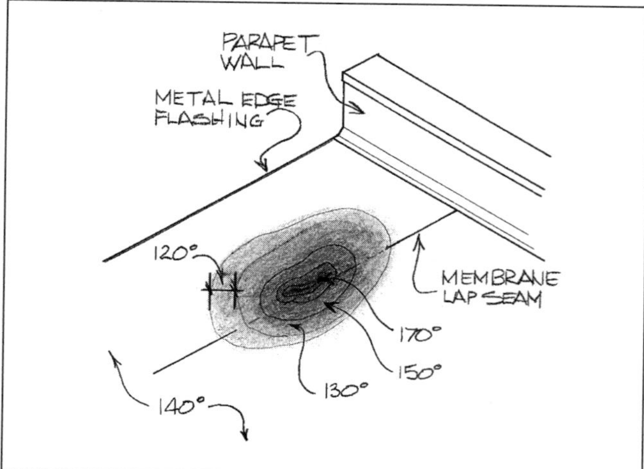

Figure 2.4 Ponded area temperature extremes. Notice that the temperature extremes increase as the size of the ponded area decreases due to evaporation. Darker areas are created toward the center of the ponded area due to a higher concentration of dust and dirt in the remaining water.

The dust, dirt, fungus, and mold which collects within the ponded areas turn these areas very dark. Even if they dry up, temperature variations within a small, localized area continue due to heat absorption of the dark areas as compared with the lighter-colored and cooler surrounding areas.

Thermal Loads and Shock. Thermal loading must be considered in other ways. Roof membrane surfaces absorb and also reflect solar radiation across a broad spectrum of light waves. The visible light seen with the naked eye is responsible for temperatures as radiant energy. Nonvisible ultraviolet light waves are responsible for accentuating, among other things, molecular reactions of materials.

Radiant energy, when absorbed by the roof membrane, causes thermal loading to roof membranes and roof assemblies. The unseen ultraviolet light causes molecular degradation of many materials, especially asphaltic compounds.

As an example, on an average 85°F summer day, with clear skies and full sunlight, temperatures under a roof-membrane surface coated with reflective aluminum coating have been recorded at 140°F. During the night, the temperature under the same roof membrane will be 10°F cooler than the 70°F ambient air temperature. (Refer to Table 2.2.)

Dark surface membranes, with black being the extreme, will experience even greater temperature differences. A temperature swing of over 100 percent in a 24-h period is not unusual for such roof systems. A cloud passing over the rooftop can cause as much as a 15 to 20°F temperature change in minutes.

With metal roofing this temperature swing is often greater and quicker. The metal roofing material reacts to the temperature change by expanding and contracting. If not properly considered and designed for, the movements of the metal panels can often cause unacceptable noise within the building interior. (See Sec. 10.1.1.)

This movement of roof systems, mainly the result of rapid cooling, is considered herein as *thermal shock*. The most exposed layers of the roof system will react first to a quick reduction in temperatures, such as can be caused by a midday summer shower. Underlying components are not as quickly affected since they are protected from rapid temperature changes by the overlying roof materials and the mass thereof.

Systems which are least susceptible to thermal shock would be roof membranes covered with gravel surfacing, being either built-up roof systems or aggregate ballasted systems. The mass of the aggregate acts as a buffer and hinders contraction from rapid temperature reduction. Naturally, an insulated concrete paver surface is the most efficient at preventing thermal shock to a roof membrane. (See Sec. 6.1.2.)

We must qualify the preceding by stating that thermal shock, as we define it here, is not considered by many roof experts to be a serious problem. We believe that thermal shock is not a serious problem but that it is a factor contributing to roof deterioration.

Any type of structural component—especially steel—which penetrates through the roof system can cause unusual stresses attributed to the temperature of the component as it compares with the surrounding roof systems. The surrounding roof membrane will move around the base of the roof penetration structure during thermal loading and/or thermal shock cycles. Damage can be prevented by the design of proper roof flashings. (See Fig. 12.1.)

Sheet metal flashings, and how they are installed and incorporated into the total system, have long been a problem area in roof systems. The problems stem from the expansion and contraction of the sheet metal flashings, which are a direct result of thermal loading. (See Sec. 12.2.1.) Thermal shock, to which the metal flashings must react quickly, can cause roof membrane stress at the flashing plies which seal the metal into the roof membrane. (See Sec. 2.3.1.)

Wind Loads. As solar radiation produces serious loads and dynamics to a roof system that are not always visible, wind loads are also often unrecognized while occurring. These factors must be recognized and taken into consideration during the design. (See Sec. 2.2.2.)

Wind loads can be minor but are normally constant with some roof membrane systems, such as the single-ply roof system that is mechanically attached. In this case, the sheet membrane, between fastener lines, will flutter and move with the breeze. The fastener and stress plate assembly will have this load transferred to it. If the fastener is installed incorrectly (at the wrong location into a metal deck such as the flute instead of the pan) or if the insulation layers are too thick and rotation of the fasteners begins, wind blow-off of the mechanically attached single-ply system can result as the fasteners fail. (See Fig. 2.5.) Also, if fasteners are attacked by corrosion due to condensation resulting from vapor drive (see "Thermal Bridging of Insulation Fasteners: Corrosion") or corrosion from elements within the roof deck, insulation blow-off due to corrosion can occur.

Wind loads can also be more dynamic and dramatic, such as during hurricanes. Factory Mutual (FM) publishes guidelines for roof system resistance to wind loss, as does Underwriters Laboratories and the major building code bodies. FM standards are probably the most referenced within the roof design community. FM Loss Prevention standards take into account the minute details such as wood nailer at the roof perimeter edge, the type of product the nailer must be from, the type of fasteners used to secure the nailer to the structure, and the type, amount, and spacing of fasteners to be used when installing flashing to this perimeter blocking. (See Sec. 14.3.3.)

Total roof assemblies can achieve wind resistance compliance with FM standards, but the designer must begin at the roof deck, specifying tested and approved decking, installed by means and methods tested and approved by FM, and including insulation products (if any), base sheets, fasteners, membranes, surfacings, and coatings. All components in that specific configuration must be approved by FM if the total system is specified to be in compliance with FM wind loss prevention requirements. (See Sec. 14.3.5.)

Most often a full system wind loss design is not used. Instead, specifications require the roof insulation layers and/or base sheet ply to be attached to the roof structure in accordance with FM requirements. As already stated, this often is not technically possible.

Catastrophic wind loss of roof systems is due to negative pressures created by high winds passing over the building top and can be aided by positive pressure created by winds entering the building interior through any open windows, doors, etc. This fluid-properties effect is the same thing that lifts airplanes off the ground and can be very powerful. During such instances, negative pressures are greatest at the corners of the roof, followed by the edges or sides, with the least amount of pressure in the center of the roof area.

The total building and the total roof system must be designed to resist both negative external pressures and any possible positive internal pressures. FM requirements and industry standards require 50 to 100 percent more fastener assemblies to be used within the perimeter and corner areas than in the field of the roof system.

Additionally, the fastener type and spacing requirements differ for attachment of base sheets and/or roof insulations. This difference is based upon height and terrain surrounding the building structure. Specifying a standard or generic fastener pattern is not correct design practice since the patterns often change. (See Fig. 2.6 and Sec. 14.3.3.)

2.1.2 Maintenance Requirements

MAINTENANCE

Will the client maintain the roof system? Most people do not think about the roof until it starts to leak. Unfortunately, experience has shown that many people and organizations fit into this category.

In such a situation, it may be possible to overdesign the roof system in some respects so that it will function effectively for an extended period of time before leaks start, and once leaks begin, it is hoped they can be confined to that roof area. (See Fig. 2.7.) This may cost

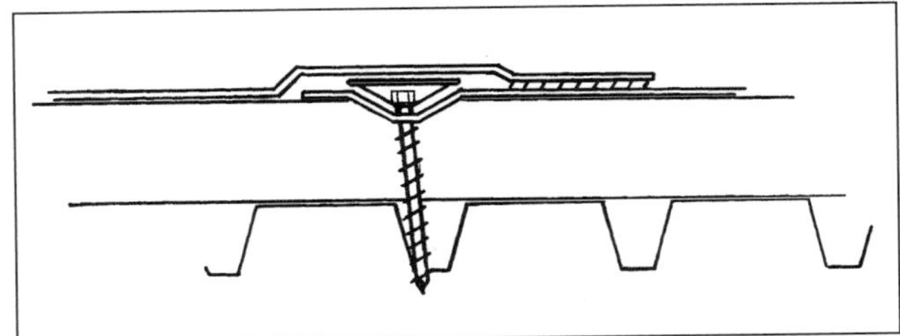

Figure 2.5 Incorrect fastener installation.

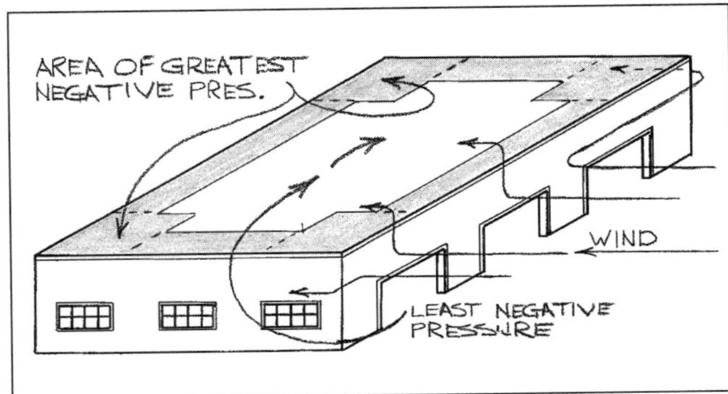

Figure 2.6 Roof pressure areas.

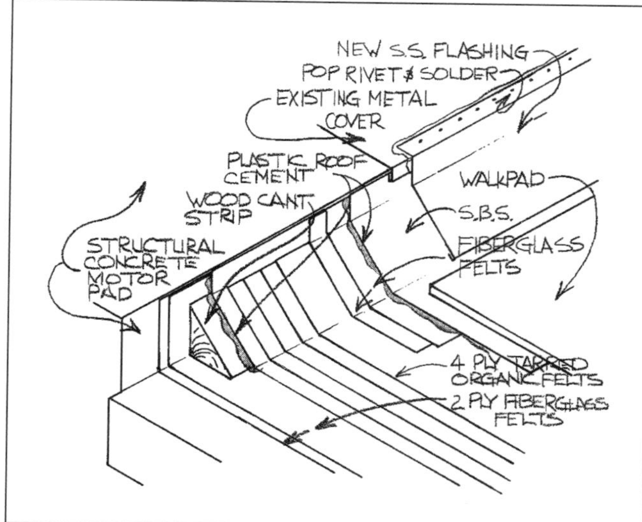

Figure 2.7 Overdesigned roof area.

more during the original construction, but when considered on a life-cycle cost basis, the extra up-front expenditure is often justifiable. (See Sec. 2.1.4.)

Some roof systems are less maintenance-intensive than others, such as metal roofing compared to the more maintenance-intensive built-up roofing. However, the less maintenance-intensive systems may be harder and more costly to repair or sectionally replace than others. This should be considered during design, based upon an evaluation of the client's roof maintenance program.

In order for the client to achieve the maximum use of the roof system, maintenance must be performed. After maintenance comes repair, and after repair comes replacement. Some (most) skip the maintenance phase, going directly to repair. Lack of roof maintenance can lead to premature roof failure and replacement.

The designer is in no way responsible for how well the client maintains the property, but a system should be designed to be as maintenance-friendly as possible. Maintenance begins with inspection. Inspection normally begins on the rooftop at the roof edges and flashing details. (See Sec. 13.1.3.)

Conforming to the total building concept, roof access should be easy, normally via a roof hatch. Regrettably, roof hatch access is often not designed into roof systems.

However, once on the rooftop, the inspector should scrutinize the edge and flashing details. All base flashings on flexible roof membranes should be with cant strip. (See Sec. 12.3.1.) On metal roof systems the base flashings are of metal, and the metal flashings should be able to expand and contract as required, while at the same time not restricting movement of the metal roof panels. Additionally, removable counterflashings are an advantage and of great benefit during the maintenance/repair/replacement procedures. Although more expensive than nonremovable counterflashings, they are more economical in the long run, allowing for complete and easy inspection, maintenance, and/or repair. The removable flashing can be removed and reinstalled. (See Sec. 12.2.9.)

Roof problems and maintenance requirements first become evident at flashing areas. This can be related to:

- Thermal shock
- Exposure to ultraviolet radiation
- Abuse by rooftop equipment service personnel
- Building component movement which is independent of the roof structure/system
- Poor workmanship on the part of the roof installer

Some of these problems can be designed out of the roof system—for example, independent movement problems—while others can have special materials incorporated into the system which help prevent failure and allow for low maintenance. Such items could include a special, tough layer of roof material applied to the outside of the base flashing which protects the underlying base flashing materials from ultraviolet radiation and/or foot-traffic abuse. (See Fig. 2.8.) Still other problems require walkways or walkpads for rooftop service personnel. However, it seems that rooftop personnel inevitably leave the designated walkway areas, and roof damage can still occur.

As designers, we must understand and appreciate the maintenance needs of the roof assemblies we design.

2.1.3 Owner Ability/Function

Will the roof need to be maintained? Some clients do not expect to be in the building for an extended period

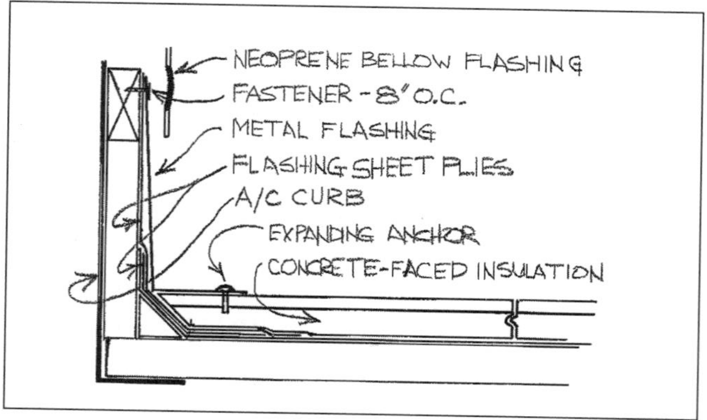

Figure 2.8 Walkpad and base flashing.

of time. For example, a retail outlet for a convenience store chain may be designed with materials that have a shorter life cycle (such as one layer of modified bitumen membrane over a ply of base sheet) than those used on a structure like a state capitol (perhaps standing-seam copper roof panels). The convenience store may have a synthetic plaster exterior wall system on metal studs applied directly over polystyrene insulation, whereas the capitol building will have granite walls. This life-cycle cost must be weighed against the client's expected occupancy period in the building.

We are in no way trying to advocate or imply that inferior roof systems should ever be designed. Nonetheless, it is a fact that some systems (the aforementioned single-layer modified bitumen over a fiberglass base to a nailable roof deck is a manufacturer-published specification) do not have the same expected life cycle as others.

In using a total building concept, the proper types of roof systems and materials should be used, not only to accommodate man-made and environmental conditions and impacts, but also to accommodate the client's long-term (or short-term) interest.

It is the owner's responsibility to biannually inspect the roof system. At a minimum, the gutters should be cleaned of all debris, the surface condition of the roof checked, base flashings around rooftop equipment inspected for damage, and the roof edges checked for signs of splitting or delamination.

Some owners of large institutions, such as school districts and state agencies, have the ability (funds) to create roof management programs which ensure that the condition of roof systems is monitored. Other owners do not have this ability, although it is still their function. In this case, a low-maintenance roof system needs to be designed.

2.1.4 Expected Life Cycle

An effective building system design can be evaluated by using life-cycle cost. The life cycle of a system, especially a system that needs maintenance, will be strongly influenced by the maintenance program—or lack thereof.

LIFE-CYCLE EVALUATION

Life-cycle cost analysis and evaluation are a complicated matter, unless you are a CPA, contractor, systems expert, maintenance expert, psychic, and economist. For persons possessing many of these skills, measuring life-cycle costs of buildings and building systems must be far easier and accurate than for the rest of us.

The life-cycle cost (LCC) of a structure or, in our case, the roof system, includes all the relevant costs associated with the system for its entire useful life. These costs include:

- Design
- Construction
- Maintenance
- Repair
- Replacement

of the roof system. Life-cycle cost analysis is useful during the design of a new roof or roof replacement system. We can compare added expected life in relation to added materials and the costs thereof. We sometimes find that increasing the materials quality (better roof felts) and amounts (four plies instead of three) may increase the construction costs by 5 percent but increases the life cycle by only 1 percent, or vice versa.

In roof maintenance and repair design, life-cycle cost analysis is very important. It does no good to spend $10,000 on roof repairs which will keep the roof watertight for only one year before another $10,000 has to be spent, when the entire roof could be replaced for $25,000. At the end of the third year, the owner may have spent $30,000 and will still have to spend $25,000 to replace the roof, throwing away all the repair work that was already done, along with his or her money.

These are extreme examples, but they are important concepts to understand for evaluating the LCC of roof systems. Other concepts that are important but outside the scope of this manual are the cost of money, discount rates, inflation rates, constant-dollar value, present-dollar values, uniform capital recovery, and cash flows. For more information and an understanding of these important concepts, see ASTM E 917-93, Standard Practice for Measuring Life-Cycle Costs of Buildings and Building Systems.

For a building with an indefinite life span, calculate:

$$\left(\frac{\text{Initial roof cost}}{\text{number of years of expected life}}\right) + \left(\frac{\text{maintenance cost over the course of one maintenance cycle}}{\text{number of years in that cycle}}\right) + \left(\frac{\text{replacement cost}}{\text{number of expected years of life}}\right)$$

This calculation produces per-year life-cycle cost, which can be compared from one roof system to another. However, the expected life span of the building is also a consideration, if the building is not expected to last the life of the new roof. As an example, a copper roof system will have a low LCC factor with a high front-end cost factor. If not allowed to achieve its full life cycle (100+ years) the LCC is increased.

Sometimes specific life expectancy of the client's building is shorter than the expected life of the roof. In such a case, divide the building life expectancy into the initial cost and do not add a replacement-cost factor. This will provide per-year roof costs. However, maintenance and repair costs may become a factor if the roof (and building) is expected to function longer than five to seven years.

Many variables and unknown factors are involved with projecting the life-cycle cost of roof systems. Maintenance and repair are very strong and dominant factors when calculating the LCC of roof systems. With proper maintenance and repair, a roof system can last much longer than normally expected. Without such maintenance and repair, the roof system will probably not achieve the expected life span.

Also, the application process and workmanship are factors in allowing roof systems to achieve the expected life cycle. Poor workmanship is sometimes hard to detect when visually examining a completed and existing roof system. Complete evaluation is a must when calculating the expected LCC of an existing roof. (See Sec. 13.1.3.)

Assumptions must be made when calculating roof-system LCC. Roof life-cycle costing sometimes seems to be more of an art than a science. For example, the person doing the analysis must determine (assume) how long the base flashings at roof-mounted equipment will last before maintenance is required and then how long the maintained flashings will last before replacement is necessary.

On low-sloped roof assemblies, the membrane flashings at the metal edge, roof drain, parapet walls, expansion joints, etc., will all have to be maintained or repaired or replaced. On metal roof systems, the surfacing finish (paint, metallic coating) will have to be maintained and then coated, and attention will have to be given to flashing maintenance at rooftop penetrations. For slate and tile roof systems, the gutters will probably need maintenance and repair at the lap joints and the roof flashings will eventually need repair, as well as probably the hip and ridge areas.

If the flashings begin to leak and are not immediately repaired to a watertight condition, damage to underlying components can occur. This damaged material—for example, wet roof insulation if saturated enough—must be replaced or damage to the roof can spread like a cancer.

This becomes a cost factor that was not programmed into the original LCC calculations. Rooftop workers, such as A/C service personnel or window washers, can damage roof flashings and membranes. This damage has to be repaired or replaced, adding costs that were not expected in the initial LCC evaluations.

Torrential and extended periods of rain, excessively hot and long summers, exceptionally cold and extended winters, and exceptionally diverse climatic conditions causing thermal shock can all affect the life-cycle span of a roof.

Some designers require a roof manufacturer's warranty for the roof system, mistakenly thinking this defines the expected life span and life-cycle cost of the roof system. It does not! Many manufacturer's warranties become invalid if periodic inspection and required maintenance are not performed on the roof system.

The information contained within this manual will help isolate problems and produce accurate answers that can be used in LCC analysis. Sometimes outside guidance is required from experts in roof LCC analysis.

Computer programs requiring little investment are available that are specifically designed for roof LCC analysis. Investment in such a program is often less than the design-hour/investigation time invested without such a program. Further information and guidance is available from:

The Roof Consultants Institute
7424 Chapel Hill Road
Raleigh, NC 27607
(919) 859-0742

2.1.5 Environmental Impact

Everything we do as individuals and as a society has an environmental impact to a greater or lesser extent. The environment must be considered in the total systems concept.

Every material we use in construction comes from a process which used energy to gather it, refine or produce it, ship it, erect or install it, and, finally, maintain it. Construction materials may or may not be from renewable resources but all consumed, at some time, energy produced from finite resources.

An environment can be global, regional, local, or immediate. The materials we specify affect one, if not all, of these areas. Some things have global, regional, and local impact, such as chlorofluorocarbon (CFC) gases which contribute to the greenhouse effect. Other items have mainly regional and local effects, such as manufacturing facilities which can pollute our air and waterways. Still others can detrimentally affect our local environment, such as closing landfills as a result of overuse or clear-cutting local forest areas for wood and paper products. On a more minute scale the immediate environment needs to be considered, and detrimental aspects can include such items as excessive noise levels within the building structure and poor ventilation.

RECYCLABILITY

As society has progressed, environmental issues have aroused greater concern. At the time of this publication, roof insulations are being evaluated for their recyclability, as are some forms of roof membranes. A material's ability to be recycled will be an issue of the future, as will the amount of energy and natural resources required to produce it.

Sometimes recycling of hazardous waste is the most acceptable manner in which to dispose of the materials. As an example, lead flashings are considered hazardous materials that cannot be disposed of in a standard landfill due to the possibility of groundwater contamination. However, lead has a salvage value and can be sold to reclaim-salvage yards.

Landfill and disposal sites have become a problem in the United States and other areas of the globe. Roofing debris takes up considerable space in a landfill, and it would probably be truthful to state that the majority of construction debris existing in landfills is roof debris.

In considering the total building, the walls, foundation, and roof constitute most of building materials used. However, of these systems, the roof is the only one that is scheduled to be periodically replaced.

Originally designing a roof system with components that are reusable is a good environmental practice. This can involve specifying items such as pipe flashing vent hoods and stacks made of copper or stainless steel which have a long life span. It can mean using an insulation system that is manufactured for installation to the top of the roof assembly, such as concrete-faced polystyrene insulation panels used to create an inverted roof membrane assembly. (See Secs. 8.1.6 and 6.1.2.) Insulation can also be laid loose under the roof membrane and the whole assembly ballasted to secure it to the building top. In this case, the insulation should be reusable.

RETROFIT

Another way to protect the environment and our resources is to design roof systems that are appropriate for retrofit purposes. In this case the existing roof system is left in place and covered over with a new system, which is sometimes referred to as *re-cover*. By this means, roof insulation is saved.

Sometimes it is more appropriate to remove the roof membrane and evaluate the underlying roof insulation layers for water contamination. After replacing wet insulation panels, new insulation can be installed over the existing insulation, thereby creating a smooth surface for the new roof system. Realize that a large percentage of roof debris volume is the insulation layers.

HAZARDOUS MATERIALS

In other cases, recovery or encapsulation of the hazardous materials is the most effective procedure in regard to both budget and the environment. Asbestos-containing materials are hazardous and require expensive abatement and disposal in limited landfill areas. It is often possible to leave an asbestos-containing material roof system in place and install a retrofit system over it. However, with retrofitting or encapsulation it is inevitable that, eventually, the hazardous material will have to be dealt with. This will occur when the subsequent top layers fail and no additional materials can be added to the system, requiring removal of all materials, including the bottom hazardous materials or it can occur when the building is demolished and the issue of hazardous materials will have to be addressed.

In the roofing industry we are faced with hazardous material daily in the form of asphalt fumes which have been classified by the EPA as hazardous, coal tar pitch fumes which are determined to contain carcinogens, and the volatile organic contaminants (VOC) regulation imposed on many of the adhesives and coatings used in roofing. Proper evaluation of the design is essential to limit the use of hazardous materials where possible, to encapsulate by retrofit or remove by abatement, and to recycle all other materials when possible.

2.1.6 Building Location

Another factor we must consider when evaluating the total building and total roof system is geographic location of the building. Building location dictates climate: whether it is extremely hot or cold, wet or dry, windy or corrosive. This can limit our choice of roof systems and types.

A roof system that is appropriate for a building in Phoenix, Arizona, may not be acceptable for a building in New York City. Thermal shock (wide temperature swings in short periods of time) will be an influence on the roof in Phoenix. A roof system that is capable of resisting a temperature of 150°F+ at the surface is required, which in turn may well become 70°F or less on the roof surface at night. We can assume that high-R-value roof insulation will be used in the roof assembly under such conditions. A possible solution would be a polymeric single-ply with insulated pavers over the surface as ballast. (See Sec. 6.1.2.)

In New York City there may be more options available for roof system selection. In New York the system must withstand higher wind velocities, longer and colder winters, with snow loads and larger amounts of rainfall. A typical built-up roof or modified bitumen roof may suffice in this circumstance, unless it is at a location such as LaGuardia Airport. In this case, a system that is capable of resisting aviation fuel contaminants and high winds, while at the same time is aesthetically pleasing (because much of the roof area at an airports is visible), would be more in order.

LOCAL CONTRACTOR BASE

Sometimes the optimum roof for the building and the climate is not feasible. You can design the perfect roof system, but if workers from Peru have to be brought in to install it, it is not the best selection. This holds true not only for the roof, but for the accessories and components that must be installed to create the total roof system.

For example, if the system will require an extensive, tapered roof insulation system that reverses in numerous locations to serve as crickets, drain sumps, etc., the technical requirements of the system may be beyond the practical abilities of the local roof workers. If you proceed with the design, one or two things can happen. First, the cost for the roof system will be out of budget. Second, the system will not be installed correctly and roof failure will result. Neither result is in keeping with good design practice. (See Sec. 15.1.)

2.2 INDETERMINATE ELEMENTS OF DESIGN

There are many forces that must be understood and designed for when dealing with roof systems. Some of these forces are predetermined (determinate) while others are not predetermined but may become forces or factors which the roof system must successfully deal with (indeterminate).

Some elements are both determinate and indeterminate—for example, wind, which is a determinate force, but becomes indeterminate when hurricane-force winds interact with the roof assembly. In many situations we place determinate elements into indeterminate categories, in order to stave off catastrophic losses in the event that determinate factors become exceptional. For the purposes of this discussion, the indeterminate elements which act upon the roof system are:

- *Precipitation* in the form of rain, snow, sleet, or hail
- *Wind* in the form of hurricanes, tornadoes, or typhoons
- *Fire* attacking the assembly
- *Movements* as can be experienced during short but extreme loading situations, e.g. roof tear-off, equipment transportation, earthquakes
- *Interior building environments* as relating to fire, but also considering other-than-normal temperatures, humidities, and occupancy
- *Roof traffic* as excessive numbers of or negligent workers can damage areas of the roof if not properly designed for

2.2.1 Precipitation

RAIN

Precipitation is a determinate factor of roof design—we know it is going to rain on the roof system. However, once in a great while, rain will fall at excessive rates. The system must be designed to:

- Withstand any rising water on the surface.
- Restrict from entry any water that is wind-driven uphill or upslope.
- Adequately dispose of the torrential rain in an expedient manner.

Various code and standard agencies use tables to calculate maximum rainfall amounts for various parts of the country. In roof design, we most often use the table published by the Sheet Metal and Air Conditioning Contractors National Association (SMACNA) to determine the maximum amount of rainfall that can be expected in a particular geographic location. Gutters, scuppers, and downspouts are then designed in proper widths, sizes, and locations to accommodate any exceptional rainfall amounts that may occur. (See Secs. 12.2.7 and 12.2.8.)

It is standard design practice to elevate the top of all base flashing a minimum of 8 in above the surface of the roof. (See Sec. 12.2.) This prevents any wind-blown rain from entering the building through the top of the flashing. Also, water had better never reach an 8-in depth across your roof or you will have more problems than roof leaks!

With a parapet wall situation, always include emergency overflow scuppers slightly elevated above the roof surface. These are secondary overflows and will prevent water from deflecting or destroying the roof structure if the primary overflows become clogged or overloaded. (See Fig. 2.9.)

In areas where freezing winter temperatures are normal, restrict gutters and downspouts from north sides of the building faces if possible. Water can freeze within these assemblies and damage the components while at the same time restricting proper flow of the water from the roof surfaces. If unavoidable, use a downspout style with an open face. (See Fig. 12.28.)

HAILSTORM DAMAGE

Hailstones, an indeterminate factor in roof design, must be a consideration in many parts of the United States. A 2-in hailstone reaches a terminal velocity of 135 ft/s, exerting 22 lb/ft^2 of force upon impact.

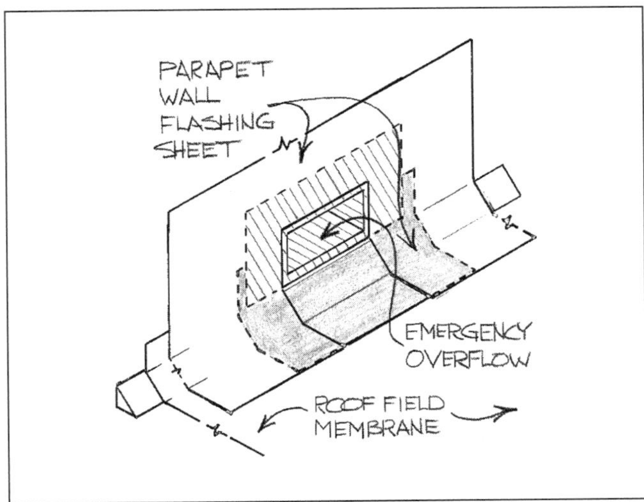

Figure 2.9 Emergency overflow scupper.

Gravel or slag surfacing is a recognized protector of roof surfaces in a hailstorm. On systems that are of smooth surface, such as single-ply polymerics, a rigid roof insulation with high compressive strengths should be used.

Skylights are often protected by the use of heavy steel wire-mesh screens or cages. Other rooftop equipment can be saved from damage by use of wire-screen protectors.

At base flashing areas, use wood cant strips, not fiber cants. Wood cants help the base flashings resist hailstone impact without rupture.

SNOW

Snow loads to a roof system are a structural concern. Every year structural failures of roof decks are attributed to snow loads. In a paper by Dr. W. Lee Shoemaker, P.E. (*Contractors Guide,* 1995), he attributes structural deck failure to snow loading in the following cases.

- The winter of 1978–1979 resulted in about 140 building failures in the Chicago metropolitan area and more than 100 failures in Wisconsin.
- During the winter of 1981–1982, exceptionally heavy local snowfalls accompanied by strong winds resulted in damage to a number of roofs in the United Kingdom.
- An elementary school library roof in Anchorage, Alaska, collapsed in January 1984 under the weight of 15 in of snow.
- A department store roof collapsed in Buffalo, New York, in January 1985 after high snowdrifts formed.
- A roller skating rink building collapsed in Richmond, Virginia, in January 1987 after a few feet of snow fell.
- A roof collapsed in Pittsburgh, Pennsylvania, following a December 1992 snowstorm, killing three employees.
- Over 50 textile and carpet mills collapsed under snow loads in March 1993 in northwestern Georgia.
- Over 100 collapses resulted from the severe March 1993 storm in the eastern United States.

The paper further states that failures encompassed all types of construction and not all failures were due to unexpected amounts of snowfall. Some of the structures were in deteriorated condition, some were improperly designed, and some were improperly constructed.

A significant problem with snow loading occurs to sloped, gabled roof decks. As the wind blows, the snow is moved from the windward side of the deck, with significant amounts being deposited to the leeward side of the roof. This results in uneven load dispersal across the building's structural system, and severe damage can occur.

A special analysis is required of metal buildings and many metal roof systems. Metal building systems are considered light construction, as compared to most standard construction systems. As such, their structural capabilities and allowances for exceptional snow loading are often marginal.

Professor Michael O'Rourke of Rensselaer Polytechnic Institute, Troy, New York, has done research in the area of snow loading, the results of which have contributed to some of the building code standards used today. Under a research project sponsored by the Metal Building Manufacturers Association and the American Iron and Steel Institute, further research is being conducted regarding unbalanced snow loading. Revised standards are expected in the future.

For roof design in snow country, eliminate as much as possible roof vents and penetrations. Snow masses sliding down the roof slope have been known to shear off vents, stacks, and even chimneys. Route all penetrations out the gable ends of the building. If this is not possible, design the vents for placement at the ridge. Always extend vent piping high enough to prevent blockage of the opening by accumulated snow, or asphyxiation of the inhabitants can occur.

For metal roof design in snow country, eliminate valleys. Snow accumulation in valleys, and the subsequent avalanche from the roof, can cause the standing ribs and seams to be bent over and disjoined. Avoid chimneys that require crickets for the same reason. In the event that valleys are unavoidable, create a wide and tapering valley of smooth metal panels without ribs or standing seams. The taper must be wide enough at all locations to prevent the accumulated snow mass from reaching any ribs or standing seams. When designed as described, the appearance of this smooth, wide, and tapering valley often detracts from the appearance of the structure.

In severe snow country many designers prefer a warm eave. This allows the ice dam that surely will form to be continuously melted by the warm roof at the eave. A warm eave is possible only if a soffit is used to completely enclose the eave overhang and warm air from the attic space is allowed to circulate to the eave.

ICE DAMMING

Ice damming at roof eaves occurs mainly when the eaves of the roof extend past the warmer attic/plenum area. Ice damming occurs as the result of a thaw-and-freeze cycle and is a more severe and persistent problem than many realize. The problem normally concerns sloped roofs, which are predominantly shingles in residential sectors and metal roof assemblies used in both commercial and residential construction.

Snow accumulates on the roof surface, and as the heat from the building interior is transferred through the roof deck, melting occurs. Heat is also transferred through snow in the infrared spectrum. As the snow water runs to the eaves it encounters the cold temperatures at the unheated eaves and freezes. This phenomenon is repeated in cycles and is further compounded by gutters which can fill with ice from the snow water.

The ice dam acts as a stop for the snow water. At the eaves location where low temperature extremes exist, the water freezes and adds to the size of the ice dam. However, when the ice dam grows to where it extends up the roof slope over the heated attic/plenum area, the water does not freeze as fast and to such an extent.

Since composition shingles, slates, tiles, etc., are water shedders and not water barriers (see Sec. 1.1) the snow water will back up under roof coverings and enter the building. In this case many people would remove the ice dam, which can lead to considerable expense and possible roof damage. Also, removing the snow and ice from the eave location only will not eliminate ice-damming problems. It will only move the ice dam upslope to the area where the snow excavation stopped. As many who live in snow country have learned, either remove all the snow from the roof slope or leave it alone.

Proper roof design can eliminate ice damming in many climates and limit it in severe climates. The design incorporates several systems:

- Ventilation
- Insulation
- Water barriers

Using these items in conjunction, they complement each other. Deleting one or more of the items can create too much dependence on the remaining systems.

Of the three, ventilation is probably the most important. The objective of ventilating the attic/plenum space is to keep the bottom side of the roof deck, and thereby the roof surface, at the coldest temperature naturally possible. This reduces the amount of snow water which reaches the eaves and freezes as it contacts the air. Experts explain that snow water can never be completely eliminated. The infrared energy of sunlight will penetrate the snow mass covering the roof, and this energy will melt the snow at the roof level. Thaw cycles will also produce snow water.

Insulation is required above the ceiling to reduce energy loss into the cold attic spaces. If budgets permit, roof insulation panels can be installed into the deck assembly and be covered with sheathing, to which the roof system is nailed. This insulation will separate the cold outside temperatures at the roof surface from the warmer temperatures within the attic/plenum area. It is not recommended to nail shingles, tiles, shakes, slates, etc., directly through roof insulations. (See Fig. 2.10.)

The third component, a water barrier, is the last line of defense. If all else has failed, any snow water reaching this barrier should be withheld by the barrier. Good design practice should always include an ice and water shield at the eave locations. This barrier is normally of a soft bitumen material from the modified bitumen family.

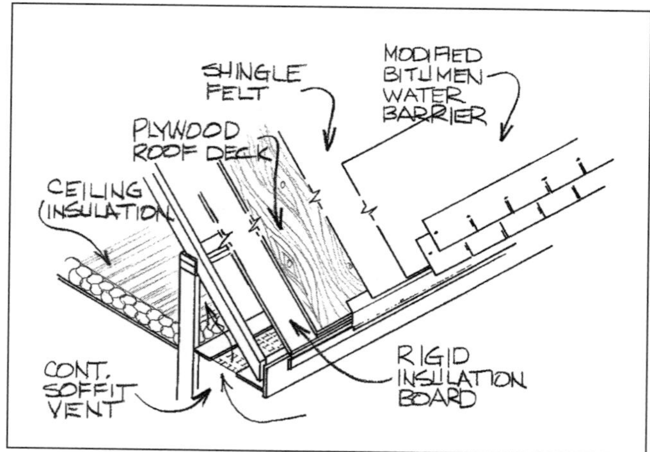

Figure 2.10 Vent/insulation attic/deck.

The shanks of the nails and fasteners which must penetrate it during shingle installation are theoretically sealed by the soft material.

The water barrier should extend up the roof slope a minimum of 24 in; however, this often is not far enough. For low-sloped roofs, the barrier may have to extend up the roof much farther. Use the barrier at valleys, chimneys, or roof penetrations where snow can accumulate.

2.2.2 Wind

Wind is a force that is usually, in some degree, acting upon a roof system. At certain times, wind forces can be extreme and such extreme forces, although indeterminate, must be designed for. Factory Mutual guidelines for wind resistance are the most common standards used in roof design.

PHYSICS OF WIND AND ROOF STRUCTURES

When thinking of roof loss under wind stress, realize that roofs are not blown off, they are sucked off. (See Fig. 2.11.) Winds traveling at high speeds create negative pressures on the roof surfaces. This is the same principle that allows an airwing to fly—faster-moving wind on top of the airfoil creates pressure that is lower (negative) on top of the surface than on the bottom surface and gives lift to the airwing.

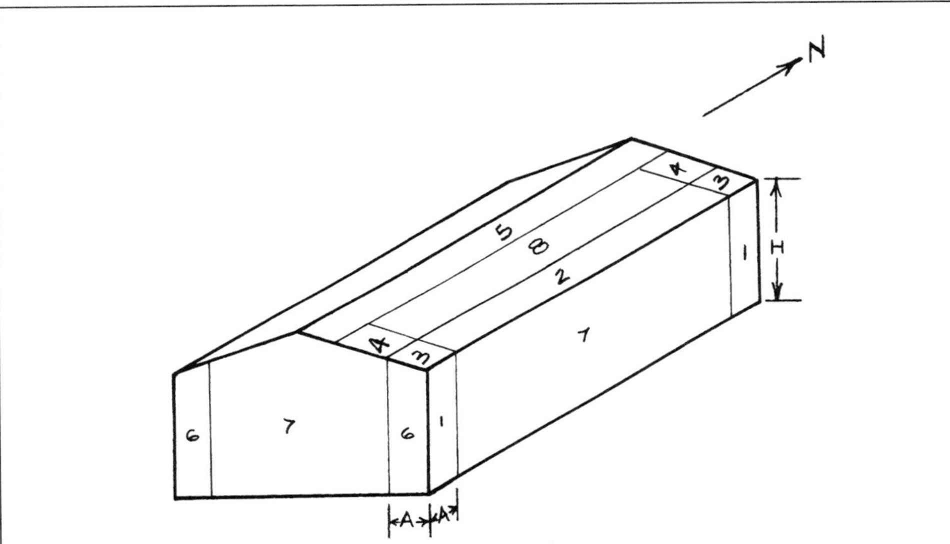

Increase coefficients (7) and (8) by 25% when openings in any wall exceed 20% of wall area.

	C_p		Wind dir. for forces on areas shown
	Flat roof	*Gabled roof*	
1 Wall Cor. Strips	−2.0	−2.0	W–E
2 Roof Peri-Strips-Eave	−2.0	−2.0	E–W
3 Roof Cor. Areas	−3.0	−2.0	NE or SE
4 Roof Peri-Strips-Rake	−2.0	−2.0	N–S or S–N
5 Roof Ridge Strip	—	−1.5	W–E
6 Wall Cor. Strips	−2.0	−2.0	N–S
7 Between Cor. Strips	±1.0	±1.0	W–E or E–W
8 Inside Peri-Strips	−1.0	−1.0	E–W

Negative sign indicates force is away from surface. Dimension A is 0.1 times least building dimension or 0.4 H, whichever is smaller.

(Adapted from Factory Mutual Loss Prevention Data Sheets, FMRC, Walpole, Mass.)

Figure 2.11 Building stress areas.

Winds at high speed, being negative pressure, create lift at the surface of the roof system. The stresses are greater at the corners of the roof, followed by the edges of the roof, with lowest negative pressures occurring in the field of the roof assembly. If the roof system has slopes exceeding a 2-in rise per 12-in run, the physics changes somewhat. (See Fig. 10.9.)

WIND DESIGN CONSIDERATION

In designing roof structures, it is important that the edge components are tightly and permanently secured to the building structure, beginning with the bar joist, purlins, etc., and continuing through to the roof insulation layers and metal edge flashings.

Special concerns of wind loss prevention design must be considered if the building has large wall openings. In the event of high-wind situations, the openings, such as window walls and overhead bay doors, could be blown open and the rush of air into the building interior could greatly accentuate the difference between internal high pressure and exterior negative pressures.

The location, height, and geography of the surrounding area have a great influence on wind design resistance. Open fields, open areas, or large bodies of water around a building will allow wind to encounter the building structure unrestricted. Trees, buildings, broken terrain, etc., will block wind forces to a degree. Also to be considered is the height of the roof above ground level. The higher the roof, the faster the wind moves, perhaps unrestricted, until it encounters the roof system.

2.2.3 Fire

An indeterminate element in design is fire. We do not ever plan for it to happen, but we must consider it in our design work. As a result of catastrophic losses from unrestricted fire on top of or within a roof assembly, fire consumption and spread are closely regulated by all model building codes.

A General Motors assembly plant in Michigan was entirely destroyed by fire in the 1950s. Had the building been constructed under today's standards, the fire might have been controlled and the entire facility probably would not have been destroyed. Originating within the facility, the fire penetrated the roof deck and caught the built-up roof system on fire. Once burning, the roofing bitumen is akin to a grease fire and is very difficult to extinguish. The fire spread across the roof system, and, as a result, the entire facility was reduced to ruin in a short time. This catastrophic loss brought the issue of fire control as it relates to roof systems under close scrutiny.

Today we design against fire from interior sources and from exterior sources. All design procedures used for prevention of such fire and fire sources are beyond the scope of this manual; however, we should emphasize that roof systems must be designed to control and restrict fire until the building occupants are safe and emergency crews have had the time needed to extinguish the fire.

Fire normally reaches a roof system from external sources and internal sources, although with torch-applied roof membranes, buildings have been set on fire during roof construction. (See Sec. 9.1.2.) An internal fire must be controlled and restricted to the space or area in the building where it began. An external fire comes to the building from burning debris that originated at another site and is blown to or dropped upon the roof surface.

INTERNAL BUILDING FIRE

For internal fires, the roof support structure must withstand the temperatures without fatigue until the fire is extinguished. The roof deck is a prime consideration in fire resistance, and with wood roof decks, this is a problem. Fire-retardant plywood was introduced to the market in recent years and problems due to delamination while in normal service have sometimes occurred.

Steel, concrete, gypsum, and some forms of preformed panel decking are fireproof or fire resistant. However, thin deck materials, such as metal decking, require a noncombustible roof insulation overlay to create a fire-resistant roof deck assembly. In the event of internal fire, the roof deck and insulation create a fire barrier that will resist the fire. If the barrier fails, flame can reach the roof membrane, which in most cases is flammable.

Rooftop access hatches and doors, as well as skylights, are to be considered when designing for fire resistance. Interior flame may be well controlled by interior finishes, such as Sheetrock or by the roof deck assembly. If the fire penetrates through roof openings, such as skylights, it has direct access to a new fuel source, which is the roof membrane. If fire escape is across the rooftop, door openings can supply oxygen and fuel for the fire.

Roof surfaces can be designed to resist flame, but not the type of large, intense flame that could come through skylights, door openings, or roof ventilators. The breaching of these openings allows fuel, being oxygen, to further contribute to the internal fire.

Often, rooftop ventilators, equipment curbs, wood curbs at expansion joints, and so on, are present. These openings often use lumber materials somewhere in the assembly and involve direct access from the bottom side of the deck. Again, flame can spread directly up these openings, using the wood curbs as fuel, and ignite the roof surface. (See Fig. 2.12.)

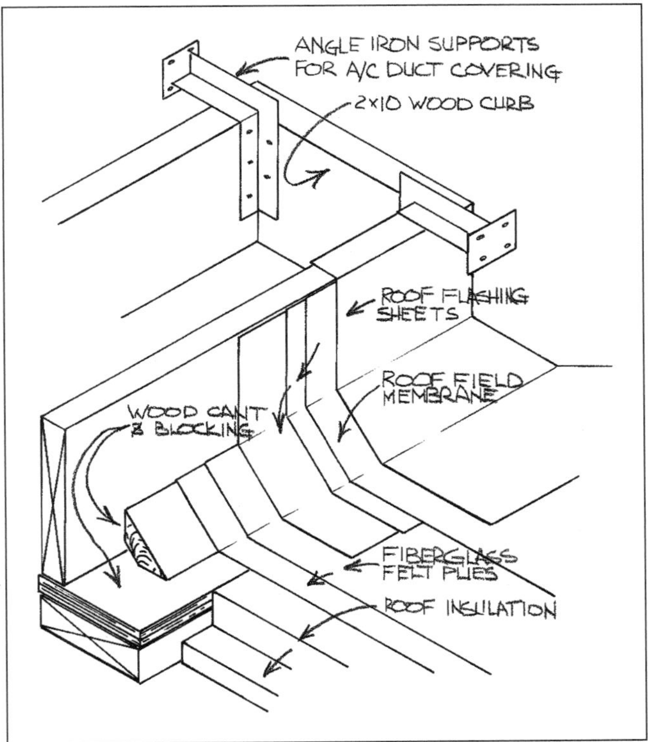

Figure 2.12 Wood roof curb.

EXTERNAL FIRE

Roof membranes are rated in various degrees of resistance to small, localized fire, using a *burning brand* test. This rates the resistance to the type of flame that is usually from blown or falling debris which comes from other sources, such as an adjacent building or from an adjacent part of the building that is burning.

Some roof membranes, such as those that are built up, are flammable. Some, such as modified bitumens, are flame resistant due to chemical additives, such as halogens. Some, such as metal, are considered noncombustible, although untreated metal can easily conduct sufficient heat to spread fire from flaming material on one side to flammable material on the other side.

A roof membrane's fire resistance can be increased by use of noncombustible surfacing, such as the gravel surfacing used in built-up roofing. Modified bitumen membranes sometimes use a clay-based asphalt emulsion coating, normally brush-applied by the roofer to the installed material's surface. Other modified bitumen products incorporate foil surfacings laminated at the factory to the material's surface.

To achieve higher fire ratings with some polymeric single-ply, aggregate ballast can be installed; the sheet can be covered with a concrete paver system, or an elastomeric coating may suffice.

In areas such as southern California where brush fires pose periodic threats to structures, materials such as tile, slate, and metal roofing are used. Their natural fire resistance makes these materials good design choices for resisting external fire hazard.

2.2.4 Movement

Building movement and subsequent roof structure/system movement are not uncommon, although in most cases they are negligible. Factors in designing roofs to accommodate roof structure movement include the use of expansion joints in the field of the roof, designing for movement of base flashings at roof penetrations, and using expansion joints, if required, at parapet/building walls. Two basic styles of design can be used with parapet walls, depending on whether the roof deck is supported by the building wall. (See Sec. 3.1.)

If the roof deck is not supported by the building, allowances for movement at the interface of the roof membrane and parapet or building wall *must* be allowed for by use of an expansion joint system. (See Fig. 3.16.) If there is no parapet or building wall, an expansion joint at the typical roof edge is not necessary—and could not be done anyway.

LOADING DURING CONSTRUCTION

Deck movement during construction will occur. However, the amount of movement is indeterminate, depending largely upon the live loading to the roof deck caused by roof materials, equipment, and personnel. Most roof deck assemblies are designed for 20-lb/ft^2 load tolerance to accommodate live loads.

During roof construction this limit may often be exceeded, but normally not to the extent that roof deck damage or failure is the result. Nor is it feasible to overdesign the deck structure to accommodate excessive loads due to roof construction, a phenomenon supposedly occurring once every 20 years.

However, roof design must consider the live load structural capability of the roof deck in regard to material and equipment loading. For example, if a single-ply roof system is to be secured to the building top with ballast, the construction crew can store too much ballast on an isolated area of the roof deck, with dire consequences.

Transporting the heavy ballast to the area of installation can damage the roof deck and/or underlying roof insulation. Damage concerns are not as great if the roof deck is structural concrete as compared with 22-gauge steel decking. After installation and uniform loading of the ballast materials, live-load concerns are negated.

Designers should carefully consider the live loads that are possible during construction. Specify, as required, weight limits which are not to be exceeded during roof storage and transportation.

SEISMIC LOADING

An indeterminate factor that some in the United States must deal with is loads placed upon building structures during earthquakes. One plausible solution to the limitation of roof damage during seismic load movements is the selection of an elastomeric roof membrane.

As the earthquake occurs, the roof deck undergoes what is termed *racking* in that it is twisted and somewhat oscillated. This is neither horizontal movement nor vertical movement but a combination of both. As the movement is transferred across the roof deck and roof membrane, the force is focused into the corners of the roof structure. At that point is where most damage will occur . . . if the building is left standing.

For earthquake-prone areas, roof membranes with elastomeric abilities are often selected. This includes modified bitumen membranes (see Sec. 9.1.3) or polymeric single-ply membranes.

Selection of the roof membrane can vary with the type of roof deck. The racking will be less severe if the roof deck is of reinforced structural concrete, and the racking will naturally be greater with materials such as wood or steel.

2.2.5 Interior Building Environments

FIRE

Fire hazard comes to the building structure from either the external or the internal environment. For external fire, the roof system can be specified so that it is fire resistant. ASTM E 108 is an often-used standard by which the external fire resistance of a roof assembly is rated.

Internal fire and the roof system's ability to resist the spread of flame are extremely important. If the fire proceeds into the roof system and ignites the roof membrane, the flame can spread across the entire roof surface. Other parts of the building, and probably the entire structure, will then be affected if not entirely destroyed.

Most commercial buildings have roof systems rated at 2-h resistance to bottom-side flame. This resistance allows enough time for the fire to be brought under control and extinguished before irreparable damage and roof deck failure occurs. Make sure the roof design allows for any openings or penetrations through the roof assembly to be resistant to flame. (See Sec. 2.2.3.)

HUMIDITY AND VAPOR CONTROL

Vapor drive is a determinate factor and must be considered in original roof design. (See Sec. 2.3.3.) However, interior temperature ranges and, therefore, humidity levels can change. Occupancy levels within the building or functions performed within the building can alter the original moisture vapor levels within the building. If changes occur and they exceed the original design parameters, damage and failure of the roof system can result. Therefore, vapor drive can be an indeterminate factor in the roof design.

As an example, a roof that covers a warehouse facility will be influenced differently if the warehouse becomes a warehouse/office facility. In this case, interior temperatures and the relative humidity of some of the interior spaces may change.

Multifamily dwellings in colder climates have historically been a problem when roof systems, and specifically the ventilation systems, were not properly designed to accommodate the interior humidity levels and subsequent vapor drive. (See Sec. 10.2.) The same can be said of hotels, office buildings, or other structures which are densely occupied by people. A person emits large amounts of humidity in the simple act of breathing.

Vapor drive can be indeterminate in that merely changing the interior temperature from 65°F in the winter to 72°F can create the need for a vapor retarder within the roof system, where at 65°F none was needed. A person who is cold-natured can destroy your roof system if this is not planned for.

ACOUSTICS

We all know that the health of building occupants is affected by the interior environment of the building. Acoustics play a part in proper building design with health considerations in mind. The roof system can greatly add to or reduce the acoustic values within the building environment. (See Sec. 2.3.2.)

Interior acoustics are normally controlled by interior finishes. Exterior noise that can penetrate to building occupants is largely a function of the exterior wall assemblies and the roof system. Exterior sound waves and the resulting vibration noise can be controlled, to some degree, by the roof assembly. Use of roof insulation reduces sound-wave transfer from the exterior environment to the building interior. Isolation of direct conduits (which can transfer vibration) leading from the rooftop to the interior occupied spaces reduces noise levels within the building interior.

Large, mechanized rooftop equipment can be isolated so that vibration and noise is not transferred to the building interior. Roof insulation can help absorb sound waves from airplanes, automobile traffic, and any surrounding industrial facilities.

2.2.6 Roof Traffic

We know that foot traffic will be present on any roof at one time or another. The indeterminate factors in many roof designs includes:

- Foot traffic that becomes excessive over the life of the roof system
- Foot traffic that was not anticipated
- Foot traffic in amounts which the roof membrane is unable to resist successfully

Roof systems are very good at resisting most normal foot traffic—"normal foot traffic" being defined as people wearing soft-soled shoes, carrying normal loads, or moving equipment on pneumatic-tired carriers, at normal speeds. A roof system cannot resist a squad of football players wearing cleated shoes and moving blocking sleds across the roof.

Roof damage can result from excessive foot and equipment traffic in the form of unanticipated numbers of workers or personnel. Extraordinary rooftop traffic can occur in response to, for example, malfunctioning HVAC or other mechanical equipment or data gathering from weather equipment. Further damage can result from standard amounts of roof traffic over fragile roof systems. Fragile roof systems can be created by poorly considered design, such as inadequate compressive values of roof insulation. (See Sec. 8.1.1.) Some roof system surfacings are inherently fragile in response to foot and equipment traffic—for example, some paint and metallic coatings on metal roof panels.

The base flashings around mechanical equipment should always have extra reinforcement. (See Sec. 12.3.) This will help prevent damage to the base flashing from workers feet, equipment, and tools. It is good practice to use solid-wood cant strips at these locations instead of fiber cants. (See Fig. 2.13.)

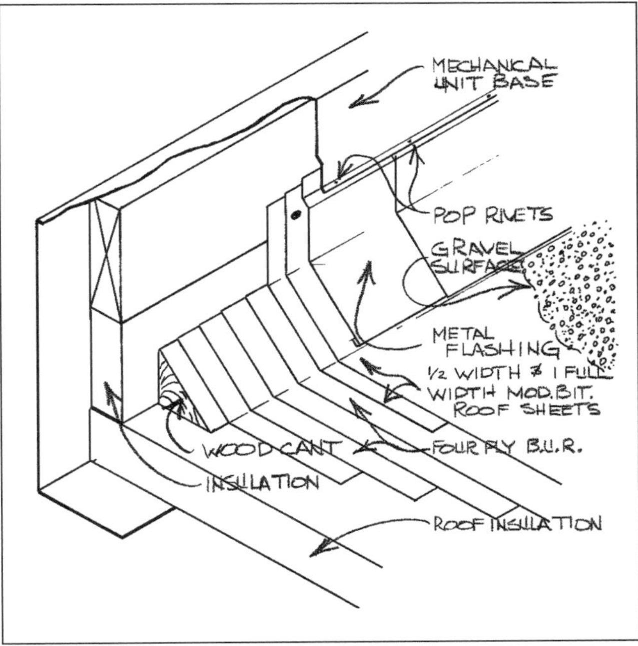

Figure 2.13 Base flashing protection.

Walkways or walkpads are also good systems to use in design (see Fig. 2.8), although workers often will not restrict their travels to these areas. Most of the service work done on a roof is around mechanical equipment. Since indeterminate factors come into play, installing roof protection systems at mechanical equipment is good design practice. (See Sec. 6.1.2.)

2.3 DETERMINATE DESIGN ELEMENTS

What most designers are aware of and what they design for (and against) are the determinate elements of design—that is, what we know to expect. However, we must understand and appreciate the complete function and limitations of the basic elements and components we are looking for in the roof system. The determinate elements of the design encompass the forces which a roof system has to deal with on a constant basis.

One of the reasons roof system design can be complex and confusing is that many different variables come into play. There is the roof deck, which can be of numerous materials, along with the consideration of the style and the manner in which it is erected or placed on the building top. There is also the roof insulation system (if any), which can be of many different types of materials or a combination thereof. Insulation is normally followed by the roof membrane, which again is selected from a wide range of material types or a combination, and is often formed on the rooftop into a monolithic unit. The entire assembly just described may then be surfaced with a protective layer of materials, such as cutback coatings, aggregates, paver units, or additional layers of membranes.

These concerns are addressed in detail in this manual. Following is a theoretical discussion of design goals as they relate to the functions of the components of the roof assembly.

2.3.1 Thermal Considerations

Most people consider an ordinary building to have four faces or walls. However, what we often forget about is the fifth wall, which is the roof. This face of the building envelope takes more abuse than any of the other building walls. Through this fifth wall, much of the energy used to heat and cool the building interior is lost or saved, but in either context, heat flow through the roof assembly is controlled by the design of the total ceiling/plenum/deck/roof assembly.

The total assembly includes all components and systems—from the interior ceiling up to the outside environment. Each material, component, and system within this assembly has a function and an effect on the overall energy flow.

Design considerations will limit the selection of materials that can be used as ceiling and ceiling insulation materials, this often being governed by building codes, materials availability and selection, and budgets and aesthetics. The insulant materials in a low-sloped roof system are often used as the major insulation component in completing the total assembly's thermal resistance capabilities.

The resistance to thermal flow of the total assembly is expressed in the total R-value of all the components. Even the outside air film on top of the roof membrane has an R-value. From a cost-analysis view, it is sometimes more cost-effective to specify ceiling panels with a higher R-value, use blanket insulation on top of a suspended ceiling, or ventilate the plenum or attic spaces. If ventilation is selected, carefully analyze all the factors required of a proper ventilation design. (See Sec. 10.2.2.) Complete and proper ventilation design has been proven to reduce heat gain through a 1000-ft^2 ceiling system by as much as 16,000 Btu per average cooling day (an average cooling day is 75 percent of a maximum design day with a 1500-cfm air exhaust).

Wind-activated or power-mechanized ventilators cannot provide proper ventilation and will do little to reduce cooling costs. Maintenance inspection must be performed to power ventilators. Also, in many parts of the country the opinion is that gravity ventilators, using natural heat convection for air movement, are a much better option than mechanized ventilation.

Due to chlorofluorocarbon (CFC) contamination of the atmosphere and the subsequent greenhouse effect, many of the roof insulation products used in the industry have been undergoing change within the last several years. HCFCs are now the predominant insulant gas used within roof insulation boards (see Sec. 8.2.1) and further adjustments can be expected in the future.

Solar reflectivity can be a significant factor in thermal resistance. If the coating placed atop the roof is a maintenance item, such as asphalt cutback aluminum pigment material (aluminum roof coating) and the coating dissipates and is not replaced, the value of the reflective coating will be removed from the total resistance equation. (See Sec. 6.1.3.)

As another example, mineral granules are often factory-applied as the top surfacing on fiberglass felt cap sheets as well as on many of the modified bitumen membranes used in today's market. As time goes on, this mineral surfacing can release from the roof sheet and affect the total thermal resistance of the assembly. (See Sec. 6.1.1.)

Situations such as these can be prevented by periodic application of aluminum roof coating. The coating will help retain ceramic mineral granules to the surface of the sheet membranes and can also enhance an external fire-resistance rating with some products.

Thermal resistances are important if a vapor retarder is used within the roof assembly. Since roof insulations are required to keep the vapor-retardant layer above dew-point temperature, if the insulation above the retarder loses insulation values, a serious failure cycle can result.

Insulation values can be compromised if insulation becomes wet due to roof leaks. It is advisable to use a roof insulation that does not readily absorb water at the location above the vapor retardant.

FREEZE/THAW CYCLES

Some roof materials are susceptible to damage in a freeze/thaw environment. Many concrete roof tiles with ceramic glaze coat finishes can be affected in such climates. The glaze coating often cannot accommodate the different expansion rates of the concrete tile body, and spalling and chipping of the ceramic glaze coating result.

Repetitive freeze/thaw cycles have a more deleterious effect on materials than do less common freeze/thaw cycles. Some geographic areas of the country experience more freeze/thaw cycles per year than do others. (See Fig. 11.5.)

Some inferior grades of roof slate can be affected in such environments. Concrete roof pavers can also experience damage due to severe freeze/thaw cycles. Both of these materials should be tested in accordance with ASTM standards to verify acceptable resistance to freeze/thaw cycles.

THERMAL LOADING AND THERMAL SHOCK

Thermal loading and shock are also discussed under Sec. 2.1.1. Thermal loading occurs when solar radiation is absorbed by the roof system. During heat absorption, roof materials will expand. Those with a higher coefficient of expansion, such as metal flashings, will expand further than will those with lower coefficients, such as roof insulations. Also, some materials within a roof system will not be loaded with the same amounts of heat energy as others within the assembly as the result of factors such as location, mass/density, and thermal resistances.

Thermal loading (absorption) is accompanied by thermal dissipation (radiation) from the materials. (See Sec. 2.3.4.) This leads to the cyclic effect of expansion and contraction. The movements of materials during the expansion-and-contraction cycle, especially that of sheet metal flashings, can cause roof damage or failure.

Thermal loading is to be anticipated and can be designed for or against. Roof insulations prevent thermal loading to the roof deck, which, if allowed, will cause thermal radiation from the deck down to the ceiling system. This radiated heat can result in excessive cooling costs.

Reflective roof surfacings, when compared with nonreflective surfacings, can prevent thermal loading to the underlying roof membrane. Common sense tells us that a dull black roof surface will absorb more heat energy than will a white or reflective roof surface.

Thermal shock is seldom considered by designers, but it can be a very powerful and destructive force. Thermal shock occurs when roof systems undergo radical and quick temperature changes. A roof temperature may be 150°F or more on a hot summer day but can be reduced to 80°F in a matter of minutes by a rain shower. Damage occurs when all components do not react to the temperature swing within the same time frame.

All components in a properly designed roof system act as one, or should act and react together in as close to a synchronized manner as possible. Thermal shock separates further than normal the mechanical properties of the different systems, materials, and components by causing some parts of a roof system to experience contraction, while other parts of the system are not contracting at the same, normally expected, rates.

Thermal shock is something all roof systems are exposed to. Older systems cannot handle the shock as well as newer systems can. Although little can be done to prevent such shock, from the standpoint of cost-effectiveness and practicality, a designer should take into account the inevitability of such natural phenomena.

The geographic area where thermal shock is the greatest is probably the desert southwest region of the United States. The daytime temperature on a roof there can approach or exceed 150°F, but the cool nights can create temperatures in the 60 to 70° range. This cycle is common and can extend for months at a time.

2.3.2 Acoustics

Acoustic principles are addressed only briefly in other sections of this manual. Following is a rudimentary explanation of acoustic behavior and influences.

Acoustics is the science of noise and vibration. Vibration can cause noise and noise can cause vibration. The roof assembly can allow either noise or vibration to enter the building and affect the occupants. This can be an important consideration in the design of certain structures, such as churches and cathedrals, mortuaries, libraries, and airport terminals.

External influences can include

- Factories and industrial facilities
- Rainwater
- Foot and/or vehicle traffic from roof terraces
- Parking garages which are incorporated into the occupied building
- Airplanes
- Entertainment centers

The noise generated by these influences is transmitted to the building through the air or attached building components. The noise is transmitted either indirectly, as noise waves through the air, or directly, as vibration conducted through attached building components, such as would be the case with overhead parking garages.

In very simple terms, noise into the building can be restricted by absorption, reflection, or disconnection. Absorption is usually the most feasible manner and is where roof components can play a vital role. A basic rule of acoustics and absorption is: the heavier the mass, or the greater the density, the more noise vibration will be absorbed. This can be accomplished with dense roof decks such as concrete, roof insulations with high density, or certain types of roof surfacings such as insulated concrete pavers.

Echo is sound waves that are reflected from a nonabsorbing surface, such as metal. Therefore you would think that metal roofing would be a good choice for controlling sound entering a building structure. However, this is not the case, since metal roofing has little density and is rigid. Sound is reflected from the metallic surface, but it is also transmitted by the vibration caused to it by the sound waves striking its surface. Metal roofing can transmit a great deal of sound to building occupants. The thicker and more dense the metal, the less the sound waves will be transmitted to other building components. Using rigid roof insulation layers installed to a structural metal roof deck and then covered by a metal panel roof system will greatly reduce noise transmitted through the metal roof panel system.

If skylights are used in the roof assembly, be aware that noise vibration will be conducted directly into the building through them. If large mechanical equipment on the rooftop is part of the design, it may be necessary to group the equipment together into one roof area. This area can then be isolated with area divider joints (disconnection), and using other special treatments to that area to reduce noise transmission into the building environment.

2.3.3 Vapor Drive

It is preferable that vapor drive considerations remain a determinate factor and do not become indeterminate per the original calculations and design. (See Secs. 2.1.1 and 2.2.5.) In the event that vapor drive reaches an unanticipated dew-point condensation level at a location within the building assembly, damage can be the result. Vapor drive is an important consideration in total building and roof design.

Understanding the dynamics of vapor drive is sometimes difficult. It can seem a complicated topic for the uninitiated. In the design process, we often rely on other professionals for the evaluation of concerns such as vapor drive and the subsequent condensation problems.

It is beyond the scope of this manual to completely explain all the dynamic and kinetic forces involved with moisture flow, vapor pressures, vapor diffusion, and dew-point condensation. However, being ignorant of the basic principles of the phenomena could hinder proper roof design. The following is a brief and simple explanation of these forces.

VAPOR PRESSURE

Beginning with the basic technology, we must understand the amount of moisture (humidity) air can hold at a given temperature. This is expressed as *relative humidity*. At 100 percent humidity, the air can hold no more moisture. If the temperature is reduced, condensation (dew point) occurs.

An example commonly used to illustrate this is that of a closed and sealed container—perhaps a glass jar—with a small amount of water at the bottom. The water at the bottom has kinetic energy which causes molecules of water to break free of the surface tension, turning, as they escape, from a liquid to a gas and becoming water vapor. (The only time molecules will not escape from the liquid is at –460°F, or absolute zero.) Some of these vaporized molecules will return to their liquid state and be added back to the water at the bottom of the jar. Left sealed and remaining at constant temperature, the air above the water within the container will absorb as many water vapor molecules as possible. An equilibrium is reached, with as many molecules of vapor leaving the liquid as molecules of vapor returning to the liquid. At this time the air above the water in the container is at its utmost saturation level, unable to retain any more water vapor, and it now has a specific *vapor pressure*. If the container is then placed into a cooler environment, where the interior air temperatures are reduced, the water vapor in the now-cool air will re-form from the gas state to a liquid state. Condensation occurs as a result of reaching the dew point, which is the temperature range at which water vapor will condense from a gas to a liquid. (See Fig. 2.14.)

Hot air can hold more moisture (water vapor) than cold air, which explains the condensation which occurred at the lower-level dew-point temperature in the preceding example. However, if the interior temperature of the container was raised instead of lowered, more moisture-vapor molecules could have entered the air above the water. Once equilibrium was reached at this elevated temperature, the vapor pressure would be greater.

Referring to the kinetic theory of gases, the only time that vapor pressure from water molecules is absent is at absolute zero. At that temperature, not enough kinetic energy is available for the molecules to break free of the surface and escape as gas. From the point of absolute zero, the higher the temperature, the more water vapor that can be present in the atmosphere and the higher the vapor pressure in a closed or semiclosed system.

VAPOR DRIVE

This law leads us to the concept of *vapor drive*. Hot air can have higher vapor pressure than cold air. In a cold climate, the air inside a building can be 70°F while the air on the outside can be 10°F. The vapor pressure inside will be greater than the outside vapor pressure, and they will try to reach an equilibrium. However, as the vapor flows from the inside to the outside in an attempt to equalize, colder temperatures will be encountered somewhere along the way. Remember what happened to the air within the sealed container when it was cooled? This explains why condensation occurs when the vapor flow encounters its dew point, which is a colder temperature. This dew-point temperature will be different for different buildings and assemblies within different environ-

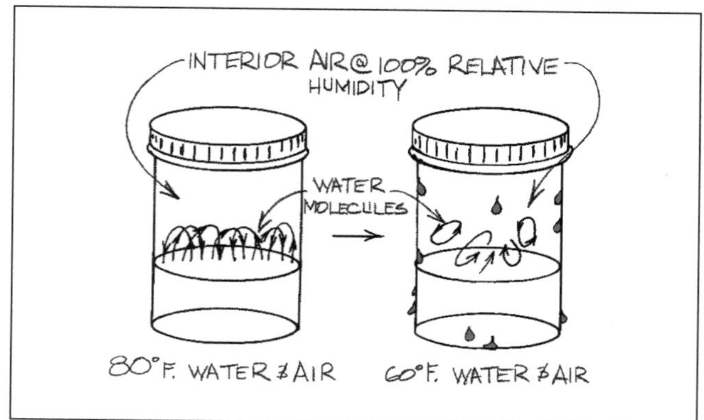

Figure 2.14 Water in cylinders.

ments. Further explanation requires an understanding of relative humidity. (See Fig. 2.15.)

Vapor pressure is seldom absolute, or 100 percent. Instead, the amount of moisture vapor that is contained within the atmosphere is expressed as a percentage, termed *relative humidity*. If the atmosphere is at complete saturation of water vapor, it is also at 100 percent relative humidity.

As a general example, if the temperature inside the building was 70°F with a 50 percent relative humidity, and the air outside the building was 10°F with a relative humidity of 30 percent, vapor pressures might be equal and no vapor drive would result. However, a problem might still exist and must be addressed.

Hot air will rise, as explained by the physical law of convection. Even though vapor pressures are assumed to be equal in the preceding example, the hot interior air will migrate toward the colder outside air. At some point it will be restricted in its overall flow and, for simplicity's sake, assume that it is stopped at the underside of the metal roof deck in the plenum/attic.

Assume the temperature on the underside of the roof deck is 35°F. What will happen? If the dew point of the interior air, which was 70°F with a relative humidity of 50 percent, is now at 36°F at the interface of the metal roof deck and air film in the plenum, what is the vapor saturation pressure level at that air temperature? Remember, none of the moisture vapor has miraculously disappeared, nor can the absolute vapor pressure of the air exceed 100 percent.

If the air temperature of 36°F has exceeded 100 percent vapor pressure somewhere along a gradient line in the travel to the metal deck, when the air contacts the cold bottom of the metal roof deck, condensation will occur on that surface. Condensation may also be occurring on components below the metal roof deck.

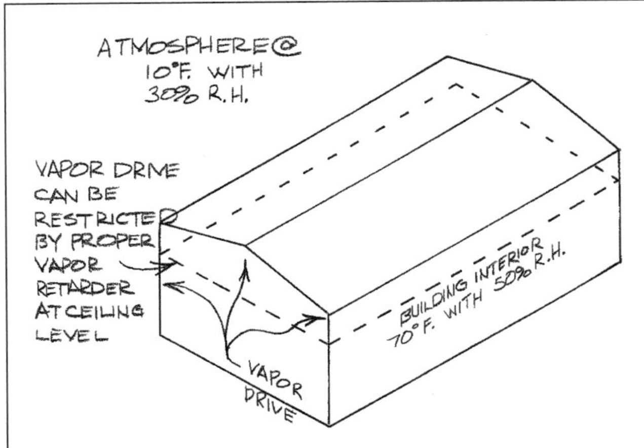

Figure 2.15 Building showing vapor drive.

Taking this example one step further, if the 35°F metal deck is not where the moisture-laden air reaches 100 percent of its moisture saturation level but is at the 30°F level halfway through the roof insulation, which is the dew-point level, problems can occur. In this instance, the vapor will return to a liquid state within the insulation layer. At 30°F, the water will freeze!

Of course, this is not a constant state of affairs. The next day when it warms up, the outside temperature may reach 35°F. If the dew-point range occurred for only a short time the night before, perhaps there was not enough condensation to create a problem.

SELF-DRYING ROOF CONCEPT

In truth, this phenomenon is now understood to occur quite often in roof assemblies. The only time it becomes a problem is when temperature extremes (and all the pressures, humidities, and drives associated therewith) remain adverse to each other for extended periods of time. These extended periods and extremes can result in unacceptable amounts of moisture being entrapped and causing severe damage to the roof and building systems.

When moisture is deposited and then evaporated within an assembly it is called many things: a self-drying roof concept, pumping, and a vapor engine. In the southern United States, this is a common occurrence. The exterior environment is mainly hot and humid, possibly 95°F with a 90 percent humidity factor in the summer months, decreasing to 30 to 40°F with a 50 percent relative humidity factor in the winter. However, during the summer months the building interior may be 75°F with 50 percent relative humidity.

Realizing that vapor drives toward cooler, and therefore lower, pressure areas during the winter, moisture from the heated building interior is driven into or toward the roof assembly. During the summer the cycle reverses, with moisture being driven out of the roof assembly into the cooler air-conditioned building interiors. In the south, for the majority of the year, the interior of a building has less humidity (less vapor pressure) than the exterior environment, creating the self-drying roof.

VAPOR RETARDANT

A vapor retarder, or vapor barrier, in conjunction with roof insulation, is used to stop vapor condensation within a roof assembly. If the vapor flow is retarded, or restricted, from reaching the level within the assembly where dew point will be realized, no problem will result. Instead, the air must retain its vapor because it cannot reach the temperature level at which it exceeds the vapor saturation level. The only time the vapor can turn to liquid is when the temperature drops low enough so that 100 percent vapor pressure level is surpassed.

To correct the problem of condensation, again use the example of the plenum-cavity, steel roof deck covered with roof insulation, into which a vapor retardant will be inserted. The design of the system must be changed to allow a layer of roof insulation to be placed on top of the metal deck, covered with a vapor retarder, which in turn is covered by another layer of roof insulation, which then has the roof membrane applied to it. (See Fig. 2.16.)

As the warm air and moisture vapor drives toward the cold exterior, the moisture vapor within the moving air will hit the vapor retarder and cannot travel any farther. So long as the crucial temperature range at which the vapor will condense is not reached, no problem will result.

The vapor retarder must be placed at a location within the assembly where the temperature range remains above dew point. This location is determined by the R-value of the roof insulations and the R-values of the other roof components.

In order to determine need and placement of vapor retarders and insulations, several calculations must be performed. The temperature at the vapor retarder must be determined. This is accomplished by using the R-values of the building materials within the assembly, from the ceiling to the outside air film. Dew-point temperatures must be determined, and a psychometric chart is often used for this purpose. A psychometric chart gives temperatures as a cross-reference between relative humidities and interior temperatures.

Once the temperature at the vapor retarder is known, it is compared with the dew-point temperature. The vapor retarder must be placed below the dew-point location. The vapor retarder must remain warmer than the dew-point temperature.

Additional insulation is incorporated into the roof assembly above the vapor retarder level, thereby restricting cold temperatures from reaching the vapor retarder lever. It is often required for roof vents to be installed into the roof assembly to vent any possible pressure accumulated within the insulation layers above the vapor retarder.

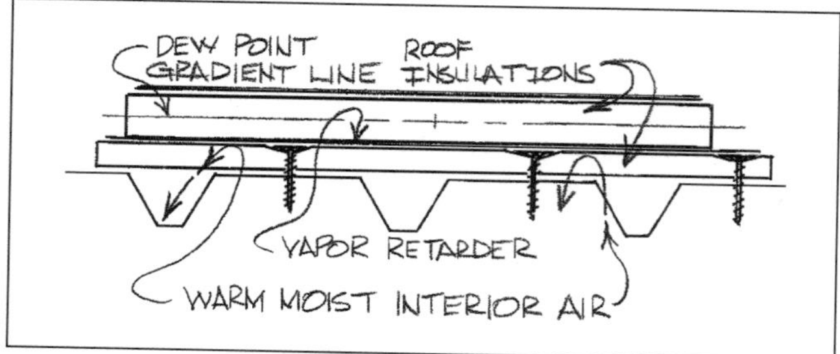

Figure 2.16 Vapor retarder in a roof system.

Many other factors are involved in a complete analysis of vapor drive and possible condensation problems within some buildings. Vapor retarders are not created perfect and some moisture will probably be driven into the assembly, where it could condense. Roof penetrations which extend through the entire roof assembly must be given careful consideration in detailing when specifying a vapor retardant.

Voids, cracks, and holes in the roof and building envelope can also allow moisture-laden exterior air into the roof assembly above the vapor retarder. If the vapor condenses to liquid above the vapor barrier, the roof system could be severely damaged or destroyed, if infiltration is extensive.

Also, a vapor retardant will act as a water barrier and keep water from roof leaks out of the building for a certain amount of time. If the owner does not carefully examine the roof system regularly, the total roof system could be destroyed before roof leakage is discovered.

Air movements within a building can carry moisture vapor to areas where it can possibly return to a liquid at a later time. The "stack" effect, common in taller buildings, can further influence air movements.

Special consideration regarding vapor drive must be given to multifamily housing, swimming pool enclosures, gymnasiums, high-rise buildings, laundries, food manufacturing facilities, food and chemical processing facilities, textile and industrial facilities, as well as other special or unusual structures where high interior and/or cold and dry exterior environments might exist.

2.3.4 Solar Radiation

RADIANT ENERGY

Radiant energy can be emitted from almost any source in the form of wavelength energy. The radiant energy we are concerned with is solar radiation.

Solar radiant comes to earth in the form of electromagnetic wave energy. This can be in the infrared spectrum, with wavelengths longer than visible light, as well as in the visible wavelength spectrum, and the ultraviolet wavelength spectrum, composed of energy wavelengths shorter than those in the visible spectrum.

We are most familiar with light energy in the visible form. This is what we can see, which is a result of reflected light energy waves. White or shiny surfaces reflect the broadest spectrum of visible light, comprising the majority of the basic color groups within the visible spectrum.

BLACKBODIES

Black surfaces reflect the fewest light waves, which accounts for their lack of color. These blackbodies are a consideration in thermal load analysis.

A *blackbody* is defined as a surface which can absorb (as well as radiate) all electromagnetic energy waves. No construction materials are blackbody radiators, although the ability to absorb and then reradiate the energy is used to categorize them in accordance with a hypothetical blackbody surface.

A material's ability to absorb energy and then reradiate the energy is expressed as a ratio, which is the difference between absorption and reradiation of energy from a blackbody surface as compared to an actual material at the same temperature.

This difference in surface temperature of the actual construction material and a theoretical blackbody is termed emissivity and expressed as *E*. Mathematically, *E* is expressed as a function of:

$$\frac{ABt}{BBt} = E$$

where BB = blackbody
AB = actual body
t = temperature

The darker the roof surface, the more wavelength energy (heat) it can and will absorb. The more reflective the roof surface, the more energy (heat) it will reflect. Likewise, the amount of energy radiated to the roof surface will always equal the amount of energy transmitted, reflected, or absorbed by the roof. Therefore, a dark roof will radiate more energy than will a reflective roof, since the dark roof absorbed more energy. This radiation can be measured as infrared radiation. (See Table 2.1.)

THERMAL LOADING OF ROOFS

The temperatures to which roof membranes are subjected are herein referred to as *ambient temperatures,* which refers to the temperature of the surrounding environment (air). Ambient temperature is seldom the temperature of the roof surface.

The temperature of a roof membrane's surface can be as much as 70°F above the ambient temperature. In a study of roof temperatures conducted by the National Roofing Contractors Association (NRCA) and Oak Ridge National Laboratories (ORNL), temperatures as high as 169°F were recorded for black surface roof membranes. At the same time and location, a temperature of 104°F—20° above ambient—was recorded for a roof membrane with a reflective white latex roof coating. Table 2.2 shows temperature extremes for roofs being monitored on a normal sunny day in Illinois.

Table 2.1 Materials emittance factors.

	Solar Reflectance, %	*Emittance*
Black asphalt shingles	3.4	0.91
White asphalt shingles	26.1	0.91
White coating	71.4	0.91
White polyester on metal roof panel	58.9	0.85
Kynar white on metal roof panel	66.6	0.85
White concrete tile	73.0	0.90
Red concrete tile	18.0	0.91
White cement shingle	77.0	0.88
Wood shingles	22.0	0.90
Black EPDM	6.2	0.86
White EPDM	68.7	0.87
White Hypalon®	75.5	0.91
Unpainted aluminum	71.3	0.04
Unpainted galvanize	60.9	0.25
Smooth asphalt	5.8	0.86

The roof membranes in the study reported in Table 2.2 are APP-base modified bitumen membranes, with the exception of one roof area which is an EPDM membrane. One APP modified bitumen roof area is uncoated, with the black roof membrane exposed. The other roof areas are coated with either solvent-based aluminum roof coating, aluminum pigmented asphalt emulsion roof coating, or white latex coating. The EPDM roof area is surfaced with aggregate ballast.

Maximum temperature extremes during the peak heating periods are important in relation to roof system function, but also to be considered are the minimum temperature extremes experienced on the roof surface during cooler periods of the night. In the aforementioned study, during the peak cooling times, the roof temperatures would decrease 10 to 15°F below ambient temperatures. The study clearly shows the physics and dynamics of heat loading and loss. On clear nights, the drop in temperature below ambient is greater than it is on cloudy nights. This is because the night sky is colder than ambient air temperatures at the roof surface. In simple terms, the heat is drawn (radiated) from the roof toward the cooler night sky in an effort to equalize temperature differentials. A cloud cover, blocking the night sky exposed to the roof surface, prevents the optimum heat exchange, referred to as *emissivity.*

Notice in Fig. 2.17 that different roof systems with different coatings have different surface temperatures at

Table 2.2 Example of temperature comparisons for a typical warm, sunny day (Aug. 11, 1991). (*Reprinted with permission from* Professional Roofing *magazine*)

Ambient	*Exposed*	*Aluminum*	*Reflective Emulsion*	*Ballasted EPDM*	*White Latex*
83°F	156°F	143°F	136°F	130°F	104°F

peak cooling times. This is due to the different emittance characteristics of the different coatings.

The study reports: "The evenings of Jan. 17 and 18 were cloudless nights. All of the roof membranes' temperatures dropped below ambient. However, the solvent-based aluminum (being the aluminum coated roof area) did not get as cold as the others. This suggests that the infrared emittance of this coating is probably lower than the others."

When calculating dew point and vapor drive, outside temperature extremes are considered. (See Sec. 2.3.3.) The ambient temperatures expected are not the temperatures which will actually exist on the roof surface. These actual roof temperatures will be dependent upon the color of the roof membrane and its emittance factor.

TEMPERATURE DEGRADATION

High-temperature extremes adversely affect roof systems and component parts. The sheet metal flashings incorporated into a roof assembly will be subjected to the roof membrane temperatures.

It is very possible for 150°F temperatures to exist during peak thermal loading and for 50°F night temperatures to exist during peak cooling. The expansion and contraction experienced by the metal flashings will be tremendous and are the main reason for roof problems at sheet metal flashings. (See Sec. 12.2.1.)

High-temperature extremes also cause roofing to degenerate. A law of physics states that for every 10°C (approximately 18°F) rise in temperature, molecular reaction doubles.

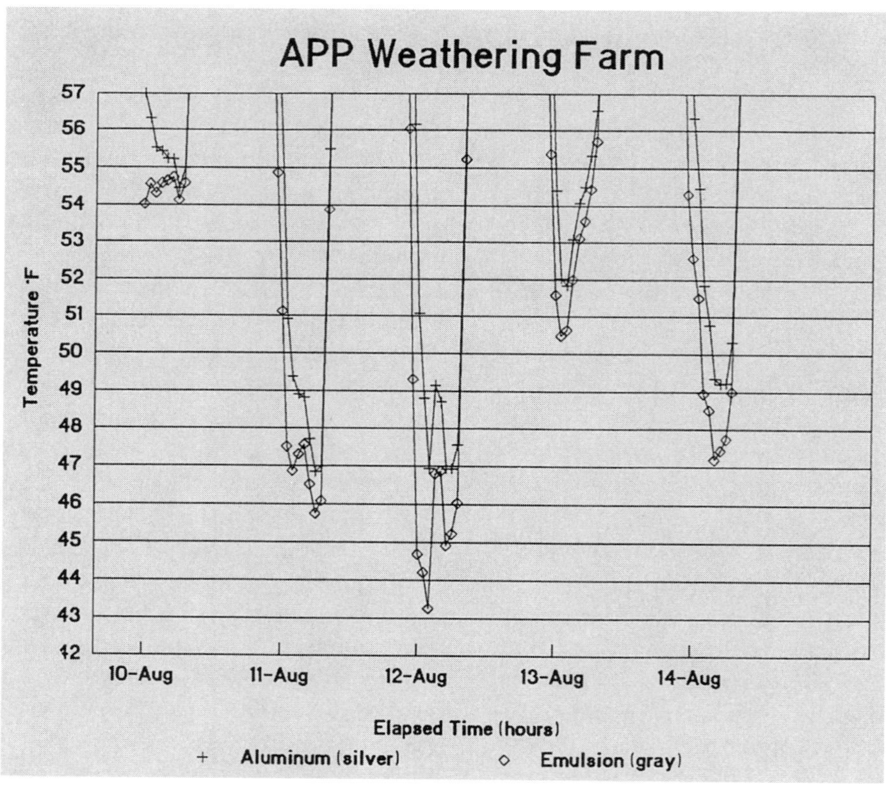

Figure 2.17 A nighttime membrane temperature comparison of the aluminum (silver color) and emulsion (gray) coatings. (*Reprinted with permission from* Professional Roofing *magazine.*)

For bitumen-based roof systems, this is evidenced by the bitumen becoming hard and brittle as it reacts with oxygen (air). This is verified in a laboratory setting using a test device and process referred to as *dark oven testing*. The higher the temperature of the oven, the quicker and more drastic the asphalt reacts, becoming brittle and hard.

ULTRAVIOLET ENERGY

Additionally, ultraviolet energy waves of sunlight cause the asphalt bitumens to degrade. The UV waves break down the molecular structure of bitumen, as well as many other organic materials. The chemical and physical reactions of organic molecular chains when exposed to short-wavelength energy (UV rays) are complex and beyond the intent of this manual. However, protecting the asphalt bitumen-based roof membranes from the UV rays of the sun is important and is one of the main functions of the roof surface materials. (See Sec. 6.1.)

UV-wavelength energy has adverse effects on almost all of the construction materials we use in roofing, to a greater or lesser extent, be they paint finishes on metal roof panels or polymeric single-ply membranes. UV degradation seldom works by itself to damage and destroy roof systems. Instead, it is the work of a combination of UV heat energy and other factors such as rain (H_2O), air (O_2), pollutants (acids), and dirt (organic contaminants).

PREVENTATIVE DESIGN

Eliminating all of the factors we discussed above, if it were possible, would result in a very long-lived roof system. Since it is not possible to eliminate thermal loading, ultraviolet exposure, air and water interaction, pollutants, and organic contaminants, as well as workmanship flaws and design error, we must instead try to limit their impact on the roof system.

If we can limit the high-temperature extremes to which a roof membrane is exposed, the molecular reaction and degradation would in turn be limited. Roof insulations play an important role in energy conservation and are a standard requirement in roof assemblies. However, the more efficient a roof insulation, the higher and lower will be the temperature extremes (thermal shock) at the roof membrane and ambient air interface. Installing a roof membrane over an uninsulated roof deck will reduce the temperature extremes at the roof membrane, but is the swap in energy loss justified?

Keeping the UV rays from the roof membrane will reduce damage caused by these rays. This is accomplished by the use of gravel and aggregates, as well as coatings and pavers. (See Chap. 6.)

A proper roof slope, eliminating any ponding water on the roof surface, will limit the effects which organic contaminants, mainly dust and dirt, can have on a roof membrane.

Acidic and corrosive atmospheres and environments are usually most detrimental to sheet metal flashings. Using noncorrosive metals such as stainless steel or copper can eliminate corrosion and premature failure at metal flashing locations.

Design error can be limited by a review and submittal process. Workmanship flaws can be limited by the services of a qualified full-time roof construction inspector.

ROOF SURFACINGS

To be emitted, energy has to first be absorbed or reflected. Gravel/aggregate is not a good reflective material, therefore the gravel/aggregate surface absorbs the radiant energy and becomes a *heat sink*. With aggregate surfacings, the emittance factor is high.

While adequately protecting the roof membrane from UV damage, the aggregate materials do not efficiently protect the roof surface from high-temperature extremes. In many cases, the gravel/aggregate can keep the roof surface at elevated temperatures until enough absorbed energy is emitted from the aggregate surfacing to reduce elevated temperatures.

Coatings are a maintenance item. They must be replaced periodically and many owners do not provide this maintenance. If and when the roof no longer has a good protective coating, dual damage can and will occur. The result is both greater temperature extremes as well as damage caused by roof exposure to UV rays.

Roof pavers have a cementitious wearing surface with an insulation material laminated to the bottom surface, which rests upon the roof surface. This system provides a continuous shield over the roof membrane, achieving the UV protection. (See Sec. 6.1.2.) The insulation material protects the roof membrane surface from extreme temperatures. This type of product would seem to supply roof membrane protection; however, there are restrictive factors.

One factor is cost, with the pavers sometimes costing more than the roof membrane installation. Also, in high-wind areas the paver system must be secured at strategic locations to the rooftop, usually with stainless steel bands. This also adds quite an expense. The best a roof designer can do is understand the external influences affecting the roof system and protect the system as well as possible.

An interesting situation to consider is a roof system installed in an Arctic region. High-temperature extremes will not exist there, so thermal loading is not a detrimental factor. If the roof surface is completely covered from the UV rays, this factor can be greatly reduced. So is this to say that a roof in an Arctic region, properly designed and protected, will last forever?

The answer is of course not. Factors such as low-temperature extremes, for extended periods of time, may affect the molecular makeup of some roof membranes. If a membrane is selected which is compatible with low temperature extremes, the roof components, such as metal flashings, will still behave differently than the roof membrane. This could lead to some stress at joining locations of the flashing and roof membrane, which the roof adhesives or membrane may not eventually be able to successfully accommodate. Also, even in pristine Arctic regions, there is pollution fallout that will probably eventually reach the membrane surface and have some effect.

If all of these factors are accounted for in this design for an Arctic environment, it can be expected that the roof system will last a very long time—if the roof does not blow off, temperatures and climate remain constant, interior building uses remain the same, the building does not experience unanticipated stress and movements. . . .

2.3.5 Durability

Durability of a material, component, or system can sometimes be accurately estimated. Sometimes our estimations are wrong. The inaccuracy of an estimation or prediction could be the result of various beliefs, sources, or occurrences.

- Sometimes our *belief* in the durability of a product, component, material, or system must be reevaluated and perhaps adjusted.
- Sometimes the *sources* from which we gathered information pertaining to the durability of a material, system, or component were not correct.
- Sometimes *occurrences* beyond our control or responsibility, such as catastrophic acts of nature, cause the material, component, or system to have less durability than it would under normal circumstances.

DEFINING DURABILITY

However, sometimes a material, component, or system fails prematurely due to acts of nature not catastrophic, and in this case we should have expected and designed against such failure. With roof systems, premature failure, or lack of durability, can have consequences that adversely affect the design professional. Durability can be defined as that which has lasting quality and permanence as can reasonably be expected.

For a roof system to have *lasting quality and permanence as can reasonably be expected,* many factors have to be considered, understood, and designed for. The intent of this manual is to help the reader understand and design durable roof systems, which requires much more information than can be presented within this section. Therefore, we shall address only the theory and physics behind what makes a material, component, or system durable or temporary. These theories and the physics of materials behavior are determinate factors in the design process and must be anticipated and planned for (or against).

The total roof system must be durable, in that it must have lasting quality and permanence as can be reasonably expected. In the event that the roof system you design fails, and in someone's opinion the failure is premature, you will have to justify to your client or possibly an attorney or a jury of your peers why the failure was beyond your control or was not premature.

- Lasting quality
- Permanence
- Reasonably expected

If you design roof systems long enough, you will eventually have to defend, explain, teach, or evaluate the concepts of lasting quality, permanence, and reasonable expectation.

- *Lasting quality* in a roof system can be evaluated by the roof's ability to be watertight.
- *Permanence* can be evaluated by its ability to remain unchanged by normal forces without the (excessive) intervention of man.
- *Reasonable expectation* can be evaluated by the industry expectations for that type of roof system.

ACHIEVING DURABILITY

The roof system is the most exposed surface of a building structure and takes the brunt of a harsh environment. Many materials, components, and systems act and react differently on a roof than they do when installed elsewhere. Therefore, analyze a material's durability in relation to the harsh roof system environment and performance, not as it has performed elsewhere.

The roof system must be durable in its resistance to:

- Water
- Foot traffic
- Movement
- Wind
- Thermal shock
- Fire
- Moisture vapor condensation
- Solar radiation

To achieve the durability required of the roof system, the physics, chemistry, and dynamics of various roof materials, systems, and components should be basically understood.

The lasting quality and permanence of most construction materials begin to diminish from the day the materials are installed. In general, this could be thought of as dissipation of the original material into a new form of material.

- Bituminous roof durability is lost as volatile oils dissipate and cohesive organic molecular chains degenerate.
- Polymeric single-ply membranes lose durability when the cross-linking of the molecular chains begins to separate.
- Metal roof panels lose durability when the protective finish is lost and the steel dissipates to rust.
- Tile and slate durability diminishes as the material changes (deteriorates) into a new substance, e.g., slate turning into gypsum.
- Roof decks fail if flexural strength dissipates due to excessive deflection and/or cyclic loads and movements (fatigue) or deterioration.
- Roof insulation durability is dependent upon the mass remaining the same under load and traffic, with dimensional stability and R-values remaining constant and not dissipating, and the original properties remaining the same even if exposed to unexpected amounts of moisture vapor.

In order for a material to dissipate and revert to another form of material, certain elements usually are required. The main elements are water, oxygen, and heat. Chemical reaction and material transformation may require all or only one of these items to be present. (See Fig. 2.18.)

Water. Water ponding for extended periods of time (72+ h) on a roof surface is prohibited under most (not all) roof material manufacturers' requirements. Water on an asphalt bitumen membrane will lead to interaction between the H_2O molecules and the long hydrocarbon chains of the bitumen. Chemical reaction will occur and the asphalt bituminous product will experience *roof rot.*

On other roof material membranes that in themselves are not chemically affected by ponding water, the area of isolated water can create other physical reactions that will cause loss of durability to the membrane system. The thermal loading of the ponding area will not be the same as the temperatures and loading of other, dry areas of the roof surface. Expansion and contraction will occur at different rates across the wet/dry areas. The seams and laps of the membrane were never intended, formulated, or designed to withstand this type of stress. (See Fig. 2.4.)

Additionally, ponding areas on roofs have a tendency to become darker than other areas of the roof surface. Once again, temperature extremes and differences from wet to dry areas will become even more pronounced as solar radiation is absorbed by the darker areas. (See Sec. 2.2.)

In ponded roof areas, water also brings with it dust and dirt from the wash-off of the roof surface, and possibly pollutants and organic contaminants. If the pollutants and contaminants do not cause a chemical reaction with the roof membrane, the dirt and dust accumulate to create what is often a very suitable sod base for vegetation growth. The root system of the vegetation can penetrate the roof membrane. (See Fig. 2.19.)

Oxygen. Oxygen is an element that most of us, fortunately, still get to deal with. It is ever present and surrounds all we do. Without oxygen in free form, many chemical reactions cannot occur. For instance, the rusting of metals is not as pronounced underwater as above in the atmosphere. However, underwater, the metal is still dissipating and chemically changing. Once above water in the atmosphere, metal objects rust exceedingly fast or fall apart in our hands.

We apply coatings to metal—whether to metal roof decking, fasteners, metal roof panels, etc.—not only to prevent water from attacking the material but to prevent oxygen from reacting with latent moisture in the air to form white or red rust.

Heat. For every 10°C (approximately 18°F) rise in temperature, molecular (chemical) reaction doubles. (See Sec. 2.3.4.) High-R-value roof insulations can increase temperature extremes on a roof surface and the chemical reaction of the roof membrane will likewise accelerate.

For most roof materials this increased temperature will lead to a shorter life than if the membrane experienced only ambient temperatures. Oxidation of bitumens increases, leading to brittle roof membranes and decreasing durability. Cross-linking of molecular chains

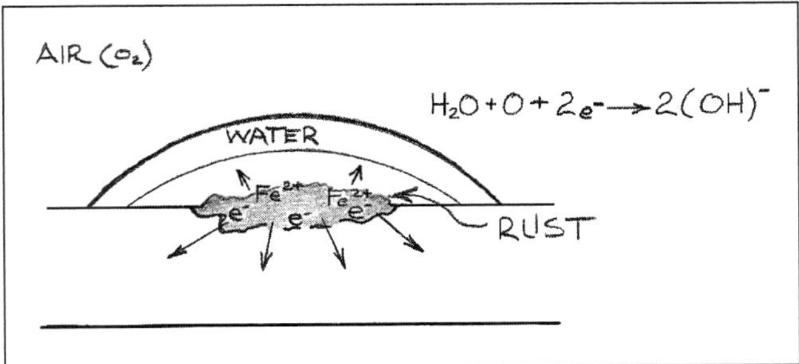

Figure 2.18 Corrosion reaction.

Figure 2.19 Rooftop vegetation.

accelerates, thereby degrading polymer-based materials such as finishes on metal roof panels and polymeric single-ply.

The detrimental effects of temperature (heat energy), water, and oxygen on roof systems vary from climatic region to region. In general comparison, it can be said that roof systems in the coastal southern regions of the United States are not as durable as the same type of roof systems in the north-central areas of the United States.

The coastal southern regions, such as Florida, experience large amounts of annual rainfall and have high humidity factors most of the year, with upper temperature extremes. Additionally, the salt air (organic contaminants) add to the loss of durability.

DURABILITY TESTING

Materials and systems testing is conducted extensively by major organizations such as Factory Mutual (FM) and Underwriters Laboratories (UL). Many other organizations, such as the following, are heavily involved with testing or testing and research results.

- Cold Regions Experimental Laboratories (CREL)
- American National Standards Institute (ANSI)
- American Society for Testing and Materials (ASTM)
- Single Ply Roofing Institute (SPRI)
- National Roofing Contractors Association (NRCA)
- Mid-West Roofing Contractors Association (MRCA)
- National Institute of Standards and Technology (NIST)
- Metal Building Manufacturers Association (MBMA)
- Asphalt Roofing Manufacturers Association (ARMA)

There are other organizations that are also involved with standards and testing, but they are too numerous to list. Also, many organizations sponsor, either independently or as joint ventures, research and testing by third-party organizations such as universities.

From test results, we are informed about how a material or system functioned during the test or research. This leads us to assume characteristics which appear to be inherent in the material or system, and enables us to make assumptions about durability.

Some testing is very scientific and closely controlled in a laboratory setting, while other testing is performed on site under simulated or actual construction processes, with visual observation and handheld measurement and calibration devices providing test results.

Fallacy. In the case of organizations such as Factory Mutual Research Corporation, data is gathered from the testing of materials and systems performance. With some test procedures, the material, component, or system being tested either passes or fails. If passed, the material, component, or system gains FMRC approval. The manufacturer of the material pays a large sum for testing. FMRC determines in house the appropriate means, methods, equipment, and parameters used in testing.

In another scenario, such as with ASTM, committees meet and decide the characteristics a material or component should exhibit when manufactured. Test procedures used to verify these characteristics are then developed over the course of many years and are adopted by the committee. After review and acceptance by the committee, the procedure is accepted or rejected by the voting membership. ASTM does no testing or research, leaving that up to qualified voluntary members of the organization.

In our effort to ensure the "lasting quality and permanence as can reasonably be expected" of the construction materials, we specify and reference ASTM, FM, UL, etc., requirements in specifications. However, as with ASTM and others, such standard compliance of materials *does not* ensure that the materials will have the qualities that will provide durability when incorporated into the roof system. The durability of one component or material is often directly affected by the performance of other materials and components within the total roof assembly. In other words, standards sometimes prescribe only the physical properties the materials should possess at the time they are sold. As such, the standard does not guarantee or ensure the performance of the total roof assembly, nor does it assure the specifier as to how long or at what level it will maintain the original properties after installation into the assembly.

Also, it is a fallacy on the part of people to believe that a material's behavior in a laboratory testing situation will be duplicated when installed to a rooftop. Materials, components, and systems function differently when installed on rooftops than they might when installed at other building locations and environments or when tested in controlled laboratory situations.

Prescriptive standards as discussed here are different from performance standards. Sometimes it is difficult for designers to discern between the two. A performance standard sets the parameters of performance that a *system* or *component* must meet, usually under adverse situations, such as a roof system when exposed to fire, high-speed winds, hailstorms, etc. In this case, if your roof system must withstand high-wind situations in order to be durable, specify a roof system in compliance with FM 1-90 standards.

Under performance standards, the designer must be cognizant of total system requirements. Realize that if one component within the assembly is substituted for another "or equal" product, and this equal product has not been tested as part of the total system, the system is no longer in compliance with the performance standard as tested and developed.

The use of standards is important, allowing us to include materials with a performance value that will meet the design parameters our system must comply with. (See Chap. 14.) Be aware that, in our endeavors to specify and design durable roof systems, a material's characteristics are defined by standards, but once installed into a system, other characteristics of the material may become obvious and adverse.

A system's performance standard is based upon the total assembly. Just because a material possesses physical properties in a laboratory setting does not ensure that the material's characteristics and properties will remain or perform the same when installed into the roof system.

CHAPTER 3

Roof Decks

3.1 ROOF DECK REQUIREMENTS

GENERAL

Roof decks are a very important component in all roof systems and a primary component of the building structure. If the deck construction and/or design is not proper, the roof will fail prematurely. No matter how good the roof is, if the deck is inadequate there will be premature failure of the roof system.

Many types of materials are used in the construction of roof decks, including:

- Metal
- Lightweight insulating concrete
- Poured gypsum
- Precast concrete panels
- Prestressed cast concrete panels
- Reinforced concrete
- Cementituous wood-fibered roof panels
- Wood

Factors that must be considered in roof deck design are:

- Deck thickness
- Material type
- Deck deflection and the loads that will be placed upon the deck
- Any anticipated building movement

The deck components that must be considered in the overall design of the roof and roof deck are:

- Perimeter details such as wood nailers and blocking
- Structural curbs and blocking for roof-mounted equipment
- Roof drains
- Attachment method of the roof deck to the roof joists or purlins

If roof insulation is to be used, consideration of the density and compressive strengths of the insulation, the R-values of the insulation, as well as plenum ventilation and vapor barriers must be evaluated. (See Sec. 2.3.3.)

The roof deck must be designed and installed properly to receive the new roof. The deck surface must be clean and smooth without any high build-ups or depressed areas. Deck panels must be set together tightly and true to the overall plane and level of the deck.

The roof deck must be designed so as to evenly transfer all loads placed upon it to the structural supports it will rest on. These loads should then be dispersed throughout the structural supports, again evenly transferring the weight loads.

All slopes of the deck should be consistent and uniform. The roof deck, depending on the type of building structure, should terminate close to or into the wall, leaving no large gaps or holes to be roofed over. Roof drains should be recessed below the plane of the deck to make the drains the lowest points on the roof deck. Wood blocking and curbs should usually be installed before any roofing begins.

DECK SUPPORT STYLES

There should be additional structural framing at all roof perimeters. This additional framing is dictated by the type of support the roof deck is rested upon. There are two types of supporting styles that decks incorporate: wall-supported or non-wall-supported.

If the deck is supported by the building walls, this is called a wall-supported roof deck. If the building and building walls move or shift, the roof deck and parapet walls will move and shift along with the building. This is because the deck is a part of the building wall, being locked and secured into it. (See Fig. 3.1.)

If the roof deck is supported by beams or subpurlins at the perimeter edge of the roof and is not locked and joined into the building wall, this is a non-wall-supported deck. If the deck terminates at or slightly into the building wall, but the building wall adds no structural support, this is a non-wall-supported deck. (See Fig. 3.2.)

The style of deck support is important if there is a parapet wall at the roof edge. If the deck is supported by the building wall, the deck, parapet wall, and building wall will move as one unit. If the roof deck is not supported by the building wall, then the parapet wall and building wall may move while the roof deck stays in the same spot and does not move, or vice versa.

There are two different styles of flashing systems that must be used at the parapet walls, depending on whether the deck is supported or not supported by the building walls. If the roof deck is not supported by the building walls, the roof deck will move independently of the building. In strong winds or during building movement or settlement, the walls may move while the deck remains stationary. This will cause a shear plane at the point where the deck intersects the parapet wall at the perimeters. The flashing system must be designed and installed to allow for this movement. If the metal flashing and the membrane flashing cannot allow for this movement, then the flashing will be torn apart and the roof will leak.

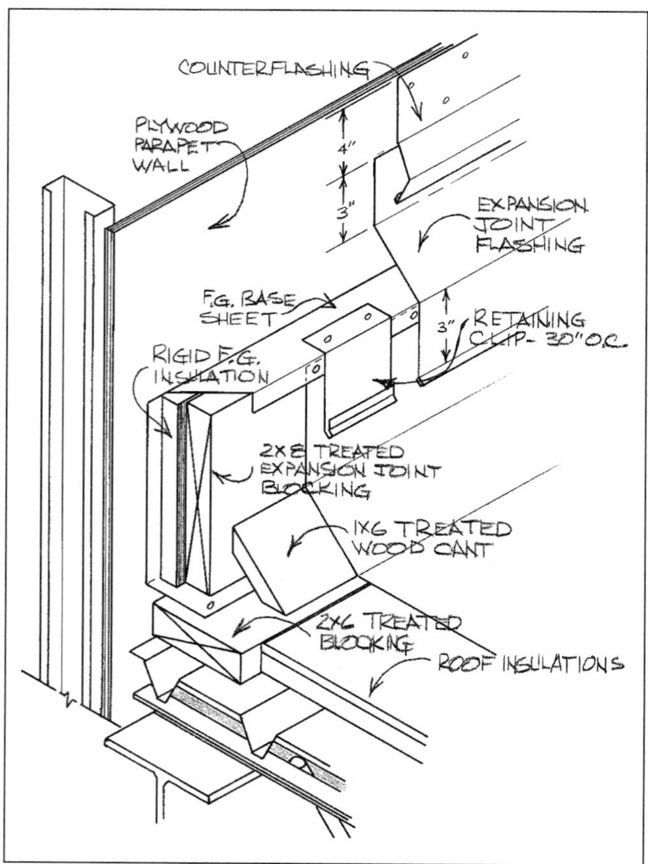

Figure 3.2 Non-wall-supported roof deck.

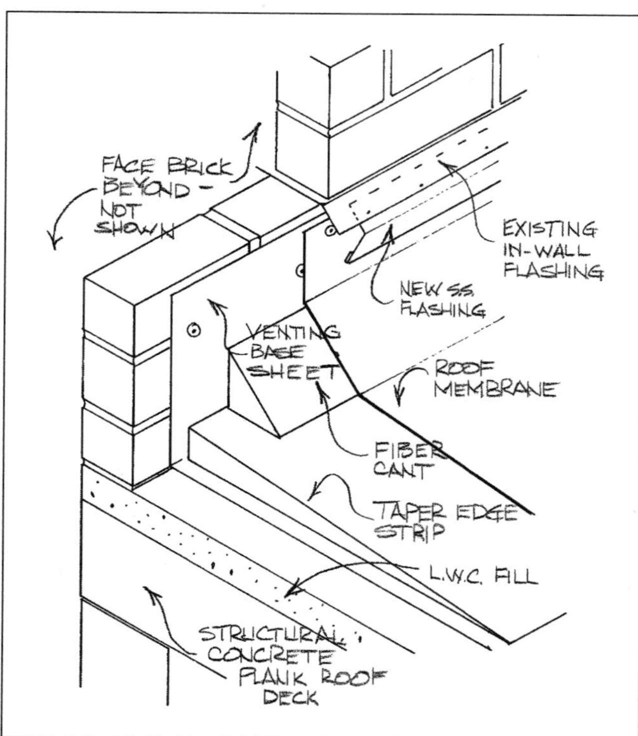

Figure 3.1 Wall-supported roof deck.

If the roof deck is supported by the building wall, there will not be a shear plane at this point. The roof deck will move along with the building because the deck is tied into the building walls.

DECK DEFLECTION

Low-sloped membrane roofs should always have a slope that will not allow water to remain on top of the roof membrane for longer than 48 h. Many material manufacturers will void their warranties if water is allowed to remain longer than this.

Many low-sloped roof decks, when designed on the drawing board, allow for a slope in the decking. Such roof decks usually have a ⅛- or ¼-in slope per running foot. However, what you end up with in the field may be different. This difference is because the designer did not allow enough tolerance for the load that will be placed upon the deck, for spans between the support beams, as well as for building settlement or fatigue of the building components that naturally occur with time.

In reroof design, ponding water on the roof surface due to improper roof slope is a common occurrence. This is corrected by the addition of roof drains into the ponding water areas and/or with a sloped roof insulation system. (See Sec. 8.1.4.)

It is required by most roof-material manufacturers—and is good design practice—to never allow more than $1/240$ for deck deflection from deck support to support. This is based upon the span between supports. If the deck is free spanning between support beams that are 5 ft on center under the deck, then $1/240$ of the 5 ft is the maximum allowable deflection. $1/240$ of 5 ft converts to ¼ in. In this case the deck cannot deflect or swag more than ¼ in under a dead load.

Many times roof drainage is restricted by improper placement of roof drains. Roof drains should be installed at the lowest area on a roof, usually in between deck supports since this is where maximum deflection will occur. Many times drains are placed close to interior load-bearing building walls or structural beams. At these walls and beams is where deflection will occur the least.

Live and Dead Loads. Live loads and dead loads are a consideration when evaluating roof decks. A dead load is a constant weight that exerts a steady load pressure to the roof deck. A dead load is the weight of the total roof assembly and will change with alterations or replacement of the roof system.

A live load is a weight that is exerting pressure and loads to the roof for a temporary time—"temporary" used in relation to the total life of the building. Snow, because of its temporary nature and because more can be added or taken away depending on weather conditions, is considered a live load. Roofing materials, when stockpiled on a roof deck prior to application, are a live load. After installation, this same material is considered to be a dead load.

A man walking across the roof deck is a live moving load. Live and dynamic loads cause most of the trouble with improper or inadequate decks. As a person weighing 150 lb walks, more than 150 lb of pressure are exerted with each step. Also, during the roofing operation, workers use roofing equipment, such as gravel spreaders, minimops, and hot luggers, some of which, when full, can weigh approximately 200 to 400 lb. This equipment can exert concentrated loads that will cause the deck to deflect more than $1/240$. The deck must have the resilience (tensile strength) to return to the original designed slope upon removal of this superimposed load.

In reroof design it is sometimes acceptable practice to leave the existing roof system in place and install a new system over it. This is termed *retrofit*. Roof retrofit may be acceptable if the combined weight of both the old and new roof systems on the building does not exceed the original design load capabilities. This is often accomplished by removing the gravel surfacing from a built-up roof and installing a lightweight metal roof system or a single-ply roof system.

However, problems can result in retrofit design if the dead load to the building support structure is increased to a point where interior building components and systems are affected. The new and increased loads may be acceptable for the roof support structure as originally designed, but additional deck deflection under the new dead load can be expected. This new load and subsequent deflections, although not a common occurrence, can be transferred to components such as the interior walls.

In reroof design, changing the existing dead load of the roof system could have drastic effects. If the load was minimal, such as 1.5 to 2.0 lb/ft^2, as with an insulated single-ply roof system, changing the roof system to a built-up roof with gravel surface will greatly increase the dead load of the roof assembly. A built-up roof with a gravel surface can weigh 4.0 to 6.0 lb/ft^2. With a 10,000-ft^2 roof area, this will increase the total dead load of 15,000 to 20,000 lb to 40,000 to 60,000 lb. The roof structure may originally have been designed to support this new dead load, but building conditions and finishes which have existed for the past 20 years may not be receptive to the new loads, deflections, and stresses which will surely occur. (See Sec. 2.1.1.)

3.1.1 Metal Roof Decks

Metal roof decks are the predominant type of roof deck assembly used in the commercial construction sector. Metal roof deck panels create the structural deck to which the roofing components are installed. Nonstructural metal roof deck panels, as used with lightweight slur deck materials, are discussed under Sec. 3.1.5.

Structural metal roof deck panels are made from cold-rolled steel, either coated with rust resistant paint or galvanized. It is recommended that only galvanized coated steel roof deck materials be used.

These metal decks come to the job site in panels that can be of different widths but are usually 30 in wide. They can be almost any length, should always be of 22-gauge thickness or better, and have ribs that are formed into them during the cold-rolling process at the manufacturing plant. The ribs can be of different depths, normally ranging from 1½ to 7½ in deep, but usually 1½ in deep.

Metal panels have three basic rib styles: narrow rib, intermediate rib, and wide rib. These ribs will extend downward and rest upon the purlins. In steel deck construction, the purlins that the ribs rest on are usually open-web bar joists.

We will refer to the ribs as the *deck flutes* and to the flat portion in between the ribs as the *deck pan*. The deck pans are usually 6 in wide, this measurement being taken from center to center of the flute opening. The deck pan can also be 7½, 8, 9, or 12 in wide.

The narrow rib will have a flute no larger than 1 in wide. The intermediate rib will have a flute from 1 to 1¾ in wide. The wide rib will have a flute from 1¾ in wide to a maximum flute width of 2½ in. The deeper the metal flute rib is and the wider the rib opening, the farther it can free-span from purlin to purlin. In comparison, if you have a wide-rib panel and a narrow-rib panel, both of the same gauge material and flute depth, the wide-rib panel will span approximately 40 percent farther than will the narrow-rib.

The metal deck panels can be either screwed or welded to the purlins, with welding being the most common method. The edges where the metal panels overlap each other should always be screwed tightly, one to the other. These screws should be spaced in between the purlins to which the panel is attached, and the screws should not be spaced farther than 3 ft on center, with centers beginning at the fastener or weld at the purlin. This prevents the decking from deflecting or moving during installation and loading of the new roof system.

The metal panels should be aligned straight and true, intersecting all walls and edges in a square fashion. A ¼-in deviation in the straight run of the metal panel is allowed for every 100 linear feet. (See Fig. 3.3.)

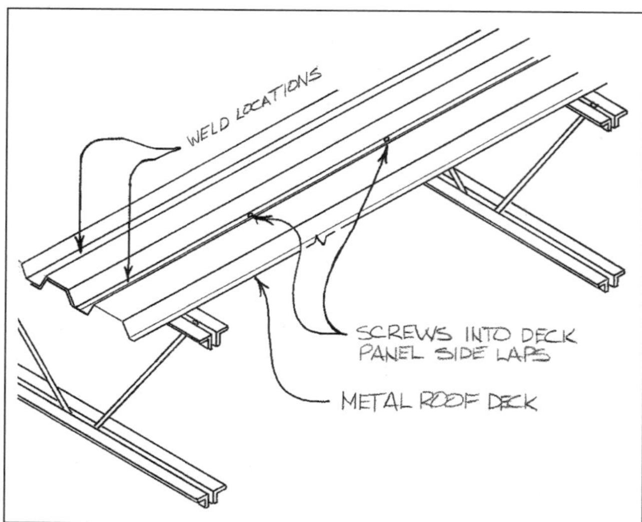

Figure 3.3 Installation of metal plate and fastener.

INSULATION

It is never acceptable to attach a roof directly to a metal roof deck, unless it is a polyurethane foam roof system. It is necessary to install roof insulation to the top of the metal deck. This insulation is normally board stock or, for nonstructural metal decking as discussed in Sec. 3.1.5, it can be an insulating wet slur fill that can be either lightweight concrete or poured gypsum.

If the insulation is board stock, the roof slope must be created by a different elevation of the purlins, which will give slope to the metal deck, or the deck can be dead-level with a tapered roof insulation system installed to the top of the metal. The tapered insulation will then create the slope. (See Sec. 8.1.4.) It is usually cheaper to create the slope with the purlins than it is to create the slope with tapered insulation.

To meet most building code requirements, and to comply with industry standards, it is never recommended that insulation be attached to the metal roof deck with bitumen or adhesives. However, a recent product on the market, a polyurethane foam–based material, has achieved certification for proper wind-resistant abilities.

Insulation must be attached using mechanical fasteners. Self-tapping screws and metal caps are the most commonly used components for attaching roof materials to a metal deck. (See Fig. 3.4 and Sec. 8.1.)

If evaluating an older roof system with a metal roof deck, or sometimes even a relatively new roof with a metal deck, you may find roof insulation attached with a mopping of hot asphalt. If the roof insulation is attached using adhesives or bitumens, the deck pan must be completely flat without any depressions across the face of the pan. A depression will not allow the insulation board to sit fully and be completely bonded to the metal pan.

Such improper attachment is the primary reason for wind blow-off. Also, this type of insulation attachment method will often allow the roof insulation panels to move under the roof membrane. When the insulation panels move excessively, cracks and splits can be the result in the roof membrane. When evaluating an existing roof and cracks and splits are observed in the roof membrane in a uniform pattern that matches the outline of the roof insulation panels, the attachment method of the insulation should be investigated.

Insulation panels must be thick enough to span metal deck flutes without breaking under rooftop live loads. Roof-insulation manufacturers enclose tables within their product literature that show the span rating for different types and thicknesses of roof insulations. (See Table 3.1.)

The side joints of the insulation panels must rest on top of the deck pan. All end joints of the panels must be staggered one from the other. All additional layers of roof insulation must be with staggered joints, with none of the

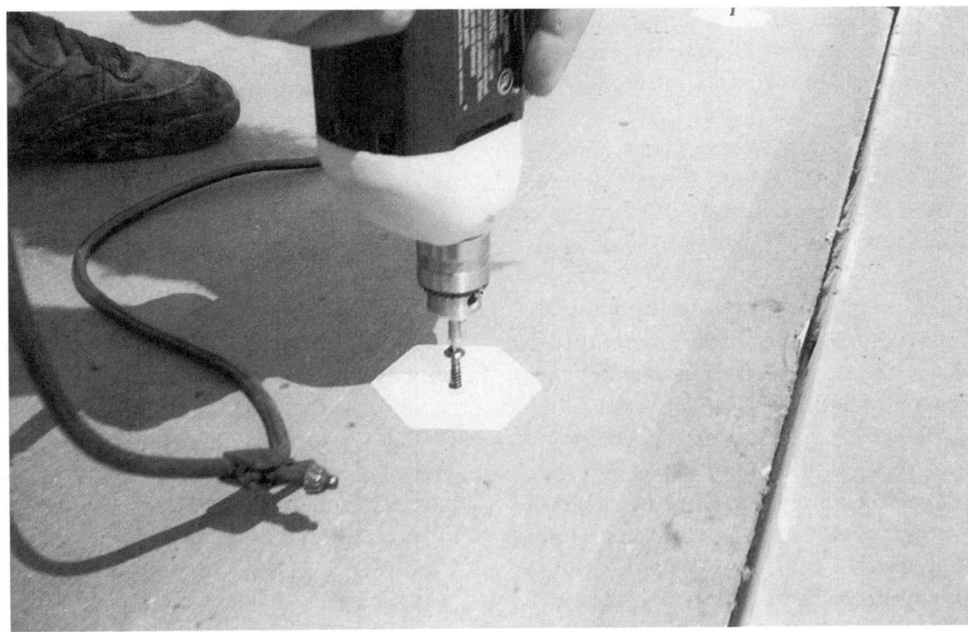

Figure 3.4 Installation of metal plate and fastener.

end or side joints in these additional layers occurring over the joints of the panels underneath. (See Fig. 3.5.)

Proper roofing practices dictate that at least two layers of roof insulation be used when covering a metal roof deck. The first layer should be mechanically attached and the second layer should be attached using hot asphalt or adhesives.

FASTENERS

Improper attachment of the roof insulation to the deck can result in wind blow-off, delamination of the roof components, and unacceptable movement of the roof system. Many types of fasteners have been created to solve these problems, including:

- Screw and plate systems
- Hand-driven barbed nails
- Toggle-bolt assemblies
- Large pop-rivet assemblies

The most popular type of fastener is the self-tapping screw. When the screw is drawn down tightly to the deck, there is very little play in the screw. In other words, the screw will not move down into the deck when pressure is placed on top of the head of the screw. This may not be true for other types of fasteners.

Screw fastening systems also have very good pull-out resistance. Factory Mutual requirements state that only

Table 3.1 A typical example of a span rating table for a perlite roof insulation (for use over metal decks).

Width of rib flute (opening)	Up to 1 in	Up to 1¾ in	Up to 2½ in
Thickness of insulation, minimum	¾ in	1 in	1½ in

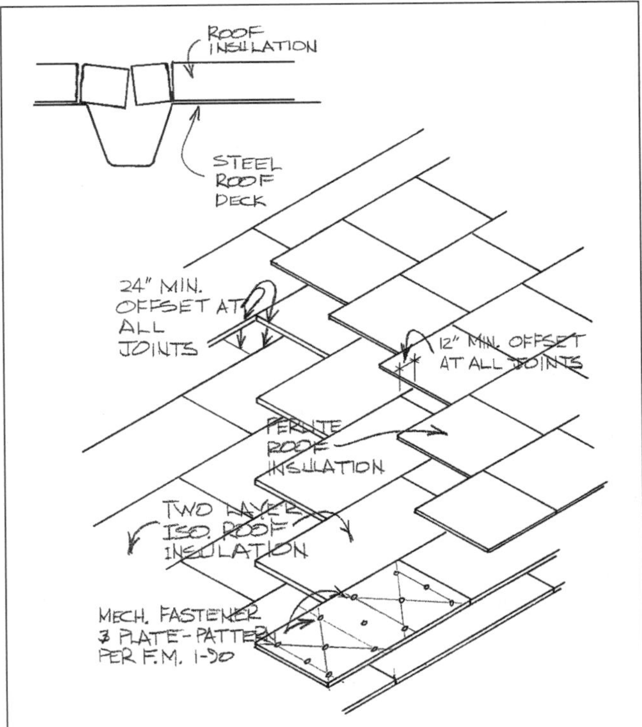

Figure 3.5 Layout schematic diagram.

screw fasteners be used in metal deck assemblies and FM Loss Prevention Data Sheet 1-28 describes the fastening patterns required to meet wind blow-off standards.

Mechanical fasteners should completely penetrate the metal roof deck. If a tapered insulation system is being mechanically attached, the fasteners may have to be of different lengths to ensure that all insulation is properly attached.

With the advent of metal decking as a predominant deck type in today's construction market, self-tapping screw fasteners became widely used. After several years, some of these fasteners failed, resulting in wind blow-off, delamination of the roof components, and unacceptable movement of the roof system.

Again, many types of fasteners have been created to solve these problems. Some screw and plate systems incorporate a locking mechanism to prevent back-out of the screw. Back-out of screw fasteners occurs in metal decks, just as nails will back out of the wood decking. This phenomenon can be traced to factors such as thermal bridging of the fastener. (See Sec. 2.1.1.)

For example, in cold climates the temperature on the fastener head will approach the outside air temperature, but the underside of the fastener, protruding through the deck, will be closer to the inside building temperature. This difference in temperatures, conveyed down the screw shaft, can cause the fastener to move and back out.

A top layer of fully adhered roof insulation, covering the bottom, mechanically attached layer of insulation, prevents this thermal bridging. Deck, insulation, roof membrane, and roof-mounted equipment movement can also contribute to fastener back-out.

Fastener corrosion has caused many problems in the roofing industry. If moisture condenses within the roof assembly or if the interior of the building has a high moisture content which attacks the exposed shaft of the screw, and the fastener is of a poor quality without a good protective coating, the fastener will rust in two. When this happens the roof is no longer attached to the deck. The fastener bottoms could start falling from the underside of the deck down into the building. (See Sec. 2.3.3.)

Vapor drive must be considered. Certain temperature differences and humidities from inside the building to the exterior of the roof can cause condensation on the underside of the deck, or even worse, within the insulation layers.

In many cases, galvanize coating did not prove effective in stopping corrosion of the fastener. We now have more sophisticated coatings, applied in multiple processes, designed especially to accommodate chemical and moisture attack.

Fasteners should be rated as noncorrosive by either FM or UL. FM standard #4470 uses the Kesternick test method, a recognized procedure for evaluating the corrosive characteristics of a metallic fastener.

Fastener heads are prone to stress. This is due to torquing during installation as well as roof component movement. The longer the screw, the more torque it will experience when being driven into and through the deck.

Also, single-ply mechanically attached membranes will flutter and move, even in a slight wind. Although this movement does not put extreme stress on the fastener head, it is constant and, in time, contributes to fastener fatigue. If the head of the screw separates from the shaft due to these problems, the roof system is no longer attached to the deck. (See Sec. 2.1.1, "Wind Loads.")

Wide-rib steel deck panels, having flute rib openings of 1¾ to 2½-in, can also present a problem with proper fastener patterns. Fasteners are required to penetrate through the deck pan and not the flute corrugation. On wide-rib panels, the proper fastening pattern may not be possible to achieve. (See Fig. 2.5.)

Another important factor coming to light is fastening patterns into decks, which are required in order to conform to Factory Mutual requirements, as well as insulation and roof membrane manufacturers' requirements. Oftentimes, many fasteners are required, in straight lines, on close centers. What happens to a metal deck that has fasteners penetrating it on 12-in centers, in rows spaced 12 in apart? What happens to a fatigued structural concrete deck that then has expandable anchor fasteners placed into it every 2 ft^2?

These are just a few of the many questions that must be considered when fastening roof materials to decking. Designers are advised to do their homework when considering fasteners. Verify that the fastener is approved by the roof material manufacturer for use in the particular assembly. Verify that there are no special considerations, such as a vapor drive causing condensation, or caustic elements within the insulation or deck assembly that will attack the screw.

3.1.2 Structural Cement Fiber Roof Decks

Structural cement fiber roof decking is composed of treated wood fibers that look like large and coarse straw. These fibers are bound together with a wet solution of portland cement or other binding agents. This wet solution is pressed and formed to desired size and thickness. The panels are usually tongue and groove, although they can also be rabbeted.

The product was first introduced to the construction market in 1949 by U.S. Gypsum. This product line was later purchased by Tectum. Today there are several manufacturers of cementitious wood-fiber roof deck panels.

The decking is hard, solid preformed panels which are installed to the purlins or subpurlins. If bulb-tee subpurlins are used, a grout must be installed around these

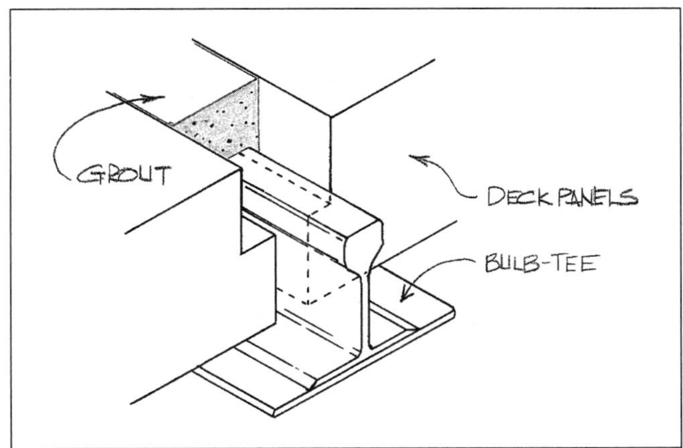

Figure 3.6 Bulb-tee and rabbeted edge with grout.

bulb-tees and rabbeted edges to the decking manufacturer's specification. (See Fig. 3.6.)

The panels are usually installed with the underside remaining exposed to the building interior. These panels provide excellent acoustical values and are often used in gymnasium areas to control sound distortion. (See Sec. 2.3.2.) The thickness of the decking panels dictates their span rating, usually spanning, between purlins, 3 to 4 ft. Thickness will also determine insulating values.

When increased R-values are required, a composite panel is manufactured using polystyrene or urethane insulation bonded to the deck panel. The insulation can also be covered by wafer or plywood sheathing to allow for installation of composition shingles, metal roofing, etc.

These cementitious panels are heavy and solid, but they will crack and split if handled improperly. These panels should never be exposed to rain and high-humidity conditions can affect their performance, although in some instances they are used in swimming pool and gymnasium areas.

If a roof is allowed to leak for extended periods of time into and onto this deck material, the cement that binds the wood fibers together will be washed out. When this happens, the decking will have no strength left. All that is left supporting the roof is wood fibers.

Special fasteners must be used to attach a base sheet to this decking. It will not retain a regular nail. Tube-type nails, wedge nail fasteners, and large nylon screw-type fasteners are acceptable for use in this decking.

Most types of roofing should not be applied directly to cementitious wood-fibered decking. A base sheet should first be attached. If roof insulation is to be used, this insulation can either be adhered in bitumen to a mechanically fastened base sheet or it can be fastened to the decking with an approved fastener that will work in this decking.

This type of roof decking performs quite well in institutional designs, such as schools and correctional facilities. The natural white finish of the deck provides good light reflectance, and the acoustic values make it a good choice for large, open areas.

The cementitious panels can be used as form boards to which a cement roof deck can be poured. Upon removal of the shoring required for the deck pour, a finished ceiling is the result. (See Fig. 3.7.)

Figure 3.7 Prison ceiling and form board. (*Courtesy of Tectum, Inc., Newark, Ohio.*)

3.1.3 Concrete Roof Decks

There are two basic kinds of concrete roof decks: the concrete panel roof deck and the structural poured-in-place concrete deck. The concrete panel decks can be prestressed, which will give them a camber, or slope.

CONCRETE PANEL ROOF DECKING

Since concrete panel roof decks are very heavy, they are supported on steel beams or concrete beams. The concrete panels require attachment and bracing to the structural beam. This is accomplished by metal plates that are embedded in the sides and bottoms of the concrete roof panel. The plates in the panel are aligned and welded to plates in the concrete support beam or directly to the steel support beam. Lateral bracing supports can also be welded to these embedded plates.

Many times when concrete panels are installed, there will be a difference in the top elevation of different panels. This difference will cause bridging of the felts or insulations. A grout must be used if there is a difference of ⅛ in or more between panels. The grout must be feathered out to create a smooth transition between the panels for the roof to sit upon.

A concrete panel can be prestressed. This stressing is done by having a strong cable placed in the deck-panel-forming mold before pouring the deck panel. After the panel is poured and the concrete hardens, the cable is pulled tighter and tighter. This pulling is done until the panel begins to rise in the center. When the proper rise, or camber, is achieved, the cable is secured and the panel is mounted to the roof structure.

Hot bitumen can come through the joints of a concrete panel roof deck. The joints should be filled in with grout or cement, or be stripped in with felt and steep asphalt bitumen.

A built-up roof (BUR) or modified bitumen roof should not be applied directly to a concrete panel roof. Roof insulation should first be applied to the roof deck or, if installing a ballasted single-ply, a separator sheet is usually required. For fully adhered single-plies, the material manufacturer should be consulted.

For BURs, the surface of the panels and the plane of the deck are normally too rough for direct application. Also, if these panels ever shift, even slightly, they will tear the adhered BUR membrane apart. If applying an insulation to the concrete panels with bitumen or adhesives, the deck must first be primed. The insulation can then be installed in a mopping of asphalt. To the top of the insulation a roof membrane can be installed.

Do not mop coal tar pitch or dead-level asphalt to a concrete deck panel. These panels will sometimes shift and the cold-flowing material will come through the joints of the panels.

REINFORCED STRUCTURAL CONCRETE ROOF DECKS

Reinforced concrete decks are poured in place. The pour is supported by form boards that are usually removed after the pour has set. This material and process is much the same as is used when pouring the slab of a building. Stone, sand, portland cement, water, and sometimes additives and curing agents are used. Wire mesh is sometimes incorporated into the pour, adding tensile strength to the completed deck. Some decks are rated as high-density structural concrete.

Certain procedures must be used when pouring a roof deck that are different from those used when pouring a building slab. The curing agents that are sometimes used may not be compatible with the roof system. They may destroy the roof components they contact. Polyethylene film may prohibit drying and cause trapped moisture in the deck to pass into the new roof.

The moisture level in a concrete deck is acceptable if a small pouring of hot bitumen does not foam and bubble excessively when poured to the deck surface. Another method is using a pane of glass and laying it on the deck surface during the middle of the day. The edges should be taped. If, after several hours, there is condensation under the glass, then there is probably too much moisture in the roof deck. In this case, a vapor barrier is required over the roof deck and venting should be provided.

It is acceptable to install a roof directly to the surface of a structural concrete roof deck. The deck should first be primed if attaching directly to it with hot asphalt bitumen.

3.1.4 Wood Decks

Before metal decks were used, wood roof decks were the most common type of decking. Wood roof decks can be plywood or wood plank. The dimensions of wood planks can range from 1 × 6 in to 4 × 12 in or greater. Plywood for roof decking should never be less than 15⁄32 in thick.

Wood planking should always be of tongue-and-groove material or shiplap material. The thickness of the planks is determined by how far they must span from support beam to support beam and the amount of load that will be placed on them from the roof and roof-mounted equipment.

All wood decking should span over at least one support beam, such as a rafter or joist. Plywood panels should have all end joints staggered. Install wood planks with end joints offset. The offsetting of the plywood or wood plank joints will help transfer the roof load evenly to all rafters or joists.

Plywood panels should bear an association's markings, normally the American Plywood Association label.

This is to certify that is has been made in compliance with most building codes and industry standards and meets Department of Commerce standards. All panels should be rated at grade C-D or better. Panels should have an exterior glue coating. An "X" usually indicates exterior glue.

Numbers are usually stamped on plywood panels. For example, a ½-in nominal thick plywood panel will have 32/16 marked upon it. This marking is the *span rating*. It means the panel will span a 32-in-wide rafter or joist system and will span a 16-in-wide floor joist system, if used in double layers on the floor.

Always use a clip to hold the side joints of the plywood together where it is spanning between supports. These are called H clips. These clips help give the deck uniform support of the roof. (See Fig. 3.8.)

You can step on one piece of plywood at the long joint between the rafters and the piece you step on will move down but the other will not. Clips will reduce this independent movement, causing both pieces of plywood to move at the same time. When clips are used, the two pieces together will not be pushed down as far as the one piece by itself.

When installing plywood panels, be sure to leave a crack between the ends of each panel. This crack should be at least 1/16 in but no greater than ⅛ in. If this crack is not left, ridging can occur when the panels expand and contract.

Ring shank nails or other fasteners that are designed to prevent nail back-out should be used when installing wood decking. Many roof problems are caused by nail back-out.

All lumber used as roof decking should be cured to a low moisture content. If green or wet lumber is used, the possibility of nail back-out as well as ridging and shrinking of the deck is greatly increased. An accepted standard for wood decking is a moisture content of 19 percent or less.

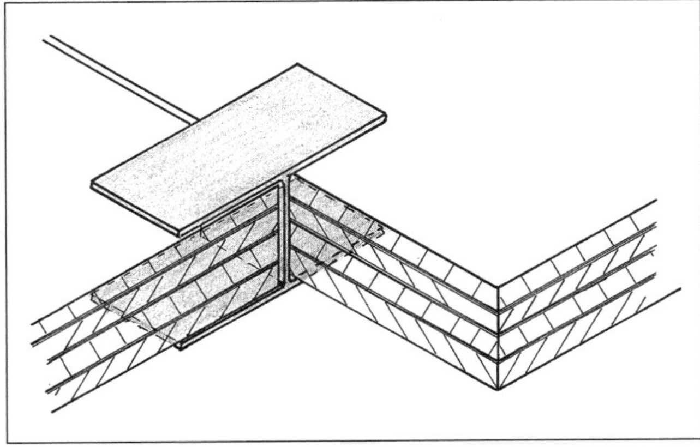

Figure 3.8 H clip.

Wolmanized lumber will often come to the job site with a high moisture content. This is because it is usually stored outside. In hot climates, if this wet lumber is installed as blocking—say as the gravel guard nailer—there could be problems. The problem occurs when the heat inside the roof system starts to dry this blocking and the wood curls and warps. If the lumber is treated, make sure the chemicals used in the treatment process are compatible with the roofing materials.

A roof system is very seldom attached directly to a wood deck. A separator sheet such as a base sheet should first be installed. Some single-plies, however, can be attached directly to a wood roof deck. In most cases it is acceptable to mechanically fasten roof insulation to the wood deck and install a roof over the insulation. However, concerns of fastener back-out through the roof membrane become a possibility. It is proper design practice to cover any mechanically attached insulation with an adhered insulation later. (See Sec. 2.1.1.)

On a composition-shingle roof system, a lightweight felt is installed to the deck. This acts as a separator sheet, keeping the turpentine and resins of the lumber from attacking the asphalt shingles. The felt also allows the shingle system to breathe and not become attached by the heat directly to the roof deck. After installation of the shingles, the felt serves little function as a waterproofer.

3.1.5 Wet-Slur Insulating Decks

GENERAL

There are several types of wet-slur, poured-in-place insulating roof deck assemblies. All of these types of decks require a base: form boards, metal decking, or structural concrete systems—over which they are poured. These types of poured-in-place decks are

- Perlite
- Vermiculite
- Gypsum
- Cellular concrete

Before any of these systems can be poured onto the substrate, several things must first be done. Wood blocking must first be attached to the deck or structural deck components. The wet-slur deck top should be level with the top of the blocking. Roof drain sumps should be set prior to the pour, as well as all equipment supports that must rest on a structural beam.

LIGHTWEIGHT CONCRETE ROOF DECKS

For our discussion here, both perlite and vermiculite roof decks are classified as lightweight concrete deck systems.

These lightweight concrete systems are formed from either vermiculite or perlite ore. The ore particles are superheated so that they expand from 15 to 40 times their original size. These expanded particles are combined with portland cement and water to form this lightweight mixture. In some cases, the ore particles are deleted and plastic foam insulation particles are substituted.

Installation. These materials are mixed together into a uniform wet slur and are pumped onto the roof deck. There must always be a subdeck for lightweight concrete.

This material, as its name suggests, is light in weight. It cannot, by itself, create a deck strong enough to install a roof over. Lightweight concrete decks are most usually installed to the tops of corrugated steel panels, which create a form deck for the lightweight material. Combined, these two components form the roof deck.

Lightweight concrete compressive strength can vary greatly, depending upon the percentages of the different materials in it. It should have minimum compressive strength of 100 lb. Its density should be between 20 and 40 lb/ft^3.

Compressive strength of a material is measured by compressing that material to ⅒ its normal thickness in a presslike piece of equipment. For example, if a piece of lightweight concrete is 2 in thick, it is compressed in the equipment until ⅒ of 2 in is pressed down by the equipment. The equipment has a gauge on it that tells how much pressure is required to compress the material to ⅒ of its thickness.

Density of a material is the weight per cubic foot of that material. If a material is rated to have a density of 20 lb/ft^3, it will weigh 20 lb/ft^3.

After the lightweight material is pumped onto the roof deck, it is screed and floated into the desired slopes and levels. This is usually accomplished by a contractor specializing in lightweight concrete pours. The thickness of the lightweight can vary, depending on the slope that is desired. The minimum thickness that should be allowed is 2 in at any location—less than 2 in and the lightweight could break apart and crumble during the roofing process.

Moisture Cautions. Since the lightweight is made with tremendous amounts of water, a curing or setting-up time is required from the time the pour is completed until the deck is dry enough to roof over. Moisture content in lightweight concrete fills is the biggest problem with this type of system. Many roofs experience failure because the roof membrane was installed too soon or improper venting of the lightweight deck was not allowed for. This causes moisture to be trapped under the roof, and blistering and ply delamination could occur.

When a wet slur is installed over a metal deck, venting should be provided to allow the moisture to escape from the pour. This is normally accomplished by sidelap venting of the metal deck panels.

A base sheet should be nailed or mechanically attached to the lightweight concrete roof deck surface, providing a suitable surface to which the roof system can be adhered. A base sheet is normally recommended when installing many roof systems, such as a built-up roof or modified bitumen roof, to the surface of a wet-slur, poured-in-place roof deck system. Upon completion of the roof membrane, moisture relief vents should be installed on top of the roof membrane surface. Moisture relief venting helps any entrapped gases to escape.

As the moisture vaporizes from the lightweight deck it will be stopped by the base sheet and roof membrane assembly. Moisture relief vents and edge venting should be incorporated into the roof system so that as the moisture rises, it will hit the base sheet and then be forced out through the edge and moisture relief vents.

Topside venting is important, but bottom-side venting is actually more critical. If lightweight concrete systems are installed over a structural concrete system (not recommended), edge and topside venting must be carefully designed and installed. (See Fig. 3.9.)

It is not recommended for roof insulations to be applied directly to the surface of lightweight concrete, but instead they should be attached to the top of the base-ply sheet. Moisture rising out of the lightweight can be entrapped in the insulation.

Also, attachment of roof insulation to the top of lightweight concrete decking can prove difficult when using mechanical fasteners and is not a recommended procedure. The use of adhesive or hot-asphalt moppings will not allow proper attachment of roof components to lightweight concrete deck systems. Roof membrane

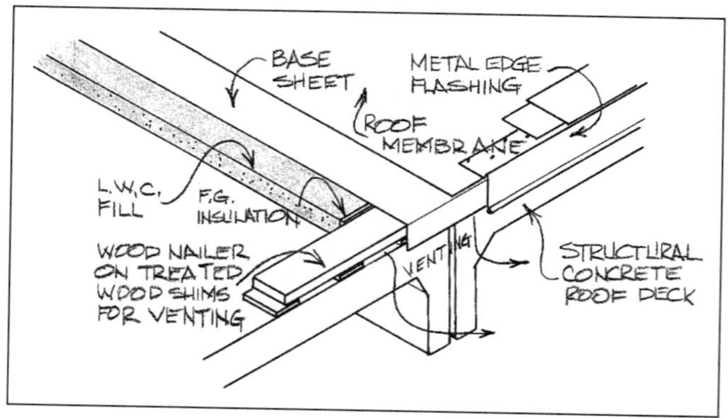

Figure 3.9 Edge and topside venting.

materials should not be mopped or adhered directly to the lightweight for the same reason.

Design Controls. If additional insulation values are desired of the lightweight concrete deck system, polystyrene insulations which resist moisture absorption can be incorporated into the pour. This is accomplished by designing the insulation panels in decreasing thickness going toward the drain or the edge. The lightweight slurry can then be poured over the polystyrene. The design must always allow for a minimum of 2 in of lightweight material covering the underlying insulation product at any location. (See Fig. 3.10.)

Depending on the temperature, humidity, and wind, it can take from 3 to 21 days for a lightweight concrete deck to cure enough so that an effective roof can be installed over it. One accepted way of determining the moisture content of a roof deck is the use of hot asphalt as an indicator. When hot asphalt is poured onto a wet roof deck, the moisture in the deck will cause it to bubble and froth. After the asphalt has cooled, it will come up easily and cleanly from the deck. If these two things happen, the deck is still too wet to roof over.

In new construction, everyone is always in a hurry. The roofing contractor will usually be pushed by the general contractor, building owner, or architect to put a roof on the building. If a roof is put on to meet a construction timetable, instead of to meet good roofing practices, the building will probably be reroofed in the near future.

CELLULAR CONCRETE ROOF DECKS

Cellular concrete roof decks could be classified as lightweight concrete systems, although they have different characteristics from perlite or vermiculite systems. Herein we classify them unto themselves, although they are still a wet-slur deck system.

Cellular concrete roof decks are usually made from a water-cement slurry which then has exact amounts of pregenerated foam added to it. The foam begins as a liquid concentrate and is created by air pressure and the use of an expanding foam nozzle which ensures that the foam is uniform. The resulting foam bubbles are completely encapsulated within the slurry. For higher-density mixes, aggregate—usually sand—is added.

The foam bubbles, trapped within the pour, create a uniform cell structure throughout the finished roof deck. This type of lightweight concrete deck has a greatly reduced drying time, approximately one-half of that required for standard lightweight concrete, making it a popular type of roof deck assembly.

Some manufacturers of the cellulating concrete material use a synthetic surfactant as a blowing agent in the wet-slur mixture. This surfactant takes the place of much of the water required with other types of lightweight concrete systems. The water volume required for perlite/vermiculite lightweight deck systems is reduced from approximately 100 gal per yard to 40 gal per yard

Figure 3.10 Cellular concrete deck being poured. *(Courtesy of Allied-Signal, Mars, Pa.)*

of concrete mix. The surfactant causes the concrete to cellulate, and the tiny cells take the place of the ore commonly used.

There is more cement used in the mixture, which gives the finished product more density and compressive strength. The downside is that there is low R-value to this material, about ½ R per inch.

Because of its low water content, and therefore its quick drying time, venting metal decks are normally prohibited with this material. It is specified for use over nonventing deck structures, such as structural concrete. In the hot southern climates, a water spray may have to be periodically applied to the top of the freshly poured deck to prevent it from curing too fast. Some single-ply manufacturers have specifications that allow their polymeric membrane to be fully adhered directly to the cured surface of this lightweight material.

Cellular concrete roof decks require less drying time, enabling roofing to start quicker. Cellular concrete will absorb less water than will other lightweight decks and is not damaged as much by roof leaks as other types of lightweight may be. Moisture relief vents are normally not required with this type of system. (See Fig. 3.10.)

GYPSUM ROOF DECKS

Gypsum roof decks are similar to lightweight concrete deck systems in that they begin as a wet slur and are poured onto the rooftop. However, they are two different materials and therefore have different characteristics. Gypsum has been used throughout history as a construction material. As early as 3700 B.C. gypsum plaster was used for construction of walls in the pyramids of Egyptian pharaohs.

Gypsum roof decks require venting, although this venting is mainly accomplished downward through the form boards. The form boards can be from a variety of material, including glass fiber, cement asbestos, mineral fiber, or gypsum. Gypsum, known commonly as Sheetrock, is the most used of the form boards. These form boards are required to give the wet slur the support it needs until the wet slur has set.

Setting time for poured-in-place gypsum can be controlled by the mixture of different components, either causing immediate setting or extending the setting time. Usually the setting of poured gypsum occurs within 10 to 15 min. Roofing can begin immediately as the material has hardened.

A gypsum roof deck is made of gypsum, a rock found in many parts of the world, and water. The gypsum material comes to the job site in the form of a powder. It is mixed in a precise ratio with the water. These materials are mixed to the proper viscosity and pumped onto the rooftop.

Gypsum decks have a density that is greater than that of lightweight concrete. The density of gypsum decks is usually between 30 to 55 lb/ft^3. The compressive strength of the cured deck is usually 500 lb/in^2.

Gypsum decks are usually poured on top of form boards which are attached to the subpurlins, and the subpurlins are usually bulb-tees. These bulb-tees have a flange, such as a metal angle iron channel. The form boards rest on this channel and are attached to it.

The gypsum is poured to the top of the form boards where it is screed and floated to the desired thickness and slope. The minimum thickness allowed for poured gypsum is 2 in with ¼ in above the top of the bulb-tee. A wire mesh is placed on top of the bulb-tees and form boards, reinforcing the gypsum deck. This mesh is galvanized stranded wire mesh. This wire must not be floated to the top of the pour and become exposed.

When a gypsum slur is being poured, a heat-releasing reaction occurs. This reaction allows gypsum decks to be poured in cold or freezing temperatures.

In today's market, lightweight concrete decks are more common than gypsum decks. Gypsum deck material will disintegrate more rapidly than lightweight if it is exposed to water for extended periods of time, as is the case with unrepaired roof leaks.

Workers installing gypsum decks must walk on the bulb-tee purlins, because the form boards will not support their weight. This can prove dangerous. Most of the other factors involved in a lightweight concrete deck must also be considered in a gypsum deck.

Lightweight concrete and gypsum decks are considered to be nailable. There are special fasteners made to go into these materials and not penetrate through the bottom of the pour. The fasteners expand as they are driven down into the pour.

3.1.6 Moisture Relief Vents

Moisture relief vents are commonly used in the roofing industry on many types of roofs, not just lightweight roof deck systems. There is some controversy in the roofing industry as to the effectiveness of moisture relief vents. These vents are not designed to vent water out from under roof systems. They will only help expel small amounts of moisture that have turned to vapor under the roof.

For moisture relief vents to perform properly, the roof system must be designed so moisture can move freely under the roof in order to reach a vent. This is accomplished by installing a base sheet or vapor barrier. The moisture cannot penetrate this barrier and enter into the roof system above. It must instead remain trapped between the roof membrane and the deck until it finds a way to get out. If it cannot get out, blistering of the roof may occur.

There are basically two types of moisture relief vents. There are vents which allow gases to pass only one way and there are vents which allow gases to pass both ways. One-way vents are usually recommended.

A one-way vent has a diaphragm in the throat of the vent that will open only one way. This diaphragm opens when pressure is created by moisture vapor building up in the roof system. The diaphragm allows moisture vapor to escape from within the roof but humidity and vapor from outside the roof cannot get in. A two-way vent does not have a diaphragm. The throat of the vent is open and will allow the passage of moisture vapor in both directions.

Moisture vapor within a roof assembly and the drive of the vapor is a complex issue. Vapor may not always rise within the roof and therefore escape through a moisture relief vent. Sometimes the vapor will drive toward the bottom of the assembly, or the vapor may drive toward the top during certain times and toward the bottom at other times. (See Sec. 2.3.3.)

There are several different ways to install moisture relief vents. Remember that a relief vent is to allow gases and vapors to escape from the component of the roof system that is suspect. Sometimes a hole is cut through the roof membrane down to the roof deck. This hole may also be through the vapor barrier, as is the case of a base sheet attached to lightweight concrete deck. Since moisture can be anticipated in a wet-slur deck system, moisture vapor must be allowed to escape. (See Fig. 3.11.)

On the other hand, it is sometimes imperative that the vapor barrier not be cut. If the vapor barrier is to restrict moisture vapor drive, cutting the barrier will allow moisture into the roof assembly.

Again, take the example of a lightweight concrete deck. To the lightweight concrete deck, a base sheet is installed. Over the base sheet, roof insulation is installed. To the top of the insulation, a built-up roof is installed.

If the base sheet were cut and the lightweight concrete exposed, any moisture that was in the lightweight could enter and contaminate the roof insulation. There are two solutions to this problem.

One is to make sure you have installed a very effective vapor retarder. This can be accomplished in many different ways—for example, installing two piles of fiberglass felts in a mopping of hot bitumen. If the barrier is strong with high vapor permeability resistance, the vapor will hit the barrier and be forced elsewhere. Proper and complete edge venting and bottom-side venting of the roof deck then become a necessity. (See Fig. 3.9.)

A second solution is available. After installation of the vapor retarder install a relief vent that does not have a cap on it. Install the roof insulations and roof membrane up to and around the pipe, using asphalt mopping or adhesives. To the top of the installed roof membrane surface you can now install a moisture relief vent directly over and waterproofing the first vent pipe that was installed. (See Fig. 3.12.)

When installing moisture relief vents, the hole that is cut through the roof insulation must be filled with loose insulation material. When installing relief vents to the top of lightweight concrete systems, the lightweight material must be removed to the form deck. The vent is then set directly over the top of the hole and sealed to the roof surface in accordance with the roof membrane manufacturer's specifications.

Moisture relief vents come in either plastic or metal. The metal ones are usually spun aluminum. Moisture relief vents should be attached to a roof like any other common penetration. Usually moisture relief

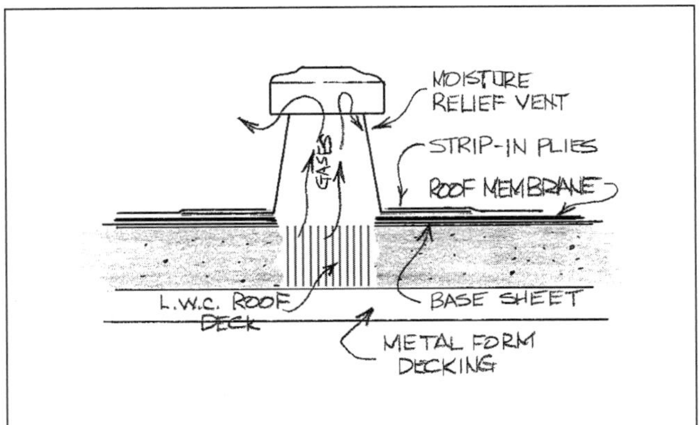

Figure 3.11 Moisture relief vent.

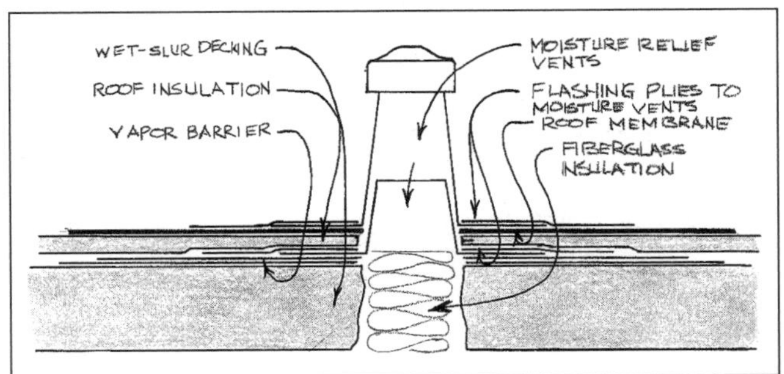

Figure 3.12 Moisture relief vent on insulated deck.

vents should be installed with one every 1000 ft^2 of roof area.

3.1.7 Expansion Joints

Expansion joints on roof systems are often improperly designed and improperly installed. For example, industry standards, which require all base flashings to terminate a minimum of 8 in above the surface of the roof, are often in conflict with material manufacturers' expansion joint details. (See Fig. 3.13.)

Expansion joints are to allow for independent movement between the areas, sections, and materials of a roof system. Area dividers, although not true expansion joints, also provide for the same. See Fig. 3.14 for an example of an area divider.

When there are two different types of roof decking on a building, there will be a difference in the expansion and contraction rates of these different materials. At the intersection of these two different decks, a roof expansion joint should be installed. When the direction of the decking is changed, an expansion joint should be installed at that point. When the interior temperature under an area of decking is different from that of the rest of the interior of the building, an expansion joint should be installed at that area.

Expansion joints are installed to the top of a structural curb which is part of the roof deck, being wood, concrete, steel, etc. The expansion joint material is usually a factory-supplied unit with elastomeric bellows. However, the bellows can also be of metal, as illustrated in Fig. 3.15.

Always design a slope to the top of the curb upon which the expansion joint sets. This prevents water

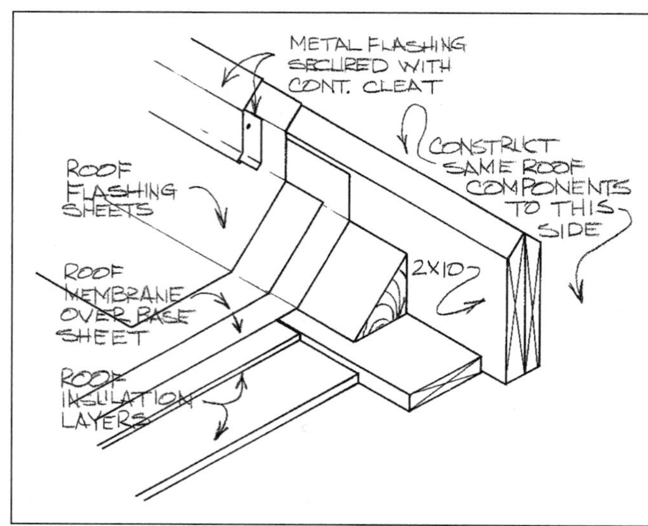

Figure 3.14 Example of an area divider.

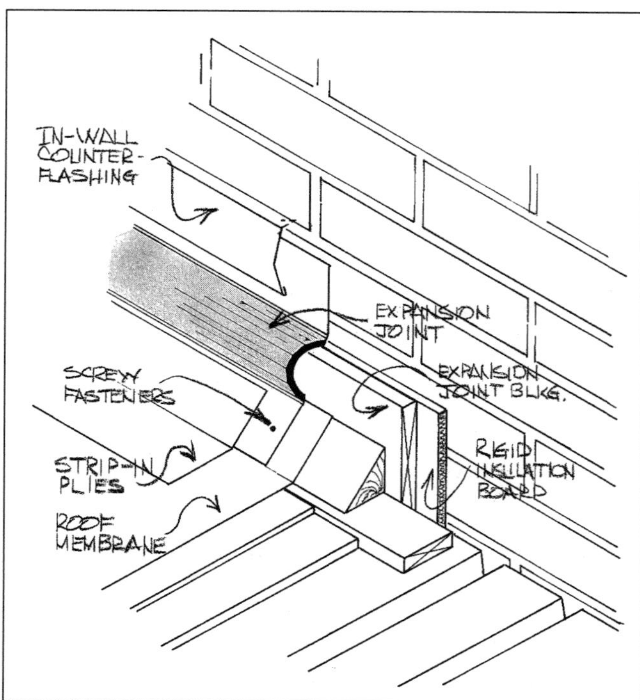

Figure 3.13 Improper expansion joint.

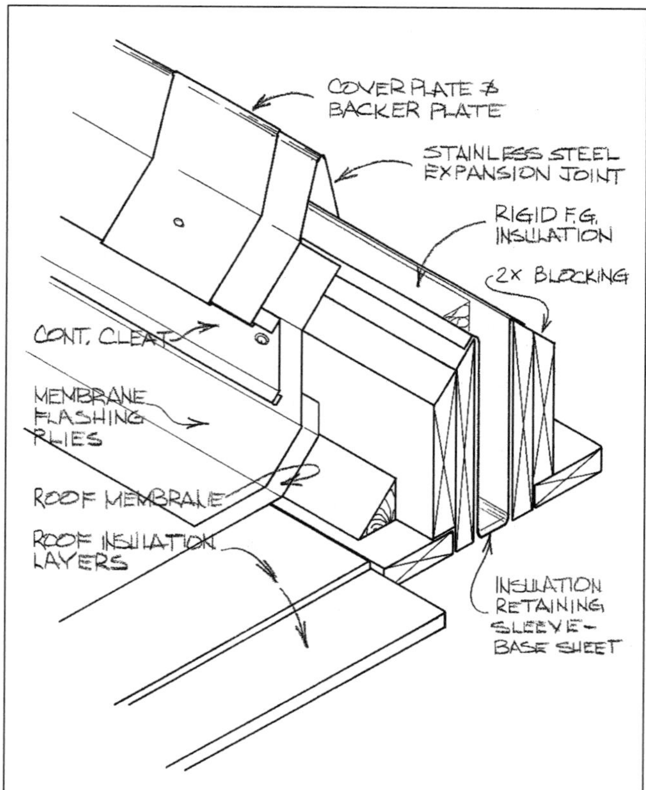

Figure 3.15 Metal expansion joint.

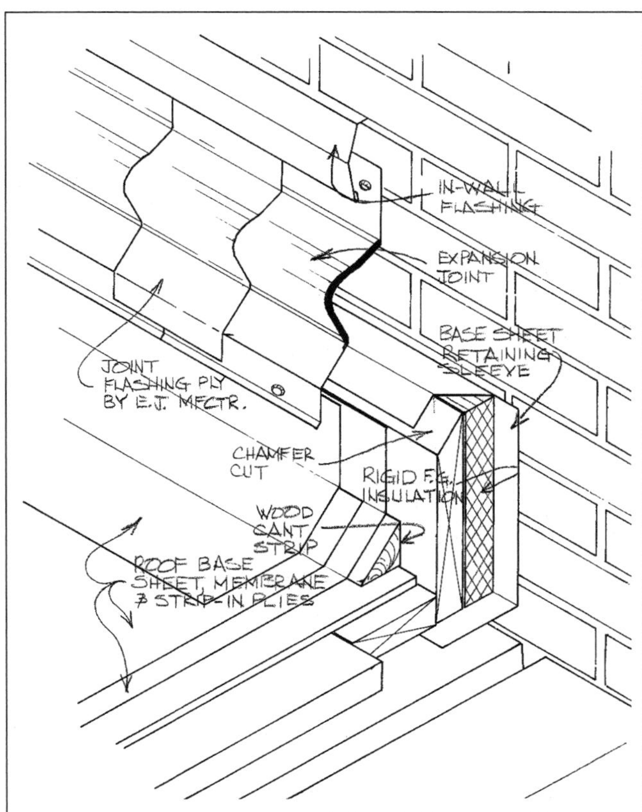

Figure 3.16 Wall and roof intersection.

from gathering on the top of the joint flange and entering through a lap seam in the joint assembly.

Where expansion joints are used at building wall intersections, specify for a positive slope to be located on the top surface of the joint. Again, this helps restrict water from entering a joint that may have become open. (See Fig. 3.16.)

A common mistake made when designing expansion joints is the termination of the joint. Often the expansion joint covering is terminated on the rooftop with a sheet metal plate being used to close off the sides of the joint where the building wall begins. Building movement will occur on the sides of the curb opening as well as the top of the curb.

The expansion joint must extend down the side of the blocking and overlap additional flashings that are part of the building-wall waterproofing (see Fig. 3.17).

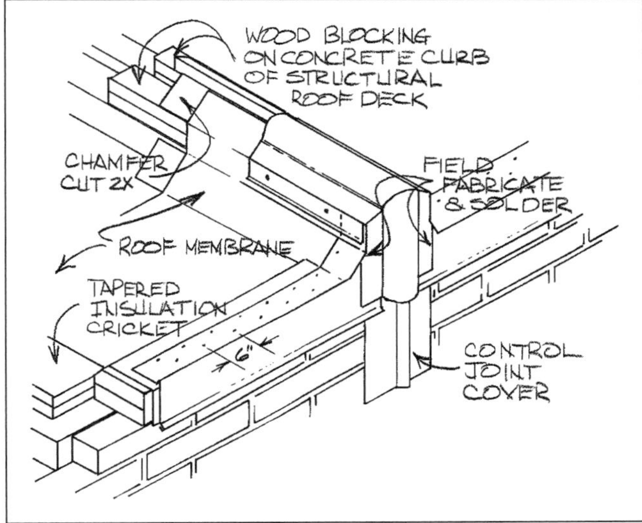

Figure 3.17 Expansion joint at termination.

CHAPTER 4

Asphalt Built-up Roof Systems

4.1 ASPHALT BUILT-UP ROOFING

GENERAL

Conventional built-up roofing can be classified into two major categories: asphalt systems and coal tar systems. Although the roofs are put on in much the same way, with the same type of equipment and workers, they are very different materials and each requires special procedures.

In this chapter we will discuss asphalt built-up roofs, often referred to as BURs. The term *built-up* is used to described the building up of a roof system by compiling layer upon layer of material until a completed roof membrane is created. (See Fig. 4.1.)

Asphalt and roof felts are the primary components of an asphalt BUR. The asphalt can be delivered to the job site in solid keg form, in which case it has to be melted in a roofing kettle to temperatures in the 400 to 500°F range, or it can be delivered to the job site in a heated tanker truck, eliminating the need for a roofing kettle. This hot asphalt is then usually pumped onto the roof

Figure 4.1 BUR being installed. (*Courtesy of Centrum Engineering, Winston/Salem, N.C.*)

by a gasoline-powered motor and piping attached to the kettle. In earlier times, it was normal to pull hot asphalt onto the rooftop in buckets, using ropes and pulleys.

Asphalt BURs can also be created from asphalt which has been cut with a petroleum distillate at a manufacturing facility, making the asphalt liquid and thereby not requiring heating. This type of asphalt material is referred to as *cold-process asphalt material* (see Sec. 4.1.5), whereas asphalt heated and melted in a kettle can be termed *hot-process asphalt, hot asphalt,* or *hot stuff.*

Asphalt by itself cannot create an effective roof system. Installing only a layer of asphalt to the top of a roof deck would result in the asphalt cracking, splitting, and crazing similar to a dried mudflat.

The asphalt layer would very shortly after installation be split at any location which experienced even slight movement, such as at the intersection of the roof and parapet walls or roof equipment stacks or flue penetrations. The asphalt may also, depending upon the type of asphalt and climatic conditions, move or creep across the rooftop from high to low roof areas.

Roof felt plies are used in the built-up roof system to eliminate these problems. Roof felt is sometimes referred to by laypersons as *tar paper* and can also be called *felt paper;* however, the term *plies* is most often used in order to also include fiberglass and polyester materials.

The roof felts act as the stabilizing component within the asphalt/felt matrix. The roofing asphalt penetrates the felt membranes, thereby fusing and bonding all the built-up layers together into one solid membrane unit. (See Sec. 7.1.)

Asphalt, in the form of natural pitch, has been used for centuries, mainly as a waterproofing element for ships, cisterns, aqueducts, roof systems, etc. (See Sec. 1.2.1.) However, the asphalt pitch was used mainly as a coating or caulk system. Many of the displacement and cracking problems as described above would occur if the pitch was used as a total roof or water-barrier system without roof felts.

The built-up roof system, with alternating layers of felt membranes and roof bitumen, solved many problems. The built-up roof did not come into existence until the early to mid-1800s. (See Sec. 1.2.2.) Coal tar bitumen was the first type of material used in a BUR assembly, with asphalt becoming the predominate bitumen type in the early 1900s.

4.1.1 Manufacturing Processes

CRUDE OIL REFINING PROCESS

Asphalt has specific characteristics which make it a unique material. These characteristics will change over time as the material is exposed on the rooftop to the elements and the environment. The characteristics can also be changed at the manufacturing facility to create products for different applications.

In evaluating existing asphalt BURs, designing new systems, or maintaining or repairing existing asphalt systems, it is important to understand the nature of asphalt material. This understanding is best begun with a quick review of the asphalt manufacturing process.

Like so many other common products, roofing asphalt is made from crude oil. When the crude oil is delivered to a petroleum or petrochemical refinery, it is processed by distillation. Distillation turns a liquid into a gas by heating the liquid and then cooling the gas back to a liquid. With the crude oil distillation process, the different substances within the base material will boil and condense at different temperatures.

The raw crude oil is heated, and as it turns into gases and vapors, it enters a series of tall columns called *fractionating* or *distillation* columns. Temperatures in these columns are hotter at the bottom than at the top. Cooler temperatures toward the top of the tower cause some of the gases to condense back to their liquid states. Different factions of the crude will condense as well as boil at different temperatures. The material faction from which gasolines are created will boil at lower temperatures than will the heavier materials, such as heating oil.

Gasoline will evaporate if left in an open container at room temperatures. Asphalt will not evaporate at room temperatures because its boiling point is higher. Likewise, asphalt will condense from a vapor back to a liquid at a higher temperature than will the lighter materials such as gasoline or jet fuels. These lighter materials are among the first materials to be taken off during distillation.

As the vapors and gases rise in the column, they cool and condense back into liquids. The liquid is then usually passed back down toward the bottom of the column. As the liquids go back toward the bottom, they pass through different levels within the column. Liquid materials may or may not be drawn off at these different levels. At the lower levels of the column where it is hotter, these liquids will again vaporize and travel back up the column, only to liquefy again. (See Fig. 4.2.)

In order for the refineries to get all the materials they can out of the crude oil, after the materials have run through these fractionating towers at atmospheric pressure, the remaining material is passed into a vacuum column. Under vacuum, the lower pressure causes boiling points of materials to be lowered.

Materials drawn off from this vacuum tower have a much higher boiling point than lighter materials such as the gasolines and jet fuels. Materials collected at the bottom of this tower, having higher boiling points than most others collected during the vacuum distillation and

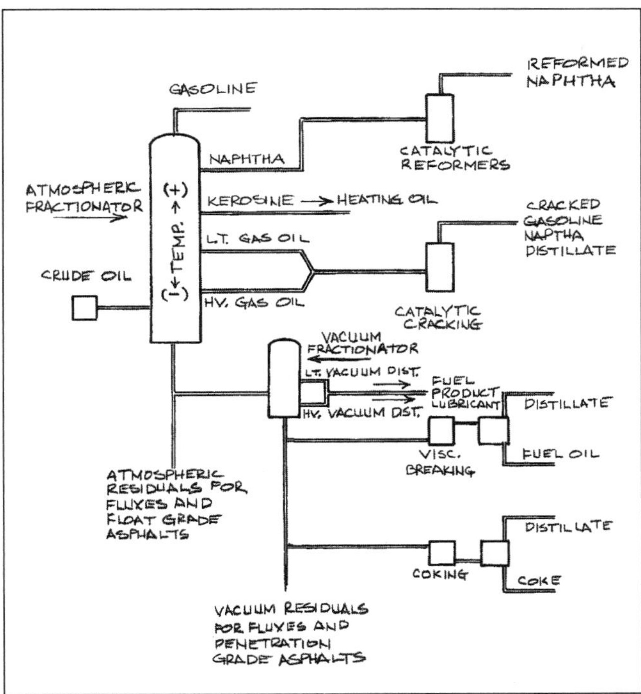

Figure 4.2 Crude oil distillation process.

fractionation, are a thick gooey black substance, called *vacuum tower bottoms*.

The temperatures, the vacuum pressure, and the types and amounts of other materials taken out before collecting this bottom material will determine what the bottom material can be used for. Paving asphalt, as well as roofers flux, come from the bottom material of the vacuum tower. Roofers flux is purchased by asphalt manufacturers and from this flux we get the different grades and types of asphalt bitumen products.

The word *bitumen* can be used to generically describe all types of asphalts and tars used in applying roofs. Bitumen, in our discussion, means the interply and the top pour material used as an adhesive to bond the roofing plies together and for installation of protective surfacing materials.

ASPHALT MANUFACTURING

The vacuum tower flux material is heated and placed into an air still column at the asphalt manufacturer's plant. In this air still, the asphalt flux is subjected to air blown through the column.

Roofers flux and asphalts are composed mainly of hydrocarbon molecules. The air induced into the blowing still will cause the hydrogen atom on the end of the hydrocarbon molecule to separate from the molecular structure. The hydrocarbon molecule that is missing a hydrogen atom will then find another hydrocarbon molecule that is also missing a hydrogen atom and the two molecules will join together. This increases the molecular weight of the asphalt. (See Fig. 4.3.)

The longer the asphalt flux is subjected to this blowing process, the more the hydrocarbon molecules will be joined together. The longer this blowing is allowed and the higher the column temperatures, the more brittle the asphalt will become.

This blowing process is what gives us four different types of asphalt: Type I, Type II, Type III, and Type IV. Type IV asphalt is blown longer than Type I.

The temperature in the tower at which the asphalt manufacturing is completed is called the *finished blowing temperature* (FBT). The temperature can be lowered if the blowing time is extended. This is an important fact in regard to heating restrictions of the asphalt in the kettle at the job site. (See Sec. 4.1.3.)

The FBT is different for the four types of roofing asphalt. The FBT will also be different for each grade of roofers flux, depending upon the crude oil source, manufacturer, and process used to create the vacuum tower bottoms.

It is possible to produce certain grades of roofing asphalt without blowing in the air still. This is accomplished by carefully controlling the vacuum tower at the petrochemical refinery, allowing the vacuum tower bottoms to be produced within specification for roofing asphalt.

4.1.2 ASTM Standards and Procedures

Over the years, experience has helped define the characteristics required of an asphalt in order for it to be effective and durable. For example, if an asphalt turns brittle at low temperatures, the roof will experience problems with cracking and splitting during the winter. If the asphalt begins to flow at moderate rooftop temperatures, it may slide off the building during the summer.

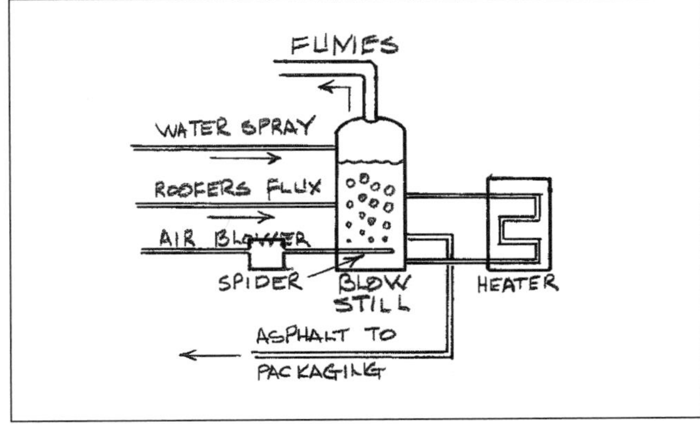

Figure 4.3 An air still.

ASTM guidelines have been developed to help eliminate these problems. These specifications, test methods, and standards attempt to keep lower-grade crude oil and inferior manufacturing processes out of the roofing industry. For example, ASTM has developed softening-point standards, different for each of the four types of roofing asphalt. When the softening point falls within this range, the asphalt should remain on the roof slope for which it is intended.

Roofing asphalt should be manufactured in such a manner as to create an end product which will comply with the ASTM D 312 standard. This standard encompasses five test procedures which the final asphalt product must meet in order to comply with the ASTM D 312 standard.

ASTM TEST METHOD D 36—SOFTENING POINT

The softening point of asphalt is determined by a test procedure called the *ring-and-ball method*. This is a simple test performed using a metal ring and a metal ball of exact sizes and weights. The metal ring is approximately the size of an eyeglass and the ball is slightly smaller than a ball bearing used in a pinball machine. The softening points of the four different types of asphalts are measured using this ring-and-ball method.

Heated liquid asphalt is poured into the brass ring and allowed to cool to ambient temperature. When this asphalt has cooled, it is trimmed and then the asphalt pad within the brass ring is placed into a beaker of liquid. The liquid can be distilled water, USP glycerin, or ethylene glycol.

The metallic ball is placed on top of the asphalt. The temperature of the liquid surrounding the ring, asphalt, and ball is slowly raised. The temperature at which the asphalt begins to flow, causing the ball to pass through the asphalt pad, is the asphalt's softening point.

ASTM TEST METHOD D 5—PENETRATION

The penetration level of an asphalt is measured using a needle that exerts pressure downward onto a sample pad of asphalt. The needle is mounted to a device that measures exactly how far the needle went into the asphalt at a specified pressure.

Asphalt penetrations are tested at three different temperatures: 32°F, 77°F, and 115°F. Naturally, the needle will penetrate the asphalt farther at 115°F than it will at 32°F. To meet ASTM requirements, the needle cannot penetrate the asphalt too far or too little, but must remain within the specified ASTM range.

ASTM TEST METHOD D 113—DUCTILITY

Ductility of an asphalt is also an ASTM requirement. One way to define ductility is to say that it is a measure of the asphalt's ability to expand to a certain limit without breaking. Ductility is determined by taking two molds that are wing-shaped, approximately 2 in × 3 in each, and placing the two molds together. These molds are then filled with hot asphalt.

When the asphalt has cooled to the specified temperature, the molds are placed into a device which pulls them apart at a steady pressure. The molds, asphalt, and device are placed into water at 77°F. The molds are slowly pulled apart. The asphalt must not break within a certain range. For example, Type I must expand without breaking to approximately 4 in, Type II slightly more than 1 in, Type III almost 1 in, and Type IV about ½ in.

ASTM TEST METHOD D 92—FLASH POINT

This test procedure uses an open cup into which asphalt material is slowly heated. An open flame is passed over the cup at different intervals as the temperature of the asphalt material is raised. Ignition will eventually occur, as the result of the flammable gases and vapors being released as the asphalt is heated. The temperature of the asphalt at which ignition occurred is the *flash point*. This test method is also referred to as the *Cleveland Open Cup Test*.

ASTM TEST METHOD D 2042—SOLUBILITY

Fillers, from base materials such as cellulose, limestone, or clay, or reclaimed materials from other products, can be incorporated into the asphalt during manufacturing in order to impart other needed properties, such as viscosity. However, fillers detract from overall quality of asphalt types.

This test procedure dissolves a specific amount of asphalt in trichloroethylene and then passes the dissolved material through a fine-mesh strainer. In accordance with the parameters of this test method, at least 99 percent of the asphalt and distillate must pass through the strainer. Most high-quality asphalt materials pass 99.9 percent of the liquid through the strainer.

JOB-SITE REQUIREMENTS

These ASTM standards have been in effect for many years and help ensure consistent quality. The asphalt could not pass these tests if too many volatile oils, asphaltenes, etc., were removed or reconfigured during the distillation process.

The ASTM specification compliance, ASTM D 312, should be stamped or printed on the side of the carton the asphalt comes in. It is also important to know the FBT, the flash point, and the equiviscous temperature (EVT) of the asphalt. This information is sometimes also printed on the side of the asphalt container. If not on the container, the information is available from the asphalt manufacturer.

When melted and prepared at the job site, asphalt should not be elevated to within 25°F of its flash point. Another accepted practice states that asphalt should not be heated to a temperature equaling or exceeding its FBT for longer than 4 h. Such excessive heating will damage the product. Excessive and extended heating can molecularly change the asphalt and possibly result in an inferior roof system. (See Sec. 4.1.3.)

4.1.3 Equiviscous Temperature

VISCOSITY

Viscosity is a term used to indicate a material's ability to flow or move. The more viscosity a material has, the less it will flow or move. For example, steel is more viscous than water. Water has less viscosity than syrup. Type IV asphalt is more viscous (less flowing) than Type I asphalt.

Equiviscous temperature (EVT) is based upon centistokes (cSt), which are units of measure describing viscosity.

$$\frac{\text{centistoke}}{\text{density}} = \text{centipoise}$$

APPLICATION TEMPERATURES

EVT is the recommended temperature range for applying hot bitumens, including asphalt and coal tar pitch. EVTs are very important when applying hot BURs. Bitumen applied too hot can result in voids within the roof system, light moppings, and incomplete film coverage of the bitumen to the roof sheets. Bitumen applied too cold can result in thick interply bitumen layers, which in turn can result in slippage of the roof system, poor adhesion of the bitumen to the felts and deck, as well as high expansion rates and low tensile strengths of the roof system. EVT ranges are the correct temperatures at which the different types of asphalt bitumens should be applied. Correct temperature ranges will limit the aforementioned problems.

Since EVTs are so important to the proper application of a long-lasting roof system, these values have been closely scrutinized, studied, and discussed within the roofing industry. In the late 1980s the studies of EVT led to the recommendation that the EVT range be changed based upon the temperature range required to achieve 125 centipoise (cP) instead of the accepted 75 cP. This resulted in an increase of the bitumen temperature at the point of application using the 125-cP requirement.

Additionally, EVT ranges are different for asphalt applied by hand-moppings from the EVT range for asphalt applied by mechanical spreader. For mechanical spreading equipment, the EVT range is based upon 75 cP, and 125 cP for hand-mopping.

EVT is a specific temperature but is considered with a differential range of 25°F either + or −, as shown in Table 4.1. So long as the hot asphalt bitumen material is being applied within the specified EVT range, the desired interaction and bonding of the roof felt and asphalt layer should be as required, assuming all other application processes are correct. Table 4.1 shows but an example of typical EVT ranges. Different asphalt products will have different EVT requirements, depending upon the crude oil source and manufacturing processes.

FELT AND ASPHALT FUNCTION

The primary element relating to the longevity of a BUR is the interply bitumen. The interply bitumen is applied either by hand-mopping or by asphalt-spreading equipment. The asphalt bitumen is applied to the roof deck surfaces as well as to the top of the roof felt ply. As the asphalt is being applied, a roll of roof felt is placed directly into the hot mopping and rolled out and into the hot mopping being applied to the roof and felt ply surface. Upon completion, all of the roof felt plies are sandwiched between asphalt layers. (See Fig. 4.4.)

The roof ply felts are incorporated into the system to provide, among other things, uniformity of the hot moppings and to give the bitumen moppings stability. The felts are not the primary waterproofer in the system.

TEMPERATURE CAUTIONS

The bitumen being applied to the roof felts must be hot enough to create fusion of the hot bitumen and the roof felts. Penetration of the hot asphalt bitumen into the roof felt must occur for fusion to result. Roof felts are normally coated and/or saturated with asphalt bitumen at the manufacturing facility, which aids in the fusion process. (See Sec. 7.1.) This fusion process has been compared to the welding of the felts by the hot mopping bitumen.

For hot-applied asphalt BUR systems it is usually recommended that the asphalt be applied at a rate of 25 to 30 lb of asphalt per roof felt ply, per 100 ft^2 of felt surface area. This is best achieved by maintaining the

Table 4.1 Example EVT ranges.

EVT	*Min., °F*	*Max., °F*
Type I	325	375
Type II	350	400
Type III	385	435
Type IV	415	465

Figure 4.4 Mopping of roof felt.

proper EVT. If a proper EVT is maintained, proper weight and thickness of the interply mopping should be the result.

Since EVTs are measured at the point of application, such as the mop cart or asphalt spreader, it may sometimes be necessary to raise the temperature of the asphalt in the kettle to where it approaches the flash point or sometimes exceeds the FBT of the product. It is accepted knowledge within the roof industry that heating of asphalt to within 25°F of its flash point can cause safety problems due to fire within the kettle. Also, heating asphalt to its FBT should be avoided. The finished blowing temperature is the temperature extreme to which the asphalt was subjected at the asphalt manufacturing plant in order to create the final roofing asphalt product.

However, the proper EVT is extremely critical to a successful BUR system. Due to cold weather conditions or distances the asphalt must be transported from the kettle across the roof to the point of application, proper temperatures may not exist at the point of asphalt application. In such cases, it is acceptable to raise the temperatures in the melting kettle, so long as the raised temperature levels do not continue for extended periods of time, at extreme temperature elevations. It has been determined that asphalt will be damaged by this heating only if allowed to continue for extended periods of time at excessive temperatures.

Excessive temperatures can cause severe damage to asphalt, resulting in what is termed *asphalt fallback*. Asphalt fallback occurs when the molecular structure of the asphalt material is changed. This change can be caused by excessive temperatures which approach or exceed the FBT used at the manufacturing facility to create the asphalt. This can result in asphalt which becomes soft (ductile) at temperatures lower than those for which it was created and specified. Lower softening points can result in the asphalt becoming brittle in the winter months and having unacceptable movement, sliding, and sluffing in the summer months.

However, it is acceptable and sometimes required to elevate the temperature of the asphalt in the kettle above the FBT, so long as this temperature is not maintained for extended periods of time, which would result in asphalt fallback. An extended period of time is defined throughout the roof industry as no more than 4 h.

Excessive temperatures within this time frame are difficult to define, however the 525 to 550°F range is the normal range that is considered acceptable as an elevated temperature extreme. The FBT for most roofing asphalt is close to 500°F. Again, the FBT can be verified through the asphalt manufacturer and will vary depending upon the crude oil from which the roofers flux came and the temperature at which the asphalt was created within the air still.

JOB-SITE HEATING OF ASPHALT

A few other items need to be explained concerning EVT and temperature at the kettle. (See Fig. 1.2.) If the kettle is having to produce great volumes of asphalt to keep up with the application rates on the roof, it may be necessary to exceed the recommended melting temperatures. In this instance, concern regarding asphalt fallback and damage is greatly reduced. This concern is negated because of the great quantities of melted asphalt being produced from the kettle. The asphalt will not remain in the kettle long enough to be heated at excessive temperatures for extended periods of time.

A thermometer in a kettle may read 550°F when great quantities of asphalt are being placed into the kettle and pulled out of the kettle at the same time. The high turnover rate of the asphalt in the kettle does not allow the bitumen to become overheated, and in truth, the reading on the thermometer is not an accurate indication of the overall heat of the asphalt.

A thermometer should be used at the point of asphalt bitumen application to verify that proper EVT is being maintained. In the event that it is not, solutions are available.

As a rule of thumb, one degree of temperature will be lost for every linear foot that hot bitumen is transported from the kettle to the point of application. This rule is approximate and will change based upon season and environment. To compensate for temperature loss, one solution is to elevate the temperatures in the melting kettle. However, this can lead to problems, as previously discussed, and should be one of the last resorts.

A realistic solution is to require the roofer to use only insulated transportation equipment, including the pipe leading from the kettle to the roof as well as the asphalt carrier equipment.

It may also be necessary to relocate the kettle several times during the roof construction. This will reduce the distance the asphalt material must be transported. For tall or large buildings, it may be necessary to place the kettle on the roof, although in case of fire at or in the kettle, catastrophic results may occur.

QUALITY CONTROL EXAMINATION OF INTERPLY ASPHALT LAYERS

The temperature of the hot mopping bitumen, at the point where it is applied into the roof system, determines the thickness of the interply asphalt bitumen layer. As stated previously, interply bitumen layers too thick or too thin will not create a proper roof membrane. Correct application temperature, being the EVT, will assure proper interply asphalt thickness.

There is a way to quickly check the interply mopping for an *indication* of the correct amount of asphalt in between the roof felt plies. The industry standard for interply asphalt weight is 25 to 30 lb of asphalt per ply, per square, which is also indicated by the thickness of the interply asphalt layer. Visual examination of the interply layers can be performed, which requires a sample, or plug, from the roof membrane system.

Within the roof sample, as a minimum, the interply asphalt layer should be approximately as thin as a dime. As a maximum, the interply asphalt layer should be approximately as thick as a nickel.

This is not an exact evaluation procedure, and some deviation in the interply mopping must be allowed for. This is merely a way to tell if there is a drastic problem with the amount of interply bitumen or felt-layer adhesion within the asphalt layers.

During construction, excessive interply bitumen can be adjusted by increasing the heat of the bitumen in the mop cart. Insufficient interply bitumen amounts can be adjusted by decreasing the heat of the bitumen in the mop cart. Always maintain proper EVT.

If the sample reveals unadhered roof felt plies and asphalt layers, or if the asphalt layers are totally unacceptable, further investigation and sampling may be required. This decision should be based upon the condition of the sample and the realization that deviations in the interply asphalt layers are common and complete adherence of the felt plies is not mandatory for a proper BUR system.

Many people within the roof manufacturing and roof construction industry discourage cutting and core-sampling of a BUR membrane, the argument being that a core cut is a possible leak in the roof membrane, created by a potentially weak area caused by a hole in what once was a monolithic membrane. Also, roofers do not like to cut open their new roof systems. Others argue that the core sample can be reinstalled, or the hole in the membrane repaired, to a condition that equals and usually exceeds the surrounding BUR membrane. Therefore, the sample area should become the strongest part of the roof membrane, not the weakest.

If it is determined that evaluation of the roof membrane plies and asphalt layers is required, roof sampling procedures should be undertaken in accordance with ASTM D 3617-95. This method describes how and where to remove, measure, and evaluate roof samples of a BUR. For a complete description of this ASTM method, see Sec. 14.2.6.

Visual examination and measuring of the interply asphalt layers and the integrity of the roof felt layers contained therein is but an indication of the makeup of the total roof system. It is not unusual to find deviations of thickness in the asphalt layers, nor is it unusual to find dry voids and unadhered areas of the roof felt plies within the sample. However, if these inadequacies are excessive, as defined under ASTM D 3617-95, corrective measures as described within the method should be initiated.

Waiting until completion of roof installation to evaluate the quality of the roof membrane is not a good practice. It is poor practice to attempt evaluation and judgment on the quality of workmanship and the future integrity of a total roof system by use of roof sample evaluation procedures. Full-time roof inspection (see Sec. 13.1.5), monitoring of EVT, and proper roof felt installation practices (see Sec. 7.1.4), help ensure a quality roof system.

4.1.4 Asphalt Characteristics of Types I, II, III, and IV

GENERAL

The four different types of asphalt all have different softening points, FBTs, and EVTs. These differences offer the designer a material which has the same basic properties but with different characteristics for each type.

For example, Type I asphalt has the lowest-temperature softening point. It will begin to flow and move at 135°F, which is in a temperature range not unusual for a roof system. This gives Type I asphalt self-healing characteristics, much like coal tar pitch. (See Sec. 5.1.) None of the other asphalt types have this same characteristic of flow at such a low temperature.

However, Types I through IV roofing asphalts all have the same basic properties. They are thermoplastic in nature. As the asphaltic material is heated it becomes liquid, and with cooling it becomes once again hard. However, even though it appears hard, it still has elasticity, even in cold-weather climates.

In the hot temperatures of summer months, even though the asphalt is softer than it is in the cold winter months, it still will not become liquid and flowing to such an extent that it is unpredictable or unusable. The special characteristics of Types I and II asphalt allow the material to somewhat flow under hot conditions, as desired and manufactured to fulfill that characteristic function.

All roofing asphalt has the property of being resistant to the environment, although not impervious to elements within the environment. Sunlight, water, corrosion, heat, etc., take their toll. However, certain characteristics of asphalt types make some types more resistant to particular environments than others. As the result of manufacturing processes and crude oil sources, these and other characteristics are differentiated among the four different types of asphalt products we use to create built-up roof systems. The specific characteristics are shown in Tables 4.2 through 4.4.

The finished blowing temperature will always fall in a different temperature range. (See Sec. 4.1.1.) The FBT will normally be slightly different for every run or batch of asphalt, due to the different chemical makeup of each batch of roofers flux. As a rule of thumb, the FBT of all four types of asphalt will be anywhere in the 450 to 550°F range. However, some grades of crude oil and the resulting roofers flux from the vacuum tower bottom

Table 4.2 Softening point per ASTM D 36.

	Softening Point Temperature	
Asphalt Type	*Min., °F*	*Max., °F*
Type I	135	151
Type II	158	176
Type III	185	205
Type IV	210	225

Table 4.3 Ductility per ASTM D 113.

Asphalt Type	*Stretch at 77°F, Min., in*
Type I	4
Type II	1
Type III	⅞
Type IV	½

Table 4.4 Penetration per ASTM D 5.

	Penetration at		
Asphalt type	*32°F*	*77°F*	*115°F*
Type I	3	18–60	90–180
Type II	6	18–40	100
Type III	6	15–35	90
Type IV	6	12–25	75

can be of such chemical composition that this temperature is lower. Also, it is possible to create an asphalt type with a lower-than-usual FBT if the blowing is continued for longer than usual.

TYPE I ASPHALT

Type I asphalt has the lowest softening point. (See Table 4.5.) ASTM requires that the ball must start to fall through the ring within the temperature range of 135 to 151°F. Type I asphalt has a typical EVT range of 350°F and a typical flash point of 475°F.

Type I is usually referred to as *dead-level asphalt*. Because of its low softening point, it should only be

Table 4.5 Type I asphalt.

Softening point	135–151°F
Flash point	475°F
EVT	325–375°F
Max. roof slope	½ in

specified for roofs with no appreciable slope, or in other words, a dead level. Since it has a low-temperature softening point, it also has a tendency to be self-healing.

At temperatures of 135 to 151°F it will begin to flow. Any small hole or split in the roof membrane surface will be filled by the flowing material. This allows roof damage to be held to a minimum until inspection of the roof locates the defective roof area and it can be repaired.

If Type I asphalt material is placed on a sloped roof, either convex or concave, it will flow of its own accord to the lowest point. In hotter climates, on roof slopes of ½-in rise per linear foot, the dead-level roof asphalt has been known to flow from the roof onto the ground, leaving behind an unprotected building, even though it is rated as acceptable for this slope.

Because Type I asphalt flows so easily, pitch dams, edge envelopes, or bleeder strips must be a part of the roof system. (See Fig. 4.5.) Pitch dams are used with coal tar pitch roof systems, which are also a dead-level material. (See Sec. 5.1.3.)

These edge envelopes are often created from roof felt material, fabricated and installed by the roof applicators. The envelope felt must not be made from perforated, translucent, or open-weave roof felts such as are fiberglass ply sheets. The envelopes are usually made from base sheet material such as #30-lb or #43-lb organic felt. Sometimes edge envelope felts are replaced by pitch dams from sheet metals. (See Fig. 5.2.)

Using a sheet metal pitch dam is a better design practice in that it is not susceptible to tear or puncture during construction and installation. If a tear, puncture, hole, or unsealed lap occurs to a roof felt edge envelope, the dead-level asphalt could leak down the side of the building wall. However, the cost of such sheet metal pitch dams is usually higher than that of edge envelopes from roof felts.

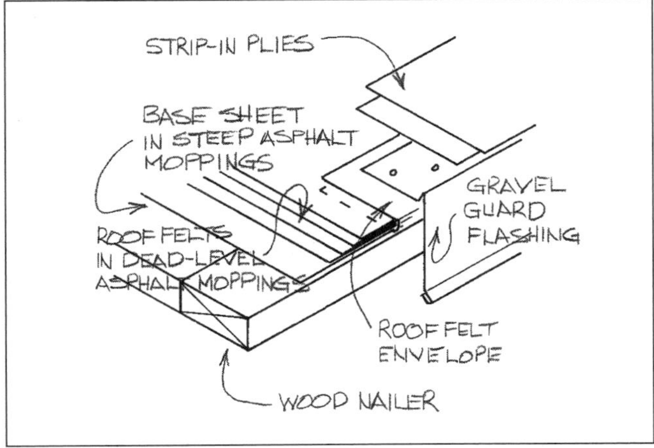

Figure 4.5 Edge envelope.

The roof felt edge envelope is created by installing the felt as one of the first components of the roof system. The envelope is usually 12 in wide and is installed with half on the roof deck and half over the edge. Roof components, such as the insulations and felts, are then installed.

After the installation of the roof ply sheets is completed, this envelope is then turned over the top of the felts and sealed to the top surface of the felts. This will act as a dam, and as the bitumen begins to flow in the heat, the envelope will stop it from going over the edge of the building.

These dams must be installed at all edges where there is a gravel guard, at all penetrations, and at all roof drains. (See Fig. 4.6.) It is sometimes impossible to create a proper envelope at some of these points, such as at roof drain sumps.

Plastic roof cement is then acceptable if the cement is applied at ⅛- to ¼-in-thick trowelings between the roof felt plies, and the area is then reinforced with a membrane such as fiberglass mesh. When specifying roof cements to create bleeder strips and edge envelopes, take great care to ensure that the work is done properly. It is a costly operation to remove roofing, metal edging, and roof drain flashings so that a proper bleeder strip can be installed.

TYPE II ASPHALT

Type II asphalt is commonly referred to as *flat asphalt*. Type II has a softening range of 158 to 176°F. (See Table 4.6.) The EVT is typically, but not necessarily 375°F. When EVT is given, it has a variance of ±25°, so Type II normally has an EVT range of 350 to 400°F. At this EVT, the product will best flow and adhere to the various roof components.

Type II is used for applying roofs to slopes up to 1½-in rise per linear foot. However, if you're designing the

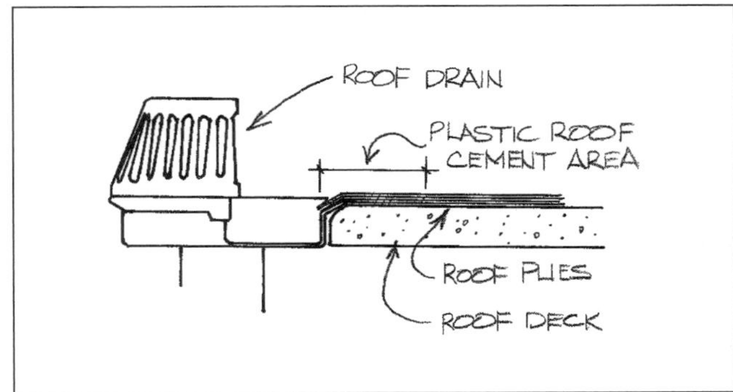

Figure 4.6 Roof drain with cement pitch dam.

Table 4.6 Type II asphalt.

Softening point	158–176°F
Flash point	475°F
EVT	350–400°F
Max. roof slope	1½ in

roof for a climate that may experience hot summers, be careful not to install this material on any roof slope greater than ½ in on 12.

Again, bleeder strips at all openings should be used with this grade of asphalt. It is not unusual for rooftop temperatures to approach or exceed 160°F in the hot summer months in many parts of the United States.

TYPE III ASPHALT

Type III asphalt is called *steep asphalt*. This material can be installed on roofs with a maximum slope of 3-in rise per linear foot. The softening point for Type III is between 185 and 205°F. (See Table 4.7.) The EVT is typically 410°F, again ±25°.

Because it has high-temperature flow, edge envelopes are not necessary for this grade. In the industry today, Type III is the most commonly used asphalt for the construction of asphalt BURs.

TYPE IV ASPHALT

Type IV is referred to as *special steep asphalt*. It will work effectively on slopes up to 6-in rise per linear foot. Type IV has a softening point between 210 and 225°F. (See Table 4.8.) The typical EVT of Type IV is 440°F.

The advantage of Type IV over the other asphalt types is the high temperature ranges it can be heated to by the roof applicators without damage. The FBT for Type IV is typically higher than that of all other types of roofing asphalt. This allows it to be heated and applied at higher temperatures than the other types. This is an advantage to roof applicators since the hotter the asphalt, the easier it is to apply to the roof surface. It can also be an advantage in cold winter months when high heat at the kettle may be required to achieve proper EVT at the point of application.

The high temperatures required and which Type IV asphalt is capable of make it a good selection for use

Table 4.7 Type III asphalt.

Softening point	185–205°F
Flash point	475°F
EVT	385–435°F
Max. roof slope	3 in

Table 4.8 Type IV asphalt.

Softening point	210–225°F
Flash point	475°F
EVT	415–465°F
Max. roof slope	6 in

when specifying SBS modified bitumen membranes. Modified bitumens must be adhered with asphalt hot enough to melt and fuse the SBS modified bitumen material of the roll into the hot mopping. Low-temperature mopping with an SBS modified bitumen can be disastrous.

CONSIDERATIONS

Sometimes it is undesirable to use Type I asphalt as the interply bitumen. If there are numerous pipe penetrations on the roof, they would demand extensive and difficult bleeder strip or pitch dam installation. In such a case, Type III asphalt can be used to create the roof system and Type I can be used as the flood coat into which the gravel is embedded. In this manner, the dead-level material on the roof-system surface will act as a self-healer. If the roof is damaged to a slight extent by foot traffic, hailstorms, vibration of roof-mounted equipment, or the expansion and contraction of metal flashings, the Type I dead-level surfacing asphalt material (because of its flow properties) will help seal up the holes, splits, and cracks created by these forces.

In the situation just described, steep asphalt used as the interply bitumen will not flow at normal rooftop temperatures, so edge envelopes and bleeder strips are not required. The roof membrane created from the Type III steep asphalt will prevent the dead-level asphalt from entering the building or going over the edge.

Asphalt's worst enemy is the ultraviolet rays of the sun. These UVs will cook the volatile oils out of the asphalt, and when these are gone, the asphalt will become hard and brittle. You can compare a dead and dried-out roof to an old car tire which has dry-rotted. The pliable elements that kept the tire flexible are gone. The old tire no longer has any tear resistance or strength left. You can bend it and it will crack.

The UVs and the heat will oxidize the asphalt, leading to loss of the volatile oils within the asphalt. Another way to consider this is to understand that UV light and the heat will cause the asphalt to get harder and more brittle. This also means that the softening-point temperature of the asphalt material has increased.

This is another good argument for the use of Type I dead level. Since the softening point of Type I is between 135 and 151°F, it will take longer for Type I to reach a level at which it is no longer effective—effectiveness being determined by the asphalt's pliability or ductility, which is a direct reflection of its softening point.

Let's take an extreme example, overstating what will actually occur. Type IV has a softening point of between 210 to 225°F. Type I has a softening point of between 135 and 151°F. As already discussed, when the asphalt oxidizes, its softening point is increased. In 10 years, because of this oxidation process, Type I asphalt might have its minimum softening point increased from 135 to 185°F. Likewise, Type IV may have its softening point increased from 210 to 260°F.

Since temperatures will seldom, if ever, reach 260°F on a roof, Type IV will have lost much of its waterproofing ability since it can no longer reach the temperature of 260°F which is now required in order for the asphalt to function most effectively. Type I, on the other hand, can reach its optimum operating range in 10 years if the temperature on the roof reaches 185°F. Service temperatures on a rooftop will normally approach the 150°F range, so the softening point of Type I allows it to operate in a temperature range that will more normally be experienced on a rooftop.

HEAT, OXIDATION, AND ROOF INSULATION

The hotter it is, the quicker the oxidation of asphalt will occur. Roof insulations will quicken this oxidation process to a certain extent. Insulation does not allow heat to be transferred through the roof deck, but instead holds the heat directly at the roof membrane.

This heat factor must also be considered when specifying the different types of asphalts on different roof slopes. Since insulation will block the heat and hold it at the roof membrane, an increase in the roof membrane temperature can be expected.

If you're specifying Type III asphalt on a slope of 3 in/ft and you have insulation under the roof, rooftop temperature may reach 50° above the ambient air temperature. You must then consider if the asphalt will flow at that increased temperature. If this is not allowed for in the design calculations, the roof may start to move.

This movement is sometimes referred to as *sluffing,* a situation where the felts and bitumen have slid, the felts are wrinkled and ridging, and the gravel surfacing is moving toward the roof edges or the drains.

Heat will also make any organic reaction go faster. As a rule of thumb, for every 10°C rise in temperature, the reaction time is doubled (10°C converts to approximately 18°F). The faster the organic reaction which oxides the asphalt occurs, the faster the roof system will wear out.

Heat may be retained within or directly under the asphalt roof membrane due to roof insulation heat resistances (R-values). However, high-R-value insulation (R-10 or greater) seems to have the same approximate temperature effects as do insulations with values of R-4. After insulation values increase beyond approximately R-4, the heat gain of the roof membrane does not increase proportionally.

4.1.5 Cold-Process Roof Systems

GENERAL

BURs, as described in the previous sections, are normally created from hot asphalt and hot-process methods. BURs are also created from asphalt products which are not heated before application into the BUR system. This type of BUR is known as a *cold-process roof system.*

The asphaltic material used in a cold-process BUR begins as the same asphalt product used for hot-process BUR systems. However, the asphalt manufacturer takes the finished product from the air still, and instead of packaging the asphalt into containers for shipment to a job site, the finished material is piped to another manufacturing station at the facility.

At this manufacturing station, the hot asphalt is blended with petroleum distillates. The distillates, being mineral spirits or similar products, create a new form of asphalt roofing product. Fibers and fillers, used to enhance the service and performance of the cutback product, are also often added.

The thermoplastic nature of the asphalt is lost in the cutback process, in that the asphalt is no longer a solid, which will become more liquid and flowing when heated and more solid and hard upon cooling. Instead, the material begins as a liquid, and as it cures and sets due to the distillate evaporation and dissipation, it becomes a solid asphaltic material. Many people are familiar with cutback asphalt materials as roof coatings purchased in 5-gal pails at the hardware store.

However, the cold-process cutback asphalt has different characteristics than does its counterpart hot asphalt. Cutback asphalts do not have designations such as Type I or Type IV. Cold-process roof systems can be put on steep slopes as well as low slopes.

Most cutback asphalt materials have more elongation characteristics than do hot asphalt products. The manufacturing process of cutting the asphalt with petroleum distillates somewhat enhances the chemical composition of the base hot asphalt material, giving it more volatile oils and changing the asphaltene structure.

This allows the cold-process material to remain more pliable than conventional hot asphalt material, retaining elongation characteristics for longer periods of time at greater rates than hot asphalt. In some cases, in addition to the distillates used to cut the material, the asphalt is also modified with polymers. The polymers can modify the cutback asphalt material to enhance the characteristics of elongation and ductility to levels greater than would otherwise be achieved.

A wide variety of cold-process cutback asphalt materials is produced for special or specific applications. For example, cutback asphalt material is produced specially for use with modified bitumen membranes (see Sec. 9.1.3) with the distillate materials and proportions changed to be compatible with the modified bitumen membranes.

Coatings specifically manufactured for application as roof coatings, with aluminum flake and pigment added, are a common cutback asphalt product, called *aluminum roof coating*. The cutback asphalt material can be blended with clay-based emulsion to create an asphalt emulsion. (See Sec. 6.1.3.)

COLD-PROCESS BUR SYSTEMS

However, regarding cold-process asphalt BURs, we mostly use asphalt cutback material created by standard methods which use petroleum distillates enhanced and strengthened with fibers. We commonly use plastic roof cement (cutback asphalt) with hot-process BUR, applying the roof cement at areas where extra strength and durability are required. Also, an entire BUR system can be created from cold-process materials.

Cold-process BUR systems are very similar to hot-process BURs, but in many respects they are quite different. They are created by using the cold-process material as an interply adhesive, but the asphalt is usually brush-applied or applied by commercial airless spray equipment instead of being hand-mopped or applied by mechanical asphalt spreader. (See Fig. 4.7.)

Multilayers of roof ply felts are used as in conventional hot-process BUR systems, but the roof plies of a cold-process system are normally polyester material or can be saturated fiberglass or asphalt coated organic or coated fiberglass felts. Saturated organic felts are not recommended for use within cold-process systems. For more information on roof felts, see Chap. 7.

Also, the cold-process system's roof felt/membrane layers, not including base sheet, can be as few as two plies and normally no more than three. In a hot-process BUR there may be as few as two and normally no more than four layers of roof felts.

The surfacing of a cold-process BUR can be gravel or mineral surfaced cap sheet, but is usually of a cutback asphalt material, such as asphalt emulsion and/or aluminum roof coating. A conventional hot-process BUR can also utilize these same coatings, but is usually a cap sheet or gravel embedded in hot asphalt mopping. (See Sec. 6.1.)

If a heavy type of roof surfacing material is specified, such as gravel, slag, or concrete pavers, a setup time for the roof membrane system is required before installation of the roof surfacing materials can be performed. The cold-process material will take anywhere from 10 to 30 days to cure and set up solid enough to allow foot traffic on the roof membrane surface. The cure time is based upon heat (evaporation of the volatile oils), humidity, and amount of cold-process material used to create the cold-process BUR membrane.

Some plastic foam roof insulations, such as polystyrenes and polyisocyanurates (see Secs. 8.1.6 and 8.1.7) may not be compatible with all cutback asphalt materials. The petroleum distillates used in the cold-process materials can attack and dissolve some roof insulation products.

ADVANTAGES

Cold-process BUR systems are extremely durable, if properly maintained. They are proven to successfully resist harsh rooftop environments, such as:

- *High and low temperature extremes leading to thermal shock* due to their pliable nature
- *Ultraviolet degradation* due to their volatile oil content
- *Foot and equipment traffic* due to the pliable nature of the asphalt and the tear and puncture resistance of the polyester felts often used

The cold-process systems require less roof maintenance and repair after longer periods of roof service time, at locations where hot-process BURs often exhibit problems, such as metal flashing lap joints, base flashings, and traffic areas.

Many experts, having years of experience evaluating and specifying cold-process systems, believe if the cold-process system is regularly recoated with an asphalt cutback material, the life expectancy of the roof system will prove exceptional.

Cold-process roof systems can be created by using as few as two roof felt/membrane plies over a properly installed base sheet. Using a modified bitumen membrane, this roof ply can be as minimal as one, which is the modified bitumen membrane itself. In cases where access is difficult for workers and hot-process BUR equipment, a cold-process roof system may prove to be advantageous.

Undesirable fumes and noise, as created by the hot asphalt being melted in the kettle, are eliminated with cold-process systems. However, the distillates within the

Figure 4.7 Cold-process BUR. (*Courtesy of Monsey Products Co., Kimberton, Pa.*)

cutback asphalt material do give off vapors that can sometimes prove undesirable or unpleasant.

The danger of hot asphalt being spilled on workers or pedestrians is eliminated with cold-process systems. Some clients, such as school districts, hotels, and hospitals, find this attractive.

DISADVANTAGES

A type of roof system not normally specified or installed, a cold-process roof system can prove to be expensive for the client as well as foreign to even the experienced roof designer. Specialty manufacturers within the United States normally market these systems directly to the client, thereby circumventing the design professional.

However, sometimes the designer determines that a cold-process system is the best choice for the client. In such a case, the help available from the materials manufacturer in preparing the construction documents often results in much of the common workload being removed from the designer. The manufacturer's representative is compensated for the time by a commission from the sale of the products.

If a designer is very familiar with all of the intricacies of cutback asphalt BUR systems, the cost disadvantage can often be eliminated. There are quality asphalt cutbacks available from many roofing material manufacturers which will provide a quality BUR system. The materials are economical and normally available through local roofing suppliers or distributors.

The disadvantage to this approach is that the designer may not have, from a large and reputable material manufacturer, the literature, specification manual, and database to reference, wherein guidelines for designing and installing products and systems are described and detailed. Liability exposure must be considered.

The base of roof contractors that are familiar with cold-process BUR systems is limited in most parts of the country. This may restrict the number of qualified bidders for a project.

The installation procedures used during cold-process roof construction are critical. A cold-process BUR is not as forgiving of application error as is conventional BUR or many other types of low-sloped roofing. Air pockets and voids within the interply and felt matrix must be limited to minute sizes and amounts. The amount of cutback interply adhesive must be much more exact than with hot asphalt interply mopping.

If a mistake is made in the application of the adhesive—e.g., not enough was applied at certain areas of the interply membrane system—or if it was allowed to cure too long before installation of the felt/membrane, or if the adhesive was not applied consistently to the required thickness, problems may result. The same can be said of conventional BUR, but as stated, the tolerance level for misapplication is lower with cold-process systems.

Foot traffic over the completed membrane must be completely restricted until the cold-process material has set up. This can take weeks to months. This also often means that base flashings and all accessory work, such as sheet metal installation and flashing, must be done as the roof application proceeds across the roof area.

Polyester or fiberglass felts, normally used as the roof felt/membranes with a cold-process system, have what is termed *memory*. In the event that the felt is stepped upon after installation into the cold-process adhesive, the felt will try to return to the original level and plane of installation. It will rise from where it was depressed by the worker's foot. At the same time the liquid cold-process interply adhesive is displaced by the pressure from the worker's shoe-sole pad. What results is an area of the roof that has no waterproofing adhesive. This phenomenon can be produced through all the felt layers. (See Fig. 7.5.)

Fiberglass felt memory is also a problem with conventional BUR, but after the hot asphalt has cooled to ambient temperature, the felt can no longer move and traffic is not a problem.

CHAPTER 5

Coal Tar Pitch Roofing

5.1 BACKGROUND

Coal tar has been used for construction of built-up roofs (hereafter referred to as BURs) in the United States for a century and a half. Coal tar pitch has always proven an effective material for roofing and waterproofing. In the late 1990s this medium is still the roof of choice for many specifiers and roofers.

People often used the word *tar* when referring to roofing, meaning to encompass all materials that are black and applied to roofs—an unfortunate misconception. Asphalt bitumen and coal tar bitumen are very different and this chapter will help clarify the differences between the materials and explain proper terminology and design practices.

ADVANTAGES

Coal tar pitch roof systems have many advantages. They are proven to have an exceptional life span when compared with other types of low-sloped roof systems. They are installed in much the same way as is asphalt BUR systems. The processes are familiar to most commercial roofers.

Having been in use for almost 150 years, we have a large and well-defined specification and materials base to draw upon. Suppliers, contractors, and material representatives are well versed in the requirements of the systems. We know where the material will work and where it will not work properly.

Coal tar pitch systems can resist ponding water to a better degree than can other types of BUR systems, and they can resist bacteria and plant growth on the roof surface. Also, pitch roof systems have a higher resistance to pollutants and chemicals than other BUR system types (cold-process built-up, hot mop built-up, modified bitumen built-up).

DISADVANTAGES

Coal tar pitch roof systems also have disadvantages. It is an extremely dead-level and moving material, requiring complete understanding of this characteristic when designing and detailing the roof slope, vents, penetrations, and roof edge details.

Although this dead-level quality is also an attribute, mistakes are often seen coming down the sides of the building and extending from the roof edges in long, black stalactite-like formations. The pitch roofing bitumen will also come through holes and cracks at roof penetrations, possibly entering the building interior. It is important that roof system design provide proper detailing to prevent pitch drippage, referred to as *bleeding*. (See Figs. 4.5 and 5.2.)

Coal tar pitch has also been recognized as a form of carcinogen, with warning labels placed on the shipping containers of the pitch bitumen material. As of the publication of this manual there has been no report of adverse, lasting effects caused to any person as the result of handling or working around coal tar pitch roofing products.

Coal tar pitch is derived from the same base product as are creosotes. Irritation of the eyes and nostrils will result from breathing the fumes and being exposed to the smoke created during heating and application of the material. Dust from the roof surface of an existing coal tar pitch roof will cause worker irritation, and for some, extreme discomfort.

In a cold season or environment, the roofing pitch becomes brittle. Roof deck or building movement, if excessive, can crack the pitch roof system, whereas other types of BURs may not be so affected. Proper design is required to accommodate this characteristic.

GENERAL

In general, coal tar pitch BUR systems can be used to effectively address life-cycle cost concerns (see Sec. 2.1.4), although the initial investment may be somewhat higher than for a conventional asphalt BUR system. These systems have proved to be effective in resisting hailstorms and foot-traffic damage.

Architecturally, the surfacings available are limited. Roof slopes cannot exceed ½-in rise per 12-in run, or less, further limiting architectural expression. In warm climates the suggested slope limitation is ¼ in:12 in.

5.1.1 Refining

Tars come from many different base products, including but not limited to coal, petroleum, wood, and oil-shale. Tar is a residual material derived from a base product during a distillation process.

Coal is the base product from which tar roofing pitch is made, thus explaining the name *coal tar pitch*. Pitches are products made from the distillation and refining of tars. The first step in obtaining coal tar roofing pitch is the distillation process of coal, which provides coal tar.

Coal must be distilled to obtain coke, an essential element in the refining and manufacture of steel and iron. Coke provides the heat used during the smelting of the iron ore, extracting oxygen from the iron ore to produce carbon monoxide gas and metallic iron.

To obtain coke from coal, the coal undergoes what is termed *destructive distillation*. This distillation takes place in an oven over a 15- to 20-h period. Normally a bank of ovens is grouped together, and these long, narrow ovens hold 10 to 20 tons of coal.

The coal is heated to temperatures of anywhere from 2000 to 2700°F, without the presence of air. This results in the coal not being consumed, but instead, giving off much of the gases and vapors that make up coal, leaving the residual material, coke.

The gases and vapors emitted during this coking process are collected in pipes. The pipes are sprayed with an ammonia water, causing condensate of ammonia, water, crude tar, and other by-products. The crude tar is collected and sent to the refining plant where it will be processed into hundreds of different products. (See Fig. 5.1.)

At the refinery the crude tar is stored in heated tanks. From these tanks it is moved to stills where the tar is heated under pressure. As the tar is heated it gives off gases and vapors. These vapors are passed into what are called *fractionating columns*, which are tall metal cylinders. These columns work much the same as the distillation columns used in the petrochemical industry. Inside these columns are many levels of trays.

Each metal tray has a series of small chimneylike perforations. Over this tray is something that looks like a metal bubble-cap. Each tray also has a line that feeds into it from the tray above, as well as an exit tube that feeds to the tray below.

As the tar gases rise in the column, they must pass through the bubble-caps. As the gases rise through this series of trays and bubble-caps, they also cool off. In cooling, the product leaves the gaseous state and returns to a liquid or semisolid state. The materials with the highest boiling points will condense at the top of the tower.

As the gases turn back into liquid, they collect in the bottom of the tray. The liquid is then passed down to the tray below through the exit tubes which connect the tray system. At this lower level of trays, the temperature is hotter and some of the liquid is turned back to gas.

The re-created gas then mingles with the incoming gases and passes back through the bubble-caps. As the combined gases rise, some will again be recondensed toward the top of the tower. This is the process of *distillation*, which is carefully controlled and is much more technical than is briefly described here.

What is desired as the end product, and what grade that end product is to be, determines what material and how much of that material will be drawn off at the different tray levels. The material that collects at the bottom of the column is drawn off as coal-tar pitch.

The longer the crude tar remains in the column and the hotter the column temperatures, the harder the pitch will be. This determines the softening point of the pitch, which in turn will be a factor in determining the grade, or type, of the pitch.

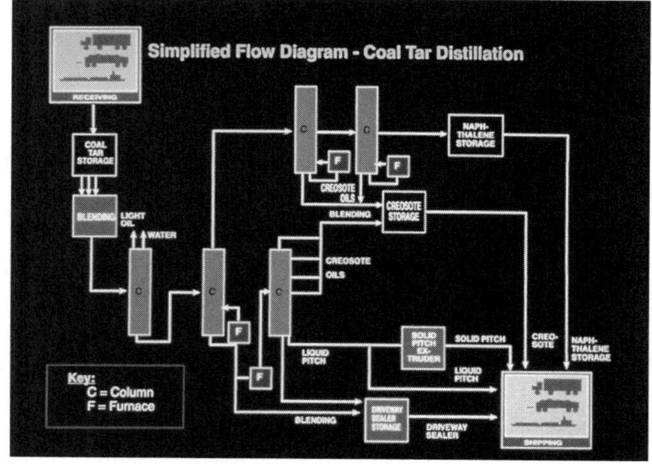

Figure 5.1 Distillation columns and refining process. (*Courtesy of Allied Signal, Mars, Pa.*)

HISTORY

Many products we use today come from the distillation of coal tars. Some products that come directly or indirectly from this process are:

- Benzenes
- Creosotes
- Urethanes
- Insecticides
- Naphthalene
- Aspirins
- Sulfonamides

However, the technically advanced tar-pitch manufacturing and roofing industry had rudimentary beginnings.

In 1845 it is reported that William Chase patented a process that coated roofs with a combination of mineral tar, clay, and red sandstone. At that time it was normal to install a flat or low-sloped roof system using ship sheathing paper coated with pine-tree tar and/or pine pitch.

According to accredited sources, during the same time, the brothers Samuel and Cyrus Warren first conceived the idea and installed composition (now called *built-up*) roof systems using coal tar. (See Sec. 1.2.2.) During that time, coal tar was a waste product created during the refining of coal to create coke for heat and gas for streetlights in Cincinnati. After further experimenting and adjustments, the brothers settled on a tar-saturated fabric for use in lieu of paper sheets. Gravel was used as surfacing instead of sand and fillers.

Other sources credit Michael Ehret as the forerunner of tar-pitch roofing systems. The U.S. Patent Office granted Ehret's company a patent in 1868 for the manufacture and construction of tar-pitch roofing systems.

Another premier manufacturer of coal tar products was the H. W. Jayne Company, which established coal tar distillation as an industry unto itself in 1887.

5.1.2 ASTM Standards

Coal tar roofing pitch must meet certain standards as set forth by the American Society for Testing Materials (ASTM). The ASTM standard is D 450 and includes seven test procedures that roofing pitch must pass in order to meet the ASTM standards and specifications.

Testing procedures used for roofing pitch are more extensive than those used for roofing asphalt. The test methods and procedures used under ASTM D 450 are described in the following sections.

ASTM TEST METHOD D 20—DISTILLATION

A redistillation test is performed, in which the finished roofing pitch is redistilled and the gases and liquids are measured and tested. This test procedure ensures that the coal tar roofing pitch is a quality product containing the volatile oils and ingredients needed to make it an effective roofing material.

ASTM TEST METHOD D 36—SOFTENING POINT

All coal-tar roofing pitch should be considered a dead-level or low-sloped material. Softening-point ranges of the three types of coal tar pitch are:

- Type I pitch: 126 to 140°F
- Type II pitch: 106 to 126°F
- Type III pitch: 133 to 147°F

The ring-and-ball method is used in this test method to verify that the softening point of the pitch material is correct. (See Sec. 4.1.2.)

ASTM TEST METHOD D 92—FLASH POINT

The flash point of all roofing pitch, as stated by current ASTM standards, is 248°F minimum. This is being revised to more closely match actual conditions. In reality, the flash point of Type I tar roofing pitch is above 374°F and that of Type III is 401°F.

This flash point is determined by a test called the Cleveland Open Cup Method. The Cleveland Open Cup Method is a simple test using a precisely shaped cup and exact heat. The bitumen is placed in an open cup and heat is applied. As the heating continues, an open flame is passed over the cup. The vapors rising from the cup, when present in sufficient quantities, will be ignited by the open flame. The hotter the bitumen in the cup, the more vapors there will be. The temperature at which the vapors ignite is the flash point of the bitumen. The development of a fire without a fire source is called the *autoignition point,* which is possibly 650 to 800°F for both asphalt and coal-tar pitch.

ASTM PRACTICE D 140-83—SAMPLING

Sampling of the manufactured product is required. Samples of the product are taken from process lines, storage equipment, shipping containers, etc. The manner, amounts, and intervals of such sample taking is specified under this sampling practice.

Also, samples of coal tar pitch are required for other test methods required under ASTM D 450. This procedure defines how to take and handle samples for testing.

ASTM TEST METHOD D 2415—ASH CONTENT

This is the standard test method used to determine the ash content of tar roofing pitch. A sample of pitch is taken and heated to 900°C in a muffle furnace or by use of other laboratory equipment. Heating is performed until the volatiles have been evaporated and the carbons have been consumed. The heating is repeated as required until only ash remains. The ash content is then measured. If too much ash remains, the coal tar pitch is not acceptable for roof bitumen.

ASTM TEST METHOD D 4-86—SOLUBILITY BY CARBON DISULFIDE

A sample of coal tar pitch is dissolved in a carbon disulfide solution. The majority of the pitch should be dissolved by the carbon disulfide. The insoluble substances and mineral matter are weighed. If too much matter remains at the end of the test, the pitch does not meet the ASTM D 450 standard.

ASTM TEST METHOD D 70—SPECIFIC GRAVITY

This test method is used to determine the specific gravity and the density of semisolid bituminous materials. Specific gravity and density of material is needed for converting volumes to units of mass as required in other ASTM standards as well as for sales transactions between producers, manufacturers, distributors, and users.

A glass container, called a *pycnometer,* is completely filled and capped with a precise stopper. By use of laboratory beakers, deionized or distilled water, and mathematical calculations, specific gravity and density of a semisolid bituminous material is determined.

ASTM TEST METHOD D 95—WATER

The amount, if any, of water in petroleum products, tars, and other bituminous materials is determined by this laboratory procedure. In refining, purchasing, selling, transferring, or using these products, the water content can be important.

The product is placed into a still, along with a water-immiscible solvent. The still has a water trap, and as the bituminous material is heated and boiled, the water separates into the trap. When the evolution of water from the product is complete, the water is removed and precisely measured. The percent of water per volume is then determined by Water % = $V/W \times 100$, where V = volume of water in trap and W = weight (or volume of sample). Normally, no more than 0.05% water is allowed.

All of the test methods listed and described above form the ASTM D 450 standard to which coal tar roofing pitches must conform. If the pitch material does not pass one of the test methods described above, the material is *out of spec*. In such a case, the manufacturer cannot state that the material conforms to ASTM requirements of D 450.

5.1.3 Characteristics of Tar Roofing Pitch

TYPES

Coal tar roofing pitch comes in three grades or types:

- Type I is referred to as *old-time pitch*.
- Type II is used only in waterproofing.
- Type III is the primary roofing pitch used today.

TYPE III

Type III was developed by the Koppers Company, a coal tar pitch manufacturer, during the late 1960s and early 1970s. Type III is a low-fuming product, with many of the chemicals which irritate the eyes and skin removed or reformulated.

Type III low-fuming pitch was developed at the request of the roofing industry labor union in order to improve the working conditions for roof applicators. Irritants contained within the smoke from the product, to which the roof applicators are constantly exposed, is reduced, making for more comfortable working conditions.

The materials removed from Type III are a guarded secret, and manufacturers will not reveal what is removed or added in processing Type III pitch. One manufacturer uses an additive in the manufacturing process. Another uses a special procedure during the distillation.

Within the industry, debate rages: Are quality and longevity equal for Type I and Type III? Some argue that volatile oils necessary to a roof bitumen's life have been removed from Type III, leaving quality and longevity deficient. Others argue that it is impossible to remove volatile oils that will hurt the performance of the pitch. This is due to ASTM standards for coal tar pitch roofing bitumen. These standards ensure softening ranges, and the redistillation test ensures that the necessary volatiles are remaining in the pitch. If too many oils, or a certain group of oils, were removed, the pitch could not meet ASTM standards. (See Sec. 5.1.2.)

TYPE II

Type II pitch is used as a waterproofing bitumen because of its low softening-point range of 106 to 126°F. This material becomes too soft, at standard roof temperatures, to be practical. Type II is normally installed under plaza decks or over subterranean rooms or buildings where the temperature is usually a constant 50 to 60°F.

The cold-flow characteristics of pitch allow Type II to self-heal in the event of small perforations or minute cracking of the waterproofing membrane. A cutback pitch material (see Sec. 6.1.3) is often used in conjunction with fabric membranes for the sealing and waterproofing of the sidewalls of these subterranean structures.

TYPE I

Type I pitch was the only coal tar pitch roofing bitumen available until the introduction of Type III. Even today, it is not exceptional to find a roof installed over 50 years ago made from Type I roofing pitch material. Properly designed, installed, and maintained, Type I has proven its long-lasting abilities.

As a designer, the author has seen limited problems with some roofs installed with Type III that were never encountered on roofs installed with Type I pitch. It was debatable if the problems were due to application error, and the reasons for the problems were never determined.

In the design practice of the author's firm, Type I pitch is used if the only reason for using Type III is to reduce discomfort to roof workers, the theory being that if Type I coal tar pitch roof systems are time-proven to last more than 50 years (if designed, installed, and maintained properly), why reinvent the wheel? Actual rooftop work experience has shown the author that the reduced discomfort level of Type III versus Type I is negligible.

However, for a Type I pitch roof system to last like they used to, you must design and install them the way it was done 50 years ago. Times have changed. Technology, practices, and even some of the materials are no longer available.

CHARACTERISTICS

All roofing pitch is dead level and is not recommended for slopes greater than ½ in on 12-in rise. In warm climates this slope factor should be reduced to less than ¼ in.

Bleeder strips (see Fig. 5.2) must always be installed as part of the tar bitumen roof system. Bleeder strips are also referred to as *pitch dams* or *edge envelopes*. They prevent the pitch bitumen from entering the building interior or "bleeding" over the edge of the roof. (See also Fig. 4.5.)

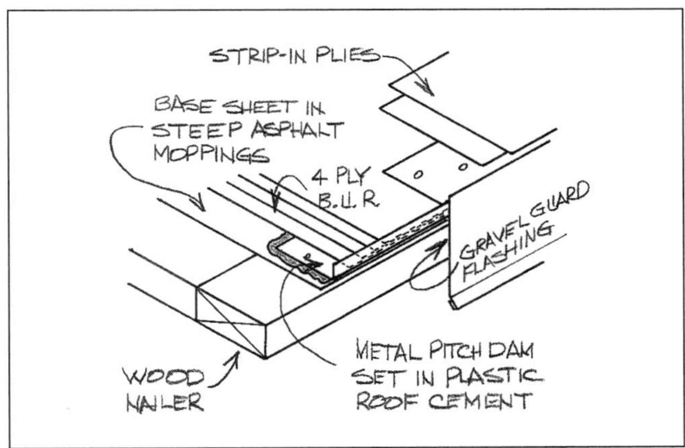

Figure 5.2 Bleeder strip.

Pitch has exceptional cold-flow ability and is often referred to as a *self-healing* material. This means that, in the event of small holes or ruptures in the roof membrane caused by foot traffic or slight roof deck movement, the cold-flow characteristics of coal tar pitch allow it to flow into the small hole or void and help seal the hole. So long as the material retains its low-temperature flow qualities, this characteristic of the pitch remains.

As stated previously, some coal tar pitch roofs have remained effective for over 50 years, with some roof systems documented to last 75 years, in place and still waterproofing a building. (See Fig. 1.5.) Main contributing factors allowing the roof to remain functional for so long are these self-healing characteristics.

Tar pitch is not the only bitumen type having cold-flow abilities. Types I and II asphalt bitumen also have cold-flow properties. (See Sec. 4.1.4.) However, cold flow as it relates to asphalt means that when it reaches its softening-point range (lowest for Type I) it will move. Coal tar roofing pitch is the only material with true cold flow. Coal tar starts to move at around 60°F, even though its minimum softening point is 126°F (Type I pitch). Therefore, in winter months, coal tar pitch can still exhibit cold-flow ability if the roof membrane absorbs enough solar heat. Coal tar roofing pitch also retains the cold-flow character longer—for several reasons:

- Its softening point is in a low temperature range, between 126°F for Type I and 147°F for Type III. It is not unusual for these temperatures to be realized on the rooftop. (See Sec. 2.3.4.)
- During the aging process of the pitch, volatile oils are cooked out by the heat and destroyed by the weather. As stated in Sec. 4.1.4 on asphalt and Sec. 2.3.4 on solar radiation, the more volatile oils that are removed, the more brittle the roof bitumen becomes. Since tar roofing pitch starts at a low softening-point range, it takes longer for the softening-point ranges to reach and exceed the higher temperature ranges experienced on a roof.
- The primary scientific reason for the basic cold-flow characteristic of tar pitch is its molecular structure. Coal tar pitch is composed of hydrogen and carbon molecules tightly bonded together in a ring formation. Due to this molecular structure, there is little internal friction and thus the molecules of coal tar move over one another more easily than do the

long, chainlike hydrocarbon molecules of air-blown asphalts.

Like asphalt, coal tars are also composed of hydrocarbons, but unlike asphalt, the carbon atoms outnumber the hydrogen atoms approximately five to one. The molecular structure of the hydrocarbon found in asphalt is an almost flat chain.

The molecular structure of coal tar roofing pitch is formed in the shape of a ring. The atomic makeup of this ring, with the large ratio of carbon atoms to hydrogen, causes this ring to be held together very strongly. (See Fig. 5.3*a* and *b*.)

This exceptional molecular makeup allows tar roofing pitch to be highly resistant to ponding water, bacterial growth, and many familiar modern chemical pollutants. Coal tar's resistance to ponding water may also be attributed to its specific gravity, which is greater than 1, being 1.22 to 1.34. The specific gravity of water is 1.0. In simple terms, tar is heavier than water.

At one time not so long ago, it was strictly forbidden to combine any type of asphalt-based product with coal tar pitch. Tarred roofing felts and tar-based roof cement were used exclusively with the coal tar pitch bitumen moppings. However, specifications and standards have changed to allow flashing systems to be constructed using asphalt materials and moppings, so long as the moppings were applied to top of the coal tar pitch membrane. Manufacturers have determined that asphalt will adhere and bind to the top of the roof felts of the pitch membrane system. It is still accepted knowledge that asphalt and coal tar pitch are not compatible, so placement of the two materials is important.

In the 1990s, a coal tar pitch modified bitumen membrane was introduced for use at the flashing areas in lieu of asphalt products. It was also used as a modified bitumen membrane roof system, as are other standard forms and types of modified bitumen membrane systems. (See Chap. 9.) The product went out of production in 1995 and at the time of the publication of this manual, it is scheduled for reintroduction to the market sometime in the near future.

5.1.4 Special Considerations

PONDING WATER

A few points should be noted about ponding water and a coal tar pitch BUR system. Some manufacturers of coal tar roofing pitch will guarantee their systems to be unaffected by ponding water. Some material manufacturers have specifications that allow for a totally water-covered roof system. This does not mean the specifier should not be concerned about substantial water ponding on a roof system.

Although a manufacturer may guarantee its roof-pitch material under ponding water, it will not guarantee the system if it fails because of deck movement. Deck movement due to the weight of the ponding water can cause the roof membrane to undergo excessive stress. This excessive weight loading can cause the roof membrane to rupture and split open. Deck movement can also cause nails to back out of wood decks and puncture the roof mat. Ponding water areas can also create a thermal shock gradient, which could lead to roof problems. (See Fig. 2.4.)

Ponding water needs consideration when specifying coal tar pitch roof systems. The building structure, the

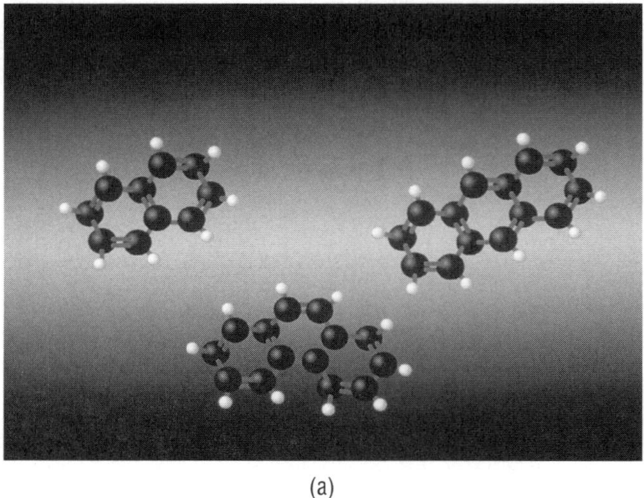

(a)

(b)

Figure 5.3 Coal tar molecular structure: (*a*) aromatic molecules; (*b*) aromatic (ring-type) molecules. (*Courtesy of Allied Signal, Mars, Pa.*)

decking supports, and the roof deck must be examined to determine if the structure can stand the weight that will be placed on it from the ponding water. If the deck movement causes roof problems, the system's warranty and guarantee usually will be void.

SURFACINGS

Coal tar pitch roofs always require surfacing, and that surfacing is normally gravel or slag aggregate. Roof pavers can be used, normally in conjunction with a separating roof insulation board. A paver surface is normally used where a waterproofing system exists for plaza decks. Roof pavers are also used for inverted roof membrane assemblies. (See Fig. 5.4.)

Roof coatings as a surfacing will not work due to the low softening-point range and subsequent cold-flow characteristics of roofing pitch. The coatings will sink into the flood coat.

INSULATIONS

Pitch is compatible with most insulations. However, polystyrene insulations can be damaged by the volatile oils in coal tar, if the volatile oils become available. For the oils to bleed from the pitch and become available, the temperature must reach the 250°F degree vicinity.

Insulation manufacturers' requirements must be adhered to when applying hot pitch to insulations. Special procedures, as outlined in manufacturers' specification manuals, must be followed in order to prevent the pitch bitumen from flowing through the cracks and joints of the insulation panels. For more information on the compatibility of pitch and roof insulations, see Chap. 8.

PRIMING PROCEDURES

When applying pitch directly to a structural concrete deck, it is not necessary to prime the deck. Pitch has enough volatile oils so that it primes itself to the deck. Metal flashings, such as gravel guard flashings which must be sealed into the roof membrane, should be primed. Coal-tar-pitch manufacturers suggest asphalt primer.

RESATURANTS

Pitch roofs are often resaturated, usually after they are 15 years old or more. The resaturation material contains extra volatile oils, blended into it at the time of manufacture. A few words of caution about resaturants:

- Pitch resaturants take a very long time to harden and set up. The resaturant is designed, by the characteristics of pitch material, to be heavy and flowing. It is these heavy and flowing characteristics that allow the resaturant to penetrate the felts and the bitumen. If a hole is causing leaks on the roof,

Figure 5.4 Plaza deck. (*Courtesy of Koppers Industries, Pittsburgh, Pa.*)

first find and seal this hole, or the resaturant will find the hole for you. In doing so, it will also find the inside of the building, after coming through the roof deck and onto the ceiling.

- If the bleeder strips have holes or splits in them, or if they are old and dried out, the resaturant can go through them and run down the face of the building. Resaturant is very liquid and will penetrate most materials, especially brick, concrete, ceiling tiles, carpets, and desktops.
- Resaturant is also a severe skin irritant. Roof workers who allow resaturant to come into contact with their skin could, depending on the extent of the contact, need burn treatment due to the action of the volatile oils and creosote on the skin. The fumes from the resaturant also cause skin irritation.

Resaturation of a tar roofing pitch system composed of fiberglass felts may not be a wise choice. The fiberglass felts are manufactured to be open-weave and are therefore very porous. (See Sec. 7.1.2.) The resaturant could pass through the felt layers and end up at places where resaturant is not needed, such as the floor of the building. Also, fiberglass felts do not resoften well. The material manufacturer should be consulted before applying resaturants to a pitch roof system composed of fiberglass roof felts. (See Fig. 5.5.)

ROOF FELT APPLICATION

Application and Heating Temperatures. As discussed under asphalt in Sec. 4.1.3, equiviscous temperature (EVT) is a crucial factor in achieving a proper BUR membrane. The EVT range must be adhered to during roof felt application in order for proper bonding and fusing of the roof felt layers, an extremely critical step in the roof application process.

The equiviscous temperature range for pitch is based upon 12 to 32 centistokes (cSt), which is a unit of measure that indicates viscosity. This often, but not necessarily always, converts to an EVT for:

Figure 5.5 Resaturation. (*Courtesy of Koppers Industries, Pittsburgh, Pa.*)

Type I: 335 to 385°F

Type III: 350 to 400°F

A problem can occur with maximum heating temperatures in the kettle at the job site and the EVT ranges at the felt application location on the rooftop. The maximum temperature to which Type III pitch can be heated in a kettle is 425°F, but with an EVT felt application range from 350°F minimum, something may be out of sync.

As hot bitumen is pumped from the kettle on the ground to the rooftop, and then transported across the roof to the felt application location, temperature of the pitch bitumen will decrease. If the construction crew raises the temperature in the kettle past the manufacturer's specification in order to maintain proper EVT at the point of felt application, the pitch can be damaged. If the temperature in the kettle is kept within specification, the EVT may not be hot enough to properly seal the roof felt layers together.

The designer must evaluate the distances the roof pitch must be transported across the roof area, as well as the ambient temperatures at the time of roof installation. Cold winter temperatures can make a big difference in comparison with hot summer temperatures.

As a general rule, anywhere from 0.5 to 1° will be lost per linear foot that the pitch must be transported across the rooftop. It is sometimes proper to specify that the roofer use only insulated pipe from the kettle to the rooftop and insulated transportation equipment to move the roof pitch to the point of felt application.

EVT and kettle temperatures can also be a problem with asphalt roof bitumens.

Felt Displacement Due to Temperatures. Fiberglass roof felts are the normal material selected today for use in BUR assemblies. (See Sec. 7.1.) However, some problems may result if certain fiberglass roof felts are used in a coal tar pitch BUR system. These problems can result from high temperatures which cause the pitch bitumen to turn "soft" enough to allow the interply pitch bitumen to be displaced from between the felt layers. The felt layers filter or sink toward the bottom of the assembly, leaving nothing but coal tar pitch bitumen on the top.

A mathematical model illustrating this phenomenon is presented in an ASTM symposium paper. Actual rooftop observations by the author confirm such possibilities. In the early 1990s most major material manufacturers discontinued their specifications for coal tar pitch systems and fiberglass felts and then reversed their policy. Once again we find coal tar specification and systems available from most major roof material manufacturers.

However, for such sinking of felts and displacement of bitumen to occur, high temperatures are required. Such temperatures may be experienced in the deep south, but seldom in the northern states. Roof insulation is also a factor. High-R-value roof insulation installed under the roof membrane will cause higher roof membrane temperatures. This phenomenon is not common, and only a few cases have been observed. The temperatures must be extreme for extended periods of time in order to cause the reaction.

Today, the fiberglass felts used in a coal tar pitch BUR systems are normally tar saturated, not asphalt saturated, with a closed weave as opposed to an open weave. Pitch migration through a closed-weave tar-saturated fiberglass felt no longer seems to be a problem.

However, if a designer is in doubt, the use of organic felt instead of fiberglass felt layers will prevent this problem. Coal tar roofing pitch will not go through the solid organic felt as it will through the weave of fiberglass felts.

CHAPTER 6

Roof Surfacings and Coatings

6.1 GENERAL

Protective surfacings are an important part of many types of roof systems. The most detrimental and dynamic forces which affect a roof membrane and cause deterioration or premature failure are:

- Ultraviolet (UV) rays of the sun
- Foot traffic
- Hailstone damage
- Thermal loading
- Thermal shock
- Wind uplift

The roof surfacing system can protect the underlying membrane from attack, harm, and deterioration by these forces and elements. The roof surfacing often plays only a small part, and in some instances no part, in the waterproofing of the total system. It instead imparts life to the roof by protecting the roof membrane from harm.

Roof surfacing materials can be applied to the roof membrane or roof sheet at the manufacturing facility. Composition shingles as used on most residential houses have ceramic granules applied at the factory. Many modified bitumen membranes have either ceramic granules or foil surfacings applied to them at the manufacturing plant. (See Sec. 9.1)

Other types of roof membranes do not specify any type of surfacing, such as most of the polymeric single-ply membranes (EPDM, CSPE, etc). These types of membrane materials are resistant to UV degradation due to the molecular structure and characteristics of the polymeric materials used to create the roof sheets. Also, most of these elastomeric membranes have enough resistance to puncture and tear that may possibly be caused by moderate hailstones and light foot traffic as to not require surface protection from such.

Coatings applied to steel roof panels are unique to other types of roof surfacings. They must have different characteristics in order to protect the metal roof membrane, although they serve the same purposes.

The paint coatings normally used must be flexible to accommodate panel expansion and contraction and survive without harm during the panel-forming process. Protecting the metal panel from rust and corrosion, the surface coating also provides architectural expression.

However, coatings to metal can also be of metallic material. Common metallic surface coatings that are applied to metal panels are aluminum, zinc, an aluminum/zinc combination, lead, and copper, as well as exotic applications such as gold and silver. (See Sec. 10.3.2.)

All roof systems created from bitumen materials—be it asphalt or coal tar pitch built-up roof (BUR) assemblies, or modified bitumen roof systems—require roof surfacings. For these roof systems we can specify a myriad of surfacing materials and systems, the most common being:

- Gravel
- Cutback asphalt coatings
- Ceramic mineral surfaced cap sheets
- Insulated concrete pavers

Every coating or surfacing has different characteristics. These characteristics can be used to enhance the overall performance of the roof system to which they are applied. For example, the very first roof warranty bond ever issued was by Barrett Manufacturing Company. The BUR system was normal for the type being installed at the time, with one exception: the surfacing was of copper sheeting.

6.1.1 Aggregate Surfacings

MATERIALS

Aggregate roof surfacing materials which are permanent and durable and which will protect the roof membrane from the UV rays of the sun and from damage caused by the impact of foot traffic and equipment are often found in:

- Crushed stone
- Water-worn gravel
- Marble quartz
- Crushed lava rock
- Crushed slag aggregates
- Ceramic mineral granules

These surfacing materials are most often installed to BUR assemblies.

The gravel material is the oldest form of roof surfacing in use today. Once spread across the rooftop and held in place by the hot bitumen layer into which it is embedded, the gravel creates a protective shield.

Crushed slag is also used effectively. The slag is lighter in weight and, due to its semiporous nature, it does not retain heat as do gravel and stone aggregates. Slag as used for roof assemblies should be blast-furnace slag or electric-furnace phosphate slag. It is gray in color.

Lava rock is obtained from solidified lava beds as can be found in the western United States. Crushed to correct size, it bonds well with the bitumen flood coat. Lava rock surfacing material is lighter in weight than roofing gravel. Due to its semiporous nature, lava rock does not retain or create a heat sink as much as does roofing gravel.

Marble mineral quartz can be used as a roof surfacing material. Being white in color, it is often considered to be a better reflectant than other forms of mineral aggregate roof surfacings. However, due to its prism shape, which is oblong and crystalline in form, sunlight may be refracted down to the roof surface instead of being reflected.

Stone crushed to the correct size can be used as a surfacing material, but is not a popular form of roof surfacing material. It often has sharp protrusions resulting from the crushing process and these sharp corners can damage the roof membrane to which it is applied.

Ceramic mineral granules are used to surface asphalt BUR assemblies and modified bitumen roof systems. Often, modified bitumen roof membranes come from the factory with these types of granules already applied. The ceramic granules are produced from small ceramic granules which have been superheated. This heating causes the granules to expand up to 30 times their original size. The granules are placed into bags or metal pails for shipping. The metal pails are often hermetically sealed to prevent the granules from absorbing moisture during shipment.

The granules can be obtained in many different colors. Composition shingles which commonly cover residential housing are surfaced with different colors of ceramic granules.

REQUIREMENTS

All gravel, stone, or slag aggregate which is to be embedded into bitumen applied to the roof membrane surface should conform to the requirements of ASTM D 1863. (See Sec. 14.2.5.) In general, the standard requires the aggregate surfacing materials to be of a certain size, because if the material is too small or too large, an effective shield covering cannot be obtained. The aggregate material must not be wet, nor can it be dirty, because the bitumen flood coat will not adhere to materials wet or dirty.

Aggregate surfacing for a BUR assembly is normally specified to be smooth, water-worn gravel. This type of gravel is procured from riverbeds where gravel layers can sometimes be found in abundance. Over thousands of years, the river-bottom gravel becomes smooth and rounded.

This type of aggregate surfacing is preferred by many specifiers because it is relatively inexpensive in most parts of the country, is extremely durable, and is of smooth profile. The smooth profile of water-worn gravel reduces damage concerns that can result from other materials which have sharp or protruding corners, facets, or edges.

However, heavy equipment or excessive foot traffic over the smooth gravel surface can still cause roof damage if the gravel is pushed down to the extent that it punctures the roof membrane. If excessive traffic is expected over the roof surface, specifying roof pads as walkways is recommended.

The gravel should be rinsed by the aggregate producer, resulting in a clean product which easily bonds and adheres to the hot bitumen top pour into which the aggregate is embedded. Specifications often refer to this requirement as *washed river gravel*.

DESIGN

Gravel Surface. Often arriving at the job site wet, the gravel is stockpiled on the roof in *wind-rows* and allowed to dry before installation. "Dry" is a relative term, and in regard to the proper condition for rooftop installation, the gravel should be dry enough to adhere into the hot pouring of bitumen.

The adhesion is field-verified by scraping or sweeping the loose gravel from a roof area and examining the embedded aggregate material. Enough aggregate should be permanently embedded in the bitumen flood coat so as to "lock" the loose overlying aggregate in place. (See Fig. 6.1.)

If the top aggregate is not locked and held in place by the underlying secured aggregate, the loose gravel will be moved by rain and/or wind scour across the smooth bitumen flood coat surface. This will leave an exposed area of the roof surface, defeating the purpose of the gravel surface system.

Normally, gravel surfacing systems will weigh between 350 to 450 lb per 100 ft^2 of roof area. This puts a relatively large amount of weight on the top of the building. A building that is 100 ft by 100 ft will have about 45,000 lb of gravel and asphalt pour as the roof surfacing. That's 22 tons!

This weight factor must be considered when designing and specifying a roof re-cover or retrofit system. Many of the single-ply systems and modified bitumen roof systems of today will allow the existing loose gravel to be removed and an insulation re-cover board to be installed over the existing cleaned roof surface.

The removal of the loose gravel may reduce the weight 150 to 250 lb per 100 ft^2 of roof area. The new roof system will often weigh less than this. This re-cover or retrofit procedure should create no problem if the building is not undergoing building movement and stress.

Other types of aggregate are embedded into a top pour of bitumen to create a surfacing system for BUR assemblies. On steeper-than-normal roof slopes, marble quartz surfacing is often selected. The prism shapes of the mineral and the density of the individual pieces help the surfacing stay in place and resist wind and rain scour.

Lava rock and crushed slag can also be installed to a roof surface in a pouring of hot bitumen. Being porous, these aggregates weigh less than river gravel. The porosity also prevents these materials from being as much of a heat sink as is river gravel. (See Sec. 2.3.1.)

Ceramic Mineral Granules. Ceramic granules are factory-applied to certain types of roof felts or roof membrane sheets. The granules vary in color, allowing architectural blending of exposed and visual roof systems with other components of the building.

These granules will often be used to surface-coat the exposed bitumen which bleeds or extends out at the edges of installed BUR membrane cap sheets or modified bitumen membrane sheets. The field-installed granules match the color of the factory-installed granules on the roof sheet. This is mainly for final roof appearance purposes.

For asphalt BUR assemblies—both hot-applied but, more normally, cold-process-applied systems (see

Figure 6.1 Gravel being installed.

Chap. 4)—ceramic granules can be applied as the protective roof surfacing system. The granules are spread into a hot asphalt top pour coating or spread into a cutback asphalt top coating. (See Sec. 6.1.3.) The cold-process materials are often asphalt emulsions or fibered or nonfibered asphalt cutback materials.

The spreading of the granules is unlike the spreading of gravel or slag into the asphalt top pour coating. Instead, granules are often applied into the asphalt top coating layer by special equipment which blows the granules out onto the roof surface or they can be broadcast by using perforated pails which are spun by the roofers. Spinning of the pails causes the granules to be dispensed in a swirl action to the roof surface.

If too many granules are applied, the loose granules will be displaced and washed into gutters and drainage systems. If too few granules are applied, a proper surfacing system will not be achieved.

The roof applicator should install the granules immediately upon opening the sealed container. If any granules become wet or are contaminated with moisture, they should be removed from the job site.

Roof Ballast Aggregate. Sometimes large gravel or crushed stone aggregates are used as ballast covering for roof assemblies, normally being, but not limited to, single-ply polymeric membranes. In such cases, the weight of the aggregate ballast holds the roof assembly on top of the building.

The aggregate ballast size selected should be in compliance with the ASTM D 448 standard. The aggregate ballast system will normally be 1½-in stone and weigh 1000 lb per 100 ft^2 of roof area.

The size and weight of the ballast are dependent upon wind uplift resistance requirements. The weight of the ballast covering can change from the aforementioned criteria, with extra ballast of larger size used in roof corner and perimeter areas (see Fig. 6.2).

When crushed stone is used as ballast in lieu of smooth river-bottom stone, a protection sheet should be installed over most types of roof membranes. This sheet is normally of polyester or fiberglass material and protects the membrane from sharp corners or projections on the crushed stone.

With a ballasted roof covering assembly, weight considerations to be imposed on the building structure are crucial. During construction and loading of the ballast from ground onto the rooftop, live loads must be considered. Roof walkways across the ballast are often required in order to access and service rooftop equipment.

6.1.2 Roof Pavers

The detrimental effects of the elements which we know to destroy low-sloped bituminous roof systems can be limited or prevented by use of an insulated roof paver. Section 6.1 lists the most detrimental elements and dynamics that affect roof membranes.

Effective roof surfacings and coatings limit the effects of these harmful actions, reactions, and occurrences. An insulated *protected membrane roof* (PMR) system will provide maximum performance in limiting and reducing

Figure 6.2 Ballasted system with wind-scour at corners.

harmful effects caused by these forces and occurrences. In general, a PMR system uses a polystyrene roof insulation, since it is nonabsorbent of and is not affected by water. The insulation is held to the roof with ballast. Often the roof membrane is laid loose, secured only at the roof perimeter, and is also held in place by the weight of the ballast. Ballast can be crushed stone, river-washed gravel, concrete pavers, or insulated concrete pavers. Insulated concrete pavers are preferred by most designers.

MANUFACTURE

An insulated roof paver is created from a top portion of latex modified concrete which is laminated to an extruded polystyrene insulation panel. (See Sec. 8.1.6.) An insulated paver could be considered a composite roof insulation material. For creation of an insulated concrete roof paver, extruded polystyrene insulation is grooved on the top face. The grooved top face is further treated with a tack glue.

A special mixture of concrete mortar, latex, and other minor additives is blended into a wet slurry. The wet slurry is poured and formed to fit the roof insulation profile. The final latex concrete surface laminated to the polystyrene insulation is normally ⅜ in thick.

Both the insulation and the concrete thickness can be adjusted by the manufacturer. Additional thicknesses of polystyrene insulation provide better insulation values. Increased thickness of the concrete facer provides additional weight and strength. Additional weight will help increase wind-resistance values. Additional strength pavers may be required for roof areas experiencing exceptional foot and equipment traffic.

Insulated pavers are manufactured with a tongue-and-groove lock on two sides (see Fig. 6.3). This lock provides wind resistance, allows straight alignment of the paver system on the rooftop, and helps hold all pavers in place.

Extruded polystyrene insulation is the only type of insulation used for this system. Polystyrene insulation does not absorb water and is therefore not affected by water on the rooftop to which it is exposed.

The latex concrete is specially formulated to resist freeze/thaw cycles common across the United States. The manner and means of attaching the concrete facer to the polystyrene insulation are important in its ability to resist such cycles and stay permanently adhered to the insulation body.

CHARACTERISTICS

The pavers, normally 2 ft × 4 ft, are covered with a latex modified concrete and are integrally locked together, forming a complete and effective shield across the rooftop. This shield surface completely blocks out the harmful rays of the sun.

Paver systems are often used over subterranean rooms and structures. The plaza at Rockefeller Center in New York City is a paver system over a subterranean room. The room is waterproofed with a bituminous roof assembly, covered with a protective insulation panel, and sur-

Figure 6.3 Tongue-and-groove lock. (*Courtesy of Lyle Hogan, P.E.*)

faced with a paver. Pavers have always proved effective in resisting foot traffic, equipment traffic, hailstones, etc.

Thermal loading and thermal shock to roof systems can be a cause of roof deterioration and failure. (See Sec. 2.3.1.) Thermal loading (diurnal cycle) occurs when roofs absorb heat during the day and radiate heat at night. Thermal shock can be caused by the sudden onset of rain to a hot roof surface or even by clouds passing across the sun. Gravel aggregate surfacings reduce thermal shock by creating a heat sink and reducing sudden temperature swings. However, the heat retained and accumulated by the heat sink can cause prolonged and elevated temperatures, which are detrimental to the molecular makeup of many roof materials.

Coatings do not create heat sinks since they do not have the mass to absorb and radiate light-wave energy. However, coatings allow thermal shock to be more radical and extensive than will occur to a roof membrane covered by a material which is a heat sink.

Thermal shock occurs due to wide temperature swings in a short period of time. In some regions this swing can be as much as 75 to 100°F in a 24-h period. The resultant expansion, contraction, and other dynamic forces can have a tremendous effect on the roof system. Additionally, thermal shock occurs to a roof system due to onset of a sudden summer shower or clouds passing across the sun.

An insulated paver will greatly reduce thermal loading and thermal shock to the roof membrane. The reduction is directly proportional to the amount of insulation laminated to the concrete facer and the temperatures at which the roof paver is to exist.

Wind-resistance characteristics are imparted mainly by the phenomenon of pressure equalization. With high-speed wind, once the negative-pressure air zone lifts the paver slightly from the roof surface, both the top and bottom surfaces of the paver experience equal pressure within 1/100 of a second. This results in no net uplift pressure on the paver. (Planes with iced wings don't fly.) (See Sec. 2.2.2.)

Additional wind resistance is provided by the interlocking of the paver system. No one unit can move without involving many others. Designers must realize that not all roof paver systems incorporate a tongue-and-groove assembly.

Finally, the weight of the paver systems comes into play. The improvement due to weight is proportional to the square root of the increased weight. The basic wind pressure equation being $p = 1/2pV^2$. V^2 is the velocity of the wind squared. In some cases additional concrete blocks are placed on top of the pavers at strategic corner and perimeter areas of the roof where wind loads will be the greatest.

Placed atop a fully adhered low-sloped roof system, paver systems should be tested and certified as being able to resist 135 lb/ft^2 negative wind-uplift pressure. Over an unadhered (loose-laid) roof assembly, with an air barrier, the paver system should be tested and certified as being able to resist a negative uplift pressure of 90 lb/ft^2. These values are obtained and verified in Underwriters Laboratories Test Method 1897.

Another method used to increase wind-uplift resistance of the roof paver system is the use of steel straps laid across the paver system and attached to the paver surfaces. The straps are secured to the building walls or other structural components of the building. (See Fig. 6.4.)

ADVANTAGES AND DISADVANTAGES

Pavers provide excellent protective characteristics that are needed by most roof systems. However, they are not a common component of roof design.

Figure 6.4 Strap assembly. This photo shows a ridge line application and metal termination at a vent stack opening. *(Courtesy of T-Clear Corporation, Hamilton, Ohio)*

Pavers completely cover the roof surface. This concerns some designers and roof installers in the event that roof leaks will have to be located and repaired. Visual examination of the roof membrane is not possible without removal of areas of the paver system. This also restricts maintenance surveys.

Others believe this complete covering is an advantage. By completely covering the roof membrane, maintenance and repair are greatly reduced since the elements and forces which cause such maintenance and repair are limited or eliminated by the complete covering of the paver system.

If the paver system must be removed, special cautions are required. When the repair is in the field of the roof, the tongue must be cut from the paver. This requires a blade approximately 2 in long, which can reach between the joints of the interlocking paver units. After removing the first row of pavers as required, the remaining pavers in that area are easily removed and reinstalled per original construction.

When the pavers are reinstalled they must be secured back into the roof at the cut line. This is accomplished by use of an 8-in-wide steel strip which is centered over the cut line and secured to the concrete face of the pavers with peel rivets. If the visual effects of the straps would be detrimental, a system exists for using a ¾-in PVC pipe to replace the tongue which was cut during the removal process.

In all cases it is important for the paver system to be properly reinstalled and secured. It may be beneficial to consult the manufacturer for an inspection of the repaired roof paver system.

The initial cost of insulated roof paver systems is sometimes five times or more the cost for gravel embedded into a top pour of asphalt, although it can be pointed out that gravel does not add significant insulation value. The labor required to install either surfacing is approximately equal, unless a strap system over the paver system is required. A strap system will increase the total paver system installation cost.

However, when considered in a life-cycle cost analysis, insulated concrete roof pavers usually decrease the total amortized roof system cost. Also, the pavers should last through several roof cycles if they are not vandalized, are not exposed to caustic or extremely polluted environments, or do not come into contact with petroleum distillates, cooking-grease discharges through roof vents, etc.

DESIGN

Insulated concrete paver systems normally weigh 450 lb per 100 ft^2 (square) of roof area. This compares with an average 450 to 500 lb per square for roof gravel on a conventional built-up roof to 1000 lb a square on a ballasted single-ply roof assembly.

Insulated roof pavers are commonly used in protected membrane roof systems (PMRSs). These types of assemblies invert the normal location of the roof membrane and the roof insulation by placing the insulation on top of the roof membrane.

PMRSs are most often used over high-humidity and elevated-temperature-extreme buildings or building sections. The inversion of the roof membrane allows it to function as a vapor retarder with the topside insulation preventing moisture condensation from occurring within the roof membrane and roof deck location. (See Sec. 2.3.3.)

Some roof designs require a vapor retarder, insulation, and roof membrane covering. It may be possible in such a design to eliminate the vapor retarder and the cost associated therewith, and to design an insulated concrete paver system instead.

The paver system will give the client more service and savings within the budget than will a vapor barrier. This would be considered a PMRS design.

Roof pavers can also be used at mechanical units and other areas of the roof where extensive foot and mechanical traffic can be expected. If roof pavers are used at mechanical units or as walkways, they should be the heavyweight 2-ft × 2-ft × 2-in pavers. These provide high strength and are very resistant to wind uplift. Lightweight pavers and insulated pavers are designed to be installed in an array which covers a defined roof section. (See Fig. 6.5.)

Although not recommended, it may sometimes be necessary to secure the pavers to the roof membrane surface, i.e., to form a walkway system across the rooftop created from insulated concrete roof pavers. Although the heavyweight paver may be more secure due to weight, only the insulated concrete roof paver can be adhered to certain membranes by use of a latex or urethane caulk or special adhesive applied to the roof insulation of the paver and the roof membrane surface. However, if the paver ever has to be removed, the roof membrane will probably come with it.

Some interlocking concrete-surfaced extruded foam pavers have been classified by UL for uplift resistance to 135 lb/ft^2. They have also been tested at the National Research Council of Canada in their 30-ft × 30-ft wind tunnel to stay in place in winds exceeding 200 mi/h. Factory Mutual has a design specification which can be used for insurance acceptance in lieu of testing since FM has no test protocol for ballasted systems. In the event that additional uplift resistance is needed, a strap system may be available from the paver manufacturer.

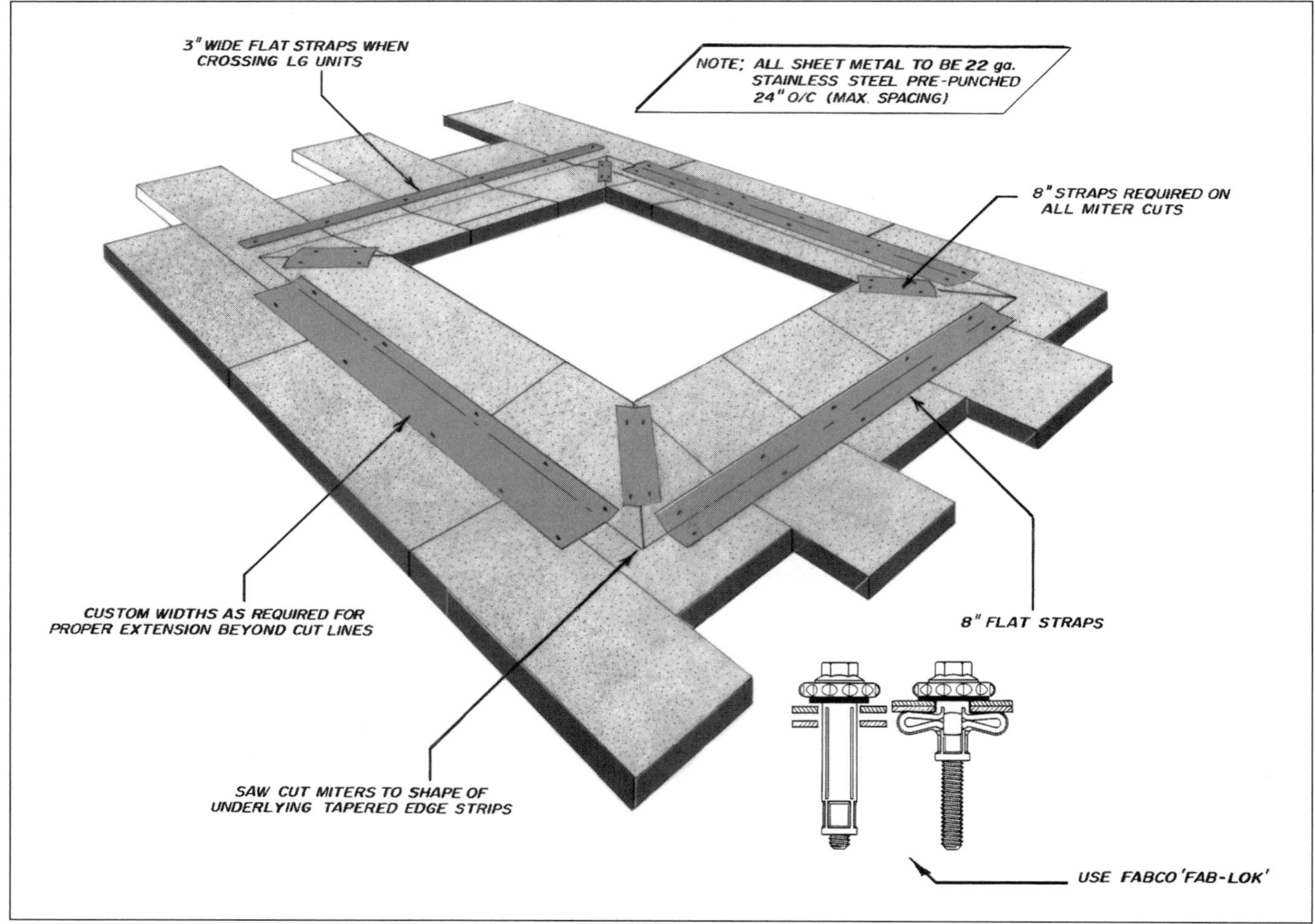

Figure 6.5 Paver at mechanical unit. (*Courtesy of Lyle Hogan, P.E.*)

When designing an insulated concrete roof paver system for use in cold regions of the United States, verify that the paver has been approved for use within that region. The U.S. Weather Index Map is used as a reference for the different regions. (See Fig. 11.5.) The concrete topping on the paver must be able to withstand freeze/thaw cycles. (See Fig. 6.6.)

Pavers are reusable. The insulation properties are therefore reusable. In the green-design philosophy becoming popular today, this aspect should not be overlooked. Roof insulation on a roof paver system is not removed from the rooftop and discarded at the landfill. Nor is energy consumed recycling the material. (See Fig. 6.7.)

6.1.3 Roof Coatings

Many low-sloped bituminous roof systems today use liquid-applied coatings as their protective surfacings. These coatings are usually cutback asphalt materials or asphalt emulsified with clay and water.

There are numerous other coatings available for roof surfacing. They can be from base products of latex, acrylics, urethanes, or coal tar, as well as from many other uncommon and exotic materials.

Some coatings are modified with polymers, allowing the manufacturer to claim exceptional elongation and durability. Some are touted as being "enhanced" or "extended" with a product which imparts durability, adhesion, abrasion resistance, etc. Some function effectively and some have not. We will address the more commonly used and accepted roof coating materials.

These coatings are created from asphalt which is diluted or cut with a petroleum distillate. The resulting cutback roof coating product is light in weight, allows visual inspection of the roof membrane, and makes roof maintenance easier.

The disadvantage to coatings is that they are usually maintenance items. The owner must have the coatings reapplied periodically. Coatings as a maintenance procedure are often applied by the owner's in-house per-

Figure 6.6 Concrete paver destroyed by freeze/thaw cycle. (*Courtesy of Centrum Engineering, Winston/Salem, N.C.*)

sonnel after a limited amount of training. The coatings can be brush-applied to the clean and prepared roof surface. For large roof areas it is often more economical to hire a contractor who can apply the coating with airless spray equipment.

Coatings are degraded mainly by the ultraviolet rays of sunlight, although other elements of the environment, such as water, pollutants, and heat, are detrimental to most coatings. Therefore, coatings sacrifice themselves to the sun while protecting the roof membranes under them. Once the coating has dissipated, the roof membrane is vulnerable to accelerated thermal loading and degradation due to ultraviolet-wavelength attack. (See Sec. 2.3.4.)

Figure 6.7 Paver system being installed. (*Courtesy of T-Clear Corporation, Hamilton, Ohio*)

MANUFACTURE

Cutback Asphalts. Cutback asphalt coatings are created from hot asphalt product as is used for built-up roofing. (See Sec. 4.1.1.) The asphalt is blended with petroleum distillates and mineral spirits. Each coating manufacturer has its own process.

The hot asphalt is piped from the oxidation column to a large metal vessel. After the asphalt has cooled somewhat, but while still in its liquid state, it is blended with the petroleum distillates. The type and amount of the distillate will help determine the viscosity of the cutback. Fibers are often blended at the same time, although some coatings are nonfibered. These fibers were often asbestos until it was labeled as a hazardous material, and today they are usually cellulose or polyethylene fibers.

The finished cutback asphalt product is placed into 5-gal pails, 55-gal drums, or bulk tanks. If spray-applying the coating, 55-gal drum containers or bulk loads are normally purchased. However, the bulk container is not functional if applying the coating by brush on the rooftop.

Aluminum Coating. Aluminum paste containing millions of small aluminum flakes can also be blended with the cutback asphalt to create aluminum pigmented asphalt roof coating. Aluminum paste used for this process can contain different amounts of aluminum, depending on the coating manufacturer product specification. Some pastes contain 45 percent aluminum, while others contain over 70 percent aluminum.

The aluminum flakes used in roof coating are manufactured in a large metal sphere. Inside the sphere are large ball bearings. The sphere is turned and rotated and the balls within roll over the aluminum flakes many times. This manufacturing process smashes the flakes out to very small and thin particles.

These flakes give the aluminum coating its brightness. Brightness is determined by the amount of flakes in the aluminum paste and by how small and how flat the flakes are.

As the aluminum coating is applied to the roof, the aluminum flakes settle and overlap. This is termed *leafing*. As the petroleum distillate evaporates, the leafing process of the aluminum flakes occurs. The leafing process should create a consistent aluminum shield over the roof surface. The amount of aluminum paste contained within the coating dictates how thick the aluminum covering will be and also provides an indication of the durability of the aluminum coating. Quality manufactured aluminum paste usually creates a brighter surface than does aluminum paste of less quality.

Asphalt Emulsion. Asphalt emulsions are made using either synthetic emulsifiers or a clay-based material as the emulsifier. In the roofing industry we most commonly use asphalt that has been emulsified with a clay such as bentonite. Emulsions are commonly made with unblown or nonoxidized asphalt.

This unblown asphalt is piped to a processing system, and while still liquid, it is blended with the emulsifier. This is accomplished by sending the asphalt through a mechanism consisting of two metal disks, aligned closely together, with their faces toward each other. The asphalt is sent between these disks in a small stream. The disks are spinning at high speeds, and as the small stream of asphalt passes between the disks, it is separated into very small globules.

Before the globules can rejoin, they are surrounded by this liquid clay solution. This solution completely covers each small bole of asphalt and keeps the asphalt particles from rejoining.

CHARACTERISTICS

Cutback Coatings. The distillates in the cutback coatings will penetrate and partially dissolve the surface of the bituminous roof they are being applied to. This action of the distillates in the roof coating allows the cutback coating to penetrate the roof membrane.

After the distillates have penetrated the surface of the roof membrane, they reverse to the surface of the membrane due to evaporation. The solids and base materials of the cutback will then take the place of the distillate.

Asphalt roof coatings can be applied to steep surfaces. This is due in part to the fibers within the coating, which keep it from slipping or sluffing. Also, the distillates which cut the asphalt to create the coating material greatly reduce the cold-flow characteristics of the base asphalt material. (See Sec. 4.1.4.)

Asphalt cutback coating material is not resistant to ponding water areas on a rooftop. Ponding water will often cause the material to experience small bubbles or blistering due to entrapped moisture between the roof surface and coating.

Coal tar pitch materials are available in cutback products. Coal tar pitch resaturants and roof cement are materials commonly used.

Further information regarding cutback bitumen products and uses is available in Sec. 4.1.5.

Aluminum Roof Coating. Aluminum pigmented asphalt roof coating has many of the same characteristics as regular cutback asphalt coatings. It is a cutback coating with aluminum flakes added. However, the aluminum flakes cannot withstand extensive foot traffic. The aluminum will be worn from the roof surface.

Also, the aluminum flakes within the applied coating are less resistant to ponding water than is the base cutback asphalt material. Ponding water areas on an aluminum-coated roof can be quickly detected by the dark area where the aluminum has dissipated from the coating.

The reflective characteristic of aluminum roof coating is one of its most important attributes. A quality aluminum coating can reduce roof membrane temperature as much as 20°F when compared to an uncoated membrane.

Asphalt Emulsion. Clay-based asphalt emulsion has better elasticity properties than does asphalt cutback roof coatings, even though the material will dry hard to the touch. The material has been used very successfully for parapet wall flashing, as well as for above- and below-grade waterproofing. Also, some manufacturers have specifications for using emulsion as an interply bitumen adhesive for roof systems.

Since asphalt emulsion's carrier is water and not petroleum, as for cutback asphalt coatings, it will not penetrate the felts and asphalt of a roof as will cutback asphalt coatings. However, emulsion will adhere to almost any type of roof surface.

Asphalt emulsion is more resistant to ultraviolet rays of sunlight than standard cutback asphalt. This is a direct result of its material base, which is clay, as opposed to asphalt. Clay is more resistant to ultraviolet attack.

Coal tar pitch emulsions are available but seldom, if ever, used for roof construction. Tar-based emulsions are most commonly used as pavement sealers.

DESIGN

The thicker a cutback coating is applied, the longer it will take for the distillates to evaporate and the longer it will take for the coating to be dissipated by the environment. It could therefore be reasoned that a thickly applied coating would function better and longer than a thinly applied coating. However, overapplied coatings may not function effectively. There are specific application rates and thicknesses for cutback and emulsion coatings, and the manufacturer's specifications should be consulted.

Applying a cutback coating in excessive amounts can create severe problems, such as cracking and crazing similar to that of a dried mudflat. Applying coatings too thin will result in an ineffective surface coating which will be soon be dissipated by the environment.

As a rule of thumb, the thinner, less viscous cutback coatings contain more distillates and fewer asphalt and binders. As the distillates evaporate, you will be left with less material on the roof. Coating quality can often be compared by referencing the percent of solids by volume in the material manufacturer's literature.

For modified bitumen membrane roof systems which require a field-applied coating, aluminum roof coatings are used, as well as a dual coating system consisting of asphalt emulsion as the base and aluminum coating as the surface finish.

Some cutback coatings are harmful to some modified bitumen membranes. Distillate attack to the membrane sheet has been known to occur. The coating materials and manufacturer should be approved by the modified bitumen manufacturer before application.

Cutback coatings will not adhere to dirty or damp roof surfaces. Require the roof surface to be clean and dry before proceeding with work. For emulsions, the surface should be clean, but a layer of moisture, such as dew, complements the application process.

As with exterior paint projects, care must be taken to prevent damage to adjacent property or automobiles from overspray or airborne coating particles. If coatings come into contact with masonry surfaces, the coatings will penetrate the porous material and removal is difficult at best.

Emulsions will not remain effective on roof areas which pond water. The ponding water will destroy the bond and adhesion of the material. Subsequent rains wash the material from the rooftop.

Emulsions should not be applied when rain could possibly occur before the emulsion material has dried. Uncured, the material is still water-soluble and will wash from the membrane surface. Curing time is dependent upon humidity and temperatures.

Likewise, emulsions must be protected from freezing temperatures. Freeze will solidify the water constituents within the material and destroy its usefulness. Also, the material must never be installed when temperatures can be expected to drop below 40°F before the material has completely cured. (See Fig. 6.8.)

6.1.4 Resaturants

GENERAL

As the UVs and the heat work on the roof system, volatile oils are cooked out. If the volatiles can be replaced, the life of the roof will be extended. Resaturation is a process by which volatile oils are added to an existing asphalt or coal tar pitch roof membrane.

Resaturation will not make an old roof new again. Resaturation is often used incorrectly to rejuvenate a roof that is beyond the hope of saving.

Resaturation is often most effective if initiated when the roof has expended 40 to 60 percent of its life cycle. This may extend the life of the roof another 10 to 20 percent beyond what it would normally have lasted.

The resaturation coating of an asphalt roof system is considered by some asphalt experts to be ineffective. Instead, asphalt resaturation is often initiated as a maintenance procedure rather than a restoration procedure. This has to do with the polarization of the asphaltenes

Figure 6.8 Coating being installed. (*Courtesy of Monsey Products, Kimberton, Pa.*)

that form asphalt and is too technical to delve into at this point.

Resaturants are made much the same way as are cutback roof coatings, except that some extra volatile oils are added. Resaturation should be used on roof areas that are difficult and costly to replace, such as a roof 200 ft in the air with pipe penetrations every 3 ft and with 6 in of high-R-value roof insulation under it. For every year the building owner can extend the life of the roof, money is saved.

It should be understood that standard cutback roof coatings will, to a certain extent, resaturate and rejuvenate a roof system. When regular cutbacks are used as a maintenance coating and also as an attempt to resaturate, the result will probably extend the life of the roof system.

Some people believe that regularly applying a coating to an asphalt roof could extend the life of the roof appreciably. If this is not true for a hot-process asphalt roof it probably holds true for a cold-process asphalt built-up roof system. (See Sec. 4.1.5.)

COAL TAR PITCH RESATURANT

With a coal tar pitch BUR system, resaturation is an accepted practice. The chemical makeup of the roof system and resaturant complement each other well. However, resaturant will not make an old roof new once again. It will only replace some of the volatile oils dissipated by the elements.

Not all coal tar pitch BUR systems are acceptable for resaturation. Fiberglass roof felts, common in today's roof industry, may not accept a resaturant well. Being of an open-weave design, the felts should be considered porous, and being fiberglass, they are not as absorbent as organic felts. (See Sec. 5.1.4.)

The pitch resaturant, by manufacturing design and chemical makeup, is heavy and penetrating. Pitch resaturant can pass through the open-weave fiberglass felts, insulation layers, and roof decking.

Organic felt BUR systems trap and adsorb most of the pitch resaturant. Fiberglass felt BUR systems may not exhibit the same characteristics.

CHAPTER 7

Roof Felts

7.1 GENERAL

In the selection of a roof type, many factors concerning the roofing plies—being roof felts, roof sheet, and/or roof membrane materials—must be considered. Throughout this chapter we will make reference to roof felts, and in many cases this is meant to encompass generically all felts, sheets, and membranes, although technically they are not the same materials and have different functions in different types of roof systems.

For example, a roof felt can be an organic felt paper used to cover a plywood roof deck prior to composition shingle installation. A roof felt can also be a fiberglass ply sheet installed into hot moppings on a built-up roof (BUR) assembly, although technically this should be referred to only as a *ply felt sheet*. Additionally, the term *roof sheet* or *roof ply membrane* is sometimes meant to reference a membrane material used as a ply sheet in a BUR system, such as a polyester fabric used in a cold-process BUR system or a modified bitumen membrane sheet used to create a modified bitumen membrane roof assembly, i.e., a modified bitumen base sheet membrane, covered by hot asphalt moppings and a modified bitumen membrane cap sheet. Terms meant to describe the various groups of felts, sheets, and membranes differ across the country. Also, *roof membrane* is a term used to describe the completed roof system of felts, sheets, or membranes and the associated interply moppings—i.e., the BUR membrane which is covered with gravel surfacing.

The many different felt materials have specific uses, for particular situations, and are used as required for a long-lasting and effective roof system. The responsibility for the design, selection, and proper application divides between the designer, the specifier, and the roof applicator to ensure that the correct material is specified and properly installed for the existing conditions.

An effective and correct BUR membrane system is created by the alternating layers of roof plies and bitumen interply moppings. For more information on the correct handling, preparation, and installation of roof bitumens, see Chaps. 4 and 5.

MECHANICAL PROPERTIES

When used in a BUR assembly, roof felts, sheets, or membrane plies:

- Stabilize the interply bitumen by joining the bitumen moppings together to form a durable roof membrane
- Provide interply bitumen mopping uniformity
- Provide tensile strength
- Can impart fire resistance depending upon the type of felt ply selected

Felt paper in a BUR can be compared to reinforcement bars in a structural concrete system, which provide strength and stability. The roof felt gives the roof membrane system tensile strength, dimensional stability, tear resistance, and flexural strength.

Roof felts alone, without interply bitumen, cannot contribute any waterproofing ability on a low-sloped BUR. Likewise, bitumen applied to the top of a building, without roof felts incorporated into the bitumen material, would experience severe problems of movement/migration, and displacement, resulting in a totally ineffective roof system.

The strength of the roof felt material is important, although, today, few roof system performance problems relating to weak and brittle roof felts are reported. In prior decades, weak and brittle asbestos and fiberglass roof felts caused problems in some areas of the northern United States and Canada. Whether using organic, fiberglass, or synthetic felt material, roof systems of bitumens and felts perform adequately if properly specified and installed.

The tensile strength of a roof felt should not be evaluated in design as an independent unit within a BUR membrane assembly. The total felt and bitumen assembly creates the roof membrane, and it is this roof membrane which must resist the environment, building movement, thermal shock and loading, foot traffic, etc. As an example, two plies of high-strength fiberglass felt may not create a system as strong as four plies of weaker organic felt.

However, some forms of roof felts resist the thermal loading of the roof membrane better than others; some resist foot and mechanical traffic better, which is in direct relation to tear and puncture resistance; while others are better suited to smooth-surface coated roof systems than others, which are better suited for gravel or covered roof surface systems.

Each type of roof felt has different mechanical properties. For example, many of the synthetic polyester-based roof ply felts have the best tear and puncture resistance of all the major roof felts, but these felts do not have the same dimensional stability after installation as do many of the other more common roof felts. Polyester felts constitute approximately 2 percent of the total roof ply felt market.

The organic roof ply felts are better suited to hot bitumen applications than are most of the synthetic polyester roof felts due to *wetting* or the ease of adhesion properties of the saturated organic felt as applied into a hot mopping of bitumen. However, fiberglass felts, also having good wetting properties, have many other favorable characteristics as compared to organic felt, making fiberglass roof felt more often selected for hot-process BUR design. Organic felts are normally used as vapor retarders or as a base sheet material, although tarred organic felts are often specified as ply sheets within coal tar pitch BUR systems.

On the other hand, polyester roof felts are often selected for cold-process BUR systems (see Sec. 4.1.5), whereas organic saturated felt is not compatible for such a design. However, coated organic felts work well with cutback asphalt cold-process roof systems because of the asphalt coating surface applied by the manufacturer to the saturated felt.

The absorbency of the dry felt mat from which the roof felt is created, the dimensional stability of the roof felt, as well as the tear strength and tensile strength of the felt are all important mechanical properties. These properties are adequately produced in the roof felts marketed by the major roof felt manufacturers. In some design situations, optimum performance of certain mechanical properties may be required. For example, if designing a BUR in a geographical region which experiences hailstorms, a roof felt which resists tear and puncture is best suited.

In other situations where minor deck or roof-substrate movement is anticipated, a roof felt with good tensile strength would be recommended. Such properties should be exhibited by the roof felt in both the machine direction and in the cross-felt direction. To further clarify, roof felts are often manufactured on conveyor belt–type systems, and, as such, the individual reinforcement strands and materials which form the roof felt become oriented in the direction of the machine. As a result of this, the tear strength is different longitudinally and transversely for organic felts and may or may not be the same for fiberglass felts because of the ability to better control fiber orientation in fiberglass felt mat manufacturing.

Adhesion. With hot mopped BUR, felt layers are not glued or stuck into the bitumen layer. Instead, they are welded and fused into the interply mopping as a result of the heat of the mopping and the amount of bitumen applied. The equiviscous temperature (EVT) of the applied bitumen is crucial (see Sec. 4.1.3) but of equal importance is the amount of bitumen applied in between the roof felt layers.

INTERPLY BITUMEN AMOUNTS

The primary waterproofing element of a BUR system, either hot-applied or cold-process, is the interply bitumen.

The amount of interply bitumen is first determined by the amount applied by the roofer to the deck or substrate. However, the amount is further controlled and defined by the roof felt as it is rolled into the freshly applied hot bitumen mopping.

1. The bitumen must be applied thickly enough to create a complete waterproofing roof bitumen layer.
2. The bitumen must be applied evenly and uniformly, in a wide enough strip so that the entire roof felt is embedded into the mopped bitumen.

These two items are best accomplished by coordination of the application of the roof felt into the freshly applied bitumen layer. An interply mopping of coal tar pitch bitumen between the felt layers will be heavier in weight than an asphalt bitumen mopping because pitch weighs more than asphalt. However the volumes, or interply mopping thickness, of the two different bitumen materials are roughly equal.

Again, the EVT should always be maintained, as this assists in determining the interply thickness of the bitumen. However, if the roof felt is not installed correctly, regardless of proper EVT, an inadequate roof system will result.

One method to help ensure application of the correct amount of bitumen, either asphalt or coal tar pitch, is to specify that enough bitumen is applied. This is best accomplished, not being specifying interply bitumen weights, which are the target amounts, but by additionally specifying for a puddle of hot bitumen of proper EVT to be present in front of the felt roll at all times during application. (See Fig. 7.1.) The size and weight of the felt roll will help spread and disperse the hot bitumen mopping layer evenly.

Figure 7.1 Felt and bitumen puddle.

FELT EMBEDMENT

The process of *brooming in* the felt layer into the hot bitumen mopping is also important. Brooming of the felt into the hot bitumen layers should always be required within the ConDocs (construction documents), for all types of roof felts and sheets. Brooming in the roof felt helps ensure complete adhesion and embedment of all of the surface of the felt into the hot bitumen mopping layer. The brooming-in process must be performed immediately behind the felt roll. A stiff-bristle broom, squeegee, or special felt follow tool is used for brooming in the felt layers. (See Fig. 7.2.)

Of importance, but often misunderstood, or ignored within both the design community and the roofing community, is the requirement to stay off freshly installed felt layers and bitumen moppings. Roof applicators often ignore this requirement, because of the difficulty of adhering to it at all times. Designers often misinterpret this requirement, prohibiting traffic across the completed roof felt membrane system—at best a difficult and costly requirement. Staying off freshly installed felt and hot interply moppings is not mandated because of the damage which might be caused to the felt by foot traffic during installation, but because of bitumen displacement and roof felt memory.

FELT MEMORY

All roof felts have a memory—some more and some less than others. The roof felt will be displaced downward into the freshly installed hot bitumen layer if stepped on by a roof worker. Upon removal of the traffic load, the felt has a tendency to return to the level or plane of original installation, often floating above the bitumen layer which was displaced by the traffic load. In such instances, the felt is no longer adhered and bonded within and to a bitumen layer. (See Fig. 7.4.)

Fiberglass and polyester felts have more memory than do organic felts. Memory problems with organic felts are minimal if excessive foot traffic is restricted from the freshly applied layers. *No problems will result from this felt memory for any type of felt after the felt and bitumen layers have cooled to ambient rooftop temperatures.* However, some roof situations require the roof installers to walk on freshly installed felts, such as at roof penetrations, parapet walls, and other base flashing areas—it is unavoidable in the practical sense. (See Fig. 7.3.)

Take these exceptional situations into account within the ConDocs. It is better to require additional or extra means, methods, and materials at felt/bitumen damaged locations than it is to require and expect roof workers to stay off freshly installed felt and bitumen layers.

TYPES

There are many different types of roofing felt paper in the industry:

- #15-lb organic felts
- #30-lb organic felts
- #40-lb category organic base sheet
- 19-in selvage organic roof sheet
- 90-lb surfaced organic roof sheet
- Type IV fiberglass felts
- Type VI fiberglass felts
- Type I fiberglass base sheet
- Type II fiberglass base sheet

Figure 7.2 Brooming in the felts.

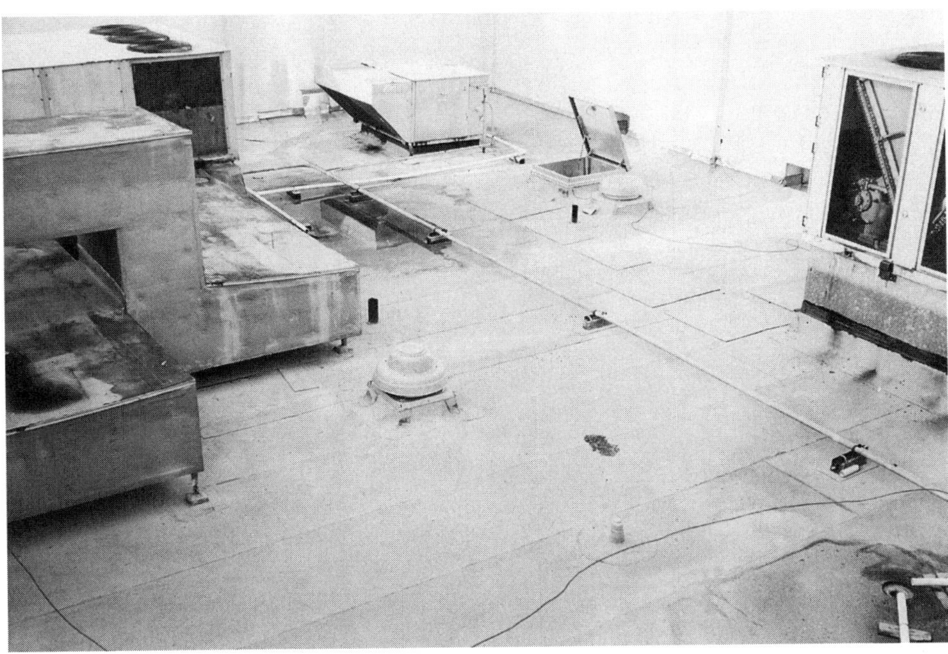

Figure 7.3 Roof with numerous penetrations.

- Venting base sheet
- Granule surfaced fiberglass cap sheet
- Spunbond polyester membrane
- Stitchbond polyester membrane

In addition, there are roof flashing sheets, reinforced with fiberglass and/or polyester membrane, used at bituminous flashing areas only.

Roof felts can be coated with asphalt bitumen, impregnated or saturated with bitumen (asphalt or coal tar pitch), or both coated and saturated.

7.1.1 Organic Felts

Organic roof felts are most commonly used today as felt underlayment in shingle, tile, and slate roof systems. However, until the 1970s, organic felts were the predominant type of roof felt used for BUR applications. Organic felts were subsequently replaced by fiberglass felts, an inorganic material. An organic roof felt is made from fibers derived from wood or paper. The fibers are obtained from corrugated paper, wood chips, saw dust, etc.

MANUFACTURE

To make organic roof felt, several different raw materials are used. Normally these are wood chips from soft timber such as pine or spruce, although sometimes hardwoods are also used, as well as paper waste from corrugated boxes and industrial paper.

Each of these different materials is reduced from the original raw form to a fibered mulch. For example, timber is run through a chipping machine, which reduces the log to small chips. The chips are saturated with high-pressure steam, which softens the chips. The chips are then screw-fed to a defiberator, which reduces the wood chips to fibers. The fibers are then transferred to a station called the *woodfiber chest,* where they are cleaned. They are then transferred to the mixing station, where the other raw materials, such as paper fibers and other minor ingredients, are mixed with the wood fibers to create the organic felt roofing sheet material.

Wood fibers are used as the basic material of organic felts. Paper fibers are used to supplement the wood fibers, adding strength, pliability, and toughness to the sheet. The different elements (wood fibers and paper fibers) are blended with water in precise quantities to form a wet slur. This wet slur is contained in a large vat, which has a screened drum rotating in it. The screen on the drum picks up the slurry and deposits it onto a moving belt. The wet slurry is pressed by rollers and vacuumed to remove the water. Another manufacturing process can also be used to form the felt mat, also utilizing a moving belt, but the wet slur is sprayed onto the belt instead of being deposited onto it.

After the initial pressing and vacuuming, the semidry mat is passed through a series of heated rollers which further dry and form it. Upon completion, the mat is wound into rolls as large as 12 ft across and 6 ft high.

This roll is then transferred to the next station, where the roofing felt will be created.

The thickness and weight of the mat, called *dry felt,* will vary, depending upon the final product desired. The thicker the dry felt mat, the more bitumen saturant it can absorb. Base sheets will be created from heavier, thicker dry felt mats, while ply sheet felts will be created from thinner, lighter dry felt mats.

The dry felt mat is cut into 36-in-wide rolls. These 3-ft-wide rolls are then:

- Saturated with asphalt to create shingle underlayment and BUR plies, which is #15- and #30-lb felt
- Saturated with coal tar bitumen to create a roof ply sheet for BUR which is #15 tarred felt
- Saturated and then coated with asphalt, creating organic base sheets
- Saturated, coated, and then surfaced with mineral aggregate granules to create roll roofing or cap sheet, which is #90-lb roll roofing or 19-in selvage roll roofing

FELT WEIGHT DESIGNATIONS

When a sheet is referred to as a "#15-lb felt," the number 15 means that the felt should weigh approximately 15 lb per 100 ft^2 (100 ft^2 also being referred to as a *square*). We say "approximately" because a #15-lb organic felt, as well as a #30-lb organic felt, comes in two classifications. One classification is for utility, light-duty use, such as composition shingle underlayment.

The felt in the utility classification will weigh considerably less than the classification states. For example, the #15 utility classified felt weighs 8 lb per square. The ASTM standard with which this type of felt material complies is ASTM D 4869-88.

When the function of the felt is temporary, as is the case with composition shingle underlayment, utility felts work fine and accomplish their purpose. However, when the roof felt must provide a durable and functioning system, such as waterproofing underlayment of a tile roof assembly, the thin utility felts are not appropriate.

The thicker, heavy-duty #15- and #30-lb organic felts should be specified where waterproofing ability and durability are required of the felt layer(s). ASTM Standard D 226-89 governs the requirements for this type of felt material. (See Sec. 14.2.2.)

The most basic and common organic felts we normally use in roofing are the #15- and #30-lb felt and #43-lb base sheet felt, which is made from a thick and heavy dry felt mat. Whereas the #15- and the #30-lb organic felts are saturated with bitumen, the #43-lb base sheet is both saturated and then coated with asphalt bitumen. This type of felt is unsurfaced from the factory, meaning that no weathering surface material, such as mineral aggregate granules, is placed on it during manufacture.

On the other hand, a #90-lb roll roofing felt is made from an organic felt mat much the same as that used for the organic base sheet. The mat is both saturated and then coated with asphalt bitumen, but it is then surfaced with mineral aggregate granules embedded into the asphalt coating. The material will weigh approximately 80 to 85 lb per square.

Selvage roll roofing is the same material as the #90-lb roll roofing sheet, except the mineral granules extend only 19 in across the sheet's surface width. Selvage roof sheets are installed by layering half the sheet over the preceding sheet, creating a finished roof with only granules left exposed.

The #90-lb and selvage roll roofing can be installed as temporary roof systems on sloped roof decks. In times past, the #90-lb roll roofing sheet was used as a base flashing sheet on BUR systems.

SATURATED FELTS

A saturated organic felt is a dry felt mat saturated with asphalt or coal tar pitch bitumen during manufacture. This process allows a bitumen solution to completely cover and thereby saturate the dry felt mat.

The asphalt-saturated organic felts are used as underlayment in a composition shingle system, as a water barrier in rigid roofing material systems such as tile and slate, or as roof felts in a BUR assembly. The function of felt under a composition shingle system is to protect the roof deck until shingle installation and to separate the asphalt shingle from the roof deck.

As a tile or slate water-barrier underlayment, a minimum of two plies of #15-lb felt are needed. However, it is often more advisable to specify at least one and preferably two plies of #30-lb organic felt as such underlayment. Use only the heavier organic #15- or #30-lb felts for water barriers, not the utility grades. For extreme situations, such as coastal regions where high-speed wind and torrential rains are expected, a base sheet system is often specified as the water-barrier underlayment.

Use of #15-lb organic felt in an asphalt BUR system requires the felt paper to be perforated with tiny holes, referred to as *perforated felt*. These small apertures allow the venting of gases caused as the hot moppings come into contact with the felt. The #15-lb felt is the only organic felt manufactured with either tar or asphalt as the saturant.

Most tar-saturated #15-lb organic felt is not perforated. Perforations may cause problems with later roof resaturation (see Sec. 5.1.4), as well as difficulty in getting the perforations to remain in the felt paper. The cold-flow characteristics of the tar pitch solution tend to close up the tiny perforations.

A #30-lb organic felt is also saturated with asphalt. The organic felt mat is thicker, allowing more saturant into the felt mat, making the finished felt product heavier.

The #30-lb felt is used most often as a water barrier in rigid roof material applications, such as in tile, slate, wood shingle, and metal roof systems. In some cases it has been used as a base sheet in BUR systems, but due to its low tear/rupture strength, this is not advisable.

COATED FELTS

Coated felts are normally used as base sheets in roof systems. As a base sheet, the felt is attached to the roof deck or roof insulation and subsequent roof felt ply sheets are applied to it.

The thick dry felt mat from which it is produced, in conjunction with the saturant and the asphalt coating applied to its surfaces, make the sheet thick and heavy duty. Coated felts normally have more strength than organic ply sheets.

Organic base sheets, referred to by ASTM as *smooth-surfaced asphalt roll roofing,* begin with an organic dry felt mat. A liquid asphalt bitumen solution saturates the raw felt mat. After the saturation process, hot asphalt is used to coat the saturated mat.

Hot asphalt is applied in small streams to the saturated felt mat. As the mat moves through a roller system, the asphalt is spread evenly across the felt. The greater the pressure of the rollers, the lighter the coating of asphalt, resulting in a lighter felt. Heavy asphalt coatings increase the weight of the felts. These heavier coated organic felts are sprinkled with talc or mica, preventing the roll from sticking together during shipping and storage. Some manufacturers use a wax-based spray instead of the mica or sand.

These felts are most often specified as a base ply felt in BURs. They can also act as a vapor retarder, helping to prevent vapor migration into the roof assembly. Base sheets also offer enough tensile strength to aid, to a small extent, the spanning of deck irregularities, referred to as *crack-bridging ability*.

Base sheets falling in the #40-lb category can be used as underlayment for slate or tile roofing and for temporary roofs and they are sometimes used as components in the construction of base flashings on BURs.

Some material manufacturers have specified BUR systems using these #40-lb-category organic base sheets as the roof plies, as well as some of the #30-lb organic coated felts as the roof plies. With hot-process BURs that use these coated felts, problems often occurred in the form of blistering and ply delamination. With cold-process BURs, the use of these felt types has proven to be effective.

Coated and/or saturated felts are available in organic as well as inorganic material. In addition to being less expensive when compared to inorganic felts, asphalt coated organic felt sheets are compatible with hot- as well as cold-process asphalt methods. However, organic felts can create some problems in certain application situations, as described in the following section.

CAUTIONS AND PROCEDURES

Saturated organic felts can absorb moisture, a process referred to as *wicking*. In humid climates, organic felts even seem to draw moisture from the air while in storage.

When organic felts contain excessive moisture, hot bitumen moppings cause blistering and ply delamination of the roof system. All felt papers must be stored in dry, rain-sheltered areas, and organic felts in particular must be kept from humid environments.

Following are guidelines to help prevent organic felt system problems:

- Never leave organic sheets unsurfaced at the end of the day if they are to be a permanent part of a BUR system. They must have a glaze coat of hot asphalt or pitch applied to the surface. This glaze coat protects the felts from moisture absorption caused by rain or dew.
- Never apply a cutback asphalt coating to a saturated organic felt as a permanent finish. The roof sheets must first be glaze-coated with hot bitumen mopping. It is acceptable to apply a cutback material directly to the surface of a *coated* organic felt since the factory asphalt coating substitutes for the field-applied asphalt glaze coating required on felts which are only saturated. However, even though not absolutely required, it is usually good practice to first apply a glaze coat of hot bitumen.
- Avoid specifying an unperforated organic sheet as a roofing ply in a BUR. In some cases, such as with a coal tar pitch BUR, this cannot be avoided. If an unperforated felt is used, care must be taken to ensure that the gases from the hot bitumen moppings are not trapped under the sheet, as this will cause blistering of the felt system. In such cases, brooming-in of the felts is critical.
- Never use a saturated organic felt as a ply sheet in a cold-process roof system.

Only in Canada do we see the prominent use of organic felts for BUR construction. Few specifications issued by major U.S. roof material manufacturers prescribe the use of asphalt-saturated organic felts as the ply sheets within a BUR. The exception is a coal tar pitch BUR where tarred organic felts are acceptable. Approximately 30 to 40 percent of coal tar pitch BURs are created using #15-lb organic tarred felts.

7.1.2 Fiberglass Felts

Fiberglass felts are manufactured from glass fiber strands and are the most common roof felt material in use today. Fiberglass felts do not wick moisture at the rate organic felts do. They have good tensile strength, which lends the roof system dimensional stability. Fiberglass felts are compatible with cold-process cutback asphalts. Fiberglass felt ply sheets can be obtained with manufacturer-applied coal tar or asphalt bitumen coating.

Fiberglass felts used as ply sheets in a BUR are not designated by numbers to indicate their weight as are organic felts. They are instead referred to as *types*. Per ASTM D 2178 there are Type II, Type III, Type IV, and most recently on the market, Type VI fiberglass ply sheet felts. Type VI is often referred to as *premier felt* by manufacturers. Type II and Type III are basically extinct.

Fiberglass base sheets are also designated as types. There are Type I and Type II fiberglass base sheets. As a general rule, in both the ply sheet and the base sheet categories, the higher the type number, the thicker and stronger the roof felt sheet.

MANUFACTURING

Two different manufacturing processes exist for fiberglass ply felts: the *continuous strand process* and the *chopped strand method*. The chopped-strand manufacturing method is also referred to as the *wet mat process*. The chopped strand method dominates the fiberglass roof felt manufacturing industry.

Continuous Strand Method. The continuous strand method is accomplished by extruding small fiberglass strands onto a moving belt in a swirl laminate pattern. The fiberglass strands are pulled or extruded directly from the molten batch material through an extruder orifice.

An adhesive agent is applied and the felt mat is further formed, then proceeds to a drying station. Upon removal of most of the moisture at the drying ovens, the felt mat is trimmed to size and wound into large rolls.

The continuous strand fiberglass roof felt offers the highest tensile strength of fiberglass roof felts. At the same time it is more porous, providing what is referred to as *wetting ability*.

An expensive manufacturing process, the continuous strand fiberglass roof felt is produced by only one material manufacturer at the time of this publication. If superior strength is required of the fiberglass felt BUR membrane, this type of felt should be considered as the roof plies.

Chopped Wet Strand Method. The chopped wet strand fiberglass felt is the most common fiberglass ply sheet in use today. The manufacturing method is similar to the continuous strand method, except the filament strands are cut into lengths instead of being continuous from the extrusion orifices.

The fiberglass strands are induced into a wet slur of water and dispersion agents. The slur is deposited onto a conveyor belt–type assembly, where the wet mat is formed and excess water expelled. A binding agent is added.

The mat is moved down the line through a drying station where the binding agent is set and any remaining moisture is removed. The completed, dry fiberglass felt mat is wound into large rolls and is transferred to the roof felt manufacturing line.

Some manufacturers introduce a small quantity of continuous strand filament into the wet chopped strand mat to provide additional tensile strength.

Fiberglass Roof Ply Sheets. Fiberglass felts are not dipped and saturated with a bitumen material as are organic felt mats. Due to the nature of the glass strands, the fiberglass mat is surface-coated, or impregnated, with either coal tar pitch or an asphalt bitumen solution.

Fiberglass Base Sheets. Fiberglass base sheets are only produced with an asphalt bitumen coating and saturant. No coal tar pitch base sheets are available. The application of asphalt bitumen is heavier for a fiberglass base sheet than for a ply sheet, and the bitumen solution often contains mineral fillers.

Hot asphalt bitumen is applied to the surface of the raw fiberglass felt mat. The mat proceeds to a roller station which spreads the applied bitumen uniformly over both the top and bottom surfaces of the roll. Depending upon the pressure exerted by the roller system and the fiberglass mat, Type I or Type II base sheets will be produced.

Mineral granules, being the same as those used to surface composition shingle roof materials, can also be introduced during this manufacturing process. The granules are deposited onto the hot asphalt bitumen surface coating on the sheet, thereby creating a fiberglass cap sheet. An organic felt base sheet surfaced with ceramic granules is referred to as a *roll roofing sheet*. In comparison, a mineral surfaced fiberglass cap sheet is lighter in weight, is not as susceptible to moisture absorption, and has better tear and puncture resistance than do organic roll roofing sheets.

The fiberglass base sheet proceeds to a cooling unit station and then to a station which places a parting agent to the surfaces of the felt. The parting agent—either sand, mica, or wax spray—keeps the bitumen coated felt surfaces from adhering to one another during shipping and storage. The final manufacturing processes involve applying ply lines to the sheet and winding into the proper length rolls.

CHARACTERISTICS

Ply Sheets. The most important characteristics to recognize and design for regarding fiberglass roof felts is their memory and the fact that they require brooming in. These topics, as discussed briefly under Sec. 7.1, are important to the proper and permanent embedment of the fiberglass felt into the bitumen mopping.

Workers must restrict foot traffic from freshly installed fiberglass felts. The stiff nature of the felt will make it rise back to the level of original installation (memory) after it has been pushed down into the interply mopping. Additionally, the freshly installed hot interply mopping will be displaced by the foot traffic. The displaced bitumen results in a dry void within the felt ply system, accentuated by an unadhered and dry felt ply at the location where the foot traffic occurred. (See Fig. 7.4.)

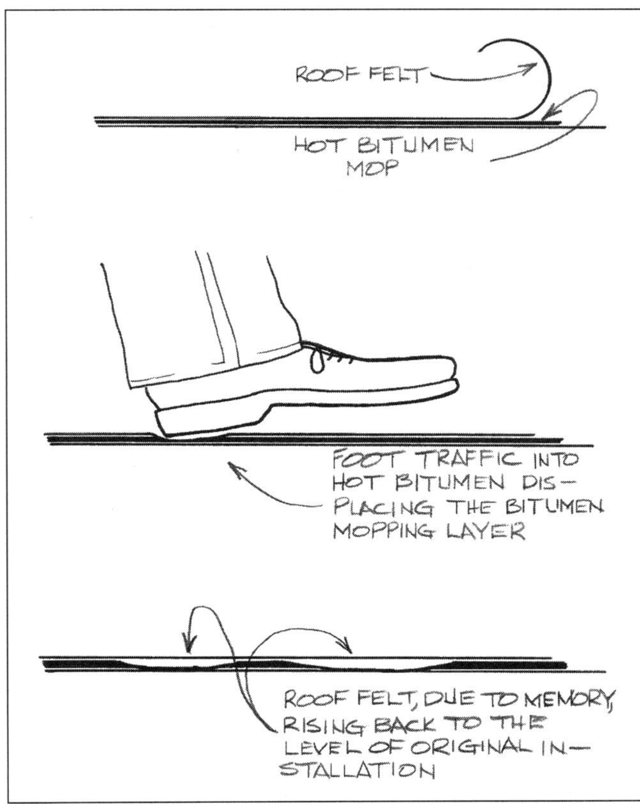

Figure 7.4 Felt memory.

Fiberglass felts are more rigid than many of the synthetic polyester felts and the organic felts. As such, they will not immediately conform as tightly to transitions caused by deck and building irregularities, cant strip faces, sheet metal flanges, etc. At cant strip and base flashing locations, as well as at sheet metal flashings, this brooming operation must be complete and diligent to adhere all of the stiff felt into the waterproofing bitumen.

Stiff-bristle brooms, squeegees, or felt follow tools are needed to help ensure that the bitumen mopping fully penetrates the fiberglass felt ply and the felt stays embedded therein. Even though a puddle of hot bitumen was present during the roll-out installation of the fiberglass felt (see Fig. 7.1), experience shows that the felt can sometimes "float" above the hot mopping due to irregularities of the roof surface, a minor inconsistency of the bitumen interply mopping layer, and/or hot gases escaping from the hot moppings. The brooming-in process is merely a quick operation performed by roof workers wherein a lightweight tool is dragged across the entire surface of the freshly installed fiberglass felt, thereby pushing the felt down into any location where the felt is not fully embedded into the hot interply mopping. Care must be taken by the roof workers not to displace the interply bitumen moppings during the brooming-in process.

Fiberglass felts are resistant to moisture absorption. This allows the membrane plies to be left uncoated at the end of the workday and, in some cases, up to several months. The exception is areas of the roof where large amounts of water can be expected for extended periods of time, such as roof drains and scupper outlets. In such cases, it is good design practice to require the completed felt system at these locations to be glaze-coated with bitumen moppings.

A smooth-surface roof system is often designed with the fiberglass ply sheet system. The surface coating selected is often aluminum pigmented cutback asphalt material. However, again the open-weave characteristic of the fiberglass ply sheet requires that a glaze-coating of hot asphalt, asphalt cutback, or asphalt emulsion first be applied to seal the felts. The aluminum coating can then be applied after the base coat application has properly cured. Sometimes an aluminum pigmented asphalt emulsion is selected, eliminating dual labor application.

Fiberglass Base Sheets. Fiberglass base sheets come in two types, with Type II being the heaviest. The heavier weight of the product is mainly due to a thicker coating of asphalt bitumen.

Base sheets are often required to separate the roof ply felts and interply bitumen from the roof deck or roof substrate. Type I fiberglass base sheet, as a result of the thin asphalt coating applied to its surfaces, may not always provide a complete separation as required.

Type I base sheet is often translucent, due to the open weave of the fiberglass mat from which it is created and the thin and often incomplete coating of asphalt bitumen applied to its surfaces.

According to ASTM Standard D 4601-95, which governs fiberglass base sheets, small pinholes are acceptable. With Type I, the holes may be more frequent and pronounced, and in such cases, with either Type I or Type II base sheet, additional felt or red rosin material may be needed to completely divorce the BUR membrane from the roof deck or substrate.

However, if the base sheet is to be used as an adhered base ply to which the ply sheets will be attached, the holes and perforations naturally occurring in the sheet may be an advantage. In such cases, Type I is probably the best selection. The holes will allow venting of the gases caused by the hot bitumen mopping. Some base sheets are also specifically manufactured with uniform perforations in the sheet.

Do not use a fiberglass base sheet as a pitch dam. (See Figs. 4.5 and 4.6.) The open-weave characteristic of the base sheet will not create an effective dam for flowing bitumens.

7.1.3 Synthetic Polyester Felt

USES

Polyester felts have many uses in the roof industry. As ply sheets, they are used mainly in cold-process roof systems, although some material manufacturers have developed specifications using hot bitumen with synthetic polyester felt for roof plies and base flashings.

A large amount of the polyester felt manufactured today goes directly to the modified bitumen and single-ply manufacturers. These manufacturers use the polyester, as well as fiberglass mats, as the inner reinforcing membrane within the polymeric-based roof membrane.

Different types and thicknesses of polyester felt are available and are used by these manufacturers. A polyester felt of thick weight and high strength will often impart these additional characteristics to the polymeric membrane within which it is used. (See Sec. 9.1.2.)

Polyester felts are very strong, having high tensile strengths and tear resistance. A two-ply polyester felt used in conjunction with cold-process bitumen, applied to a proper surface such as a base sheet, is considered by many to be a 20-year roof system.

The cold-process adhesives saturate the membrane during application. As the completed system cures over time, it acquires high resistance to foot traffic and hailstorms.

MANUFACTURING

Polyester felts can be manufactured by one of two process styles: *spunbond* or *staple fiber*. Spunbond polyester is sometimes referred to as *stitchbond polyester*.

The spunbond process is a continuous filament needle-punched fabric formed into thousands of nonending continuous filament strands. Fibers are laid down in multiple overlapping layers providing strength in all directions. The web is mechanically interlocked by needle-punching, using thousands of barbed needles. The fibers are bonded together with resin binders and heat.

The staple fiber process is a short fiber, needle-punched fabric. The short fibers are uniformly laid down and interlocked by needle-punching. The fibers are bound with resin binders and heat.

Needle-punching the fibers provides a stable internal bonding mechanism, which prevents delamination and adds to tensile strength.

The fluffier and thicker the mat, the more adhesive it absorbs. The stiffer the mat, the more problems it has bridging irregularities on a roof surface. Stiff polyester membranes exhibit more memory problems during application than do the softer membranes.

Thickness usually determines the weight of a polyester felt, commonly designated in ounces or grams per square meter. Thin and stiff felts will weigh between 1½ and 2½ oz/yd^3. Thick and fluffy membranes can weigh between 8 and 10 oz/yd^3. Some polyester membranes fall into the middle of these ranges.

You cannot intermix hot and cold applications of polyester. They use very different finished mats and the respective field applications have very different, specific guidelines. Even within the cold-application polyesters, there are fabrics with very different hand and usages.

Although needed, generic classification designating various grades and types of polyester felt has yet to evolve in the roofing industry. In addition to varying thicknesses, some polyester felts are stiffer than others. These manufacturing variances lead to different tensile strengths and elongation properties.

7.1.4 Design and Specification

DESIGN SELECTION

For low-sloped roof systems using a roof felt membrane, the designer has three basic categories of roof system to select from:

- *Conventional built-up* roof assembly, which today normally uses fiberglass roof ply felts in hot bitumen moppings
- *Modified bitumen built-up* roof assembly, where underlying roof felt plies in bitumen mopping are

covered with one or more membrane sheets of modified bitumen

- *Cold-process built-up* roof system using asphalt cutback adhesive as the interply adhesive

The modified bitumen assemblies are referenced under Chap. 9.

It is the designer's obligation to determine which of the systems available is best suited to the building needs. Criteria will include such items as fire-resistance ratings and wind-resistance ratings. In such cases, it is the total roof system that must be designed to resist such forces, with not only the roof felts, but also the insulation layers, fasteners, roof deck type, and roof surfacing being properly selected for such compliance. The major roof material manufacturers usually publish these systems and material configurations in their specification manuals.

If the roof system is expected to be subjected to stresses greater than normal, a roof felt with high tensile strength should be selected. Tensile strength of roof felts should be determined in accordance with ASTM D 146-90, which includes ASTM Test Method D 828 for evaluation of tensile strength. (See ASTM standards for roof felts.)

Above-normal stresses can be expected due to:

- Extreme temperature fluctuations, leading to thermal stress
- High-temperature extremes, leading to thermal loading
- Foot traffic across the roof surface
- Roof deck or substrate movement
- Hailstones

Exceptional thermal stresses can be expected in geographic regions where the roof system will be subjected to high-temperature extremes during the day in the summer and cold extremes at night in the winter. An average annual ambient temperature difference of 85°F or more may lead to extreme annual thermal stresses on a BUR membrane. (See Sec. 2.3.1.)

However, the material used to surface the roof can create greater or lesser fluctuations in the short-term temperature variances to be experienced by the roof membrane. For example, a gravel surfaced membrane will experience less thermal shock (see Sec. 2.1.1), since the gravel acts as a heat sink and temperature stabilizer. However, the gravel heat sink will create higher temperatures to be endured by the roof membrane during summer months, leading to thermal loading. (See Sec. 2.3.1.)

High-performance roof insulations can also create thermal loading and thermal stress problems. The thermal loading and/or thermal stress is a common occurrence with roof systems. It is a design problem only when the forces become extraordinary.

Stesses can be accommodated not only by high-strength felts, such as Type VI fiberglass roof felts, but they can also be accommodated by use of numerous plies of felts with less strength. For example, a two-ply fiberglass felt membrane may not have as much strength as a four-ply organic felt membrane.

Another solution common to today's roof design practices is the use of a fiberglass cap sheet or a mineral surfaced modified bitumen membrane sheet as the roof surfacing. These materials are adhered in the hot bitumen mopping to the top of the BUR felt membrane and add strength to the total felt membrane system.

Other stresses which can be designed for by the proper selection of roof felts are rooftop foot traffic and hailstorms. The resistance of the roof membrane to these forces is related to the puncture and tear resistance of the roof felts, as well as the roof surfacing selected.

Since the roof surfacing is the first line of defense, it is usually more important. Concrete roof pavers and walkpads can prevent damage to the roof caused by rooftop traffic. (See Sec. 6.1.2.) However, walkpads can sometimes be dimensionally unstable and have been known to cause severe damage to some roof membrane systems. (See Fig. 7.5.) Hail damage can be minimized by the use of gravel or stone ballast. However, impact forces can be transferred through these materials and components, at which time the roof membrane must be able to resist the minimized forces. Additionally, gravel or stone ballast makes roof membrane investigation difficult and can hide hail damage during visual inspection.

In regions or instances where the roof membrane can be subjected to surface impact it is not advisable to design a roof felt membrane which has a low tolerance for such impact. Although preferably minimized by proper selection of roof surfacing material, the impact can be repetitive and therefore damaging.

Hot-Process Built-up Roofing. For hot BUR systems, the selection of the felt types and amounts is a relatively simple manner. Roof material manufacturers offer system specifications which state the type of roof felt to use, the type of asphalt to use, and the type of surfacing to apply, as well as the amount of each component or material.

Usually, but not always, the designer should not substitute materials or components that are foreign and not approved by the manufacturer, but should comply with the material manufacturer's guidelines, materials, and specifications. If specific code or owner requirements concerning fire or wind resistance are needed, such as pertaining to FM or UL, the total roof system must be in compliance with such. The material manufacturer's rep-

Figure 7.5 Damage to roof membrane system from walkpad.

resentative or reference literature is often helpful with design selection.

In hot climates such as those common to the southern and desert areas of the United States, it is not advisable to design a BUR system using fiberglass felt with interply mopping of coal tar pitch or dead-level asphalt bitumen. These bitumens, due to their cold-flow nature, may transpose themselves through the open weave of the fiberglass felt. It may be more appropriate (or safe) to use a tar-saturated organic felt for a coal tar pitch BUR system, or in the case of an asphalt BUR, change to Type III or Type IV as the interply mopping bitumen.

Cold-Process Built-up Roofing. Synthetic polyester felt resists thermal loading, thermal stress, and movement better than other, more common roof felts. However, it can be considered an exotic felt material, seldom used in a conventional BUR assembly. (See Sec. 7.1.3.)

Polyester felts, predominantly used as a reinforcing membrane within modified bitumen and polymeric single-ply membranes, are also used to create cold-process BUR systems. The interply bitumen can be hot process but is more often cold process, applied using cutback asphalt as the interply adhesive. (See Sec. 4.1.5.)

Success has been evidenced using cold-process asphalt adhesives and polyester felt membranes in BUR assemblies in areas experiencing high traffic, numerous penetrations, and caustic environments. However, with cold-process BUR systems, there is not the same tolerance for applicator error as with conventional BUR systems.

Also, the system cost per square foot can be considerably higher for cold-process polyester felt BUR than for conventional BUR systems. Additionally, finding contractors familiar with the materials and required installation processes is sometimes difficult.

Since the system is more exotic than many other BUR systems, there are not as many existing industry standards and guidelines to aid in the design process. Normally a three-ply polyester membrane, installed over a fiberglass or organic base sheet, with all plies in a complete brush- or spray-applied coating of asphalt adhesive, will provide 20+ years of service.

There are several large and reputable material manufacturers within the United States that market cold-process roof systems. Warranties are available on the systems, and the sales and technical staff can assist with selection and specification of the roof system.

QUALITY CONTROL SPECIFICATION

Handling and Storage. Roof felt rolls must always be stored on the ends and never flat on their sides. If stored on their sides, the roll will become elliptical, and in losing the roundness of the roll, they will not install correctly into bitumen moppings.

Roof felts must never be in contact with water or moisture prior to installation into the roof system. A dry roof felt is extremely crucial to a proper BUR system. Moisture can condense under plastic coverings used to protect the roof felts while on pallets at the job site. This can cause problems if the plastic and moisture condensate is allowed to come into contact with the roof felt rolls. Such condensation is a result of the dew point being reached on the interior of the plastic coverings which act as a vapor barrier as well as a protective covering. Such condensation problems can be eliminated by providing air flow around and through the stored felt rolls.

Waterproof but air-permeable canvas coverings eliminate condensation problems, but they must be installed correctly to prevent the wicking of water through the canvas covering in direct contact with the felt rolls. Storage of roof felts in a job-site container, such as a trailer, can eliminate these problems, but such storage adds expense to the project.

Application. Two processes must be accomplished by the roof installers at the same time: the spreading of the bitumen and the application of the felt roll into the bitumen mopping. With a cold-process BUR system, felt installation procedures are not as time-critical as with a hot-process conventional BUR system. See Sec. 4.1.5 for more information on cold-process BUR systems.

Regarding hot-process BUR, certain requirements must be adhered to by the roof application crew:

- Roof felt plies must be installed immediately into the bitumen mopping—an essential requirement.
- The amount of bitumen being applied must be adequate and complete.
- The hot bitumen mopping must be of the correct temperature, which is the very important equiviscous temperature range (see Sec. 4.1.3).
- The felt application worker cannot step or walk on the felt layer as it is being applied and setting up in the hot mopping layer.
- The roof felt must be broomed in by the roof workers to ensure that the felt is completely embedded into the bitumen mopping and to help eliminate any entrapped gases and voids (see Chap. 14 for field-examination procedures).
- All felt runs installed into bitumen should be straight and true, with no more than a 1-in deviation per 100 linear feet of felt run.
- Any fish mouths must be immediately cut and the cut felt set into the hot bitumen. The cut is then covered with additional layers of roof felt.
- A puddle of hot bitumen should always be present in front of the felt roll during application.
- No felt should touch felt, which requires a complete mopping of the interply bitumen to separate the felt layers.

CHAPTER 8

Roof Insulations

8.1 GENERAL REQUIREMENTS

In almost every new roof or reroof installed today there is roof insulation incorporated into the system. While this reduces heating and cooling costs, it also causes problems such as accelerated membrane deterioration, thermal shock, and stresses due to expansion and contraction on the roof membrane.

There are many kinds of roof insulation available. Several new types have recently appeared and several old types have been phased out. Like so many other things in the roofing industry today, this segment is in change, reevaluation, reformulation, and redevelopment.

The main types of roof insulations are:

- Cellular glass
- Composite board
- Fiberglass
- Perlite
- Phenolic
- Polyisocyanurate
- Polystyrenes
- Wood fiber

These insulation materials are manufactured in panel form. They range in size and thickness from a minimum of ½ in thick to maximums of 4 to 6 in. They can be a minimum of 2 ft × 4 ft in length and width to 4 ft × 8 ft maximums. (See Fig. 8.1.)

Some of the biggest problems concerning insulation that face us today are:

- Dimensional stability
- Chlorofluorocarbon contamination of the atmosphere
- Compatibility of insulant materials with other materials of the roof system
- Off-gassing of insulations into the roof system
- Thermal drift

In order to avoid and compensate for these and other potential problems, an understanding of the basic prin-

Figure 8.1 Insulation being installed. (*Courtesy of Atlas Energy Products, Atlanta, Ga.*)

ciples and requirements of roof insulation materials is required. Following is a brief review of the characteristics and properties which make a good roof insulation, what roof insulation products are supposed to do, and what they are not supposed to do.

R-VALUES

A roof insulation should have a high R-value while at the same time remaining as thin as possible. This R-value should remain constant throughout the life of the system and not undergo what is termed *thermal drift*. Thermal drift occurs when an insulation begins to loose its R-value or its heat transmission resistance capabilities. (See Sec. 8.3.)

COMPRESSIVE STRENGTH

A roof insulation must have good compressive strength as well as adequate density. You could not install regular batt insulation, such as used in the attic of a home, to a roof deck and then install a built-up roof system over it. The insulation is too soft and would not supply a solid, rigid deck for the roof to be attached to. The fiberglass batt insulation lacks proper compressive strength and density for a roof substrate.

DIMENSIONAL STABILITY

The insulation panels should have dimensional stability. If the insulation changes shape due to shrinkage, curling, or warping, this will cause the joints of the individual insulation panels to ridge or separate. This can cause a bituminous roof membrane to crack or split at these ridging locations.

At one time the urethane (polyisocyanurate) insulations occasionally had trouble with warping, curling, and shrinkage, especially if exposed to moisture or high humidity. Some facers laminated to these insulation panels at the factory shrank after a period of time. This in turn caused the edges of the board to curl.

Other insulation panel types have been known to curl and warp after installation. This is because they expand in the heat; as the joints push against each other due to the expansion, a ridging effect becomes visible through the roof membrane. The probability of this happening is increased if the roof is leaking or if the insulation boards get wet during application. A good roof insulation panel will not readily absorb moisture.

ATTACHMENT

The insulation must be able to be attached to the roof deck in a manner to meet code and industry requirements, such as the wind uplift resistance requirements of Factory Mutual. It must be manufactured true and uniform in order to be installed to the requirements of these and other code bodies.

Fluted, 22-gauge steel roof decks (see Sec. 3.1.1), the predominant type of roof deck specified in today's construction market, must be installed within a ¼-in tolerance per 100 linear feet. Screw and plate fastener assemblies which are used to attach the insulation panels to this roof deck must penetrate only the top pan and are not allowed into the fluted area. (See Fig. 2.5.)

Crooked runs of the steel roof deck panels will cause the roof insulation panel edges to fall over the flutes. Such a situation will result in an unacceptable attached insulation and roof assembly. (See Fig. 8.2 and Sec. 3.1.1.)

Industry standards require additional fasteners at the corner and perimeter areas of the roof deck, usually 50 percent more and sometimes 100 percent more. Negative air pressure is greatest at these areas and the additional fastening secures the roof system to the roof deck. (See Sec. 2.1.1 and Fig. 2.6.)

Roof insulation layers are sometimes fully adhered with adhesives or bitumens to underlying base sheets (see Sec. 7.1.2), roof decks (see Sec. 3.1.3), or a mechanically attached layer of roof insulation. This requires the roof applicators to fully "walk in" the adhered panels as they are applied. Without such diligence on the part of the roof worker, an unattached system can be the result.

All insulation panel joints must be offset from any underlying panel layer joints. The minimum offset requirement should be at least 12 in. This requires accurate layout by the installer and hopefully a detailed set of drawings by the designer.

MULTILAYERED ASSEMBLIES

It is always good design practice, but sometimes not mandatory, to use a multilayer roof insulation system under the roof membrane. Such a case is a mechanically attached polymeric single-ply system, in which the fasteners used to secure the roof sheets must lie directly under the roof membrane. (See Fig. 8.3.) Therefore, isolating the head of the insulation fasteners in a multilayer insulation assembly would not isolate the fastener head used to attach the single-ply membrane sheets. These

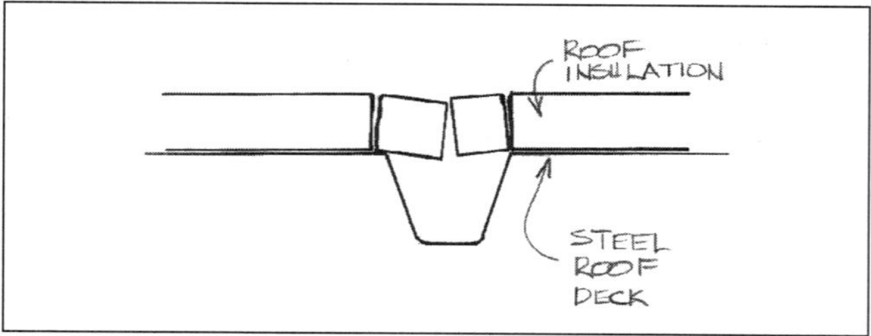

Figure 8.2 Insulation over deck flute.

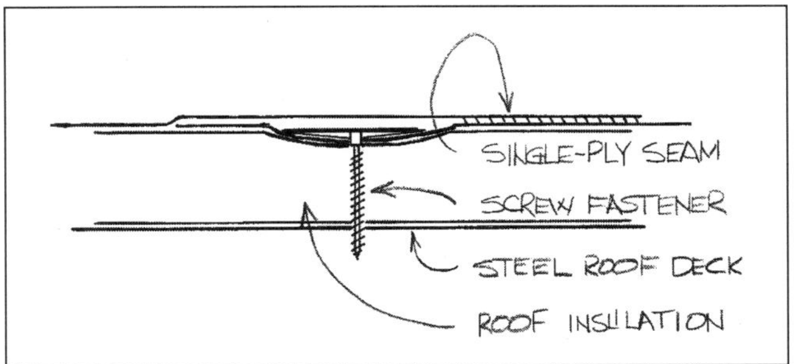

Figure 8.3 Mechanically attached single-ply system.

membrane fasteners must, by the design of the single-ply mechanically attached system, lie under the roof sheet and be exposed to temperature differentials.

Fastening. However, for fully adhered roof membrane systems, such as built-up roofs (BURs), which incorporate a mechanically attached roof insulation, a two-layered (dual) insulation system is normally required as good design practice. Such a two-layered insulation system is typically required with an asphalt, coal tar pitch, or modified bitumen BUR system over a steel deck.

If the head of the insulation fastener assembly lies directly under the roof membrane, the temperature variance along the shaft of the screw fastener will be of such difference, from top to bottom, to possibly cause fastener back-out. The fastener backing out of the roof deck will in turn create holes in the overlying roof membrane. (See Sec. 3.1.1 and Fig. 2.2 for a complete discusion of fastener back-out and multilayered insulation requirements.)

Single-layer insulation design is sometimes acceptable if the insulation panel is being fully adhered to the roof deck or a mechanically attached base sheet. In such a case, insulation fasteners are not required since the bitumen mopping is the securement component. However, be aware that some types of roof insulations have a tendency, in some situations, to off-gas when installed in hot bitumen moppings. (See "Design Practices" as follows in this section.) A single-layered insulation system which can possibly off-gas during installation should be compensated for by additional insulation layers.

Vapor Pressures. Hot bitumen moppings, being either asphalt or coal tar pitch, will range anywhere from approximately 350 to 450°F. The heat of such moppings can draw moisture from the insulation panels, where it will be released as a vapor. If the released moisture vapor is entrapped under the fully adhered roof membrane, ply delamination and blistering can occur.

MOISTURE CONTAMINATION

Insulations can become contaminated with moisture for various reasons. In humid environments some insulation materials, or the facers laminated to them, can absorb moisture vapor from the moist, humid air. Insulations can also be exposed to moisture by the early morning dew when stored overnight on a rooftop and not correctly covered, ventilated, and protected by the roof applicators.

Insulations can become wet or damp during transport from the manufacturer to the material distributor or to the job site. In turn, some material distributors neither correctly store nor completely protect all roof insulations from damaging weather. Also, some high-density insulation materials, such as perlite and wood fiber, are manufactured with an extraordinary amount of binders and fillers which contain latent moisture. (See Secs. 8.1.3 and 8.1.8.)

DESIGN PRACTICES

In our opinion, good design practice assumes that moisture vapor will be released from insulation panels when being installed with hot bitumen. A multilayered insulation system helps allow such gases to pass from areas where vapor pressure is increased and be absorbed by insulation in areas where vapor pressure is normal and therefore less. When the vapor gas pressure is equalized within the insulation layers or allowed to pass through the layers to a venting substrate or component, harm to the roof membrane is prevented.

Gas vapor pressure will travel to areas of less pressure. If gas vapor is drawn to and through the surface of an insulation panel by hot bitumen moppings and an avenue to lower-pressure areas is available, the created gases will attempt to travel to that area. For example, if an insulation layer is mechanically attached with a screw and plate fastener assembly to a venting deck, such as a steel deck, and a subsequent top layer of insulation is being attached with hot bitumen moppings, any excessive gas vapor pressure will probably equalize as it is driven back through the mechanically attached insulation layer and out into the atmosphere interface at the steel deck.

Fully adhering an insulation layer over a nonventing roof deck, such as structural concrete, and covering with a fully adhered roof membrane, such as a built-up roof, requires careful design. In such a case, allow for any possible gas vapor pressure created during installation to equalize somewhere in the assembly.

Fiberglass roof insulation material is susceptible to vapor flow in such a situation. However, it has an organic facer which can, if contaminated by moisture due to improper shipping, storage, or installation, entrap and hold moisture which will be released by hot bitumen moppings. If a roof assembly is being fully adhered to such wet facers on any type of insulation, not just fiberglass, blistering will probably occur.

However, fiberglass roof insulation is very beneficial in absorbing any moisture vapor into the stranded glass-fiber matrix of the board stock. Perlite and wood-fiber insulations, not manufactured as high-density materials, also work well for absorbing and dispersing vapor pressure.

Therefore, multilayered insulations serve more than one purpose. They isolate the head of the roof insulation fastener from temperature differentials and extremes, thereby eliminating fastener back-out. Multilayered insulation systems can also allow for pressure equalization within the insulation assembly, thereby reducing the risk of roof blistering. Multilayered systems can also provide additional tensile strength to the roof deck. The redundancy of the multiple layers can also help correct deck irregularities or any holes or gaps existing within the layers of the multilayered system.

COMPATIBILITY

The roof insulation must be compatible with the membrane and membrane adhesives, and not disintegrate from the hot mopping bitumens, torch flames, or single-ply and cold-process adhesives. For example, polystyrene insulations are not compatible with many of the EPDM adhesives used in the past.

Also, high-density wood fiber and perlite insulations are not always compatible with hot bitumen moppings. (See Secs. 8.1.3 and 8.1.8.) When encapsulated between nonventing materials, such as a structural concrete roof deck and a top roof membrane covering, the high-density insulation can release vapor gas which cannot escape or equalize pressure. These gases in turn may possibly cause blistering of the hot bitumen built-up roof covering.

Roof insulations must carry appropriate fire ratings. Some are combustible and may have problems meeting all insurance bureau or building code requirements.

8.1.1 Characteristics and Values

Each insulation type has different characteristics which in turn provide the material with different values; i.e., some insulation materials have good noncombustibility characteristics which provide low smoke and flame development rating values. Others are combustible and must be placed between noncombustible materials in order to achieve desired fire-resistant ratings for the total roof assembly.

COMPRESSIVE STRENGTH

Compressive strength values of a roof insulation material are an indicator of the insulation's ability to resist roof traffic and weight. Compressive strength is determined in a test which compresses the insulation until either 10 percent or 5 percent (depending on test method and insulation type) of the material has been pressed down. The amount of pressure required to compress the material is measured and that pressure is the compressive strength.

The equipment used in this test is a delicate and sophisticated presslike device capable of operating in compression while measuring applied forces. If a 1-in piece of insulation is being tested, the press will exert force onto the 1-in-thick insulation until 10 percent of the 1-in thickness is compressed, although some tests evaluate insulation at a 5 percent consolidation factor.

Some materials are tested till they yield. This is because they will not compress but will instead shatter or break. This yielding will take place when cellular glass insulations, structural concrete, etc., are tested. The pressure required to make the material yield is its compressive strength.

DENSITY

The density of an insulation is an indicator of its weight. The density is the weight per cubic foot of the material; i.e., if the density of fiberglass insulation is 9 lb, then a cubic foot of the same material will weigh 9 lb.

HIGH-DENSITY INSULATION

Some wood fiber and perlite insulation materials are manufactured as both standard and high-density material. High-density wood fiber and perlitic insulations are a minimum of ½ in thick and can be 4 ft × 4 ft but are more normally 4 ft × 8 ft.

The minimum ½-in thickness of high-density wood fiber and perlitic insulation requires additional fibers and binders to be incorporated into the insulation panels in order for it to be handled and applied without breaking. These fibers and binders are more excessive in the high-density insulation materials than in the standard materials and can release gas and vapor when hot bitumen is applied to the insulation panel. While their dimensional and insulation values are unaffected and acceptable for roof use, this gassing characteristic may cause problems with some hot process BUR systems. (See Secs. 8.1.3 and 8.1.8.)

WATER ABSORPTION

Some roof insulation materials are more water absorbent than others. Some are more and some are less damaged and susceptible to change by moisture than are others.

Materials Selection. This aspect of the different materials is important when considering insulation for use within a self-drying roof assembly. We now understand that in many cases across the United States, due to vapor drive, roof insulations have moisture condensation within the layers at certain times of the year and at other times the moisture is driven from the insulation materials. (See Sec. 2.3.3.)

Most roof insulations of today have proven successful in resisting this dynamic force, if and when it occurs. However, some insulations may prove better at long-term stability than others under excessive and intensive wet-dry cycling. If excessive and intensive wet-dry cycling is expected, it may be prudent design practice to incorporate a vapor retarder to prevent the drive of moisture vapor into the insulation assembly.

However, vapor retarders can act as a water barrier. If a vapor retarder is installed within roof insulation layers, the insulation above the vapor retarder should have a high resistance to water absorption. (See Fig. 8.4.)

With such a design, if the roof membrane begins to leak, the water will not readily find its way through the vapor retarder, but will instead be trapped in the insulation layer(s) between the roof membrane and vapor retarder. We theoretically assume that the roof leak will be minor and that it will be detected during the semiannual roof inspection.

Therefore, the roof insulation should be able to resist major damage from such roof leakage. Most roof insulations can successfully resist minor leakage for short periods of time. However, if the roof leak is extensive and has occurred for an extended period of time, major damage will probably have occurred to most roof insulation materials.

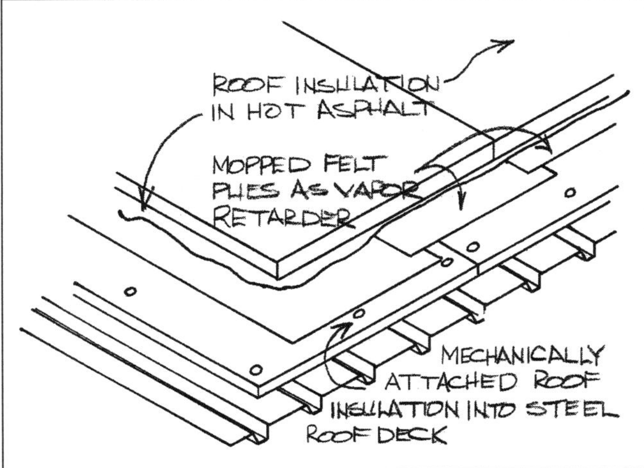

Figure 8.4 Vapor retarder and insulation assembly.

Insulation selection for this type of design can become difficult with fully adhered BUR systems. Plastic foam insulations, such as polyisocyanurates (ISO) and extruded polystyrene, resist water absorption better than other types, such as perlite and wood fiber insulation. However, it is against recommended practice to install hot bitumen moppings directly to the surface of such plastic foam insulations. Fiberglass insulation can be another option, but if it becomes wet, the glass fibers can consolidate, resulting in lost insulation value and possible inadequate support for the roof membrane. Design options available may be installing a loose-laid modified bitumen or polymeric single-ply system over a nonabsorbent plastic foam insulation, such as extruded polystyrene, and then ballasting the roof and insulation layer(s) to the building. (See Sec. 6.1.2.)

Hazards. In the event that wet insulation is discovered under a roof membrane, it must be determined if removal is necessary. Wet roof insulation can cause:

- Roof deck deterioration
- Ridging of insulation due to accelerated and exceptional expansion and contraction
- Energy loss through the wet and heat-conductive material
- Roof fastener corrosion
- Roof rot in some roof membranes

Cautions. Damp insulation will, in many cases, be acceptable within a roof assembly if it can dry out. Wet insulation must be removed. Therefore, the difference between *wet* and *damp* is determined by the ability of the insulation to return to a dry condition while still retaining its compressive strength, dimensional stability, and thermal values.

This ability to dry out is directly related to roof venting design, accomplished either by metal roof decking, which can vent air through the side and end laps, or wood edge blocking which can be designed to vent. (See Fig. 3.9.) We also can use roof vent assemblies to allow or create moisture venting from within the roof assembly.

Moisture Relief Venting. Moisture relief venting to dry out wet roof assemblies may be overused in the roofing industry. It should be clearly understood that moisture relief vents are effective only for allowing small amounts of moisture vapor to escape from small areas of the roof assembly. (Refer to Sec. 3.1.6 for more information on moisture relief vents and procedures.)

There are one-way vents and two-way vents. A two-way vent has an open flue which allows moisture to pass freely from the inside to the outside. Air can also pass from the outside to the inside, carrying humid air from the outside atmosphere into the vent flue and possibly into the insulation assembly. One-way vents have a diaphragm in the flue and allow vapor pressure to pass only from the interior of the vent to the outside atmosphere.

As a minimum, one moisture relief vent should be installed per every 1000 ft^2 of roof area which requires venting. However, more vents may be required to accommodate roof areas which are on the borderline between damp and wet.

Determining the effectiveness of moisture relief vents in allowing roof insulation drying versus the removal of wet roof insulation can be a difficult decision. The decision is further complicated by the expense of the major roof repair work required for insulation removal. A certain amount of liability exposure goes with the decision, if moisture relief venting is determined by the designer to be appropriate and effective for the long-term life of the roof system.

If the insulation is *damp,* moisture relief venting should work. If the roof insulation is *wet,* ***insulation removal is required***. As a general rule of thumb, but not an exact scientific procedure, dampness and wetness of roof insulation material can be determined by a simple test procedure.

Evaluation. Place a paper cloth or tissue (which is more sensitive) on the insulation material when pressed down. If moisture is transferred into the paper or tissue, dampness definitely exists.

Wetness can usually be determined by visual observation combined with touch. If water or dampness is transferred to your hand or fingers during touch, it can be assumed that the insulation is beyond dampness and falls within the wet category.

Another more accurate way to determine the level of moisture contamination is by use of moisture scan or moisture probe equipment. Further information on these procedures is available in Sec. 13.1.3.

If the roof insulation is damp, installing moisture relief vents will probably expel the entrapped moisture and return the insulation system to a normal condition. The procedures of cutting holes in the roof membrane and insulation system in order to install the moisture relief vents varies. The procedures and requirements are dependent upon the type of membrane and insulant system.

DIMENSIONAL STABILITY

All roof insulations should comply with ASTM test methods which confirm the insulation panel's dimensional stability under normal roof conditions. However, when evaluating existing roof systems and problems, dimensionally unstable roof insulation materials may be encountered.

Different types of roof insulations can become dimensionally unstable for different reasons. For example, a polyisocyanurate (ISO) insulant panel, covered with an organic felt facer, can become dimensionally unstable if the organic facer on one side of the panel becomes wet and the organic facer on the opposite side does not and the panel is not properly fastened.

The dimensional change of the panel in such a situation is further propagated if the wet facer side is subjected to heat extremes to which the other dry side is not, such as could be the case with the wet facer side lying directly under the roof membrane. On the other hand, if the same ISO insulation panel is covered with a fiberglass strand facer, dimensional change in the panel is less likely. This is due to the different facer reactions with heat and moisture.

Dimensionally changed, or changing, roof insulation is usually obvious through the roof membrane surface. Ridging areas are sometimes obvious as long straight runs across the roof surface, occurring at the side edges of the underlying insulation panels. Ridging of roof insulation is less obvious on gravel-surfaced roof systems than on single-ply or smooth-surfaced roof assemblies.

Some roof insulations can become dimensionally unstable due to excessive moisture condensation within the assembly as the result of vapor drive. Still other types of insulation proved dimensionally unstable under normal rooftop conditions, regardless of ASTM compliance.

A dimensionally unstable roof insulation will ruin a roof system. It is always good design practice to have the roof membrane manufacturer approve, in writing, the roof insulation to be used within the roof assembly.

INSULATING VALUES

These values are indicators of the ability of an insulating material to resist heat energy transmission. All roof insulations have specific resistance to heat energy transmission. These resistances are expressed, in several different ways, as:

K-values
C-values
R-values
U-values

Each value is an indication of this resistance, expressed in a different manner. To begin with, all these values express the resistance of heat flow. This is measured in heat energy, which in turn is measured in Btus. A Btu is the amount of energy it takes to raise the temperature of 1 lb of water 1°F.

K-values. The K-value of a material is the amount of heat energy transferred through a 1-in-thick piece of material that is 1 ft^2 in 1 h when there is a difference of 1°F from one side of the material to the other. In other words, if you have a 1 ft^2 piece of material, and the material is 1 in thick and on one side the temperature is 70°F and on the other side the temperature is 71°F, the K-value will tell you how much heat is transmitted through the material in 1 h.

This K-value is the indicator of heat conductivity. The formula for computing K-value is:

$$K = \frac{\text{Btu}}{\text{square feet} \times \text{inch} \times \text{hour} \times \text{degrees F}}$$

C-values. Heat conductance is also measured by C-value. C-values are used for indicating heat transmission through material that is of any thickness—not just 1 in thick, as K-value indicates.

If the material is 1 in thick, the C-value and K-value will be the same. If a material's K-value is known, the C-value can be determined by dividing the thickness in inches of the material into the K-value:

$$C = \frac{K}{\text{thickness in inches}}$$

Many materials also have an aged C-value. This aged value predicts what the insulation values of the material will be in years to come. Many insulating materials will lose some of their heat-resistant properties through diffusion of the insulating gas that is contained within closed cells of the insulation panels. As the insulating gas leaves and/or air and moisture enter the cells, the thermal efficiency of the material will be reduced. (See Sec. 8.3.)

R-values. R-values are a material's thermal resistance to heat transmission. Where the C-value tells a material's heat conductance, R-value tells a material's heat resistance. It is the same resistance value, expressed in reverse.

$$R = \frac{1}{C}$$

and

$$R = \frac{\text{thickness in inches}}{K}$$

U-values. Sometimes U-values are taken into consideration. U-value should always be the designer's problem to determine, not the constructor's. This indicates the total system's resistance to heat transmission.

U-values take into consideration all components of the roof, insulations, air spaces, and ceiling finishes. U-values can be determined for building walls and floor systems as well.

To get the value of *U,* the R-values of all components within the system need to be known. When the R-values are known, they are added together and then divided into 1.

$$U = \frac{1}{\text{total } R}$$

Tapered Insulation R-value Formulas. It is sometimes necessary to determine an insulation system's R-values, but the insulation system is tapered or sloped. Almost all insulations can be manufactured to a certain slope. This slope can be ⅛ in, ¼ in, or a combination thereof. Tapered perlite insulation usually proves to be the least expensive form of tapered or sloped panels, if R-value is not considered.

A tapered insulation system can be used to eliminate water from ponding on roofs, to form crickets that will force water toward drains, and to eliminate ponds that occur only on some areas of the roof.

For computations, tapered systems are considered to be either one-way sloped or two-way sloped. A one-way slope is where the tapered insulation slopes in two or fewer directions. For example, a tapered insulation system can create slope into a roof drain in the middle of the roof. The slope can come from both the north and the south sides and still be considered a one-way slope.

At these two roof sides the tapered system will be the thickest. If the tapered system has a slope of ¼ in per foot, this also means it is getting ¼ in thicker with every foot proceeding from the roof drain toward the roof sides.

This one-way slope can also be designed to shed water from the center of the roof to the edges. This will create a ridge in the center of the roof, where the tapered insulation will be the thickest. The insulation will taper down from this center ridge to the edges and will be thinnest at the edges. (See Fig. 8.5.)

To calculate the average R-value of a tapered system, you must know the average thickness of the insulation. You can then determine the R-value for that average thickness of insulation. The formula for calculating the average thickness of a one-way sloped system is:

$$\frac{\text{Maximum thickness} + \text{minimum thickness}}{2}$$

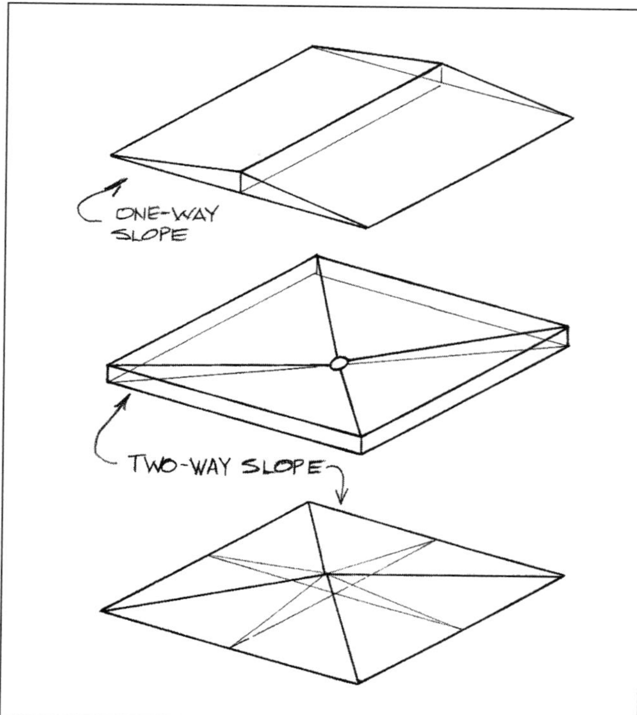

Figure 8.5 One-way and two-way slopes.

A two-way sloped system is one that slopes from all four sides. Let's use the same illustration and say there is a roof drain in the center of the roof. A two-way tapered system is one that slopes into the drain from all four sides. The other way, where the water needs to go over the edge, would create a peaked point in the center and slope to all four sides of the roof.

To determine the average thickness of the tapered insulation on a two-way sloped system, you subtract the minimum thickness from the maximum thickness and multiply by ⅔. To this figure you then add the minimum thickness. This will give the average.

$$(\text{Maximum thickness} - \text{minimum thickness}) \times .66 + \text{minimum thickness}$$

8.1.2 Fiberglass Insulation

MANUFACTURE

Fiberglass insulations are made from spun glass. The glass material is made by combining sand, soda ash, limestone, and other minor ingredients and melting at temperatures of 2500°F. The molten liquid is forced through equipment which extrudes it as tiny strands of glasslike material.

This glass is spun until it is light and fluffy. The spun glass is then combined with adhesives, compressed, and covered with facers. The facer is normally of an organic felt material which is coated with asphalt. The final process is cutting the roof insulation into the required sizes.

CHARACTERISTICS

Fiberglass insulation thermal resistance is created by two factors. One is the small pockets and voids created within the panel when the spun glass is compressed and faced. The second is the length of the strands themselves.

First, air will not transfer heat well, although this is a relative statement. Air is a much better conductor of heat than is Freon, but air will not conduct heat as well as will copper and other metals. Therefore, the small pockets of air within the insulation act as an insulator.

Second, the strands are long and heat is transferred through these strands. The strands do not run directly from one side to the other, but make long crooked paths from one side to the other. One strand that is 2 in long may never reach from one side to the other in a 1-in-thick piece of fiberglass insulation.

Heat is dissipated as it makes the long, crooked journey through the strands. The glass fibers themselves do not conduct heat well. The air pockets, the long strands, and the poor conductance of the glass fibers all help make fiberglass roof insulation an effective thermal barrier. (See Table 8.1.)

PRECAUTIONS

Compressive Strength. When fiberglass insulation is used, care should be taken to avoid rolling heavy equipment over the installed membrane. The lower compressive strength range of the fiberglass does not allow much tolerance.

Due to the same compressive strength concerns, it is not recommended for insulation fasteners to be installed directly under the roof membrane when using fiberglass insulation. The fiberglass insulation can compress slightly due to the traffic load, but the fastener will often remain stationary. The fastener head can then puncture the roof membrane. Instead, good design practices should be followed and a dual-layered insulation assembly designed. (See Sec. 8.1.) In such a case, the bottom layer of fiberglass roof insulation is mechanically attached. The subse-

Table 8.1 R-values of fiberglass insulation.

Thickness, in	*R-Value*
¾	2.78
15/16	3.70
1 1/16	4.17
1⅝	5.26

quent top layer of fiberglass insulation is adhered to the bottom layer with adhesives or, most commonly, hot asphalt bitumen moppings. An alternate type of insulation with higher compressive strength values can also be substituted as the top layer, giving the roof a better resistance to traffic loads.

Moisture Absorption. Fiberglass insulation fibers will not *absorb* moisture because they are glass, but the insulation panel will *retain* moisture. Water can be held within the stranded glass fibers. If this happens and water is being held in excessive quantities under the roof, several things will occur.

In addition to blistering and deck deterioration when there is entrapped moisture under a roof membrane, fiberglass insulation will also expand and contract at greater rates than normal. The roof membrane will then undergo stresses and strains it cannot accommodate.

With fully adhered roof membrane systems, the joints of the wet insulation panels can be seen as ridges on the roof surface, running through the area of the wet insulation. Always attach the fiberglass insulation tightly to the roof deck.

Fiberglass insulation will not readily deteriorate from water and roof leaks as will other types of roof insulations. If the material can be dried out and the water saturation has not been extensive for long periods of time, the insulation material should return to a serviceable state.

Drying out of installed roof insulation can be accomplished only by proper venting design. This is accomplished either during the initial roof system design (see Fig. 3.9) or by installation of subsequent roof moisture vents. (See Sec. 3.1.6.) This does not mean that wet fiberglass is of no concern. Since this insulation always has a facer, this facer can possibly become irreversibly damaged by the moisture. In this event, the facer could become dimensionally unstable, could delaminate from the insulation, or both.

Excessive water saturation within a fiberglass insulation system can deteriorate the binder that holds the fiberglass strands together. In such cases the insulation must be removed and replaced. Also, because of the nature of the stranded fiberglass, water will spread quickly through the insulation panel system and contaminate large areas of the system.

Unlike some other types of roof insulation, fiberglass insulation is slightly more forgiving of water contamination. This means if a leak occurs on the roof and some of the insulation becomes damp, it may be possible to vent the roof properly and dry the insulation out to its original state. However, if the water has saturated the insulation and caused the glass fibers to consolidate, original R-values will be lost.

Determining the difference between "wet," "damp," and "saturated" is an important judgment call. For the designer, a certain amount of liability accompanies the decision to leave wet or damp insulation in place and dry out with venting systems. (See Secs. 8.1.1 and 13.1.3 and Table 8.2.)

DESIGN REQUIREMENTS

Retrofit. Fiberglass insulation is often specified as a retrofit insulation assembly. In such cases, the insulation is installed to the top of an existing roof system and a new roof is applied to the top of the insulation panels. In a roof retrofit situation, the fiberglass panels will mold to contours and any irregularities of the existing roof surface very well. Sometimes the panels are attached to an existing roof surface in hot asphalt moppings and, due to the ability of the panels to conform to contours, the roof insulation system becomes fully adhered by the hot moppings.

This process can eliminate concerns of roof fastener heads being installed directly under the roof membrane covering. By attaching a thin layer of fiberglass roof insulation to the top of an existing roof membrane with hot asphalt or other adhesives, the cost of a dual-layered insulation system is eliminated.

However, for such retrofit design to be effective and durable, proper design practices must be followed:

- Never allow a retrofit roof system to be installed over underlying wet roof insulation layers.
- Never fully adhere insulation layers to rotted or deteriorated roof membrane areas.

Table 8.2 Typical physical values (will vary).

	Values	*Test Method*
Compressive strength	12 lb/in^2 at 2.5% deformation	ASTM C 165
Tensile strength (perpendicular to board)	100 lb/ft^2	ASTM C 209
Break load (min.)	20 lb/f	ASTM C 203
Flame spread	20 (unsurfaced board)	ASTM E 84
Water absorption (% volume max.)	10%	ASTM C 209
Smoke development	20 (unsurfaced board)	ASTM E 84

- Verify that the existing roof membrane to which a new system is being retrofitted is compatible with the hot bitumen or adhesive mopping.
- Verify that the existing system is properly attached to meet wind resistance standards.

Code and Industry Compliance. Fiberglass insulation is acceptable for use on all types of roof decks and can meet Factory Mutual wind resistance requirements when attached to the various decks.

The bottom sides of the panels are usually unfaced, thereby allowing the noncombustible fiberglass to be used as part of a fire-rated roof assembly. The flammable facer is used as the base to which the roof system is attached.

In a multilayered roof assembly, fiberglass panels can be selected as the top layer of insulation. Being installed over a hard and rigid insulation panel, such as polyisocyanurates or perlite panels, they are often attached to the underlying panels in moppings of hot asphalt. Of concern with such design is the amount of rooftop traffic to be expected, not only during the life of the roof system, but during the initial construction. Remember, fiberglass insulation has low compressive values and thus cannot support heavy loads across the roof membrane surface.

Applying fiberglass insulation panels as the top layer in a dual-layered system, this design configuration helps compensate for any gases which are released from the bottom layer of roof insulation when hot asphalt is applied to their surface. Any such gassing is dispersed throughout the glass fiber matrix of the fiberglass insulation assembly layer with no ill effect. The equalized pressure therein usually eliminates any blistering problems related to such off-gassing which can occur with some insulation materials. However, severe blistering problems can occur if the fiberglass insulation board or organic facer have been contaminated with moisture prior to installation.

8.1.3 Perlite Insulation

MANUFACTURE

Perlite insulations are made from expanded perlite ore. Perlite ore is strip-mined, sifted, cleaned, and sorted to get the proper size ore particles.

The small ore particles contain 2 to 6 percent water by volume. The perlite ore is placed in a furnace operating at 1700°F. At that temperature, the water vaporizes and causes the ore particle to pop, much like popcorn.

This expanded perlite is then combined with cellulose and other fillers, some asphalt, as well as other minor ingredients. These materials are formed into a wet mulch. The mulch is deposited onto screens, pans, or racks and placed into a furnace for drying.

After drying, the board stock is cut to proper length and width size. The face of the perlite board will be treated with a bituminous solution to reduce asphalt absorption and increase bitumen adhesion. The expanded ore is the primary insulating component of the insulation panels.

CHARACTERISTICS

The insulation is inexpensive, rigid, and dimensionally stable, and has good compressive strength. Asphalt and many other adhesives will attach well to it. Perlite roof insulation is rated as nonflammable.

Perlite insulation resists moisture absorption. However, if water is present in large quantities (such as when a roof is leaking and the water is held on and under the perlite by a structural concrete deck), the perlite insulation will absorb this water. When this happens, the binders of the insulation material deteriorate, causing the material to turn to the consistency of something similar to mud.

Perlite does not have as high R-values as do many of the other insulations. However, it usually costs less per inch thickness than many other insulation types.

Cant strips are manufactured from perlite material. This is mainly because of its low cost, ability to be easily mold-formed by the manufacturer, and ability to resist fire. This resistance makes it a safe component to be used with flame-applied modified bitumen membranes. (See Fig. 8.6.)

See Table 8.3.

PRECAUTIONS

When evaluating an existing roof system with perlite roof insulation, be aware that roof leaks can severely damage the insulation. In most cases involving reroof

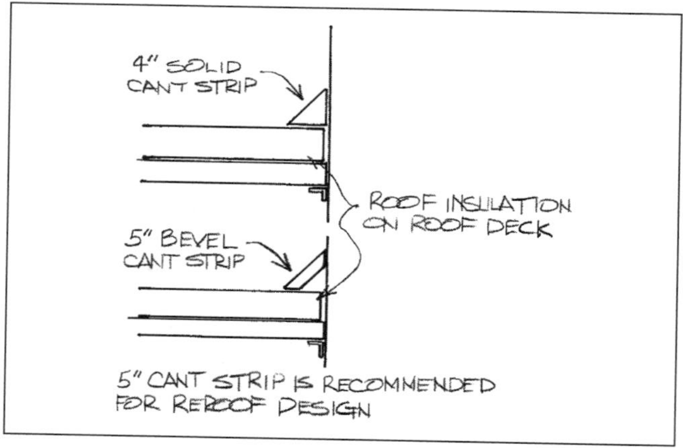

Figure 8.6 Cant strip/insulation.

design, the total perlite insulation assembly is removed and disposed of.

Dust and small, loose particles from the insulation will be created when the perlite is being cut by the roof installers. This dust can hinder bitumen attachment to the insulation surface. The roof workers need to clean the perlite insulation surface before proceeding with roof ply installation to the perlite insulation system's surface.

Perlite retrofit insulation, also classified as high-density insulation due to its additional binders within the board stock, can off-gas when applied into hot bitumen mopping. Such gassing can cause blistering and premature failure of the roof membrane.

DESIGN REQUIREMENTS

Retrofit Perlite Insulation. The binders within perlite roof insulation panels are important in helping to hold the material together. In the thin retrofit panels, being ½ in thick, additional binders are required, which also increase the density of the perlite panels. These binders are cane fibers, wood fibers, etc. They contain moisture.

When hot bitumen, such as asphalt, is applied to the surface of the high-density retrofit perlite panel, the binder fibers can release their moisture. Since these thin retrofit panels are often used as the top layer in a dual-layer insulation system, a roof felt is often mopped directly to the surface of the panel. This can entrap any released gases between the roof sheet and the top of the perlite panel.

To comply with industry standards it is required that the roof felt be fully adhered to the top of the panel in most parts of the United States. Spot mopping only portions of the top of the panel would allow gases to travel between the felt and insulation interface and vent out of the roof assembly, but an improperly attached assembly could be the result.

Moisture relief venting will not prevent blistering due to any off-gassing of the insulation panels. Since the felt is fully adhered to the surface of the insulation panel, vapor pressure cannot be fully relieved by the vents.

There are solutions available. The insulation material manufacturer suggests keeping mopping bitumen temperatures low, between 250 and 300°F. This heat reduction should limit off-gassing, but would violate roof industry requirements of proper EVT when installing roofing felts. (See Sec. 4.1.3.)

Another solution practiced by roof designers is the use of an insulation material which will help absorb and equalize vapor pressure differences. This can be a thicker layer of perlite insulation which is not of a high-density nature, or fiberglass insulation, or, most common in today's roof design industry, a layer of polyiso (ISO) insulation. In theory, the underlying insulation material will absorb any created gases as they drive to an area where they can most easily equalize, being the insulation board stock as opposed to the felt membrane and retrofit insulation interface. (See also Sec. 8.1, "Design Practices.")

Another design option is to use ¾-in-thick perlite insulation instead of the ½-in-thick high-density board. The additional cost is usually minimal. The designer must consider if the additional thickness will affect the height and thickness of other roof components, such as wood nailers at the roof perimeter edge, roof drain levels, or scuppers.

8.1.4 Tapered Insulation

Almost every type of roof insulation material can be obtained in a sloped and tapered panel. A tapered sys-

Table 8.3 Typical physical values (will vary).

	Values		*Test Method*
Compressive strength	Regular 35 lb/in^2 at 5% consolidation	High-density 20 lb/in^2 at 5% consolidation	ASTM C 165
Laminar tensile strength	4.0 lb/in^2	4.9 lb/in^2	ASTM C 209
Flame spread	40	40	ASTM E 84
Smoke development	40	40	ASTM E 84
Water absorption, % volume—2 h	1.5 max.	3.5 max.	ASTM C 209
Product density, lb/ft^3	9	11.14	ASTM C 209

tem is required to add slopes to the roof deck or modify and enhance existing slopes. Tapered insulation is used as crickets to force water away from parapet and building walls and to eliminate ponding water areas. (See Figs. 8.5 and Secs. 12.16 and 12.18.)

Good design and installation practice requires all joints of insulation panels to be offset one from the other in a multilayered system. However, with a tapered insulation system this is not always practical and few problems are reported relating to this noncompliance. (See Fig. 8.7.)

In reroofing design, tapered insulation systems are normally required more than in new construction design. In most new construction design today, the proper slope is normally incorporated into the roof deck assembly. Tapered insulation may still be required in new construction design to shed water at roof drains, building and parapet walls, etc.

Perlite material is usually the most inexpensive of the tapered insulation materials, although its average R-value is usually less than that of other types of materials. If additional R-value is required of the design, it is usually more cost effective to overlay the tapered perlite system with an additional layer of insulant material. This overlay can also eliminate any irregularities present in the tapered system, such as gaps between panels, cuts not made true and accurate by the installers, and missing portions of the smaller and thinner panels.

Tapered insulation assemblies can be complicated when used to cover the entire top of the building. Reverse slopes, crickets, existing equipment height, roof drains, etc., can cause problems with the continuous layout of the intended slopes.

Good design practice should include a complete schematic drawing of the tapered system. Such a drawing will allow the designer to evaluate and accurately consider elevations of the tapered system at different locations across the roof insulation system. Verify that the insulation is not extending too high at roof access doors and hatches, rooftop equipment stands, in-wall metal flashings, etc. Often a schematic drawing of the tapered system is available at no charge from the insulation material manufacturer.

Figure 8.7 Tapered insulation system.

8.1.5 Cellular Glass Insulation

Cellular glass insulations are made from a form of crushed glass and a cellulating agent. This crushed glass and cellulating mixture is placed in a mold and put into a furnace. The mixture is brought to 950°F, at which point it begins to melt as the cellulating agent evaporates. This leaves an expanded material made up of millions of tiny cells. Each small cell contains an inert gas that does not readily transfer heat.

Cellular glass insulations are very rigid and have a high compressive value. The insulation has a low moisture absorption rate and will retain its original insulation values well. Cellular glass insulations are not widely used in the roofing market because, although they have excellent characteristics for an insulation board, they are more expensive than most other types of insulations.

Cellular glass insulation is often used in high-humidity areas such as pulp wood processing plants. The closed-cell nature of the glass-based product makes it resistant to the moisture vapor drive often associated with these facilities. Cellular glass insulation has a high resistance to moisture absorption, making it a good choice for a roof system where leaks may go undetected for extended periods of time. Cellular glass is accepted as being able to receive hot bitumen moppings to its surface without damaging off-gassing occurring. This makes it acceptable for use as the top layer in a dual-layered assembly where a hot mopping of roof felts is required.

8.1.6 Polystyrene Insulations

EXPANDED POLYSTYRENE

Polystyrene insulation material is made in two different processes. There is *extruded* polystyrene and there is *expanded* polystyrene. Expanded material is often referred to as *EPS* by people in the roofing industry and is known to the general public as *Styrofoam,* which is a registered trademark of the Dow Chemical Company.

Manufacturing. Expanded polystyrene is manufactured from small beads of polystyrene that are impregnated with a blowing agent, usually pentane or butane. These small, slick beads look like sand in their unformed state.

The beads are placed into a preexpander and then heated with steam, often more than once. This steam heat causes the beads to expand up to 40 times their original size.

These expanded beads are placed into holding bins and allowed to off-gas and stabilize. The large stabilizing bins can be likened to large bags, with many holes in the side to allow for the passage of air. The expanded beads are left in these bins overnight, allowing the gas that is the blowing agent to mostly dissipate from the beads.

After off-gassing and stabilizing, the expanded beads are placed into a forming mold. In the mold, the beads are heated with steam and once again expanded. The heat softens the beads, and the expansion, being restricted by the forming mold, forces the individual pellets to be joined together.

The more beads placed into the mold, the more density the large block—or *billets,* as they are called—will have. For example, if 500 lb of bead material are placed into the mold, the resulting billet will be heavier than if only 250 lb of bead material were placed into the mold.

The billet produced during each of the different processes will have the same overall dimensions, but one will weigh twice as much as the other and therefore have a higher density. Compressive strengths of this material are directly related to density.

Billets can be produced in many different sizes, but are usually 12 to 16 ft long by 4 ft wide by 3 to 5 ft tall. After the billet leaves the mold, it is often required that the billet be allowed to stabilize for dimensional reasons. This depends on what the product will be used for.

As the billet leaves the mold, it is still warm from the manufacturing process. The heat required to fuse the beads together will also, to a small degree, have affected the individual beads that form the billet. This causes the billet as it leaves the mold to be slightly larger than it will be after it has cooled and the beads have again stabilized.

A curing time is required for the freshly produced billets, and can be for short periods of time or up to six weeks. This is dependent on the manufacturer, equipment, chemical composition, quality of the raw material, as well as its end use. For example, if the end use of the product is to be underlayment for a wall plaster system, such as EIFS, the board must be completely stable. This material has had few problems in the roofing industry related to dimensional stability.

Finally, the billet is trimmed and cut into the appropriate size and thickness. This is done with a thin, hot wire and produces insulation panels of varying thickness and size. On the other hand, extraordinary shapes can be formed of this material in several different ways. Coffee cups are made from expanded polystyrene and are formed with a vacuum process.

Characteristics. The expanded polystyrene insulation derives its main insulating characteristics from the expanded beads, which also contain small cells. These cells within the beads contain mainly air. There are also minute voids between the beads, which allow the intrusion and passage of air.

Air will conduct heat and reduce thermal resistance. The more moisture the air contains, the greater will be the conductance of heat. The R-value of EPS can be increased or decreased and is mainly determined to a certain point by its density. The more dense it is, the tighter the beads are formed together, helping eliminate the intrusion of air.

Polystyrene insulations have proven to have acceptable dimensional stability. However, it is sometimes costly to get a high density in this material. For roofing applications, expanded polystyrene should be manufactured with a 1.7- to 2.3-lb density and compressive strength of 25 lb/in^2. (See Sec. 8.1.1.)

In some cases, the standard material will prove to be too weak for roofing applications, especially if there is going to be extensive foot and mechanical traffic on the completed roof assembly. For EPS insulations under these conditions, a compressive strength exceeding 25 may be in order.

See Table 8.4.

Design Requirements. Expanded polystyrene insulation is not compatible with hot bitumen moppings, torch flames as used with some modified bitumen membranes, or hot air as used in some single-ply applications—it will melt. If hot bitumen must be used, specify that low temperature extremes be used as application temperatures.

Normally, polystyrene insulations, both expanded and extruded, are used in ballasted roof assemblies. With ballast securing the roof assembly to the roof deck, adhesives and fasteners are not required to secure the insulation.

Expanded polystyrene insulation will absorb and retain moisture. If this insulation has been subjected to extended periods of water contamination, removal is required.

Table 8.4 Typical physical values (will vary).

	Values	*Test Method*
Compressive strength	10–25 lb/in^2	ASTM D 1621
Flexular strength	25–75 lb/in^2	ASTM C 203
Flame spread	10	ASTM E 84
Smoke development (1-in thickness)	15–75	ASTM E 84
Water absorption % volume—max.	1–4%	ASTM C 272

Cold-process asphalt cutback adhesives are not compatible with polystyrene insulation materials. The petroleum distillates within the cutback material can dissolve the insulation panel much as gasoline will dissolve a Styrofoam cooler. Also, verify compatibility of single-ply membrane adhesives with the polystyrene materials.

EXTRUDED POLYSTYRENE

Manufacture. Extruded polystyrene, unlike EPS, is a combination of both liquid and solid materials at the beginning, not bead material. A polystyrene resin is melted. Other materials are added to the molten mixture which give the final product certain characteristics, such as fire resistance and color. This molten material then has a blowing agent combined with it, causing the batch material to expand.

This mixing of the materials and blowing agents is done at elevated temperatures and pressure. As it expands, it is extruded through an orifice which shapes and forms it. This process is compared to shaving cream as it is dispensed from the can. The shaving cream can is the extruder, with the shaving cream being the polystyrene.

Many times, the materials created by the two different processes are confused with each other. Expanded polystyrene, referred to as EPS, is formed from expanded beads which have small cells of air trapped within the beads. Extruded polystyrene has no beads, but is formed with small cells within the board, and each cell contains an inert gas.

Characteristics. Extruded polystyrene usually has a higher R-value per inch of thickness than does expanded polystyrene. This is due in part to the skin which is formed on the board surfaces during the extrusion, which helps keep air out. Also, closed cells formed within the insulation board during manufacture contain an insulating gas. Extruded polystyrene will usually have a higher density and compressive strength when compared to expanded polystyrene.

See Table 8.5.

Table 8.5 Typical physical values (will vary).

	Values	*Test Method*
Compressive strength	15–60 lb/in^2	ASTM D 1621 (valve at yield)
Flexular strength	60–140 lb/in^2	ASTM C 203
Dimensional stability % change—max.	2.0	ASTM D 2126
Flame spread	5	ASTM E 84
Smoke development	45–175	ASTM E 84
Water absorption % by volume—max.	0.10–0.05	ASTM C 272

Design Requirements

Protected Membrane Roof Assemblies Extruded polystyrene insulations are used to create inverted roof membrane assemblies. In these assemblies the primary insulation is placed on top of the roof instead of under it. This inversion of the insulation, and subsequent surfacing normally used to secure the insulation, protects the roof membrane, resulting in the generic terms, *protected roof membrane system* (PRMS) or *inverted roof membrane assembly* (IRMA).

Extruded polystyrene works well in this type of assembly because of its low moisture absorption rate, but expanded polystyrene, because of its bead form and resulting water absorbency, could be ineffective and should not be specified for this application.

The extruded insulation usually has a concretelike paver as a facer, providing the weight needed for a ballasted assembly. This concrete surface also protects the polystyrene from the UV damage and foot traffic. (See Sec. 6.1.2.)

Cautions. Many single-ply adhesives and no petroleum solvents should be allowed to come into contact with polystyrene materials. This reaction would be the same as pouring gasoline onto a Styrofoam cooler. Cutback bitumen adhesives, such as plastic roof cement, can also cause damage due to petroleum distillates within the cutback materials.

If extruded polystyrene is installed on the rooftop in PRMS, and this roof is in a chemically caustic environment, problems could arise. The insulation manufacturer should be consulted.

Polystyrene insulations, both EPS and extruded, are flammable. Most polystyrene insulation has a flame-retardant chemical added, thereby qualifying for use in accordance with local building codes. Verify that the polystyrene insulation being considered in the design meets the flame spread requirements.

It should also be noted that polystyrene insulations have a melt point in the 150 to 300°F range. This requires special handling and application procedures when applying hot bitumens to its surface.

8.1.7 Polyisocyanurate Insulation

One of the most popular types of roof insulation is polyisocyanurate insulation. This material is made from polyols and isocyanurates, as are urethane insulations. Isocyanurate insulation is a urethane insulation. Polyisocyanurate insulation is also known as *isocyanurate, polyiso,* as well as *ISO* insulation. It is referred to as ISO from here on.

ISO is a second-generation urethane. When urethanes first came on the market there were many problems, including dimensional stability, facer delamination, as well as the material continuing to off-gas even after it was installed under the roof.

Today, quality control during the manufacturing process and the technology are greatly improved. The raw materials used in the chemical makeup of the board stock are better. The science has also been improved and is much better understood today.

There is a difference between ISO insulation and urethane insulation. Urethane insulation is made by combining polyols and isocyanurates in approximately equal amounts. The polyols can be either polyester or polyether, or a combination of the two. The isocyanurates normally used are prepolymers of TDI or polymeric MDI.

Whereas there are equal amounts of polyols and isocyanurates in urethane, in polyisocyanurate insulation there are larger amounts of isocyanurates in relation to the polyol. This excess causes the isocyanurate to react with itself, creating isocyanurate structures as well as urethane structures within the insulation.

The polyols employed in ISO are mainly polyester-based and the isocyanurates are mainly polymeric MDI.

MANUFACTURING PROCESS

ISOs at one time were made by combining chlorofluorocarbons (CFCs), usually Freon and polyols and isocyanurates together. There are other materials added, such as surfactants and sometimes minute amounts of water. Today we substitute HCFC for CFC.

The proportion of these various materials, or the recipe, will change from manufacturer to manufacturer, and will also be changed depending on what type of facer the ISO is to be adhered to. Some facers require a wetter slur than others. Some facers require the ISO material to be more aromatic and tacky for adhesion to the facer. The facer on an ISO insulation panel is extremely crucial to its long-term performance.

ISO boards are manufactured in four different processes:

- Slab-stock
- Press injection
- Horizontal injection
- Vertical injection

In roof design, ISO created by the horizontal injection process is mainly used and often referred to as *restrained rise*. This process involves an extruder head which discharges the ISO material for forming. The material is expelled from the extruder onto a bottom facer. At one time, the facer was organic felt-based material. This was followed by stranded fiberglass facers, which are today followed by facers combining felt, asphalt, and stranded fiberglass. The facer can also be many other type of materials, such as wood, organic felts, or other types of insulation boards. See Sec. 8.2 for information on composite roof insulations.

The ISO material is extruded from the mixer onto the facer material. This facer is traveling on large, heated iron plates, called *platens*. This platen system may be 100 ft long. It has been described as a long track such as you may see on a bulldozer, but larger and longer. As the bottom facer is carried past the extruder head, the liquid ISO material is placed onto the facer.

As the liquid ISO is carried down the line, it begins to rise. This is due mainly to the blowing agent gas, with its low boiling point, starting to react.

Also, as the polyols and isocyanurate are mixed, a reaction occurs, causing heat. The reaction, in conjunction with the heated platen plates, causes the gas trapped within the ISO material to further react. This creates the necessary blowing of millions of tiny cells which are permanently trapped within the material.

As the liquid material starts to rise, a top facer is aligned, also on a heated platen system. The expanding ISO material comes into contact with the top facer and steel plates and by this restrained rise method the ISO insulation board is faced and formed to proper thickness and density. At the end of the line, the material is trimmed and cut to the required length.

ISO can also be produced in a free rise method, creating bunlike billets. This is called *free rise* because there is no plate to restrain the growth of the material. The growth is controlled, among other things, by the exact mixing of the material components and the amount of material expelled from the extruder head in relation to the speed of the line.

The manufactured ISO billet is placed onto and between a protective coating, usually plastic wrap. The wrap provides protection during shipping and handling. The billets are usually between 20 and 30 in thick. The ISO material is then cut from the large billets to the required size and thickness.

The advantage to this process is the tolerance of the board stock, which is very exact. There is little or no difference in the thickness or size of a board cut from a billet of ISO material.

This type of ISO board is often used in the metal building industry, in the chemical industry, and for industrial applications. Pipe coverings and vessel insulation are just two of the applications where expanded ISOs are used.

In the past, ISO insulations had the chlorofluorocarbon gas Freon contained in each of the internal cells, providing the insulating characteristics. Today that CFC gas has been replaced with HCFC gas in order to reduce the ozone depletion of the atmosphere.

HCFC gas does not transfer heat readily. The entrapped gas within the closed cells of the ISO insulation is the main insulating element.

CHARACTERISTICS

ISO insulation is one of the most popular types of roof insulation in use today. Designers find its R-value, in relation to cost, to be superb. It offers good to excellent dimensional stability, is resistant to water and moisture, can be used in a fire-rated assembly, and has good compressive strength. (See Table 8.6.)

With foil-faced or organic felt–faced ISO insulation, in some environments and application situations, curling and warping of the panels may be experienced. It is most common in today's market for ISO to be faced with stranded fiberglass or a combination of fiberglass strands, organic felt, and asphalt.

DESIGN

ISO is resistant to water absorption, although not rated as nonabsorbent. It is therefore often used as the only insulant material under a single-ply polymeric membrane system. Single-ply systems often sweat, with moisture vapor condensing on the bottom side of the membrane.

The ISO insulation panel itself will not be adversely affected by minor amounts of this occasional moisture condensate. However, ISO panels always require that a facer be applied to the top and bottom surfaces to provide dimensional stability. Some facers become delaminated in the presence of moisture. The fiberglass/felt/asphaltic facers used today resist this moisture and prevent the moisture from reaching the facer-ISO interface. This water-resistant type of facer also resists moisture absorption.

If the facer has a tendency to absorb moisture—even moisture present in the air of a humid environment—blistering problems with fully adhered roof membranes can result. With the first-generation ISO of years ago, blistering of BUR membranes was a problem. This problem was addressed by the establishment of an industry standard requiring the ISO to be covered with an additional layer of nonfoam insulation material such as perlite or wood fiber insulations. The subsequent roof membrane is adhered to this top, nonfoam insulation material.

Table 8.6 Typical physical values (will vary).

	Values	*Test Method*
Compressive strength	20–25 lb/in^2	ASTM D 1621
Dimensional strength	<2% ln. change	ASTM D 2126
Flame spread	25	ASTM E 84
Water absorption % volume—max.	<1%	ASTM C 209

CAUTIONS

A problem with ISO insulation, as well as other types of plastic foam insulation, is that it will undergo thermal drift. The thermal drift is due to loss of the past-used CFC and present-day HCFC gas from within the cells. Insulating values are also diminished when this gas is not lost, but is instead contaminated and diluted by the infusion of air into the cell structure.

Thermal drift is important to the designer when evaluating certain situations, such as the long-term energy efficiency of large, heavily insulated roof systems. For further information, see Sec. 8.3.

Some adhesives are not compatible with ISOs. Cutback asphalts may eat into the board and partially dissolve it in some cases.

Due to potential off-gassing of some ISO insulations, it is today an accepted roof industry practice never to attach a BUR system directly to the surface of the ISO insulation panel. This includes hot- and cold-process asphalt BUR systems, coal tar pitch BUR systems, and most types of modified bitumen roof systems.

As a minimum, a base sheet felt must first be installed, usually with screw and plate fastener assemblies, over the surface of the ISO panels. However, this is not recommended practice since it allows the fastener assembly to lie directly under the installed roof membrane covering. (See Fig 2.2.) It is usually proper design practice to cover the mechanically attached ISO insulation with a fully adhered second layer of insulation which is compatible with bitumen moppings.

8.1.8 Wood Fiber Insulation

Wood fiber insulation is very common throughout the roofing industry. This material is often used as recovery boards during a reroofing (retrofit) process. These insulations boards have good compressive strength, are dimensionally stable, and are relatively inexpensive. This type of insulation is often referred to as HD (for "high-density") fiber base insulation or asphalt-impregnated sheathing. Asphalt-impregnated sheathing (A&I board) may or may not be appropriate for roof applications, often being manufactured only for building wall applications. (See Table 8.7.)

Table 8.7 Typical physical values (will vary).

	Values	*Test Method*
Compressive strength	20–25 lb/in^2	ASTM D 1621
Dimensional stability	<2% ln. change	ASTM C 2126
Flame spread	25	ASTM E 84
Water absorption % volume—max.	<1%	ASTM C 209

MANUFACTURING

Wood fiber insulation is manufactured from wood or cane fibers, fillers, and binding agents. Sometimes asphalt is also included in the solution. These materials are combined into wet mulch. This wet mulch is placed upon screens or trays and then into dryers. This is basically the same process perlite insulation undergoes during manufacture.

The insulation properties of this material come from the air spaces created within the board during manufacture. These pockets space out the fibers and fillers. In a ½-in-thick board, heat may have to travel ⅝ in to get from one side to the other. This is because heat will be conducted along the fibers. As the heat passes around and next to these air spaces, some of the heat is dissipated. This allows the heat to be lost in its travel from one side of the insulation panel to the other.

As the wood fiber insulation leaves the dryers, it can either be coated with asphalt or left uncoated. This material will absorb and retain water, its main protector against water infiltration being the asphaltic skin coating applied to it during manufacturing. Wood fiber is supplied with asphalt saturant coating applied to one side, to five sides (the top and all four edges), and to all six sides.

DESIGN USES

The insulation is normally specified and used in ½-in-thick panel stock and is normally 4 ft × 8 ft in length and width. In decades past, the material was more commonly produced in thicker and smaller panels, such as ¾ in × 2 ft × 4 ft.

Because of its economical cost and low R-value, it is considered to be a utility insulation material. It is most often used to:

- Create a smooth surface to which a roof can be attached, such as applying to a rough surfaced structural concrete deck before installing the roof membranes
- Separate fastener heads from the roof membrane in a dual-layered insulation system, where the bottom insulation material is the main insulant
- Act as a recover insulation board in retrofit roof assembly where it is used to create a smooth substrate surface over an existing, in-place roof system

CONSIDERATIONS

Many problems can be experienced with this material if it ever gets wet. Water will migrate through this board, with the board acting as a sponge. Large areas of roof insulation, and therefore the roof system, can quickly become ruined if roof leaks are experienced for extended periods of time.

Since this material is made from wood fibers, it is flammable. If this insulation is being used with a torch-applied roof system, such as a modified bitumen membrane, the chances of a fire atop the building is an important consideration.

Half-inch wood fiber insulation is usually considered to be high-density material, although evaluation of ASTM C 209 test results show little if any density difference in some manufacturers' wood fiber insulations, regardless of thickness.

The bottom insulation layer should normally be mechanically attached to the nailable roof deck. A top layer of wood fiber roof insulation can then be fully adhered to the bottom mechanically attached layer with hot asphalt mopping. The top of the installed wood fiber insulation is then surfaced and sealed with additional hot asphalt moppings and roof felt.

This type of assembly is commonly used with success. However, if a nonventing roof deck is part of the design or if there are concerns regarding offgasssing of the bottom roof insulation layer, it is advisable to contact the primary material manufacturer of the roof assembly prior to completion of the roof design. (See Sec. 8.1, "Design Practices.")

When used as a retrofit panel over an existing roof assembly, off-gassing is not such a major concern, although it is still present. It seems that the gases, if released from the panel by the hot mopping to the top of the panel, have a tendency to be equalized by the free air space between the bottom of the insulation panels and the top of the in-place and retrofitted roof surface. (See Fig. 8.8.) However, in such a case, the fastener heads used to attach the panel to the existing roof system lie directly under the new roof membrane. Fastener back-out is often experienced with such design. (See Secs. 2.1.1 and 3.1.1.)

8.1.9 Phenolic Insulation

Phenolic roof insulation was developed in the early 1980s. It is made from phenolic resins, organic acids, and blowing agent. The blowing agent is Freon, which is also the main insulating component.

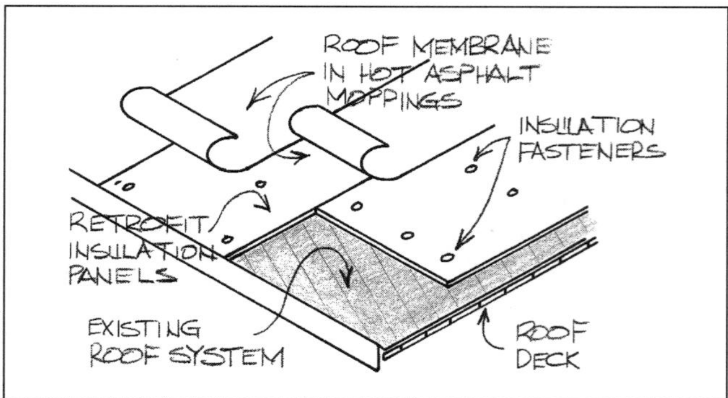

Figure 8.8 Mechanically attached retrofit insulation system.

Phenolic foam is no longer produced as a roof insulation. In the presence of water, the acids within the panel attacked steel roof decks. In the event of roof leaks or moisture condensation at the steel deck and insulation interface, this reaction proved extremely detrimental.

Phenolic insulation was made basically the same way as ISO insulation. The various materials were blended, injected with the Freon, and extruded between facers. As a rule, phenolics have heavier R-values than do ISOs, urethanes, or extruded polystyrenes.

CHARACTERISTICS

One of the biggest advantages of phenolic insulation is that it does not experience the thermal drift that other plastic foam insulations do. Material manufacturers of the product guaranteed this aspect of the insulation. Phenolics also have exceptional fire resistance.

The reduction in thermal drift is because the Freon gas inside each of the millions of cells is incompatible with phenolic polymer resin. The Freon will off-gas very little as time goes on, because the Freon wants nothing to do with the phenolic material of the board.

Also, the cell walls in the phenolic insulation resist cracking and rupturing better than many other plastic foam insulations. The Freon is trapped more permanently within each cell. Also, the cell structure of phenolic insulation hinders the infusion of air molecules into the board. All these factors allow the board to better retain its original R-value.

CAUTIONS

Acids used in the manufacture of phenolics were the main cause of trouble in the past. When the phenolic insulation materials were first being introduced, the acids attacked mechanical fasteners and destroyed them. This was somewhat corrected by substituting lower acids for the higher acids used in the previous formulations.

However, if moisture was introduced at an interface of steel or metal and phenolic insulation, the acidic reaction resumed. This has caused phenolic foam to be pulled from the roofing market.

8.2 COMPOSITE ROOF INSULATIONS

All the major types of roof insulation can be combined together to form what is termed *composite roof insulation*. Composite roof insulations are made from a composite of one or more different types of roof insulations or materials.

The core and main insulating component is usually plastic foam such as ISO, urethane, or extruded polystyrene. The facer can be any combination of wood fiber insulation, perlite insulation, plywood, gypsum, or metal panel, to name a few. The facers can be on one side or both sides.

As the foam insulation leaves the extruder, the facers are applied. As the foam finishes setting and expanding, the facers become a permanent part of the insulation panel. Delamination of the facers can occur if the insulation panels get wet or proper quality control is not maintained at the manufacturing plant.

Different types of facers can be selected to give the board better compressive strength or tensile strength. The facers will also protect the plastic foam from solvents that may attack it or heat that would destroy it. Certain types of facers can be selected to give the insulation system a higher fire rating. Impermeable facers have proven to greatly reduce long-term thermal drift.

THERMAL DRIFT

At one time during the early to mid-1980s thermal drift was a very controversial topic. The term *thermal drift* is used to generically describe the phenomenon by which an insulation material slowly loses its insulation value.

At one time this was an important topic. However, with today's insulation, we are seldom concerned with thermal drift. Thermal drift in current insulations appears to be minimal and, in most design situations, not a consideration.

However, in some design situations it may be required to evaluate large roof systems, with extensive layers of high-R-value roof insulation. Long-term energy efficiency may be a large concern of the client. In such a case, it is important to be aware of thermal drift.

Also, understanding what affects or has affected insulations, why they were so affected, and what caused the effect is important in the overall understanding of the nature of insulations.

Plastic foam insulations are most susceptible to long-term thermal drift. Plastic foam insulations are those which incorporate a gas, such as CFC or HCFC, or air as the insulant entrapped within cells within their matrix.

This includes ISO, polystyrenes, phenolic, and cellular glass materials.

In the 1980s the National Roofing Contractors Association (among others) sponsored a study to evaluate in-place samples of plastic foam insulations. Samples from eight different roofs were tested. The samples were an average of three years old, the youngest 15 months in service and the oldest 51 months in service.

Findings from the testing laboratory showed that the insulations were 19 to 28 percent less efficient than what was projected by the insulation manufacturers. Another problem was also uncovered by this test. Some of the samples were from a multiple-layer insulation system. The findings showed that the insulation panels installed on top and directly under the roof membrane experienced more thermal loss than did the insulation panels on the bottom of the system. This thermal decay is linked to the heat and heat cycles that insulation must go through. On black membrane roofs it can be expected that thermal drift will be more significant than on white or reflective roofs.

The NRCA recommends that, for ISO and urethane foam insulations, a service-life R-value be used for calculation of R-values of the insulation over its expected 20-year life cycle. This R-value is 5.6 per inch thickness of insulation. Some people do not believe this is a conservative enough figure.

The Society of Plastics Industries, Inc., prepared a very informative report, entitled "Rigid Polyurethane and Polyisocyanurate Foams: An Assessment of Their Insulating Properties." This report is complete and thorough, containing information dating back to the 1980s, when many of the plastic foam insulations were introduced. This report concludes that nonpermeable facers, such as foil, are the strongest deterrent in reducing thermal drift. Nonpermeable facers retard the flow of air into the insulation and help restrict the CFC gas (predominantly in use at the time of the report publication) from diffusing out.

The report disputes that a single aged R-value or K-value be used, since this would generically combine plastic foam insulations. Since all insulations are not created equal, other factors should be used to calculate the long-term insulating characteristics of the insulation component.

SPI contends that the following factors are important considerations, each attributing to thermal resistance or contributing to thermal drift. They are:

- Initial insulating power of the foam
- Foam density, the thickness of the cell walls
- Size and orientation of the cells
- Type of foam and polymer
- Thickness of the foam
- Temperature and humidity the foam is exposed to during use
- Uniformity of the foam at the interface between the foam and the facing

Information from the SPI report, and other sources, confirms this. Thermal drift is mainly caused by infusion of air into the insulation board, although diffusion of the blowing agent into the board stock and into the atmosphere is a factor.

The CFC gas used up until the early 1990s is mainly Freon, which is often compatible with the polymer resins that compose many of the plastic foam insulation materials. Studies have shown that much more of the Freon is absorbed into the polymer resins of the board than is released into the air.

Today the HCFC gas can also be compatible, to a greater or lesser extent, with the polymer that constitutes the board stock which is the insulation panel. Compatibility or noncompatibility of the gas with the insulation panel polymer is dependent upon the chemical makeup, manufacturing procedures, etc., of individual insulation manufacturers.

The densities of the plastic foams are important factors of thermal resistance. The polymer by which the closed cells are surrounded is a much better conductor of heat than is the gas entrapped within each cell. This would lead to the assumption that lower-density boards, which reduce the polymer mass, would result in better insulating qualities of the insulation board. This is not true after a certain point. Low-density insulation materials have thin cell walls. These cell walls are easily ruptured, allowing air in and CFC or HCFC out.

Cell size, cell shape, and cell orientation within the insulation is a factor in initial insulating power. However, these items do not seem to increase or decrease thermal drift.

The heat that the foam insulation is exposed to will affect the rate of thermal drift. The hotter the temperatures, the faster the thermal drift phenomenon will occur. However, the end result of the drift will be the same after a 2- to 3-year period, no matter if the drift takes 2 months or 2 years. Thermal drift seems to stabilize within a 2- or 3-year period, but samples evaluated after 22 years still show that a very slight degree of thermal drift was still occurring.

With HCFC insulant gas, thermal drift does not seem to be as drastic as compared with CFC gas. Also, in the 10 to 15 years since thermal drift was a large issue, insulation manufacturing science and technology has progressed. Formulations, polymers, and manufacturing processes are superior to those used a decade and more ago. Therefore, thermal drift within plastic foam insulation is not as great.

However, it is important to realize that thermal drift is a factor that will always be present in insulations. As a matter of fact, it can be said that all insulations, not just plastic foams, experience thermal drift.

Over an extended period of time, fiberglass insulation will experience thermal drift resulting from the slow compaction of the fiberglass fibers due to gravity and the weight of the overlying roof system. Perlite and wood fiber insulations will lose insulation efficiency due to the infusion of humidity into the board stock as well as degradation of the panels, which will reduce and eliminate the air cells within.

CHAPTER 9

Modified Bitumen Membranes

9.1 GENERAL CHARACTERISTICS AND USES

Certain polymers can modify, and therefore change, the chemical makeup and characteristics of asphalt or coal tar pitch bitumen. This modification creates a new form of roof material. This material, known as *modified bitumen,* is one of the most successful roof innovations of the late twentieth century.

Modified bitumen roof membranes are quite widely used all over the United States. Originating in Europe (mainly Italy), the majority of all roofing applied in Europe is done with modified bitumen materials.

This roof material is sometimes referred to in slang as a *rubber roof,* although it most certainly is not. Modified bitumen membranes are more correctly referred to as *modified bitumens, mod bits,* or *MBMs.* They are sometimes grouped with single-ply elastomeric roofs. However, these modified bitumen roofs contain much more asphalt bitumen than polymeric modifiers.

Modified bitumen roof systems do not have the characteristics, installation requirements, maintenance requirements, or specification and design guidelines used for polymeric single-ply systems. Also, they are normally designed and installed in a multiple-ply system, not a single-ply system. We, therefore, believe that a category unto themselves for modified bitumens is correct.

MBM materials are most often composed of asphalt, reinforcing fabrics incorporated into the roof sheet during manufacture, and polymers used to modify the asphalt. Modified bitumen roofing material is normally supplied in roll form, usually 100 ft^2 per roll, and is approximately ⅛ in thick.

MBM TYPES

The most common polymers used to modify the asphalt bitumen are atactic polypropylene (APP) and styrene butadiene styrene (SBS). There are also SBR, EIP, and SEBS polymer modifiers.

Coal tar pitch bitumen can be modified with Tardyne™ polymers, creating an MBM compatible with coal tar pitch built-up roof (BUR) systems. This modified bitumen material, introduced in the mid 1990s, is also appropriate for use as a complete MBM roof system.

Modified bitumen material is also produced in a keg form, looking much the same as keg asphalt or coal tar pitch. It is also handled and installed much the same as keg asphalt roof material.

INSTALLATION PROCEDURES

In general, modified bitumen membranes are either heat-welded or installed with adhesives. They are normally fully adhered to base felts, insulations, or roof decking.

They can, however, be specified as a ballasted system wherein only the side laps are sealed and aggregates or pavers are placed over the unsecured roof membrane to secure the system in place.

APP modified bitumens are normally applied with an open-flame torch process. The roll material is melted and each sheet is welded/melted to the roof deck and to each other. Hot-air welding equipment can also be used in lieu of the open-flame torches. APP can also be obtained in a peel-and-stick form whereby it is self-adhered to a properly prepared roof deck or substrate.

SBS modified bitumen sheets are normally installed with hot asphalt moppings. They can also be installed with asphalt cutback cold-process adhesives. Like APP membrane materials, SBS can also be produced in a manner which allows the roll good to be heat-applied with torch flame or hot air. Coal tar pitch modified bitumen can be installed with hot pitch moppings or applied with open flame.

Keg-form modified bitumen material is from the SBS family. It is installed similarly to hot asphalt BUR systems in that it is melted in a kettle at a job site and applied via hot moppings to the roof surface. Roof felts are incorporated into the hot moppings, with the result being a monolithic MBM BUR system.

The other types of polymer modified asphalt and coal tar pitch bitumen membranes will normally fall into one of the aforementioned categories. APP and SBS modified bitumen membranes are the predominant types of modified membranes specified in today's roof construction market.

SURFACINGS

Different types of surfacings are required for some of the MBMs. Hot asphalt or coal tar pitch bitumen is incompatible with APP membranes. Therefore, in order to apply a gravel surface to the installed APP membrane system, a thick layer of asphalt emulsion surfacing is required into which gravel aggregate can be embedded.

APP modified bitumen membranes are often supplied unsurfaced from the manufacturer. Gravel surfacing, as previously mentioned, is seldom used. Instead, it is most common to surface the APP membrane with an asphalt cutback aluminum roof coating. Sometimes, it is recommended for an asphalt emulsion to first be applied as a base coat for the aluminum coat finish. (See Sec. 6.1.3.)

APP can also be supplied with a ceramic granule surface. SBS modified bitumens, on the other hand, normally come from the manufacturer with a ceramic mineral surfacing, such as that used to surface asphalt composition shingles.

SBS membranes are compatible with hot bitumen mopping. As such, the SBS sheet membrane is normally installed by hot asphalt mopping. It therefore can be surfaced with asphalt and aggregate, although the factory-applied mineral surface usually suffices.

Keg-form modified bitumen roof system material can also be surfaced several ways. After the material has been melted and applied, the roof applicator surfaces the completed roof system with gravel aggregates or ceramic minerals.

CHARACTERISTICS

SBS membrane materials are more flexible than APP membranes. They resist cold weather extremes due to their exceptional cold flex abilities.

APP membranes do not react well with cold temperatures. Extensive foot traffic across the roof surface or impact to the APP surface from tools and equipment can split the APP membrane during low-temperature periods.

However, SBS membranes are normally more susceptible to deterioration by heat and ultraviolet rays of the sun than are APP materials. The factory-applied mineral surfacing helps provide long-term protection from sunlight for the SBS membrane.

With torch-flame-applied MBM systems, close detail work can be achieved at roof flashing areas. However, the open flame presents a fire hazard. Also, with torch-flame or other heat-welded systems, the integrity of the system is greatly dependent upon the lap seam. Such seams, being 3 to 4 in wide, require proper and diligent application procedures on the part of the installer.

With adhesive-applied MBM systems, such as SBS membranes installed with hot asphalt mopping, if the seam is compromised the adhesive still can provide a watertight bond for a period of time. Some people think that this characteristic of the hot-mop-applied MBM system allows it to be more forgiving of applicator error than are heat-welded systems.

Modified bitumens have been used in applications ranging from pond liners to roofing on extra-steep inclines. Manufacturers issue 10- to 20-year warranties to cover material and labor.

CAUTIONS

Some inferior MBMs have existed, do exist, and will exist within the marketplace. Inferior MBMs are difficult to detect with the naked eye. Selection of a large and reputable material manufacturer does not always ensure a quality product.

Filler content within an MBM is an important consideration. Excessive fillers, while reducing manufacturing cost, create a membrane that, when in the field, often cracks, splits, and delaminates. Filler content and filler products used within the MBM material are often difficult to obtain from the material manufacturers, since it reflects their recipes, which are usually a guarded secret.

The placement and consistent location of the inner reinforcing fabric included within most MBMs is important. This fabric, discussed in detail later, is crucial in providing dimensional stability and tensile strength to the membrane.

The inner fabric should be at a consistent location within the MBM sheet. It should not deviate from the top of the membrane toward the bottom or vice versa. This placement can be checked by cutting a section through a membrane sheet and visually examining.

Most MBM materials are made with an asphalt bitumen base, with the polymer modifiers constituting a small percentage by volume of the material. Asphalt quality and type is imperative for a quality MBM product.

Only unblown or nonoxidized asphalt should be used in the manufacture of MBM. This type of asphalt is available in limited supply, in comparison to standard ASTM D 312 asphalt as used in BUR construction.

New polymer types are being introduced for use in numerous roof materials and applications. Proceed with caution when considering new polymeric blended and modified bitumen materials. Rooftop exposure is difficult to reproduce and duplicate in a laboratory. Reactions and life span on a rooftop have in the past proved many products unsuitable, even though they function well in laboratory testing.

9.1.1 Selection and Uses

Each type of modified bitumen membrane and application has advantages and disadvantages. Design selection is dependent upon:

- Roof deck and/or roof insulation type
- Number of roof penetrations and detail areas
- Capability and experience of local contractors with different MBM types
- Desired life expectancy of the roof system
- Roof maintenance allocation by the owner
- Budget

ROOF DECK/INSULATION TYPE

For combustible roof decks or insulation systems, a flame- or heat-applied membrane can create fire concerns. If such an MBM is selected over a combustible roof deck or insulation system, a base sheet or roof felt system installed in the hot asphalt mopping is prudent. The asphalt and felt layers, in conjunction with nonflammable perlite cant strips at base flashing areas, help create a fire barrier. However, in a case where the hot asphalt equipment and crew are on site to install felts and hot asphalt, it is often more prudent to install an SBS membrane than an APP membrane system.

DETAIL AREAS

Roof penetration and detail areas are best sealed with a heat-applied MBM. This can be with APP or the not-so-common heat-applied SBS membrane. However, since detail areas are very susceptible to flame penetration, fire hazard with a combustible roof deck and/or insulation system is again a concern. If the detail areas can first be sealed with roof ply layers, the hazard of fire is reduced.

CONTRACTOR EXPERIENCE

Roof contractor expertise with MBM differs from region to region. This often goes hand in hand with the MBM type required to function effectively in that particular geographic area.

For example, in the northern United States and extending into Canada, torch-applied SBS membrane is most common. However, this type of MBM is little used in other areas of the United States.

It is sometimes a grave mistake to specify a roof system based only on the merits of the roof materials' characteristics. Proper application by local contractors is required for a successful installation.

LIFE EXPECTANCY

Some MBM materials can be expected to last longer than others, when combined together in a proper sequence and manner. This life expectancy is often reflected in the price the contractor must pay for the MBM material.

Life expectancy can be increased with additional layers of MBM, either incorporated into the main field of the roof system or strategically located at flashing and stress areas. SBS membranes are sometimes used as a cap sheet over a two- or three-ply BUR system.

Life expectancy of the MBM roof system can also be increased by coatings applied to the surface of the completed roof system. This can mean additional layers of coating materials applied to factory-surfaced sheets, such as aluminum roof coating applied over factory-applied ceramic granualized sheets.

The life expectancy of an MBM is greatly reduced by ponding water. It seems to be increased with the slope of the roof deck. The lower the slope of the roof deck, the shorter the life expectancy when compared with a steeper-sloped deck and MBM system.

PREVENTATIVE MAINTENANCE DESIGN

Some MBM systems are less maintenance-intensive than others. Applying aluminum roof coatings periodically to a low-sloped MBM system can become costly over a 15- to 20-year period.

MBMs with a factory-applied ceramic granule finish, although more costly than unsurfaced sheets, prove more cost effective from a life-cycle cost view. Sometimes, applying an aluminum or other reflective coating to a ceramic granule–surfaced sheet can further decrease life-cycle cost.

Ceramic mineral granules will in time dissipate from the surface of the sheet as it ages. As the granules are displaced by rain, wind, and/or release due to aging of the sheet, the sheet membrane is left exposed to the elements and the sunlight. It rapidly ages at this point.

Applying a coating when the MBM system is new will help protect the sheet from aging, thereby extending the life cycle. The coating will help bond the granules to the sheet more effectively and for a longer period of time. It is also more cost effective to have such a coating applied at the time of construction than it is for the owner to enter into a contract at a later time for this specific task.

Few owners, although well-intentioned at the time of construction completion, allocate funds, personnel, or time to roof inspection and maintenance. It is therefore often advisable to design extra-durable flashing areas, walk areas, equipment service areas, etc. (See Sec. 2.1.2.)

BUDGET CRITERIA

Modified bitumen roof systems can be designed and specified to meet many budget criteria. An APP membrane system, torch-applied over a base sheet mechanically attached to a thin insulation recover board, can be considered an inexpensive utility roof system. Such retrofit assemblies are published in MBM manufacturers' specification manuals, often qualifying for a manufacturers' warranty bond.

Other systems, budget allowing, can be multiple layers of MBM with the top cap sheet of metallic factory surfacing. Such metallic factory-applied surfacings include aluminum and copper foils. These systems can be designed to provide an exceptional number of years of service, although sometimes the costs of such systems require more roof budget allotment than other types of systems might.

We often find MBM systems competing on a heads-up level with conventional BUR systems. Sometimes a two-ply BUR membrane is specified, to be covered with an MBM cap sheet. The cap sheet substitutes for the additional one- or two-roof-ply and gravel surface which would be required to achieve a complete BUR system.

ADDITIONAL CONSIDERATIONS

We also have available from this wide selection of material types (just in case it is not complicated enough) SBS and APP base sheets. These are always smooth surfaced and used as an underlying roof ply in a modified bitumen roof system. This allows for a multilayered MBM system which can utilize different application processes for the same roof system.

This is sometimes advantageous to quality control, production schedules, and budget. For example, in a reroof situation, it is advisable to cover and waterproof each day's work, but numerous pipe and roof penetrations will make the production schedule slow and expensive. A solution to this situation can be specifying an SBS base sheet installed in hot asphalt mopping. This process of application is quick, saving labor and increasing watertight production time when compared with torch-applied MBMs in the same situation.

Since SBS is compatible with asphalt and asphalt cutback materials, roof cement can be used at the end of the work day to ensure that no holes, gaps, or leaks are left at the numerous roof penetrations. It can be expected that the flashing areas will not be perfect or permanently watertight at this point, but an effective night seal can be economically obtained. However, the final and top SBS ply can be specified to be a torch-applied SBS modified bitumen material. The top cap sheet, being torch-applied, will bond and blend well with the bottom asphalt mopped SBS base sheet.

This accomplishes several goals. The roof applicator can remove the existing roof system and achieve a watertight seal at the end of each day with the new, partially completed roof system. The roof crew can proceed across the roof, removing roofing and debris, creating a clean work area for subsequent application. Nightly tie-in costs to waterproof the old and new roof are minimized.

By torch-applying the final layer, which is the cap sheet, the numerous roof penetrations and flashing areas can be minutely addressed by the roof applicators. Proper and long-term seals can be expected at all flashing areas. Production time is minimized by the roof contractor. Threatening weather does not stop production of the cap sheet since there is no risk to the building interior because no roofing is being removed.

An aesthetically pleasing roof system with long continuous runs of the cap sheet can be produced. The nightly tie-ins of the underlying SBS base sheet are not evident. Long, continuous roof membrane runs, with end laps staggered, also create a better roof system.

9.1.2 APP Modified Bitumen Membrane Systems

Like all other forms and types of roofing, APP modified bitumen membrane is unique unto itself. Unlike most other types and forms of roofing, modified bitumen roof materials are relatively new to the U.S. roofing industry, making the debut on a national level in the early 1970s.

In the beginning, they were not completely understood by many, including material manufacturers, roof applicators, and specifiers. Mistakes—some major—were made by all. Today, we are all more appreciative of the complexities of the material than we once were. An understanding of the chemical makeup of the material, leading to the requirements of proper manufacturing procedures and techniques, was one of the first steps required to produce a roof membrane which could function effectively in all regions of the United States. As stated previously, modified bitumen technology was imported from Europe.

Today we are still in a learning curve. This is evidenced by current National Roofing Contractors Association (NRCA) studies evaluating proper coating materials and the curing time required before coating of APP modified bitumen membranes. Also, as of the publication date of this manual, there still are not complete standards and test methods for evaluating different types of modified bitumen membranes by ASTM.

APP MODIFIED BITUMEN RAW MATERIALS

A brief overview of what APP modified bitumen material is and where it comes from is necessary. First there is propylene, a product derived from crude oil at the petrochemical refining plant. These short propylene molecules are joined together to form longer molecular chains, resulting in polypropylene. Depending on the exact formation of the new molecular chain, isotactic polypropylene or amorphous polypropylene can result.

Isotactic means the chain structure is formed in a random, nonconstant, and different configuration. Isotactic is also referred to as *itactic*.

Amorphous molecular chains are constant and of exact configurations. Amorphous is usually referred to as *atactic*. Atactic polypropylene (APP) polymer is the modifier used to create APP modified bitumen membrane roof materials.

Isotactic polypropylene, or IPP, is used in performance-grade impact-resistant materials, such as the bumpers on automobiles. Originally APP was a byproduct removed from the isotactic polypropylene. For a long time, there was no use for the APP. It was considered a waste product and was disposed of, either by burying it or stacking it in open fields or warehouses. Today, manufacturers specifically create large quantities of APP for the purpose of MBM manufacture.

MANUFACTURING PROCESS

Each manufacturer creates MBM differently, but the basic process is similar. Unblown, nonoxidized asphalt is melted in a large tank at the plant. APP polymer and 70 to 80 percent by volume asphalt are blended together to form modified bitumen material. Also in this mixture may be fillers, such as calcium carbonate (talcum) and other agents, as well as small amounts of itactic polypropylene.

A fabric, either fiberglass, polyester, or in some cases both types of fabrics, runs through this tank of hot modified bitumen mixture. The fabric is passed over, under, and through a series of rollers within the tank of hot mixture. The rollers control the amount of hot modified bitumen mixture applied to the reinforcing fabric, at the same time providing penetration of the modified bitumen into the fabric. The roller system also ensures that an even and uniform coating of modified bitumen material is applied to both sides of the fabric.

After the reinforcement fabric(s) has been impregnated and coated sufficiently to create a modified bitumen roof membrane sheet, the sheet exits the solution tank and is cooled, usually in a trough of water. After cooling, lines are applied to the completed roof membrane sheet to allow alignment by the roofers in the field.

The sheet is then cut to the right length for use. A thin sheet of material such as polyethylene may be laminated to the bottom side of the finished membrane, or the sheet good can be dusted with sand, talc, or mica granules.

The laminate sheet, talc, sand, and/or granules keep the roll from adhering to itself during shipping and storage. Like composition shingles, the modified bitumen material may still adhere to itself if left in direct sunlight or high-temperature conditions.

The sheet is then rolled up tightly, banded and/or wrapped, palletized, and prepared for shipping. This is a continuous process, from the application of modified bitumen mixture to the reinforcement membrane until palletization of the finished goods.

Inner Fabrics and Placement. The fabric placement within the roof membrane sheet is important. This location of the inner fabric determines, among other things, how the sheet will react to heat and adhesives used in the field for application. By adjusting, tilting, and setting the rollers of the system, the manufacturer can cause the reinforcement fabric to be produced in the center of the MBM sheet or closer to the top or the bottom of the finished membrane.

With APP being torch-applied, the reinforcement will be placed closer to the center or top of the roof membrane. This protects the reinforcing fabric from heat damage during application.

In an MBM to be applied with hot asphalt, usually SBS, the reinforcing fabric may be closer to the center or bottom of the sheet membrane. After the mopping asphalt and SBS sheet have been laid, the reinforcing fabric is closer to the center of the waterproofing components, which are the SBS and the asphalt. If the SBS is to be torch-applied, the scrim will be placed closer to the center or top. Again, this protects the inner reinforcing membrane from heat damage during torch application.

Second, while the modified bitumen sheet is being run over the rollers repeatedly during the manufacturing process, the inner reinforcing fabric can be stretched and pulled. This will occur with polyester fabrics much more than it will with fiberglass.

If the stretching is excessive, the roof applicator must lay the MBM sheet flat on the roof and allow it to relax. Failure to relax the sheet fully may cause buckling and wrinkling of the roof membrane, as well as separation of the lap seams as the roof ages.

It may not be possible to fully relax the sheet in the field due to the excessive stretching of the inner fabric during manufacture. After a period of time, the MBM may shrink, causing severe problems. When MBMs were first introduced to the United States, field relaxation of the MBM sheet was a normal requirement of many of the manufacturers. Some of the MBM systems still shrank after installation. Due to advanced technology, an understanding of the manufacturing process, and the dedication of manufacturers to modified bitumen production, this requirement is now almost nonexistent. Few MBM failures are related to shrinkage.

Computerized equipment assists plant personnel in mixing, blending, and producing quality products. Polyester fabrics are now of better quality, with more suppliers, than a decade ago. As with any other manufactured roof product, problems have occurred, and will continue to occur with MBMs because of manufacturer error. However, the major U.S. modified bitumen manufacturers have dedicated the equipment, personnel, and budget to producing, marketing, and warranting a quality material.

The reinforcing fabric in the MBM sheet is a main component giving the membrane sheet its elongation and tensile strength. Tensile strength, in simple terms, is a material's ability to withstand tension, brought on by bending, movement, stretching, and pulling of the roof membrane, without breaking. For example, steel beams have good tensile strength.

Elongation indicates a material's ability to be stretched and is measured by the point at which a material breaks or yields or is deformed. A rubber band has good elongation properties.

Modified bitumen material alone does not have enough tensile strength or elongation properties to make it a universal roof material, suitable for application in many different situations. The inner reinforcing fabric is used to enhance tensile strength and elongation properties. Fragile, brittle, and inferior scrim membranes can be a factor in allowing a modified bitumen sheet to prematurely crack and break under normal rooftop conditions.

Some manufacturers offer different weights of inner scrim fabric in MBM sheets. Usually the heavier the scrim, the greater the cost of the MBM roof sheet.

An MBM with thick reinforcing fabric is sometimes selected because of its ability to better withstand foot traffic, building movement, or excessive weather conditions. Sometimes a closer look at structural alterations to the building or protective surface to the MBM system may instead be in order.

MANUFACTURING AND QUALITY CONTROL PROBLEMS

Some difficulties can occur during the manufacturing process. These problems are limited and vary from manufacturer to manufacturer, and, as time has passed, many have been eliminated. The main problems have been and in some cases still are:

- Quality of the raw materials
- Proper blending of the raw materials
- Application of the hot modified bitumen compound to the reinforcing fabric
- Excessive stretching of the polyester reinforcing fabric (called *necking*)
- Position of this reinforcement within the final product

Some manufacturers may reclaim APP stored outside or underground as a waste product. The end product will not be of the same quality as modified bitumen membrane material made with APP that was carefully produced and handled.

The blending of the asphalt, other materials, and modifiers is a very crucial step. This is where most manufacturers admit that problems begin. Enough time must be allowed for the mixing and blending. The separate materials must be added at the right amount and at the right time to create a quality end product.

The blending of the materials can be checked using a fluorescent microscope. A sample from an in-process batch mixture is examined under this microscope. A trained chemist can quickly determine, by the alignment of the molecules, if the asphalt has accepted the modifiers. The modifiers should be evenly and uniformly dispersed throughout the mixture, showing that the batch has acquired the needed homogeneous qualities. (See Fig. 9.1.)

Problems will arise if inferior equipment is used for the dipping and rolling process of the reinforcement fabric in the modified bitumen solution tank. First, the MBM material can be applied to the membrane in an uneven coating. This can result in areas of the final MBM sheet that are too thin or too thick, as well as causing the inner reinforcing fabric to be too close to the top or the bottom of the finished sheet.

Surfacings. Many APP modified bitumen manufacturers offer a roof sheet with a factory-applied surfacing. Ceramic granule surfacing is the most popular factory-applied finish, although there are some MBMs with other surfacings, such as aluminum or copper foil.

Figure 9.1 Molecular view.

MBMs also come unsurfaced from the factory, requiring a field-applied finish. Asphalt cutback coatings are most commonly used to surface APP MBMs after they are applied—i.e., aluminum roof coating. These coatings react virtually the same way on an MBM system as they react on a conventional BUR surface. However, we are beginning to understand that, for an aluminum asphalt cutback roof coating to be durable on an APP modified bitumen roof system, an additional layer of asphalt emulsion is sometimes advantageous. (See Sec. 6.1.3.)

This is especially true for recoating an existing MBM system which has an existing aluminum roof coating. It is recommended that the asphalt emulsion be nonfibered. The emulsion should be installed at manufacturer-recommended rates, usually 1.5 gal per 100 ft^2 of roof surface. It should completely dry and cure, normally for 5 to 10 days, depending on humidity and temperatures, before application of the aluminum roof coating. The aluminum roof coating should be of high quality, with the appropriate amount of aluminum flake content.

With a cutback coating, care must be taken to avoid ponding water, chemical environments, foot traffic, and other roof surfacing cautions. Some manufacturers publish lists of approved coatings for their MBM systems.

Other surfacing can be applied by the roofer, including acrylics and granule and gravel surfacings. Most manufacturers do not specify hot asphalt to be used with APP modified bitumens; therefore, a gravel surfacing can be installed into asphalt emulsion, as can ceramic granules.

With MBMs supplied with a ceramic granule surface, special requirements are advised at base flashing areas. Base flashings normally consist of multiple layers of MBM. A better job is achieved if smooth surface APP is specified as the underlying flashing plies. This allows the granule surface MBM to be torch-applied to a smooth modified bitumen sheet. It is more difficult for the roof applicator to achieve a complete solid seal between two sheets, both surfaced with ceramic granules, than it is to adhere a top sheet with granule surface to an underlying, nongranule smooth surface sheet.

CHARACTERISTICS

APP has good weathering characteristics. Its resistance to the ultraviolet rays of the sun can be rated as good to excellent. When properly blended with asphalt bitumen, these weathering characteristics are imparted to the MBM.

However, a surface coating must be installed and maintained to the top of the MBM system. Without such a protective coating, the membrane system will be prematurely destroyed by the ultraviolet rays of the sun.

APP modified bitumen membrane systems, normally installed by open flame or sometimes by hot air, have a softening-point range and certain flow characteristics. The flow of the material is dependent upon the softening-point range of the material.

Many manufacturers of MBM offer a winter-grade and a summer-grade MBM. Each grade has a different softening-point range. Higher softening-point temperature ranges are used during hot summer months; lower softening-point membranes are used during the cold winter months. The different formulations assist the roof applicators in obtaining the proper flow of the bitumen compound during installation. (See "Specification and Design.")

APP membranes can become brittle at low-temperature extremes. Do not specify an APP membrane for the cold northern climates when extensive foot traffic can be expected on the roof surface during the winter or when the roof assembly can be expected to undergo excessive movement.

APP MBMs, as well as most other MBMs, have very low water permeability rates. They are an excellent choice for below-grade waterproofing assemblies. The torch-grade materials are used successfully for waterproofing vertical sidewalls of underground structures.

SPECIFICATION AND DESIGN

Today, open flame is the most common way of installing APP modified bitumen roof systems. These flames are normally produced by propane-fueled torches. The torch can either be hand-held or a series of torches can be mounted onto a piece of equipment. This mechanical equipment is pulled or pushed by the roof applicator.

MBM roof systems are installed by laying and adhering the modified bitumen membrane roll to the roof surface with the heat from the torch flame. At the same time, the roll being installed is heat-fused to the lap edge seam of a previously installed roll.

As the membrane sheets are torch-heated, the modified asphalt melts and the lap seams are fused together, joining one sheet to the other. The melted material looks very much like hot mop asphalt.

MBM sheets usually overlap one another about 3 to 4 in at the lap edges. At end lap seams, the sheets normally overlap a minimum of 6 in. The seamed edges of the MBM system are the most important element in long-term waterproofing of the roof system.

As heat is applied to the MBM sheets, the modified bitumen compound is melted from both sheets, causing the two sheets to be fused together. This melting causes what is referred to as *flowout* at the lap edges. When welding two pieces of steel together, this is called a *bead*. The flowout at the seams of the MBM material is a most important factor and a main indicator of good installation.

Care must be taken not to overheat an APP, thereby damaging the inner reinforcing fabric. The large torch used to apply and seam the rolls of modified bitumen together puts out a flame of 1300+°. At that temperature, overheating can occur quickly.

As the roofer is pushing the roll forward, a flowout of modified bitumen compound should come from between the two sheets at the side-lap edges. The compound flowout must not be too wide or too narrow. If too much heat is applied to the two sheets, the flowout will be too wide. If not enough heat is applied at the correct point, the flowout bead will be too small. Manufacturers differ in their particular requirements, but a flowout bead of ⅜ to ½ in is acceptable.

The lap seams are very important. A wide flowout bead is an indication of a weak lap. In this case, the material that was supposed to be keeping everything together and waterproof now extends out beyond the lap, doing no good at all. Also, as this overheating occurs, the inner fabric often becomes too hot. The inner fabric, especially if it is polyester, cannot withstand excessive overheating. It can become weakened and often wrinkles. If this happens, the reinforcing fabric is no longer able to serve its full purpose.

Not enough flowout is also an important indicator of trouble ahead. First, the two sheets did not get hot enough, possibly leading to false welding. A false weld makes the lap edges of the two sheets appear bonded together. However, after they have been in the field for a period of time, due to thermal shock, building movement, or relaxation of the new roof system, the two sheets that looked welded together may come apart. Second, improper application techniques, resulting in insufficient heat being applied, prevent the MBM material of the two sheets from becoming liquid enough. The compound of the lap edge seams must become liquefied so as to mingle and blend completely together.

Also, without a flowout bead at all places along the lap seam, a void in the lap seam is created. At that point, the two sheets may be 95 percent welded together, but that leaves a 5 percent area that is not completely fused together. What starts as a small void can in time become corroded and enlarged by wind- and rain-driven abrasive particles on a rooftop. As the dirt and small particles are moved around, they will start to eat at the seam. The dirt will act as a corrosive and attacking element up under the lap at the void. Moisture within these voids, which experience freeze/thaw cycles, will also help to enlarge the void. Any of these factors will contribute to premature lap failure due to improper application.

SPECIFICATION

- Require all membrane sheet runs to be straight, within 1-in tolerance, per every 50 linear feet.
- Require a flowout bead to be present at all seam locations. The flowout bead should not be more than 1 in wide.
- All base flashings should be 100 percent adhered to the underlying sheet flashing membranes and to any roof curbs. No voids, gaps, or bridging of membrane materials should be present at base flashing locations.
- Require that a weighted roller, designed for use with modified bitumen membrane roof systems, be used at all metal flashing locations where the MBM is adhered to the sheet metal flashings. A 100 percent bond should be required between the metal flashing and membrane at all locations.
- Caulk and/or roof cement will become ineffective if the torch flame heats the metal flashing and, in so doing, "cooks" the caulk or adhesive. If caulk is required in the design at crucial areas, specify for the torch flame to be kept from the area where such caulk is installed, and instead heat only the MBM sheet to be installed at that area.
- Completely and heavily prime all metal flashings with cutback asphalt material in order for the MBM to adhere to the metal flashing.
- Do not specify or design any caulk or roof cement to be exposed on any surface to which an APP membrane is to be installed.

Design

- Eliminate all sheet metal flashings if possible, using instead cant strips and bituminous base flashings.

- Do not rely on the solder joints of sheet metal flashings for any reason with a torch-applied system. The heat of the flame will melt the solder joints and allow the solder to contaminate the seal at that point; i.e., where a scupper must pass through a parapet wall, require watertight sealing of the scupper hole with MBM before installation of the scupper.
- Metal edge flashing should employ cover and backer plates. (See Secs. 9.1 and 12.2.6.)
- MBM roof systems cannot resist deck movement as can polymeric single-ply systems such as EPDM. Do not design the MBM to substitute for expansion joints and area dividers.
- All MBM base flashings should terminate a minimum of 8 in above the roof surface.
- Use smooth surface MBM for underlying flashing plies. Adhere granule surfaced MBMs, if used, to the smooth surface sheets.
- Water should not pond for longer than 24 h at any location on an MBM system.

SAFETY CAUTIONS

Open flames are usually used for installation of APP membranes. This creates certain risks on wood-structured buildings. This risk is increased when roofing older buildings where wood components are cured or dry-rotted.

Some buildings have caught fire during reroofing. In the past, this situation has led to trouble with insurance carriers covering roofers working with an open flame. It is often advisable to require written verification from the insurance carrier that such open-flame work is included under the contractor's liability insurance policy.

Safe construction practices dictate that there must be at least one fire extinguisher per torch at all times. Extinguishers should be kept close to the work on the rooftop. If a roof fire starts, 10 extinguishers in trucks scattered around the job site could prove useless. What started as a small fire can easily spread to an attic, plenum space, or parapet wall, beyond the fire extinguisher's capability.

Most fires start at pipe penetrations, parapet walls, roof drains, or scuppers. It is at these locations that work is mostly details, being accomplished by holding the flame close to the roof material and the object being waterproofed. These detail areas may have exposed, or partially exposed, wood decking, nailers, or cut edges of roof insulation panels. Wood at these areas may be somewhat deteriorated, since roof penetrations and detail areas are where most roof leaks have occurred in the past.

In reroofing, wood fiber roof insulation is often used with a modified bitumen membrane system. The insulation is used as a recover board, being installed over the existing roof. Wood fiber insulation board is flammable and smolders and burns if ignited.

The edges of the insulation panels are the most vulnerable part of the board, especially if it is a field-cut edge. Often, the roofer cannot know that the insulation is burning, since the material can smolder for hours until enough heat has built up to cause it to flash into flame.

The roofer might cover up smoldering board unwittingly and leave the work site at the end of the day. By the next morning, the roofer could well return to a burned-down building and an upset, fiery-tempered customer. Require that a fire watch be posted a minimum of 1 h after all torch-application procedures have ended.

9.1.3 SBS Modified Bitumen Membrane Systems

MANUFACTURING

The other popular form of modified bitumen uses the styrene butadiene styrene (SBS) polymer as the modifier. The SBS modified bitumens are made by the same batch manufacturing process as is APP. Like APP, SBS modified bitumens usually have a fiberglass or polyester inner reinforcement fabric, or the fabric can be a combination of both.

CHARACTERISTICS

However, SBS membranes have different characteristics than APP modified bitumen materials. SBS modified bitumens have a much better low-temperature flexibility than do APP membranes. SBS withstands building movement and thermal shock better than APP. SBS can be installed in a mopping of hot asphalt, a process most roofers are familiar with.

The SBS polymer is a synthetic rubber, giving the SBS good low-temperature flexibility and elongation properties. This rubber polymer also causes SBS modified bitumens to have a low melt point but different flow characteristics when compared to APP.

SBS modified bitumen membranes are manufactured with more asphalt than are APP modified bitumens, and for this reason they are considered by some to be more susceptible to weathering and ultraviolet degradation than APP.

INSTALLATION

Although SBS modified bitumens can be heat-welded with either an open flame or hot air, they are commonly installed using hot asphalt bitumen. Other installation processes use a cold-process asphalt-based adhesive, a self-adhering membrane sheet, or SBS in a solid keg form which is melted at the job site and installed by a hot-mop process.

Heat-Welding. If flame or hot air is used to install SBS modified bitumen, care must be taken to avoid applying too much heat to the membrane. SBS material, when installed properly, will not flow as readily as APP modified bitumen material. Applicators must be aware of the different flow characteristics of the two materials.

Overheating by the torch flame or the hot air stream will cause the material to experience excessive flow. The excessive flow of the modified bitumen compound will cause too much of the modified bitumen material to flow out from under the sheet membrane. This lack of modified bitumen compound under and in between the sheet membrane layer(s) can reduce the ability of the roof to function effectively as a system.

SBS modified bitumen membranes must be specially designed and manufactured and specifically created for heat-welding procedures. The placement of the inner reinforcing membrane fabric within the membrane sheet is at a different location level within the roof sheet than it is if the sheet membrane is manufactured for bitumen adhesive application.

With MBM sheets manufactured for heat-application procedures, the inner reinforcing fabric is normally located toward the top of the sheet. For MBM sheets manufactured for hot asphalt mopping application, the inner fabric is normally located more toward the bottom of the sheet membrane.

Torch flame or hot air can damage an inner reinforcing sheet fabric located close to the bottom of the sheet membrane, as is the case in most MBMs manufactured for hot bitumen application. If the reinforcing fabric is damaged by the heat of the torch flame or hot air stream, the total roof system can be compromised. However, a contradictory note is in order here. In Europe, the common manner of installing MBMs is with cold-process adhesive under the main body of the sheet membrane, with the lap edges of the installed sheet being sealed by hot air.

Depending on heat, humidity, and adhesive composition, cutback asphalt cold-process mastics can take from 24 to 72 h to form a bond that will not be affected by heavy rains and water. Hot air or sometimes hot iron sealing of the laps or self-adhering lap edges on modified bitumen sheets allow the roof to become immediately waterproof.

In Europe, where heat sealing of the lap edges is common, with MBM roof systems being the predominant roof type specified and installed, techniques, tools, and modified bitumen membranes are adapted to this procedure. In the United States, where workers commonly use open-flame torches, the techniques will probably not be the same as those used in Europe.

Cutback Asphalt Cold Process. SBS, and in Europe some APP modified bitumens, can be attached to properly prepared roof substrates using cold-applied asphalt cutback mastics. In the United States, we normally only apply SBS modified bitumen material in cold-process mastic adhesive.

The lap edges of the sheets are normally sealed by the same cold-process mastic, although, as stated above, hot-air welding of the seams may be appropriate if workers are properly trained and the equipment used is of the proper type and regulated correctly.

Before applying modified bitumen membranes with cold-process adhesive, the manufacturer of the sheet membrane and the manufacturer of the adhesive should be consulted. Some modified bitumen manufacturers market both the modified bitumen and the adhesive.

Cold-process adhesives are applied by brush, squeegee, or spray equipment. Spray equipment allows some contractors to install as much modified bitumen, cold-applied, per day as others do using mop-applied hot asphalt.

Oils in the cold-process adhesive attach to the asphaltenes in the modified bitumen during application. The main concern here is the solvents that are the cutback agent in the adhesive. Many failures of the cold-applied modified bitumens are directly linked to improper adhesive or improper application of a correct adhesive.

Solvents are used to create liquid cutback asphalt adhesive. These solvents are responsible for adhesion of the cutback adhesive into the modified bitumen membrane. If the adhesive contains too great an amount of solvents or distillates, damage can occur to the modified bitumen by the attack of the solvents on the sheet. If too much adhesive is applied, even if it is the correct adhesive for the modified bitumen membrane, the solvents become trapped within the system and cannot flash off. This can also cause solvent attack on the roof sheet.

Not enough solvents in the adhesive or insufficient application of the adhesive will result in insufficient solvents to allow the bonding of the adhesive and modified bitumen material.

Hot Bitumen Process. The most popular method of installing SBS is the use of hot asphalt as an adhesive. This requires the SBS membrane to be installed using many of the same techniques and procedures as used when installing a cap sheet roofing ply on a BUR system.

High-range equiviscous temperature (EVT) must be maintained at all times when installing SBS modified bitumens. (See Sec. 4.1.3.) The mopping asphalt must be hot enough to melt some of the SBS from the modified bitumen sheet. By maintaining the upper-range temperatures in the EVT scale, some of the SBS modified bitumen material will be melted from the roof sheet and become mixed with the mopped asphalt.

As *overheating* is the worst aspect of torch-applied modified bitumens, the worst thing with a hot asphalt–applied SBS is *underheating*. There must be mixing and adhesion of the hot asphalt and the SBS material. Most manufacturers require that the mopping temperature of the asphalt, at the point of application, be maintained above 400°F.

Self-Adhering Modified Bitumens. Self-adhering modified bitumens have been available for many years and may become more popular as time goes on. Manufacturers claim quickness and ease of installation and offer both APP and SBS formulations. SBS is by far the most accepted and popular type of self-adhering modified bitumen.

The roof deck surface must be properly prepared for adhesion of the self-adhering membrane. This is accomplished by using a special base sheet, coated roof insulation panels, or primers. These components should be supplied by the manufacturer of the self-adhering modified bitumen membrane.

A release film is attached to the back of the pressure-sensitive modified bitumen. After the membrane has been properly placed and aligned to the roof surface, the release paper is removed. As the modified bitumen comes into contact with the specially prepared surface, it immediately adheres.

The lap edges on top of the rolls usually have a release film. After the film on the back has been removed and the roll is adhered, the film on the lap edge is removed and the seams of the sheets are mated. Some systems use an adhesive applied to the lap edge in lieu of or in addition to the self-adhering surfaces. A roller is then used on the top of the sheet to ensure complete and watertight adhesion.

This method is much like the adhering and seaming of some single-ply membranes. Likewise, protection of the seam from dust, dirt, and contaminants can be a problem, as well as visual verification of the complete bonding of the two sheets.

Keg-Form SEBS. SEBS modified bitumen material is available in keg form from some manufacturers. This allows the roofer to melt the modified bitumen in a kettle at the job site. The roofers then mop modified bitumen material directly to the prepared roof deck, similar to applying a conventional BUR.

Some manufacturers have a special product line encompassing both felts and this modified bitumen material in keg form. The ply sheets, usually two or three, are normally polyester but can be fiberglass. This process combines new technology with old-time practices. This type of application has several advantages.

- The system is completely monolithic, being totally assembled in the field.
- The system has no lap edges to be carefully sealed as in the other forms of MBM systems.
- All flashings are as one with the field membrane.
- Extra modified bitumen material can be placed by the applicator where additional wear, tear, and strain is expected.
- The bitumen, modified with an SEBS polymer, is more forgiving of roof deck movements, thermal shock, etc., than is an asphalt BUR system.

However, this procedure has the same inherent problems and concerns of conventional BUR as discussed in Chap. 4.

SURFACINGS

SBS modified bitumens must have a protective surfacing. Most SBS sheets come from the manufacturer with a factory-applied weathering surface, such as ceramic granules. Many modified bitumen manufacturers also allow gravel surfacing to be field-applied in a pouring of hot asphalt. Again, high-range EVT must be maintained to allow the SBS sheet to slightly melt and blend with the top pouring of hot asphalt.

It is sometimes required to resurface older SBS modified bitumen systems. This can be accomplished by use of an asphalt cutback adhesive, such as MBM manufacturer-approved asphalt roof coating or asphalt emulsion. New ceramic granules can be installed into the coating.

CAUTIONS

Since asphalt is a critical component of this roof system, it is advisable to install this type of roof system only on areas that are compatible with hot asphalt systems. You should not install this type of roof on areas that pond water or experience chemical or pollutant contamination, or directly to roof insulations damaged by hot asphalts.

For MBMs with a coal tar pitch base, it may be possible to install the membrane in situations not compatible with the standard form of asphalt-based MBM. Consult the MBM manufacturer.

In cold geographic regions or during the winter months, it may be difficult to properly install hot-mop-applied SBS membranes. Upper-range temperatures of the hot mopping bitumen may be difficult to achieve and/or maintain at the point of membrane application.

Current volatile organic content (VOC) regulations may pose some problems with cutback asphalt adhesives used to install SBS by a cold-process method.

Check with the material manufacturer and all building codes. Also, for cold-process applications, obtain written approval from the MBM manufacturer regarding type and brand of adhesive selected. Correct application rates and amounts of adhesive should also be provided by the manufacturer.

For heat-welding of SBS membranes, select only SBS membranes specifically manufactured for such applications. If heat-welding the seams of an SBS designed for and installed by hot bitumen or cold-process adhesive, obtain written permission for such from the MBM manufacturer. Also, have the manufacturer provide the means and methods for such application techniques.

SBS modified bitumen membranes cannot tolerate ponding water. Ensure that there is a positive slope at all locations on the roof deck to which the MBM is to be installed.

SPECIFICATION

Steep asphalt, either Type III or Type IV, should be used when installing SBS with hot asphalt. Type IV asphalt will provide higher EVT ranges, and therefore is often more advantageous. (See Sec. 4.1.4.)

If a low-sloped or dead-level asphalt is used, the asphalt could bleed from under the sheet and from between the laps. Low-sloped asphalt could compromise the quality of lap seams and, since the weight of some SBS membranes approaches or exceeds 100 lb per square, slippage and sluffing could occur with Type I or II asphalt.

When designing a roof with hot-mopped bitumen and SBS modified bitumen, specifying cold-process adhesives for adhering the SBS to parapet walls is sometimes advantageous to the overall quality of the system. When flashing parapet walls, it's difficult to place enough hot asphalt onto the wall, to keep the asphalt hot enough till the sheet is placed to the wall, and to place the sheet on the wall quickly before the hot asphalt runs off the wall. Cold-process adhesive eliminates some of these problems.

It is also sometimes feasible to allow application of SBS in mopping of hot asphalt bitumen, then use the SBS with cold-process adhesives at all the flashing areas. This can reduce the risk of failure due to poor application of hot asphalt at these critical areas. Many think that by use of a cold-process material, the method is easier, more accurate, and more efficient around penetrations, edges, and curbs.

In lieu of cold-process adhesive, torch-applied SBS can be used at roof detail areas. This also allows for meticulous work at these areas. However, be aware of the potential fire hazard when using open flame. (See Sec. 9.1.2.)

Require all metal flashings to which the MBM must be adhered to first be primed with a heavy and liberal coat of asphalt primer. Care should be taken not to allow excessive primer to spill onto the SBS roof sheets where the distillates within the primer could possibly cause damage to the roof sheets.

DESIGN

Eliminate all metal flashings mounted to the roof surface if possible. Substitute, when possible, base flashings with a cant strip. Roof design for an SBS modified bitumen system is similar in discipline to that for a built-up roof system.

Avoid all ponding water areas on top of an SBS roof system. Use tapered insulation assemblies to create saddles, crickets, roof drain sumps, etc. (See Sec. 8.1.4.)

SBS modified bitumen base sheets are available and should be used at all areas and locations where additional strength and pliability is required. In most cases, one layer of modified base sheet substitutes for two plies of fiberglass roof felts.

CHAPTER 10

Metal Roof Systems

10.1 GENERAL

METAL ROOF TYPES

There are many types and forms of metal roofing. There are copper roof systems and roof systems of lead. These systems are formed from the metal into panels, usually by the roofers, and installed with cleat and clip fasteners to the roof deck. (See Sec. 11.3.) Lead and copper have been used for centuries as roofing materials and are credited as being the longest-lived form of roofing in the world.

There are metal shingles of copper, steel, and aluminum. These shingles are usually factory-made and installed using cleats and clips for attachment to the roof deck and to each other. (See Fig. 10.1.) Lead and copper roofing as well as metal shingle roof systems are normally installed to sloped roof decks since they are water shedders, not water barriers. Water-shedding systems rely on the gravity-induced flow of water to prevent roof leaks while water-shedding systems rely on the seal and waterproof integrity of the roof covering to restrict water entry. A built-up roof (BUR) is a water-barrier system, while composition shingles as normally used on residential housing are a water-shedding roof system. (See Secs. 1.3, 10.8.2, and 10.8.3.)

Some types of metal roofing can be installed as either a water-barrier or water-shedding system using metal panels. As an example, sheet copper can be cut, formed, flat-lock-seamed, and soldered to create a low-slope or dead-level flat water barrier system. (See Sec. 11.3.5.) These flat-lock solder-seam roof systems were more prevalent at the turn of the century, when they were used as plaza decks and even as tank liners for reflection pools.

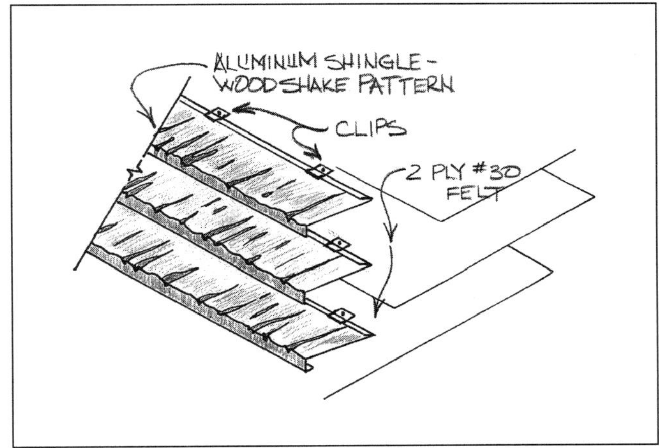

Figure 10.1 Aluminum shingles.

MODERN STEEL ROOFING

This chapter mainly concerns coated-steel roof systems as used today in the commercial and industrial market, although some of the systems as discussed herein are used in the residential sector. Coated-steel roof systems are becoming a dominant form of roof system.

In the distant past, metal roofing was used mainly in agricultural and rural settings as roof coverings on barns, sheds, farmhouses, etc. The style of metal panels was usually corrugated or V-crimp with a galvanized coating.

In the mid-1900s metal buildings as total systems began to be introduced to the commercial and industrial sector. These systems were marketed and manufactured from a single source and usually included all structural components, including the steel framing, building walls, doors, roofing, and sometimes even the insulation and light fixtures.

These building systems are often very economical. The building envelope, including the roof, have proven to have a long life cycle with very low maintenance requirements. It is therefore easy to understand why people would desire such an effective, long-lived, low-maintenance roof system on their buildings. The logical assumption was (is) that the metal building roof system would provide excellent service for other building types as well.

The roofing for metal buildings is often a rib profile panel, using screws with a gasket head to attach the panel to the underlying steel purlin. The gasket head provides the waterproof integrity for the fastener. These panels were referred to as *R-panels*. They were normally the same panels used to clad the building walls of the metal building. (See Fig. 10.2.)

Metal roof panels with exposed fasteners are still popular, usually having lower construction costs than the concealed clip fastened panels. The downside to using exposed fasteners with a metal roof panel is the repair and maintenance cost often required due to fastener seal failure.

Today we see structural standing seam roof panels, fastened to the roof structure with concealed clips, used extensively in commercial and industrial applications. The advent of this type of metal roof panel can be credited with making the metal roof system one of the fastest-growing segments of the roof industry. (See Fig. 10.3.)

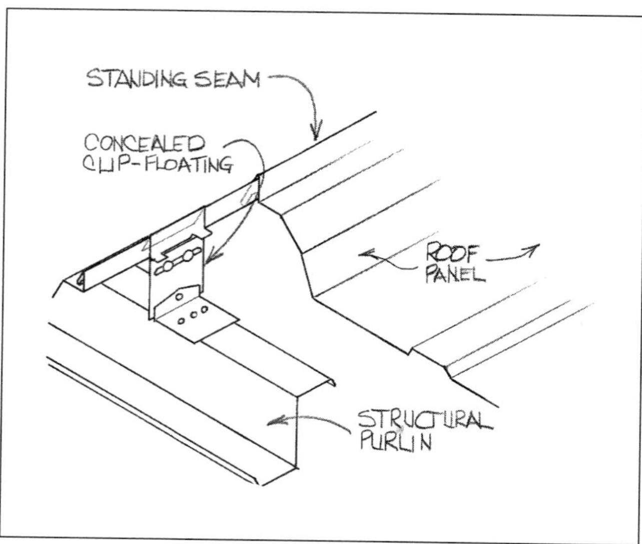

Figure 10.3 Concealed clip on structural standing seam roof panel.

GROWTH OF METAL ROOF INDUSTRY

In 1985 the number of metal roofing systems being specified was far lower than in 1995. This can be attributed to two factors. The first factor is dissatisfaction with low-slope roof systems' performance, either in terms of life span when compared with optimum-performing metal roof systems or life-cycle costs of many nonmetal low-sloped roof systems. Membrane low-sloped roof systems require maintenance and often repair to achieve a 15- to 25-year life cycle.

Metal roof systems *can* exist for 40 years without being plagued by roof leaks. A low-sloped bituminous or polymeric roof system can also achieve the same life cycle, often with low maintenance and repair costs; however, historically, this target is seldom achieved.

This leads to the second factor: architectural style and expression. Low-sloped membrane roof systems, such as BURs, were seldom visible from the ground. Emphasis was transferred to the building line.

A metal roof system can be designed with a low slope, concealing the roof from ground view and continuing to allow the building line to be dominant. However, a metal roofing system can also be designed as a key visible element of a building structure.

The colors and styles of metal roof panels available are very diverse, providing architectural expression and style not available with most other commercial roof system designs. Architects can now successfully make the roof a focal point of the building.

The search for the better mousetrap has led to the metal roofing system, whereby it is hoped roof performance will be enhanced. Additionally, metal roofing systems have lent themselves to greater architectural expression and style.

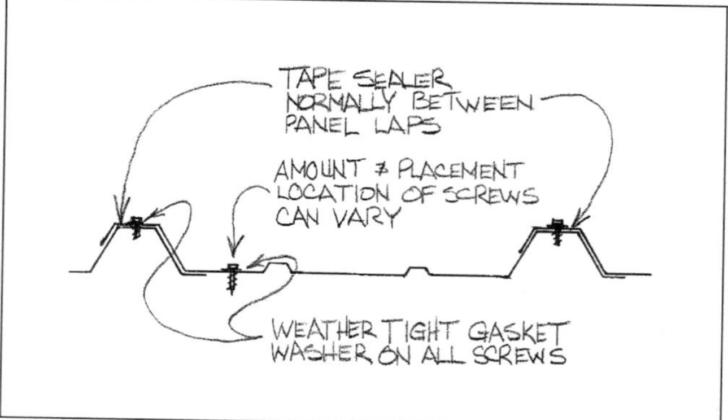

Figure 10.2 R-panel with exposed screws.

DESIGN PROCESS CAUTIONS

One other factor may be a consideration when a designer is selecting the type of roof system for a project, and, after some deliberation, we have decided to discuss it. This factor is the perceived ease of design involved with a metal roof system.

First it must be understood that as yet there are few accepted standard details within the metal roofing industry. Each manufacturer's panel style, size, and configuration is different. Thus different components are required at attachment areas, flashing areas, eaves, ridges, rakes, valleys, etc., dependent upon the manufacturer of the metal roof system.

It has been observed that some designers are using a submittal process to design the metal roof system, especially in reroof situations. In such cases, the drawings are often limited to a Site Plan or Roof Plan. On the Roof Plan, dashed lines may be used to show where valleys, hips, ridges, rakes, eaves, ventilators, and rooftop equipment is to be located. Often no other drawings are produced by the designer.

The specification is a short form listing the performance requirements of the completed roof system. Requirements usually include wind uplift resistance of the system, type of coating finish on the metal panels, any warranty requirements of the completed system, and roof slope of the system.

The roof contractor, in conjunction with the material manufacturer, then submits drawings and specifications showing and listing the structural framing plan, attachment means and methods, flashing details, and other design and installation requirements of the roof system.

Since the structural framing plan is often an engineered system provided by the manufacturer, the designer sometimes saves consulting engineer fees. Since the standard details as published by the metal roof panel manufacturer are used in the submittal document, the designer is supposedly alleviated of this design burden.

We do not intend to imply that a submittal process is not required or should not be necessary with metal roof system design. It is often required since many details and requirements differ from one manufacturer to the next. However, by being so far out of the design loop, many professionals are probably heading for trouble. Knowledge and understanding of the roof products and systems by the designer are diminished with the submittal process as described.

In this scenario, the designer is adding little value to the project. In truth, a competent owner can perform the submittal function described. Perhaps the only reason for an owner to engage the services of a professional designer in such a case is to have available design liability of the professional in the event that problems arise in later years. Maybe we should ask whether we are selling our services or our design liability insurance?

Just because a manufacturer provides engineered drawing, and the contractor installs the systems to the material manufacturer's details and specifications, and a watertight warranty is provided by the material manufacturer to the owner, does not mean there will not be problems and perhaps failure with the roof system. Nor can a designer avoid all responsibility in such a case.

Metal roofing is not the magic cure for problems in the roof industry. Metal roofing is not simple to install. Metal roofing systems are not easier to design than other forms of commercial roof systems. There are special concerns and problems with metal roof systems not experienced with other forms of roof systems.

10.1.1 Design Fallacies and Misconceptions

Metal is the oldest form of roof material in existence if you include copper roofing, some of which is still functioning after being erected centuries ago. Metal roofing has been successfully used in the United States for over 100 years. This has led to perceptions and misconceptions concerning modern-day metal roof systems, which are very different from metal roof systems used in the past. In fact, modern metal roofing is a relatively new industry. Some people believe this form of roofing is the answer to all the problems that have plagued the roofing industry.

Many building owners, designers, facility managers, and contractors believe metal is the magic roof. This is due to the misconceptions that, since most of the metal roof system is preengineered, roof problems relating to design considerations are limited. Another misconception is that the standard details published by the metal roof panel manufacturer will be adequate to address situations occurring with the roof system. All manufacturers of roof materials (which are used to create total systems) publish standard details. This ranges from single-ply polymeric membrane manufacturers to built-up roof material manufacturers to composition shingle manufacturers. Any competent designer, owner, or manager realizes that these details are but a guide to be used in the design process.

Specification of work addressing metal roof panel system installation is often ambiguous, incomplete, or inadequate. Many people seem to feel that since most of the components used to create the metal roof system are premanufactured, installation of the components is simple and not a major concern within the project.

The possibility of bottom-side condensation on the metal roof panels is often ignored or improperly addressed. Such condensation is a major reason for the premature failure of metal roof systems. Any problems or failures relating to bottom-side condensation are not covered under warranty by metal roof system manufacturers. (See Secs. 10.2 through 10.2.2.)

Some people believe that all roof problems can be solved by a material manufacturer's warranty. A coating warranty is furnished by most metal roof panel manufacturers and can extend from 10 to 20 years. This type of warranty is usually referred to as a *nonperforation warranty.*

A weather-tightness warranty is also available from manufacturers, with time of coverage varying from 2 to 10 years and in some cases, 20 years. However, these warranties have many exclusions, as do most warranties issued by other roof material manufacturers. If you rely on a warranty to ensure a successful design and long-lived system, beware! (See Sec. 15.3.3.)

PREENGINEERED SYSTEM

Metal buildings can be successfully preengineered. This is because most of the components of the metal building system are supplied from one source and those which are not can be readily adapted to the metal and steel structure. Outside imput, above and beyond building structure engineering, is needed for site and soil investigation, geographic and climatic condition designs, and requirement specification pertaining to local building codes.

Skyscrapers, on the other hand, cannot be successfully preengineered. Most of the building components and systems will come from varied sources, and materials can completely differ one from the other. An architect is needed to blend the various materials together into a total building system.

Metal roof systems can be successfully preengineered if a simple metal roof system is being installed to a metal building facility under a new construction process. In such a case, the metal roof panels will be supplied from the same source as the structural framing and building envelope components. The roof system is but a part of a total preengineered package.

When we consider a reroof, roof retrofit, or design of a metal roof to a structure which is not being erected at the same time and supplied from the same manufacturing source, preengineering acceptability of the roof system is a fallacy.

For example, rake flashings up the gable ends of a nonmetallic building structure, such as block wall, may have to be specifically designed, fabricated, and installed to accommodate the building and the roof structure. In other instances, the various components supplied by metal building manufacturers or by metal building component suppliers can be extremely varied. The designer is needed to select and blend the various components together into one system. The roof system must then act and react correctly with the total building system.

A total system design concept is required. (See Sec. 2.1.) The designer must evaluate expected foot and equipment traffic across the roof surface in the years to come. A proper coating finish is then specified to resist such traffic. Dead loads and live loads must be anticipated and designed for, especially snow and wind loads.

Annual temperature extremes must be evaluated and designed for, especially in the flashing details. Expansion and contraction of metal panels and flashings is the major cause of roof leaks and one of the major reasons for system failures with metal roof systems.

With retrofit design, the material manufacturer seldom if ever engineers the attachment sequence, location, and procedures for the new roof framing to the existing structure. Also site and building specific, and seldom if ever addressed by the material manufacturer, are insulation or ventilation requirements for the new roof system.

STANDARD MANUFACTURER'S DETAILS

To produce a roof design which consistently uses the material manufacturer's standard details for all components and systems installation is probably going to create roof problems. Before we delve into this topic, we need to understand where metal roofing is, where it came from, and who participates within the industry.

Metal roofing has experienced a tremendous growth rate in the past decade. Being from the metal building industry, many metal roof suppliers, manufacturers, and often the contractors are still in a learning curve regarding metal roof systems as applied to structures other than preengineered metal buildings. Some manufacturers have done their homework and make a dedicated effort to test and evaluate their systems using both laboratory and rooftop experience. Some participate in educational seminars and roofing industry associations, serve on committees, etc. Unfortunately, some manufacturers do not, although the weak are being weeded out, with the strongest surviving.

Understanding and designing for the dynamic and kinetic forces involving many metal roof system detail areas is difficult for most of us. Being able to create a standard detail that successfully addresses these situations as they exist on every rooftop is impossible.

Also, it is important to realize that many metal roof system manufacturers began marketing their products on a regional level, not a national level. Details for flashing and attachment often address the region wherein the manufacturer first entered the marketplace. Therefore, standard details as published by the metal roof panel manufacturer may not be correct for the geographic area in which the system design is being used.

Detail and flashing areas are sometimes excluded from manufacturers' warranties as they pertain to watertightness. Problems arising from drainage and roof accessories are also normally excluded.

INSTALLATION OF THE COMPONENTS

Proper detailing and specification can limit problems relating to poor installation. Some people believe that since the majority of all metal roof system components are premanufactured, installation is simple and trouble free. The installation (workmanship) of roof systems, including metal roofing, will always be an area of great concern and of roof problems.

The metal roof industry is very diverse. Different manufacturers have different installation requirements for their materials and systems. Design and installation requirements also vary for water-shedding panels to water-barrier panels as well as structural panels as compared with nonstructural (architectural) panels.

Installation requirements are listed in the specification portion of the ConDocs. If in doubt as to all the items to list in order to achieve a proper installation, list what is not acceptable.

Realize that the commercial roof industry has been slow to get on board regarding metal roof systems. Many contractors have just recently begun to train workers in the craft of metal roof panel installation. We believe it will still take years for the industry to balance between the demand for the metal roof system and the supply of qualified workers.

This is not to imply that qualified personnel are not available within the application field. However, it is not unusual to find a crew of commercial membrane roof applicators installing a metal roof system. These people have been trained in and spent the majority of their work lives installing membrane roof systems. They understand waterproofing principles quite well, but lack a total understanding of metal roof material characteristics and requirements.

On the other hand, it is not unusual, and is in fact most common, to find a metal building erection crew installing metal roof systems. However, realize that these people are trained to install metal panel systems to preengineered buildings. They understand the principles and characteristics of metal panels quite well, but lack an understanding of roof forces and waterproofing requirements often required for nonstandard applications.

Composition shingles are premanufactured and yet there are sometimes leak problems with these systems. Single-ply membrane systems and modified bitumen roof systems are premanufactured, yet they are not free of installer-related problems. Do not believe that metal roof systems, just because they are of premanufactured components, are magic and somehow avoid problems that also affect other roof system types.

BOTTOM-SIDE CONDENSATION

As stated previously in this section, bottom-side condensation is a major concern with metal roof system design. Many new uses and applications for metal roof panels are being discovered. As of yet there is no uniform standard which can clearly be used to determine ventilation requirements of all types of metal roof system installation in all situations.

The many variables introduced when reroofing or retrofitting an existing facility can especially lead to inadequate bottom-side ventilation. This in turn causes condensation on the bottom of the metal roof panels, as well as on the structural steel members in contact with the panels. (See Sec. 10.2.)

Concerns of bottom-side condensation on the metal roof panels are greatest with a metal roof system installed over an existing roof deck or roof system. This configuration creates an attic space or plenum which entraps and holds air that is often warmer than outside air. Warm air holds more moisture than does cold air. (See Sec. 2.3.3.)

When the warm and moisture-laden air within the roof cavity contacts the cooler metal panel underside, moisture vapor is condensed from the warm air onto the cool metal panel. This can be prevented with air exchange within the cavity.

Replace the warm moist air with the cooler and drier air from the outside environment. The air must move across the metal roof panel underside in a continuous and complete wash. The recommended air exchange rate is a minimum of three times per hour, although many experts within this field are strongly advocating air exchange a minimum of five times per hour. However, even with air exchange of five times per hour, ventilation standard recommendations by such organizations as ASHREA and FHA may not be fully realized.

MANUFACTURERS' WARRANTIES

Several types of warranties are offered by metal roof manufacturers. However, as of yet, the available warranties with metal roof systems have not reached the levels or extents of coverage claimed by other commercial roof system manufacturers.

There are warranties available for material only, which are the most common. There are also warranties available for labor and material, referred to as *watertight warranties*. Often, a labor and material warranty is issued by the contractor. Some material manufacturers issue watertight warranties, with exclusions, for a fee.

Material warranties on components are probably more implied than expressed, which is usually to consumer advantage in case of litigation. Components used in the metal roof system include such items as the metal roof panel body, the clip fasteners, screws, and structural framing components.

One concern is the weathering components of the metal roof system, mainly being the coating finish on the metal panel. Manufacturer warranties can extend from 2 to 20 years on the finish, while some finishes for roof panels are not expressly warranted at all.

Be aware that often a coat finish warranty does not guarantee the finish to stay as new, but instead warrants certain limits of failure the finish will not exceed. Metal panel manufacturers can list the extent of acceptable degradation the finish coat can achieve under warranty time and terms.

This limit of degradation sometimes extends to what is termed a *nonperforation warranty*. It covers leakage due to the panel rusting completely through (from the top side). Failed panels are often replaced under a prorated system, based upon warranty coverage time. Manufacturers' liability is limited to prorated panel costs which may or may not include such items as delivery costs to the job site.

Metal panels can also be warranted for characteristics of the coating at the time of manufacture and the resistances created by the characteristics. Chalk, fade, adhesion, blistering, and impact resistance are some of the main characteristics normally referenced in a warranty. (See Sec. 14.2.8.)

If, during the warranty coverage time, the finish degradation exceeds these limits, the manufacturer is under obligation to correct deficiencies under the means and terms of the warranty. This correction is often limited to cost per square foot, material only, or by means and methods which are totally at the manufacturer's discretion.

Finish-coat warranties are voided if installed in corrosive environments (aggressive atmospheres as caused by contamination or containment of salt spray, chemical fumes, etc.). Finish-coat warranties are also voided in the event of "excessive" foot and equipment traffic or applicator error or misuse during installation.

For a designer to assume that manufacturers' warranties will address problems of an inadequately thought-out and designed roof system resulting in leakage, rusting, paint peel, fading, etc., is a frequent misconception.

NOISE

Within the last several years we have learned of several metal roof applications where the system is unacceptable due to noise generated by the metal roof panels. The noise is a result of long and continuous panels moving due to expansion and contraction within the fixed concealed clip fastener or which results as the panel bottoms move over some substrates, such as plastic foam insulation board. A loud popping noise is produced as the panels expand and contract.

In cases where the panels bind within the clip fastener, the noise is usually a result of the clip fastener attempting to hold the panel stationary. This adverse situation between clip and panel can be the result of the clip being improperly installed, either out of line with the panel side laps or overdriven into insulated steel roof decks. However, these types of noise-related problems can often be avoided by proper specification and design of both metal panels and concealed clips.

Many metal panel manufacturers offer two types of clips to be used to secure the panel to the roof structure. One is termed a *fixed clip* and the other is a *movable,* or *floating, clip*. The floating clip is two-pieced and allows for additional movement of the clip with the panel. Good design practice often requires specifying the floating-clip assembly, especially if long and continuous panel runs are being designed. (See Figs. 10.4 and 10.5.)

Noise generated by friction as the panel body expands and contracts on top of roof insulation can be easily solved by design. One solution is to use a slip sheet of red rosin paper applied between the insulation layer and metal roof panel system. The metal panel will slide across the slip sheet with little resulting friction and noise. Another solution may be available by specifying a high-floating clip as compared to low-fixed-clip assemblies. The high-profile clip elevates the metal roof panel system above the insulation layer. With some nonstructural metal roof panel systems, this design may not be an option.

Designers must remember that the longer the metal roof panel, the greater the area of movement due to expansion and contraction. A 100-ft-long panel will expand to greater length and contract to lesser length than will a 10-ft-long panel. Many owners and designers require a continuous panel with no lap seams. On long roof runs this can create additional design concerns due to the extent of movement which will occur during thermal cycles. It often is better design practice to eliminate long continuous-run panel lengths and instead use transverse lap seams.

10.2 METAL ROOF CONDENSATE CONTROL

GENERAL

Condensation occurs on material surfaces as a function of dew-point temperature being reached. Moisture

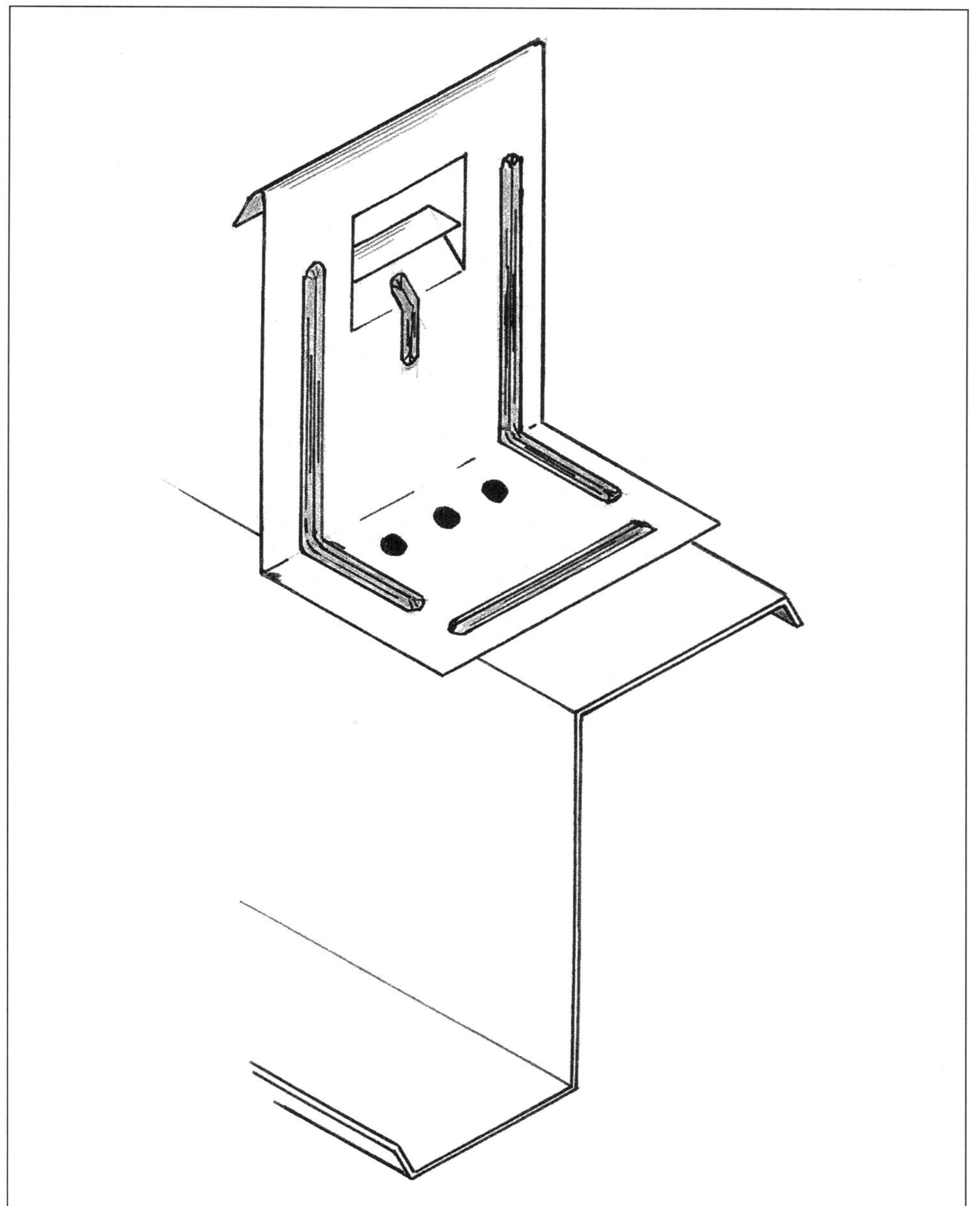

Figure 10.4 Fixed clip.

vapor in warm air (attic/plenum air) will turn to a liquid when coming into contact with a cool surface (bottom of metal roof panels).

Metal panels, as well as all other materials, absorb and then reradiate heat energy. *Infrared emittance* or *emissivity* is the term used to describe the reradiation. The more emissivity a material has, the more energy it will radiate.

On cool, clear nights the emissivity of a metal roof panel is the greatest. As temperatures drop the lowest just before dawn, the panels may be as much as 20°F below outside ambient temperatures.

The panels are cooler than other components within the attic/plenum, further accentuated because of emissivity. (See Sec. 2.3.3.) The warmer and more humid air within the attic contacts the cool metal panel and the moisture vapor within the air is released as a liquid, gathering on the bottom side of the cooler metal panel.

When moisture condenses on the underside of the metal roof panel system, the condensate is often trapped between the metal roof panel and the purlin which supports the panels. (See Fig. 10.6.) This entrapped moisture, often present for extended periods of

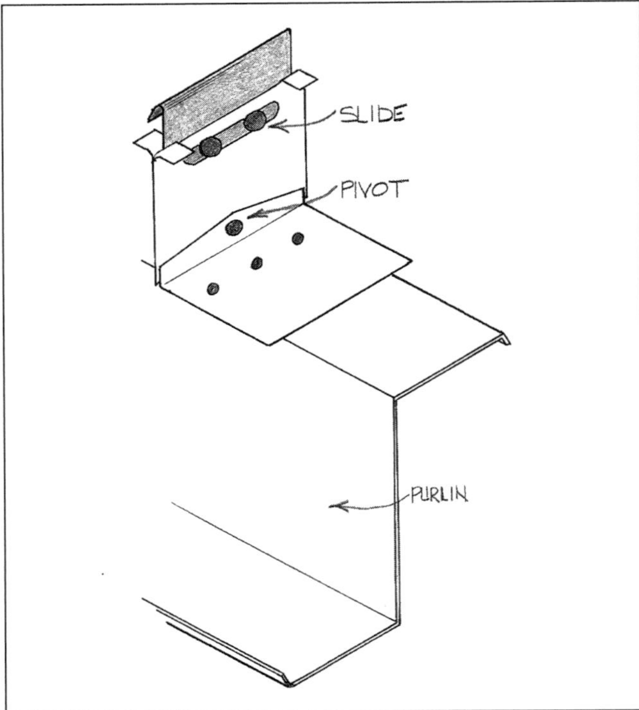

Figure 10.5 Floating clip.

time, can cause premature roof failure. It can be prevented in accordance with Sec. 10.2.2.

When metal panels sweat on the underside there develops a strong possibility that they will rust through from the bottom side. No relief is available from the material manufacturer since warranty excludes coverage due to perforations occurring from the bottom side of the panels.

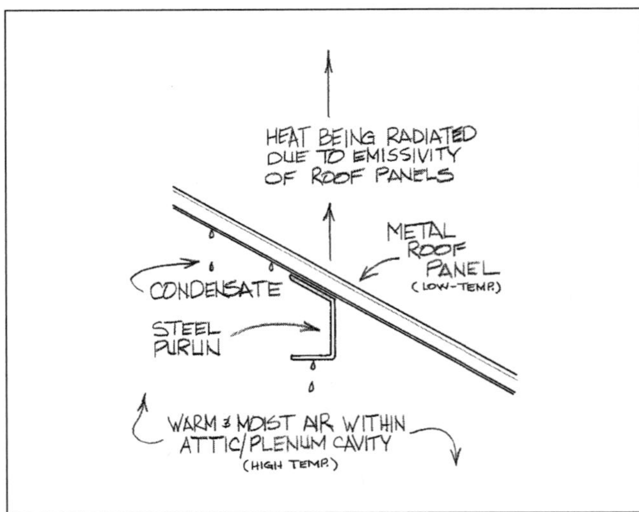

Figure 10.6 Bottom-side condensate conditions.

VENTILATION

By replacing the warm, moist air of the attic cavity with outside air flowing in a continuous wash across the bottom of the roof deck or the metal panel underside, dewpoint temperature at the air and metal interface will not be reached. (See Sec. 2.3.3.) The American Society of Heating, Refrigeration and Air Conditioning Engineers (ASHRAE) Fundamentals Handbook or the Federal Housing Administration Minimum Property Standards are the documents and standards normally referenced by building codes for ventilation and humidity control of an attic cavity.

Chapters 20 and 21 of the ASHRAE Fundamentals Handbook address humidity control, and therefore condensation problems, within an attic cavity. ASHRAE suggests the problem is best controlled, not with ventilation alone, but by vapor retarders and building design which restricts and directs vapor drive. This is probably the best solution, and reduces the many problems, variables, and unknowns of ventilation design discussed later in this section. However, in the real world, such complete control by a vapor retardant of this powerful force is often not practical or possible.

"Loose construction" of a building allows infiltration and passage of air from and to many locations within the building envelope. In the past, this loose construction allowed metal roof systems to breathe, or ventilate, without excessive condensate concerns.

As an example, picture the rustic house situated far into the woods or hills. Perhaps your great-grandmother or great-uncle lived in such at the turn of the century. These houses were often built of rough-sawn lumber plank siding, with little or no insulation, no vapor retarder material, no air-conditioning, and a corrugated metal roof usually installed on wood lath, all of which was exposed to the interior of the house. This loose construction allowed the entire house to breathe, and any minor condensate occurring on the bottom of the metal panels was of little concern.

Today we use tighter construction methods. With metal roof design, especially roof retrofit design, we often entrap moisture within the attic cavity, which requires ventilation design for removal.

VAPOR RETARDERS

Metal roof systems often use the principles of vapor retarders in conjunction with ventilation. Many metal roof systems exposed to the building interior use a vapor retarder which covers a fiberglass blanket insulation. The fiberglass insulation batt is installed directly under and next to the metal roof panel with the exposed underside of the insulation often covered by a vapor-retardant sheet—often vinyl. Building occupants receive the benefits of a brighter building interior due to the white reflective nature of the vapor retarder, which is the exposed interior finish of the metal roof system.

The lap edges of the vapor retarder seldom retard dynamic moisture movement. The methods used to join the lap edges vary, but often one sheet edge is rolled with the adjoining sheet edge and then stapled together. In theory we know that vapor drive can force humid air through this loose connecting joint of the vapor retarder. Therefore, in theory, this vapor retarder should not be totally effective. However, in practical applications, the design works quite well. During research on this topic we could not find any major metal roof manufacturer reporting condensation problems when an insulated vapor retarder was installed to an exposed building interior area.

The explanation offered by one technician was that apparently air movements through the large building area under the metal roof system must be adequate to allow required ventilation. Since this design is usually for metal building systems, ventilation can be related back to the loose construction of the building envelope.

Overhead doors in warehouse or bay areas of the building, rake and eave trim flashings, as well as roof ridge vents usually installed atop metal buildings apparently provide enough air intake and exhaust to prevent condensation on the underside of the metal panels. Additionally, even though the vapor retarder is not airtight, it apparently functions well enough to restrict harmful amounts of humid air from the metal roof panel underside.

For a vapor retarder to become a vapor barrier there must be no penetration of the barrier. In the application as described above, even if all side laps could be sealed airtight, the fastener assembly used to attach the metal roof panel to the purlin would penetrate the barrier.

Another important consideration, as shown in Fig. 10.7, and only in recent years being addressed by the industry as a whole, is thermal bridging of the purlin and metal roof panel. The insulation blanket is compressed where it crosses the purlin. This renders it ineffective as a thermal insulation at that location.

The metal purlin exists in the warm humid space of the building interior. Without a thermal block, it will be supercooled by the thermal bridge of the cool roof panel transferring the temperatures through the compressed and ineffective fiberglass insulation blanket. In such a case, the purlin often begins to sweat as the moisture in the warm air condenses on the cool surface of the purlin.

This reaction can be eliminated by the use of thermal blocks when such insulation and vapor retarding design is required. (See Fig. 10.8.) Available through most suppliers of metal roof systems, the thermal blocks are inexpensive and easy to install. However, the thermal blocks are not available for all types of roof panel style and configuration.

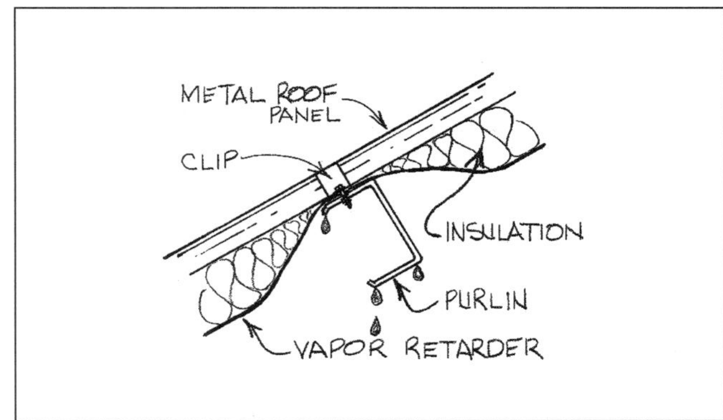

Figure 10.7 Compressed insulation at purlin.

Many metal roof systems are not exposed to the building interior. They are instead part of an attic or plenum area. This attic/plenum area is created by the metal roof and a ceiling system, an attic floor, or an existing roof membrane system which is left in place and covered with the new metal roof system.

This type of metal roof system design does not place insulation next to the metal roof panels. Instead, insulation is normally placed atop the attic/plenum floor or ceiling system. Any vapor retarder system required is normally installed at the attic floor or ceiling level and below the insulation layer.

It is usually recommended to use a vapor retarder with a metal roof system. Proper ventilation design is sometimes not possible, due to roof size, slope, or configuration, and inability to incorporate an effective ventilation design for the attic/plenum cavity requires a vapor retarder.

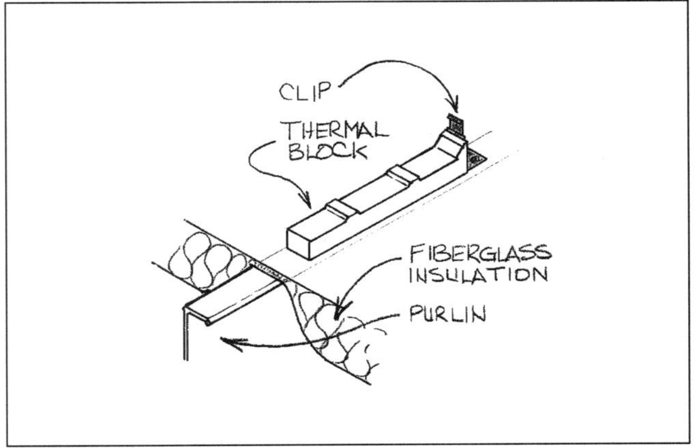

Figure 10.8 Thermal block.

The vapor retarder must be airtight. The design should address all locations where the vapor retarder sheet will be penetrated by piping, wire, or other items which lead from the building interior through the retarder layer and into the attic cavity. Also of concern should be the edge of the retarder sheet where it is lapped and joined together and where it terminates into or at a building wall.

However, with metal roof retrofit design there is normally no vapor retarder installed. The existing roof membrane (being retrofitted over) may possibly serve as such, if it is not split or ruptured, or if all splits, tears, and ruptures are repaired prior to covering over with the new metal roof system. However, an airtight membrane is usually a watertight membrane, therefore, such roof repair would often be extensive, expensive, and impractical.

10.2.1 Ventilation Standards

Studies and research projects concerning ventilation requirements have been extensive. Some people have devoted their working lives to the study of ventilation and, by their own admission, still encounter situations where the best solution to the problem is not practical and/or possible.

Any ventilation standard, requirement, or practice guide must involve air exchange within the attic/plenum cavity. This can be accomplished only by intake and exhaust of air from the cavity.

Intake and exhaust of air, a simple statement, becomes a complex process. To understand how to determine ventilation system requirements for a building, and specifically a metal roof system, we must first understand why ventilation system requirements can be different for each building and roof system.

Note: Some design requires ventilation mainly to address condensation control which is usually most pronounced in winter months, while other design is more concerned with energy savings, being the reduction of attic/plenum temperatures during the summer months. For most parts of the country, a ventilation system designed to provide cooling of the attic cavity during summer months will more than adequately provide proper condensation control during the winter months. However, ventilation design which can control condensation during the winter is often far less than what is required to provide adequate cooling within the attic cavity during hot summer months.

CONSIDERATIONS

Some of the major factors influencing the amount of roof ventilation required per building are:

- Geographic location of the building which dictates mean low and high wind speeds, temperature extremes, and therefore the thermal loading of the roof covering and attic cavity, which in turn can influence vapor pressure and humidity levels within the attic cavity
- Humidity levels to be expected within the attic cavity, either due to vapor drive from the building interior or from humidity created by components encapsulated within the attic cavity during construction (such as damp roof insulation and roof membrane covered by a metal roof retrofit system)
- Location of the vents, which sometimes require less-than-optimum placement
- Other factors such as slope of the roof deck or roof system and obstructions within the attic cavity which may hinder air flow

Geographic Location. Geographic location dictates average annual sustained wind speeds. The stronger the wind (the faster the wind speed), the greater will be the pressure created at vent openings. Therefore less net free vent space area of the total ventilation system is required in areas with greater wind speed than in areas with lower wind speed. Net free vent space area is not the size of the vent assembly, but is instead the amount of unobstructed opening provided by the vent.

The specific location of the building must also be analyzed. If the structure is surrounded by buildings, trees, or other structures which prevent or hinder wind flow, the influence of wind and pressure areas created by wind will be affected.

Geographic location also dictates the climatic conditions within which the building, roof structure, and ventilation system must exist and function. Cold winter days with heated building interiors as well as hot humid days with cool, clear nights will create maximum condensation opportunities within an improperly vented attic cavity. Thermal loading of the metal roof panels and attic cavity, and the humidity levels of the exterior environment are determined by the geographic location of the building.

Humidity Levels. Vapor pressure and vapor drive are a function of humidity levels and temperature extremes. The ventilation system must be designed so that it is adequate to remove humid air from within the attic cavity before it can condense.

Low humidity levels within the air cavity, combined with moderate temperature differentials between the cavity and the external environment, will require a minimal amount of air exhaust flow from the cavity area. On the other hand, high humidity levels and severe temperature extremes will require more intake and exhaust from the attic/plenum area.

Another important fact which designers must realize, but often ignore, is the amount of latent moisture that is entrapped within an attic cavity when a metal roof is retrofitted over an existing low-sloped membrane roof system. Such a reroof design process seldom investigates accurately or completely the amount of wet roof material existing.

If the existing roof system wasn't leaking, it probably would not be in the process of being replaced. In metal roof retrofit design, the new structural support system and metal roof panel system is installed directly over, to, and through the left-in-place roof membrane and any rigid roof insulation layers. Previous roof leaks will usually have caused moisture to be entrapped within the existing roof system.

When this existing system is encapsulated within the new metal roof system attic/plenum cavity, the moisture can create exceptionally high humidity levels within the cavity. In such a case, complete ventilation of the cavity is required.

Ventilation Component Placement. As fully discussed in Sec. 10.2.2, intake and exhaust vent locations are critical in achieving proper and complete ventilation of the roof cavity. It is also stated that optimum placement is sometimes not possible or practical.

To achieve optimum ventilation, 50 percent of the vent area must be located in a negative pressure area and the other 50 percent of the vent area must be located within a positive pressure area of the building structure, providing a *balanced* ventilation system. (See Sec. 10.2.2.) Air flow must wash across the entire underside of the roof deck, leaving no dead air spaces.

However, in metal roof system design, we often cannot provide intake vents of the correct size (net free vent area) in the proper location (continuous at the eave/soffit). Sometimes there is no eave or soffit with a metal roof system. Additionally, gutter or fascia flashings are normally used at the eaves where the intake vents could possibly be located, thereby blocking or restricting any vent area at that location. *Vent area is measured in net free space of the vent cover through which air can pass, not the size of the vent component itself or the opening into which the component is installed.*

Roof Slope. The lower the slope of the roof system, the more difficult it becomes to maintain proper air flow within the roof cavity. Common sense tells us that it is harder to move air under a dead-level flat surface than it is to move air under a steeply pitched surface. Steep slopes allow convection forces of heated air to assist with upward air movements.

Metal roof systems are often designed with a low slope. This often crowds the available air space within the cavity due to purlins, air duct and equipment, insulation layers, etc. Complete air flow through the cavity as required can be hindered by such obstructions.

To help offset the negative effects of low roof slope and crowded attic/plenum areas, we often select for use power ventilation equipment. Power ventilation leads to other concerns.

Being thermostatically controlled, power ventilation equipment sometimes will not function when needed for air exchange. The air exchange is needed, not for temperatures reached within the cavity, but for moisture content of the attic cavity air and temperature of the metal roof panel. Also, anything mechanical is subject to failure and requires maintenance service. If the equipment ceases to function, will the maintenance personnel know it?

Also, as demonstrated in Sec. 10.2.2, power ventilation is not effective ventilation design. Air flow across the entire underside of the roof system will not be achieved with power ventilating fan equipment. (See Fig. 10.15.)

GENERAL REQUIREMENTS FOR VENTILATION

Outside air must be taken into the roof cavity, where it flows across the underside of the roof and is expelled at the highest point of the roof structure. Correctly designed, the intake air will flow on the underside of the roof deck, continuous across the roof structure.

Many metal roof system designs do not provide for this continuous wash of air across the underside of the roof deck. Some designs cannot provide for such; some could, but do not. Some metal roof systems will exist trouble free regardless of inadequate design; some will not.

If proper and continuous ventilation is so important, then why do some metal roof systems without such correct ventilation design exist free from condensation problems? A nationally recognized ventilation expert's reply was that "a little ventilation, in the correct area, goes a long way. Loose construction, although perhaps unintentional in the original design, but incorporated into the final work, can provide adequate ventilation in certain geographic areas and climates." This may be an adequate explanation but not an adequate design procedure. Instead, we need to understand current standards, requirements, and recommendations for attic/plenum cavity areas.

The following information within this section discusses air-exchange rates recommended for the attic/plenum cavity. Once the rate of exchange has been determined, proper design of the ventilation system is essential in achieving the design rate of air flow. Therefore Sec. 10.2.2, which discusses such design requirements, is fundamentally linked to this section.

We shall consider the two basic ways in which ventilation requirements of metal roof systems are determined. One consideration is for ventilation to control condensation within the roof cavity. Another consideration is for ventilation to control heat build-up within the roof cavity during summer months, thereby reducing cooling costs. It is generally suggested that proper design to provide optimum cooling ventilation will also provide adequate condensation control ventilation.

DESIGN REQUIREMENTS FOR CONDENSATION CONTROL

A ventilation design practice normally used within the metal roofing industry is exchange of the total air volume within the attic cavity of three times per hour, minimum. For metal roof retrofit design, where an existing roof membrane is being roofed over by the new metal roof system, it is recommended that air exchange within the cavity be increased to five times per hour. Many experts think that air changes of five times per hour are required in such situations due to the possibility of encapsulated moist materials which could exist within the existing roof system being covered by the new metal roof system.

Retrofit Ventilation. There is no air exchange standard which directly addresses all the variables involved with a metal roof retrofit system—and probably never will be. The biggest unknown is the amount of latent moisture which can be released from the left-in-place roof system. Excessive moisture within the newly created attic/plenum cavity will require excessive ventilation.

Also of importance is air movement through the cavity. Often C-channels and Z-channels installed for support of the metal roof can block air passage.

With such metal roof retrofit design (see Fig. 10.9), care should be taken to ensure that maximum and correct air flow through the attic/plenum cavity is achieved. Again, as a minimum, enough air should be exhausted from the cavity to equal three air changes per hour, with five changes per hour recommended.

This recommendation will only address condensation problems and have little effect in controlling energy savings during cooling periods. With both retrofit design and new construction design which creates an attic cavity, insulation is placed at the attic/plenum floor or ceiling level. The metal panels normally are not insulated.

The air flow should be continuous across the underside of the metal roof panels. The ventilation system should be balanced, using positive and negative pressure areas of the building. Section 10.2.2 addresses design considerations and problems of metal roof and roof retrofit design.

Targeting air changes of five times per hour should nullify entrapped moisture which can be within the roof membrane and insulation layers of the low-sloped roof

Figure 10.9 Roof retrofit. (*Courtesy of MBCI, Houston, Tx.*)

system which was retrofitted. With such moisture, the air cavity will be subjected to higher humidity levels than would normally be expected if such moist material were not present within the cavity.

Clearly understand that the designer must investigate the condition of a membrane and insulation assembly before retrofitting with a metal roof system. Industry standards prohibit wet roof insulation, which can retain large amounts of water, from being enclosed within a metal roof system. (See Sec. 13.1.3.)

Metal roof retrofit creates the most difficult ventilation design processes and decisions. Retrofit design requires adapting a metal roof system to a building structure not originally designed for a metal roof system. The ventilation system must then be fitted into the metal roof system which was fitted, by design, to often unusual situations created by the building structure.

Metal Roof Cavity Ventilation. Usually less difficult than with retrofit design, air cavities created by a metal roof system designed as original to the building normally require air exchange within the cavity of three times per hour, minimum, to control condensation. Design is less difficult since vent areas at the eaves and ridge can be designed and installed economically and efficiently. (See Sec. 10.2.2.) Also, obstructions within the cavity can be limited to provide and allow for complete air flow across the bottom of the metal roof panels.

Humidity levels to be expected within the attic cavity are easier to determine than with a retrofit design. Also, potentially damp materials are not being enclosed within the cavity. Humidity levels within the cavity, caused by vapor drive from the building interior, can be controlled to some extent by vapor retarders placed at ceiling level.

Recommendations within the ASHRAE Fundamentals Handbook can be referenced for vapor retarder design requirements. However, we recommend that such vapor retarder design be supplemented with attic cavity ventilation.

The essential design elements for creating an effective ventilation system which will control condensation within an attic cavity must be followed. For either metal roof retrofit design or new construction metal roof cavity design, the air exchange through the cavity should be continuous across the underside of the metal roof panels. This is best accomplished the majority of the time by ventilation design per Sec. 10.2.2.

DESIGN REQUIREMENTS FOR COOLING-COST CONTROL

It is accepted practice to design a ventilation system which addresses cooling of the attic cavity during hot summer periods. Such ventilation will usually be adequate to provide acceptable ventilation during cold winter months when condensation possibilities are greatest.

Ventilating for cooling-cost savings instead of condensation control is important, even when fiberglass batt insulation is installed to the top of an existing retrofit roof surface, ceiling panels, or attic floor. The thicker the blanket insulation system, the more important proper ventilation is in controlling energy savings during hot summer periods.

The insulation will become heated during the day. During the night, without proper ventilation of the attic cavity, all the heat will not dissipate from the insulation. During the next day, additional heat is absorbed by the insulation layer. This cycle will continue and place unnecessary demands on the HVAC system cooling the building interior.

The entrapped heat is radiated from the insulation, both upward toward the attic cavity and down toward the building interior. The occupants of the building may feel warmer than the actual air temperature within the building because of the radiated heat. The thicker the blanket insulation layer is, the more heat it can store and radiate to the building interior. Proper ventilation design can prevent the insulation from becoming a heat sink.

Building code ventilation requirements may vary for different areas of the country, and design may require more or less ventilation per roof structure depending upon job-specific requirements. Usually, as a minimum, we should try to provide a ratio of net free vent area to attic floor space of 1:300. This almost always exceeds the minimum requirement of air exchange within the attic/plenum cavity of three times per hour, as discussed above.

This minimum requirement is effective only if the ventilation system is balanced, per Sec. 10.2.2. At least 50 percent of the net free vent area must exist within a positive pressure area, and 50 percent must exist within a negative pressure area.

Net free vent area is used to described the square inches of unobstructed vent opening through which air can pass. Wire-screen or slotted vent coverings mechanically restrict air flow through the vent openings. Therefore, the net free area of a slotted soffit vent cover which may be 6 in wide by 18 in long, having a total area of 108 in^2, may have a net free area of only 60 in^2.

Even if proper ventilation design principles of net free vent area and proper vent location placement are followed, inadequate ventilation for cooling-cost control can result with the aforementioned minimum requirement of 1:300.

Wind direction, wind speed, maximum thermal loading and maximum thermal cooling of the roof covering, humidity levels without and within the building, and especially vent performance are all factors influencing air movement requirements and performance.

Some experts within the ventilation industry have advocated a ventilation ratio of 1:96 instead of 1:300. This correlates to 1 ft^2 of net free vent area per every 96 ft^2 of ceiling area. This usually correlates to 1.5 ft^3/min (cfm) of air exhaust from the attic cavity per 1 ft^2 of ceiling area under optimum conditions.

This may be the very best requirement for attic ventilation. Such cfm air exhaust from an attic/plenum cavity will indeed result in the maximum cooling of the cavity during the summer as well as provide maximum moisture removal during cool and cold periods.

Research conducted by universities and private industry has shown that increasing attic ventilation exhaust from 0.3 cfm to 1.5 cfm/ft^2 of ceiling area decreased the heat gain through the ceiling of a 1000-ft^2 house by 16,000 Btu during an average cooling day.

However, this ventilation requirement is often not practical to obtain with natural ventilation system design. Natural ventilation is that which utilizes no power-mechanized equipment or wind-turbine vent louvers, which spin with wind force and extract air from the cavity.

A building 20 ft wide by 50 ft long, with a gable ridge 5 ft high will have 2500 ft^3 within the attic cavity. An exhaust rate of 1.5 cfm per 1 ft^2 of ceiling area results in a total air exhaust from the attic cavity of 90,000 cfh. (See Fig. 10.10.) This results in an air change within the attic cavity 36 times per hour. Although this ventilation system can be designed on some residential structures, it is not practical and often not possible on commercial building structures. Once the width of the building exceeds 50 ft, the mechanics of ventilation and effectiveness decrease rapidly.

Additionally, this requirement can only be achieved with ventilation systems of the correct size (net free vent space area) installed at the correct locations (soffit and ridge) in the proper amounts (continuous at both locations). (See Sec. 10.2.2.) Commercial metal roof system and building configuration often do not allow for such design.

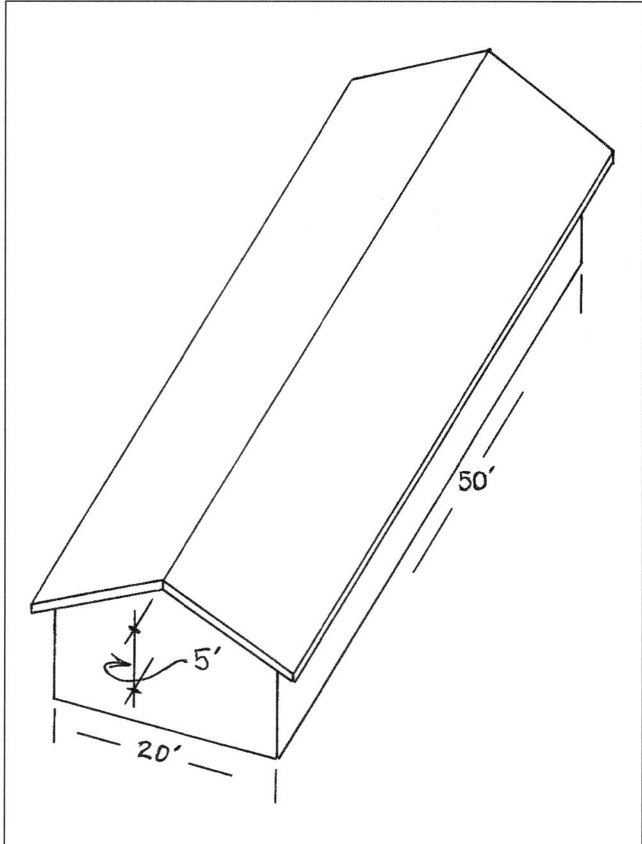

Figure 10.10 Attic plan with 2500 ft^3.

HIGH-HUMIDITY BUILDING INTERIORS

Accelerated ventilation cycles per hour must be used for high-occupancy buildings or for situations where unusual vapor pressure is being created within the building interior. The excessive moisture-laden air will drive from the building interior toward the metal roof in an effort to escape into the less humid environment. When the moist air contacts the cooler metal panel underside, condensation will probably occur. (See Sec. 2.3.3.)

10.2.2 Ventilation Design

Research has shown that ventilation of the attic/plenum cavity is best accomplished by using natural convection and wind forces which create positive and negative pressure areas. Intake at the eaves and exhaust at the ridge is the optimum design. Power roof ventilators and ventilators which spin by wind force and exhaust air are ineffective in achieving the maximum ventilation required for cooling and condensation control.

With optimum ventilation design, the intake area is continuous at the eaves or soffit and the exhaust area is continuous at the ridge. The net free intake area, per eave, should be the same as the net free exhaust area at the ridge.

This design will allow for all of the deck underside to be vented by fresh outside air. Briefly stated, in order to achieve the ventilation required for *maximum* savings regarding cooling costs of the building interior, and therefore *maximum* condensate control ventilation, air flow through the exhaust should equal 1.5 cfm per square foot of attic floor/roof deck area.

This maximum rate of air flow is often impossible to achieve outside of residential housing design. When a building exceeds 50 ft in width, the effective mechanics of ventilation design dramatically decrease.

To achieve maximum effectiveness of air exchange rate the designer should use two natural forces: wind pressure and thermal effect. Wind pressure is caused by even slight wind striking the building structure. Thermal effect is caused by differences in temperatures experienced within the attic cavity. Hot air rises and cold air falls.

Thermal effect is only a small factor in ventilation design. Air has mass, and once air is in motion it has a tendency to stay in motion unless otherwise affected. Air mass will not move in the proper direction in sufficient quantities without correct intake and exhaust design. With correct ventilation design, the air mass will be moved by wind pressure resulting from negative and positive areas created by the placement of the vent systems.

Wind pressure has a much more powerful effect than does heat convection of air. In fact, hot air can be easily forced to flow down toward the cooler areas of an air cavity due to negative and positive pressure areas occurring at vent openings on the structure.

DESIGN THEORY—WIND PRESSURE

Wind, when striking a structure, flows around the structure. This flowing causes areas of positive and negative pressure. Being the same Venturi principle as used with airwings, the designer can use this force to create air movements and ventilation within the roof cavity.

Different areas of positive and negative pressure will be created around the building structure, depending upon the direction of the wind. As wind direction changes, the positive and negative pressure areas move. It is therefore ineffective to design a ventilation system based upon prevailing winds. The prevailing wind direction can shift as much as 20 to 30° within seconds, and continue to shift for extended periods of time. As the wind changes direction, even slightly, the pressure at vent openings changes. In some cases, this causes an exhaust vent to become an intake, or vice versa. Figure 10.11 demonstrates the basic principle of natural ventilation design. Air will always move from a positive pressure area to a negative pressure area. Because of this principle, air has been documented as moving through one part of a vent and exhausting through another part of the same vent.

In a study begun in 1961 and continuing through 1975, air movements within attic cavities were closely monitored and analyzed. The study, in conjunction with extensive research conducted at the University of Illinois, resulted in a better understanding of venting requirements, venting products, and air movements due to thermal and pressure effects.

The research project analyzed the four major types of venting systems used for attic/plenum spaces:

- Soffit venting
- Roof louver venting

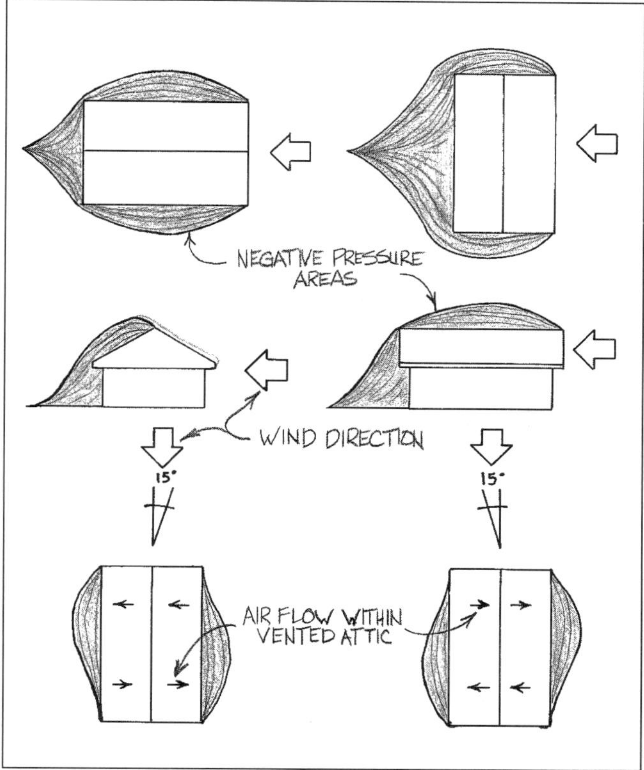

Figure 10.11 Pressure areas of buildings in windstream.

- Gable-end venting
- Ridge venting

Since the study demonstrates air movements in relation to vent types and locations very well, we list a brief summation of the findings as follows.

LOUVERS

Figure 10.12 shows that roof louvers alone are totally ineffective in removing heat from an attic space or in the removal of moisture-laden air. Air movement is limited directly between and below the louver vents. Air movement with such design results from opposing pressures at different louvers or from air infiltration into the attic space as a result of loose construction. No air movement results from thermal effect as many would believe.

SOFFITS

Figure 10.13 shows air movement within a roof cavity with soffit vents to be minimal. Most movement occurs across the lower attic cavity regions. When wind direction is exactly parallel to the ridge, in accordance with positive and negative pressure areas, wind will enter the soffit vents on the downwind end of the building. At the upwind end of the building air from the roof cavity exits

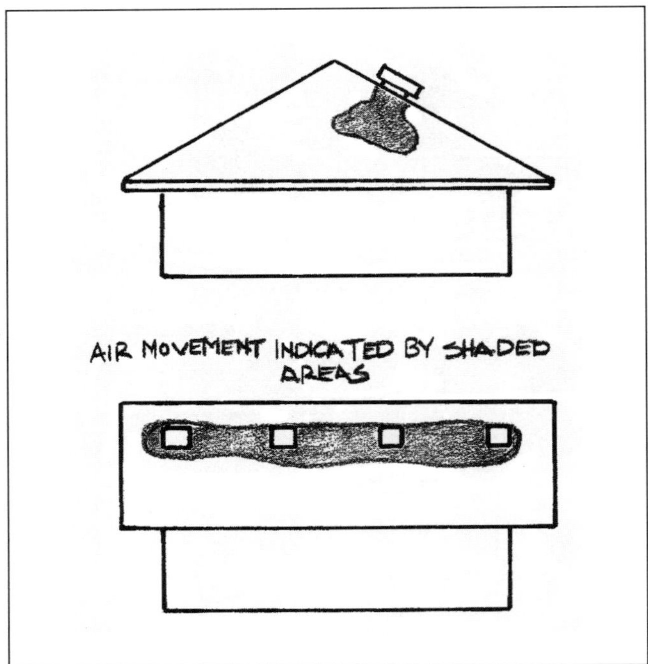

Figure 10.12 Roof louver venting.

the soffit vents. Air will always flow from positive to negative areas. Figure 10.11 also demonstrates this principle, although the air stream is not striking the building exactly parallel to the ridge.

GABLES

With an attic cavity vented only by gable louvers, effective ventilation cannot be achieved. When wind is parallel to the ridge, as shown in Fig. 10.14, the wind movement occurs mainly across the deck areas. Removing moisture-laden air from under metal roof panels will not be achieved, possibly resulting in condensation. When wind direction is perpendicular to the ridge, both positive and negative pressure is created at different locations across the louver face. The louver is acting as an intake and exhaust at the same time. Air movement is limited to the gable-end areas of the structure.

Each of these ventilation designs above does little to prevent excessive heat build-up within attic cavities. Combination of these systems, as shown in the following sections, still cannot produce the required ventilation effects.

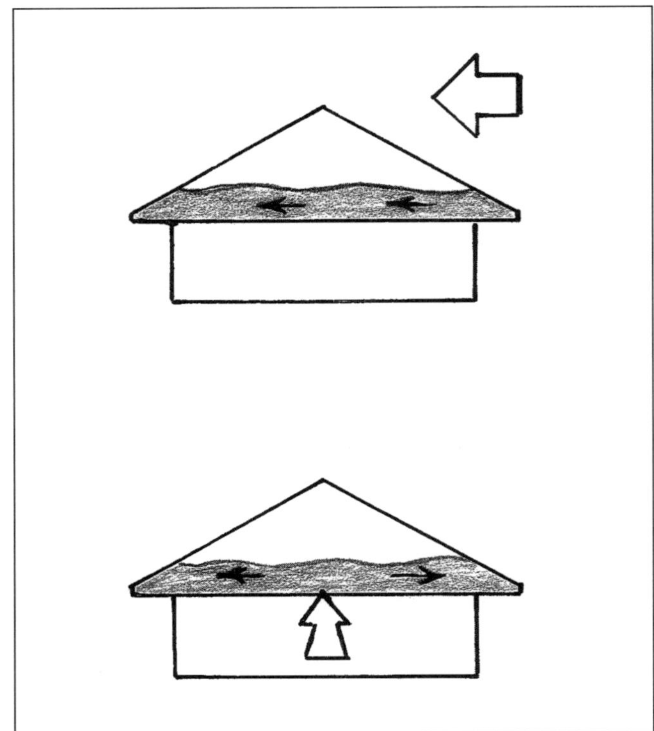

Figure 10.13 Soffit venting.

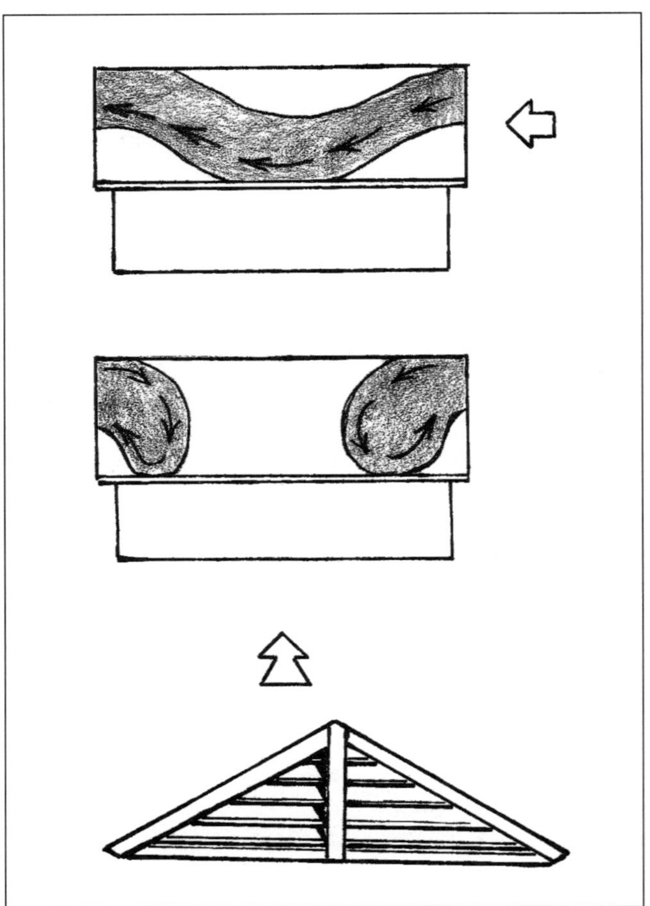

Figure 10.14 Gable louver venting.

COMBINATION VENT DESIGNS

Louver and Soffit. Roof louvers with soffit venting would seem to provide what many of us have considered adequate attic cavity ventilation. Air can enter at a low roof area and be expelled from a high roof area, with the assumption that air movement will be caused by the force of convection (hot air rises). As illustrated in Fig. 10.15, this design is inadequate.

It is impractical to install enough roof louvers to provide adequate air exchange, at the proper locations required, to prevent excessive heat build-up within the roof cavity. Instead, it has been found that air movement is confined to small areas near the louvers and to the area above the attic floor as shown. Air moving across the attic deck does not significantly reduce heat radiated down into the building interior.

With such design, the majority of hot air does not leave the attic cavity, but instead becomes a large mass of hot air stagnated within the cavity. The hot air area is of such magnitude, with enough latent heat, to radiate heat through the deck or ceiling and insulation layers covering such.

Moving currents of air across a deck or ceiling are proven to have little effect on cooling costs when such heat radiation is present. However, if the deck or ceiling is insulated, a ratio between insulation R-value and volume of moving air can be calculated to achieve heat removal from the insulation by the moving air current. This will be effective only if the insulation is thick enough and air flow is constant across the insulation layers.

In such a case, the heat being radiated by the air space to the insulation layer will be restricted and somewhat absorbed by the insulation layer. The cooler air moving across the insulation surface will remove the heat from the insulation layers. However, such design will have little effect on condensation control within the attic cavity.

Gable and Soffit. This design also utilizes high and low vent areas, and also is ineffective. In regard to cooling, this combination design is no more effective per square foot of vent area than gable venting alone or soffit venting alone. (See Fig. 10.16.)

Regarding moisture-condensate control, the effective cfm exhaust per square foot of vent area is usually less for this combination than for either type of the previously discussed vents used alone. Maximum ventilation is achieved by this combination design only when wind direction is parallel to the ridge. In such a case, the combination increases air flow by as much as 50 percent. However, since air is still stagnated at the roof deck in many areas, condensation can still occur.

Ridge and Soffit. A ridge and soffit vent combination is the best way to achieve proper ventilation design.

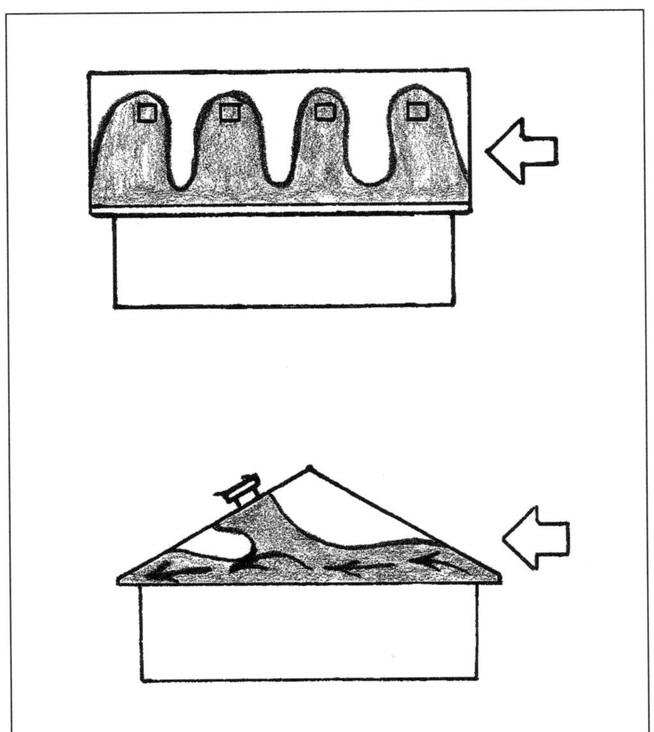

Figure 10.15 Soffit and louver venting (actual size).

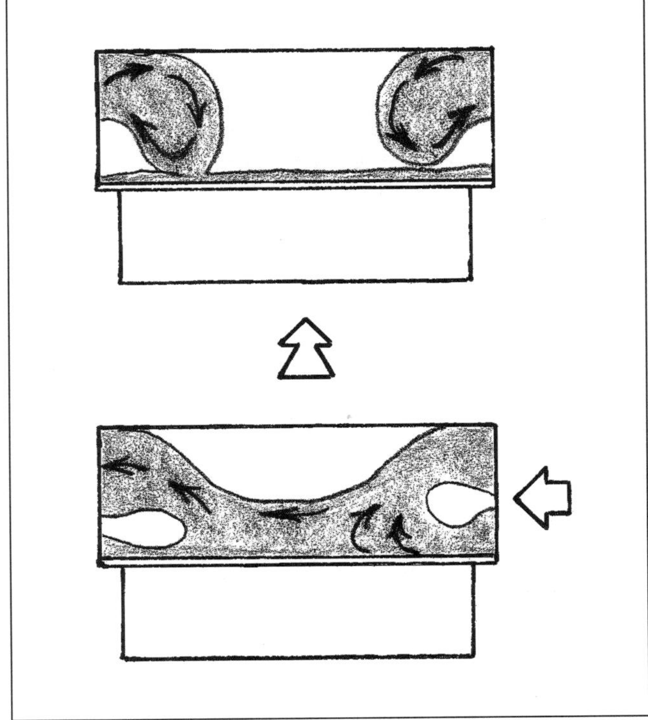

Figure 10.16 Gable and soffit ventilation (actual size).

This design provides the optimum balance between intake and exhaust of air into and out of an attic cavity. This balanced ventilation design utilizes both air pressure and thermal effect under the widest range of wind and weather conditions. (See Fig. 10.17.)

A balanced ventilation design must provide:

- Adequate net free area of vent opening
- Intake vents at the lowest points and exhaust vents at the highest point of the roof with approximately equal areas of vent space located within both positive and negative areas
- Continuous vent components in both high pressure and negative pressure areas.

Designing a continuous ridge vent of proper configuration and continuous eave/soffit vent on both building sides will provide adequate and balanced ventilation. Cooling costs will be lowered and condensation will be limited to no effect.

The configuration of the ridge vent is important in obtaining a consistent negative pressure area. An external baffle on the ridge vent assembly will create a negative pressure area regardless of wind direction. In the event that wind direction is exactly parallel to ridge, wind passing over the ridge assembly opening will create a negative pressure area and draw air from the attic cavity. (See Fig. 10.18.)

Without such an external baffle, wind can enter the ridge assembly, creating a positive pressure area instead of the required negative pressure area. In such a case, complete ventilation of the entire deck/roof underside may not be accomplished.

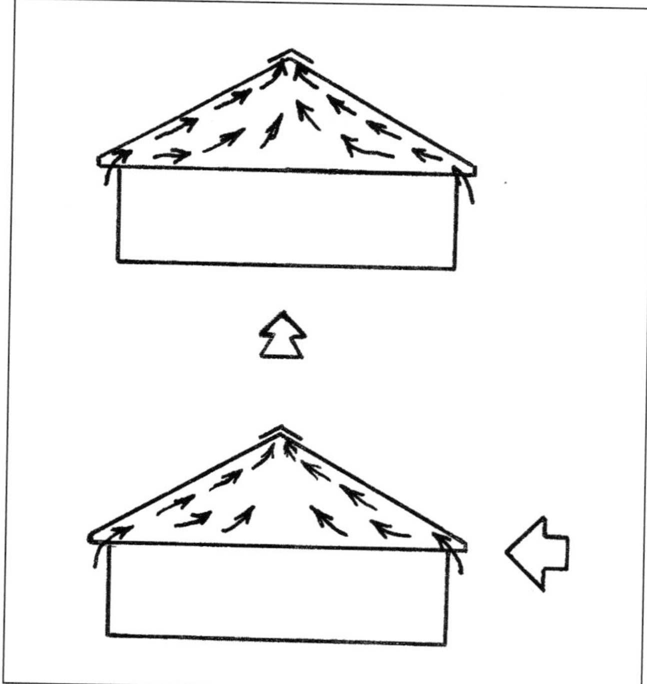

Figure 10.17 Ridge and soffit venting.

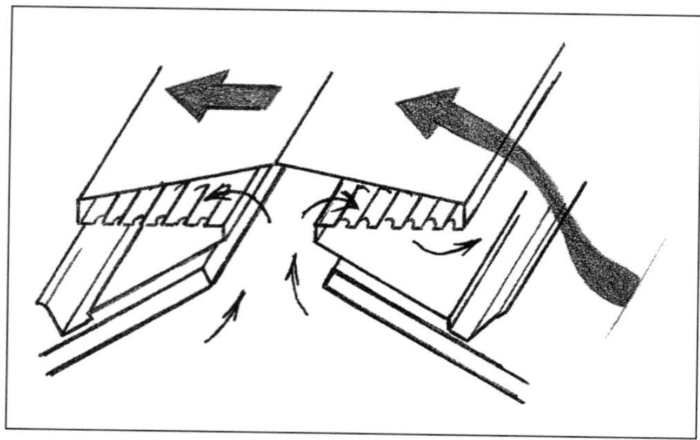

Figure 10.18 Ridge vent with baffles.

VENT AREA CONSIDERATIONS

There are many considerations in the calculation of venting requirements. Some vents do not work as efficiently as others, even though they may have the same amount of net free vent opening. One influence of vent component efficiency is the configuration or style of the component. (See Fig. 10.18.)

Also, the design of the vent cover as furnished by the manufacturer is to be considered in design selection. Vents with a screened cover or with small, round perforations through which the air intake must pass often become clogged with dust, dirt, and insulation fibers.

Vents furnished with small louvered slits, ⅛ in × 1 in, provide maximum net free area and the added advantage of an opening that effectively resists insect entrance and dust and fiber obstruction. The amount of net free vent area used in ventilation design calculations must remain the same throughout the life of the building.

The louver formed along the edge of the slit directs air flow to the maximum advantage. Beware that this type of louvered vent, if turned in the wrong direction by the installer, can direct water into the attic/plenum area of the building. (See Fig. 10.19.)

The efficiency with which vents perform is also affected by where they are placed, in that they should exist in both positive and negative pressure areas, and are equally balanced between these different pressure areas.

Vent components must be selected which provide the required amount of net free vent area. If the soffit area of the roof overhang is small and narrow, then a vent with maximum net free area per linear foot will be required. Vent efficiency must also be considered.

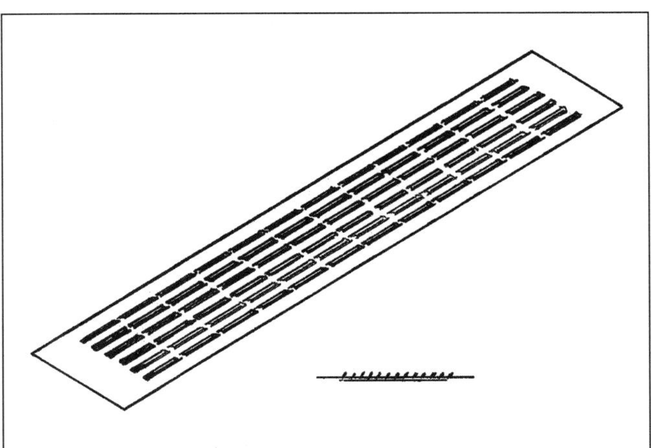

Figure 10.19 Louvered soffit vent.

The amount of pressure created by wind speed is a factor in vent area requirements. The average wind speed to be expected at the building location should be considered. The faster the wind speed, the more powerful will be the negative and positive pressure areas created at the vent openings.

It is recommended that the designer plan for wind speed which is less than the average for the area in which the building is located. This will provide adequate ventilation even during periods when winds may be calm. Also make note of building surroundings, in that trees and tall buildings will restrict the average wind speed for that geographic location.

Optimum design for critical situations (where excessive moisture and temperature extremes are expected, and where cooling costs are also a consideration) should target exhausting 1.5 cfm of air per every square foot of roof deck or ceiling floor area. However, as stated previously, this is often impractical or impossible. This optimum requirement is easier to achieve on a simple and small residential house than on larger commercial structures. The designer must determine if ventilation will be designed to accommodate minimum or maximum levels, meaning summertime cooling (requiring maximum ventilation), or only moisture removal to prevent condensation (requiring a lower ventilation rate).

The type of equipment selected as the ventilation components is a factor of the ventilation design. Equipment considerations involve where the vent openings are located as shown in Table 10.1. Equipment considerations also must take into account the efficiency of the air flow through the vent.

If practically possible, the humidity levels to be expected within the attic cavity should be determined. Exceptional humidity within the cavity will require higher ventilation rates. The same holds true for exceptional heat gain and possible retention within an attic cavity area.

10.2.3 Calculation

VENT COMPONENT EFFICIENCY

Efficiency of the ventilation equipment is dependent on how well air flows through the vent component, which can also be stated as how well air flow acts and reacts at vent openings. Unfortunately, we do not know of an international or national rating system used throughout the industry to rate the efficiency of air flow through ventilation equipment.

Vent efficiency is related to the velocity of air immediately after passing through the net free vent opening area as compared to wind velocity as it strikes upon or passes by the vent component. Simply stated, this the ratio of wind velocity through the vent to atmospheric wind velocity.

As a general guide only and an example of possible vent efficiency, Table 10.1 lists vent component efficiency. This table is taken from a study produced during the mid-1970s.

The volume of air which flows through a vent is evaluated on the formula:

$$Q = EAV$$

where Q = air flow, ft^3/min (cfm)
A = net free area of vent opening, ft^2
V = wind velocity, ft/min
E = effectiveness factor of vent

Table 10.1 Effectiveness E factor of vents.

Type of vent or louver	*Range of* E *during test*	*Mean*
Roof louver only	0.14–0.6	0.2
Gable louvers only		
Wind parallel to ridge	0.6–0.8	0.7
Wind perpendicular to ridge	0.1–0.4	0.2
Average		0.4
Soffit louvers only	0.2–0.4	0.3
Roof and soffit louvers	0.2–0.3	0.2
Gable and soffit louvers		
Wind parallel to ridge	0.4–0.6	0.5
Wind perpendicular to ridge	0.2–0.4	0.3
Average		0.4
Ridge vent and soffit louvers	0.4–0.5	0.4

E = ratio of velocity through the vent to wind velocity.

VENT SYSTEM EFFICIENCY

The efficiency of the vent components dictate how well the total vent system will function. The effective cfm of flow through vents is evaluated by the formula:

$$EC = \frac{D}{T}$$

where EC = effective cfm
D = volume of attic, ft^3
T = time for replacement of all attic air, min

As stated in Sec. 10.2.1 proper ventilation can eliminate not only condensation within an attic/plenum cavity, it can also drastically reduce cooling costs during summer months. It often is possible to increase ventilation capacity or air movement through the cavity with little additional expense.

Tests conducted have established attic air and floor temperatures attained when different vent system designs, at different prevailing wind speeds, are used. The correlation of the data from the tests established the effective cfm ($EC = D/T$) per square inch of net free vent area. (See Table 10.2.)

GUIDELINE FOR VENT SYSTEM AREA REQUIRED

As mentioned previously, extensive testing and research have been conducted by private industry as well as by universities, and such research led to publication of the reference chart in Table 10.2. The chart reflects the effective cfm ventilation rate per square inch of different vent systems as it relates to wind velocity.

Also referenced is the ventilation rate during both summer and winter conditions. This illustrates the thermal effect of air convection in the summer as opposed to winter. When wind velocity is at 0, convection still causes air movement with a ridge/soffit vent system. However, as air speed increases, convection influence diminishes.

All of the information within this section leads to proper ventilation design. Determining ventilation requirements is a factor of building location and prevailing wind speed at the roof, ability of the air to flow freely within the roof cavity, ability of the air to provide a continuous wash across the entire underside of the roof deck assembly, which is directly dependent upon location and size of vent components.

For those who wish to use a scientific approach, we provide the following mathematical formula. Vent area required can be determined from the formula.

Table 10.2 Effective cfm per in^2 vent area.

	Wind velocity (mi/h)					
Vent system	*0*	*2.5*	*5.0*	*7.5*	*10*	*15*
Summer						
Roof louvers only	0	0.153	0.306	0.459	0.612	
Soffit louvers only	0	0.173	0.347	0.520	0.695	
Gable louvers only	0	0.208	0.416	0.624	0.832	
Roof louvers plus Soffit vent	0	0.163	0.326	0.435	0.660	
Gable louvers plus Soffit vent	0	0.208	0.382	0.555	0.728	
Ridge vent plus Soffit vent	0.40	0.48	0.695	1.00	1.32	
Winter						
Roof louvers only	0	0.063	0.076	0.090	0.118	0.109
Soffit louvers only	0	0.097	0.125	0.153	0.181	0.278
Gable louvers only	0	0.104	0.139	0.194	0.250	0.364
Roof louvers plus Soffit vent	0	0.083	0.111	0.167	0.222	0.333
Gable louvers plus Soffit vent	0	0.118	0.146	0.167	0.187	0.219
Ridge vent plus Soffit vent	0.222	0.347	0.66	1.00	1.32	1.96

$$VA = AF\left(\frac{CF}{CV}\right)$$

where VA = total vent area, in^2
AF = area of attic/plenum floor, ft^2
CF = cfm of exhaust desired per ft^2 of floor area
CV = cfm of air exhaust per in^2 of vent area for type of vent system and wind velocity selected for the design (see Table 10.2)

For those who do not wish to use a formula, Table 10.3 can aid in determining ventilation requirements. Both formula and table are to be used as a guide only.

10.3 NOMENCLATURE

METAL INDUSTRY TERMS

Acrylic Coatings: A thermoset coating based on resins from acrylic and methacrylic esters or acids, which are typically cross-linked with amino or epoxy resins.

Age Hardening: The loss of formability of a material with the passage of time.

Aluminizing: Application of aluminum or aluminum silicone alloy to steel by the hot-dip process.

Anodizing: Aluminum coating process by electrolytic oxidation which results in a thin film of aluminum oxide of extreme hardness (aluminum anodic oxide coating). A wide variety of colors is possible by dye-coloring impregnation during the anodizing process.

Back Coat: The coating applied to the back side of the panel strip during the coating process, serving both aesthetic and mechanical functions. This coating is faced inward, away from the exterior environment.

Blister: 1. A defect in the metal produced by gas bubbles either on the surface or from beneath the surface when the metal is hot. 2. A defect in the coating usually caused by trapped solvent. 3. A failure of the bond between the coating and the metal surface due to interface oxidation, delamination of differential elasticity during fabrication, temperature fluctuations, etc.

Table 10.3 Vent area required per ft^2 of attic floor area.

Vent area required, in^2/ft^2 of attic floor area			
Vent system	*Summer*	*Winter*	
	1.5 cfm	*0.4 cfm*	*1.0 cfm*
Roof louvers only	3.3	4.4	11.1
Soffit louvers only	2.9	2.6	6.5
Gable louvers only	2.4	2.0	5.1
Roof louvers and soffit vents	3.1	2.4	6.0
Cont. soffit and cont. ridge	1.5	0.4	1.0

Burnishing: A change of gloss created by friction between two surfaces.

Burr Up: A condition resulting from the cutting of metal so that the lip resulting from the cutting action faces up instead of down.

Calendered Film: A film processed through a series of rollers to create a smooth and/or glossy finish.

Camber: Deviation of the straight line of the edge of a metal panel or strip.

Center Buckle: An out-of-flat condition caused by the stretching of the metal, resulting in a sheet longer in the center than at the edges.

Chalking: A loose, powdery surface condition occurring to finishes as a result of degradation of the finish binder by ultraviolet rays from sunlight.

Coil Coater: A large piece of equipment that applies paint or other liquids as the finish to metal coils. Essentially consisting of support rollers for the metal strip, drying ovens, and paint application stations, it can also emboss metal coil strip.

Coil Set: The tendency of metal strip to retain the curve of the coil from which it came.

Color Match: A situation where the difference between a color and a color standard cannot be detected visually or by instrument. Instrument testing, color standard, and allowable deviations are agreed upon between buyer and seller.

Conversion Coating: A chemical treatment causing reaction with the metallic strip which converts the strip surface to a nonmetallic, nonconductive surface for improved paint adhesion and corrosion resistance after coating.

Corrosion: The electrochemical degradation of metals due to reaction with the environment.

Cratering: A surface-coating defect related to metal surface tension. Characterized by small pockmarks or indentures surrounded by a ring of coating material projecting above the general plane of the coating.

Cross-Linking: The union of high-polymer molecules by introduction of primary or secondary chemical bonds.

Crown: Increased thickness of the metal in the center of the strip with decreased thickness at the sheet edge.

Ductility: As referred to within the metal industry, the property of metals which allows them to be mechanically deformed without fracture when cold. Usually measured by elongation and reduction of cross-sectional test area as determined in a tensile test.

Elastic Limit: Maximum stress a material can withstand before becoming permanently deformed.

Elongation: Increase in length which occurs before a material tears or fractures when subjected to stress, expressed as a percentage of the original static length. A measure of ductility.

Embossing: Creating patterns into the metal by depressing the metal surface using a pattern roller, often done during the coil-coating process.

Ester: A product created by the reaction of organic alcohol and organic acid.

Fading: A color change involving the loss of pigmentation appearance; lightening or weakening of a color; a change in hue.

Fatigue: Fracture of the metal surface due to repeated and fluctuating stress.

Ferrous: Related to iron (from Latin *ferrum*).

Fingernail Test—Adhesion: A test wherein an experienced quality control technician places a fingernail at a scribe line on the metal finish and attempts to peel the finish from the panel.

Fingernail Test—Mar Resistance: A test wherein an experienced quality control technician attempts to mar the surface of the metal panel finish with a fingernail.

Floating: A coating defect evident in nonuniform or nonhomogeneous coloring of the surface when inspected under magnification, usually resulting from inadequate dispersion of pigment within the coating or incompatibility of one or more pigments within the coating vehicle.

Fluting: Appearance of creases or sharp parallel kinks which occur in the arc when metal is formed cylindrically.

Foil: Metal which is no more than 0.005 in thick, any width.

Galvanizing: A coating of zinc applied to steel. Application may be electrodeposition or hot-dipping.

Gloss: The image reflection of a surface, related directly to the smoothness of that surface. Luster or shininess.

Gloss Meter: An instrument used for measuring gloss, usually at 60° from the horizontal.

Hardness Pencil: A method used in determining the hardness of a paint film, in which a series of drawing pencils, each having been calibrated for hardness, then sanded to form a flat, cylindrical edge, are held at a 45° angle and pushed with a downward and forward motion against the panel being tested. The hardness pencil which fails to cut the film is the hardness of the film.

Hot Dip: A process in steel mill practice by which ferrous alloy base metals are dipped into molten metal—normally zinc, aluminum, tin, or terne—and used for the purpose of fixing a rust-resistant coating.

Impact Test: This test uses a steel ball of an established diameter and weight dropped from varying heights to determine the impact values. It is most commonly used to determine adhesion and flexibility of a coating.

Interleaving: Placing a paper or film between pieces of metal to prevent damage to the finish during shipping and handling.

Matte Surface: A finish with low luster or gloss.

Nonferrous: Metals or alloys which are free of iron.

Oil Can: A localized out-of-flat condition often seen as buckles toward the center of an otherwise flat sheet.

Orange Peel: The uneven finish of a surface resembling the surface of an orange.

Plastisol Coating: Themoplastic coating of pigmented dispersions of finely divided polyvinyl chloride resins in suitable plasticizers. The resin particles are solvated by the plasticizer and fuse to a continuous film during a baking process.

Polyester Coating: A thermoset coating using the condensation products of polybasic acids and diols (dihydric acid) and generally cross-linked with amino resins.

Reflectance: The ratio of reflected to incident light or radiation.

Retrofit: Installing a new building system over the top of an existing, in-place system.

Rockwell Hardness Test: A standard method of measuring the hardness of metals, expressed as a number relating to the depth of residual penetration of a steel ball or diamond cone.

Roll Forming: An operation of forming metal strip into building panels by use of a series of steel rollers of definite size and setting which progressively bend the sheet to the desired style and configuration.

Salt Spray Test: A test process by which metal is exposed to a water and salt spray, either continuously or intermittently, to evaluate its resistance to corrosion.

Silicone Polyester Coating: Thermoset coating based upon the product of the reaction between an organo-siloxane-intermediate and a suitable polyester resin and further cross-linked with amino acids.

Silicone Resin: Any of a large group of copolymers based on a structure consisting of alternate silicon and oxygen atoms with various organic radicals attached to the silicon.

T-Bend Test: Bending of metal 180° with an internal diameter equal to xt where t equals metal thickness.

Tensile Strength: The breaking strength of a material when exposed to a stretching force. Normally determined by placing a specimen into the jaws of the tensile machine and gradually separating the jaws until the specimen tears or breaks, at which point pounds/inch or tons/inch required to break the specimen is the tensile force.

Thermal Resistance: In the metal industry, the ability of a coated product to retain its physical properties after 16 h of exposure at a specified temperature.

Viscosity: The internal resistance to flow exhibited by a fluid.

Wash Coat: A coating applied to the back of the metal strip during the coil-coating process. Not to be confused with backwash, the wash coat prevents damage to the finish coat and prevents corrosion on the back side. Not closely controlled during application.

10.3.1 Metal Roof Panel Types and Characteristics

TYPE DEFINITION

In years past we could classify the types of metal roof panels used in roof applications as structural panels and architectural panels. Even today these terms are still sometimes used. However, times have changed, and these two basic classifications can no longer be used to accurately describe a group or type of panel.

The term *structural panel* refers to a roof panel which spans from purlin to purlin, often spaced on 5-ft centers. Structural panels require no roof deck for support since the panel itself has structural capabilities. A structural roof panel, in essence, is the roof deck and the roof covering.

In the past when referring to a structural panel as used in commercial roof application, you were probably referring to one of the types shown in Fig. 10.20. Today there are even more styles of roof panel which are structural.

- A structural panel system must be watertight. Since no roof decking is included in the design, a waterproofing membrane underlayment is not possible.
- In the past and even today, as a general rule, structural panels are primarily functional and secondarily aesthetic. Usually a structural panel is selected for a low-slope application where the roof system is not a prime focal point of the building structure.
- A structural panel system is considered a water-barrier system. As a water barrier, the laps and connections of the panels can withstand water which may temporarily cover the joints.

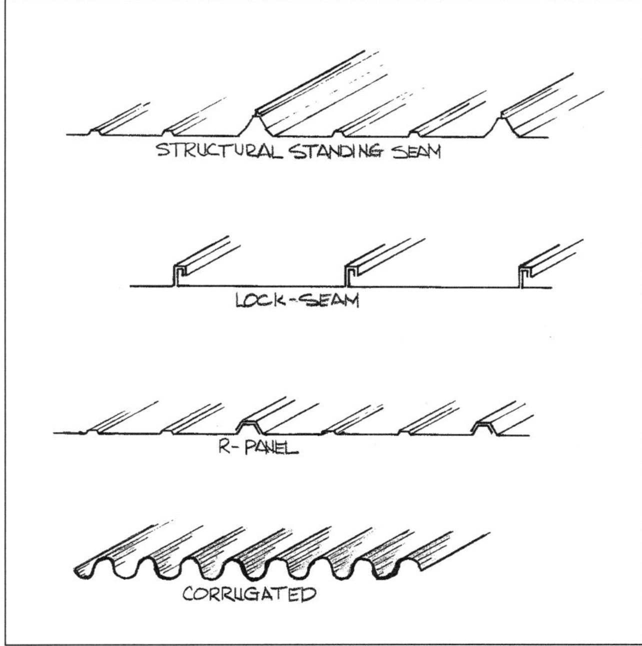

Figure 10.20 Structural panel types.

The distance a metal panel can free-span is dependent upon the gauge thickness of the metal and the style of the panel. The more breaks and bends—i.e., the ribs and seams—used to form the metal panel, the stronger it will be. Engineering load tables are usually included in each material manufacturer's manual, listing load ratings, spanning capabilities, etc.

The same principles of strength apply to sheet metal flashings and metal roof decking material. However, metal roof panels do not provide the same strength to a building structure as does metal roof decking.

Metal roof decking, by the method and manner of attachment to the structural roof framing, provides lateral load resistance to a building. Metal roof decking stiffens the entire building structure. By the manner and method of joining structural roof panels to the building's roof frame, even though they may be referred to as structural, the metal roof panels cannot impart significant structural strength to the building.

In the past, if a metal panel was not structural, it was probably architectural. The architectural panels had different characteristics and requirements from the structural panels.

- Architectural panels did not have structural capabilities, often being formed of lighter-gauge metals without as many crimps and bends within the panel. As such, the architectural panels required a solid deck for support.
- Architectural panels were water shedders, not water barriers. The lap seams and joints of the panel could not resist water flooding the area. Thus the panels were installed on slopes of at least 3-in rise per 12-in run and required a waterproof membrane layer under the panels.
- Architectural panels probably got the designation from the fact that they were used to accent architectural expression, extending from the fact that they were required on roof slopes which were usually visible from the ground. The panels came in a variety of colors and gloss, normally with concealed fastener clips used to secure the panel to the roof deck.

Today many of the above requirements have been blended. Many architectural panels today are also structural. As such, the architectural panels require no roof decking and therefore have no waterproofing underlayment. Likewise, many structural panels appear architectural, with defined, thin lines, concealed fasteners, and a wide selection of available colors.

Perhaps one way to define categories of metal roof panel types would be as structural and nonstructural, or perhaps deck and nondeck panels. Yet, this terminology would indicate little to nothing of the waterproofing design, installation procedures, or limitations of the panel. Therefore it is becoming common within the industry for panels to be referred to only as either water-shedding panels or water-barrier panels. Sometimes the term *hydrokinetic* is used instead of water-shedding and the term *hydrostatic* used in lieu of water barrier.

Water-barrier panels prevent water infiltration through the laps, seams, and joints, even if covered for short periods of time by water. Water-shedding panels rely on the slope of the roof to prevent water from submersing laps and seams.

WATER-BARRIER SYSTEMS

Low-sloped flexible membrane roof systems, such as built-up or modified bitumen roof systems, are water barriers. The roof membrane, by design and construction, is a barrier against water. These membrane barrier systems will withstand water over the surface, in theory, up to 8 inches in depth, which is the minimum recommended height of base flashings. (See Sec. 12.3.)

A metal roof system which is a water barrier can also withstand water over its surface, in theory, up to the height of the flashing tops and as much load as the roof can support before collapse. However, there are many differences between a flexible water-barrier membrane and a rigid water-barrier membrane.

Metal roof systems cannot tolerate ponding water, in any amount. Metal roof systems experience far greater thermal movement than flexible low-sloped membranes. Flashing design situations for metal roof systems are far different from those for flexible membrane systems.

Just because a metal roof is a water barrier does not mean it should be subjected to water level over the seams and laps. A minimum slope of ¼ in is required for most types of water-barrier systems.

The structural standing seam is a type of water-barrier panel often used. The trapezoidal seam elevates the standing seam usually 3 in above roof plane. (See Fig. 10.20.)

Caulking. The seam atop the structural panel is waterproofed by caulk sealant placed within the seam. The caulking used with water-barrier systems is essential in keeping the system permanently watertight.

Caulking is factory-applied to the panel at all crucial locations. Roofers install caulk as required in the field. The caulking is installed to create a flexible waterproofing gasket between panels and within joints and seams. This requires the metal pieces to be compressed. When compressed, the metal pieces force the caulk into a uniform gasket which will stay flexible and waterproof. The caulking used is specifically formulated for this purpose. It is noncuring if installed in compression and not exposed to sunlight.

On water-barrier panel systems designed for low-roof-slope applications, detailing at flashing areas as well as caulking placement and use are critical. There is no redundancy factor at the flashings as with base flashings of a built-up roof. (See Fig. 12.41.) If a mistake is made in application or design—even a small one—roof leaks are a likelihood. See Sec. 10.4 for additional flashing detail requirements.

Foot and Equipment Traffic. Water-barrier systems are often installed on commercial and industrial buildings with low roof slopes. As such, we often find roof-mounted equipment. Equipment usually requires servicing, which requires workers, which leads to rooftop traffic, which can lead to roof damage.

The finishes on metal panels are especially susceptible to damage from foot and equipment traffic. (See Sec. 10.3.2.) Walkway systems are available and elevate foot traffic above the roof surface. However, an added expense is created not only by the purchase of the walkway equipment, but by the flashing installation cost, as well as possible roof maintenance at the walkway support flashing areas.

WATER-SHEDDING SYSTEMS

Metal roof panels used as water-shedding systems rely mainly, but not totally, on gravity to keep the building watertight. The steeper the slope, the faster the water will be moved down the surface.

Theory. However, water does not always move downhill. Wind blowing or gusting directly into a roof slope can cause water to run uphill when being pushed by the wind. Water can run sideways, up and into a metal panel seam, by wind blowing across a roof surface.

Also, a runoff rate ratio will exist between rainfall intensity and roof slope. After a certain rate of rainfall is reached, water will begin to gather on the roof panel at the lower downslope end of the roof structure. The steeper the slope, the more intense the rainfall required to create the water backup. The lower the slope, the less rainfall required.

There truly is no minimum slope requirement for water-shedding systems. If the panel runs are long (i.e., 100 ft), the amount of water which can collect on the lower end of the panel is greater than if the panel runs were short (i.e., 20 ft). Therefore, a roof slope of 3 in per foot (the normal industry-recommended minimum slope for architectural water-shedding systems) may be adequate for the 20-ft panel run system, but the same slope for the 100-ft panel system may be inadequate if it is installed in a torrential-rain, high-wind area. On the other hand, the 100-ft panel run system slope may be adequate in the torrential-rain, high-wind area if it has high rib seams. The seams and joints where the panels are joined, if high enough above the floodplane on the roof surface, may not be affected by wind-blown rain and water build-up.

Waterproofing Underlayment. Properly designed, correctly installed, and in normal conditions, water-shedding roof panels should not allow water through the laps and seams. However, if your design practice is not in Utopia, Texas, a waterproofing membrane under the water-shedding panel system is recommended.

A good design practice is to create a waterproofing underlayment that makes the building watertight before installation of the metal panels. The underlayment is normally of organic felt. (See Sec. 7.1.1.) Specify and verify installation of the underlayment to a condition making the building leakfree in a rain, even though the metal roof system is not installed.

Before installation of the metal roof panel system, require the waterproof underlayment to be covered with a slip-sheet paper, normally red rosin paper. The paper will prevent the metal panel from adhering to the roof felt underlayment. During the expansion and contraction cycles of the metal roof panel, an underlayment adhered to the moving panels will be torn.

Do not rely on the underlayment to permanently prevent roof leaks. If water penetrates the metal roof system in sufficient quantities, roof leaks will probably occur. Installation of metal roof panels causes the underlayment to be penetrated numerous times by clip fasteners, screws, and/or nails.

Also realize that even small amounts of water, if continuously repeated through a leak area of the metal roof system, can damage and probably destroy most underlayment. Moisture from the roof leak can remain trapped in the leak area for extended periods of time. Without being able to dry, deterioration of the metal panel from the bottom side may then be imminent.

Additional water-barrier underlayments are a common design practice at areas where the metal panel system may experience occasional flooding due to exceptional heavy rains, wind-driven rain, obstructed valleys and troughs due to leaves and debris, and ice dams which cause snow water to back up and pond. Valleys, crickets, and saddles behind chimneys and eaves in snow country usually require an additional waterproofing underlayment.

Again, do not consider this underlayment as the primary system in achieving a waterproof roof system. It should function only as the last line of defense in an area which should be waterproof the majority of the time. This waterproofing underlayment is normally of a polymeric modified bitumen membrane material. In theory, the modified bitumen material, being soft and pliable, will seal off the holes created by nails and screws. This sealing at the fastener shank by the modified bitumen underlayment should be further enhanced by the heat of summer months.

Capillary Action. In addition to water being forced upslope or sideways by wind, water will travel against the force of gravity due to capillary action. In grade school, capillary action is demonstrated by holding two flat pieces of glass together and partially dipping them into a beaker of colored water. The water will travel between the glass pieces and easily rise above the water level within the beaker.

The same water action can occur between two pieces of metal held tightly together. At the laps and seams of a water-shedding roof system, care must be taken to prevent capillary action. As described above, the seams and laps at the end of long panel runs are susceptible to leaks due to capillary action. Also, ice damming at roof eaves can cause water to be sucked into the lap seam and cause roof leaks as a result of capillary action. (See Sec. 2.2.1.)

Water infiltration due to capillary action can be prevented by capillary joints incorporated into the metal panel seams. These joints, by separation of the metal pieces, stop capillary action. These capillary joints are ineffective if water levels rise above the break. (See Fig. 10.21.)

Some panel profiles will not allow capillary joints. An example is a vertical leg standing seam as shown in Fig. 10.22. For profiles not allowing capillary joints, caulking is required within the laps and/or seams.

Caulking, if of the right type and placed correctly in a lap or seam which will keep the caulk in compres-

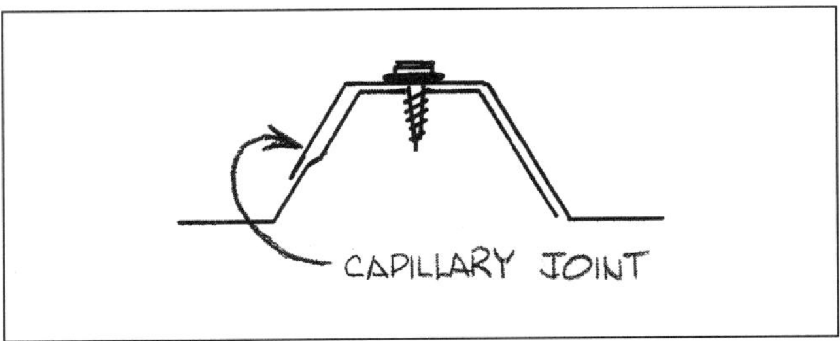

Figure 10.21 Capillary joint.

Figure 10.22 Standing seam capillary joint.

sion, can create a water-barrier system from a water-shedding system. On areas of the roof where water may flood over the lap or seam, design of such waterproofing is advisable.

Air Infiltration. Water-shedding seams and laps are often not airtight. Sometimes roof leaks occur in water-shedding metal roofs and there seems to be no deficiency with the metal panel system. In such a case, it may be due to air and water infiltration through the laps and seams.

Water can sometimes be sucked through the laps or seams of the panels by positive and negative pressure differentials. Section 10.2.1 demonstrates how differing pressure areas always exist around a building structure. During a rain, wind velocities often increase, thereby increasing pressure differentials across the building and roof plane.

If a positive pressure exists on one side of the roof and a negative pressure exists on the other side of the roof, the pressure can try to equalize itself through the interior space of the building. The interior space of the building often exists at lower pressure than does the area of the roof experiencing wind gusts, which create high-pressure areas. The higher pressure levels are due to the higher wind speeds during the rain.

At the same time another area of the roof may be experiencing below-normal air pressure, again due to high wind speeds created by the rainstorm. Air within the building interior, existing at higher pressure than the low-pressure area of the roof, will try to flow and equalize the negative pressure area on the roof. The air flowing from the interior to the low-pressure area further accentuates the lower-than-normal pressure of the building interior. The high-pressure area of the roof will try to equalize the negative pressure building interior.

Although not common, this phenomenon has been known to occur, causing inexplicable roof leaks. During a rain, water is moved into the lap seam by the inrush of air through the seam. Capillary action aids in continuing the movement of the water to the building interior.

10.3.2 Coatings

Coatings are essential to the successful life of the metal roof panel system. On steel panels the coating must remain intact to prevent corrosion of the steel. On noncorrosive metal panels, such as aluminum, coatings do not prevent panel deterioration but must remain intact to maintain the initial design appearance of the roof system.

COATING PROCESS

Both metal types are prepared in much the same way so the coatings will permanently adhere. The first process is a highly concentrated wash of an alkaline-based chemical, sometimes applied in conjunction with mechanical brushing. This process will remove oils, dirt, and surface grease.

For galvanizing, steel panels are then completely dipped into a solution of molten material. This molten material can be of several different mixtures. If galvanized finish is required, the molten material is zinc. The liquid zinc cools on the sheet surface and forms a protective coat. A galvanized finish can also be applied to steel using an electroplating process, although the hot-dipping method is the most preferred for durable finish.

The molten material can also be a combination of zinc and aluminum, commonly referred to as *Galvalume,* a trademark of B.I.E.C. The solution is usually 55% aluminum, 43.5% zinc, and 1.5% silica, although steel panels are sometimes coated with 95% zinc and 5% aluminum metal. Steel panels can also be coated with a complete solution of aluminum and are referred to as *aluminized steel.*

If a painted surface coating is then desired, the metallic-coated metal is chemically prepared to receive the paint. This chemical preparation will vary, depending on the type of base metal, either aluminum or steel, and the type of surfacing the metal panel has on it, either zinc galvanizing, zinc and aluminum, or pure aluminum finish. Aluminum-coated sheets will be treated with chromates. Zinc-coated sheets will be treated with complex oxides, zinc phosphates, or chromates.

After surface preparation, the metal is run through a continuous processing machine, referred to as a *coil coater,* wherein the paint coat finishes will be applied to the metal surface. Most metal is fed into the machine from a large coil. After the painting and coating process is complete, it is recoiled for shipment to the next processing station or plant.

The base metal can also be primed and then: coated with a finish paint, have a finish paint system laminated to it with adhesives and heat, or be embossed with patterns to simulate wood grains, stucco, etc. These steps are all accomplished as the metal is moved through the machine in a continuous process. Application of the coating finishes to the metal is very carefully controlled. This process has greatly improved with the advancement of modern technology and computers.

Briefly described, the coil coating process begins with a large metal coil being placed on an arbor at the beginning of the feed line. This new coil is joined to the preceding coil that is in the coil coating machine with a specially designed punch press which laps and interlocks the two coil sheets together.

The metal moves into the machine line where it first comes to a chemical bath solution. Here it is cleaned of contaminants and prepared to receive subsequent coatings. The metal strip then advances on down the line to the next process, where the primers and finish coats are applied. These liquid coatings are applied by roll coaters which are accurately designed and automatically controlled, resulting in the application of a precise and uniform film coating to the metal. Both primers and finish coats can be applied during this phase of the process.

Sometimes, instead of being applied as a liquid, a film coating is laminated to the metal using adhesives. The adhesives can be applied to the metal surface during the coating step of the process or as part of the lamination sheet. The coatings applied are referred to as *laminates*.

The metal advances to the oven curing station of the coil coating process. The metal is exposed to heat, and the coatings are allowed to completely cure. If a laminated process is required, it is usually applied during or directly after this step. After the metal strip leaves the ovens it is cooled using water and air quenching systems.

If a pattern is desired, it is embossed into the finished metal at this time. Some metal also has a plastic film coating applied at this phase, which protects it during shipping, fabrication, and application. The film is removed as the metal panels are installed at the job site. This helps ensure that the finished product is clean, bright, and without scratches. As the metal strip exits the machine, it is rewound into a large coil and is ready for shipment.

COATING TYPES

There are numerous types of organic coatings. A good background in chemistry is helpful for a comprehensive understanding of organic coating characteristics. The metallic coatings are fewer and easier to understand.

Each different type has certain advantages and disadvantages. Coatings are either of metallic-based or organic-based materials. Aluminum and zinc coatings are the most common metallic coatings.

METALLIC COATINGS

Aluminum coatings are a barrier coating. This coating is all that is between the base metal and the weather. When the aluminum coating is scratched, chipped, or worn off, the metal underneath is exposed and can begin to deteriorate.

Zinc coatings, on the other hand, are a barrier which is sacrificial. Zinc is water-soluble, so a zinc-based (galvanized) coating will eventually be dissipated, or sacrificed, from the surface of the base metal. However, if the zinc coating is scratched or chipped, the sacrificial action will help protect the exposed base metal underneath. You could refer to this coating as being self-healing to a small degree.

Since the zinc galvanized coating is sacrificial, the quality and thickness of the coating is important for long-term protection. G-60 and G-90 are the most common grades of zinc coating applied to steel sheets, with G-90 producing better long-term corrosion control.

A popular coating in corrosive atmospheres is aluminum-zinc, usually referred to as Galvalume, which is a B.I.E.C. registered trade name for the product. Aluminum resists chemical pollutants and oxidation better than zinc. Zinc, being sacrificial, will compensate for minor damage to the coating finish. Galvalume coatings are designed and marketed as blending the best characteristics of both.

Compatibility. Compatibility of these metallic coatings with other metals and caulking materials is a consideration. Copper and lead are the most common compatibility problem we most often encounter.

Lead flashings, such as roof jacks, should be avoided with metallic coating types in most environments. If possible, design roof flashings of the same material as the roof panels.

Aluminum-based coating material will not accept solder. Some flashing situations may be best served by the permanent seal of a soldered joint. An alternative may be a factory-supplied flashing piece which is sometimes available to accommodate the situation. If such is not available, caulking of the flashing is then inevitable. Low-sloped roof systems and field-applied caulking to create a watertight flashing component must follow the guidelines within Sec. 10.4.2.

Any exposed copper lines on air-conditioning units must be insulated and covered watertight. Condensate from these A/C units must be piped across the panels so that the copper-rich condensate will not destroy the panel coating.

In roof replacement design, we often encounter existing lead or copper flashing and accessory components. These should be removed and replaced when installing a metallic-coated roof panel. Any downspouts or gutters made from copper- or lead-coated steel should not be allowed to come into contact with metallic-coated metal roof panel systems. Additionally, no water discharge from such gutter or downspout systems should be allowed to spill onto metal roof panels not of copper or lead materials.

Water runoff from other roofs that are made from or coated with lead or copper must not be allowed onto roofs with galvanized, aluminum, or Galvalume metallic coatings. Copper will cause a quick and disastrous reaction with zinc- and/or aluminum-coated metal. However, we often find that no reaction occurs when runoff from these metallic-coated panels is fed into or onto lead or copper materials.

For example, a copper gutter system, being expensive and ornate, can often be left in place when installing a metal panel other than copper above it. The water runoff from a galvanized or aluminum-coated panel will usually have little effect on the copper. However, if water from the copper gutter splashes onto the metal roof panels, reaction to the metal panel will occur. Care must also be used to completely separate the copper gutter accessories, such as hanger supports and brackets, from the metal roof materials.

CAULKING

Caulking materials are available in a wide selection of types. Caulking technology is ever changing, with new products and formulations being introduced. Not specifically, but as a general rule, silicone-based caulk material is not compatible with the type of metallic-coated roof panels discussed. Urethane-based caulking is normally acceptable.

Roof design should limit the use of caulk to the greatest extent possible, relying instead on the mechanics of water flow, seaming of lap joints, and factory-applied sealants within the panels when required. Therefore, when caulking is required to be field-applied, it is crucial that the material bonds to the metal surface.

Be aware of the fact that coated metal panels usually have an oil residue applied at the factory. The residue must be removed via an approved solvent in order to allow the caulk to completely adhere and bond to the metal surface. Priming is often required by the material manufacturer. Surface preparation has always been an important step in caulking application.

ORGANIC COATINGS

Organic, barrier coatings are formed from polymers. A polymer is created from monomers. A monomer is a short molecular chain, and when five or more monomers are joined together, the result is a longer molecular chain, having a higher molecular weight, and referred to as a *polymer*.

Usually, the higher the molecular weight of the polymer, the better it will withstand the environment. Higher molecular weight can be accomplished by joining more monomers together, which creates a bigger, more complex molecular chain. Coatings begin to experience trouble when the polymeric molecular chain is broken down and separates.

In organic barrier coatings, there are *thermosetting* and *thermoplastic* coatings. The molecular chains in thermosetting coatings normally cross-link with each other. This creates a three-dimensional polymeric chain that is very tightly joined together and also has very high molecular weight. A thermoplastic coating does not cross-link. Instead, the polymers are merely entangled one with the other.

This may be a little confusing, but it is very important in understanding coating performance. It has to do with what is termed *molecular filter*. A thermosetting polymer coating, three-dimensionally cross-linked with high molecular weight, creates a tighter filter through which moisture and contaminants must penetrate to reach the base metal.

A thermoplastic polymer coating normally is not three-dimensional. It has lower molecular weight, and therefore the molecular filter properties of this type of coating are more open. This increases susceptibility to the elements of the environment.

Resistances and Reactions to the Elements. Different coatings will resist different external forces better than others. In designing a metal roof system, the environment, foot traffic, and long-lasting appearance must be considered.

The coating finish must be evaluated for its ability to withstand high humidity, corrosion, and abrasion as well as the coating's ability to remain on the metal without cracking during the panel forming process. In addition, the coating's color and gloss must be evaluated for its resistance to chalking and fading.

Ultraviolet radiation can result in a white film appearing on the coating surface, referred to as *chalking*. This is the result of the UV rays, along with rain and dew, breaking down the molecular structure of the polymers of the coating. As the polymer molecules are broken, water and sunshine can penetrate the coating and eventually reach the base primer or the metal panel itself.

This is a natural phenomenon and all coatings will eventually fail. The properly formulated and applied coatings, correctly selected by the designer for the specific environment, should last their expected life cycle before chalking, fading, or other failure is evident.

With the darker-colored panels, fading and chalking of the colors is more evident than with the lighter-colored ones. Additionally, light-colored panels can be economical since colored pigments are not needed.

Water sometimes will penetrate into the coating system and become trapped between coating layers. This shows up as small blisters on the paint coating finish.

Moisture will also dissolve small amounts of the low-molecular-weight polymers as well as water-soluble elements within the coating's pigment and additives. Also, the entrapped moisture can act as an electrolyte in the galvanic corrosion cell process. The hotter the temperatures of the environment, the more rapid and severe the deterioration of the coating.

Coatings must be designed to resist man-made pollutants. These pollutants will differ from area to area. If designing a metal roof in a polluted area, or if trying to determine why a roof panel failed prematurely, investigate the pollutants in the area. Some pollutants are not easily detectable by the nose or eye, but even in small amounts can dramatically and severely affect a coating system not manufactured to resist that group of pollutants. Unfortunately, all parts of our country have polluted air, to a lesser or greater degree.

Coastal areas of the country create special concerns. Salty air is very corrosive and can permeate throughout the metal system. Raw cut edges of metal panels, even if concealed, can corrode from salt air.

Coating Types. There are many different organic coatings used as barriers to protect the metal panel. The most common are:

Alkyd-amine
Thermoset acrylic
Acrylic film laminate
Acrylic latex
Polyester
Silicone polyester
Vinyl plastisol
Solution vinyl
Vinyl organosol
Poly-vinylidene fluoride
Poly-vinyl fluoride film laminate
Poly-vinyl chloride film laminate

The coatings we refer to here are basic categories of generic coatings in which most coatings will be included. In order to evaluate and select the best coating type for a particular application, a chart has been prepared by members of the coil coating industry. (See Table 10.4.)

It is strongly emphasized that Table 10.4 is for general reference only. It can greatly assist the designer in selection of the type of coating needed to resist job-specific forces and elements. After the generic type of coating is selected, the designer should consult the manufacturer of metal panels with that particular coating. The manufacturer will have technical data which specifically lists the characteristics of the coatings used with their product.

Needless to say, all coatings are not equal. Discrepancies can be found within each generic category of coating, varying from metal manufacturer to manufacturer.

Regarding Table 10.4, the numeric rating system was established by criteria. The committee responsible for rating the various coatings followed these guidelines:

- Each type of coating should be rated as a general class for each property. For example, vinyl coatings have flexible films, providing high rates in forming properties, impact resistance, embossing, etc. Epoxy-type coatings, when rated, have poor resistance to chalking, and therefore are rated low for exterior durability, especially in colors and tints.
- The rating of each coating should be in terms of performance as a coil coat finish and not in terms of maintenance finishes or other uses involving the same generic type of coating.
- A fair rating for each generic type of coating performance must be made. To achieve this it is necessary to compare the performance of one type of coating to that of the others. A more valid appraisal can be made by review of the rating given another class of coating.
- For rating purposes, assume all the various coatings are pigmented for the best durability.
- The ratings assume two-coat systems on aluminum or galvanized steel. While a change in substrate will change certain characteristics, since the ratings are comparative, the change will normally remain relative and constant within the group of coatings tested.
- For rating purposes, assume all the various coatings are applied at equal film thickness (1.0 mil dry film). Exceptions are the plastisols and vinyl laminates, which may be applied at heavier films for embossing purposes.
- The following rating key should be used to rate all properties:

  5 = excellent
  4 = very good
  3 = good
  2 = fair
  1 = poor or not possible

The information in Table 10.4 was current at the time of publication of this manual (1997).

Table 10.4 Coil coating finishes—Technical Bulletin No. IV-1, comparative properties and performance chart.

	Resistance and durability properties										*Weathering properties*							
Generic coating type	*Impact resistance*	*Mar resistance (fingernail test)*	*Metal marking resistance*	*Resistance to pressure mottling in coil*	*Solvent resistance (aliphatic hydrocarbons)*	*Solvent resistance (aromatic hydrocarbons)*	*Solvent resistance (ketone or oxygenated)*	*Grease and oil resistance*	*Stain resistance (household agents and foodstuffs)*	*General chemical resistance (acids, alkalis, etc.—spot tests)*	*Resistance to water immersion*	*Humidity resistance*	*Abrasion resistance*	*General corrosion resistance (industrial pollution)*	*Corrosion resistance (salt spray)*	*Gloss retention (5 year Florida, 45° south)*	*Chalk resistance (5 year Florida, 45° south)*	*Color retention (5 year Florida 45° south)*
Epoxy-ester*	1	NA	NA	NA	4	4	3	NA	NA	NA	4	4	NA	NA	NA	NA	NA	NA
Epoxy*	1	NA	NA	NA	5	5	4–5	NA	NA	NA	4–5	4–5	NA	NA	NA	NA	NA	NA
Alkyd-amine	2	2–3	3	3	4	3	3	2–3	2–3	2	2	3	2	2	2	1–2	1–2	1–2
Polyester	3	3–4	3–4	4	4	4	3	4	3	3	3–4	3	3	3	3–4	2–3	2–3	2–3
Solution vinyl	4	3–4	3–4	3	4	3	1	2	3	3	3	3	3	3	3	1–2	1–2	1–2
Organosol—vinyl	4	2	2–3	3	3	3	1	2	2	3	2	3	3	3	3	1–2	1–2	1–2
Plastisol—vinyl	4–5	2	2	2–3	3	3	1	3	2	3–4	3	4	4	3–4	3	2	2	2
Thermoset acrylic	2–3	4	4	4	4	4	4	3	3	3	4	4	3	2–3	2–3	3	2–3	2–3
Silicone acrylic	2	4	3	4	4	4	4	3	3	3	4	4	3	3	3	3	3	3
Silicone polyester	2–3	3–4	4	4	4	4	4	3	3–4	3–4	3	4	3	3–4	3–4	3–4	3–4	3–4
Poly-vinylidene fluoride	4	3	3	3–4	4–5	4–5	4	4	4	4–5	5	5	3–4	3	3	4–5	4–5	4–5
Poly-vinyl fluoride film laminate	5	3	3	4	4–5	4–5	4	4	4	4–5	4	4	4	3	3	4	4–5	4
Poly-vinyl chloride film laminate	4	3	2	2	4	3	1	4	4	4	4	4	4	4	3	2	3	3
Acrylic film laminate	4	3	3	4	4–5	4	3	4	4	3	4	4	4	3	2	3	3	3
Acrylic latex—waterborne	3–4	3	4	4	4–5	4–5	3–5	3	3	4	2	2	2–3	3	3	3–4	3–4	3–4

	Application and cure						Physical properties					
Generic coating type	*Thermoplastic*	*Thermoset*	*Ease of application*	*Cure temperature PMT*	*Color and gloss retention (doubletime in oven)*	*Unit finishing cost range*	*Film hardness—pencil*	*Film flexibility—T-bend*	*Film adhesion*	*Ability to achieve high gloss (above 85 units 60°)*	*Ability to fabricate after aging*	*Adaptability to embossing (with metal)*
Epoxy-ester*		✓	4	420	NA	L	NA	2T	3	NA	3–4	3–4
Epoxy*		✓	4	435	NA	L	NA	2–3T	4	NA	3	4
Alkyd-amine		✓	4	435	2	L	F-H	2T	2	4	1–2	2
Polyester		✓	4	435	3	M	F-H	1–3T	3–4	5	3–4	3–4
Solution vinyl	✓		3–4	400	2	M	F-H	1T	3	3–4	4	4
Organosol—vinyl	✓		4	400	2	M	F	1T	3	2	4	4
Plastisol—vinyl	✓		2–3	400	2–3	MH	HB	0T	2	2	4–5	5
Thermoset acrylic		✓	4	440	4	LM	F	3T	3	4	3	3
Silicone acrylic		✓	4	450	4	MH	F-H	3T	3	3–4	3	3
Silicone polyester		✓	4	450	4	MH	F-H	2T	3	4	3	3
Poly-vinylidene fluoride	✓		4	465	4	H	H-2H	1T	2	1	4	4–5
Poly-vinyl fluoride film laminate	✓		4	400	NA	VH	F-H	1T	3	1	4	4
Poly-vinyl chloride film laminate	✓		4	400	NA	H	H	1T	1	3	4	4
Acrylic film laminate	✓		4	400	NA	H	H	2T	2	3	4	4
Acrylic latex—waterborne		✓	2–3	430	4	MH	HB-F	2T	3	2–3	4	3

*Primer

10.4 FLASHING DETAIL CONSIDERATIONS

At the time of publication of this manual, there is a cry for manufacturers' standard details. When a metal roof leaks, it is often at flashing detail areas. Unusual detail design situations are often encountered in reroof or retrofit design and could be aided by standard details. Also, designers could more easily address flashing-specific design by using standard details. In today's market there are many varied designs for each flashing detail area, depending upon manufacturer and type of panel. A flashing design for one material manufacturer's panel must be changed for use with another material manufacturer's panel.

Most manufacturers' panels differ from one another in the profile, with either different heights of seams or different widths of panels, or different sizes and spacings of stiffening ribs, with different manners and means of sealing at the lap seams and often different styles of clips used as concealed fasteners to secure the panels to the structure. Additionally, the same panel type can have several profile dimensions, even though they come from the same manufacturer. Therefore, the detail that worked well at a flashing with one type of panel will not necessarily work with a variation of the same panel, once again requiring specific selection and design.

When the designer is responsible for a project involving public funds, it is normally required that bid offering not be limited to a specific manufacturer. This creates quite a problem with metal roof systems since the detail flashing designs can vary so widely from manufacturer to manufacturer. As we have done repeatedly throughout this manual, we once again strongly suggest that it is good design practice to evaluate and design each flashing situation specifically for the roof system, building structure, climate, and exposure to which the roof system will be subjected.

Because of the complexities of designing metal roof flashing details, especially on some of the low-sloped metal roof systems, and the importance of keeping the roof watertight, it is hoped that standard details will soon be made available to help the designer. This is needed because the many forces which act and react with a metal roof are far different from what our experience and training with flexible membrane roofs has taught us.

However, the many varied styles of metal panels, the expansion and contraction considerations which will be different for each material type as well as different per each flashing area, and whether the roof panels are installed as a water-barrier or water-shedding system will all have a great influence on the flashing design. Standard details which can address the majority of the flashing situations we encounter with metal roof systems will be extremely difficult and perhaps not practical.

The following sections offer examples of what could be considered standard details, even though that is not our main intention. Time and space constraints prevent including all flashing areas which will be encountered in metal roof system design. Instead, the following text and illustrations will concentrate on the strengths and possible weaknesses of the detail as designed and why, in our opinion, the detail works or will not work in a durable manner.

By understanding the principles and forces involved, a designer should be able to select the best total roof and flashing system as offered by a manufacturer. Using the manufacturer's standard details is usually less expensive than custom-designing flashing systems, although we find that it is often necessary to modify or alter some items within the manufacturer's design offering. Be completely aware that changing or adapting a manufacturer's design without written consent, in many cases, will void or limit the manufacturer's responsibility in the event of roof leaks or failure. This is particularly true of "watertight warranties" issued by material manufacturers. (See Sec. 15.3.3.)

Many of the following figures are generic adaptations of material manufacturers' flashing designs. In our attempt to demonstrate a means and method by which designers can evaluate and then select the best flashing system design, it is necessary for us to use what is commonly available across the United States to all designers. It is not our intention to critique manufacturers' designs. It is instead our intention to further the understanding of metal roof flashings and systems. We demonstrate a thought and evaluation process which we believe designers can successfully use when considering the metal roof and flashing system.

Material manufacturers' flashing designs vary for a number of reasons. The designer must understand a few of the important aspects of different flashing system designs.

Many manufacturers started out designing and producing metal roof systems for a specific geographic area. As time passed and the metal roof system market grew at incredible rates, these manufacturers expanded into other regions and climates. In some cases, their designs have not been refined or broadened to include all the geographic locations and differing climates in which they are now sold and installed.

For example, some details (which we illustrate) have worked quite well in the dry southwest regions. The same flashing detail would be totally ineffective in the rainfall-intense Gulf Coast region. Likewise, a metal roof flashing detail which works fine in Miami, Florida, would not be cost-effective in Tucson, Arizona, since it is probably overdesigned for a dry, inland area.

At press time, the National Roofing Contractors Association (NRCA) had recently released their first attempt at generic, standard details for metal roofing. A large and unbiased, committee-driven organization and effort, their attempt is commendable. However, the contents in the following sections may sometimes be opposed to NRCA recommendations as well as specific material manufacturers' minimum design requirements. Not being committee-driven, and attempting to address adverse climatic conditions, the author expands, in more specific (and sometimes biased) terms, upon issues and solutions which we believe are relevant.

Standard, generic guidelines for metal roof panel flashings are much different than for bituminous or sheet metal roof flashings as published by the NRCA and roof membrane manufacturers. Again, this is due to the broad difference of styles, shapes, and configurations of metal roof panels; the varying regions wherein they are used which place different design and erection considerations and restraints on metal roof and flashing systems, and, in general, the lack of experience of the metal roof manufacturing and application industry.

Metal flashing systems are often custom-designed by someone within the manufacturer's organization, based upon their experience of metal roof systems, standard practices, and application standards. Such experience is often garnered from local or regional practices. This independent design furthers the problem of different flashing system design among manufacturers. Most manufacturers understand and agree that the flashing design as published in their literature is for guidance only and can be adapted to satisfy job-specific requirements. Once again, we state that our purpose is to show the designer how to evaluate and possibly adapt flashing design to meet the needs of a specific project.

Many of the principles and forces to be considered with metal roof flashing design are referenced in other chapters of this Manual. Forces of expansion and contraction (Secs. 11.3.1 and 12.2.1), metal flashing design principles (Sec. 12.1.6), and water-shedding design of metal roof panels (Sec. 11.3.2) are discussed elsewhere, but contain key information which is inherent to the requirements of metal flashings on metal roof systems.

Metal roof systems usually require metal flashings. Adhering and sealing a metal flashing to a metal roof panel is more complicated than many realize. The design and application process is less forgiving of error than is, for example, the sealing of a modified bitumen flashing sheet to a BUR surface. There is no redundancy of additional layers as there is with a modified bitumen BUR base flashing system. With metal roof flashings, we must rely on the gravitational flow of water or a single layer of tape sealant or caulk to keep the system watertight.

However, general waterproofing principles as used with flexible membrane roof flashing systems can sometimes apply to metal membrane roof flashing systems. The sealing adhesive (caulk) between the flashing and metal roof membrane must be continuous and of correct material to create the waterproof seal. The flashing must be of correct size, extending onto or under the metal roof and up any flashing structure to correct width and height. The metal flashing component must be of correct gauge thickness to adequately compensate for the girth width of the metal flashing. The metal flashing must be designed, fabricated, and installed waterproof and in a manner to blend with the roof panel system and not fight against it during expansion and contraction cycles.

10.4.1 General Requirements of Flashings

SUPPORT

All flashing structures, be it a plumbing soil stack, ductwork, or other equipment penetrating through the roof panel must be supported and firmly secured stationary below the roofline. We must already plan for the metal roof panels moving and the metal flashing moving, and we do not need added surprises of the flashing structure moving, due to snow loads, wind, etc. Also, we sometimes need to attach flashing components to a solid and secure structure.

We often need to attach roof panels or metal flashings at various locations around a roof penetration. The design must therefore include proper framing support completely around the opening through which the flashing structure will extend. When the flashing detail is designed, refer to the structural drawings and verify that the structural framing at the penetration is of adequate size and at the proper location to allow any needed fasteners to be installed.

PANEL OBSTRUCTION

If the flashing structure obstructs water flow through the flat pan portion of the panel, water backup can result. Although many water-barrier systems can supposedly resist this action, it is better to avoid the situation if possible.

If the structure is going to obstruct more than 50 to 60 percent of the pan width, design a flashing which extends completely across the pan to the adjacent pans on each side of the flashing. This requires more time, material, and, therefore, expense, except when leaks begin.

This procedure must be weighed against the possibility of water backup. Water will back up behind a square structure (fan curbs) more easily than it will at a round structure (soil stack). Also consider foliage surrounding the building. Leaves will gather behind flashing structures and very effectively restrict water flow.

Crickets, or saddle flashings, are always a consideration, although we seldom see them installed on metal roofs at flashing structures. Again, this is a judgment call by the designer since they require time, materials, and expense. Crickets are not required if the designer is sure that water will not back up behind the flashing structure to an extent that waterproofing seals or laps will be compromised.

CAULKING AND SEALANTS

If caulking is a key ingredient in keeping the flashing system watertight, make sure it is the proper type of caulk as recommended for use by the panel manufacturer. Get it in writing from the manufacturer.

Make sure the caulk will permanently stay in compression between the roof panel and the flashing component. Compression causes the caulk to become a waterproofing gasket. This gasket is essential to waterproofing. (See Fig. 10.26.)

Like all caulk sealant systems, the caulk thickness has a range of minimum and maximum thicknesses in which it is most effective. Overtightening or undertightening flashing to the roof surface can cause the caulk gasket to be ineffective.

In some cases, it is manufacturer-recommended and accepted practice to date to use sealant tape in lieu of caulk. In panel laps seams, tape works quite well in restricting water entry (see Fig. 10.2). At transverse panel seams, specify an additional row of sealant tape . . . just to be sure.

Require written approval of the caulking type and manufacturer from the metal panel manufacturer. Also require written instructions for metal surface preparation prior to application of caulk. There usually will not be any requirement, but . . . just to be sure.

On crucial flashings which have to be shop-fabricated by the contractor, we suggest soldered corners and laps. The argument against such is that the rest of the roof system is waterproofed at essential locations with caulk or tape sealant, so why solder now?

Caulk and tape sealant used at other roof flashing locations work on the principle of compression created by the two pieces of metal screw fastened together, which forms a gasket and creates a watertight seal. (See Fig. 10.26.) The laps of the shop-fabricated flashing unit will often not be able to produce such an effect. Soldering is permanent, although caulking may work, if expertly applied in a correctly fabricated lap. But . . . just to be sure.

Also, at some 90° flashings which have to turn a 90° corner, a metal piece will have to be installed to fill the gap created by the cut required. (See Fig. 10.23.) If designing this flashing piece for a BUR, soldered corners would be required. No less should be required of a metal roof flashing.

METAL FLASHING MATERIALS

If soldering is to be performed, the flashing components must be either galvanized steel, stainless steel, copper, or lead-coated metal. The coating from a painted metal roof panel must not be removed to allow for a solder joint. Rust and deterioration is a strong possibility in such a case, even if the solder joint is shop- or field-painted. The paint coat finish cannot be reapplied to the same standard as is performed at the factory.

Compatibility of materials is always a consideration. Technically, no metal is compatible with another. Instead, some combinations of metals are more compatible than are other combinations. The environment in which the metals will exist is a prime consideration. (See Sec. 12.2.3.)

If flashing components are to be shop-fabricated by the contractor, the metal must be compatible with the metal roof panels. Considerations also include sealing requirements of the laps, guage thickness requirements, and the final appearance of the flashing component on the roof system.

For example, if a bright blue metal roof panel system is being installed and is very visible, a fan curb flashing existing in the middle of the roof should aesthetically blend with the rest of the roof. Fabricating the curb from the same metal stock that the roof system is made from would be advantageous but not correct design. Fan curbs are normally required to be of heavy 18-gauge

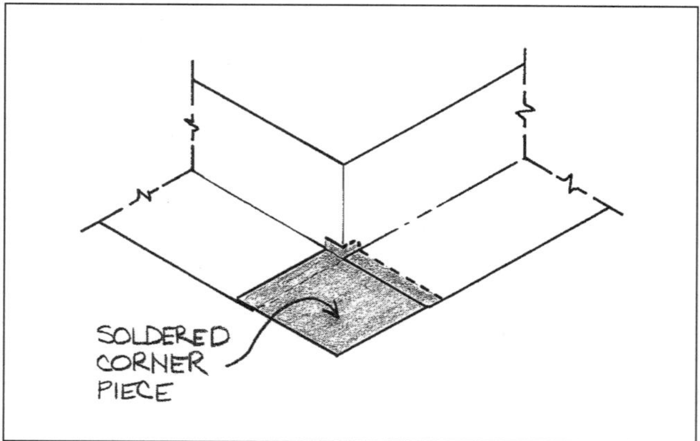

Figure 10.23 Soldered corner base flashing.

metal, and roof panel metal stock seldom exceeds 22-gauge, and is more often 24-gauge material. The fan curb may need to be soldered, and the paint coated metal stock as used for the roof will prevent soldering of the flashing piece.

If soldering is required to create a permanent watertight flashing for the situation just mentioned, galvanized steel could be soldered and shop-painted, but the color will not last. Stainless steel could be used and would not require painting to prevent rust; however, a bright and shiny flashing may not be the visual effect desired.

One solution may be to create the curb flashing from stainless steel, soldering and making it as watertight as required, and then cladding it with blue roof panel metal for visual effect. The blue cladding metal need only be attached with rivets above the water floodplane level.

Regarding rivets, which are commonly used to secure flashing joints together, painted rivets are available to match the color of the paint coated panels. However, we often find that the mandrel is steel, and in some environments the steel mandrel will rust. After time, rust stains can appear on the metal roof or flashing system.

An option is specifying either stainless steel or aluminum rivets, which have the same mandrel type as the rivet. However, the rivets will probably not be available in color.

ROOF PENETRATIONS

Avoid roof penetrations on metal roof systems.

Consider installing any vent or fan through a building side wall, thereby eliminating the roof flashing. Sometimes vent exhaust pipes can be manifolded together, reducing the number of roof penetrations and the resulting flashing. Building code requirements and restrictions apply.

If the roof design will require numerous penetrations of flashing structures, strongly consider a different type of roof system. If a different type of roof system is not an option, then use a steep-sloped metal roof design instead of a low-sloped system. Even if the metal roof has a slope allowing for water-shedding design, use water-barrier design principles at flashing structure penetrations. (See Sec. 10.3.1.)

Designing rooftop A/C units should be avoided. If unavoidable, make sure the condensate is piped in PVC to the eave and over the roof edge. The A/C condensate contains copper ions which will discolor and often destroy many panel coatings.

Plumbing vent stacks must never be installed through a lap seam, but must instead penetrate through the flat pan of the metal panel. Manufacturer-supplied neoprene or silicone collars are used to seal the pipe penetration to the metal roof panel. If the pipe diameter exceeds 50 to 60 percent of the metal panel width, a curb is required to extend across the entire panel width, thereby directing water flow to the unobstructed panels on either side of the pipe penetration.

Avoid roof penetrations on metal roof systems.

REQUIRED MANUFACTURERS' FLASHINGS

Eave, rake, ridge, and gutter flashing is supplied by each metal roof manufacturer. These components are coated with the same paint or metal as the roof panels. The components are fabricated to fit with the roof panels to create a watertight system.

Designers usually specify these manufacturer-supplied flashings. If specially designed flashings are determined to be required, they can often be ordered through the manufacturer or can be fabricated by a local contractor.

Special design of a specific flashing—for example, a gutter—may be required because the metal roof panel manufacturer does not provide a gutter having the required characteristics. This can be related to inadequate allowance for emergency overflow, too broad or too narrow a face, or the need to match existing, in-place gutter at other locations on the building.

Also, designers must closely examine and evaluate manufacturer-supplied flashings. Some do not provide for all requirements of a proper roof design. It may be necessary to modify the manufacturer's flashing design.

An example can be a rake flashing which the manufacturer shows as being attached to the roof panel and to the building wall. (See Fig. 10.24.) This design does not allow for movement—which will occur and cannot be stopped—of the metal roof panel as well as the rake flashing. Requiring a continuous cleat will allow the rake flashing to be firmly secured to the building wall while at the same time allowing movement of the rake flashing at the building wall. (See Fig. 10.25.)

10.4.2 Flashing Design Theory

GENERAL

Some metal roof systems can withstand water flooding and covering the seams and laps, and are referred to herein as water-barrier systems. Other types of metal roof panel systems cannot and rely on gravity to prevent water flooding of the panel system. These types of systems are referred to as water shedders.

The roof panel styles are different for each category, with structural panels dominating the water-barrier panel systems. Structural panels do not require a roof deck for support but instead span from purlin to purlin for support. The absence of a roof deck prohibits a

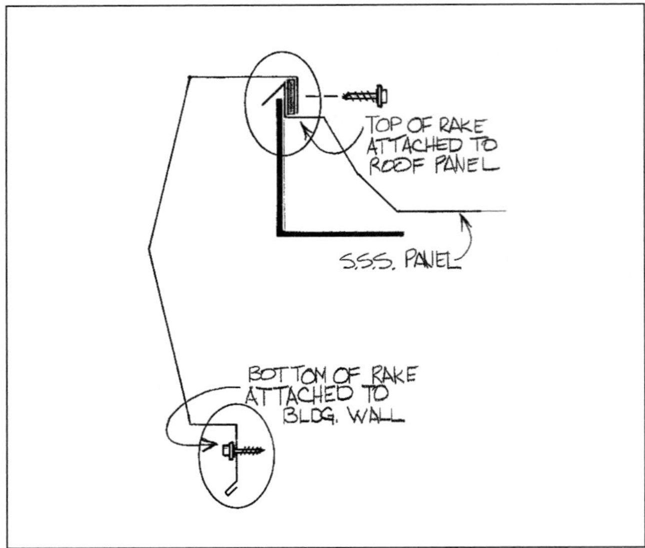

Figure 10.24 Fixed rake flashing.

waterproofing felt or membrane layer under the roof system. Structural panels are most often used for industrial and institutional applications.

Water-shedding panels are usually, but not always, nonstructural. As nonstructural, they require a roof deck for support and are most often used for architectural applications where the roof is a visible component of the building structure. Visibility requires slope, which produces the gravity effect required for water-shedding systems.

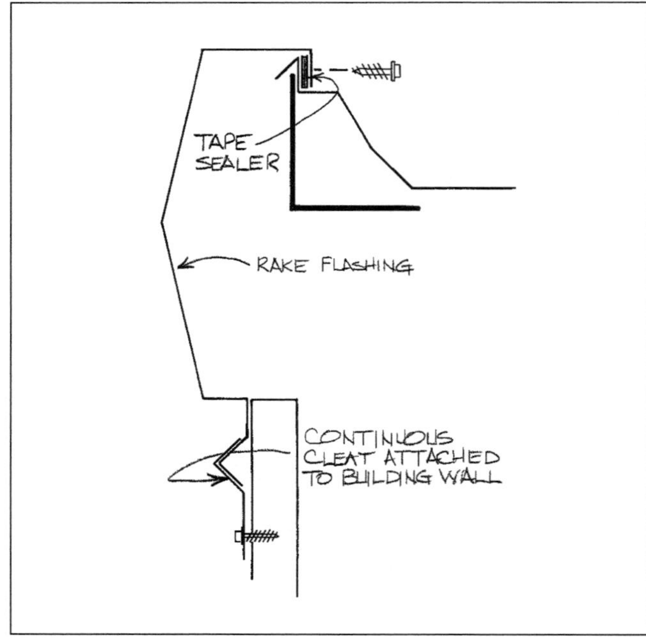

Figure 10.25 Rake with cleat.

However, some water-barrier structural panels are also used for visible architectural applications because of their pleasing appearance on certain building structure styles and they may be required even on a steep-slope roof (>3:12) with long panel runs from ridge to eave. Long panel runs can cause water to back up and flood the roof panel laps and seams. (See Sec. 10.3.1.)

Many flashings are designed and installed differently for water-shedding and water-barrier panel systems. At other times they are similar. Sometimes flashings on a water-shedding system must be designed and installed as a water barrier. Sometimes on water-barrier systems the flashings can be designed only as water shedders.

In the remaining portion of this section we will examine the most commonly used flashings for metal roof systems, both water shedding and water barrier. Many of the figures are adapted from material manufacturers' design manuals; some are variations of commonly used flashing details within the industry for a particular panel style, while others are examples of design adaptation to create what we believe is a better solution.

Some of the key factors to consider when evaluating or designing flashings are:

- The ability of the flashing to allow for movement of the metal roof panel system
- The ability of the flashing to restrict water entry in severe conditions after extended periods of time
- The ability of the flashing to remain secured in place even during tremendous stress periods, e.g., strong winds and snow loading
- The ability of the flashing detail, as designed, to be built correctly in the field by the roofer

In our design practice we often adapt, modify, or completely redesign some flashing details, depending on building and site conditions and service required of the roof system. We feel comfortable in doing this. However, be completely aware that when a material manufacturer's details are changed, the designer usually takes full responsibility for the adequacy and correctness of the design. If problems occur due to improper design of the flashing, the material manufacturer has no responsibility.

It is good design practice to thoroughly evaluate the flashing details of a particular system. After defining the project requirements of either a water-shedding or water-barrier system, the next selection parameter requirement is usually the flashing design compatibility. (See Chap. 15.) If there appear to be too many inadequacies, selection of another system from the manufacturer's offerings or selection of another manufacturer may be advised.

If a weather-tightness warranty is required from the material manufacturer, changing or altering flashing details should be done only upon written approval by the material manufacturer. Manufacturers' warranties do not guarantee there will be no problems with the completed roof system; they may provide some relief in the event of problems, or they can possibly increase the liability position of the designer. (See Secs. 10.1.1 and 15.1.3.)

It is always a good design practice to work with the technical/design department of the material manufacturer during the material selection and roof design process. Address all detail and flashing areas on the drawings and within the specifications. Obtain written approval and acceptance from the manufacturer of the roof detail design prior to construction. (See Sec. 15.1.3.)

TAPE SEALER AND CAULKING

Many flashing details used with metal roofing heavily rely on the waterproofing ability and permanence of butyl tape sealer, urethane, or butyl-based caulking. To provide the required longevity and service, the design and application of these materials are different from what we normally use for other construction applications.

Many flashings use either tape sealer or caulking in compression, hidden from the sunlight and elements. Sunlight will rapidly destroy these material types. Compression is required to transform the materials into a waterproof gasket system.

Correct and permanent compression seal is directly related to the rigidity (tensile strength) of the steel flanges between which it is installed. To better understand waterproofing design by compression, consider tape sealer placed between two pieces of light-gauge aluminum, such as is used in the manufacture of soft drink cans. In such a case, screw fasteners or pop rivets, no matter how closely spaced together, will not create enough compression to produce a water-barrier seal. This is because the tensile strength of the thin metal is not adequate to transfer and spread the stress created by the fasteners uniformly across the materials joined together.

However, consider two pieces of structural angle iron with tape sealer placed between. When the two angle iron pieces are fastened together, the tensile strength of the iron angle will most definitely compress the tape sealer to create a watertight seal. Always consider this when evaluating or designing a water barrier using tape sealer or caulk. (See Fig. 10.26.)

Designing a compression seal using a metal roof panel of 24-gauge material and a sheet metal roof flashing of 26 or 24 gauge may not provide the tensile strength required to permanently and adequately create a compression seal for water-barrier design. We therefore always try to incorporate, at some location within the compression seal system, a heavy-gauge steel flashing to impart tensile strength to the other components.

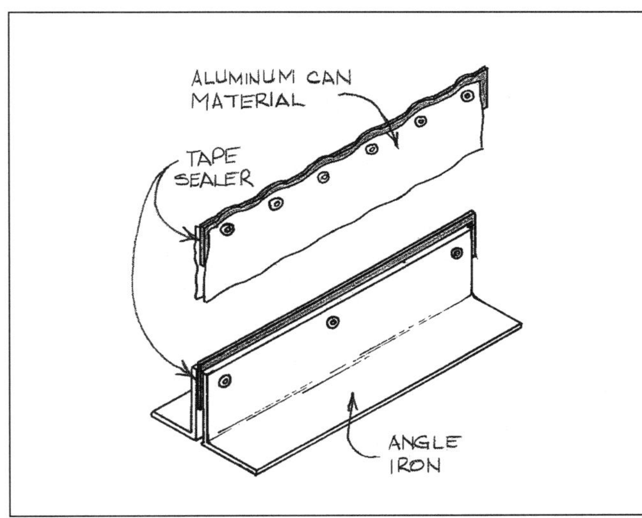

Figure 10.26 Tape sealer in different compressions.

10.4.3 Parapet Rakes

The flashing detail shown in Fig. 10.27 illustrates a structural water-barrier panel abutting a parapet wall or building wall. There are several items which, in our opinion, do not satisfy the requirements of a proper flashing design. One concern is the metal wall flashing which is attached to both the metal panel and the building wall.

During thermal cycles the occurring expansion and contraction movement of the "floating" metal roof panel will be somewhat restricted by the metal wall flashing. Since the wall flashing is secured to the metal roof panel and to the building wall, it cannot float with the roof panel movements that will surely occur.

Also, since the tape sealer is located in the flood plane of the roof panel system, its performance is critical as a water barrier. Stress caused by the panel movement restriction will be concentrated at this tape sealer location. The amount of movement stress at the wall flashing and tape sealer location is dependent upon the length of the metal roof panel and the annual temperature extremes to be experienced by the roof assembly. (See Sec. 12.2.1.) The more excessive the roof panel movement, the more stress is transferred to the tape sealer location.

If a screw fastener becomes unsecured due to a "wallowing-out" effect where it penetrates through the metal roof panel, or if it backs out due to the same cause of stress movement, the tape sealer is no longer in

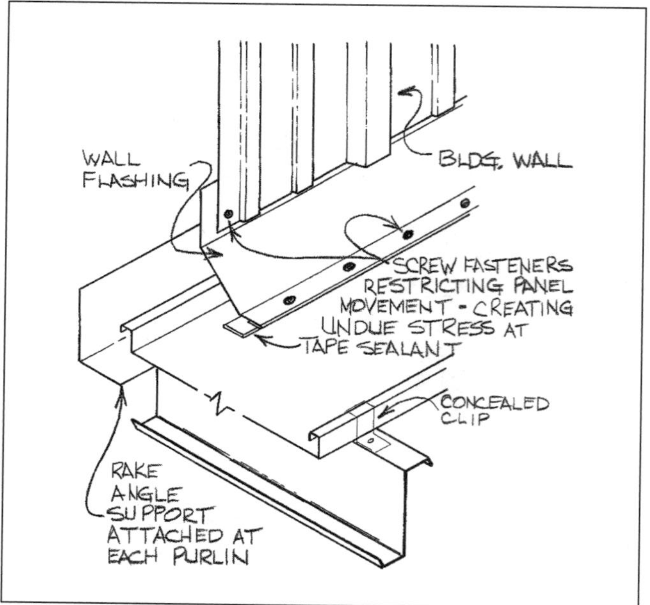

Figure 10.27 Rake flashing at parapet/building wall.

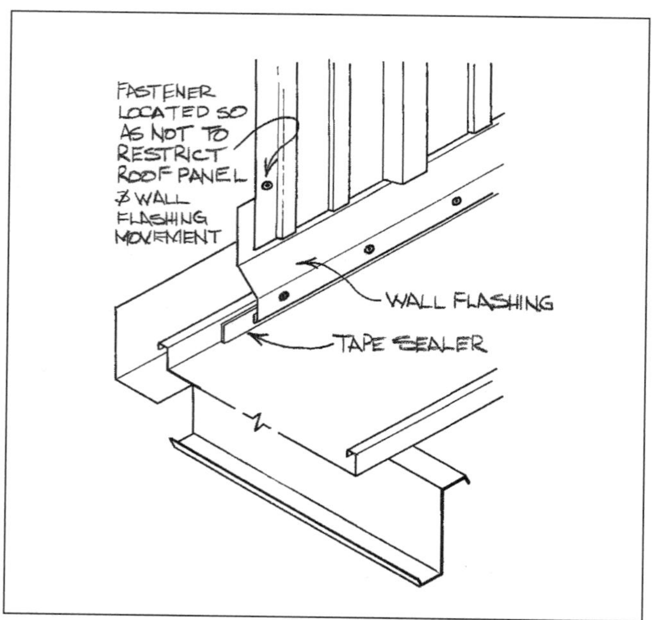

Figure 10.28 Moving the tape seal location.

compression and leaks can occur. Some manufacturers' details attempt to compensate by extending the rake angle support, normally 16-gauge steel, under the roof panel far enough so that the screw fastener penetrates the wall flashing, metal roof panel, and the rake angle support. Being permanently fixed to the purlins, it is hoped that the heavy-gauge steel support angle will help restrict panel movement and provide the backup support needed to hold the tape sealer in compression.

However, in our opinion, this is illogical. We have learned to allow for panel movement, hence the concealed floating clip fastener which allows for roof panel movement. Tying to restrict such movement, especially at a flashing detail, may not be the best design solution.

One design option is to move the tape seal location. The detail drawing in Fig. 10.28 locates the tape sealer to the vertical leg of the metal roof panel. This accomplishes several purposes. It moves the critical tape seal out of the panel flood plane. A water-barrier system is now also using water-shedding design principles. Additionally, relocating the wall fastener to be above the top flange of the metal wall flashing will allow the wall flashing to move unrestricted with the roof panel movements. It can now "float" with the metal roof panel, eliminating undue stress at the tape sealer location.

However, there are still some problems with this design. One consideration is the ability of this parapet rake area to resist negative wind uplift pressure. Roof eaves, ridges, rakes, and parapet rakes experience high levels of uplift force during strong winds. (See Sec. 2.2.2.) The design in Fig. 10.28 does not provide for additional securement as required to resist the negative pressures induced by high-speed winds.

Another consideration is roof slope which determines water-barrier or water-shedding design requirements. If the roof slope is low-pitched, the system must be a water-barrier design. Even though the tape sealer is located above the metal roof panel pan, a low-pitched roof slope will still place it in the flood plane. Water can flood, cover, and even extend above the exposed fastener heads.

Therefore, the compression seal of the tape sealer is once again critical. In Fig. 10.28, the tape sealer is held in compression by the wall flashing and roof panel flanges. These materials are normally of 26-, 24-, or possibly 22-gauge metal. The tensile strength of light-gauge sheet metal components may not be adequate to properly and permanently hold the tape sealer in compression well enough to create a water-barrier seal during water flooding conditions. (See Sec. 10.4.2.)

Figure 10.29 incorporates all the design elements required of a proper parapet/building wall flashing detail. The critical waterproofing tape seal location is moved to the vertical leg of the roof panel seam. The wall flashing is pinned to the building wall and hem-locked to the roof panel. The hem-lock provides for independent movement of the flashings and roof panel. The caulk lip of the upper wall flashing can be deleted and extend up and under metal wall panels, as shown in Figs. 10.27 and 10.28. A rake angle support is used as a backer to provide the necessary tensile strength required at the tape sealer location. The rake angle sup-

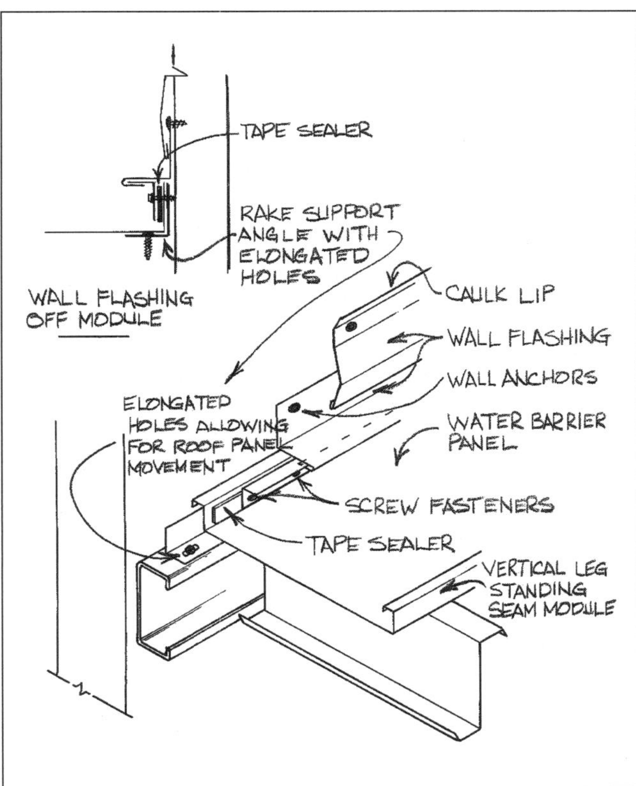

Figure 10.29 Wall flashing detail with all the proper design elements.

port will also provide the necessary strength to resist negative pressure caused by strong winds.

Of key importance to this detail, and seldom seen in the metal roof industry, is the manner in which the rake angle support is attached to the structural steel purlin. The rake angle is manufacturer-supplied with elongated holes through which a special fastener is placed. The fastener is special-shaped to allow the support angle to float with the movements of the roof panel.

NONSTRUCTURAL CONTINUOUS PANELS

Sometimes the metal roof panel selected does not allow for panel lapping, therefore requiring all panels to be continuous from eave to ridge. This often prevents the roof contractor from shop-fabricating breaks (bends) into the rake panels, since most sheet metal shop breaks (metal bending machines) are 10 ft long. If the roof panels exceed 10 ft in length, fabricating breaks into the panel is possible only at the metal roof panel manufacturing plant. This becomes important if the roof panel seam configuration does not allow flashing details as depicted in the preceding figures. Different-shaped panel seams which prevent panel overlapping are shown in Figs. 10.30 and 10.31.

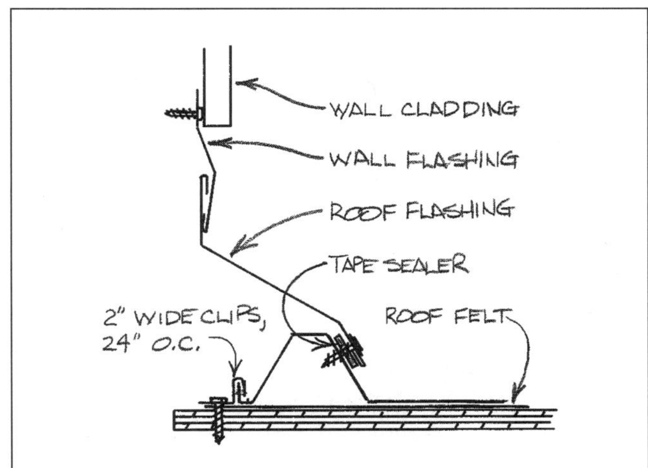

Figure 10.30 On-module wall termination of panel seam that prevents panel overlapping.

The parapet/building wall rake flashing detail in Fig. 10.30 fulfills the requirements of a proper flashing detail. Since this style of roof panel is used only as a water shedder, the tape sealer is out of the water flood plane. Even though the tape seal may not be in continuous and full compression because of the light gauge of the roof panel and sheet metal flashing, again the water-shedding requirements of the roof system design will keep the seal out of the water flood plane.

The roof flashing is secured only to the roof panel seam. The flashing is unsecured at the top, allowing for unrestricted roof panel movement.

In the field, the roof installer bends up the fastening leg of the roof panel, to which clips are hem-locked and then fastened to the roof deck. This lock and fastening allows for roof panel movement while at the same time

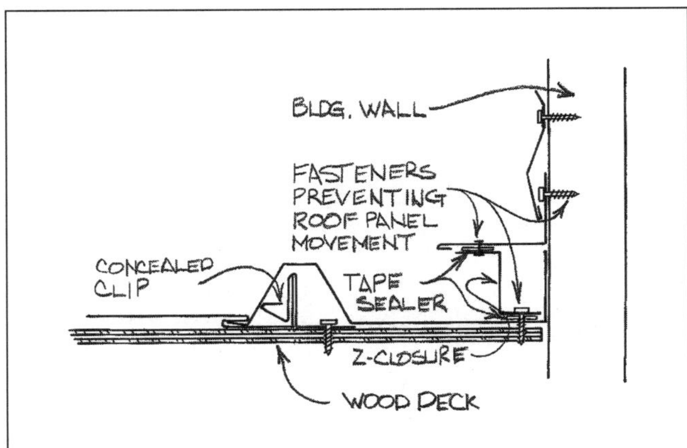

Figure 10.31 Off-module wall termination of panel seam that prevents panel overlapping.

providing additional hold-down strength at the critical rake area.

Another parapet rake detail used when this type of panel finishes off of the roof panel seam module is shown in Fig. 10.31. The Z-closure is sealed by tape sealer to the metal roof panel. Even though the tape sealer is in the water flood plane, the roof slope should provide adequate drainage to allow the seal to function.

The Z-closure is fastened through the metal roof panel and into the roof deck. This will restrict independent panel movement. This will probably function adequately if the panel run is not too long. Again, a long panel will expand and contract more than will a short panel run. Notice that the roof panel is further secured in place by the fastening of the upper leg of the Z-closure to the wall flashing.

After considering this manufacturer's detail, we offer an alternative detail design for this situation as shown in Fig. 10.32. However, there are some possible problems with the design.

The first problem may be buildability by the roof installers if the roof panel is to be bent and formed in the field. We show a 1½-in-high vertical dogleg panel seam. This can be formed by use of sheet metal tongs which will create the vertical leg 2 inches in height. A 2 × 2 or 2 × 4 is then placed next to the vertical leg and the seam is bent over the top of the board by use of a rubber mallet.

The result is a formed 1½-in-tall vertical dogleg seam. A professional roofer experienced with metal roofing can create this detail; however, we have been informed by metal manufacturers that workers skilled enough to create field flashings are the exception instead of the rule.

Another consideration with the detail is panel movement being restricted by the hem-locks of both the Z-closure and the wall flashing. If the locks are crimped tight to the metal panel, and the panel undergoes excessive movement cycles, binding of the panel to the closure may result. It is therefore imperative that the dogleg of the vertical seam be large enough to fully and permanently engage the Z-closure and that the hem-locks are not tightly crimped to the vertical panel seam.

This can be accomplished by making the horizontal dogleg larger than ½ in. This will require the vertical leg to be longer, which can create a problem in the field since most hand tongs used by roofers will not allow for more than a 2-in bend. One solution is to procure hand tongs which will allow for an extra-tall vertical seam, even if they have to be built by the contractor. (See Fig. 10.33.)

Another option to be considered by the designer is having the vertical dogleg seam created by the manufacturer during panel fabrication. Manufacturers can break and form flashing bends onto panels during panel forming.

However, the detail in Fig. 10.33 is for a rake termination, not a rake starting detail. It is almost impossible to lay out a job accurately enough to predict where in the panel layout run this termination will occur. Therefore, most often it must be built in the field.

10.4.4 Rake Flashings

Rake flashings are required at gable-end situations. The style, components used, and waterproofing integrity vary greatly from material system manufacturer to man-

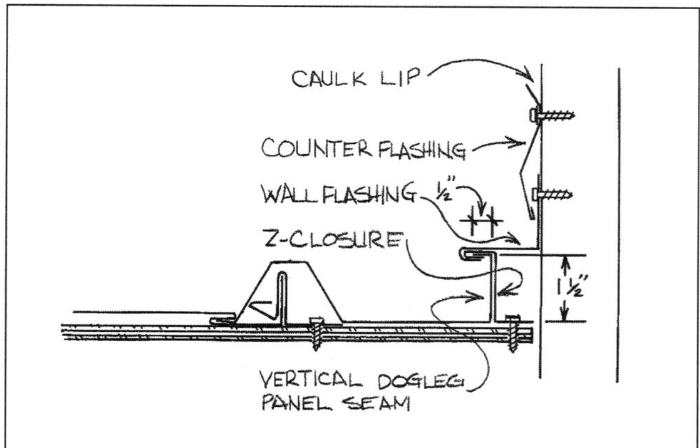

Figure 10.32 Alternative detail design for off-module non-lappable panel.

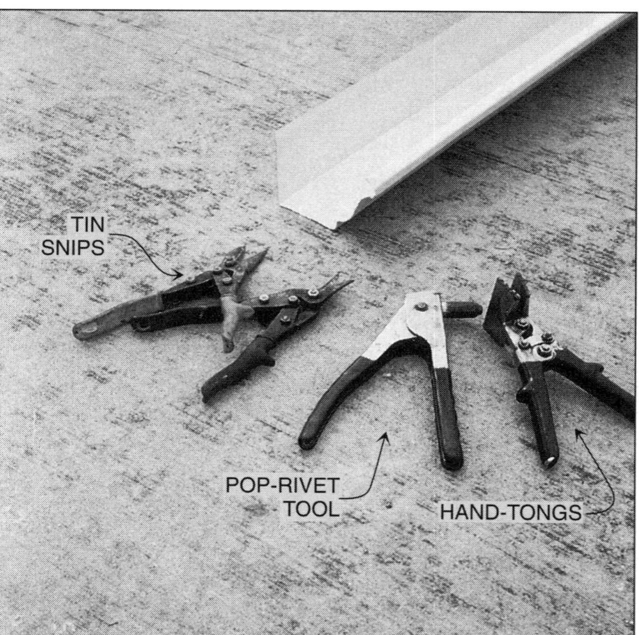

Figure 10.33 Hand tools.

ufacturer. Figure 10.34 shows typical rake flashing details as used over a solid roof deck.

The two styles of rake flashing depicted are *floating* and *fixed*. Panel types, both structural and nonstructural, which normally use this detail are also shown. These details are normally used for water-shedding roof systems, although they have been used for water-barrier panel systems.

The fixed rake flashing does not allow for movement of the roof panel, which will surely occur. Also, the important tape sealer is located in the flood plane of the roof panel. Although a steep roof slope should allow this design to function adequately, we still question if such detail is in keeping with good design practice.

Perhaps the advantage of the fixed rake to the floating rake is the economic savings due to the simpler construction. For small roof panel runs of 15 ft or less, this fixed rake detail should work adequately.

However, in our design practice we always use the floating rake detail . . . just to be sure. The floating rake detail takes the tape sealer out of the flood-plane level. The C-closure provides wind uplift resistance needed at this area of the roof.

However, there can be problems with this detail design. It is imperative that the C-closure not be attached by the pop rivets which secure the tape sealer between the metal roof panel leg and the 90° external metal flashing piece. See expanded view. If the roof panel is attached to the C-closure, the rake will no longer float, but will instead be fixed to the C-closure.

Buildability is a consideration. The C-closure needs to fit somewhat close to the roof panel's vertical turn-up leg. The dogleg atop the C-closure must fully engage the external flashing piece in order to provide perimeter edge securement to the rake flashing system. However, if placed too close, the roof installer may also drill a hole through the C-closure and attach the roof panel to the closure, restricting panel movement.

Also, the tape sealer may not be held in proper compression throughout the flashing system. Since the nonstructural panels are supported by a solid deck, we often use 26-gauge material for the roof panels. Flashing pieces are also often made from the same-gauge material. The thin-gauge materials will not have as much tensile strength as heavier-gauge metal. We must rely on the water-shedding slope of the roof to prevent water entry through any deficient area.

For your consideration, a rake flashing detail which either begins or ends on module is shown below. It is a structural panel, therefore it can be installed on purlins although it is often installed to a solid deck. It is also referenced in Fig. 10.34.

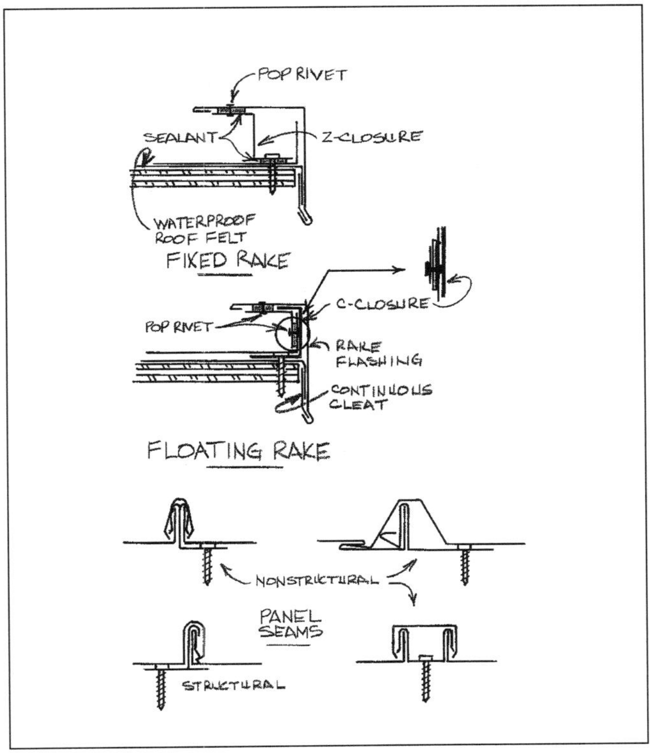

Figure 10.34 Typical rake flashing details over a solid roof deck.

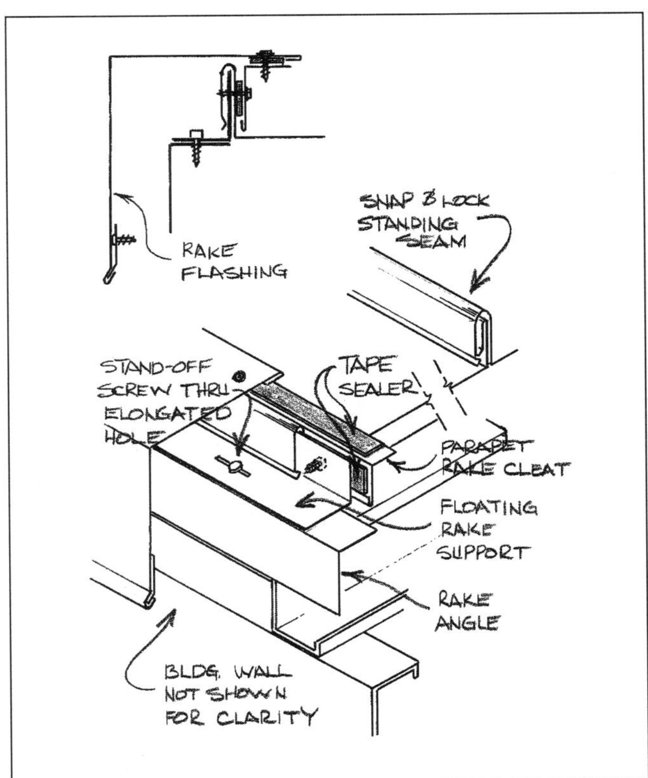

Figure 10.35 Rake flashings on module.

The detail shown in Fig. 10.35 allows the flashing and roof panel to move independently by a different design. Once again, the stand-off screw fastener, through elongated holes in the rake angle, allow for panel and flashing movement. Additionally, the rake angle and floating rake support are of heavy-gauge steel. This provides the additional strength required to secure the roof during high wind conditions.

For finishing the roof system off module, instead of on module as shown, the roof panel must be bent to a 90° angle at the floating rake support location. All components are then installed as shown.

In review of other rake flashing designs we evaluate Figs. 10.36 and 10.37.

In some geographic locations with low annual rainfall amounts and moderate to low wind speeds, this detail has functioned fine. However, it would appear that strong winds could easily cause convexing of the roof panel, causing it to slide and lift from the starter strip flashing. Also, as time passes and the caulk hardens and/or loosens from the metal, water entry under the metal roof system will be imminent. For such a detail design, the waterproofing felt(s) underlayment is crucial.

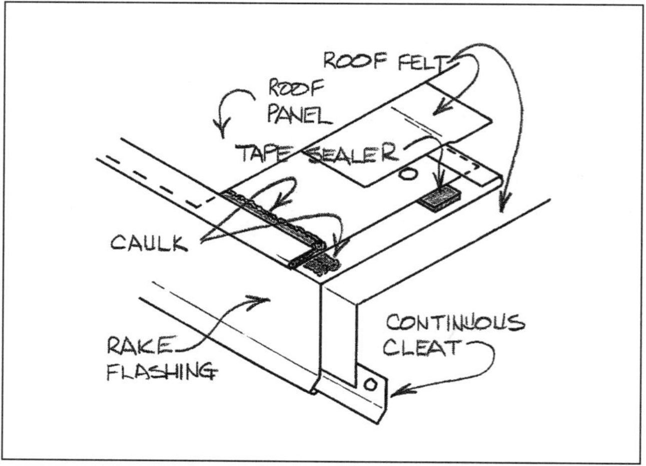

Figure 10.36 Starter strip rake flashing.

In our personal opinion the detail shown in Fig. 10.38 is best suited to most all rake detail situations. The roof panel can move independently, not being fastener-attached at any rake location. We are not concerned with allowing for movement of the rake flashing since it has no waterproofing function that lapping of the rake flashing end pieces cannot accommodate.

The rake flashing is secured to the building structure by use of the continuous cleat. The roof panel is secured to the rake flashing by use of a hem-lock turn on the roof panel. This detail will resist strong negative pressure uplift experienced at rake edges.

If the building is out of square, this detail will still work. Perhaps the disadvantage to this detail over some others is buildability. We have been informed by some metal manufacturers that many metal roof erectors do not have the talent or patience to correctly and aesthetically create this detail in the field.

Figure 10.39 shows a common type of commercial roof panel. Normally referred to as a structural standing seam panel, it more accurately is described as a structural trapezoidal seam panel. This panel is often used on roof slopes of ¼-in fall per running foot. However, we highly discouraged this minimum slope requirement, and suggest it is better design practice to require a ½-in:12 roof slope—just to be sure.

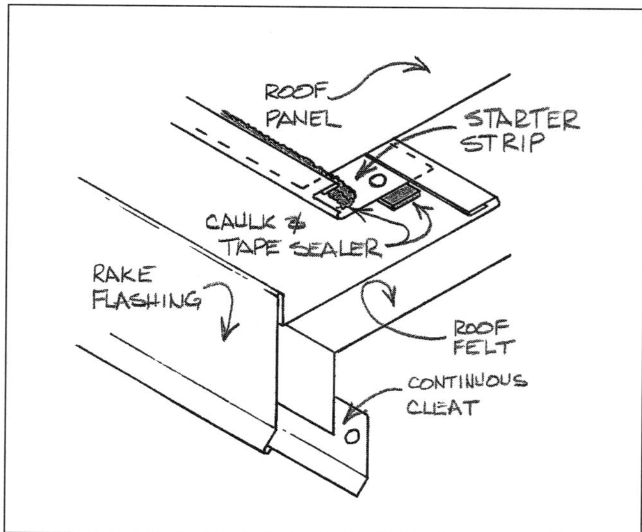

Figure 10.37 Starter strip rake flashing off module.

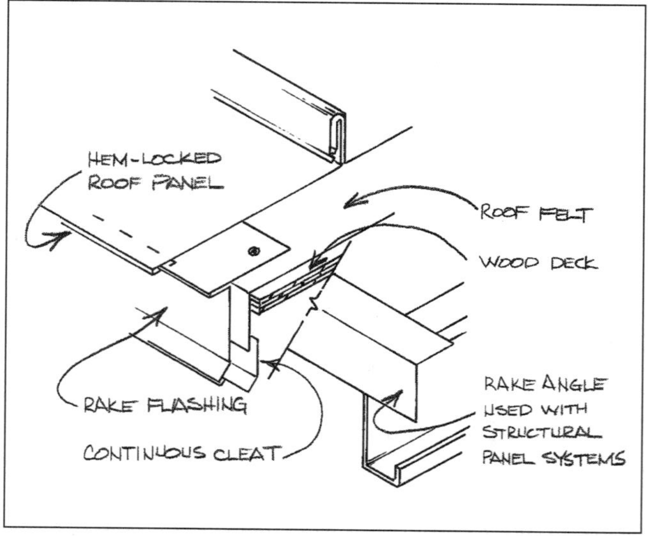

Figure 10.38 Hem-lock rake flashing.

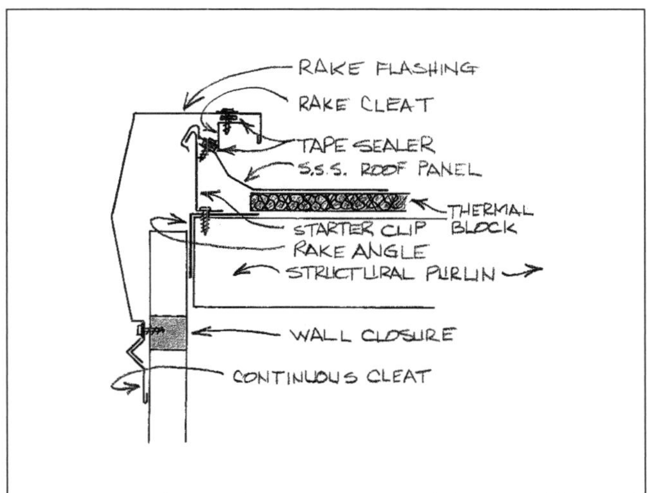

Figure 10.39 Rake flashing—fixed structural standing seam.

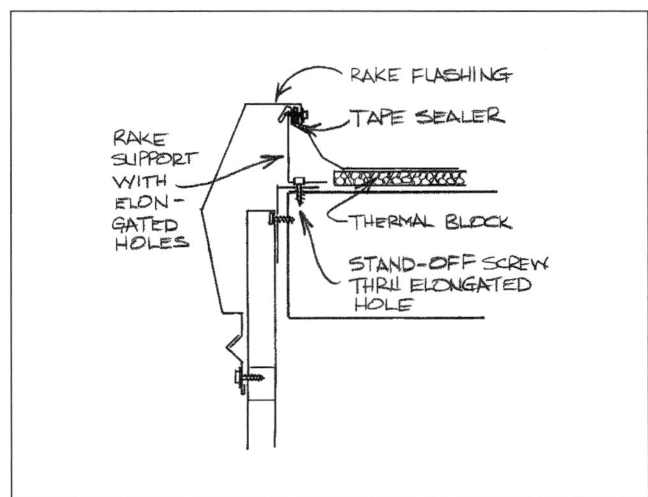

Figure 10.40 Floating rake flashing.

We have purposefully shown the screw fastener at the bottom of the rake flashing to be penetrating into the building wall. This one item creates a fixed rake flashing, wherein independent movement of the roof panel is restricted. By moving the screw fastener to the continuous cleat, a floating rake is created.

A single small item such as this can jeopardize the waterproof integrity of this detail. On a low-sloped roof surface, water can easily flood or be wind-driven to the tape sealer location. If the seal at this location has been compromised due to expansion and contraction, stress leaks may occur.

Also note that this detail compresses tape sealer between light-gauge sheet metal, being the roof panel and the rake cleat. Under panel flood conditions, which is not uncommon when this panel is installed to low-slopes, the seal may not be adequate or may not be durable for extended periods of time.

Another detail using the same type of roof panel provides for independent movement in that it is a floating rake system. (See Fig. 10.40.) A stand-off screw through elongated holes in the rake support allows the roof panel to move without being restricted by the rake flashing. Movement can also be provided at this location by other types of floating clip fasteners.

In addition, the tape sealer is compressed between the light-gauge steel of the roof panel and the heavier gauge rake support. This provides optimum compression of the tape sealer, creating a watertight barrier.

Both details (Figs. 10.39 and 10.40) show rake flashings on module. However, when finishing off the roof panel run, the rake edges seldom coincide with the roof panel module. A detail such as shown in Fig. 10.41 is then needed.

Again we have opted to show a detail using a stand-off screw through elongated holes in the rake support angle which create a floating rake assembly. This detail, or others like it, will work fine when the module terminates within allowable distances from the rake edge.

However, we often encounter situations where the module terminates more than 6 in from the rake edge. In such a case, this detail is unacceptable. The rake flashing will be too large for proper design unless made from heavy-gauge steel. Heavier gauges in paint coated steel are usually not available. We therefore use details such as shown in Fig. 10.42.

By using a stand-off screw through elongated holes in the rake angle and cleat, a floating rake detail is created. However, the critical tape sealer, although properly compressed, is in the flood plane of the roof panel.

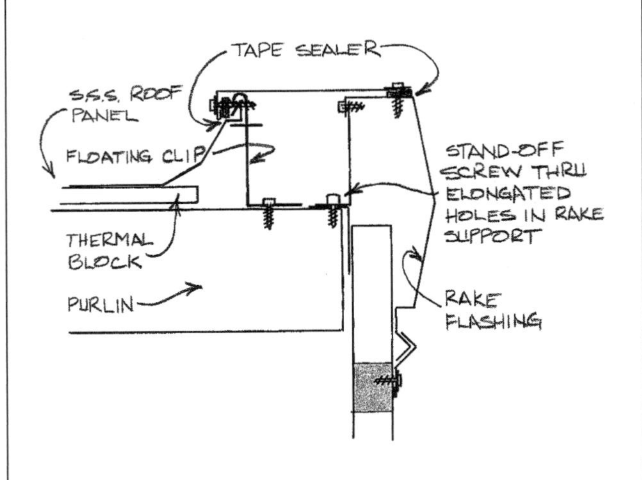

Figure 10.41 Rake flashing off module.

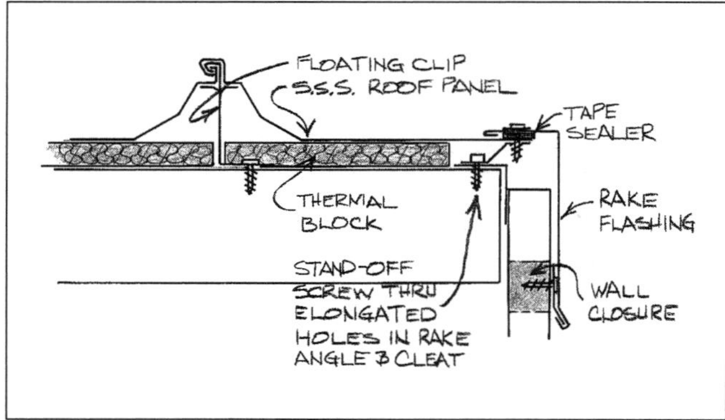

Figure 10.42 Rake flashing in flood plane.

In such a situation, other options may be considered. It may possible to design a rake detail using the principle as shown in Fig. 10.38. However, if a roof panel strengthening rib occurs at the hem-lock location, field fabrication of the hem is very difficult. Additionally, a structural trapezoidal seam panel is often specified to be of 22-gauge steel, further increasing the difficulty of field-forming.

Additional options may be a variation of the detail as shown in Fig. 10.35. However, such detail design will often place both tape seal locations in the flood plane of the roof panel. If the roof panel run is short, or if the slope is 1:12 or greater, this may not be a concern.

10.4.5 Eave Flashings, Gutters, and Ventilation Design

GENERAL

Every roof will have an eave, therefore eave flashing details are common. Eaves will have all the water from the upslope washing across them, exposing them to more water flow than other roof components as well as making the eaves more prone to being a water flood-plane location, especially in the event of ice damming. We also must consider and analyze eave details in their ability to resist negative pressure uplift caused by strong winds. (See Fig. 2.11.)

In the following section we investigate and analyze some typical eave flashing details as used in the metal roofing industry. As a general rule, we try to design eave details to address several problems which, in our opinion, we consider important:

- Avoid exposed fasteners at the eave if possible and practical.
- Provide for uplift resistance as required by code, geographic location, and industry standard to resist any possible strong winds.
- If a low-slope is being used, ensure that water running off the eave will not cling to the roof panel underside due to capillary action and travel upslope and enter the building.
- If the roof panels are not fixed at the eave (normally by use of exposed fasteners), ensure that enough allowances are made for panel expansion and contraction at the eave location since this is where all longitudinal panel movement will occur.
- Use every option available to provide air intake at the eave to allow for proper attic/plenum cavity ventilation. (See Secs. 10.2 through 10.2.3.)

GUTTERS

We have opted to omit gutter details on most of the figures in this section in order to enhance clarity of the eave detail. However, such omission does not imply that gutters are unimportant or do not cause roof system problems. Quite the contrary, gutter systems on metal roofs often fail to perform and function as needed—in many cases, long before the roof panel system begins to experience problems.

One problem we often see is gutter lap joints leaking. If the building wall is metal, as is often the case, consistent leaking for extended periods of time will alter the color of the wall panels as a drip-line stain.

Water dripping from leaking gutter laps for extended periods of time (even after the rain has stopped) are usually a result of clogged downspouts or partially obstructed gutters. Another cause can be lap joints located at a low area of the gutter system.

Gutters are usually supported and attached to the structural roof framing and/or to the metal roof panels. As such, the horizontal plane and level of the gutter is dictated by the existing construction. Workers normally have no way of adjusting the level of the gutter in a practical and cost-effective manner.

If the gutter stands water there is usually little that can be done. Dust and dirt will accumulate within low water-standing areas. Rain turns the dirt to mud, which remains moist for extended periods of time.

This standing water and associated moist dust/dirt/mud, and any leaking joints, often cause premature failure of coated-steel gutters. Coated steel cannot resist detritus effects caused by standing water. To make matters worse, if the gutter lap joints leak for extended periods of time, the raw, uncoated edge of the steel gutter lap joint is probably also being exposed for extended periods of time to water and moisture. Rust will begin at the lap joints, accelerating leaking, accelerating rusting, and so forth.

If budget allows, and if the same coating is available, it is good design practice to specify a noncorrosive metal as the gutter system. This can be either aluminum or stainless steel, both of which are normally compatible with paint coated steel panels in most situations. Verify compatibility with the metal roof panel manufacturer (in writing).

Gutters on metal roof systems are seldom manufactured, designed, or installed in keeping with accepted sheet metal industry standards or accepted practices. (See Secs. 12.2.1, 12.2.2, and 12.2.7.) Being fixed to the roof structure and/or the roof panel, they cannot expand and contract as required. (See Fig. 10.43.)

An additional problem is created if the gutter has to be replaced and it is prehung to the roof structure as shown in Fig. 10.43. An option available in such a case is removal of the exposed fasteners at the roof panel eave. The gutter can then be slid out from under the existing roof panels. This is possible only if the prehung gutter has not been attached to any framing or support members before application of the roof panel. Normally the erection crew secures the gutter in place before starting roof panel layout and installation.

If the gutter is attached with a fastener which cannot be accessed except by removal of the roof panel, other procedures are required. Such procedures may be field-cutting of the back side of the existing gutter and sliding a new gutter under the cut flange piece or sectional replacement of the failed gutter section(s). Either process is costly and often unsightly.

Another rule of gutter design, often ignored with metal roof systems, is never allowing the face of the gutter to be higher than the rear flange of the gutter. If downspouts become clogged or closed with debris or ice, and water backs up within the gutter, it will flood over the rear flange and enter the building. Designing the face of the gutter to be lower than the rear will allow water to spill over the face before it enters the building.

As a minimum on low-sloped roofs, the front gutter face dimension should be 1 in lower than the rear face dimension. On steeper-sloped roofs, the front and rear faces should equal the roof slope line. (See Sec. 12.2.7.) However, on low-sloped trapezoidal seam roof panel systems, designers and building owners wish to hide the unsightly open end of the trapezoidal seam. It is common practice to use the face of the gutter to hide the panel and seam end from view. This problem can be addressed with the proper design and installation of a specific style of gutter as shown in Fig. 10.44. Such gutter design allows any water flooding the gutter to escape over the rear face and be shed onto the building wall.

Also, the gauge of the metal from which the gutter is fabricated is important. The gauge should be as required for gutter girth. (See Fig. 12.26.)

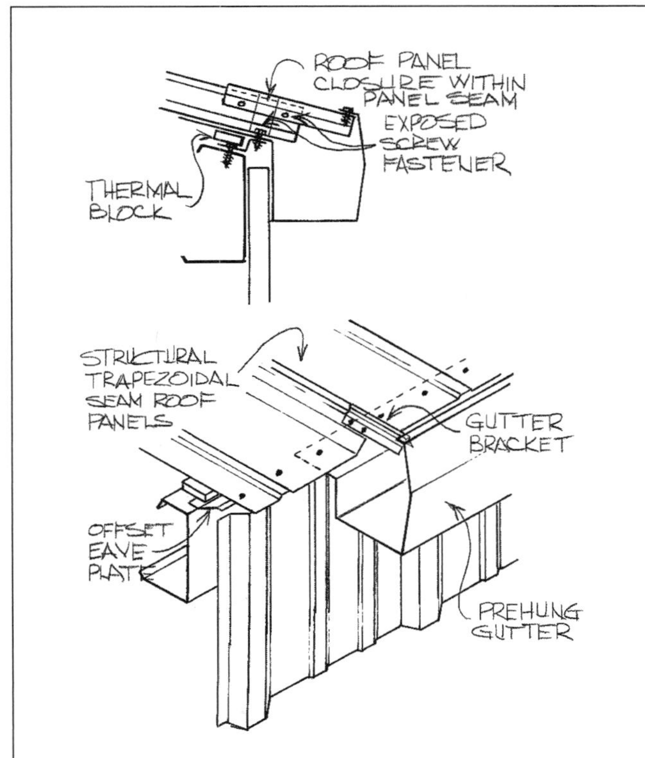

Figure 10.43 Improper gutter at fixed eave.

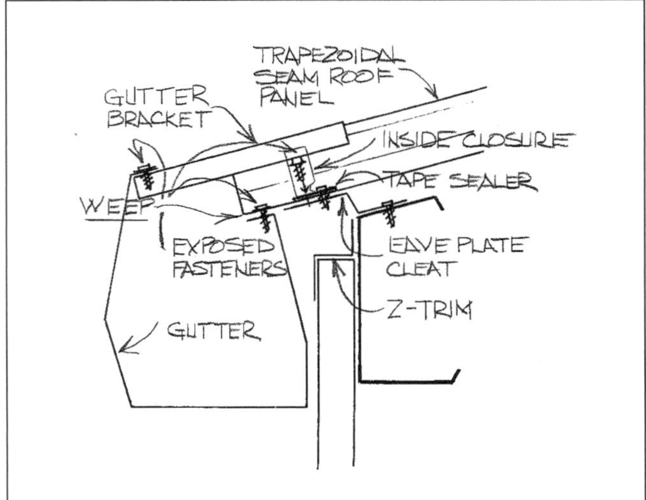

Figure 10.44 Gutter with weep at fixed eave.

EAVE FLASHINGS

Figures 10.45 and 10.46 show eave flashing wherein no exposed fasteners are used to secure the roof panel to the building structure. This detail is easily created by the erection crew if the panel type being installed has no stiffening ribs in the flat panel area. A structural trapezoidal seam roof panel (see Fig. 10.45) is seldom installed in this manner due to the stiffening ribs. Many other panel types can be installed in this manner.

If this detail is used, the roof panels must be fixed at the ridge or hip location. As such, linear movement during thermal cycles will occur at the eave. Care must be taken to allow enough space between the roof panel hem and the eave flashing cleat to allow for the annual thermal movements which will surely occur. (See Table 12.2 and Fig. 12.7.)

The selection of either eave detail as shown in Figs. 10.45 and 10.46 is dictated by roof slope and potential ice damming at eaves. If the roof slope is 3:12 or greater, the detail in Fig. 10.46 is acceptable. If the roof slope is less than 3:12, or if ice damming is probable, the detail in Fig. 10.45 is required.

For roof panel profiles which cannot use the hemlock at the eave, the panel is normally fastened into support members at the eave. Fastening at the eave requires that the hip or ridge flashing detail be designed so that the roof panel can expand and contract during thermal cycles.

Figure 10.47 shows a normal design often used to fix and secure the roof panel eave to the building structure. The expanded view within the figure shows how one metal roof panel manufacturer has designed to provide for the eave to move while at the same time using exposed screw fasteners for attachment.

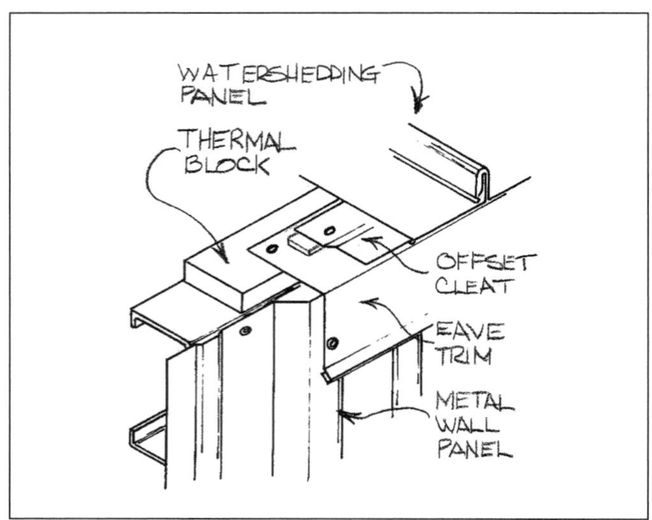

Figure 10.46 Floating eave on offset cleat.

VENTILATION DESIGN

(See Secs. 10.2 through 10.2.3.) Ventilating metal roof systems is essential. Proper ventilation requires air intake at the eaves and air exhaust at the highest point on the roof, usually the ridge. Without ventilation, mois-

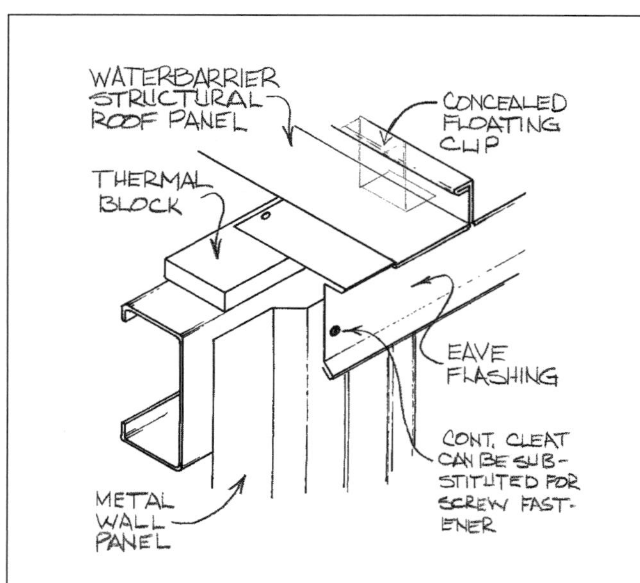

Figure 10.45 Hem-locked floating eave.

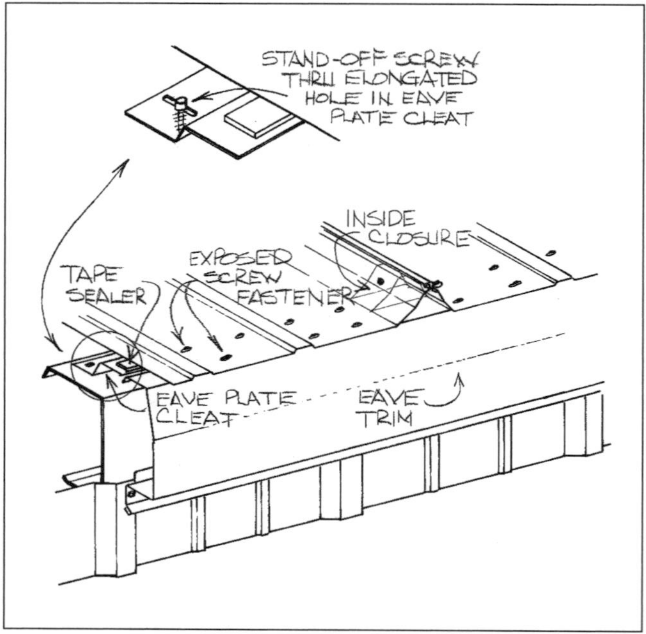

Figure 10.47 Fixed eave.

ture can condense on the underside of the roof panels, possibly causing rust and premature roof panel failure. Metal manufacturers' warranties offer no relief to the designer or building owner in the event of panel failure due to bottom-side condensation.

The ability to *properly* ventilate a commercial/industrial metal roof system is difficult at best, and sometimes not practical or possible. Roof size, slope, and configuration can prevent proper air ventilation amounts from

- Entering a continuous eave soffit
- Traveling along the entire bottom side of the roof system
- Expelling through a continuous ridge vent assembly

However, even a little ventilation, in the right pattern and places, will achieve the desired results, which are removal of moist air before it can condense and cause harm. The figures that follow show some design options available.

Figure 10.48 depicts a ventilation design which can be used for metal roof retrofit design. In retrofit design, where the existing roof system is left in place, ventilation is crucial. The designer must investigate and establish proper means for attachment of the components and systems shown. Special consideration should be given to securing the wall panels and the soffit vent. The design, securement, and attachment of the new retrofit system will normally be in accordance with engineering specifications and metal roof system manufacturers' requirements.

In addition, calculations should determine the approximate amount of air flow and air exhaust required for the roof design. The designer should also determine the amount of net free area of the soffit vent and the vent efficiency. (See Sec. 10.2.3.) This calculation process should also be performed for new construction ventilation systems, as shown in Fig. 10.49.

In new construction design, the designer should evaluate and further define the attachment and securements needed for the ventilation system as shown in Fig. 10.49. The figure does not show a ceiling system nor an attic cavity/plenum area. If the insulation system is clad in a vapor retarder, and the retarder is exposed to the building interior (no ceiling or attic/plenum), and the building is loose construction, eave ventilation is normally not required.

Allowing air into the eave location will do absolutely no good if the air cannot be exhausted at the highest point of the roof panel. Figure 10.50 depicts a generic design of a ventilating ridge assembly.

In our opinion, this ventilating ridge assembly, or a variation thereof, should be included in every metal

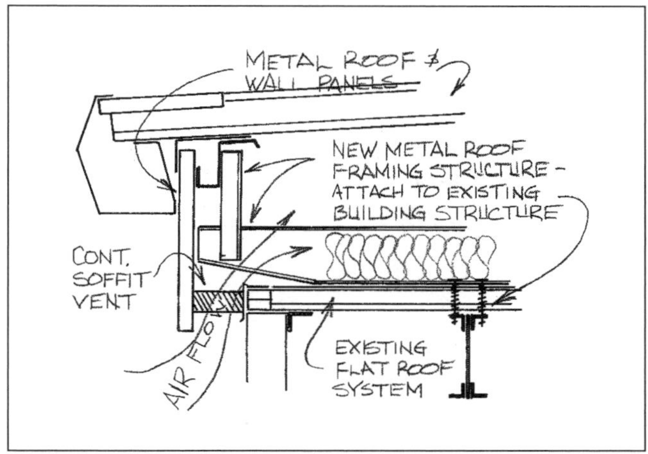

Figure 10.48 Ventilation design—retrofit. (*Adapted with permission of Prevent—Division of CTI Building Systems, Liberty, Mo.*)

roof design. The other option available is ridge ventilators, as often used on commercial warehouse-type metal buildings. In cold climates, building owners or occupants sometimes prefer ridge ventilator equipment because the equipment can be provided with a damper. In winter the damper is closed to prevent loss of heat from the building interior. (Winter is when ventilation is most required.)

This dampered ventilation equipment will work well with the roof and building system only if the metal roof is insulated on the bottom with a vapor-retardant faced insulation. The roof insulation vapor barrier must be exposed to the building interior and the building must be of loose construction.

If the building has an attic or roof cavity/plenum area, ridge ventilating equipment will not be totally effective

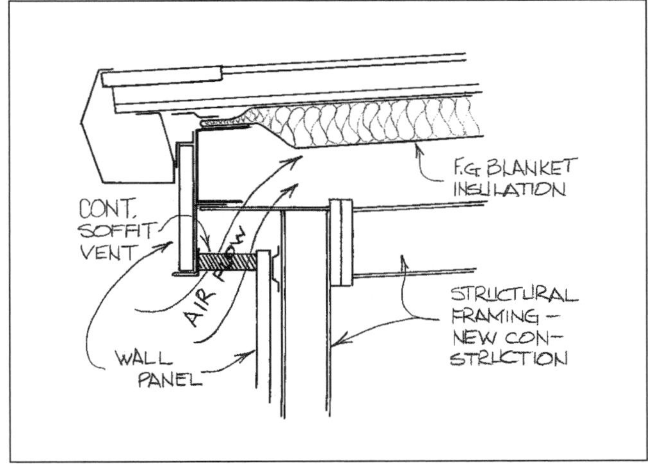

Figure 10.49 Ventilation design—new construction.

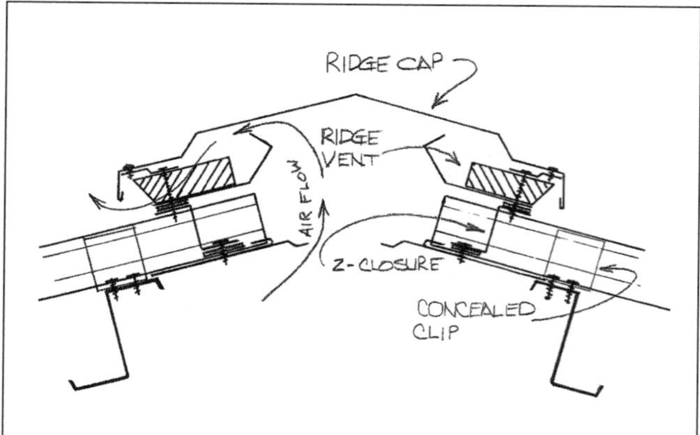

Figure 10.50 Venting ridge—floating.

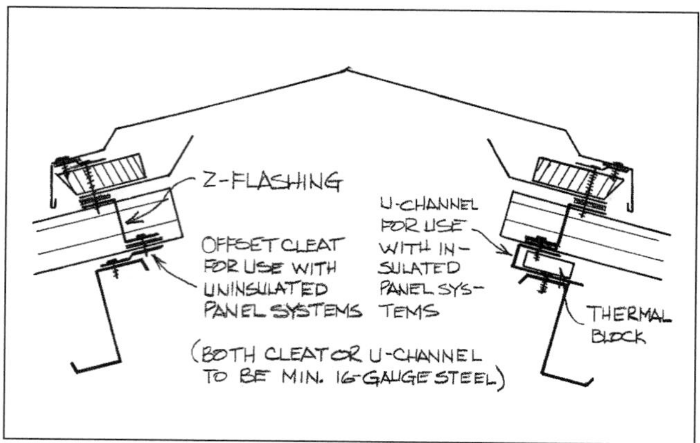

Figure 10.51 Venting ridge—fixed.

in removing moist air from the attic cavity. In essence, the ridge ventilating equipment will function as roof louvers and can be effective only if they are installed almost continuously at the ridge. Such design will not be as cost-effective as the ventilating ridge system shown. (See Sec. 10.2.2.)

10.4.6 Ridge Flashings

Ridge flashings are a common system on many metal roofs. They are fairly uniform in design and components throughout the industry.

Consideration must be given to attachment design of the metal panel roof system. If the eaves are unfixed and floating, then the ridge or hip areas must be fixed to the building structure. Without fixing the roof panel at some point, it can slide from the roof structure.

In our opinion, it is best to leave the eave floating and unfixed, if possible or if practical. (See Fig. 10.45.) This requires the hip or ridge area to be secured to the roof structure. Figure 10.50 shows a floating hip, in that it is unfixed to the structure. This would then require the eave to be secured to the structure as shown in Fig. 10.47.

Sometimes structural panels are left unsecured at the eave. Figure 10.51 details how a ridge can be fixed to the structure to accommodate such design.

Notice that an offset cleat is shown as well as a U-channel member. These different support members will be used depending on if the roof panel system has batt insulation installed under it.

For insulated metal panel systems, a high floating clip is used. Therefore, the U-channel compensates for the height of the clips used throughout the panel system. We also recommend using thermal blocks at purlins whenever insulating a metal panel system.

The offset cleat is appropriate for use when the metal panels have not been insulated. It holds the panels off the purlin approximately ⅜ in, which equals the spacing creating by the low clips used throughout the panel system.

Both the offset cleat and the U-channel must be a minimum of 16-gauge steel to provide adequate support. In addition, the gauge of the ridge flashing must be evaluated. This design may require a larger-than-normal ridge cap. The larger the girth of the flashing component, the heavier the gauge required of the metal from which it is formed.

Attaching a ridge or hip flashing to a solid deck is the same as is shown in Fig. 10.51. The structural purlins are replaced by the solid deck. The Z-flashing is placed onto a strip of tape sealer and screw-fastened through the metal panel into the solid deck.

10.4.7 Valley Flashings

Valleys are common, although not mandatory, for every roof system. The style of the roof design (hip, gable, shed) and shape of the building dictate whether the roof will be configured and shaped so as to require a valley(s). On commercial and industrial metal roof systems where standing trapezoidal seam or R-panel roof systems are more often used, we use fewer valley details than with the architecturally designed metal roof panel systems.

A valley receives all the water from the roof panel area it services. All this water is directed within the valley until it is discharged from the roof area. If a valley is obstructed or blocked by leaves or other debris, or by ice dams and/or snow, water can flood over the waterproof valley flashing system and roof leaks can occur. Even unobstructed valleys can leak in a torrential rain if the flood plane of the valley design is exceeded.

As with tile and slate roofing valleys, metal roof valleys should always be tapered, with the bottom of the valley exposure larger than the top. The possibility (probability) of valley obstruction, length of valley run, normal rainfall amounts, and slope of valley dictate the tapered exposure of the valley required from top to bottom. Consult with the metal manufacturer or the manufacturer's representative for local practices.

In most cases it is good design practice to include a waterproof membrane under the valley flashing. Based upon probability of water flooding at the valley, the underlayment can be of minimum resistance (#30 organic felt) to maximum protection (modified bitumen membrane). We suggest covering any waterproof underlayment with a slip sheet of red rosin paper. If this slip sheet is not used, the metal flashings can become hot enough in the summer months to adhere to the underlayment. When expansion and contraction occur to the metal valley flashing, it will tear the adhered underlayment, rendering it an ineffective water barrier.

Some climates and some valley design may not require either the underlayment or slip sheet. However, it is the last line of defense against water infiltration into the building system, so just to be sure. . . .

Realize that the seams of the roof panel which extend into the valley flashing are not watertight. Even though they may be sealed with caulk by the roof installers, in our opinion it is good design practice to assume that these locations will allow water to pass. There are also other locations and components within a valley flashing system which can allow water to pass if the flood plane rises over it. Regardless of caulks, closure gaskets, and water-barrier panels, experience has shown that a valley flashing should always be considered a water-shedding system, not a water-barrier system.

Figure 10.52 shows a valley flashing joining roof areas of different pitch slope. Notice that the flood-plane level requires the valley flange on the low-slope side to extend farther than on the steep-slope side.

We also suggest that it is good design practice to use two rows of tape sealer under the continuous cleat instead of the single row as shown in most manufacturers' details. The tape sealer will provide a watertight seal around the pop rivets or screws used to attach the cleat to the valley flashing.

Additionally, we recommend a hemmed lip at the side lap edges of all valley flashing pieces. The hemmed lip is just one more item to help restrict water to the valley flashing.

Figure 10.52 also shows a piece of tape sealer within the hemmed lips. This is not customary in the metal roof industry, but we use it to help keep the hemmed lip in an open position. During construction there is usually a lot of foot traffic in a valley area. If the hemmed lip is closed due to foot traffic, it loses much of its ability to perform.

In such case, it is important that the tape sealer be installed with the factory-applied release paper side up,

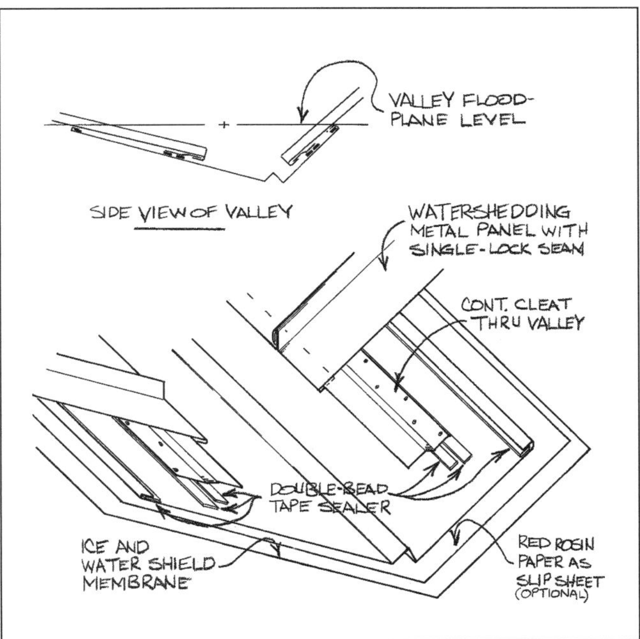

Figure 10.52 Valley flashings on solid decking.

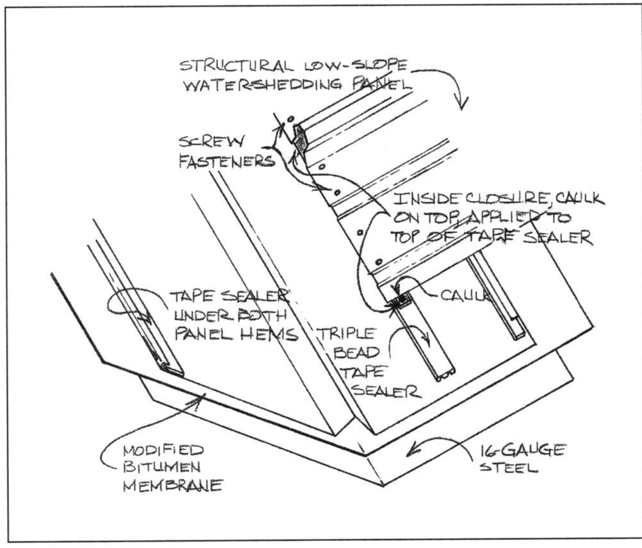

Figure 10.53 Valley flashings using exposed fasteners.

and this release paper should not be removed from the tape. This process will require the hemmed lips to be fabricated more open than is normal to allow for installation of the tape sealer. The roofer must close the hem after tape sealer installation.

Figure 10.53 shows a valley flashing installed with exposed fasteners. If possible, this design should be avoided in geographic areas subject to torrential rains or for design where the valley flood-plane level may rise above the screw fastener level.

Even though the exposed screw fasteners penetrate the tape sealer, and an underlying 16-gauge steel plate is used for support and provides the required strength to create a proper compression seal of the tape sealer, we think that in adverse situations this design may not be permanently waterproof.

CHAPTER 11

Tile, Copper, and Slate Roofing

11.1 GENERAL REQUIREMENTS

GENERAL

Of all types of water-shedding roof systems, tile roofing, slate roofing, and copper roof systems have historically been proven as the longest-lived. It is not unusual for tile and slate roof systems to remain intact, with little maintenance or repair, for 75 to 100 years. Copper roofing has been recorded as lasting as long as 1000 years, but practically speaking, we can expect a life span of 100 to 400 years.

In general, the steeper the slope, the longer these systems can survive. All of these systems are water shedders, not water barriers, and therefore a waterproofing underlayment is often required. The flashing details are critical for long-term performance. None of these systems are very forgiving of design or application error.

Being long-lived and expensive, we seldom find these types of systems on utility construction systems. Concrete and cementitious fibered roof tiles and panels are sometimes installed to some moderate to upper-scale housing, restaurants, and so on.

Tile and slate systems are heavy, normally weighing from 800 to 1200+ lb per 100 ft^2 of roof coverage. Some slate roof systems can exceed 5000 lb per 100 ft^2 of roof coverage. This requires a structurally sound and capable roof support system and deck. If reroofing with tile or slate, the entire structural system of the building should be investigated.

All flashing materials must have the same life expectancy as the roof material. It is not advisable to build materials into these types of roof system which will require maintenance and replacement every 20 years. For this reason, lead or copper flashings are used. In addition, all lumber at flashing areas should be treated against decay.

All fasteners and nails are often required to be of copper or stainless steel, although in some arid parts of the country hot-dipped galvanized nails are acceptable. Rivets and nails used to attach metal flashings must be of the same materials as the flashings. Solder is used in lieu of caulking.

Foot traffic must be restricted from tile and slate roof systems, and prohibited to minimum for copper systems. When designing these types of systems for schools, dormitories, and so on, beware of possible access locations to the roof system, and try to restrict entry at those points.

FLASHINGS

Waterproof integrity of these roof systems is strongly dependent upon the metal flashings. The flashings on copper tile and slate roofing should always be of permanent-type material, with copper being the most common.

Among the most common mistakes made with the metal flashings are:

- Improper attachment of the flashings
- Improper size and length of flashings
- Improper joining of the flashings to each other
- Improper design of flashing systems

Flashings should always be attached with a cleat, which attaches to a hemmed lip of the metal flashing and secures it to the roof deck or structure. Never nail through a flashing to the structure, thereby creating a nail hole in the flashing. (See Fig. 11.1.)

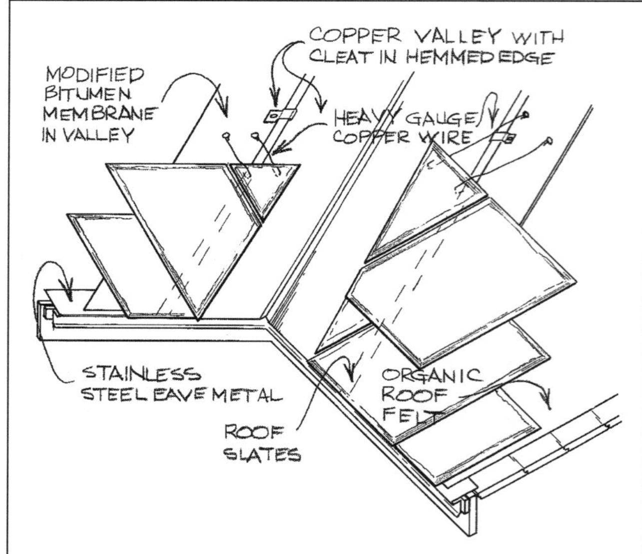

Figure 11.1 Copper valley flashing.

Valleys. In a valley location, the metal flashing should normally be made from a 24-in-wide sheet of metal. This allows enough material for a crimp to be created in the center and hemmed edges to be created on both sides of the flashing, while still leaving enough metal extending up and under the slate or tile to catch windblown and/or backing up water.

The same general rule applies to valleys of copper roof systems. However, waterproofing principles of design differ as shown in Sec. 11.3.

Valleys and other water troughs should be tapered wider at the bottom than at the top. This helps shed any leaves or debris which might accumulate in the valley trough areas.

If the valley trough is located under overlying trees, expect water leak problems. The fallen leaves will accumulate in the valley trough and create a water dam. Water flow will be restricted because of this created obstacle and in many instances will back up over the top of the valley flange and enter the structure. Correct design for such situation entails a steep roof slope with wider than normal valleys, allowing for an exceptionally wide tapered valley.

Step Flashings. Step flashings inserted between each course of slate or tile shingle is the most permanent way of waterproofing a base flashing location, if the roof slope is steep enough. The step flashing should extend a minimum of 6 in under each roof tile or slate panel and up the building wall a minimum of 4 in.

For lower slopes, we recommend step flashing as well as hemmed base flashing. Any water that penetrates the step flashing system will be caught and directed from the roof by the pan of the hemmed base flashing.

The step flashing over the hemmed base flashing also helps keep the base flashing pan clear of debris. Excessive debris, such as leaves, dust, and so on can block the water flow in the base flashing pan and cause roof leaks. (See Fig. 11.2.)

Caulking—even modern material rated as lasting 20 years, 50 years, 100 years, or until the next Ice Age—should not be used to seal and waterproof flashing on these types of roof systems. Eventually the caulking will fail.

Instead, proper design and installation techniques learned over the centuries should be used to install and join the metal flashings. This includes joints hemmed and locked together instead of merely lapped, with cleats, clips, and solder as and if required.

Independent movement due to expansion and contraction must be allowed for by design at all locations of the metal flashings. For instance, do not ever solder a base flashing metal to a valley flashing for waterproofing at that location. These two pieces will move independently, and the solder joint, experiencing too much stress, will often break.

Improper design of metal flashings is often directly related to misunderstanding, or ignorance, of the basic principles of water-shedding systems. Water runs downhill unless stopped or redirected, at which time it will travel in opposition to gravity until that directing force or obstacle is removed, at which time it will resume the downward journey. It will always resume the downward journey until it is in the water table or aquifer.

Many times it is not practical or possible to keep water from under the roof materials of a slate or tile roof

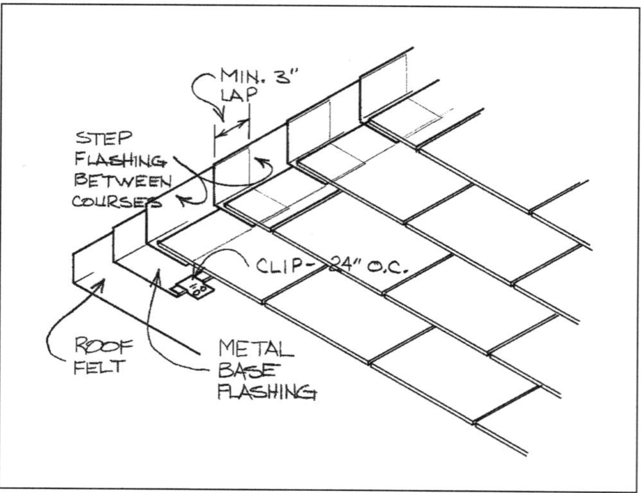

Figure 11.2 Step and base flashing.

system. In this case, metal flashing must be installed under the rigid roof panels to catch and restrict the water to the desired path and location. The metal flashing is designed to eventually direct the water back up and onto the surface of the roof panels or into a gutter or water trough.

Base flashing at a building wall abutting a tile roof assembly is a good example. The flashing should be designed to direct water only within the metal flashing pan until it is fed out onto the top of lower tiles or until it is fed into a gutter, valley, or trough. (See Fig. 11.3.) Where trees are present the design shown in Fig. 11.3 is not recommended, since the base flashing trough can become obstructed with leaves and debris. Instead, refer to design principles as shown in Fig. 11.2, using step flashing in conjunction with a base flashing trough.

Wind can blow rain uphill to undesired locations, such as over the top of metal flashings or through the side joints of slates. Once the water is at that undesired location, it is no longer directly influenced by the wind and will resume a downward path, often into the structure.

Also, realize that the water can continue to be forced in a direction opposed to gravity, even though it is no longer directly influenced by the wind since it is up and under the roof materials. Water outside on the roof surface is still being blown uphill and sideways by the wind, pushing the water that is already under the roof materials.

Wind-induced roof leaks are not uncommon, and will occur mostly at areas and locations where water is concentrated in heavier than normal amounts. These can be, but are not limited to, areas such as valleys, where water from all roof planes collects in order to be fed from the roof.

In valleys, small pieces of slate or tile are often required to finish the course extending into the valley. Nailing the small piece would cause the nail fastener to penetrate the metal valley flashing, which would probably lead to a wind-induced roof leak. The hole created in the valley flashing would be covered by the tile or slate, but rising or blown water could enter through the hole in the flashing caused by the nail.

Such cases require the small roof piece to be suspended into the valley location on a copper or stainless steel wire. The wire is nailed to the roof deck out of the valley, above the location where the tile or slate will go. The other end of the wire is secured through a hole in the tile or slate. (See Fig. 11.1.)

The roof piece, being hung on the wire, is thereby suspended in place within the valley without making a hole through the valley flashing. A small bead of caulk is sometimes used to attach the small piece to an adjacent roof piece.

Wind-induced leak problems can also occur at metal flashing areas which restrict the flow of water. This can be a cricket flashing behind a chimney which is not designed to a steep enough pitch or is not large enough to separate the oncoming flow of water from the base flashing. (See Fig. 11.4.)

The flashing design in Fig. 11.4 is inadequate, and will allow water rushing down the roof slope to be forced or driven under the in-wall counterflashing and over the top of the base flashing. Correct design uses a saddle cricket with a horizontally level ridge, thereby moving the in-wall and base flashings out of the flood plane of onrushing water, as well as creating a steep enough slope at the chimney and flashing interface to

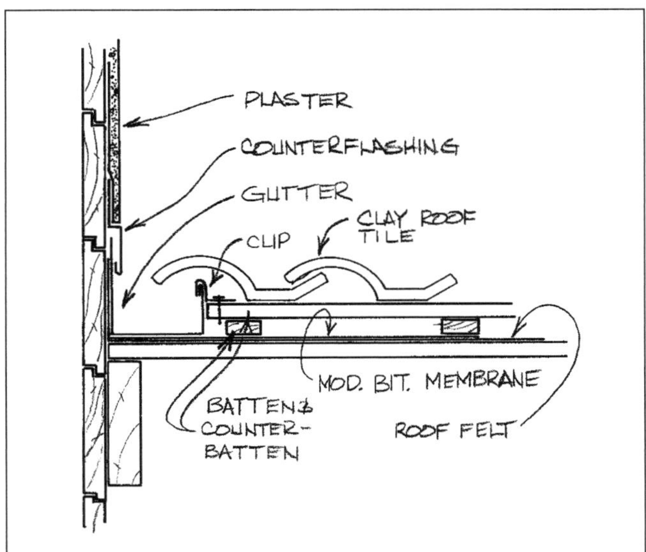

Figure 11.3 Concealed gutter trough at building wall.

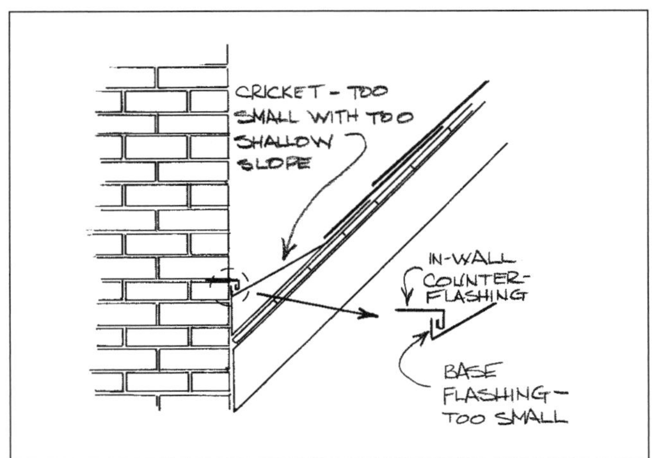

Figure 11.4 Improper cricket.

prevent water from gathering in excessive amounts. The low slope shown in Fig. 11.4 will allow excessive amounts of water to gather and back up behind the chimney before being directed around the chimney and back out onto the roof shingles. Additionally, the vertical base flashing as well as the in-wall counterflashing flange should be a minimum of 4 in tall, further preventing wind-driven rainwater from rising over the top and entering the building.

UNDERLAYMENTS

With tile and slate roofing systems, a waterproofing underlayment is mandatory. With copper roof panels an underlying waterproofing membrane is not as essential, since the panels form a watertight (not waterproof) seam at the side lap edges and the steep slope design prevents windblown rain from accessing the roof deck. However, a roof felt is still normally installed to the roof deck, if for no other reason but to protect the building interior until the copper roof panel installation can be completed.

It must be noted that in different regions across the United States these requirements differ. In certain areas tile, and even slate, roofing has proven durable and effective without roof felt and waterproofing underlayments. Some tile and slate roof systems still exist from the nineteenth century that are installed directly to lath stripping over an undecked attic, much the same as wood shingles are installed. Regarding copper roof panel systems, in some parts of the country which normally experience torrential rains and high winds, a double layer of roof felt is used as an underlayment, in conjunction with extra underlayment materials at valleys, eaves, saddle crickets, and so on.

Over the years the design community and material manufacturing industry have opted to include waterproofing underlayment as a common design practice. The underlayment is of different materials, depending upon its function and the service life required. For example, one layer of #15-lb organic felt, as commonly installed to a wood roof deck prior to the installation of composition shingles, is the minimum underlayment ever to be used, and will be acceptable for a steep slope tile, slate, or copper roof system being installed in a dry, arid geographic location. On the other hand, an underlayment of two layers of #30-lb organic roof felts, or layer(s) of organic base sheet (see Chap. 7), or in some extreme circumstances a layer of modified bitumen membrane (see Chap. 9) may be required for a roof installed in regions where torrential rains and high-speed winds are common.

Additionally, for hurricane-susceptible areas (torrential rains and high-speed wind), the waterproofing underlayment often protects the building interior in the event of roof blow-off, so long as the underlayment stays attached to the roof deck. The underlayment also protects the building interior in the event that tile or slate is broken or displaced due to fallen tree branches, hail storms, and so on.

It is good design practice to specifically design water-barrier underlayments at valleys, crickets, roof eaves in snow country, slope transitions, and so on. The water-barrier underlayment is usually of a modified bitumen material, some of which is specially formulated and marketed as water-barrier underlayments for roof systems. This underlayment acts as the last line of defense at times when exceptional wind and rain is experienced or when valleys and troughs become temporarily obstructed with debris.

Underlayment water-barrier design must never take the place of proper water-shedding design principles. The roof system must be designed and installed as if there was no additional water barrier under the roof. The water barrier must be designed and installed as if there was no overlying roof covering.

11.2 TILE ROOFING

GENERAL

Tile roofing has been a predominant type of roof material in North, Central, and South America for centuries. There is more tile roofing manufactured and installed in South and Central America than in North America.

Tile roofing is considered to be very durable. Manufactured from the correct material, in a proper manner, it can last 100+ years. It is not uncommon to reroof a building using the same existing tile.

In such a situation, it is often the roof felt underlayment and/or the metal flashings which deteriorate and start to leak. Decking begins to rot . . . tiles shift over the weak decking . . . water starts to enter into and under the system at greater rates . . . and the roof leak deterioration process accelerates.

In order to correct bad roof felts, metal flashings, or rotted decking, the existing roof tiles must be removed to access the underlying components. These internal systems are refurbished or replaced and the existing tile is reinstalled. It is sometimes (often) necessary to obtain new or replacement tiles of the same style, by the same manufacturer, to supplement any tiles that are damaged and/or which are broken during construction.

CLAY ROOF TILE

In early America clay roof tiles were supplied to the geographic area by a local foundry, which probably also produced firebrick, chimney pots, and sometimes pottery utensils and cookware.

The early twentieth century saw the creation of clay tile manufacturing firms dedicated to producing roofing tiles to be distributed over a larger area. The predominant manufacturer emerging during this time was the Ludowici Celadon Company. In 1926 an antitrust suit was brought by the Federal Trade Commission against Ludowici Celadon Company. The company was allowed to continue operations under a consent decree and has continued since that time.

Today, the market offers many manufacturers of clay tile roof products. We often find imported clay tiles being specified in lieu of domestically manufactured tile products.

Some clay tile roofing products, both imported and domestic, are top quality; some are not. When selecting and specifying a clay tile, confirm that it has been tested and passed ASTM C 1167-94.

Some clay tiles can resist certain geographical environments; some cannot. Tiles are classified into *grades*. The grades reflect the clay tile's ability to resist cold and freezing weather. Spalling and failure of the clay tile in cold climates will result if not manufactured to resist freeze-thaw cycles. The three grades of tile reflect this freeze-thaw resistance. (See Fig. 11.5.)

CONCRETE TILE

The raw materials for concrete roof tiles are more common than those used in clay tiles. Portland cement, lye, sand, and other minor ingredients are used in the mixture to create concrete roof tiles.

Concrete roof tiles are today manufactured and distributed by large firms located throughout the United States. However, in the early to mid-1900s it was not uncommon for local contractors to manufacture and install their own concrete roof tile.

In-house manufacturing of concrete tile diminished after World War II due to the utility, lower-cost housing popular in this era. This type of housing could not normally support the dead load of the concrete tile roof system, approximately 600 to 800 lb per 100 ft^2 of roof area.

Also, increasing labor costs for roof workers needed to make the tile, and inefficient equipment and methods, restricted the local roof contractor from competing economically with concrete tile manufacturing facilities.

Today there are numerous manufacturers of concrete tile roof products. Most manufacturers have production facilities strategically spread across the United States to help reduce shipping costs.

Styles of concrete tiles are not as varied as with clay tiles. Also, the finish of a concrete tile will be applied differently than clay tile.

Finishes on concrete tile will either be *inherent*—completely through the tile—or the finish will be applied in a *slurry coat* to the top of the tile. Slurry coat finishes are not recommend for cold climates where freeze-thaw cycles are common.

Concrete tiles provide a long-lived roof system, close in appearance to clay tile roof systems. However, the cost of materials and installation is usually less. Concrete tile roof systems are not as complex in detail design as some clay tile roof systems. They are not as difficult to install, in most cases, as clay roof tiles.

11.2.1 Clay Roof Tile Systems

MANUFACTURE

The base products from which the clay roof tile is manufactured are crucial to its proper function and durability. Fireclay is the main ingredient in clay roof tiles, being combined with shale and other minor ingredients.

All clays are not the same. The geographic location from which the clay comes is important to the quality of tile produced.

The clay is extracted from the ground and blended at the manufacturing plant with shale and water. The blending is accomplished by a *pug mill* at the manufacturing facility.

A pug mill is a large vat in which paddle mixers are used to completely blend all elements together into a homogenous state. In olden times the pug mills were run by horses and mules; today they are electronically operated and controlled by computers.

After blending is complete, the semiliquid material is extruded through a die and onto a conveyor system. The conveyor carries the tile material through a process where the tiles are cut to proper length.

The tiles continue to be transported down line to a dryer assembly location. At this location, or during transport to this location, the glaze material is applied. Some tiles are left unglazed. Glazing is an important aesthetic consideration, as well as a functional consideration in freeze-thaw climates.

After leaving the drying station, tiles are transported and stacked into a kiln. In the kiln the temperatures can exceed 1000°F, depending on material composition of the tile, glazing requirements, geographic location for which the tile is destined, and so on.

After the kiln firing process, the tiles are removed, wrapped, palletized, and shipped. The packaging process is crucial in reducing damaged and broken stock.

However, this manufacturing process could not have always been as complicated as it is today, or even as it was in the early twentieth century. Clay tile roofing originated in Asia, with clay tile roof systems being archeologically documented as early as 3000 B.C.

In Central and South America, and possibly in the southwestern United States, clay tiles were manufactured from earthen clay, formed over the person's thigh. The tiles were then dried in a wood-fired kiln.

PRODUCT REQUIREMENTS

When clay tile products are heated and fired in a kiln, a process known as *vitrification* occurs. Vitrification occurs to glass when it is created by the heating process.

Heating in the kiln is required to create the proper molecular bonding of the elements and compounds within the clay tile material. When properly fired, vitrification of the clay roofing tile is achieved.

Vitrification causes the clay tile to acquire important properties. The important qualities the clay roof tile must have upon completion of the firing process are:

- Resistance to water absorption
- Resistance to damage from freeze-thaw cycles
- Strength
- Resistance to efflorescence
- Resistance to water permeability
- Acceptable appearance
- Adherence of glaze coating, if any
- Dimensional accuracy
- Accurate and constant weight of tiles

Freeze-Thaw Cycling. One of the biggest problems which can be experienced with a clay tile is *spalling* due to freeze-thaw cycles. This is assuming it is a quality product and no unusual deficiencies occur, such as efflorescence, cracking due to weak material, and so on.

A national weathering map in Fig. 11.5 shows regions within the continental United States. Different grades of tile are required within the cold, weathering regions as compared to the warmer, less-weathering regions. Grade 1 tile resists freeze-thaw cycles. Grade 3 tile cannot resist freeze-thaw cycles.

- *Severe weathering,* with extensive freeze-thaw cycles, is indicated by a 500 or greater rating. Only Grade 1 clay tile should be used in these regions.
- *Moderate weathering,* with some freeze-thaw cycles, is indicated by a 50 or greater rating. Only Grade 1 or Grade 2 clay tiles should be used in these regions.
- *Negligible weathering,* with few if any freeze-thaw cycles, is indicated by a less than 50 rating. All grades of tile can be used within these regions.

The weathering index is calculated from the average annual freezing cycle days and the average annual winter rainfall.

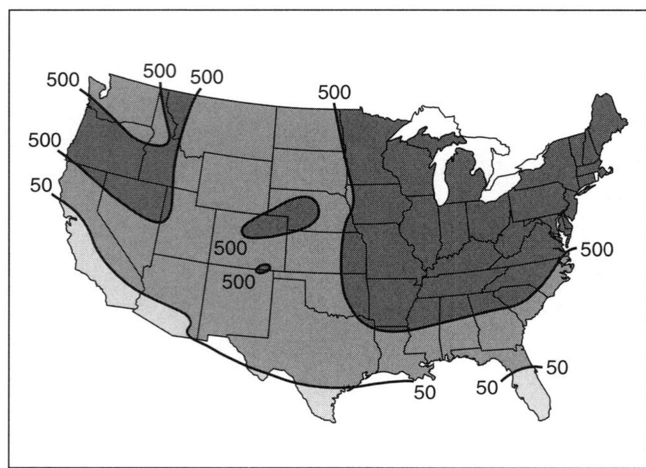

Figure 11.5 U.S. weathering index zone map. Only Grade 1 tile should be used in regions rated 500 or greater. Only Grade 1 or Grade 2 tile should be used in regions rated 50 to 500. Grade 1, 2, or 3 tile can be used in regions rated less than 50.

Water Absorption. Under ASTM Standard C 1167:

- Grade 1 tiles can have no more than 6 percent maximum water-absorption rate when 5 tiles are tested and averaged. One tile taken from a batch or lot of Grade 1 classified tile can have no more than 8 percent water-absorption rate.
- Grade 2 tiles can have no more than 11 percent maximum water-absorption rate when 5 tiles are tested and averaged. One tile taken from a batch or lot of Grade 2 classified tile can have no more than 13 percent water-absorption rate.
- Grade 3 tiles can have no more than 13 percent maximum water-absorption rate when 5 tiles are tested and averaged. One tile taken from a batch or lot of Grade 3 classified tile can have no more than 15 percent water-absorption rate.

Glaze Coatings. Another consideration in freeze-thaw regions is the *glaze coating* applied to some tiles. How well it is adhered and bonded to the tile is a prime consideration.

The same ASTM Standard C 1167 addresses this concern. In no case should any tile have a glaze coating with an adherence strength of less than 100 lbf/in^2 (689 kPa).

Another consideration, unable to be directly addressed by ASTM standards, is the ability of the glaze coat to function with the clay body of the tile. This is a consideration in any climate, regardless of freeze-thaw cycles or extreme temperatures.

The coefficient of expansion of the glaze must be compatible with the coefficient of expansion of the clay roof tile. If it is not, crazing, cracking, and peeling of the glaze from the tile surface can result.

If the manufacturer of the tile is in bankruptcy, or is a foreign manufacturer—not dedicated to the U.S. market, your client, or yourself—little recourse may be available. Glaze-coating chips on the ground and an interesting color pattern on the roof may be the result in such a situation.

In a freeze-thaw region, it is highly advisable to use only glaze-coated tile time-proven to resist the environmental extremes of such regions. *Time-proven* in this instance means 20+ years of actual installed roof exposure.

Caution is required because accelerated weathering can be experienced by a clay (or concrete) roof tile with a partially deficient glaze coating in a cold climatic region. If the glaze coating cracks or even crazes, moisture can migrate between the coating and the tile surface, interface, or into the minute cracks caused by crazing. A freeze will expand entrapped moisture and cause the glaze coat to spall from the tile.

Breaking Strength. Some tiles are not a strong as others. In a case where gutters must be regularly cleared, or other traffic can be expected on or around the tile roof system, a strong tile should be specified. Also, in situations where tree overgrowth and possible falling branches, hail storms, kids throwing baseballs onto the roof, and so on, may be expected, a strong tile is prudent.

The style of the tile is a factor in determining its strength. Clay roof tiles are categorized into three types:

- *Type I.* High profile.
- *Type II.* Low profile.
- *Type III.* All others.

High-profile tiles normally have the highest transverse breaking strength. This value is addressed in ASTM C 1167 and should normally be found in the manufacturer's literature.

CHARACTERISTICS

Clay roof tiles are rigid, hard, heavy, and unforgiving of design or application error. They are a water shedder and not a water barrier. Heavy rains and high winds will cause water to penetrate the lap edges of the tile panels. The steeper the slope, the less water penetration will occur.

Also, head lap of the tile will reduce water infiltration. *Head lap* is how far the head of the tile extends under the overlapping tile above. The portion of the tile left exposed is called the *exposure*. (See Fig. 11.6.)

On steep slopes the exposure can be greater, resulting in less of a head lap. On low slopes, the exposure needs to be less. In regions with torrential rains and/or high-speed winds, a minimum 3-in head lap is usually good design practice.

Roof slope is important to the way a roof tile functions. Tile cannot function effectively, for extended periods of time, on slopes less than 4-in rise per 12-in run. It is good design practice to install tile on a minimum 6/12-in slope.

Most prestigious structures with requirements for a long-term waterproof tile roof use roof felt underlayment to shed any water infiltrating the tile roof covering. It is good design practice to assume that a tile roof system will leak from the day it is installed.

A contradictory note is in order at this point. Although we normally consider tile not to be waterproof, but to be instead a water shedder, it is possible to find tile roof systems which have functioned quite well, for extended periods of time, without a waterproofing layer under them.

In fact, many of these types of tile systems are installed without a roof deck, being instead installed directly to purlins or laths. You can stand in the attic and see the bottom of the tile roof system.

Some tiles can be manufactured to be more watertight than others, with lips and edges that help with water-shedding characteristics. In addition, and very important to note, these tiles are normally installed on steeper roof pitches, in regions with moderate rainfall, often on structures incorporating lofts and high ceiling exposed areas. Rural farmhouses, barns, warehouses, and utility construction buildings may be good examples.

Also, if you examine the purlins or laths closely, you will normally find evidence and traces of moisture. In

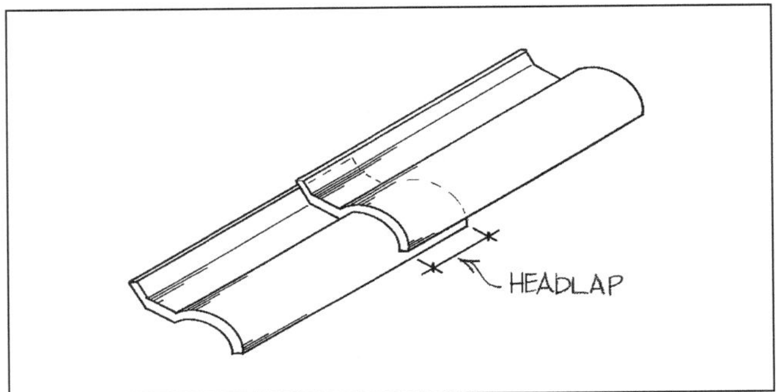

Figure 11.6 Tile head lap and exposure.

such situations it may take years or decades for a roof leak to become a problem.

Leaves and debris on a tile roof will restrict and change its water-shedding characteristics. Clogged valleys will cause roof leaks. Debris in the flutes and rolls of a tile will cause water to back up and enter a tile roof system.

Tile roof panels should be *hung* from the nail fastener. Tiles should never be nailed or otherwise tightly secured to the roof deck. This requirement can often produce *tile rattle* when small, lightweight tiles are hung on steep slopes.

We most often experience tile rattle on the sides of dormers clad in tile roofing. Tile rattle can be eliminated by the use of mastic at the top head lap of each tile, usually by the nail head location. This secures the tail lap of the subsequent overlapping tile tightly to the nailed tile underneath. (See Fig. 11.7.) Tile rattle on a windy night, at a client's bedroom, leads to morning phone calls.

Tiles are difficult to displace from roofs in moderate to gusting winds. However, in strong winds, such as can be experienced in flat open areas or in coastal areas, tiles can be blown from the roof surface.

The resistance of a roofing tile to strong winds is attributable to its weight and rigidity. However, this weight and rigidity makes it a very formidable and damaging ballistic projectile if displaced from the roof in a high wind. Also, once a small section of tile is displaced, those remaining have a tendency to catch wind at the voided area and also be blown from the roof deck.

Hurricane clips are a normal requirement in high-wind areas. The clips hold the tail of the tile down to the tile roof surface, allowing the tiles to better resist high-wind conditions. (See Fig. 11.8.)

In areas such as Florida, where hurricanes and high winds are anticipated, tiles are often set into a complete bed of cement mortar. The roof deck is waterproofed with roof felt underlayment and covered with a slur of cement mortar, into which the roof tiles are immediately placed. Recent hurricanes have proven this method not to be as durable as expected, and it is no longer an accepted design practice. Instead, foam set is being evaluated as an attachment medium, as well as using screw fasteners instead of nails to attach the tiles.

SPECIFICATION REQUIREMENTS

Verify the region you are specifying tile roof in is compatible with the grade of tile specified. Use the national weathering index map (Fig. 11.5).

Specify a minimum of two layers of #30 organic felt as the waterproofing underlayment. It is often better design practice to use #43 organic base sheets, or combination of #30 organic felt and #43 organic base sheet. (See Sec. 7.1.1.)

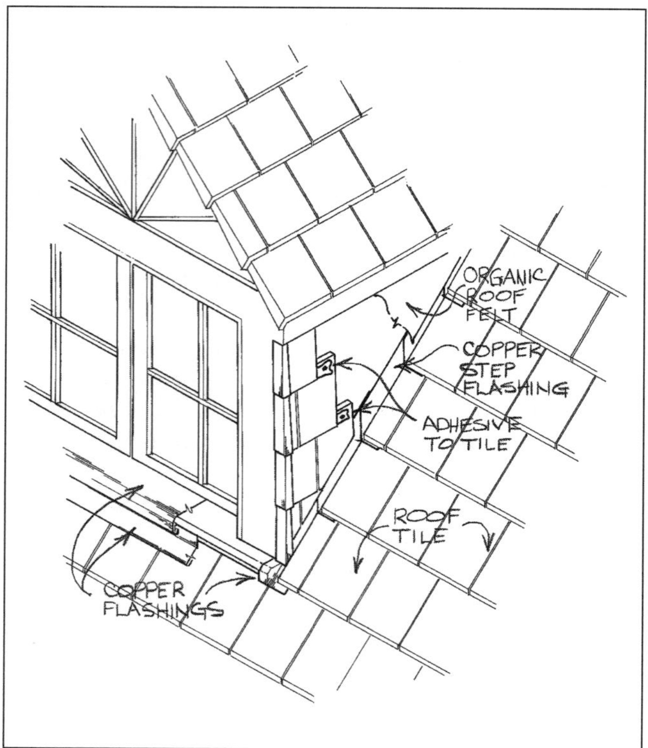

Figure 11.7 Side of a dormer clad in tile.

Specify only noncorrosive metals be used at flashings and as fasteners. Lead, copper, and stainless steel are most common. Aluminum can be used; however, soldering is not possible to aluminum. Do not rely on caulking to provide a watertight joint for the life of the roof. Instead, use soldering materials and practices. (See Sec. 11.3.5.)

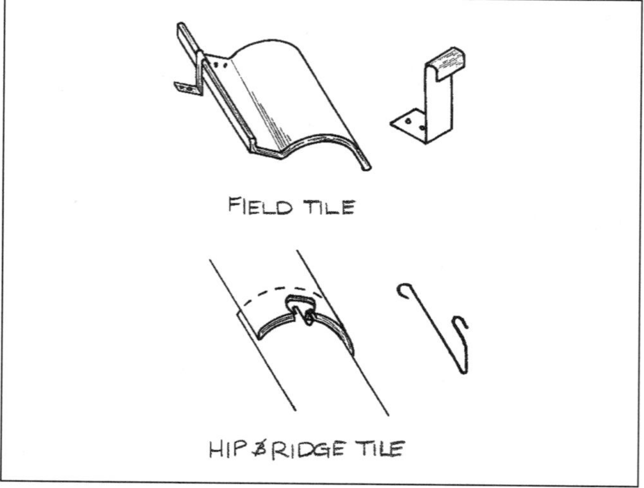

Figure 11.8 Hurricane-clipped tile.

Mortaring ridge and hip tiles in place is an important waterproofing phase. Require clay tiles to be soaked in water immediately prior to installation into the mortar at the hip and ridge locations.

Clay roof tiles are rigid, and as such require careful alignment and placement in order for waterproofing of side lap lips, rolls, and curves. Require all runs of tile to be straight, accurate, and consistent, one with the other. The alignment can be checked visually, and during visual inspection, no curved or crooked rows, courses, or runs of tile roof panels should be evident.

DESIGN

Since it can be assumed that all tile roofing will leak at some time during its service life, a waterproof felt underlayment system is required. This felt system should shed water into or over any metal flashings.

The metal flashings should then restrict any moisture from entering the building. Metal flashings are often designed to catch water and direct it from the roof system.

At locations where excessive water can be present, at areas where waterproofing is crucial, and/or at areas where roof leaks are common, install a layer of modified bitumen membrane. The membrane best suited to sealing around the shaft of the nail fastener is SBS modified bitumen membrane.

Metal flashings become hot during the summer months, which can cause the underlying modified bitumen membrane to adhere to flashings. Cover any modified bitumen membrane with a slip sheet, such as red rosin paper, or an additional layer of roof felt. (See Fig. 11.9.)

Good design practice allows for a batten system to be installed on top of the roof felt underlayment. Tile roofing is attached to the batten system, normally 1 × 2 or 1 × 4 pressure-treated lumber. The batten system should be elevated to allow water to pass freely under the battens.

A procedure which can also seal the nail holes in the waterproofing felt layers caused during attachment of the batten system is good design practice. In Fig. 11.10, composition shingles are folded in half and placed under the batten system to elevate it above the felt layers on the roof deck.

A troweling of plastic roof cement is placed on top of the felt layers and the composition shingle is placed into the cement material. The batten is subsequently laid on top of the composition shingle and nails are used to secure the batten to the roof.

The nail penetrates the wood 1 × 2 batten, the composition shingle, the roof cement, the roof felt, and, finally, the wood roof deck. The roof cement seals the composition shingle to the roof felt and seals the nail holes in the waterproofing felt layers.

Cutting clay tile requires special saws and blades, is time consuming, and is therefore expensive. Also, cut tiles on a roof can be unsightly and can create possibilities for leaks.

It is possible to design rafter run lengths so that whole tiles are used from the eave to the ridge. (See Table

Figure 11.9 Felt membrane underlayments in a valley. Additional roof felts to be installed over deck area extending into valley flashing.

Figure 11.10 Batten system on top of felt underlayment.

11.1.) Also, valley tiles can be manufactured to the slope and angle of the valley systems, providing a closed tile that is pleasing in appearance.

11.2.2 Concrete Roof Tiles

GENERAL

Concrete roof tiles have started to make an impression in the roof community, becoming widely marketed and used in the early 1970s. However, concrete roof tiles have been in existence for perhaps as much as 150 to 200 years.

The main ingredient in concrete is *portland cement.* Portland was discovered, mined, and first put to use in the Portland area of England. It can therefore be assumed that concrete roof tiles originated in England as a direct result of portland cement.

Concrete tiles are a common roof material in areas of Florida and the southwestern United States from New Mexico to California. Many of the design and installation requirements of clay roof tile systems also apply to concrete roof tiles.

However, concrete tiles are normally used on more utilitarian and common structures, such as residences, restaurants, commercial buildings, and so on. Clay tile is used more on churches, cathedrals, museums, and so on.

Concrete tile often costs 25 percent of the cost of clay roof tile. It often provides faster installation by the roof applicator. Galvanized steel nail fasteners and galvanized flashings are often specified in lieu of copper nails and flashings.

It therefore is often less expensive than a clay tile roof system, yet the life expectancy of a concrete tile roof system can be estimated at 30+ years, with some concrete tile manufacturers offering a limited 50-year warranty.

As with clay tile roof systems, the waterproofing felt underlayment system and flashing work is crucial to a long-lived system. A batten system is always good design practice. (See Secs. 11.1 and 11.2.1 and Fig. 11.10.)

Table 11.1 Rafter runs.

Correct rafter lengths for full-length tiles.

Based on 2″ projection at eave of roof

Course	*Rafter*	*Course*	*Rafter*
1	11¼″	7	72¾″
2	21½″	8	83″
3	31¾″	9	93¼″
4	42″	10	103½″
5	52¼″	11	113¾″
6	62½″		

Spanish tile sizes	
Length	13¼″
Width	9¾″
Average length exposure	10¼″
Average width exposure	8¼″

In high-wind areas additional fastening is required. Hurricane clips (see Fig. 11.8) normally satisfy this requirement.

Concrete roof tiles can be very susceptible to freeze-thaw cycles and damage caused thereby, resulting in spalling of the tile. Very few concrete tiles can be successfully installed in cold climates. The number and extremes of freeze-thaw cycles which a concrete tile can resist is directly dependent upon its moisture content and the glaze coating applied to the tile surface.

As of the publication date of this volume, there is no standard for concrete tiles as published by ASTM. Some code bodies and organizations reference concrete tile requirements; however, these requirements are normally specific to the geographic location wherein the code organization exists, and may not be generically applicable for all concrete tile. As a minimum, a standard should list guidelines of moisture content, strength of tile, surface application tolerances, and so on.

MANUFACTURE

Concrete tiles are mainly composed of portland cement, sand, and other cementitious fillers and binders. Natural oxides are sometimes used to color the roof tile.

The materials are mixed in a hopper, water is added, and a wet cement slur is created. The slur is extruded into aluminum pallet molds at high-speed production line facilities.

The tiles are moved to a drying location where much of the water is removed, leaving the tile in the final shape. Shapes and style of concrete tiles can be varied, but most common are:

- Flat tile
- Single S tile
- Double roll tile

A glaze coating is sometimes applied at this phase, being an additional slurry layer of concrete providing a vivid color range. For tile with color pigmentation throughout the entire tile, a clear or tinted latex coating can be applied in lieu of a glaze coat.

The concrete tile is then forwarded to a kiln drier. The kiln operates at lower temperatures than those used in the clay tile industry. Humidity is also elevated and monitored within the kiln for drying concrete tiles.

Upon leaving the kiln, the tiles are palletized and prepared for shipment. Pallettization is important in keeping the tiles from damage during shipment.

SPECIFICATION

In the near future it is anticipated that ASTM will have approved a standard specification for concrete tiles.

Color or glaze of tiles can vary from batch lot to batch lot. If different shipments are required, probably resulting in different batch lots, verify color continuity.

In high-wind areas, or in earthquake regions, specify hurricane clips, nose clips, tile clips, and so on. These clips will hold tiles on the roof if loosened from the deck during earthquakes or will hold the end of the tile down, and resist blow-off, during high winds. Require the clips to be of noncorrosive and strong metal, such as stainless steel. (See Fig. 11.8.)

For earthquake areas, tile roofs are currently being evaluated and tested for attachment to the roof deck with stranded wire instead of with nails. Consult the tile manufacturer for specifications for wire tying. Use strong, noncorrosive wire, such as stainless steel.

In hot, humid areas, require that all lumber directly related to fastening the tile, such as the batten system (if any), hip and ridge nailers, and so on, be treated to resist decay. (This does not apply to the roof deck.) In dry, arid regions, such as the desert southwest, untreated lumber usually functions acceptably.

Nails and fasteners used to attach the concrete tile should be of materials per local practice and custom. If not copper or stainless steel, at a minimum nails should be hot-dip galvanized. Electroplated galvanized nails often rust and fail.

Recent studies and surveys indicate that fully mortar-set tile systems do not resist high winds significantly better than nail-on systems. Nail-on systems, installed on a batten system with hurricane clips at each tile, can survive hurricane winds and keep the building dry as well as or better than fully mortar-set tile systems.

For emergency facilities, such as hospitals, fire stations, and so on, take extra care in specifying and designing the tile roof system to remain watertight in an emergency. It has been found that extensive tile damage and loss can be experienced from windblown projectiles in the air stream during high-wind conditions.

In this case, the roof tiles will be displaced from the structure when they are broken into several pieces by wind-driven projectiles, no matter how well they are attached. The waterproofing felt underlayment and the metal flashing system then become the only waterproofing elements.

The roof felt layers should be of long-lasting material, such as coated base sheets, heavy organic felts, roll roofing materials, and/or modified bitumen membranes.

In cold regions, verify that the concrete tile has been successfully used in that region for an extended period of time. Freeze-thaw cycles and spalling of the tile surface is a consideration.

In cold regions subjected to freeze-thaw cycles, avoid using tile with a surface coat treated by the slurry process. Minute failure of the slurry coat, such as crazing, spider webbing, and cracking, can cause tile spalling. In cold regions, always specify an ice dam underlayment at eaves, valleys, saddle crickets, and so on. The ice dam water barrier is normally of modified bitumen material. (See Sec. 2.2.1.) In snow country, avoid designing valleys into the roof system if at all possible. Large sliding snow masses within a valley will easily displace tiles. If valleys are required, make the valleys exceptionally large, with wide tapers from top to bottom.

Require the concrete tile to be presoaked in water prior to installation into any mortar, such as at the hip and ridge locations. Mortar at the hip and ridge locations, since it is normally exposed and a visual component of the roof system, is normally colored with an oxide. This oxide should be supplied by the tile manufacturer. Require the roof applicator to prepare a sample for approval before application to the roof. The recipe (ratio of oxide to mortar) should be consistently followed by the roof applicator.

DESIGN

The roof felt and sheet metal flashing must create a waterproof system on top of the roof deck before installation of tile begins. If the felt and metal flashings cannot withstand the environment without the tile as a waterproofer, the system will probably leak. (See Secs. 11.1 and 7.1.1.)

In high-wind areas, it is often good design practice to hurricane clip each ridge and hip tile, in addition to setting in a full bed of cement mortar. It is also sometimes advisable to include concrete adhesive additive into the mortar mix, if acceptable to the tile manufacturer.

In regions where high-speed winds can occur, and where heavy rains are not unusual, batten systems elevated from the roof deck are often good design practice. (See Fig. 11.10.)

11.3 COPPER ROOF SYSTEMS

Copper is one of the oldest forms of roofing we have in existence. The copper roof on the cathedral in Hildesheim, Germany had remained untouched by human hands since it was installed in 1230 A.D. Allied bombing destroyed the cathedral and the copper roof during World War II. Copper flashing on the Parthenon was still in existence and functioning as of last report.

MATERIALS

Copper roofing is formed from flat sheets of copper. The sheet goods can be of different thicknesses, denoted by weight per square foot; that is, 16-oz copper weighs 16 oz/ft^2. We normally use 16-, 20-, and 24-oz copper in roof applications. Copper plate material normally begins at $\frac{3}{16}$-in thickness.

We have *cold-rolled copper* and *hot-rolled copper*. The rolling process used to manufacture the copper sheet metal gives the copper material different temper and elasticity characteristics.

Hot rolling of the copper to create a flat sheet metal material creates a soft temper product. This is useful when custom fitting copper sheet to rolled, domed, or curved surfaces. Hot-rolled copper, also more commonly called *soft temper copper*, behaves similarly to sheet lead. It can be malleted to form for unusual shapes and conditions.

Cold-rolled copper, also referred to as *hard temper copper*, is used for most roof applications. The hard temper stock far better resists the stresses and strains of expansion and contraction that are ever-present on a copper roof assembly.

Copper sheet can be coated with lead. The resulting product, referred to as *lead-coated copper*, offers benefits to the architectural designer:

- The lead finish is as durable and permanent as copper. It will take a paint coat easily and hold the coating for a durable time.
- The copper sheet to which the lead is laminated provides stiffness needed for many applications which is not provided by pure lead sheets.
- The weight of the lead-coated copper roof is far less than that of a pure lead sheet roof system. Yet with a lead-coated copper system, the appearance and weathering of a lead sheet roof system can be achieved.
- Lead will not form a staining patina as copper will. Lead-coated copper flashings are often used on stone, marble, stucco, and concrete works.

Roof systems created and formed from copper sheet metal can also be created from another popular form of sheet metal, referred to as *terne-coated metal*. Terne-coated metal is either 26- or 28-gauge steel coated with a complete layer of lead-based material.

This terne-coated steel sheet acts and reacts much the same as copper, with lower coefficient of expansion rates. However, most of the same principles of design and application apply to both copper and terne-coated metal.

Copper and terne-coated metal adapt very well to architectural, water-shedding, and water-barrier roof systems. The material is easily formed and worked in the field by the roof installers, and will easily take a solder joint if required. Terne-coated steel must be painted, but the lead-coat surfacing makes it a very durable material. Copper forms its own natural finish and is one of the most durable roof materials in existence. Other metals normally will not conform to the bends required to create the double-locks, hooks, and multirolled cleats often required at the seams and flashing locations. Fracturing and breaking of the metal often occurs if a pliable metal is not used.

DISSIMILAR METALS

Different metals can react and deteriorate when in contact with each other. The deteriorating reaction requires the presence of an *electrolyte,* such as moisture with a small amount of acid present. This electrolyte is almost always present, in varying degrees, with metal systems used on a roof or exterior assembly. In such cases a galvanic reaction occurs, and the less noble (or possibly both) of the metals is destroyed.

Table 11.2 lists a metal's ability to resist electrogalvanic reaction when in contact with a dissimilar metal. The metals are listed in increasing nobility.

When two metals in this list are in contact, and an electrolyte is present, one will deteriorate the other. The one with the highest number, or *nobility,* will prevail, and the metal with the lower number will be destroyed. For example, when steel (3) is in contact with copper (8), deterioration of the steel will occur. The closer different metals are in the series, the less reaction there will be.

If a steel gutter is used to collect rainwater from a copper roof, the deterioration will be immediate. However, a copper gutter can be used to collect water from a steel roof system, and no reaction will occur, so long as the copper does not touch the steel roof.

However, the table shows that copper and lead are incompatible, yet we use lead and tin to create solder, which is successfully used on copper metals. We also use galvanized coatings, which are a combination of zinc and lead, to coat steel and iron.

With solder material, the ferrous tin elements are successfully entrapped within the lead compound, thereby reducing the incompatibility of lead-tin solder with metals. Also, lead is very close to copper in the electrochemical series.

With a coating applied to a metal, even if the coating is incompatible with the base metal, reaction seldom occurs. This is due to the coating sealing the surface of the base metal, restricting water, moisture, and electrogalvanic reaction.

Avoid using any type of metal other than copper or high-copper alloys with copper roofing. This includes nails, rivets, screws, or other fasteners. We often see problems with copper systems directly related to this noncompliance.

If it is not possible to avoid dissimilar metals, separate the metals so that they cannot come into contact, or form an electrogalvanic bridge, with each other.

Stainless steel, not listed in the electrochemical series, has little reaction with any of the metals. Use stainless steel nails, rivets, and fasteners where extra strength is required of the copper roof system. Use stainless steel nails in other situations, such as when attaching a copper roof system through insulation layers to a steel roof deck. The stainless nail is neutral, and an adverse reaction between the steel deck and the copper will not occur.

Table 11.2 Dissimilar metals.

1. Aluminum	5. Nickel
2. Zinc	6. Tin
3. Steel	7. Lead
4. Iron	8. Copper

11.3.1 Expansion and Contraction

The dynamic force of expansion and contraction is the main reason for roof problems and roof failures when dealing with copper roofs, metal roofing, or sheet metal flashings. It can be restricted but not stopped. Provisions for the force must be allowed for, especially with copper roof systems. Do not try to stop it—acknowledge that it will occur, and direct it.

All building materials will expand and contract, some more and some less than others. Metals have different rates of expansion, expressed in *coefficient of expansion* rates. The greater the temperature differences a material is exposed to, the greater will be the linear change in dimension of the material.

Table 11.3 shows approximate linear changes in 8-ft lengths of different metals when exposed to a temperature difference of 150°F.

With a section of copper gutter or a copper roof panel 10 ft long, the change in its length can be expected to

Table 11.3 Expansion/contraction rates of 8-ft lengths of metals.

Metal	*Expansion, in*	*Approximate expansion, in*
Steel—soft	0.0878	5/64
Iron	0.0956	6/64
Steel—hard	0.1051	7/64
Monel	0.1104	7/64
Copper	0.1411	8/64
Aluminum	0.1843	12/64
Lead	0.2331	15/64
Rolled zinc	0.2492	16/64

be approximately ⅛ in from winter to summer, if there is a temperature difference of 150°F during the annual cycle. Such a temperature difference is not uncommon due to emmissivity. Further information on this phenomena can be found in Sec. 2.3.4.

A designer is often required to know the amount of expansion and contraction that will occur to metal roof components. A good example is a 50-ft-long copper gutter assembly built into the eave section of the roof.

This type of gutter design is referred to as a *built-in gutter*. The built-in gutter assembly is placed into an opening at the eave in the roof deck structure. Therefore, it is not able to freely expand and contract since it is restricted by the roof frame.

A gutter expansion joint will be required in the center of the 50-ft section to reduce the stress of expansion and contraction on the other joints of the gutter. The expansion joint will also allow the gutter assembly to move without causing unacceptable stress due to the confines of the built-in frame in which it is installed.

A quick review of Table 11.3 shows that the 50-ft copper section can be expected to expand and contract (change linear dimension) approximately ¾ in during annual cycle. Due to the critical nature of the design, a more accurate assessment of the gutter movement is required.

An expansion joint will be required in the center of the gutter assembly. (See Fig. 11.11.) The expansion joint will be designed to allow movement of the gutter section. However, we must accurately know how much the gutter will expand and contract during annual cycles.

In the following calculation we will also examine a most important fact of expansion joints on metal systems. Very few designers or installers take into consideration the temperature existing at the time of installation of the metal assembly.

If installing metal components during cold winter months, allowances must be made for the expansion which will surely occur to the component or system when the hot summer months arrive. In the hot months, materials need to be installed close together, because in the cold months, they will contract and spread apart.

Also, since the expansion joint systems incorporate lips and flanges that all the components slide on to accomplish the expansion/contraction movement, the lips and flanges must be of proper size to allow for such movement from year to year. The original placement and location of the metal components into the expansion assembly are dependent upon current temperatures at time of assembly. (See Fig. 11.12.)

Taking the example of the gutter as stated previously, a calculation of movement to be expected and the amount of space to allow for such expansion and con-

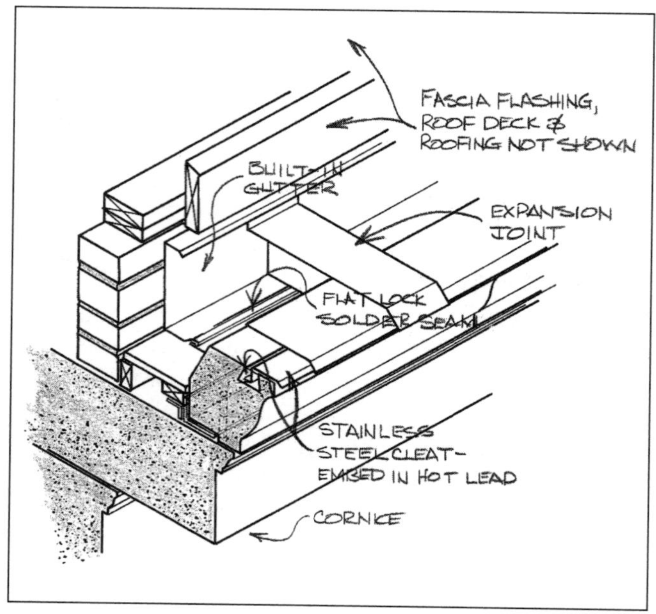

Figure 11.11 Built-in gutter expansion joint.

traction follows. We will use a 90°F day in summer as installation temperature and a 50-ft-long gutter assembly.

Coefficient of expansion rate for copper is:

0.0000098/°F, rounded off to 0.00001

Minimum design temperature is −20°F

Maximum design temperature is 150°F

Contraction temperature difference = 90° − (−20°) = 110° (90° is the temperature at installation)

Expansion temperature difference = 150° − 90° = 60°

Total contraction CN = 50 ft × 0.00001 × 110 = 0.055 ft = 0.66 in = ⅝ in

Total expansion EX = 50 ft × 0.00001 × 60 = 0.030 ft = 0.36 in = ⅜ in

A minimum of ¼ in clearance is required between gutter ends. This will occur during maximum expan-

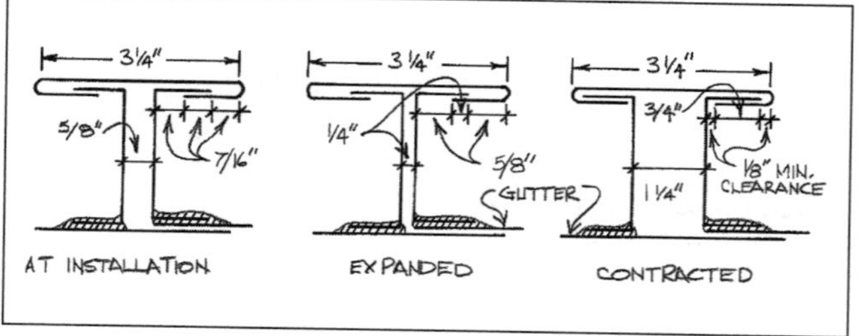

Figure 11.12 Cross-section of an expansion joint at different times of the year.

sion CL_x as shown in Fig. 11.12. Therefore, the required clearance CL_l of the gutter ends at time of installation is:

$$\tfrac{1}{4} \text{ in} + \tfrac{3}{8} \text{ in} = \tfrac{5}{8} \text{ in}$$

During periods of maximum contraction, gutter ends clearance CL_c, as shown in Fig. 11.12 is:

$$\tfrac{5}{8} \text{ in} + \tfrac{5}{8} \text{ in} = 1\tfrac{1}{4} \text{ in}$$

Therefore, total relative movement of the gutter ends is 1 in, with each end at the expansion joint moving ½ in during the annual cycle.

A ¼-in allowance for the lap of the expansion joint cover cap and the top flange of the gutter ends when fully expanded is required, and ⅛ in must be allowed for the lap of these components when fully contracted. The dimension of these components is very important and can be determined by the following:

Length L of the top flange is:

$$\tfrac{1}{4} \text{ in} + \tfrac{1}{8} \text{ in} + \text{CN} + \frac{\text{EX}}{2} = \tfrac{7}{8} \text{ in}$$

Width of expansion joint cover cap K is:

$$2(\text{CN} + L + \tfrac{1}{8} \text{ in}) = 3\tfrac{1}{4} \text{ in}$$

Fold back of joint cover cap is:

$$K - \frac{CL_c}{2} - \tfrac{1}{8} \text{ in} = \tfrac{7}{8} \text{ in}$$

A lengthy process of calculation, but most people would not have assumed such rates of expansion with a 50-ft section of copper gutter. Without allowing for expansion and contraction of such dimensions, the expansion joint would have failed.

If the top expansion joint cover flange was not of correct size, it could have been displaced when maximum or minimum lengths of gutter were reached. A roof leak could have then occurred.

We use the example of the built-in gutter to demonstrate a point, although built-in gutter assemblies are seldom designed anymore. (Most of the built-in gutters installed in recent decades leaked, usually due to inadequate design and improper installation.)

In copper roofing, as well as other types of metal roofing, exposed nails and fasteners are not used. Instead, the panels and components are hooked and locked one to the other, using hidden cleats, lock strips, and edge strips. The same rates of expansion as previously demonstrated must be considered in the design of such lock joints. (See Fig. 11.13.)

11.3.2 Design Considerations

GENERAL REQUIREMENTS

The Copper Development Association publishes the following requirements for design considerations:

- Provide suitable, durable nailing surfaces for all copper work (preferably wood).
- Provide asphalt saturated roofing felts (15 or 30 lb per 100 ft^2) as a leveling and cushioning medium over wood decks.
- Provide rosin sized building paper (4 to 6 lb per 100 ft^2) as a slip sheet between copper roofing pans and the roofing felts.
- Use copper cold-rolled tempered to ASTM B370; minimum weight of 16 oz/ft^2.
- Provide 16-oz copper cleats at least 2 in wide and long enough to permit folding the ends back over the nail heads.
- Secure all cleats with at least two copper, commercial bronze, or silicon bronze large-head slating nails of the ring-barb type, not less than 12 Stubbs gauge and a minimum of 1 in long.
- Where wood screws, machine screws, and bolts are required, use silicon bronze or stainless steel series 300 alloy.
- Where riveting is required, use flathead copper tinner's rivets or copper pop rivets with brass mandrels (preferably closed end).

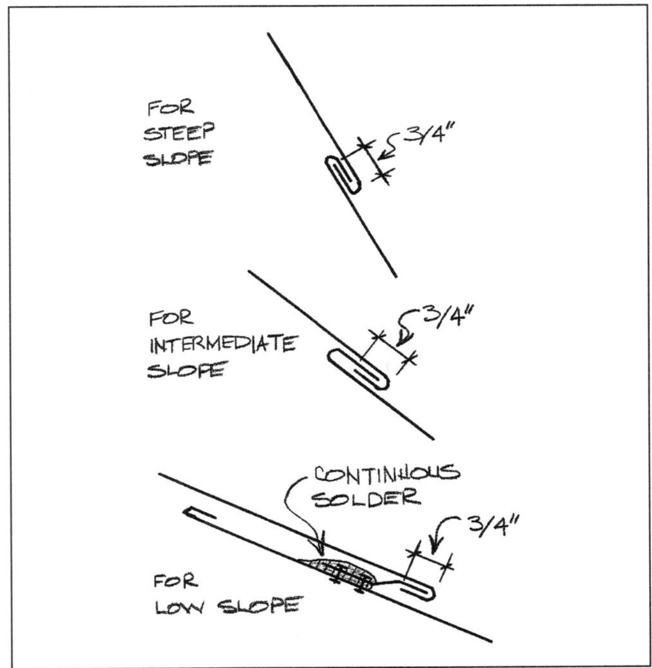

Figure 11.13 Hook lock of copper roof panels.

- For longest service life, use plain copper. Use lead-coated copper only where the gray color is desired, or where runoff staining of light-colored material is to be minimized.
- When soldering plain copper, use 50-50, tin-lead solder. When soldering lead-coated copper, use 60-40, tin-lead solder. Mechanically clean the copper and coat the surface with liquid or paste flux conforming to ASTM B813-91. Pretin the edges of the copper panels for a width of 1½ in prior to soldering. When soldering is completed, flush the joints with warm water to remove all flux residue.
- Where appearance is critical, consider using compatible sealants rather than solder for high visibility roofing, fascias, and flashing applications.
- Use fixed cleats for standing-seam pans less than 10 ft long. Use expansion cleats for standing seams greater than 10 ft long or when eave-to-ridge seam length exceeds 30 ft.
- To retard the natural oxidation and patina formation, apply a clear lacquer coating. Contact CDA for a clear coating report.
- To accelerate the natural oxidation and patina formation, apply an accelerant or use prepatinated, factory-finish sheets. Contact CDA for the latest information.
- Where copper abuts a dissimilar metal such as aluminum or steel, separate the two metals by painting with bituminous coating.
- Wherever possible, adhere to the details and specifications as published in the latest edition of the CDA *Copper in Architecture Handbook*.

WATER SHEDDING BY DESIGN

The hook-lock joints used throughout copper roof assemblies allow for movement. They also provide water shedding without sealing by caulks or solder. The top of the panels or flashing is bent into a hook which locks into the underlying panel, which is then held tight to the roof surface with a hidden cleat. This eliminates all exposed fasteners.

It is possible to find copper roof systems installed 100 years ago that do not have any solder joints at all. All waterproofing was accomplished by properly bending, lapping, cleating, and hooking the metal panels and flashings. In the event that sealing of a joint was required, such as in a built-in gutter system, white lead paste was used instead of solder.

In some situations it is required that solder be used to permanently seal and waterproof a component. This procedure should be a last resort after all water-shedding design options have been considered. Solder is mandatory for flat-lock solder seam panels, and is often required in gutters and at flashing locations.

On low-sloped roof systems, wind-driven rain can be blown into the hook-lock joint and enter the roof system. Capillary action of water can also cause water migration into the roof assembly at joint locations. In such cases alternatives other than solder to seal the lap joint should be used. (See Fig. 11.14.)

Solder cannot resist powerful forces of expansion and contraction, so it must be applied in a location and manner so as not to be subject to movement of adjoining panels. A solder joint should be designed to fuse two pieces of metal together, and this one-piece assembly should then be allowed to expand and contract as one unit, and not have stress focused on the solder joint.

If unavoidable, try to eliminate or reduce the force of movement which will occur at a solder joint. The joining of roof panels to flashings should not use solder. Terminating a panel or flashing at a location with a solder joint should be prohibited.

The strip-pan method shown in Fig. 11.14 allows the overlying panel to be hooked onto a cleat, while the underlying metal extends up the roof slope far enough to prevent any rising water or windblown rain from entering into the roof system. The cleat must be continuously soldered and sealed to the main metal component.

The slope of the roof is a consideration in copper roof style selection.

- Batten-seam roofs function effectively on roof slopes of 4 in rise per 12 in run and greater.

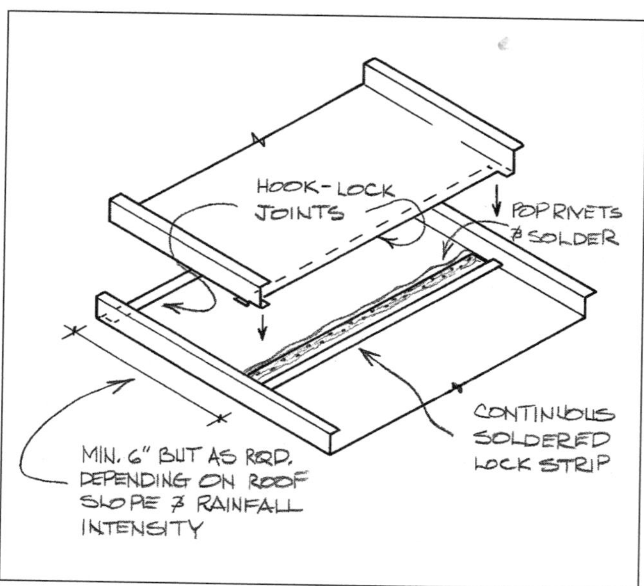

Figure 11.14 Copper roof strip-pan method.

- Standing-seam, double-lock systems function well on slopes of 3 in rise per 12 in run and greater.
- Flat-lock soldered seam roofs are used on slopes as low as ¼ in rise on 12 in run.

ROOF STYLES

Copper roofing has probably been used on every type of roof structure, from extremely steep slopes to water-covered tanks, such as reflection pools. There are many styles of copper roofing available from manufacturers, such as corrugated panels, copper shingles, and copper panels.

However, copper roofing panels are most commonly created from flat stock sheets or from coil stock, either in a sheet metal shop or at the job site by roll forming or portable break equipment. The sheets are formed into partial shapes, with the final forming done on the rooftop.

The sheets can be formed to many different shapes and styles. The double-lock standing-seam roof system is the most common style of copper roof designed today. These panels are installed and locked together in the field by the roof applicators. (See Fig. 11.15.)

Copper roofing, in addition to being designed in a standing-seam style, can also be designed using batten style, flat-lock seam style, Bermuda style, sawtooth style, and other more exotic, custom styles. We most often select either standing-seam, batten, or flat-lock style. (See Figs. 11.16 and 11.17.)

MATERIALS

Tensile Strength. *Soft temper* copper is available that has malleable characteristics similar to lead sheet. This soft copper product is used in applications where the metal must be field-formed to unusual shapes and structures.

Only *hard temper,* also referred to as *cold-rolled,* copper should be used for most roof panel applications. Different tempers of cold-rolled copper are available.

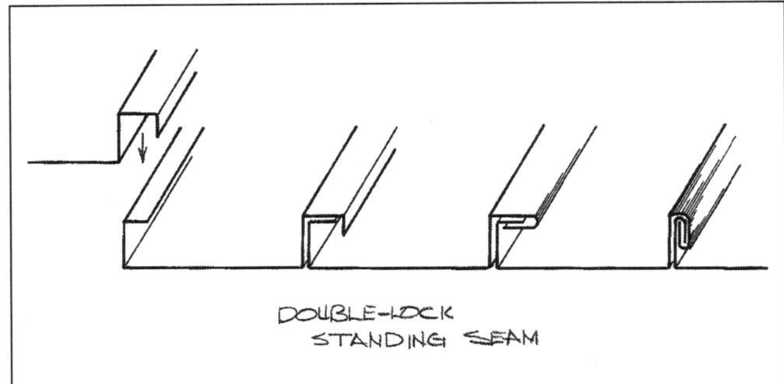

Figure 11.15 Double-lock standing-seam process.

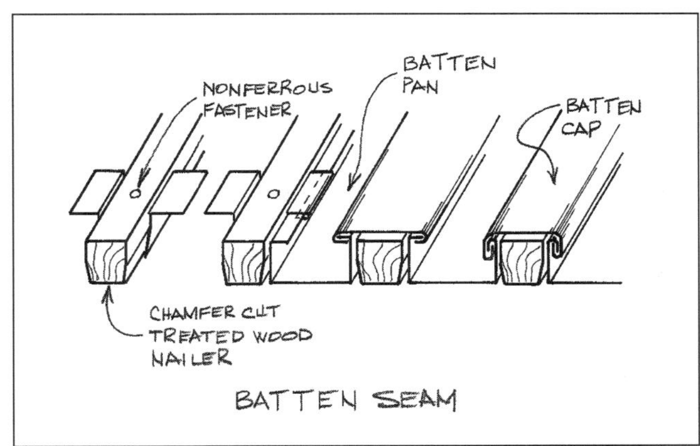

Figure 11.16 Batten-seam process.

The roof panels are normally created from either 16-, 20-, or 24-oz copper, although other weights (thicknesses) of copper sheet are available.

Forming. Copper roof panels are sometimes created at the job site by *pan-forming machines,* also referred to as *roll-forming machines.* Roll formers extrude a finished roof panel in a continuous length manufactured from a coil of copper metal. The coil can be of varying widths, normally 24 in, and be of different lengths, normally 50 to 100 ft long. The panel, in theory, can be as long as the coil, although long panels are difficult to handle without bending and subsequent damage.

The advantage to such forming equipment is savings of labor and the elimination of transverse panel seams

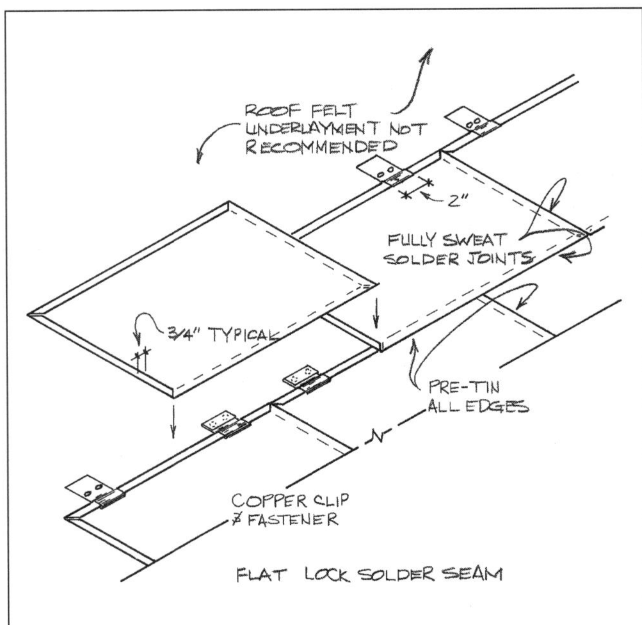

Figure 11.17 Flat-lock solder seam process.

every 10 ft, as is a normal for panels formed with a 10-ft-long sheet metal break. However, long and continuous roof panels create design considerations including, but not limited to:

- Expansion and contraction clearances for the panels
- Expansion cleats
- Fixed cleats
- Oil canning

Strength. Additional strength and stiffness may be required of the copper roof panel system, either to resist possible wind pressure uplift forces due to high-speed winds or to eliminate unsightly oil canning. This can be accomplished by increasing the thickness of the copper, which also increases the weight. Since copper is sold by the pound, with 16-oz copper weighing 1 lb/ft^2, increasing the weight of the copper stock from which the roof panels are to be made will increase the construction cost. Another solution may be to use standard 16-oz copper, and decrease the spacing between the side seams; that is, reduce the standing seams from 24- to 18-in spacing.

Due to the original width of the copper stock, this may not always be practical in that too much waste can be created, therefore making it more cost-effective to use the next heavier weight copper stock. Another option may be increasing the number of transverse seams within the roof system. (See Figs. 11.13 and 11.14.) Transverse seams add rigidity to the roof panel and decrease oil canning. Also, the rear hem of the underlying panel can be cleated to the roof deck, increasing wind resistance of the panel roof system. However, transverse seams increase labor costs, so once again consider material costs for heavier copper in relation to the labor expense of creating and installing transverse seams.

Hook-lock seams give rigidity to sheet metal components. The more frequent their spacing, the more rigid and stiff the panel becomes. Always stagger horizontal joints. (See Fig. 11.18.)

At areas where high wind stress can be anticipated, such as eave overhang locations, use stainless steel flashings as the cleat component. (See Fig. 11.18.) The stainless steel is compatible with copper and other metals. It provides the strength required to hold the panel ends to the roof structure.

Copper roofing takes much more time to install than most other types of roofing. It also requires proper design to allow the roof, the flashings, the roof structure, and all roof penetrations to function together properly.

Copper roofing requires skilled craftsmanship. The roof installer must understand the dynamics and material characteristics of all materials and components encountered on the roof.

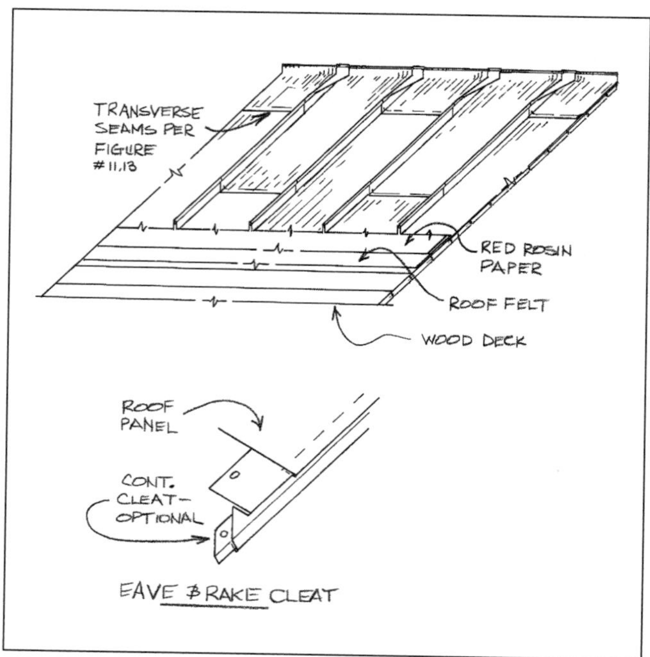

Figure 11.18 Transverse staggered seams of standing-seam process.

Life-cycle cost analysis usually shows copper roofing to be one of the least expensive roof systems to own. Properly designed and installed, copper roofs are usually maintenance free for hundreds of years.

However, it is one of the most expensive types of roof systems to purchase. It is not unusual for a simple copper roof to cost \$10.00/ft^2.

11.3.3 Batten-Seam Roofing

Batten-seam roofing provides a dignified appearance with ornamentation, creating very deep shadow lines and bold definitions on large roof areas. This style of roof works well, with a pleasing appearance, on large roof areas such as mansards or gabled roofs. It is often specified for public buildings, churches, terminals, and so on.

The style of batten, with the edges chamfered, provides for lateral movement of the individual panels. (See Fig. 11.16.) Annual temperature extremes and temperature at time of installation must be properly considered. The battens must be of treated wood, heavy copper, or copper alloy.

Spacing of the battens is an architectural consideration, within limits. The battens cannot be spaced further apart than a full-width sheet can span. This span includes the roof field, the sides of the batten, and all formed locks used to secure the panels to the roof structure.

The size of the roof sheet from which the roof panels are to be made must be 3 in greater in width than the space from center to center of the battens. That is, if the copper stock is 24 in wide, the battens must be spaced apart 21 in on center.

For spans exceeding 21 in between battens, the copper stock is often required. For larger spans between battens, 24-oz copper or greater is required. In addition, the panel lengths may have to be reduced from the standard 10-ft length to perhaps 5 ft to provide additional strength for the larger span roof panels.

Batten-seam copper roofing allows for expansion and contraction of the copper. If installing the system in cold weather, allow a ¼-in clearance at the pan and batten strip.

DESIGN CAUTIONS

Do not stop a batten strip short of an eave, valley, or other such termination. This will create an area at the end of the battens which must be sealed and waterproofed by soldering the adjoining flat pans together (since they are not separated by a batten). This will eliminate the independent movement needed by the individual pans. Extend the batten over the edge of the valley, gutter, or eave as shown in Fig. 11.19.

In areas such as valleys, which can experience water backup due to ice dams or leaves and debris obstruction, use the method of soldered cleat as shown in Fig. 11.19. The valley metal must extend far enough upslope to always be above any rising water level.

In considering the expansion and contraction of the copper roof panels, realize that the top leading edge of the panel, because it is cleated and fixed to the roof deck, will not move as the bottom of the panel does. The movement will occur at the lock joint of the overlying pan. Consider thermal movements at the top of the panel run where they join ridge battens and at eaves where they lock onto a hook strip. See Fig. 11.18 for eave hook strip.

11.3.4 Standing-Seam Roofing

Standing-seam roofing is the most economical in application cost of the three major types of copper roof systems. The seams normally stand 1 in high after being double-locked to each other. These seams break up the expanse of the roof, but with less-defined lines than are created by the batten strip roof system.

The double-lock seam provides lateral movement of the copper panels, The hook lock used at all lap locations provide for longitudinal movements.

Exposed fasteners are not permitted. Soldering is restricted to a minimum.

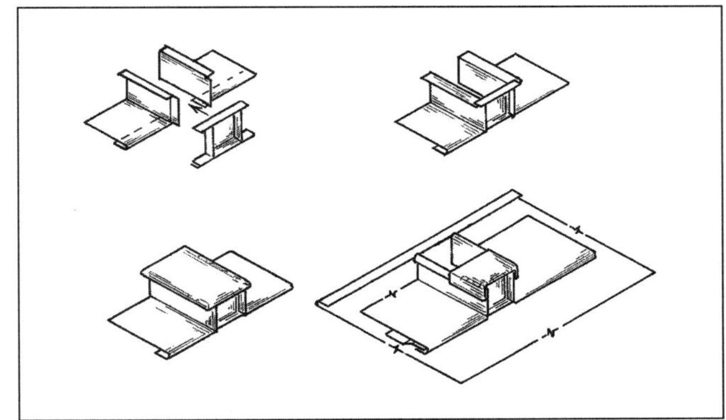

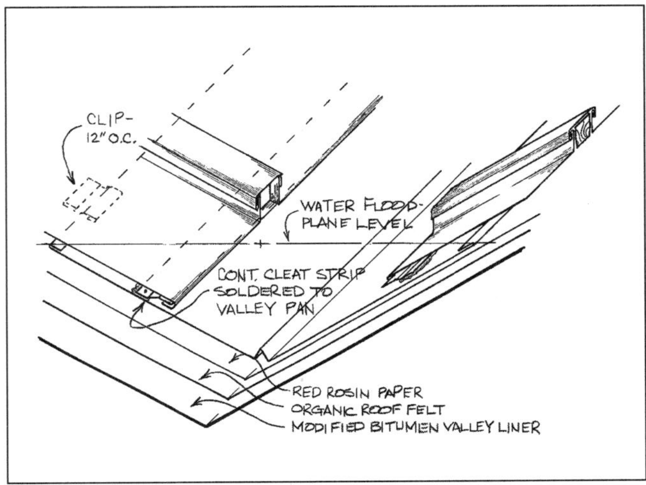

Figure 11.19 Batten-seam details at a valley.

The panels are normally shop-formed, with exception of the final locking process. At the job site the roof installers lay and cleat the unlocked panels to the roof. (See Fig. 11.15.)

Hand-held seamers are used to bend and lock the panels together. A mechanized seaming machine is also available for use. The mechanized seamer is useful for long seam runs which are not interrupted by transverse panel seam joints. Such long panels are created by pan-forming machines.

Long panel runs have advantages and possible disadvantages. Transverse seams give strength to the panels. The 180° turn of the panel tops and bottoms, used to hook the panels together and to the roof surface, give rigidity and strength to the panels. The lap joints also act as small expansion-control joints.

However, each panel joint is a possible leak area. Applicator error at such a crucial location can cause other roof problems, such as separation of the panels during an expansion and contraction cycle or roof leakage.

Long and continuous panels can be formed to almost any length by a pan-forming machine. This method is often used for coated steel architectural panel systems. The elimination of transverse seams saves application time and reduces roof leak potential.

However, the expansion and contraction rate of each panel must be closely and carefully analyzed. For a 40 ft copper panel run, the expansion and contraction rate can be conservatively estimated at ¾ in. The way, manner, and means by which such a long panel is hooked at the eave or valley locations, and how it is terminated at the ridge or hip locations, will affect the roof system's long-term performance.

Also, because rigidity is not provided by transverse seams every 10 ft, heavier copper may be required of continuous panel systems. However, this increase in material cost may balance out when compared with labor savings due to lack of transverse seam installation.

Normally, for seam spans 20 in on center or less, 16-oz copper is acceptable. For seam spans greater than 20 in on center, 20-oz copper is required. For large seam spans approaching 30 in on center, heavier copper may be required, with additional transverse seams.

The seam spans are dictated by the width of the copper stock from which the panels will be made. For standing seams to finish 1 in high, the copper sheet must be 3¼ in wider than the seam spacing.

The panels should be clipped to the roof surface every 12 in on center by a minimum 2-in-wide clip. Two copper nails should be installed through each clip. For high-wind areas, the clip spacing should be closer together. (See Fig. 11.20.)

Most roof leaks with a double-lock standing-seam panel system normally occur at locations where a seam or panel is terminated. This problems can be reduced by use of the pan finish at hips, ridges, and walls. (See Fig. 11.21.)

At valleys, use the strip-pan method (Figs. 11.14 and 11.19) if rising water, windblown water, or ice dams can be expected. In all other cases, the manner of installation for a valley area as shown in Fig. 11.22 is acceptable. Today, seams are normally terminated standing, and not folded under as shown. Folding under and hooking the standing seam is the more difficult of the two methods.

11.3.5 Flat-Lock Solder Seam Roofing

Whereas all other types of copper roof systems are water shedders, relying on roof slope and the flow of water across the roof surface, flat-lock solder seam copper roofing is a water barrier. A truly unique roof, solder seam roofing can be used as the waterproofing system on:

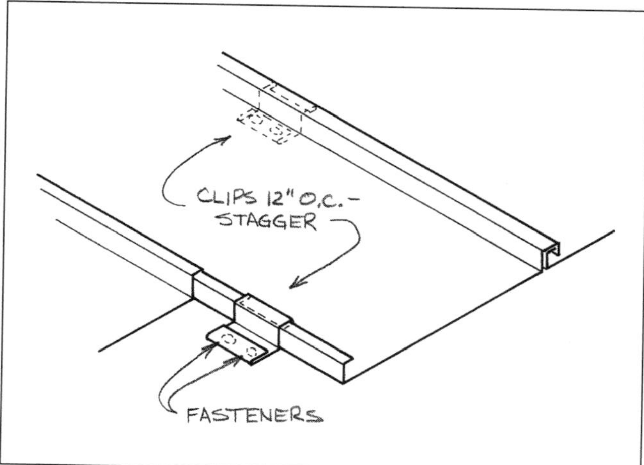

Figure 11.20 Clips at a standing-seam panel edge.

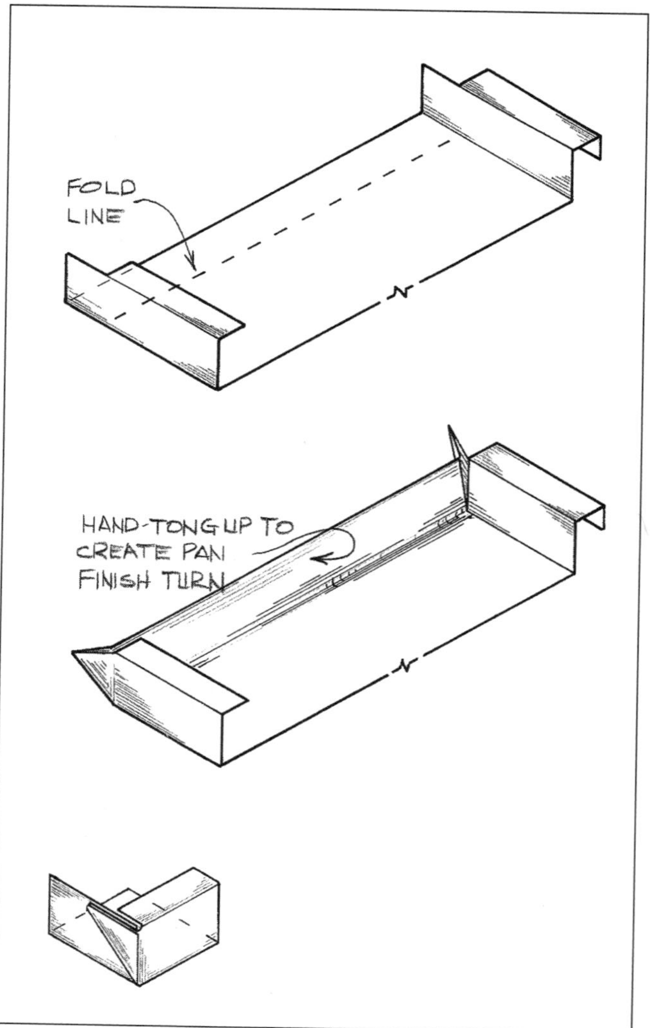

Figure 11.21 Pan finish process.

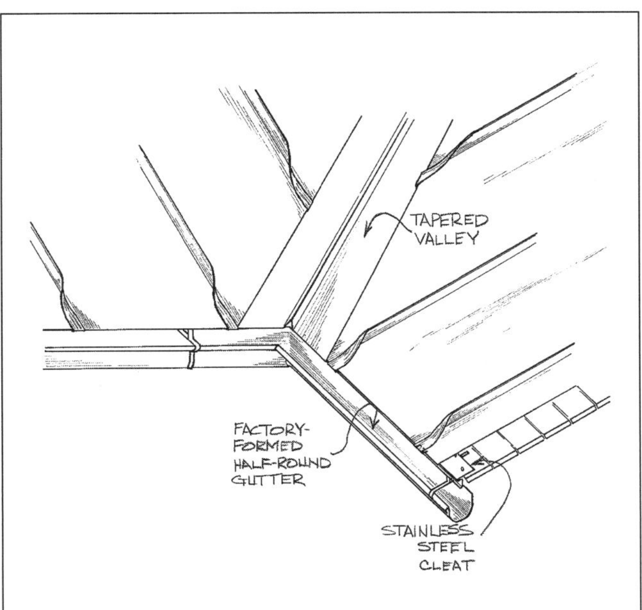

Figure 11.22 Valley within standing-seam roof.

- Water-cooled roofs
- Roof gardens and pools
- Low-sloped roofs
- Roof terraces
- Sunken gardens

The design and method of application of a flat-lock solder seam is simple to understand, but in today's industry, little used. We are sometimes required to use the solder seam in other types of copper roof systems, at areas such as built in gutters, base flashings, and so on.

SOLDERING

Solder is pulled into a joint by heat. The heat is produced by copper soldering irons, held to the joint being soldered by the sheet metal worker. Heat can also be produced by a gas flame, a practice common today.

All of the metal to be sealed by the solder must be uniformly heated. This includes, imperatively, all of the metal extending into and through the laps and joints. The heat is applied at low temperatures slowly.

This process, referred to as *sweat soldering,* allows all of the metal being soldered to become uniformly heated. The solder turns to a liquid and is drawn to the heated metal surfaces.

The metal joints or lap surfaces into which the solder is sweated must be touching. The solder is heated and turned to a liquid. It is sweated into the areas where the metal is lapped, locked, and touching.

Solder is conveyed into the lap joint or seam much the same as water will move into two touching surfaces due to capillary action. In order to understand and appreciate the techniques and mechanics of a permanently sealed solder joint, this capillary action must be understood.

Although solder is not water, when it is heated and melted, it is a liquid. The heat of the touching metal pieces, when uniformly and completed heated, draws the liquid solder in between the metal surfaces. Upon cooling the solder returns to a solid state, leaving a thin layer of solder acting as a bond between the metal surfaces soldered.

The solder, being a combination of lead and tin, will move to an extent with the expansion and contraction of the metal pieces soldered together. However, tensile strength imparted to the solder joint is more important than the elongation abilities of the joint.

The seam must be strong in order to resist and absorb the movement of the metal components soldered together. The solder seal must not be torn apart by the movement of the metal materials. If the solder is ruptured, torn, or comes apart from the metal surfaces to which it was attached, roof leaks will happen.

PRETINNING

Pretinning is essential in obtaining the correct solder joint with a flat-lock seam. Pretinning also provides the tensile strength required of the solder joint. (See Fig. 11.23.)

The most important aspect of a successful and proper flat-lock solder seam is pretinning. The pretinning is required to create a complete solder joint, permanently watertight.

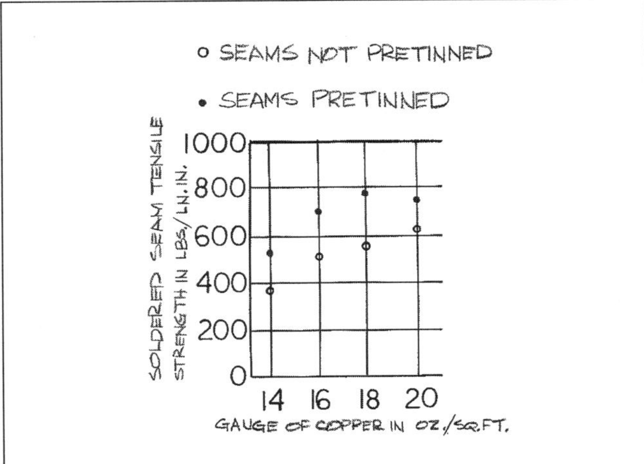

Figure 11.23 Tensile strength comparison of soldered seams—seams pretinned and not pretinned.

Any time copper is to be soldered, whether a lock seam or a lap joint, pretinning is highly recommended. *Pretinning* is the process by which a layer of solder is carefully and completely adhered to the surface of the metal before the soldering process. Soldering in earlier times was referred to as *tinning,* since block tin was often used as the solder material.

When the flat-lock seam is formed, the solder cannot effectively penetrate all the folds of the lock seam. The pretinning places solder up and within the folds. When the flat-lock seam is heated, the solder on the various faces within the folds of the seam turns liquid.

The solder bonds and seals all of the internal faces of the lock seam together. As Fig. 11.24 shows, this pretinning process greatly increases the tensile strength of the soldered lock seam.

Pretinning should be performed at the copper manufacturer's mill or in the shop, where the sheet edge can be dipped into the molten solder. A heavy and uniform coating of solder can be best obtained by this method. However, today we most often see laps pretinned at the job site, if pretinning is performed at all. It often is not.

PANELS

The roof panels are locked and malleted flat with a rubber or wooden hammer. They are then soldered at all seams. These flat-locked solder seam panels are rectangular in shape, normally 18 × 24 in with a ¾-in locked edge. The lock edges are turned under at the bottom and on one side, and turned over at the panel top and one side. The lap seams should be in the direction of the water flow.

All pretinned lap seams of the roof panels are sweat soldered watertight before the end of the work day. However, soldering a unit tight to an adjacent unit violates the primary rule we learn in coppersmithing roofs—allow units to move with expansion and contraction.

However, when designed and installed properly, a flat-lock solder seam roof system can withstand both standing water as well as thermal movements. This is a direct function of the cleats used to secure each panel (being a total of eight upon completion), the tension of the solder joints, and the expansion joints required per roof area.

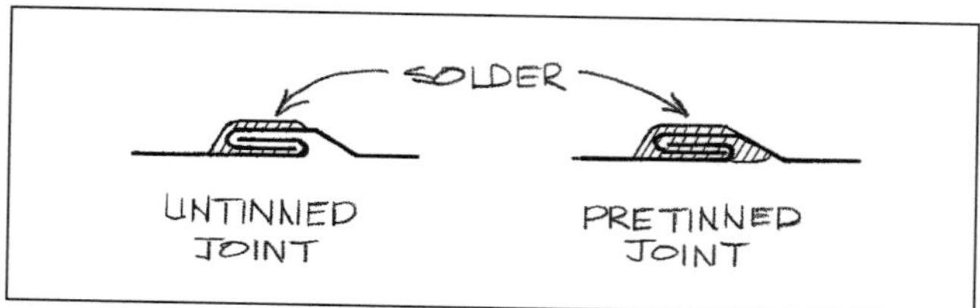

Figure 11.24 Pretinning and solder results.

Each piece of roof panel, being secured by the 8 cleats, and stiffened by solder seams on approximately 23 percent of its area, acts as an individual unit and absorbs its own thermal stresses. The cleats disperse the tension evenly in all directions.

Under expansion each sheet buckles slightly. The total expansion of a 24-in-long panel, when exposed to a 170°F temperature swing, is approximately 0.04 in. Under contraction, which is always less than expansion, the cleats confine the tension to each panel.

However, not all stresses are confined to individual panels. The panels, being soldered one to the other, act and react with each other, creating total system movement. This total system movement must be allowed for with expansion joints.

The flat-lock solder seam roof system is divided into squares when can be circumscribed by a 50-ft circle. Each area is enclosed by expansion battens as shown in Fig. 11.25. For 24- × 18-in panels, each square of roof area should be 37 × 36½ ft, resulting in 780 panels without waste.

We expect *green design* to become more popular as time goes on. With green design will come outside terraces and roof gardens.

Copper roofing is an excellent choice as the water barrier in such design. Roots will not penetrate its surface or joints. It can resist the acids and alkalis present in such systems. It is permanent. (See Fig. 11.26.)

However, finding qualified applicators for such systems may be difficult. Finding more information on design of flat-lock solder seam roofing, or the other

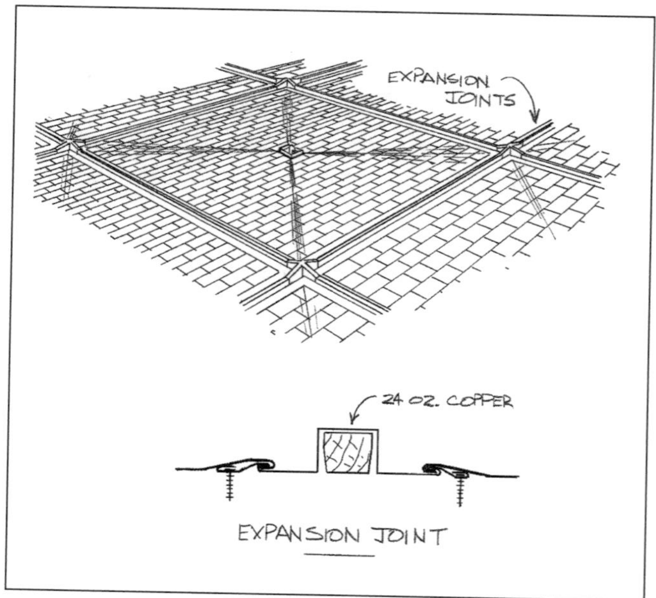

Figure 11.25 Solder seam roof system with expansion joint.

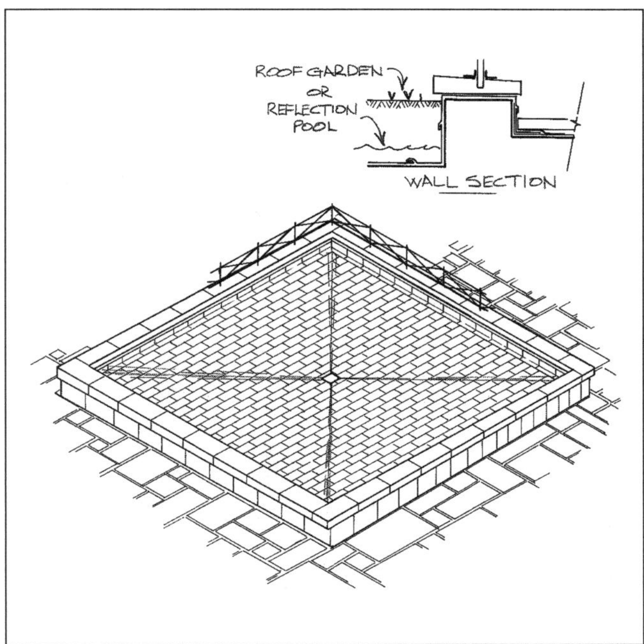

Figure 11.26 Rooftop garden or pool system.

types of copper roofing used today, can be obtained from:

Copper Development Association, Inc.
260 Madison Avenue
New York, New York 10016
(212) 251-7200

11.4 SLATE ROOFING SYSTEMS

MATERIALS

Slate roof materials evolve over millennia, created from clays and fine silts deposited on the floors of ancient seas and oceans. Time and geological pressures transformed the silt and clay into shale, which was then further transformed into slate, mica, chlorite, and quartz.

Slate as used for roofing is normally found in the United States close to the Appalachian mountain chain. Not all slate is acceptable for roof material, since the minerals from which it is created, the extent and length of geological pressure, as well as other factors, directly influence its strength, flexural, and weathering characteristics.

The colors of roof slate are different, varying from region to region and quarry to quarry as a direct result of the geological forming process and mineral content. The porosity and water-absorption rates of slate are also a result of this process, and further define acceptable and nonacceptable roof slate materials.

MANUFACTURE

Slate is quarried from the ground in much the same manner as other stone. The quarried block of slate has two distinct characteristics which allow it to be formed into roof shingles by the quarrier—the slate *grain* and slate *cleavage planes.*

The forming and creation of slate shingles is performed by hand, much the same as it has been done for centuries. The grain and cleavage planes allow the slate block to be hand-split to desired sizes.

In the manufacturing process, the quarried slate block is taken and hewn by splitting along the grain to obtain a semiuniform, oblong, rectangular block of slate suitable for further forming. The rectangular block is then cut into appropriate lengths to obtain the approximate length required for the final shingle product. This cutting is today normally performed by a wet-saw process.

This cut and sized block is taken and split along the grain lines running within the block, to obtain the approximate width of slate shingle desired as the final product. The cleavage planes, running horizontally, allow the block to be split and resplit until the desired thickness of slate shingle is obtained. (See Fig. 11.27.)

A final trimming process shapes the shingle to accurate size and shape and produces the traditional rough edges on the slate. Holes are punched into the shingle, with quality manufacturers creating a small countersunk hole on top of the shingle to receive the nail head used for installation.

In earlier times, the holes were punched by the slate applicators. The hole location dictates the exposure of the slate shingle during installation. For some applications the nail hole location will vary, base upon the style of slate roof system or a required exposure which may be other than standard.

CHARACTERISTICS

Color. Slates come in a variety of colors. Since slate roof systems are often a very prominent architectural consideration on a structure, color selection is important. The most common colors are:

- Gray
- Blue-gray
- Black
- Green
- Purple
- Red
- Mottled or variegated

These colors are often supplied in varying shades and luster.

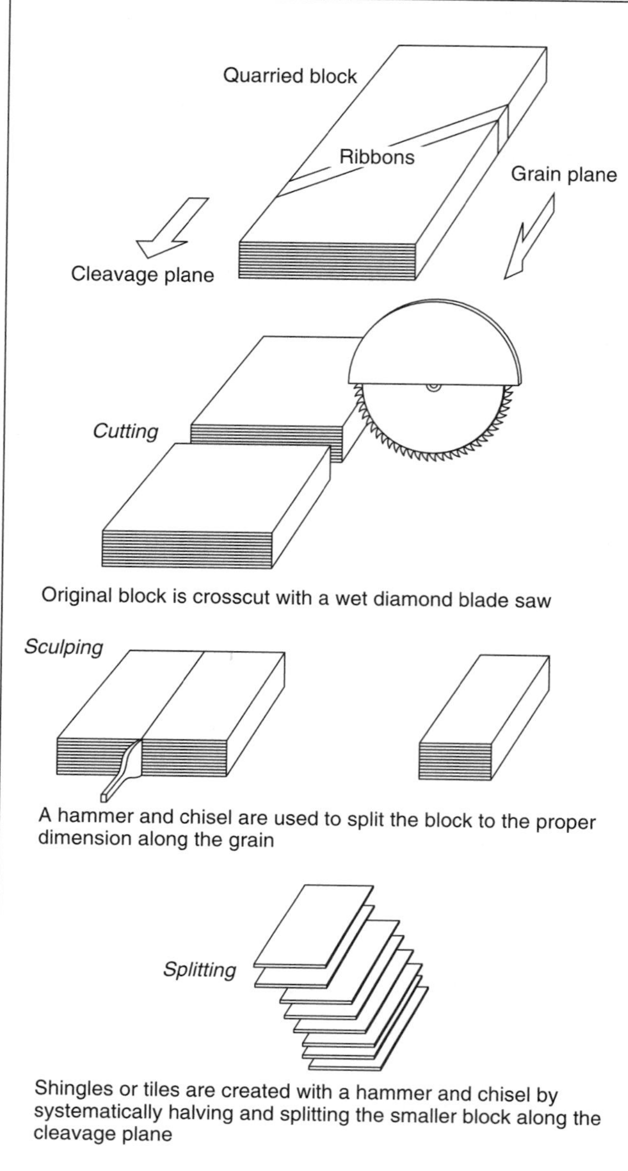

Figure 11.27 Slate splitting process. (*Courtesy of U.S. Government.*)

We more often replace or repair an existing slate roof than specify slate for new construction. In renovation work, especially historic, it is mandatory that the original color, and therefore normally the type, of slate be used to duplicate the original assembly.

In general, a deep blue-black slate is obtained from Maine and Virginia, and was obtained from the Peach Bottom district of York County, Pennsylvania. Gray and black slates normally come from the Virginia region, having a lustrous appearance due to high mica content. Lehigh and Northampton Counties of Pennsylvania produce grayish-black slate. Purple, green, red, and mottled slates are obtained from the New York–Vermont region. Red, an extremely rare and expensive slate, is only obtainable from the New York region.

Roof slates are also classified into *fading* and *unfading* categories. Nonfading slates retain their original color and shades. Fading slates will change color and hue.

For example, the *weathering green* slates obtained from the New York–Vermont region will experience a color change in approximately 20 to 50 percent of the slates per lot. Upon exposure to the atmosphere the fading slates will change to soft orange-brown, gray, and buff shades. This reaction is due to fine-grain disseminated pyrite within the slate.

It was not unusual in earlier times to blend colors of slate to create geometric patterns, words, or even dates on the roof. Different colors could also be blended to create a variegated-color roof system.

Life Span. Color of the slate does not normally indicate its expected life span. The region from which the slate originally came is a better indicator, based upon the centuries these regions have been supplying roof slate and the record of durability of the slate provided by that region.

Some slate, still in service today, was supplied by a quarry no longer in commercial production. The Peach Bottom district of Pennsylvania produced slate lasting approximately 200 years or more. Hard-vein slate of Pennsylvania can be expected to remain in service for at least 100 years. These slates are no longer available, with many of the quarries being covered by water from the TVA project.

Also, circa 1880 there were three quarries in the United States providing firebrick red slate. Today, only one exists. The most rare and expensive of all slates, red slate can be expected to last over 100 years.

New York–Vermont region slates can be expected to last 125 years.

Buckingham, Virginia, slates can be expected to last 175 years or more.

Pennsylvania soft-vein slate can be expected to last at least 50 years.

Quality. As previously stated, different quality slates, as related to durability, will come from different geographic locations and quarries. In addition, the quality of slates produced from the same region and the same slate vein can vary, and is often dependent upon the quality control procedures used by the slate producer.

Sorting and culling out of imperfect pieces should be performed at several stages during production. Culling creates waste for the producer. Another important aspect, which should normally require rejection by the slate producer, is directional uniformity of the grain within the slate. If the grain does not run consistently parallel with the long dimension of the slate, an inadequate roof shingle results. Inferior slates often have the grain pattern running in a transverse direction to the slate shingle. Grain directionality can be verified by using a bunsen burner to heat the slate until it breaks. The break line will normally be along the grain, allowing visual verification of slate acceptability.

Weathering. Roof slates, although endowed by nature with a long life span, eventually deteriorate, flake, and delaminate. The delamination of the stratified layers, along the cleavage plane, is due to gypsum forming within the slate panel.

Gypsum is formed primarily as a reaction of calcites and iron oxides, due to the wet-dry and hot-cold cycles of the environment. As the gypsum is formed, it expands.

Gypsum is water-absorbent. The increase in moisture absorption accelerates the gypsum-forming reaction. As the gypsum forms, usually in the top surfaces first, thin layers of the slates delaminate.

This delamination occurs on the underside of the slates as well as on the top surface, although the surfaces exposed to the environment usually deteriorate at a faster rate. Because the deterioration occurs to both the top and bottom surfaces, it is not feasible to remove deteriorating slates and flip them over for reinstallation.

The deterioration is a natural and slow process and does not mean the slate roof system has reached the end of its life cycle. Flaking and delaminating slates on a roof indicate that the system is approaching the end of its life cycle. Monitoring and inspection on a regular basis should be the next step, followed by repairs and maintenance as required.

A simple process is used to determine if a roof slate panel has deteriorated beyond service life. The process is called *sounding*. Sounding is performed by holding the slate panel lightly in your hand and tapping it with a hammer.

If the slate is still intact and serviceable, a clear ringing sound will be heard. If the slate is delaminated within the mineral matrix, often not detectable by visual examination, a dull sound will be heard.

This sounding process is the same principle used to find cracks and separation in a structural concrete roof deck. With a concrete roof deck, a large and heavy steel chain is dragged across the roof. When the chain crosses a crack or separation in the deck, a dull sound is produced, different from the clear, ringing sound produced by dragging the chain across a solid and intact concrete deck.

So it is with a slate panel having delaminated interior layers, or a slate that has a hairline crack. An experienced slate applicator normally taps each slate before installing it to verify that the slate is completely intact.

Hairline cracks, not visible, will cause the slate to split and fall from the roof system after installation, sometimes years after. If not sounded before application to the roof deck, an experienced slater can often tell by the way the slate sounds and feels during nailing if a problem with the individual slate exists.

When evaluating an existing slate roof system that has deteriorated, it must be determined if the deterioration is extensive enough to require total replacement or whether repairs are in order. *Slate roofs should always be repaired when possible.* Far too many slate roof systems are replaced when they should have been repaired.

As a general guideline, if 20 to 25 percent of the slates on the roof are in need of replacement, reroofing is in order. Less than 20 percent, the roof should be repaired by installing new (or used) slate into the location where the bad slate was removed. See Sec. 11.4.2.

11.4.1 Design and Specification

DESIGN

There are three classifications of slate which can be selected for use in the roof design:

Standard slate. Commercial grade slate, commonly used for slate roof systems, approximately 3⁄16- to 1⁄4-in thick. Standard slate has a smooth finish, and is uniform in length and width, with square cut ends and sides.

Textural slate. Has a rough, or textured, surface due to the composition of the slate, which upon splitting at the manufacturing facility separates not in a clean and smooth surface layer, but into a rough surface.

Graduated slate. Can have either a smooth or textured surface, although normally are from textural slates. The slates graduate in size, thickness, or both, with larger and thicker slates installed at the bottom eave, decreasing in size and thickness as courses are laid to the ridge top.

The slate roof is often an aesthetically important and apparent building system, contributing to the overall building design and character. The style of slate selected, being any of the three described, imparts aesthetic features to the building. Color of the slates and pattern of installation are also important design considerations.

The architectural styles prevalent during the late nineteenth century and early twentieth century were greatly responsible for the height of slate production and installation in the United States. During this period strong emphasis was placed on the roof lines of a structure, with slate being the material which best complimented these architectural styles.

Today, many of these slate systems are nearing the end of their service life. A resurgence in slate roof design can be expected.

Many structures having aged slate roof systems will be historical in nature and/or designation. It is therefore architecturally responsible and proper to consider roof *restoration* instead of simple replacement.

If the roof system is being replaced in its entirety, design and specify materials as similar to the original as possible. In most cases this can be done by performing research to determine the type of slate used originally, what quarry or region it was obtained from, the type of metal flashings used, the style of ridge and hip assembly used, and so on. Increasing the service life and durability of the roof system can often be accomplished by upgrading metal flashings—that is, from galvanized steel to copper or lead-coated copper—or by designing better valleys, saddle crickets, and so on. (See Sec. 11.1.)

Accessing the roof and visually examining the system will answer many questions. However, be extremely careful, since slates are often loose and can slide from the roof when walked upon. Slates are also slick, especially if moss-covered or wet. Aged slate roof systems may also have weak and deteriorated decking. Since these roofs are normally high and steep, inspection should be performed carefully and slowly, often requiring high-reach equipment.

Old and original slate or slate pieces can sometimes be found in the attic. The original installers sometimes placed original drawings, specifications, contractors, and workers names—perhaps even a descriptive history of the installation—in the eaves or soffits within the attic. (P.S.—You, in turn, should do the same.)

Roof Design Process. In reroof (restoration) design, the style and type of slate roof system is already dictated, if you desire to maintain the original concept. The biggest challenge with this type of design is duplicating the means and methods used as much as 100 to 150 years ago.

Much of the art of slate installation has been lost to the vast majority of the roof industry. There are some applicators versed in application styles and methods, although the manner in which we install slate today is not always the same as it was installed in earlier times.

Unless there is an extremely intricate design involving valleys, dormers, roof accessories such as a cupola, or metal flashing systems, modern day design and application methods will be similar enough to reproduce the original effect. If there are intricate roof components or accessories, a competitive bid process for the construction is not always advisable

Sometimes a design-build approach is best. In this case a contractor specializing in or very experienced with historic slate roof systems is located. With technical assistance from such a contractor, a set of ConDocs is produced.

It is sometimes difficult to determine how systems or components were originally designed and installed until the demolition of the component or system. In such a case a record can be made during demolition (dismantling), and drawings and specifications prepared and issued to the contractor for recreating the original design of the component or system. Again, this eliminates a competitive bid process.

Roof Design Styles. We often find multicolored and decorative slate roof systems installed on the mansard roofs of Second Empire style buildings and on the steep slopes of Gothic Revival and High Victorian Gothic style structures, as well as the turrets and cupolas of Queen Anne style buildings.

The multicolored effect can be achieved in two ways: mixing various colors of unfading slates, or by the use of weathering slates. With weathering slates, sometimes also referred to as *fading slates,* 20 to 50 percent of the slates will change color and shade after installation.

Decorative design can include sawtooth patterns created by use of different colored slates. Decorative design can also be obtained by using thick, heavy, and irregular width and length shingles, decreasing in size, thickness, and exposure as the slates progress toward the ridge. This style is called *graduated.* If roofing is to be installed on a round or circular surface, such as a cupola, graduated slate is required to compensate for the decreasing deck surface area as the slate progresses up the slope.

To compliment Tudor style and Collegiate Gothic style buildings, a graduated textural slate was often used. The rough surface of the textural slate, combined with the different size slate progression, created the quaint and rustic English appearance desired of these architectural styles. With this style of roof, the butt-end corners were often trimmed to create a more rustic appearance. (See Fig. 11.28.)

Roof slates come in many different lengths and widths. (See Table 11.4.) This is a design consideration relative to appearance and construction cost. Smaller slates will provide denser pattern of line. Smaller slates also require more slate panels per square of roof area to be covered, increasing labor cost for installation.

ROOF SLOPE AND SLATE

Slate roofing, like all other types of rigid roofing materials, requires slope to shed water from the roof surface and proper lap of the adjacent and overlying panels to restrict windblown rain. Slate roofing normally requires a 3-in head lap and a minimum 3-in offset of all overly-

Figure 11.28 Slate roof on Tudor-style structure. (*Courtesy of Evergreen Slate Co., Granville, N.Y.*)

ing panel joints. Minimum roof slope for a slate roof system is 4 : 12. (See Fig. 11.29.)

On low roof slopes the head lap of the slate is increased. This requirement is a matter of judgment on part of the designer; however, on slopes lower than 8 in rise per 12 in run, head laps are normally increased. In regions where heavy and torrential rains can be expected, lower slopes may require head lap of more than 3 in. On steep slopes, such as the side of a dormer wall, the headlap can be decreased to 2 in.

Head lap variances will increase or decrease the weight per square of the slate. A *square* of roof slate is the amount of slate required to cover 100 ft^2 of roof area.

Design Weight. Different thickness of slate have different weight. (See Table 11.5.) Some slate installed in the Bavarian regions of Europe can be as much as 2 in thick, weighing as much as 8000 lb per square. In reroofing design, if the thickness of slate is increased, verify through structural engineering methods the capability of the structure to support the weight.

Older structures are often fatigued. In reroofing, extensive rework of the wooden support structure is often necessary in order for it to support the new slate roof system for an additional 100+ years.

Roof slates can leach and retain moisture when they reach the state where gypsum is forming within the stratified slate layers. This often causes the wooden roof deck and support members to remain wet or damp for extended periods of time. This can occur even if the structure is not experiencing extensive roof leaks to the building interior.

Waterproofing Design. Slate roof panels, when installed with proper head lap per slope requirement, and with proper offset of side joints, are virtually waterproof. This is best demonstrated by the ability of slate to be installed to a 1 × 4 lath system, without a solid roof deck or roof felt layers, and maintain a watertight building.

However, properly installed slate still has the potential of leaking. Roof leaks can occur at locations where water is centralized in great amounts, such as valleys and crickets. Strong winds, combined with torrential rain, can cause water to be blown between the laps of the slate system.

It is therefore common practice to install a roof felt under the slate system, normally an organic #30 felt. (See Sec. 7.1.1.) Due to the number of holes created in the roof felt during nailing of the slate, this felt cannot be considered a waterproof barrier. However, it will help shed small and inconsistent amounts of water if such passes through the slate system.

At areas where the possibility of water passing through the slate system can be more consistent, additional and heavier layers of roof felt need to be installed. These are under the valley system and at base flashings by chimneys and dormer walls, as well as any ice dams needed for the colder climates. Today, this roof felt is often replaced by modified bitumen membrane sheets.

Table 11.4 Sizes for standard 3⁄16-in slate.

Size of slate, in	*Pieces per square*	*Exposure with 3-in head lap, in*
26 × 14	89	11½
24 × 16	86	10½
24 × 14	89	10½
24 × 13	106	10½
24 × 12	114	10½
24 × 11	125	10½
22 × 14	108	9½
22 × 13	117	9½
22 × 12	126	9½
22 × 11	138	9½
22 × 10	152	9½
20 × 14	121	8½
20 × 13	132	8½
20 × 12	141	8½
20 × 11	154	8½
20 × 10	170	8½
20 × 9	189	8½
18 × 14	137	7½
18 × 13	148	7½
18 × 12	160	7½
18 × 11	175	7½
18 × 10	192	7½
18 × 9	213	7½
16 × 14	160	6½
16 × 12	184	6½
16 × 11	201	6½
16 × 10	222	6½
16 × 9	246	6½
16 × 8	277	6½
14 × 12	218	5½
14 × 11	238	5½
14 × 10	261	5½
14 × 9	291	5½
14 × 8	327	5½
14 × 7	374	5½
12 × 10	320	4½
12 × 9	355	4½
12 × 8	400	4½
12 × 7	457	4½
12 × 6	533	4½
11 × 8	450	4
11 × 7	515	4
10 × 8	515	3½
10 × 7	588	3½
10 × 6	686	3½

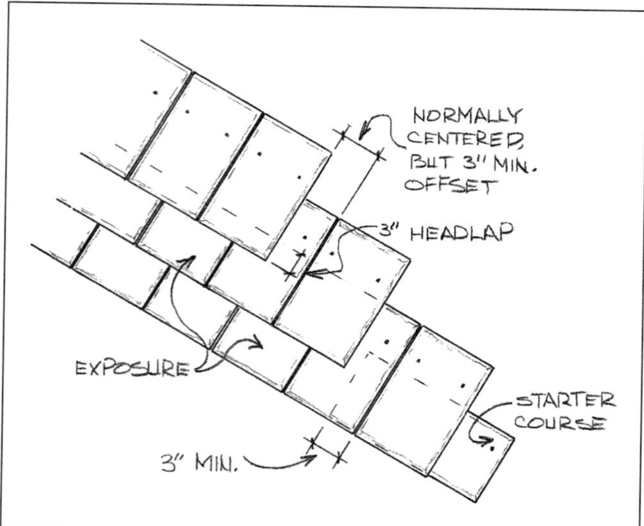

Figure 11.29 Slate exposure and head lap.

However, do not rely on the waterproofing felt membrane to maintain the waterproof integrity of the roof system. Felts and membranes deteriorate due to heat, water, and age. The felt membrane underlayment will not last the 100 to 150 years that the slate can be expected to last. The felt membrane will help restrict water that should infiltrate the slate system due to unusual occurrences.

SPECIFICATION

Specify slate to be manufactured in accordance with ANSI S-1. This ensures uniformity and quality of slate shingle.

Slate should be manufactured with the grain. Cross-grain slate shingles do not have the strength or durability of slate shingles made with the grain.

Table 11.5 Slate weight.

Slate thickness, in	*Weight per square (with 3-in head lap), lb*
3⁄16	700
3⁄16	750
¼	1000
⅜	1500
½	2000
¾	3000
1	4000
1¼	5000
1½	6000
1¾	7000
2	8000

Slate should be consistent in thickness. This requires the cleavage plane to be consistent within the rock block the slate is manufactured from. It also requires proper culling, and extensive waste, at the manufacturing facility.

If restoring the roof with all new slate, specify the same type slate as existing. If possible, obtain slate from the same quarry region as the slate original to the structure.

Specify only nonferrous nails, fasteners, and metal for flashings. Copper is the most commonly used material. Use minimum 16-oz copper or lead-coated copper, 26-gauge stainless steel, 26-gauge terne-coated steel, or .040 aluminum. Aluminum is discouraged because it cannot be soldered. In areas of high abuse or limited access, such as valleys, crickets, and so on, use heavier metals.

Follow procedures and requirements as outlined for metal works in Chap. 12.

Require pretinning of all solder joints. Restrict the use of caulking for waterproofing metal flashings.

Specify construction process for all other work associated with or accessible only by the roof. This can include repointing or plastering of chimney chases, repairing skylights, lightning protection systems, window glazing, and so on. This should be completed before roofing is installed at these areas.

All head lap of slate should be 3 in, except on low roof slopes where it should be increased.

All vertical joints of the slate should be offset a minimum of 3 in from any vertical joint of an overlying or underlying vertical slate joint.

All installed slate should be free of defect. All slates should be sounded by the roofer before installation to the roof deck.

SYP decking, nominally 1 in thick, is suitable for roof decking replacement in the event that deteriorated lumber is found. Treated lumber sometimes warps.

Install no warped or distorted slates. Store slates on edge, under cover, on pallets, per manufacturers' recommendations.

Allow no roof demolition to begin until roof slates are on site or in the contractor's possession. It sometimes takes up to one year for delivery of some special slates. A 4- to 12-week delivery after order is not unusual for most slates.

11.4.2 Slate Roof Repair

To repair or not repair; that is oft the question. The decision is based upon facts discovered about the existing roof system.

If possible, it is best to determine from which quarry region within the United States the slate originally came. This is a good indication of the expected life span of the slate roof materials. (See Sec. 11.4.) This information is seldom obtainable without an original bill of lading, or some other proof of slate origin. A few experienced slate roofers can tell by eye, or it may be possible to obtain the opinion of a slate producer.

Knowing the accurate installation date is very helpful. However, the actual installation date is often opinion by the current resident or occupant of the building.

If these facts are unobtainable, or unverifiable, the decision must be made solely upon discovery and investigation of existing component and material conditions. Not to fear, this is normally all you have to go on anyway.

INVESTIGATION

Investigation often begins in the attic of the building. Signs of structural damage, such as deteriorated wood supports or decking, is often found by chimney penetrations, valley locations, and eaves.

The type of nail fastener used during roof installation may also be evident during the attic investigation. Ferrous nails in humid, wet, and corrosive atmospheric environments often do not last the life span of slate roofing. If the nails are steel, rusting and subsequent slipping and displacement of the slate can be expected in such an environment.

In such cases there is little that can be done to repair the slate roof. Removal and reinstallation of the slate is often the only solution, at which time copper or stainless steel nails should be used.

During the attic investigation old slate shingles used during the original work may be found. If so, this provides a good comparison of a "new" slate and the weathered rooftop slate. Sometimes original drawings and/or specifications of the work can also be found, helping to establish type of materials used and construction dates.

To investigate the actual condition of a slate roof, you normally have to access a portion of the roof. The roof is normally steep. The slate roof system is normally old, and may be covered with slippery moss or algae growth. In addition, roof leaks could have deteriorated the roof structure and/or decking. A lift truck or other mechanical lift is often the best and safest way to closely examine a slate roof. *Be careful!*

Roof leaks and deteriorated components normally first occur at flashing locations, such as valleys, built-in gutters, dormers, chimneys, crickets, and so on. If roof leaks are isolated to these locations, and if flashing failure is the cause of roof problems, and if the slate shingles themselves are in good condition, repairs are often the best solution.

If roof leaks are isolated to random areas of the roof, and are not extensive, it is often due to broken, cracked, or missing slate shingles. In such a case repairs are often the best solution.

If roof leaks are isolated to southerly exposures of the building, roof replacement to these roof facades may be the best solution. The remaining facades should be closely monitored and scheduled for replacement in a timely manner. Roofs deteriorate on southern exposures quicker than on other exposures.

All of the preceding items are relevant to the overall condition of the slate shingles. Slate shingles deteriorate in a stratified delamination process. (See Sec. 11.4.) It is useless to try and repair a slate roof system whose shingles are decayed, weak, water absorbent, and delaminating along the cleavage planes.

If any shingles are loose it is possible to *sound* the shingle. Sounding of a slate shingle is performed by tapping it lightly with a hammer. A clear ringing sound is produced when a solid, non-delaminated slate shingle is so struck. If it is possible to so test any of the existing slate shingles, the result will help in the repair-or-replace decision.

Normally, if approximately 25 percent of the slate shingles are damaged or deteriorated, repair is not cost-effective. In such a case roof replacement is often the best solution.

PROCEDURES

Metal Flashing Repair. Proper roof system design and good roof installation practices will prevent untimely roof leaks and problems, on any type of roof, in any location. Easy to say—hard to do.

An experienced slate roofer may not be a good coppersmith or sheet metal worker. A good sheet metal worker may not be a qualified waterproofer. Problems can arise if the very exceptional person, qualified at both crafts, is not present during roof installation.

Often, two different crews are used to install the slate and to install the metal flashings. Sometimes the metal flashing work required is not so complex that the slate roof workers cannot properly install the flashings.

The roof system designer must understand:

- The nature of the materials being installed
- The geographic and environmental conditions in which the materials and systems must function
- The manner in which the components, materials, and system will interact one with another
- The means and manner in which the roof applicators will perform their work

Considering the preceding, problems can arise at areas of the slate roof system where different components and skills are required in the construction process. This is often at metal flashing locations.

To correct roof flashing problems it is normally required that slate shingles be removed to access the metal flashing components. Enough slate shingles should be removed to prevent breaking and cracking of the adjacent shingles by workers during the repair procedure.

The defective materials, being either the flashings or the shingles, are removed and discarded or they may be repaired in place. New materials are properly formed and installed.

For example, if a copper valley location is experiencing roof leaks, the cause of leaks should be determined before work proceeds, if possible. The roof leaks could be due to improperly installed slate shingles, broken shingles at the valley, cracked and open lap joints of the valley sections, or something as simple as a valley obstructed by tree branches, leaves, or other debris.

If the slate shingles are cracked, displaced, or improperly installed at the valley, then metal flashing work is not required. Instead, roof slates are removed and new slate roofing, properly cut and formed, is installed into the valley.

However, if the metal valley is the cause of roof problems, more extensive work is required. In such a case the slate shingles should be removed the entire length of the valley run, normally in a strip 2 to 3 ft wide per each side of the valley. (See Fig. 11.30.)

The metal valley is removed and new waterproofing felts installed to the deck. The new felts or membranes must be installed into the roof felt underlayment system in a water-shedding manner.

New metal valley flashing, preferably copper or stainless steel, is fabricated and installed. Slate shingles are then reinstalled into the valley flashing.

Examine the removed materials. Confirm the cause of the roof problems and verify that the procedures being used to correct the problems are correct and durable. Design new flashings in accordance with time-proven methods. (See Secs. 11.1 and 12.1.1.)

Such repair procedures are time-consuming and expensive. Several considerations must be addressed by the designer in order to best serve the client.

1. If the roof area to which the extensive repair work is being performed is small, it may be prudent to remove the slate from the entire roof area and restore that area in its entirety. At the least, it is prudent to request price structures from contractors for both procedures.
2. If one valley (or other metal flashing) area is failed, will others soon begin to experience problems? After

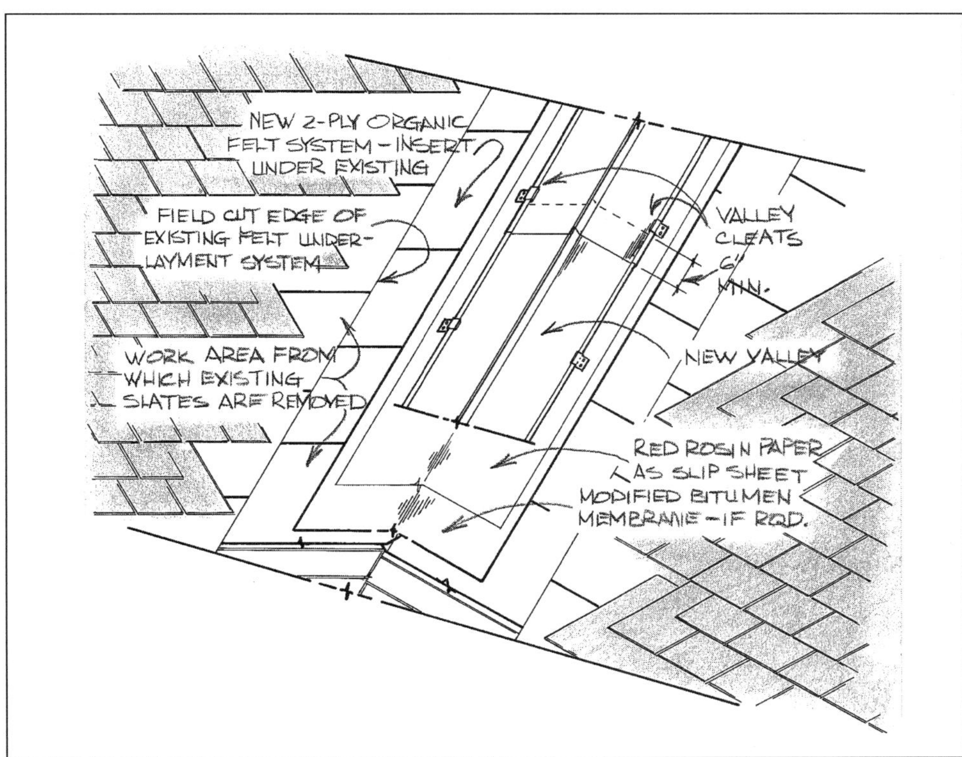

Figure 11.30 Valley repair on a slate roof.

all, they were probably all installed in the same manner, by the same workers, at the same time.

Mobilization and setup on a steep, tall slate roof is a large expense to the roof contractor. It is more cost-effective to have all work done at one time than to continually call contractors to return and perform additional repair work.

3. Metal flashings usually join areas of roof together, such as valley flashing which joins and seals different roof slopes and intersections. Metal flashings also seal the base of a building component into the slate roof system, such as flashings at a chimney chase, dormer, or building wall. If work will be required in the future to the building component above the slate roof surface, require such work at the time of roof repair.

Building components with mortar joints, paint finishes, or other materials requiring periodic maintenance which exist at the roof repair area should be evaluated. Maintenance, refinishing, and repair should be perform to any building component at the time of roof repair, if access to that building component will require working on or over the new repair area. Also, evaluation of the condition and the future accessibility of any roof area above the repair location should be considered.

Slate Shingle Replacement. Slate roofing is repaired by careful removal of the damaged slate. Slate removal is performed by a slate tool referred to as a *ripper*.

The ripper is a long, thin, flat bar that can be slid under the damaged shingle. When in place, the roofer manipulates the ripper to either cut the nail shank holding the shingle in place, or to pull the nail from the deck and from under the slate shingle. In either case, the nails holding the damaged slate in place are removed, allowing the slate shingle to slide free and be discarded.

To reinstall a slate shingle into the space created by the removed shingle, a simple process is used. A copper or stainless steel strap or wire is attached in between the vertical joint of the exposed existing shingle head lap. The metal is long enough to extend past where the bottom edge of the new shingle will be. (See Fig. 11.31.)

A new replacement slate shingle is slid into place, into the same location as the removed shingle. The metal wire or strap is then bent up and over the bottom edge of the newly installed slate.

The wire strap secures the slate shingle from sliding down the roof. The existing shingles that overlay and are adjacent to the clipped-in slate shingle secure it against wind uplift.

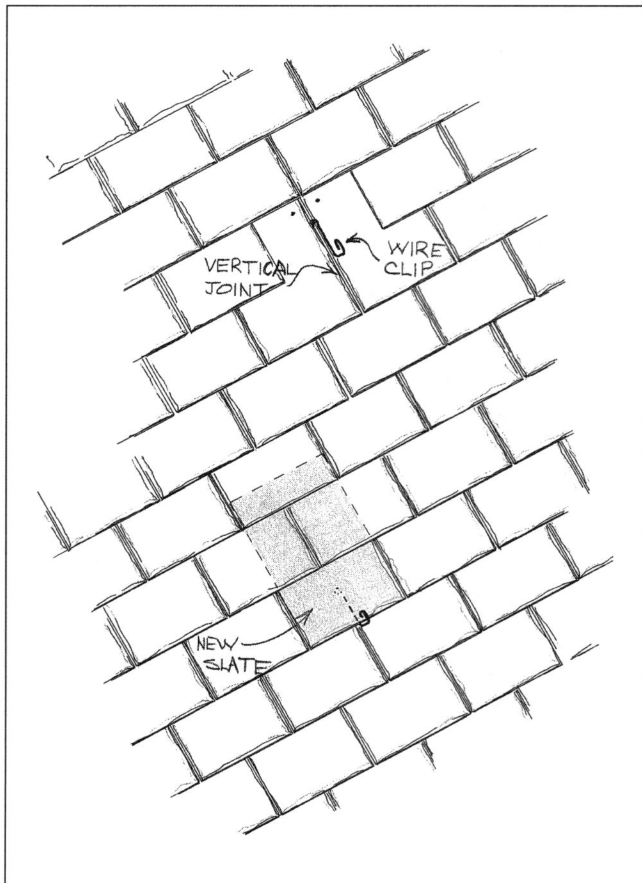

Figure 11.31 Repair with clipped slate.

Sectional Roof Repair. It is sometimes in the client's best interest to initiate a controlled-schedule roof replacement program. Often, the architectural style of the building incorporates numerous roof facades, making this process even more feasible.

The are advantages and disadvantages with sectional roof replacement. Completed costs, contractor responsibility, and, therefore, liability are of concern.

With sectional roof replacement total capital outlay is divided into units. Being divided into two, three, or more roof areas, the cost per area is sometimes easier for the client to absorb than the cost for entire roof replacement.

Also, with sectional replacement, existing conditions which may not be visually evident are discovered and subsequent design and budget on other sections can reflect such discovery. Change orders and surprises are limited on other sections.

The roof slate from the section being replaced can be salvaged. Salvaged slate in serviceable condition can be stored and used as repair materials on the other sections of the roof.

The salvaged slate, being the same size, color, and texture as that existing elsewhere, blends with the remaining roof system. This can help extend the life of the remaining roof system, eliminating unpleasant appearance and material costs for repair slates.

Disadvantages to sectional roof replacement are also to be considered. Normally, the square foot cost is more for phased roof construction than for total replacement at one time. There is a greater waste factor, which also relates to increased square foot cost.

An important consideration is the location where the new roof section joins the existing, in-place roof section. For example, if a roof section is being replaced on a hip roof, the new section usually terminates at the hips.

In such a case, the two hips of the section to be reroofed are removed. A new hip system must be installed. The hip, ridge, valley, and other flashing or detail areas are the most expensive aspect of slate roof construction costs.

When the other hip roof areas which adjoin the newly replaced hip roof section are roofed, the newly installed hip roofing and materials must be removed and reinstalled yet again.

This includes the often custom-cut slate covering the hip, as well as any underlying wood strip nailers, metal and felt flashings, and metal clips and/or ties. Often, these materials are destroyed in the removal process and must be created again.

It is better design practice to extend new roofing past any such hip onto the adjoining hip area. When reroofing is required to the adjoining hip areas, all that has to be removed, and possibly wasted, is the roof field slate. This prevents rework of the more expensive hip detail areas. (See Fig. 11.32.)

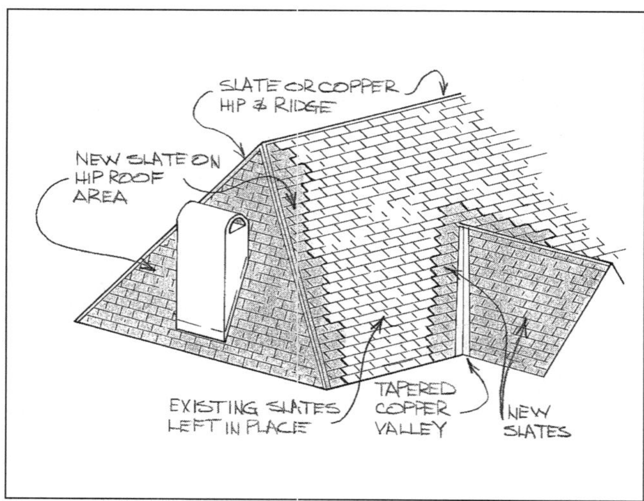

Figure 11.32 Sectional replacement on a hip roof.

Such practice should also apply to valley and ridge locations. Extend new roofing past the valley or the ridge. During demolition and roofing of the adjacent roof sections, it is hoped that the valley or ridge work will not have to be removed and wasted.

Evaluate and possibly confer with the contractor on the feasibility and proper attachment of slates at the connection lines. Field slate which must be joined to previously installed, existing work often requires some clipping of slate, as shown in Fig. 11.31. Wind loads and, possibly, slate blow-off are concerns in some situations and are dependent upon roof configuration and tie-in locations on the roof.

Contractor responsibility for any roof problems can be of concern. In the event that a replaced roof area leaks, the contractor may contend the leak is from a section yet to be roofed.

Also, if each construction phase is competitively bid, more than one contractor may work on the roof system. In the event of problems, it may difficult to assign responsibility.

Color continuity of the roof slate may be a concern if the construction project is phased through many years. Slate is quarried from the ground, following the vein of slate. Color contrasts may occur in the vein as quarrying progresses.

CHAPTER 12

Roof Flashings

12.1 GENERAL

All roof systems must have roof flashings. Many roof leaks and roof failures are directly related to these flashing systems. Failure can be traced in most cases, not to the material used, but to the design of the flashing system or the manner in which it was installed.

It is not practical, and perhaps it's impossible, to list and illustrate all the different flashing situations that will be encountered on the various roof systems and building structures existing or which will exist. It is therefore extremely critical that a designer understand the purpose, mechanics, and theory of flashing and roof membrane interface.

FLASHING PURPOSES

The roof flashing is used to:

- Seal the roof membrane into a building wall (base flashings, counterflashings)
- Terminate the roof membrane (metal edge/gravel guard)
- Seal penetrations through the roof membrane (pitch pans, pipe flashings)
- Conduct or direct water from the roof (gutters, downspouts, scuppers, drains, valleys)
- Seal and waterproof roof structures (parapet copings, vent and chimney hoods)
- Allow for expansion of roof areas (expansion joints)
- Seal the interior of parapet walls (parapet wall flashing)
- Divert water from building wall interior (through wall flashing)

FLASHING MATERIALS

Metal flashings are created in the shop from sheet metal or formed in the field from lead or soft temper copper. Bituminous flashings are created on the rooftop from roof sheets, felts, membranes, and adhesives. The materials which can be used are numerous. With sheet metal flashings, materials may include:

- Aluminum
  - paint coated
  - metallic coated
  - anodized
  - mill finish
- Copper
  - lead coated
  - soft temper (hot-rolled)
  - hard temper (cold-rolled)
- Lead
- Monel
- Stainless steel
  - terne coated
  - mill finish, dull or bright
- Steel
  - metallic coated (galvanized/aluminum)
  - paint coated
- Zinc alloy

With membrane flashings, the makeup can be as varied as the materials available for roof construction. The membrane flashing is often created from the same type of material as the roof membrane.

In Figure 12.1, components are identified for future reference. It also shows the base flashing composed of bituminous membranes, roof ply sheets, cant strips, hot-process bitumen mopping, and asphalt cutback adhesive.

The counterflashing over the bituminous base flashing is stainless steel sheet metal flashing. Caulking is used to create a gasket seal and exposed seal of the sheet metal bonnet flashing.

12.1.1 Flashing Design Theory

The roof flashing must be compatible with the roof system, to the extent possible. The flashing must complement the roof membrane, creating the strongest and most durable area of roof system, not the weakest link in the chain. For example, in the past it was not uncommon to find a base flashing created from a 90° bent sheet metal flashing, sealed to the roof membrane with additional plies of roof felt. (See Fig. 12.2.)

In such case, the metal flashing does not complement the roof membrane because it is not compatible. Metal and bituminous material have totally different characteristics. It fought against the roof membrane every day during the expansion and contraction cycles created by the temperature differences on the rooftop. Roof leaks can be expected of this flashing system design. This design requires high maintenance time and cost.

MEMBRANE FLASHING

Today, we always try to eliminate metal flashing from the rooftop. We substitute the membrane flashing as shown in Fig. 12.1 or something similar. With such design there is the basic roof membrane, with all roof felt and membrane layers and plies, extending up the cant strip face and out of the normal water level, created during rains, on the rooftop.

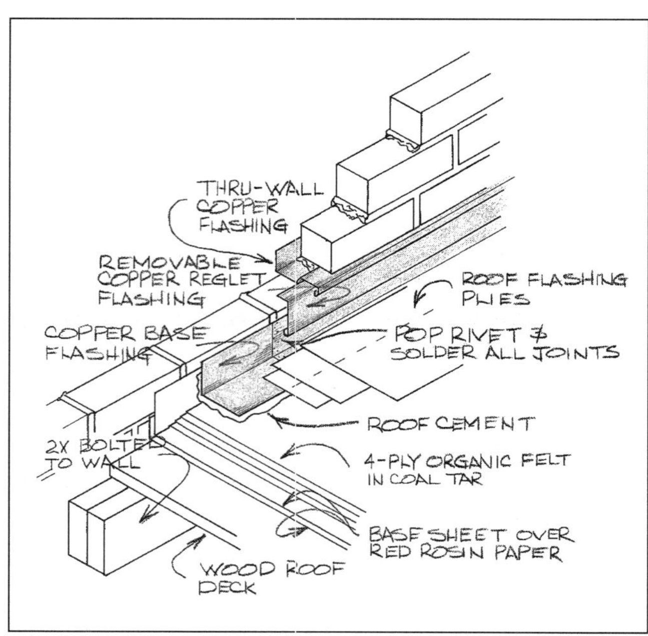

Figure 12.2 Metal base and counterflashing.

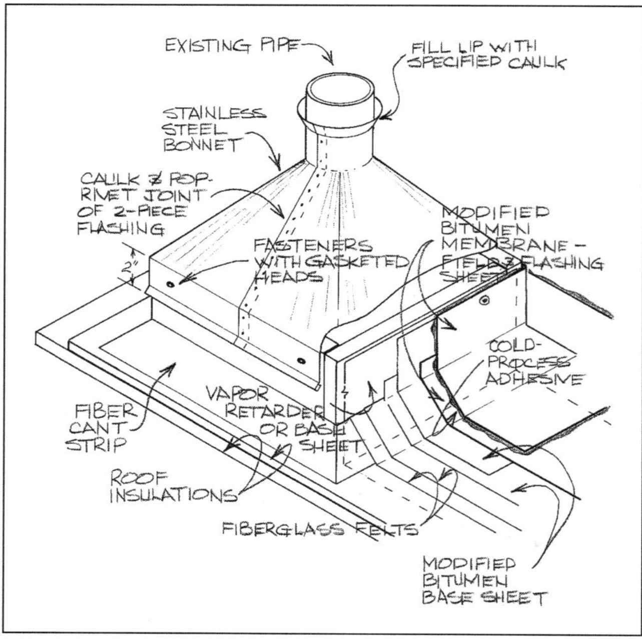

Figure 12.1 Pipe penetration with bonnet and base flashing.

Additional roof plies, membranes, and bitumen layers are added at the cant strip area. This provides the durability required to absorb movement caused by thermal expansion of the roof system, live loads occasioned to the roof structure, building movement, and provide environmental resistance required of a flashing system. Upon completion of installation of these additional materials, a membrane base flashing is created. The membrane base flashing is compatible and complements the roof system. It is now the strongest link in the chain, not the weakest.

In addition to providing additional strength, the flashing plies can also be considered sacrificial. Deterioration of the exposed top ply can be expected. Roof maintenance and repair will normally be needed to the base flashing at some time during the life of the roof.

Cant strips are always required with bituminous membrane systems. The roof felts and membrane sheets are not able to make a 90° bend. If so installed, the roof membrane will crack or rupture at the angle break line. Also, unacceptable bridging of the membrane in the 90° corner will occur. The cant strip divides the 90° bend into two 45° angles.

Sometimes, membrane base flashings are installed to equipment curbs that may experience movement from the equipment mounted upon them, such as a roof exhaust fan. This movement, although slight, is repetitive and can cause damage to the membrane flashing over time.

For such design, it is appropriate to incorporate a dry sheet against the curb upon which all the other plies and adhesives of the membrane flashing will be built. This unadhered roof sheet will be mechanically attached at some location, usually the top, and acts as a slip sheet. This helps isolate the base flashing membrane from any movement of the equipment curb. (See Fig. 12.3.)

With membrane flashings—specifically, built-up and adhesive-applied modified bitumen systems—we believe cold-process adhesives are much more effective than hot moppings of asphalt bitumen. At base flashings which are expected to be exposed to and resistant of unusual stresses, cutback asphalt mastic or plastic roof cement is very helpful.

The adhesive material can normally be applied under the final surfacing sheet. The mastic will remain soft and pliable longer than hot asphalt bitumen, allowing the flashing system to better accommodate movement and rooftop abuse. (See Fig. 12.1.) Verify compatibility of the adhesive with the flashing membrane.

Special Note. On polymeric single-ply roof systems, the membrane flashings are normally of the same type of material as the roof membrane. However, cant strips are often not required. The flexural ability of the membrane allows for a 90° bend without adverse effects. Fasteners are installed at the base of the angle turn to eliminate bridging of the membrane in the 90° corner.

Many other flashing details, specific only to polymeric membranes, are used with these types of systems. Additionally, details of one manufacturer often are not approved for use by another material manufacturer.

Due to the complexity and specific requirements of the polymeric single-ply membranes, we do not reference or discuss such systems within this manual.

SHEET METAL FLASHINGS

It is sometimes impossible to keep sheet metal flashing from the rooftop, such as in the case of metal edge or gravel guard flashings. In these instances, expect and plan on the dynamic forces that will surely occur and will affect the roof and flashing system. (See Sec. 12.2.1.)

Elevate the metal edge flashing on wood nailers. This will keep any delaminated, split, or cracked membrane roofing at these areas from the plane of water on the rooftop during rains.

Always design backer and cover plates at all metal edge joints. This disperses concentrated stresses to two lap joint locations instead of concentrating stress to one lap joint location found in such lap joints without cover and backer plates. Also, pliable sealant layers within the cover and backer plate system restrict water entry. (See Fig. 12.4.)

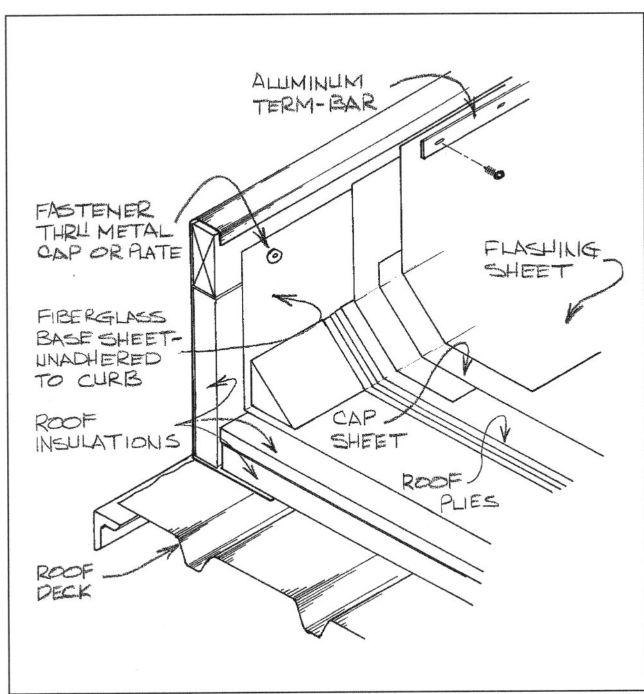

Figure 12.3 Isolated base flashing and curb.

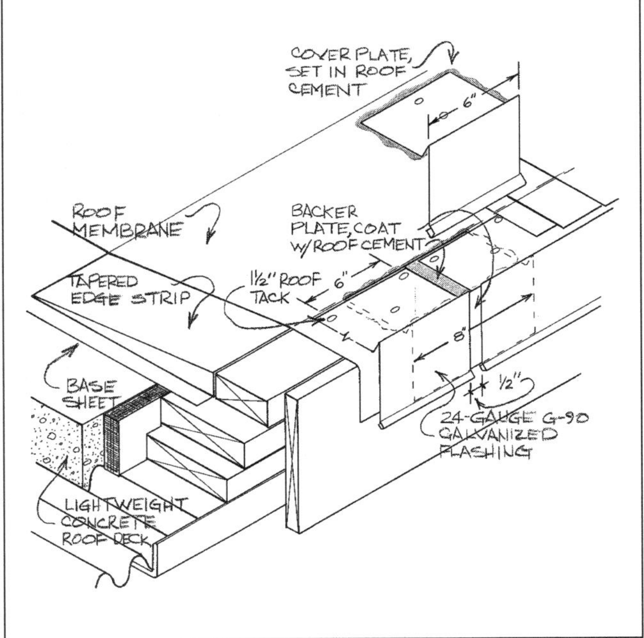

Figure 12.4 Metal edge on wood nailer with backer–cover plate.

The most damaging forces of sheet metal flashings against which to design are expansion and contraction of the metal. Such forces are normally evidenced at the lap joints. Lap joints of metal flashing components are where most roof leaks originate. (See Fig. 12.10.)

At one time, in an effort to reduce this damaging force, it was a common practice for some designers to require all the lap joints of the sheetmetal flashing to be soldered tight. This will only work correctly, for an extended period of time, if the solder joint is optimally created, resulting in a complete and proper solder bead with high tensile strength. Expansion joint assembly must be included within the flashing system. (See Fig. 12.11.)

On a rooftop, doing meticulous work in what often can be considered as less than the best working conditions, quality of solder work sometimes suffers. Also, when soldering a joint installed over a bitumen roof membrane, the lap joints can become contaminated with dirt and bitumen oils. Also, for the solder joint flashing system to function effectively, expansion joint provisions must be designed and built into the metal flashing system. The expansion joints must be included a minimum of every 50 ft and sometimes less.

Failed solder joints which have split and opened, allowing water to enter the system, are not uncommon. The amount of stress imposed on the joints during the expansion and contraction cycle is more significant than many realize.

With the advent of high-performance elastomeric caulks, soldering of lap joints is not as prevalent as in the past. Also, technology and information have led designers to understand and use better design solutions.

If sheet metal flashing must be applied to a roof surface and it is not possible to elevate on wood blocking (see Fig. 12.4) and/or not feasible to include cover and backer plates within the metal flashing system, at least set all of the metal in a bed of plastic roof cement or appropriate elastic adhesive. (See Fig. 12.5.) The cement or adhesive creates a pliable bed of mastic sealant. If the metal flashing leaks, the sealant bed provides a line of defense which can often keep the water from penetrating farther into the roof system.

In such cases, it also good design to use plastic roof cement or appropriate cold-process adhesive to seal the flashing plies to the metal. The bituminous cutback adhesive will remain pliable, allowing elasticity between the movement of the metal flashing and the flashing plies. (See Fig. 12.5.)

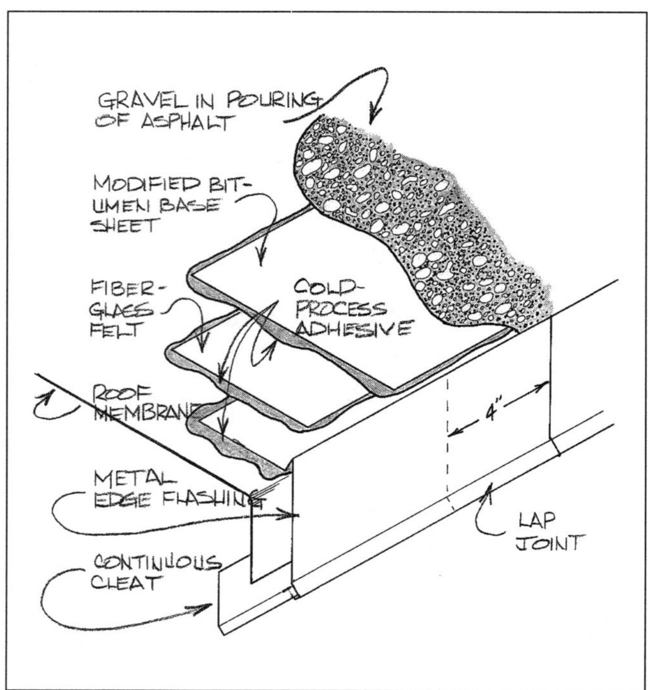

Figure 12.5 Metal edge set in cement and sealed with cold process.

MISCELLANEOUS METAL FLASHING DESIGN THEORY

For critical design situations, where leaks must absolutely be restricted or where they can be expected to occur, the entire length of the metal flashing flange should be set in roof mastic. Again, the mastic provides a water barrier that will help restrict the passage of water if the flashing leaks. As shown in Fig. 12.5, this is sometimes required of the metal edge/gravel guard flashing system which is not elevated on wood blocking.

In the design of metal flashings, a 4-in dimension is very common. The amount of metal flange extending out onto the roof membrane, to be sealed by the flashing plies is normally 4 in. The usual minimum dimension required for faces of metal flashings which are exposed is 4 in. The amount of lap between metal flashing pieces is normally 4 in.

Almost all minimum dimension requirements of metal flashing are 4 in, which provides the safety factor required to restrict water traveling horizontally as a result of blowing wind or from capillary action.

Four inches of metal edge flange on a gravel guard or other flashing system provides an adequate amount of metal for the roof membrane to adhere to. A flange larger than this can cause adhesion problems between the flashing plies and the flange. A flange greater than 5 in is never recommended because this much metal may move excessively and cause splitting or delamination of the flashing membrane plies from the flange.

In the design of metal flashings, it is almost always required that the primary roof membrane system be installed before installation of the metal flashings. Although not required, it is good practice to achieve a watertight roof system before installation of metal flashings.

The flashings are then installed to the top of the roof and sealed, normally by use of materials the same as or similar to the roof membrane. Sometimes the flashing seal is further reinforced by application of mastic to the roof surface into which the metal flashing is set.

An important function of the metal flashing is to keep the roof system secured to the building top and to remain in place, waterproofing a roof structure, even in high winds. This is accomplished by use of the appropriate gauge or thickness of metal flashing and by the type of fastener and spacing of same.

The thicker the stock from which the sheet metal flashing is created, the stronger it is. The closer the spacing of the fasteners used to attach the flashings, the more wind-load stress it can resist. Also, ring shank nails have more pull-out resistance than smooth shank nails.

12.2 SHEET METAL FLASHINGS—GENERAL

Metal flashing design, manufacture, and installation can be a specialized field. It is a craft unto itself. Understanding terms used to express materials type, thickness, finish, and style is important.

WEIGHTS, THICKNESSES, AND GAUGES

Sheet metal flashing systems and components are created from flat stock or coil stock material. The flat stock material is in sheet form, where the flat sheets are normally:

4 ft × 10 ft (48 in × 120 in)
3 ft × 10 ft (36 in × 120 in)
4 ft × 8 ft (48 in × 96 in)
3 ft × 8 ft (36 in × 96 in)

Sheet metal flashings can also be created from coil stock. Coil stock sheet metal is delivered in a large coil, normally 50 to 100 ft long. The total length of the coiled metal is dependent upon the thickness and weight of the metal. The thicker the metal of the coil stock, the more it will weigh. Excessive weight makes the coil difficult to handle during shipping and shop-forming.

The coil stock can be supplied in a variety of widths. Generally, the widths are in increments that are normally used in the sheet metal industry, such as 18, 24, 32, 36, and 48 in. Coil stock seldom exceeds 36 inches in width, and is normally of thin to moderately thick material. Thick sheet metal does not adapt well to coil.

Metal comes in different thicknesses. This thickness is referred to as gauge, weight, or decimals of inch.

Gauge. In 1893, Congress passed an act establishing a standard gauge for steel and plate iron and steel. The act was for the purpose of ensuring uniformity, particularly in connection with determining import duties levied by the government on iron and steel sheets and plates.

This gauge system designated that a section of iron or steel 1-ft^2 and 1-in thick should weight 640 oz. (Today, steel is accepted as weighing 652.8 lb per ft^2/1 in) Therefore, each U.S. Gauge Number represents a certain number of ounces and a corresponding multiple of 640ths of an inch in approximate thickness. Due to inconsistencies encountered in the U.S. Standard Gauge Table in converting from weight to thickness, a gauge table known as the Manufacturers Standard Gauge for Steel Sheets is used, having a definite thickness equivalent for each gauge number.

Today plate metal is usually ordered in a decimal equivalent which corresponds to the gauge number. In the roofing and sheet metal industry certain types of sheet metals are still referenced in both gauges and decimal equivalents.

Decimal Equivalents. Metal thickness can be described in decimal equivalents of inches. Sheet metal normally results in the decimal being in the thousandths. Aluminum has historically been described in thousandths of an inch. See Table 12.1.

Table 12.1 Metal thicknesses.*

	Inch (fraction)	*Inch (decimal)*	*Gauge (B&S)*	*Lb/ft²*
Aluminum	1/64	0.016 (0.015)	26	0.22
	1/32	0.031 (0.032)	20	0.45
	3/64	0.047 (0.050)	16	0.70
	1/16	0.062	14	0.90
Copper	1/64	0.016	26	0.75 (12 oz)
	1/48	0.022	22	1.00 (16 oz)
	1/32	0.032	20	1.50 (24 oz)
	3/64	0.048 (0.050)	16	2.25 (36 oz)
Galvanized steel	1/64	0.015	28	0.78
		0.018	26	0.91
		0.024	24	1.15
	1/32	0.030	22	1.40
		0.035	20	1.65
Stainless steel	1/64	0.015	28	0.65
		0.018	26	0.78
		0.025	24	1.05
	1/32	0.031	22	1.31
		0.037	20	1.57

* Some values are rounded to the most commonly used equivalent.

The normal thicknesses used for aluminum flashings are 0.025 in, 0.032 in, 0.040 in, and 0.050 in. However, 0.016 in is sometimes used, as is 0.125 in. Because it is so thin, 0.016 in is used only in noncritical utility construction where little to no stress is expected. Metal of 0.125 in is thick and is normally supplied as extruded aluminum.

When aluminum and other sheet metal materials become so thick they cannot be formed on standard equipment found in the normal sheet metal shop, the metal flashing is supplied by a manufacturer. The manufacturer extrudes the material from a forming machine—hence the term *extruded.*

Weights. Some flashing materials' thicknesses are described in weight. This includes copper and lead. The weight per square foot of the material is used to describe its thickness. Common terminology would be 2-lb lead or 16-oz copper.

Table 12.2 Coefficient of expansion rates.

Flashing material	*Coefficient of expansion*	*1/64-in increase in 10-ft length per 100°F increase*
		0 1 2 3 4 5 6 7 8 9 10 11 12 13
Galvanized steel	0.0000067	>>>>>>>=
Terne	0.0000067	>>>>>>>=
Monel	0.0000078	>>>>>>>>=
Copper	0.0000094	>>>>>>>>>=
Stainless steel	0.0000096	>>>>>>>>>=
Aluminum	0.0000129	>>>>>>>>>>>>>=
Lead	0.0000161	>>>>>>>>>>>>>>>>>>>=
Zinc	0.0000174	>>>>>>>>>>>>>>>>>>>>>=

12.2.1 Expansion and Contraction

TEMPERATURE CONSIDERATIONS

Expansion and contraction are powerful dynamic forces, resulting from temperature differences which occur over the annual cycle. They cannot be stopped, but they can be expected and planned for. The force results in linear dimension changes, and therefore movement, of all building materials. Metal flashings exhibit more movement than many other nonmetallic building materials such as wood and plaster.

Different metals will change dimension lengths at different rates. This movement can be calculated for the different metals using the coefficient of thermal expansion for each metallic material. See Table 12.2.

The amount of linear change is a function of temperature difference. If the temperature to which the metal was exposed never changed, the dimension of the metal would never change. However, the greater the temperature differences during the life of the metal component, the greater will be the movement and linear change of the component.

We normally design for movement of metal components based upon the coefficient of expansion for that particular type of metal and the temperature differences it will experience over the course of an average year. This temperature difference is based upon the coldest winter temperature and the hottest summer temperature. The temperature difference between the two is an important quotient in calculating expected movements.

For critical design situations, where the movement expected may be greater than normal and/or the amount of movement which will occur must be accurately known, the temperature of the metal component itself should be considered, not the ambient temperatures. This actual material temperature is sometimes far greater than the ambient temperatures, due to the principles of blackbody radiators and emissivity. (See Sec. 2.3.4.)

The temperatures within and under a roof membrane will often be far hotter or colder than the surface temperatures of the membrane, which in turn are not the same as the ambient temperatures existing at the same time. The temperature variations are a result of heat absorption and radiation. The membrane type, surface color and condition, and thermal resistance values of the substrate (roof insulation, wood blocking) over which the roof and metal flashings are installed are factors.

As an example, it is not unusual for a stainless steel gutter to reach a temperature of 120 to 130°F during a sunny day when the ambient temperature is 90 to 95°F. A copper gutter can also experience such a temperature difference but the difference will change as a patina forms on the copper surface, resulting in different absorption and radiation of heat.

Also to be considered in metal flashing design are the temperature and season at the time of installation. This becomes critical if a metallic expansion joint is being designed and installed.

Metallic expansion joints are usually required in gutter systems. However, long and continuously joined sections of metal flashing, with the joining method not providing expansion at each joint of the flashing system, also require expansion joints.

For gutters, an expansion joint is required a minimum of every 50 ft. This joint may be required to open and close as much as 1 to 2 in over the annual cycle.

If the metal flashing system is being installed in either the cold or hot season extremes, the expansion joint opening must be set either closed or open. The spacing will be dependent upon temperatures at the time of installation. (See Figure 12.6.)

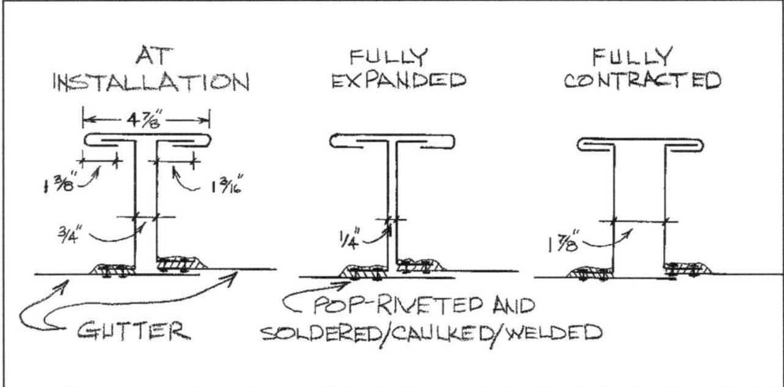

Figure 12.6 Joint opening of expansion joint at different temperatures.

CALCULATIONS OF MOVEMENTS

(See also Sec 11.3.1.) To calculate the annual movement of a metal flashing, the temperature extremes in which it will exist must be determined. This number is then multiplied by the coefficient rate for the material being specified. This factor is then multiplied by the length of the metal flashing component. The result is multiplied by 12, representing 12 in. The final result provides the decimal equivalent of 1 in, and tells how much movement can be expected for the metal flashing.

For example, a gutter system may have the lap joints every 10 ft pop-riveted tightly together. The design allows no appreciable free movement at the joints. The gutter is of aluminum, is 90 ft long, and is being installed in Houston, Texas. The gutter will be split in half by an expansion joint, since no section longer than 50 ft can be designed without an expansion joint. (See Fig. 12.7.) The movement to be expected per each of the resulting two 45-ft-long sections is calculated as follows.

Winter temperature extreme—ambient	20°F
Design temperature extreme—actual	10°F
Summer temperature extreme—ambient	100°F
Design temperature extreme—actual	130°F

130°F (Summer temperature extreme—actual)
−10°F (Winter temperature extreme—actual)
120°F (Annual temperature difference—actual)

120°F (Annual temperature difference)
× .0000129 (Coefficient factor for aluminum)
0.001548

0.001548
× 45 ft (Length of gutter section)
0.069660

0.069660
× 12 in
0.835920 in = ¹³⁄₁₆ in movement per section per year

or

= 1⅝ in movement total for entire gutter section

Each gutter section can be expected to expand and contract (grow and shrink) slightly more than ¾ in from the coldest period of winter to the hottest period of summer. This simple calculation allows the designer to consider if one expansion joint, or possibly more, is needed.

MOVEMENT DESIGN

As the gutter system extends past a corner, the corner section becomes stationary, not allowing movement. It is attached to the building and all movement will be forced away from this fixed point and, in this case, to the expansion joint. If the gutter does not extend around a corner, design should fix the gutter to be stationary at the corner.

Movement should never be allowed at a sheet metal flashing corner. With gravel guard, metal edge, gutter, and coping systems, the corner turn pieces are pop-riveted and sealed tight and closed.

The last consideration is the expansion joint opening required to accommodate the movement. The time of year the gutter system is installed is now crucial for the design. Theoretically, if the gutter and expansion joint were being installed on the hottest day of the year, a ¼-in opening would be left between each gutter section. (See Fig. 12.6.) A minimum of ¼ in is always required as the opening between flashing systems within an expansion joint. Likewise, if being installed during the coldest day of the year, the opening created between the gutter ends would be 1⅝ in + ¼ in.

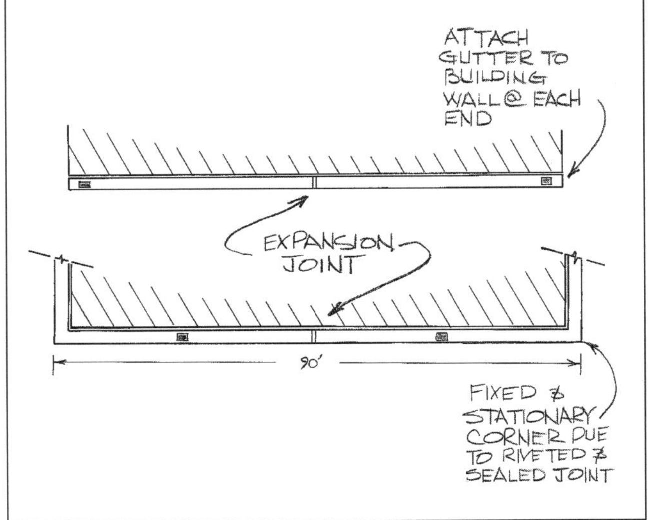

Figure 12.7 Different gutter system configurations.

12.2.2 Expansion Joint Design

GUTTERS

Continuing the discussion from the preceding section, gutter installation will probably be at some time between extreme temperature days. The clearance between gutter ends at the time of installation CL_I must be determined, as well as how wide the expansion cover flange must be and the how wide to design the flange of the gutter ends.

The expansion temperature difference EX and the contraction temperature difference CN express the size of the expansion joint opening at the time of installation as it relates to the maximum dimension changes which will occur during the annual cycle. EX shows how much further the metal will expand after installation as the temperature increases to its expected maximum. CN is how much the metal will contract after installation.

Using the previous example of the gutter, a calculation of movement to be expected and the amount of space to allow for such expansion/contraction is as follows. We will use an 80°F day in spring for the installation temperature.

Coefficient of expansion rate for aluminum = 0.0000129 per °F

Minimum actual design temperature = 10°F

Maximum actual design temperature = 130°F

Contraction temperature difference = 90° − 10° = 80° (90° is the assumed superheat temperature of the metal flashing at installation, although the ambient air temperature is 80°F.)

Expansion temperature difference = 130° − 90° = 40°

Total contraction CN =
[90-ft gutter section]
× 0.0000129 coefficient of aluminum
0.001161
× 80° contraction temperature difference
0.09288
× 12 to convert to inches
1.11456 in = **1⅛ in = CN**

Total expansion EX =
[90-ft gutter section]
× 0.0000129 coefficient of aluminum
0.001161
× 40° expansion temperature difference
0.04644
× 12 to convert to inches
0.55728 in = **½ in = EX**

These two distances indicate how much the total 90-ft section of gutter will expand and contract after it is installed at the present temperature of 80°F (90° superheat). As previous calculations show, total expansion and contraction of the gutter system is approximately 1¾ in, with each 45-ft section moving one-half this distance, or approximately ⅞ in.

The clearance of the gutter ends at the time of installation CL_I must therefore be:

$$EX + \tfrac{1}{4}\text{ in} = CL_I$$

½ in EX (additional expansion distance required between gutter ends)
+ ¼ in (minimum clearance between gutter ends required when fully expanded)
¾ in CL_I (clearance at time of installation)

The total clearance between gutter ends that will be exhibited when the gutter sections are fully contracted will be:

$$CN + CL_I = CL_C$$

1⅛ in CN
+ ¾ in CL_I
1⅞ in CL_C (clearance between gutter ends when gutter is fully contracted)

The width of the expansion joint cover cap and the gutter flanges must also be accurately determined. If they are too large, or too small, the movement of the gutter will displace or distort them, possibly leading to leaks.

The gutter end flange must allow for ¼-in lap of the cover cap when fully expanded and ⅛-in clearances when fully contracted, as in Fig. 12.6. The following calculation is made to determine the length of the gutter flanges:

$$\tfrac{1}{4}\text{ in} + \tfrac{1}{8}\text{ in} + \frac{(CN + EX)}{2} = L$$

¼ in (expanded)
+ ⅛ in (contracted)
⅜ in

1⅛ in CN
+ ½ in EX
1⅝ in (total contraction of entire gutter system)
× 0.5 in (half for each gutter flange)
1³⁄₁₆ in
+ ⅜ in (from above)
1⁹⁄₁₆ in *L* (length of top gutter flanges)

The width of the expansion joint cover cap is determined by the following:

$$2(CN + L + \tfrac{1}{8}\text{ in})$$

1⅛ in CN
1⁹⁄₁₆ in *L*
+ ⅛ in (clearance when fully contracted)

$2\frac{7}{16}$ in
$\times\ 2$
$4\frac{7}{8}$ in *K* (width of expansion joint cover cap)

The last item to determine is how far to hem-fold the cover cap over and under to the gutter flanges. This is determined by:

$$K - \frac{CL_C}{2} - \tfrac{1}{8}\text{ in} = H$$

$4\frac{7}{8}$ in K
$-\ 1\frac{7}{8}$ in CL_C
3 in
$\times$ 0.5 (for each of the two gutter flanges)
$1\frac{1}{2}$ in
$-\ \frac{1}{8}$ in (for clearance during maximum contraction)
$1\frac{3}{8}$ in *H* (hem-fold both sides of cap *K*)

Gutter systems are where this type of expansion control joint is most often required. The design process illustrated here becomes simple after it has been performed several times. (See Fig. 12.8.)

METAL EDGE AND COPINGS

Any time a metal flashing is installed, it will move. The longer the flashing system or piece, the more movement to expect. The amount of movement and the harmful effects can therefore be restricted by reducing the length of the flashing.

This is best accomplished by dividing the flashing system into individual units. A 100-ft gravel guard system can be divided into ten 10-ft lengths. The overall expansion and contraction forces of the 100-ft-long system will then be dispersed to each of the joints between the 10-ft pieces.

In truth this will occur whether designed for or not. The only way to keep the movement that occurs at each joint from becoming harmful is to:

- Join each lap together, so that they cannot move independently, or
- Design each joint as an expansion control system.

On metal flashing systems which are nail-fastened in place, such as gravel guards, it is much more advisable to allow movement to occur at each joint instead of trying to isolate the force by moving it in line to a specific area. Therefore, on many of the designs common to sheet metal roof flashing systems, it is good practice to use an expansion system at each lap joint. This is accomplished by use of a backer plate and a cover plate, as shown in Fig. 12.4, or by other means such as a standing seam as often used on copings. (See Fig. 12.9.)

With a single lap at each metal flashing joint, all the stress of the movement will occur at the lap joint. This movement involves both pieces of adjacent and overlapping flashing pieces. (See Fig. 12.10.)

A cover plate provides two lap joints for the movement to occur over. This reduces the stress by half from what it would be with a single lap. Roof membranes can better resist a force reduced by half than absorb and resist the total stress force created by a single lap.

A lap joint designed with a cover and backer plate is also more watertight. It is true that water entry is

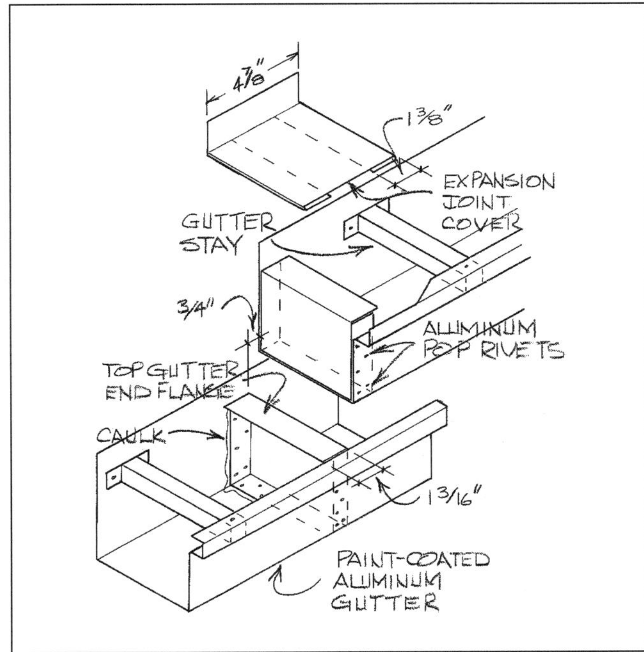

Figure 12.8 Gutter and expansion joint.

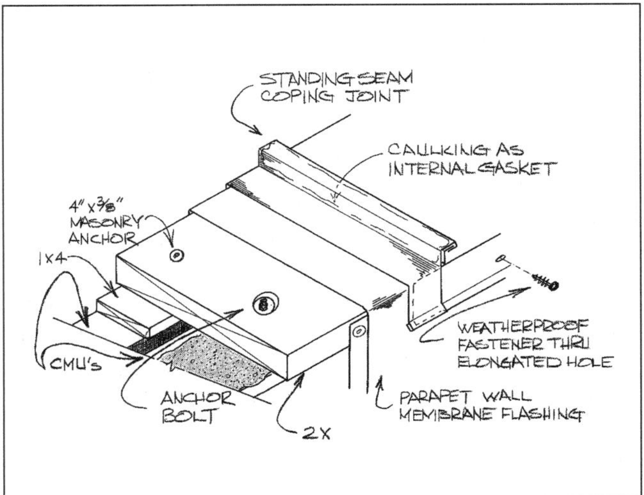

Figure 12.9 Standing seam joint on coping.

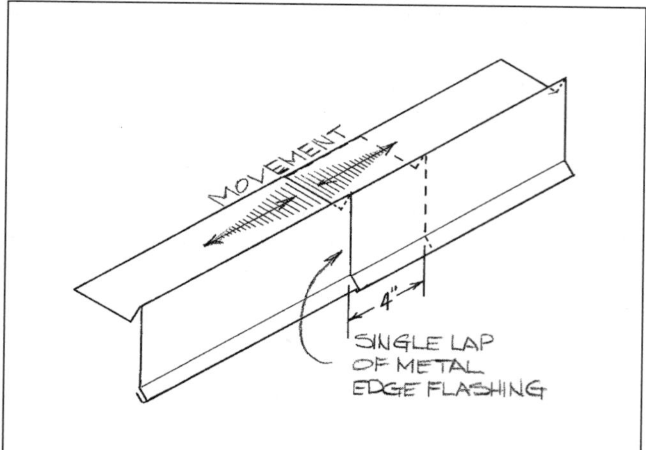

Figure 12.10 Metal edge lap seam showing movements.

increased from one location to two lap locations; however, the path which the water must travel to reach a vulnerable part of the system is greatly increased.

Water must enter through a lap in the cover plate. It must then travel through several inches of mastic sealant before it reaches the opening between metal flashing pieces. It must pass through this opening and then travel through several more inches of mastic sealant installed over the backer plate.

If a cover/backer plate system leaks, it is usually from water traveling a path directly down the side edges of the cover plate. Following this path it can be forced under the flashing plies and to the rear of the metal flashing flange, where it can enter the roof system if proper precautions are not taken. (See Fig. 12.11.)

The backer plate is centered over the area where the ends of metal flashing pieces will occur. The backer plate is covered with mastic, normally plastic roof cement. The mastic should be wide enough to extend several inches past the edge of the backer-plate flashing in all directions out onto the roof membrane.

The metal flashing pieces are then set to the roof, with the ends of the metal flashing centered over the backer plate and bed of mastic. The metal flashing pieces are set with a joint opening between the pieces. The size of the opening is dependent upon the temperature extremes to be experienced by the metal flashing and the type of metal the flashing is created from. However, ¼ to ½ in is usually adequate to compensate for movement which will occur at this expansion joint.

The ends of the flashing pieces are then covered with a bed of roof mastic, extending 6 to 8 in past the end lap edge of each flashing piece. A cover plate is set into the bed of mastic. The cover plate must center over the joint opening between the metal flashing pieces.

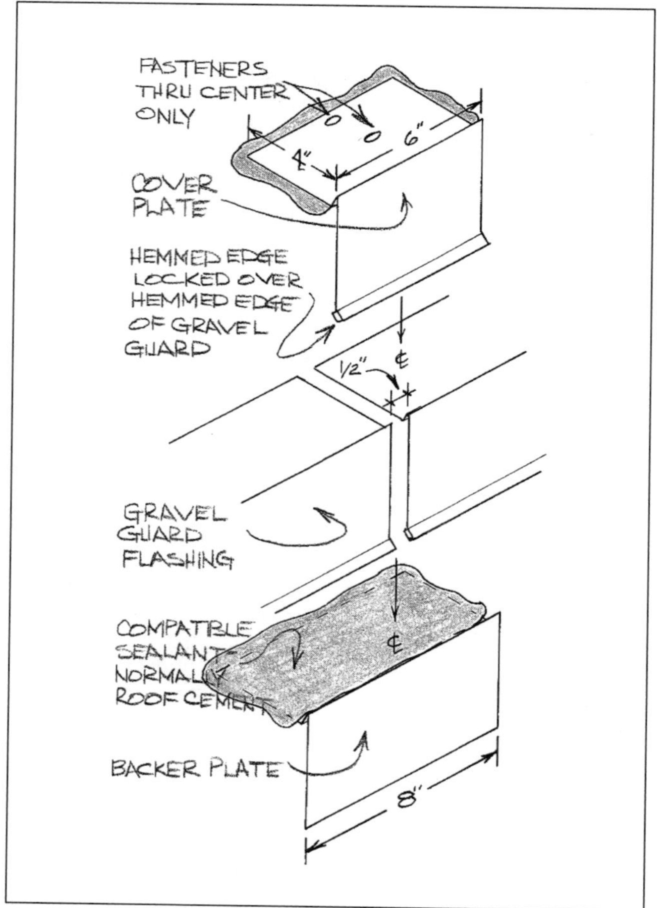

Figure 12.11 Cover and backer plates on metal edge.

The cover plate can only be attached with fasteners driven through its center so that the cover plate is attached through the underlying backer plate only. This process allows the end pieces of the metal flashing to slide during expansion and contraction within the sleeve created by the backer and cover plate.

This type of expansion joint is commonly used on coping which covers the top of parapet walls and should always be used on metal edge and gravel guard flashing systems installed to the top of a membrane roof assembly.

ROOF EXPANSION JOINTS

Roof expansion joints are required to allow movement of the roof structure independent of adjoining building walls, roof areas, or structures. Expansion joints are also used to absorb movement stress at specific locations due to a direction change of the roof deck. (See Fig. 12.12.)

Many designers specify expansion joints with sheet metal flanges and flexible bellows. This unit comes pre-

Figure 12.12 Premanufactured expansion joint.

manufactured, and installation by the roof worker is relatively easy.

Roof expansion joints can be formed from sheet metal flashings. These types of flashings are more intricate and difficult to design and install as compared to the premanufactured units. (See Fig. 3.15.)

With metal expansion joint flashings, there are no flexible bellows of neoprene or EPDM to deteriorate or be damaged by foot traffic. The metal can be of material that is long-lasting, therefore the expansion can be reused during reroofing in the future.

Also, for unusual design situations involving numerous slope and radius changes, the level of design and installation necessary to create a properly functioning expansion joint system may be as difficult for premanufactured units as for shop-formed metal units.

12.2.3 Dissimilar Metals

Different metals can react and deteriorate when in contact with each other. The deteriorating reaction requires the presence of an electrolyte, such as moisture with a small amount of acid present. This electrolyte is almost always present, in varying degrees, with metal systems used on a roof or exterior assembly. In such a case, a galvanic reaction occurs and one, or possibly both, of the metals are destroyed.

The following is a simple table which ranks a metal's ability to resist electrogalvanic reaction when in contact with a dissimilar metal.

1. Aluminum
2. Zinc
3. Steel
4. Iron
5. Nickel
6. Tin
7. Lead
8. Copper

When two metals in this list are in contact and an electrolyte is present, one will deteriorate the other. The one with the highest number will prevail, and the metal with the lower number will be destroyed. For example, when steel (3) is in contact with copper (8), deterioration of the steel will occur.

If a galvanized steel gutter is used to collect rainwater from a copper roof, the deterioration of the gutter system will quickly occur. However, a copper gutter can be used to collect water from a galvanized steel roof system and no reaction will occur, so long as the copper does not touch the steel roof.

However, the table shows that copper and lead are incompatible, yet we use lead and tin to create solder, which is successfully used on metals. We also use galvanized coatings, which are a combination of zinc and lead, to coat steel and iron.

With solder material, the ferrous tin elements are successfully entrapped within the lead compound, thereby reducing incompatibility of lead tin solder with metals. Also, lead is very close to copper in the electrochemical series, and the closer different metals are in the series, the less reaction there will be.

With a coating applied to a metal, such as lead to copper or lead/zinc to steel, even if the coating is incompatible with the base metal, reaction seldom occurs. This is due to the coating sealing the surface of the base metal, restricting water, moisture, and electrogalvanic reaction.

If it is not possible to avoid dissimilar metals, separate the metals so that they cannot come into contact, and form an electrogalvanic bridge, with each other.

Stainless steel is not listed in the electrochemical series because it has little reaction with any of the metals. Use stainless steel nails, rivets, and fasteners where extra strength is required of the metal flashing system.

12.2.4 Sealants

CAULKS

Caulking is used extensively in today's market—and will continue to be. There are many different kinds, suitable for many different purposes.

SOLDER

Solder is created from a mixture of lead and tin. Some solder is a 50/50 combination of these elements, some is 60/40, and some can be 95/5 for extraordinary applications. We normally use 50/50 solder, but if soldering to a lead surface, such as lead-coated copper sheeting, use 60/40 solder.

Solder should be applied to flashing joints which are not to experience movement. Movement from expansion and contraction, if greater than the tensile strength of the soldered joint, will break and rupture the solder joint. A solder seam with a minimum of 350 lb/in^2 tensile strength will prove adequate for rooftop applications.

Let us consider 16-oz (0.0216 in thick) copper sheet flashings to be joined at the lap seam with a solder joint. The heat of soldering will completely anneal the sheets, reducing the elastic limit of the copper from 28,000 lb/in^2 to approximately 10,000 lb/in^2. Therefore, a 1-in length of the metal seam can sustain a maximum stress of 10,000 × 0.0126 × 1, resulting in a sustained stress load capability of 216 lb/in^2. The amount of lap necessary between the two sheets, which will be completely soldered together, is determined by:

$$\frac{216}{350} = 0.616 = \tfrac{5}{8} \text{ in solder seam}$$

In this case, a ⅝-in lap of the flashing sheets, with a proper bond of solder within the lap, will achieve the maximum stress resistance required for the joint to be effective.

Understand that such force is not exerted continuously to the solder joint. The joint can withstand higher stress loads for short durations of time, up to 800 lb/in^2 for 60 h.

Also, the solder joint should connect to other flashings which have expansion joint capabilities or should be used for small pieces of flashing which, not having appreciable length, will not build up high, sustained stress loads.

The slow and complete heating of the metal seams is crucial to a proper solder joint. The solid bar of solder will turn liquid by the heat of the flame or soldering iron and is transferred into the lap joint. The liquid solder will follow the heat of the soldering equipment as it is moved down the lap seam. This process is referred to as *sweat soldering* and is the only way to achieve a fully soldered joint.

Another important requirement of specification is to require all joints which are to be soldered to first be pretinned. Pretinning prepares and coats the edges of the metal with a layer of solder, a minimum of 1 in wide per lap edge.

The pretinned sheets are then laid, lapped, and field-soldered. Pretinning ensures a complete bond between the flashing pieces and results in far fewer problems with solder joints. (See Sec. 11.3.5 and Fig. 11.24.)

The laps of the metal flashing pieces to be soldered must be held tightly and continuously together. For solder to fully sweat between the pieces, the metal surfaces within the lap must touch. Pop rivets are used to accomplish this purpose. Rivets are often installed ½ in on-center, sometimes in dual rows down the lap edge of the solder joint. This allows the solder to sweat fully between the joints.

Rivets should be a minimum of ⅛-in diameter and should be the shortest length as required to fasten both flashing sheets together. Rivets should be of the same material as the metal flashing or they can normally be stainless steel.

12.2.5 Wind-Load Design

The wind-load resistance of a metal flashing is a function of its gauge or thickness and its means of attachment to the building and roof structure. To a lesser degree, the style to which it is formed plays a role, in that some designs create a stronger or stiffer flashing.

Any vertical face of a metal flashing, which is visual and exposed to the environment, is the most susceptible part of the flashing during wind stress loads. As the dimension of this face increases, the thickness of the metal also must be increased.

As wind strikes the side of the building wall or roof structure, such as parapet walls, it will be forced upward as well as down and horizontally. The face of the metal flashing extending over and down the wall will catch the wind.

Also, as wind traveling up the wall reaches the top of the roof where the flashing is located, the windstream will bend back into a horizontal flow direction. This, in addition to the wind already traveling horizontally over the roof, wall, and flashing, creates a great deal of negative pressure at the flashing location.

It is accepted practice for any flashing having a face dimension of 5 in or greater to be held to the building or roof structure face with a continuous cleat. The continuous cleat fully engages the hemmed lip of the flashing face. As the face dimension is increased, so is the thickness of the metal flashing. In geographic areas where high-speed winds can be expected, such as coastal regions, a continuous cleat and thicker-than-normal metal is often good design practice.

The hemmed edge lip should not be bent past 30°. The less it is bent, the fuller it will engage the cleat; the more it is bent, the easier it becomes to displace the hemmed edge from the cleat. (See Fig. 12.13.)

Roof systems seldom blow off in the center, leaving the edge attached. Roof blow-off normally begins at the edge and proceeds from there. If the edge of the roof can stay on, the roof will normally survive high winds. If the metal edge flashing stays secured to the building, the roof will stay secured.

With roof gutter and downspouts mounted to the side of a building wall, wind stress is also a consideration. The larger the flashing component, the more surface area it has to catch wind. Therefore, it must also increase in thickness, and therefore strength, as it increases in size.

The thickness of the metal must also increase with the size of the flashing for appearance reasons. This is discussed under "Flashing Size, Gauge, and Design" below.

The manner in which a flashing is attached is crucial for proper wind resistance. Normally, the metal edge/gravel guard is attached with nails spaced 6 in on-center in two staggered rows. The nails should be ring-shanked to increase pull-out resistance. (See Fig. 12.13.)

The location of the fastener through the flange is also important in regard to long-term waterproofing. The fastener creates a hole through the flashing and into the roof. If the fastener is placed too close to the outside face of the flashing, the distance water has to travel to reach the hole, if the roof plies fail at the flashing face, is not acceptable.

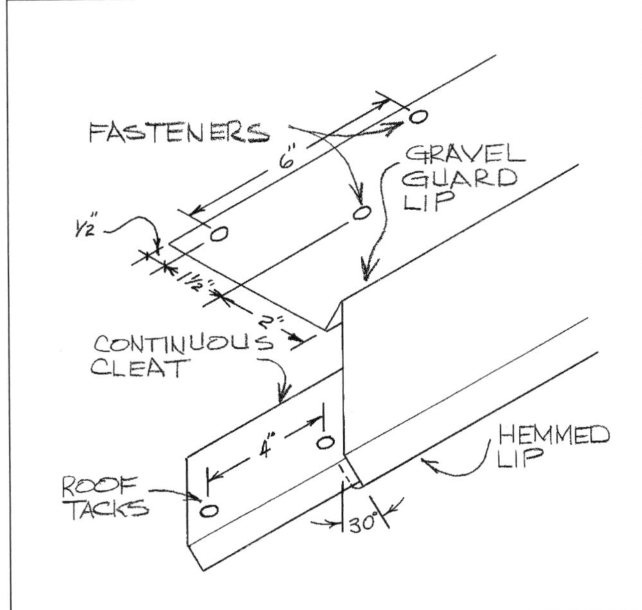

Figure 12.13 Metal edge with continuous cleat.

If the fasteners are placed too far to the rear of the flashing flange, not enough of the flange is secured down and tight to the roof surface. In a wind, the flashing will have too much movement and can become displaced.

FLASHING SIZE, GAUGE, AND DESIGN

Total size of exposed metal flashings must be considered when specifying the thickness of the metal. As a general rule: the larger the flashing, the thicker the metal.

Total size is referred to as *stretch-out* or *girth*. Girth is the total width of the flashing when stretched out flat, from outside edge to outside edge.

Larger-girth flashing must be of heavier and thicker material to resist environmental forces, such as wind and rain load, and to create a pleasing appearance. Large, flat surfaces of thin metal have a tendency to deflect and warp in and out down the large face surface. This is referred to as *oil-canning*. For example, a piece of 26-gauge steel metal edge flashing with a face dimension of 8 in would be very unsightly due to oil-canning. Also, even with a continuous cleat holding the bottom hemmed edge of the flashing to the building wall, it would not be able to resist wind load properly. A thick 14-gauge steel flashing would be more appropriate for such a design or 0.080-in extruded aluminum. The extraordinary thickness of each of these metals would make the flashing rigid. They would also be costly and hard to cut and work in the field.

With such a design situation, other more practical solutions are available. The most economical solution may be to create a two-piece flashing system. (See Fig. 12.14.) This could consist of a metal edge with a face dimension of 4 in. A metal fascia with an exposed 4½-in face could be installed under the metal edge flashing to complete the required 8-in face dimension of the flashing system. In most circumstances these flashings could be of 26-gauge steel or 0.032 aluminum. In Fig. 12.14, a hemmed edge is used to provide stiffness to the bottom fascia metal.

Another option, as shown in Fig. 12.14, is the use of a two-piece flashing system, using a continuous cleat to secure the metal edge flashing to the roof structure. In high-wind areas, this design would be the best option.

The stiffness of a flashing is related not only to the thickness of the metal from which the flashing is created but also from the characteristics of the metal itself. Some metals are stiffer than others. In technical terms, this is referred to as *tensile strength*. (See Table 12.3.)

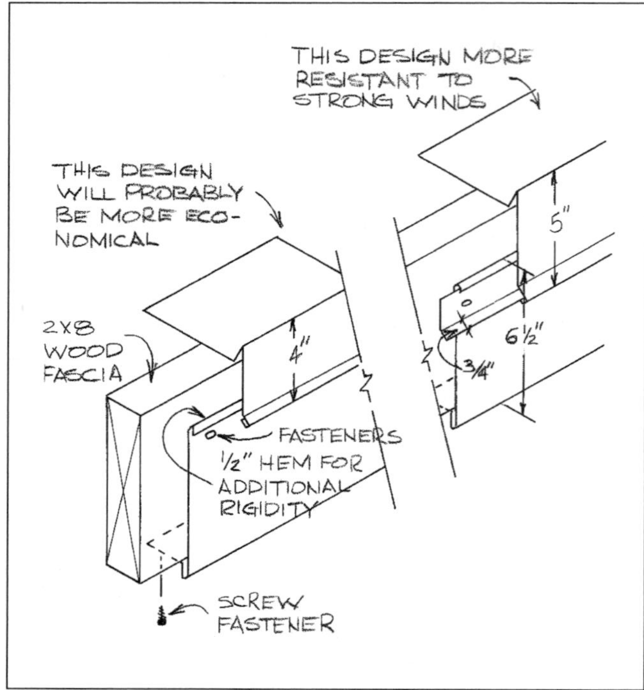

Figure 12.14 Metal fascias.

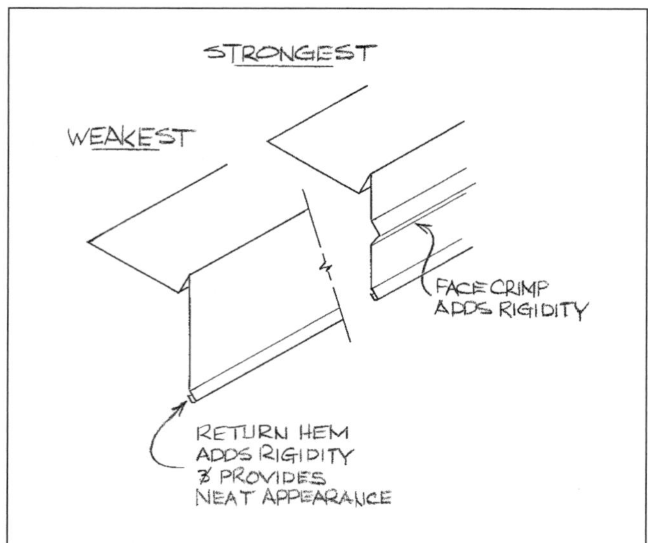

Figure 12.15 Design styles of metal edge flashing.

Due to different tensile strengths, aluminum flashings must be much thicker than stainless steel flashings to achieve the same wind-load resistance. In the sections which follow, the minimum thickness of each type of material for each type of flashing and face dimension will be listed.

Stiffness can also be added to metal flashings by use of crimp bends, referred to in the sheet metal industry as *breaks*. When a piece of metal is bent, it is referred to as *breaking*.

Oil-canning of metal flashings can be reduced or eliminated by use of breaks incorporated into metal flashings. This also provides some architectural effects. If the thickness of a metal flashing is marginal in regard to the girth required for the metal flashing component, a crimp break through the face will provide additional rigidity.

However, wind resistance may not always be increased by such breaks. In Fig. 12.15, the face break will eliminate unsightly oil-canning, but a negative-pressure wind area will try to pull the flashing away from the building. The crimp break as shown adds strength to resist bending and deformation in a longitudinal direction, but adds no resistance strength for load acting in a transverse direction across the face of the flashing piece.

Table 12.3 Tensile strength of metals.

Material	*Tensile strength, lb/in²*
Aluminum	22,000
Copper	36,000
Galvanized steel	50,000
Stainless steel	80,000+

A continuous cleat is most effective in adding resistance in a transverse direction, in that it secures the bottom edge of a flashing to the building wall. If the bottom edge can remain secured and in place during wind loading, and the top flange is secured tightly to the roof structure, optimum wind-load resistance is achieved.

However, crimp breaks through the face of metal prove beneficial in reducing other design problems. An example is a coping which is acceptable in regard to the gauge of metal selected for the girth of the flashing piece. However, there are long-term design concerns relating to durability of resistance to wind load and possible deformation of the metal coping due to roof traffic across the parapet wall by workers in the future. Even though the coping material selected is of proper and adequate-gauge thickness for the girth, the design could be considered marginal in the likely event of such forces.

Strength can be added to the coping by designing a slight crimp break through the center of the coping top. This will give the coping added rigidity on this top face. (See Sec. 12.2.9.)

It should be understood that such crimp breaks do not compensate for inadequately designed metal flashing components. They are marginal in effect, and only complement a properly specified flashing.

Hems to the bottom of exposed metal flashing pieces should always be required. This creates a neater appearance, adds stiffness to the metal flashing, and does not leave the cut edge of the metal directly exposed to the environment.

12.2.6 Metal Edge Flashing

All roof system design normally requires metal edge flashings. For a roof system with a gravel surface, the metal edge is called a *gravel guard flashing*. A lip extending up on the outside edge of the flashing retains loose gravel on the roof, hence the term *gravel guard*.

Smooth-surface roofs, being those coated with asphalt cutback or other types of liquid material, or mineral-surfaced roofs, such as modified bitumen membranes factory-surfaced with ceramic granules, do not require gravel guard flashing. The raised gravel guard lip would restrict water at the roof surface edge. This could cause unacceptable ponding or standing water on the roof surface.

RAISED-EDGE BLOCKING DESIGN

Metal edge flashing should be elevated on wood blocking at the roof edge. The blocking should be a minimum of 2 × 6 lumber, treated to resist decay. The blocking is the nailer to which the metal flashing is attached. It elevates the metal edge flashing from the water present on the roof surface during rains. This design results in higher construction costs than metal edge installed on wood blocking not elevated above the roof surface.

If the roof slope is designed to force water to the roof edge, scuppers must be included in the wood blocking/metal edge flashing system. Scuppers must be of the proper amount and size to allow water to flow from the roof surface without being restricted and backing up.

Another important fact to realize, sometimes incorrectly excluded from the roof design, is crickets between the scuppers. As the water flows down the roof to the edge, it must be directed to the scupper outlets. This requires special sloping of the roof deck itself at these locations, or more often, requires a cricket system of tapered roof insulation between the scuppers. (See Fig. 12.16.)

This cricket system leads to other design considerations. As the insulation tapers from centers to scupper locations, it must decrease not only in width but in height. The top of the wood blocking at the roof edge must maintain the same level as the tapering cricket at the roof edge. If a wet-slur roof deck is being installed during original construction, this is not difficult. The deck erector can float the crickets to the correct slope and thickness, easily matching the top of the wood blocking.

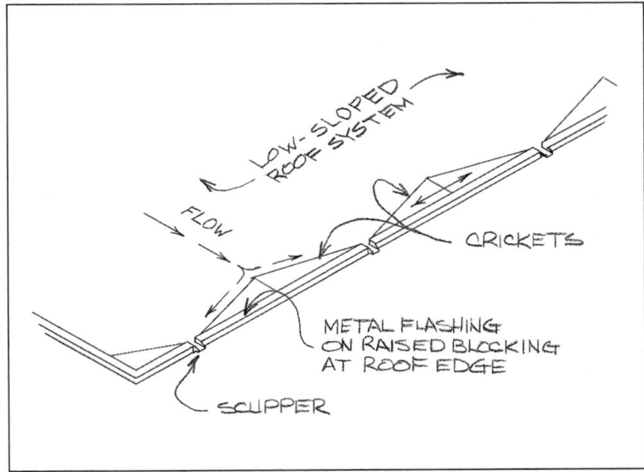

Figure 12.16 Crickets between scuppers.

However, if a tapered insulation panel is required, design decisions must be made. Either the back side of the tapered insulation must remain a constant 1½ in high to match the top of the 2 × 6 nailer, or the blocking must also decrease in thickness, equaling the tapered insulation, as it approaches the scupper outlet.

For the blocking to remain level, without a taper, the back side of the insulation cricket must remain constant, equaling the height of the blocking. This process requires the roof installer to field-bevel and shape the insulation panels, thereby field-creating a tapered insulation cricket system. (See Fig. 12.17.)

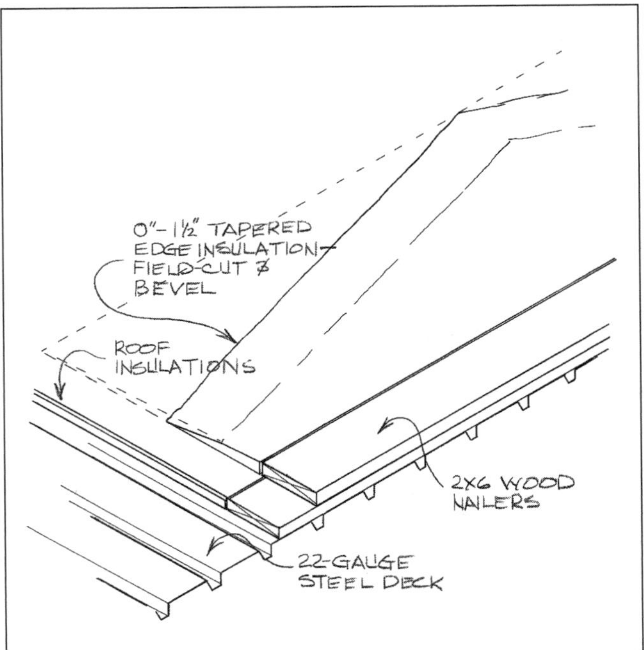

Figure 12.17 Field-beveled, tapered-edge crickets.

This option does not require tapered insulation panels to be specified. Instead, tapered-edge panels are specified, normally 2 ft wide × 4 ft long with a backside dimension of 1½ in tapering to a front-side thickness of 0 in. This is referred to as 0- to 1½-in tapered-edge insulation.

The tapered-edge insulation panel should be made from perlite material or some other type of insulation material which is easy to field-bevel and form. The roof installers must not only cut and form the tapered edge to increasing/decreasing widths, they must also taper the surface of the panel to create a smooth transition from the roof surface to panel surface.

Another option is available. This design requires the wood blocking to taper. The blocking is of three 2x's ripped to proper taper. The 2x's are then attached to each other tightly with wood screws. The tapered blocking is then covered with ½-in plywood.

This process requires field layout and calculations. Rough carpentry skills are required to accurately cut three 2x's to equal heights. Also, the amount of screw fasteners must be adequate, but not excessive, or the 2x tapered blocking will be split. (See Fig. 12.18.)

The scuppers can be soldered into the metal edge system, or, more appropriately for most designs, scuppers are joined into the metal edge flashing system using cover and backer plates. If a modified bitumen membrane system is specified, avoid using the type of membrane which is installed with open flame. At the scupper locations, the open flame will often melt the solder and contaminate the seal.

Realize that all the water from the roof surface will pass through the scuppers. Scuppers must be designed

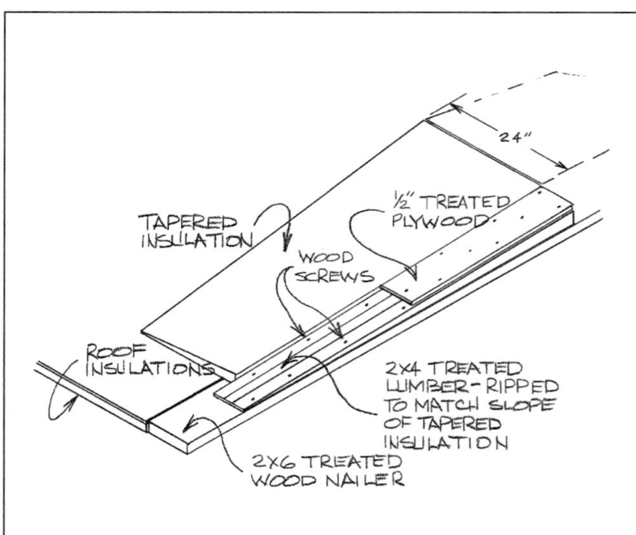

Figure 12.18 Tapered blocking.

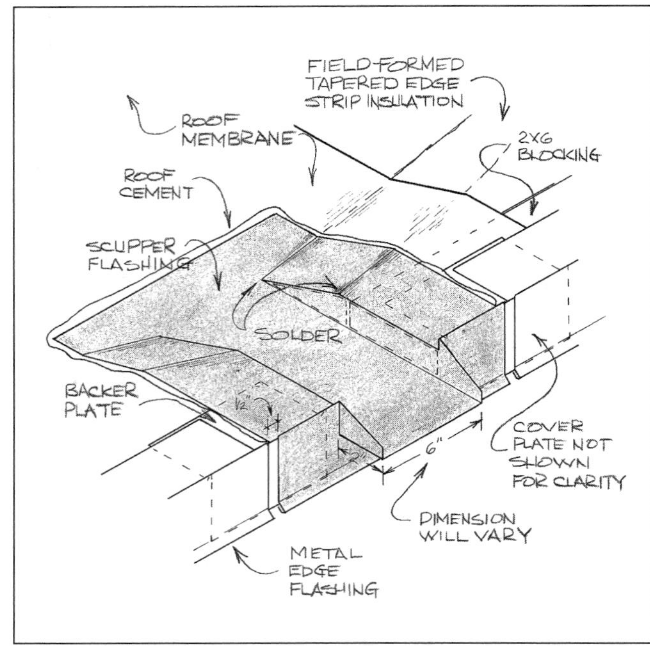

Figure 12.19 Scupper through raised blocking.

carefully and installed correctly, or roof leaks will occur. (See Fig. 12.19.)

A third option is available and is sometimes illustrated in other reference guides and manuals. It consists of beveling the wood nailer. This design is not recommended by the author. The 45° chamfer cut provides approximately a 2-in cant face. For most roof membranes, this is not enough face area to allow the roof plies and membranes to turn and form to the cant face. Unacceptable bridging of the roof felts and voids can occur at the beveled blocking unless the roof applicator exercises extreme care and diligence at these locations. (See Fig. 12.20.)

NONELEVATED METAL EDGE FLASHING DESIGN

In actual practice, we seldom see elevated metal edge design. The metal edge is often designed to be level with the roof surface (probably due to budget restraints) and, as stated earlier, this is not the best design practice.

For such design, it is good practice to require the metal edge be set into a complete bed of roof mastic. The flashing is then sealed into the roof system with additional roof plies or membranes.

In addition, cover and backer plates in roof mastic should be included in the design. The first ply used to seal the metal edge into the roof is sometimes applied into roof mastic. (See Fig. 12.5.) Verify compatibility, design and specification of all roof mastics with membrane material manufacturer.

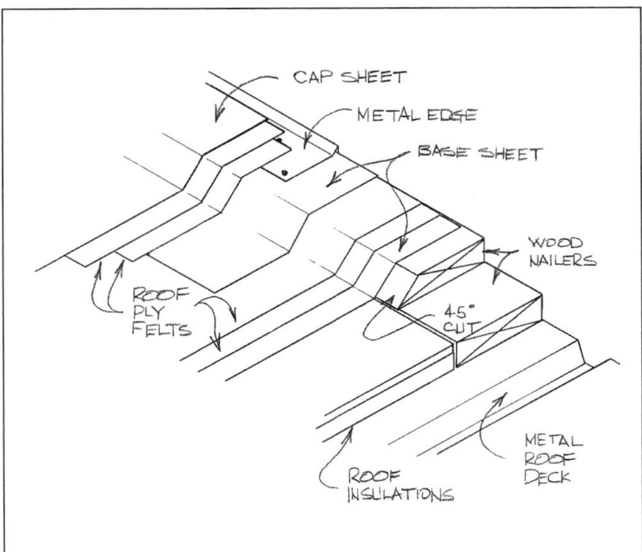

Figure 12.20 Beveled blocking.

DIMENSION AND THICKNESS

The larger the face dimension of the metal edge flashing, the thicker the metal must be. This allows the metal flashing to resist wind load and to provide proper and acceptable appearance. Thick metals resist oil-canning better than thin metals. We are normally concerned only with the face dimension, since the roof flange is always approximately 4 in wide.

However, thick metal as an edge flashing in a bituminous roof system can cause problems. Thick metal, such as extruded aluminum, is far more rigid than thinner-weight metal. Of course, this is why it is used for metal flashings with wide surface dimensions.

The fasteners used to attach a thick metal edge often cannot resist the movement caused by expansion and contraction of the thick metal. With an extruded aluminum metal edge system, it is not unusual to have the nail fasteners back out ½ inch in a 24-h period after installation. This is not due to extraordinary linear changes in a thick metal flashing as compared with a thinner weight metal. The coefficient factor is the same. (See Table 12.2.) Instead, it is due to the fact that the thick metal is not as elastic as thin metal.

As thin metal expands and contracts, not as much stress is put on the fastener as compared to the amount of stress related to a thick metal flashing. With thin metal flashing, as it expands, the metal between the fasteners will convex. During contraction, the fasteners can resist the tension stress.

For large face dimensions of metal edge systems, it is better design practice to use a two-piece flashing system, as shown in Fig. 12.14. If required, use the thick metal flashing as the bottom fascia.

Whenever thick metal is used, always require slotted holes in the metal, through which the fastener is placed. As movement of the metal occurs, the slotted hole will allow it to slide under the fastener head. This will successfully avoid fastener back-out due to stress loading of the fastener.

If thick metal is required of the metal edge system, other design options should be considered. The design shown in Fig. 12.21 does not require roofing plies to seal the metal into the roof. It is easily inspected and maintained. Avoid aluminum since aluminum cannot be soldered at the scupper locations, if required.

Thick metal and *thin metal* are relative terms. As a rule of thumb, if a sheet metal shop can break (bend) the sheet metal on a standard sheet metal break, it is not too thick to require special design considerations.

Table 12.4 is a general guide. In most cases, the size of the flashing face in relation to the indicated thickness of metal will work adequately. Different practices will be experienced from geographic region to region. Loads due to service workers or high winds may require heavier metal than shown.

For metal edge flashing with a face dimension of 5 in or greater, a continuous cleat is required. The cleat must be fastened to the building wall 8 in on-center. It must engage, a minimum of ⅜ in, the hemmed edge of the metal edge flashing. The cleat and hemmed edge should not exceed a 30° angle break. (See Fig. 12.13.)

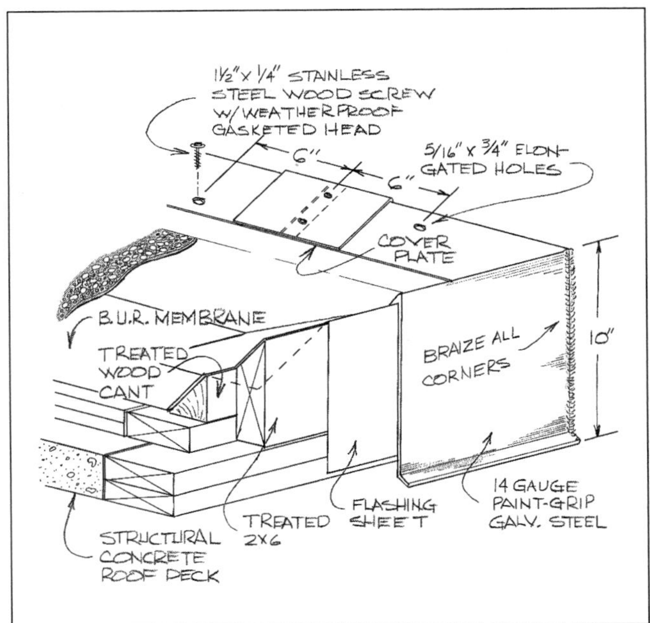

Figure 12.21 Extruded metal edge on wood cant.

Table 12.4 Face dimension/gauge required for metal edge flashings.

Face size	*Galvanized steel*	*Stainless steel*	*Copper*	*Aluminum*
4 in	26-gauge	26-gauge	16 oz	0.032 in
4–5 in	24-gauge	26-gauge	16 oz	0.032 in
5–6 in	22-gauge	24-gauge	20 oz	0.040 in
6–7 in	22-gauge	22-gauge	20 oz	0.040 in
7–8 in	20-gauge	22-gauge	24 oz	0.050 in

ADDITIONAL REQUIREMENTS

It is important that all of the metal edge flange be primed prior to sealing with roof plies or membranes. It is better to require the priming operation after the metal edge flashing is installed. This allows the fastener heads to also be coated with primer.

Primer should be applied in a heavy coating. The metal should not be visible through the primer. Primer must be completely dry before application of roofing plies, membranes, and adhesives.

Attach metal edge flashing tight to the roof membrane, using barbed roof tacks or ring-shank nails. See Fig. 12.13 for standard fastening pattern and cautions.

The lap joint of the metal edge flashing is critical in regard to long-term waterproofing. For most standard metal edge flashings, a cover and backer plate is recommended. (See Fig. 12.11.)

If a cover and backer plate cannot be used with the design, the joints can be lapped 4 in with roof cement or other compatible mastic between the joints. (See Fig. 12.5.)

12.2.7 Gutter and Downspouts

The function of a gutter is to collect the water from the rooftop and feed it to a downspout. The downspout deposits the collected water at a specific area on the building grounds.

The gutter and downspout system is visible and therefore architectural style of design affects the building appearance. However, style complements function, not vice versa.

Without proper consideration, calculation, and design, the gutter and downspout drainage system will not function correctly. Malfunctioning gutter and downspout drainage flashing systems are evidenced in:

- Sections of the system becoming loose and falling or hanging from the building
- The systems becoming clogged with debris or ice and overflowing the gutter edge, sometimes penetrating the building interior
- Gutter lap sections leaking
- Gutter system being destroyed due to electrolytic corrosion

Gutter size is determined by the amount of rainwater it must accommodate. This is determined by rainfall charts and calculation methods based upon data from the U.S. Weather Bureau. This information is collated and published by the A.I.A. in Architectural Graphic Standards. Local plumbing code references also normally have the information required to determine correct size of gutter and downspout drainage systems for that locality. Due to the availability of information contained in numerous publications elsewhere, the calculation means and methods of determining gutter and downspout sizing is not contained herein.

GUTTERS

The ability of a gutter to properly handle maximum rainfall amounts is a function of its width. Width is the bottom dimension of a gutter.

Gutter width is sometimes oversized in order to accommodate large downspouts. The larger the downspout, the more gutter area it will service, thereby reducing downspout used.

The gutter is designed with a depth-to-width ratio of 3 to 4. The depth is the face dimension of the gutter, measured from top to gutter bottom. (See Fig. 12.22.)

After determining the correct size gutter required for the roof area and geographic location, the gutter face dimension should be 75 percent of the gutter width. As a minimum, the face dimension should be 1 in lower than the rear face dimension of the gutter. On sloped roofs, the back and front faces should equal the roof

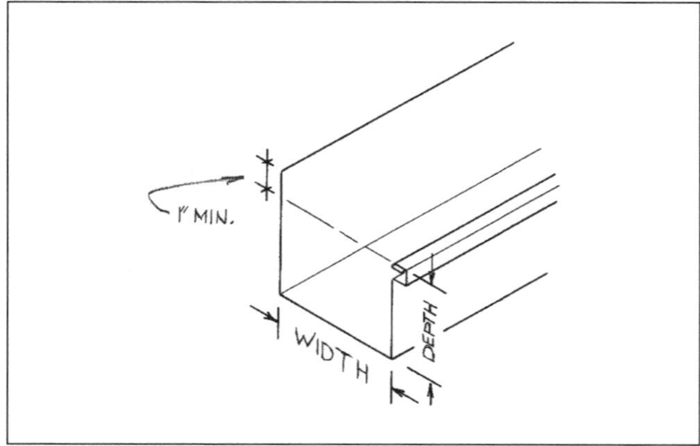

Figure 12.22 Gutter showing width and depth.

slope. This requirement is important. If the gutter or downspout systems become obstructed, water will flow over the lower outside face of the gutter. If both front and rear faces were equal in height, overflow water would also exit over the rear face of the gutter and possibly enter the building interior.

GUTTER SUPPORT

Rectangular Gutter. It is normally good design practice to support the gutter system within gutter brackets, sometimes also referred to as *straps*. These brackets are attached to the building wall blocking and allow the gutter to be cradled and supported by the brackets.

The alignment elevation of the support brackets also provides slope for the gutter system. Gutters are often designed and/or installed level.

Gutter systems should be designed with a positive slope which directs the water to the downspout openings. If specifying paint-coated steel or galvanized steel gutters, this requirement is mandatory for a long-lived gutter system. Standing water often occurs within a horizontally level gutter system. Such standing water will prematurely destroy the finish and allow deterioration of the base metal.

Proper design practice prohibits attaching the gutter to the brackets. Fixing the gutter to the brackets will restrict or conflict with expansion or contraction. Gutter brackets can be incorporated into the top gutter bead to hold the gutter in place and prevent wind blow-off.

In Fig. 12.23, a continuous cleat is used at the top rear face of the gutter. This provides support and helps secure the gutter system in place. If bracket supports are not included in the design, a continuous cleat is the next-best option. The cleat will help hold the gutter in place but will not provide support. However, it is not necessary to use a continuous cleat if bracket supports are used.

Gutter spacers are always required. The box type spacer as shown in Fig. 12.23 is suggested. The box-type spacer will provide strength and deflection resistance in the event that ladders are placed against the gutter for roof service work in the future.

Spacers are need to help stabilize the front face of the gutter. Flat strap spacers can be used, but will only provide strength against convex movement of the gutter face. Spacers should be attached to the gutter only, and not be fastened through and attach to the building wall blocking behind the gutter system.

Brackets and spacers can be installed on either 30- or 40-in centers, depending on the support values needed for gutter load. Using 30- or 40-in centers, each gutter lap can be covered by the bracket, if 10-ft sheet metal stock material is used to create the gutter. Spacers should be offset from support brackets.

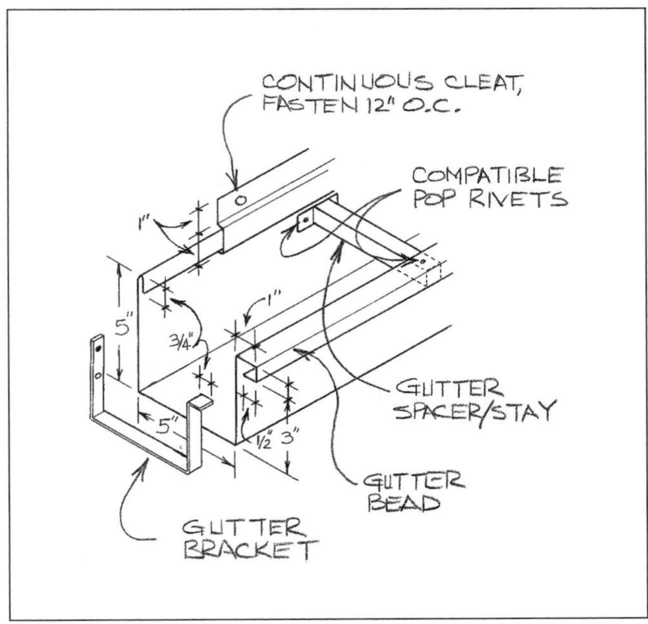

Figure 12.23 Gutter bead/stay/strap/bracket.

Spacers should be, as a minimum, the same thickness of material as the gutter. They should also be of the same material as the gutter. Brackets used to support the gutter should likewise be of the same material as the gutter. The minimum thickness required for brackets is shown in Table 12.5. In no case should a bracket be less than twice the thickness of the gutter metal.

In situations where gutter support brackets are not a consideration and a continuous cleat is not used, the gutter is usually attached to the building wall with fasteners at the top of the rear face. Elongated holes should be created in the top rear face for the fastener shank. The elongated holes will allow the gutter to expand and contract while also preventing undue stress on the fasteners.

The fasteners should be nonferrous and compatible with the gutter material. (See Sec. 12.2.3.) These fasteners should be spaced closely, the centers determined by gutter size and anticipated load.

Again, brackets to support commercial gutters are the recommended design. Using fasteners at the top rear face to hold the gutter up and to the building can possibly lead to problems. The exceptions to this rule are light, utility, and/or residential gutters. These units are usually premanufactured from a material manufacturer or they can be formed at the job site in a continuous length, referred to as a *seamless gutter*.

Ogee Gutter. Such gutter is usually of 0.025 aluminum or 26-gauge galvanized steel. A round ferrule with an aluminum spike, supplied by the gutter manufacturer is used to attach the gutter directly to the building fascia.

Table 12.5 Gutter bracket sizing.

Gutter girth, in	*Aluminum*	*Stainless steel*	*Copper*	*Galvanized steel*
<15	3/16 × 1	1/8 × 1	1/8 × 1	1/8 × 1
15–20	1/4 × 1	1/8 × 1½	1/4 × 1	3/16 × 1
20–24	1/4 × 2	1/8 × 2	1/4 × 1½	1/4 × 1½

Creating an elongated hole in the top rear face of the gutter is still suggested. However, due to the thin metal from which these gutters are usually made, fastener stress is not as significant as with thicker sheet metals.

Any metal edge flashing will be notched around the spike and ferrule. Gutter spacers are still recommended with ogee gutters. (See Fig. 12.24.) Water loads and debris can force the face of the gutter away from the building, exerting pressure on the spike and loosening it from the building face.

On shingle-type roofs, the spacers often extend under the shingle where they are attached to the roof deck. They are pop-riveted to the front gutter bead.

Half-Round Gutters. Half-round gutters, like ogee gutters, are normally supplied by a manufacturer. The gutter supports are also a stock item with the manufacturer.

Half-round gutters are normally used for sloped-roof design. It is possible to successfully use the half-round gutter for a low-sloped roof system when installed into a bracket support. In such a case, the metal edge would extend over the rear face of the gutter.

For hanging half-round gutters, the strap hanger is normally of 1/16- to 1/8-in-thick metal. For bracket-supported gutters, the bracket is of plate metal. A spring-type wire clip is used to secure the bracketed gutter shown in Fig. 12.25. For the hanging half-round gutter, the strap is continuous around gutter.

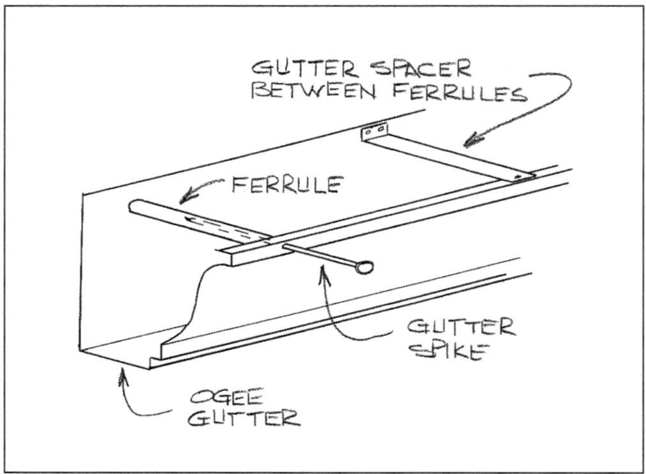

Figure 12.24 Ogee gutter/ferrule/spike/strap.

GUTTER SIZE

In gutter material selection, the entire girth, or stretchout, of the metal is considered. Since gutters are large, the sheet metal from which they are fabricated is often of heavy, thick stock.

Gutter size is relative not only to the amount of rainfall it must collect, but also to the size of the downspout needed to direct the water from the gutter to the ground. The bottom width of the gutter must be large enough to accommodate the proper-size downspout required to handle the maximum water volume collected by the gutter system.

Gutter and downspout size are determined by use of charts and calculations readily available in numerous other manuals; thus, we will not include them here. Instead, we will deal with other principles of gutter selection and design not readily available or clearly and accurately explained in other sources.

When gutters exceed the size and metal thickness shown in Table 12.6, many sheet metal shops will not have the equipment required to bend and form the metal. Special break-forming equipment is required.

When gutter girth requires metal to be greater than 14-gauge steel or 0.080-in aluminum, the metal can be classified as plate material not sheet metal. As such, the metal plate is usually welded instead of soldered. Special design is required to support and secure the heavy gutter system to the building.

GUTTER DESIGN

Style. Style is normally selected either to enhance building appearance or to be as economical as possible. Economy can complement style in sheet metal design.

Sheet metal normally is supplied in 24-, 36-, or 48-in-wide stock material. The total girth of a sheet metal component should achieve a multiple of a standard width listed in Table 12.6. For example, designing a 19-in-girth gutter will result in 5 in of metal as waste (or "drop," which is slang for the piece that drops to the

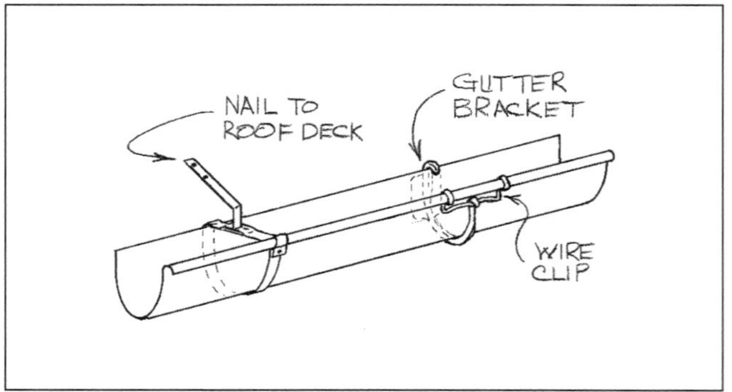

Figure 12.25 Half-round gutter assembly.

Table 12.6 Minimum metal thickness for gutter.

Girth, in	*Aluminum*	*Copper*	*Galvanized steel*	*Stainless steel*
<15	0.032	16 oz	26-gauge	26-gauge
15–20	0.040	16 oz	24-gauge	26-gauge
20–24	0.051	20 oz	22-gauge	24-gauge
24–30	0.063	24 oz	20-gauge	22-gauge

shop floor) from a 24-in-wide piece of sheet metal stock, equaling a 20 percent waste factor. In such a case, the building owner is normally paying for the entire 24-in sheet metal stock, the cost of such being calculated into the construction price by the sheet metal contractor. In some cases the drop can be used to create accessories to the flashing system, such as metal edge, gutter spacers, or downspout straps.

When designing sheet metal flashings, consider the entire girth of the component and the stock material from which it will be created. If designing a 19-in-girth gutter, the style of design can be adapted to create a 20-in-girth gutter, perhaps adding a larger gutter bead on the face, a crimp break through the face, or a higher rear face. Perhaps it is possible to decrease the size of the gutter to an 18-in girth. This will result in no waste, since two gutters can be created from one piece of 36-in-wide stock.

Style of design influences the gutter system stiffness, which in turn can influence the selection of material type, load conditions of the gutter system, and support requirements of the gutter. The more horizontal crimp breaks included in the design style, the stiffer the gutter (or other sheet metal systems) will become.

Therefore, styles A through C, as shown in Fig. 12.26, may require a thicker metal, with more gutter support than normal, especially if exceptional loads can be expected within the gutter. Exceptional loads can be a result of snow, ice, service workers, etc. Style F, due to more horizontal breaks, is stronger and may not require thicker metal and supports for the same situation.

DOWNSPOUTS

Factors to be considered in downspout design are:

- Dimension of downspout needed to drain maximum waterfall from gutter
- Style of downspout design
- Ice forming within downspout
- Vacuum created by exceptionally long downspout systems
- Turns and bends required of downspout
- Outlet tube connecting downspout to gutter
- Location of downspout
- Attachment of downspout to building wall

DOWNSPOUT STYLE

The design style of the downspout is normally dictated by the gutter style. We seldom use a round downspout with a rectangular box gutter. (See Fig. 12.27.)

Ice forming within the downspout is an important style consideration in cold climates. A downspout with an open face is preferred for severe climates. Styles D, E, and F, due to ice-forming forces, should be considered for cold climates.

Round and corrugated downspout styles A, B, and C are usually manufacturer-supplied, although for large gutter and downspout requirements, style B can be shop-formed. As such, outlet tubes to be installed into the gutter as well as hanger brackets are usually accessories supplied by the downspout manufacturer. These styles are normally used in residential design, along with ogee and half-round gutters, although they are also common with copper roof system design.

DOWNSPOUT SUPPORT

Downspouts need support to resist lateral loads from wind and vertical loading due to obstructed and clogged piping. Lateral loads can be expected. It is hoped that weight load due to obstructed downspout piping never occurs, but it should be anticipated. In cold climates, ice can form and obstruct an otherwise clear feed pipe.

In cold-climate regions, ice load can be expected and should be designed for, not only with additional strapping but with larger and fewer downspouts.

As a minimum, downspout strapping should be installed 40 in on-center, with a strap at the bottom and at the top of the downspout. Strapping is attached to the building wall and should be designed to keep the downspout off of the wall a minimum of ½ in.

Downspout straps, as a general rule, should be two gauges thicker than the downspout material. The fasteners used to attach the strap to the downspout and to the wall should be of the same material as the downspout or should be compatible with the downspout metal. Lead expanding anchors are normally specified for attachment to masonry walls.

Designing a strap system which must be removed from the building wall in order to change or service a downspout should be avoided, as shown in style A in Fig. 12.28. Screw fasteners are normally used to attach the downspout to the strap; they should be noncorrosive and of minimum length so as not to aid in downspout obstruction.

Strap design styles are numerous. Figure 12.28 depicts only a few of many available from a sheet metal con-

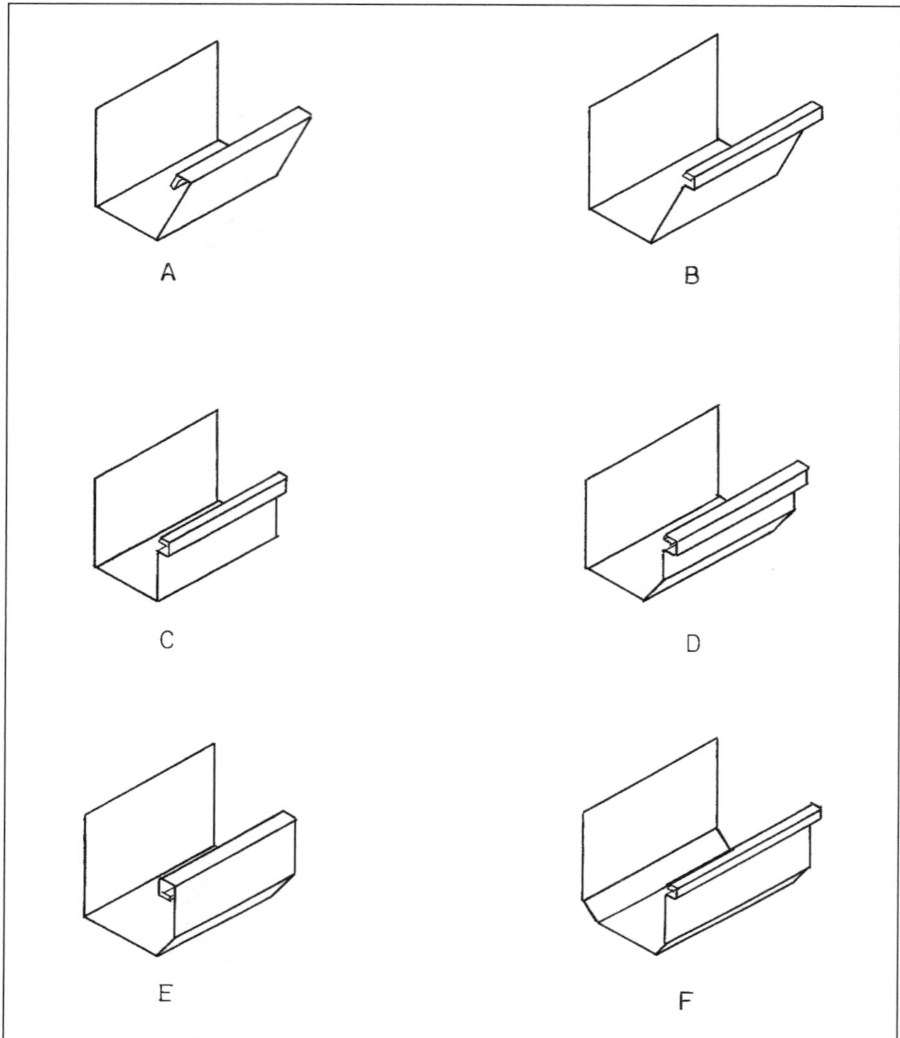

Figure 12.26 Gutter styles.

tractor. Ornate downspout straps can be selected from downspout manufacturers' catalogs.

DOWNSPOUT LOCATION

Since gutter should never be longer than 50 ft per section, a minimum of one downspout per 50 ft is a general design guide. However, if the one downspout becomes clogged, the gutter may fill with water and damage or displacement will occur. If possible, always include two downspouts per gutter section.

Downspouts should be placed at the lowest points of the gutter. Since many gutters are designed to be level (not suggested design practice), water flow and subsequent low areas may be difficult to determine.

In such a case, other rules apply to help determine downspout location:

- Never expect water to effectively turn an inside or outside corner to reach a downspout. Downspout should be placed close to the corner in such a case, unless the gutter slope is away from corners, as it should be with a sloped gutter system.
- Place the downspout opening a minimum of 6 in from gutter ends or the expansion joint. Enough room must be allowed for work and fit of the outlet tube into the gutter bottom.
- In cold climates where freeze cycles can be expected, try to eliminate or restrict downspouts from the northern exposure of the building.
- If the downspout is to be secured rigidly to the outlet tube, the tube and downspout must be at a location where the gutter is fixed and nonmoving. If

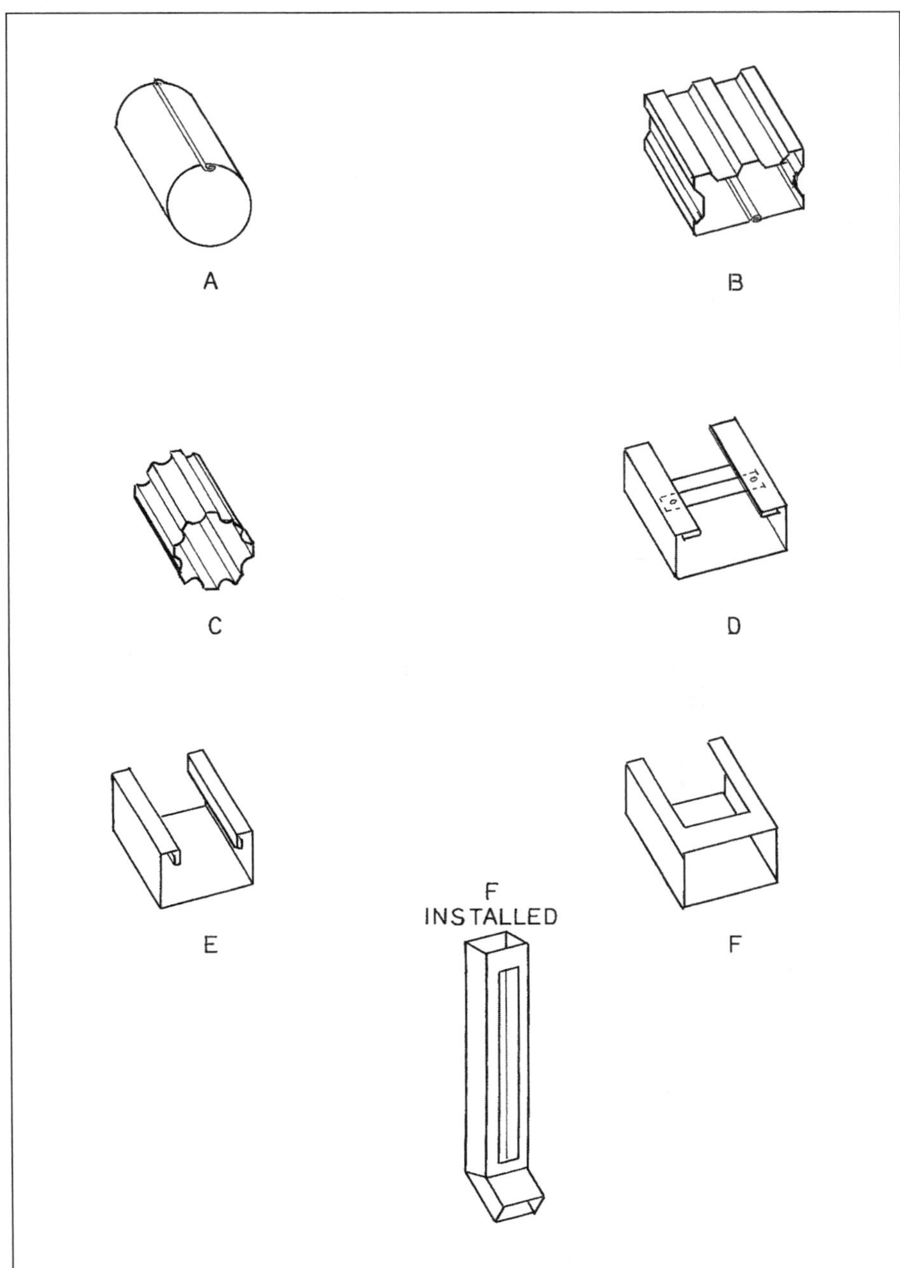

Figure 12.27 Downspout styles.

the gutter experiences movement and the downspout is secured tightly to the outlet tube which is moving with the gutter, the joint between tube and spout will be compromised.

- An oversized downspout can be used to collect water from two outlet tubes. This is accomplished by designing two downspout openings on either side of a gutter expansion joint. A funnel or conductor head is used to conceal the outlet tubes and feed the water to the oversized single downspout.
- Never allow a downspout to be located directly under a lap in the gutter. Sealing of the outlet tube into and through a lap joint is difficult.

OUTLET TUBES

It is preferred that the outlet tube be positioned across the entire gutter bottom. This allows it to more effec-

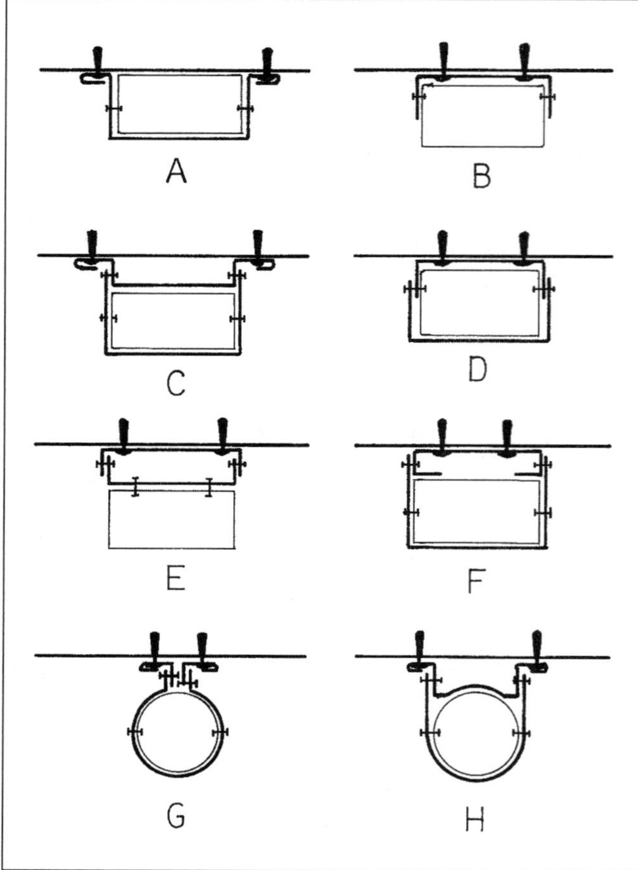

Figure 12.28 Downspout bracket styles.

tively drain the gutter than if it was positioned with longest sides parallel to the gutter bottom. However, downspouts, because of appearance concerns, are normally positioned as in style B in Fig. 12.29. If maximum drainage is a concern, a more effective gutter outlet is to use the design shown C.

Properly designed gutter systems will move with expansion and contraction cycles. If the downspout is firmly attached to the outlet tube, as shown in A in Fig. 12.30, as the outlet tube moves with the gutter, the downspout must also move or risk damage.

Design can place the outlet tube and affixed downspout at a location where the gutter is attached to the building and therefore stationary. Concerns of movement transfer from the gutter to the downspout are thereby eliminated.

The best design solution is not to attach gutter outlet tubes to the downspout. As shown in B in Fig. 12.30, the gutter outlet can move independently and not affect the downspout.

Additionally, good design practice is also adhered to in that the opening at the top of the downspout provides venting for the downspout pipe as well as emergency overflow. In the event of a clogged downspout, the emergency overflow will help allow water to escape and hopefully not overload the gutter system.

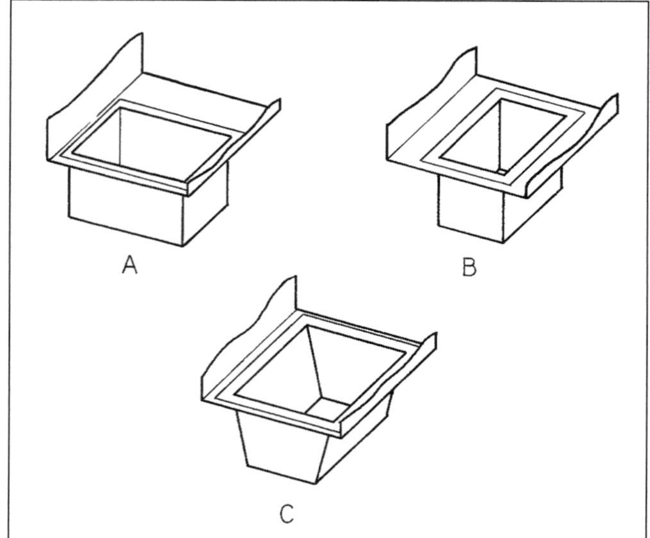

Figure 12.29 Outlet tube styles.

DOWNSPOUT DESIGN

After determining the size of the downspout piping required, the location where they are to be installed, the style to use for the pipe design, the type of gutter outlet to use, and the manner in which they will be attached to the building wall, other considerations are still required.

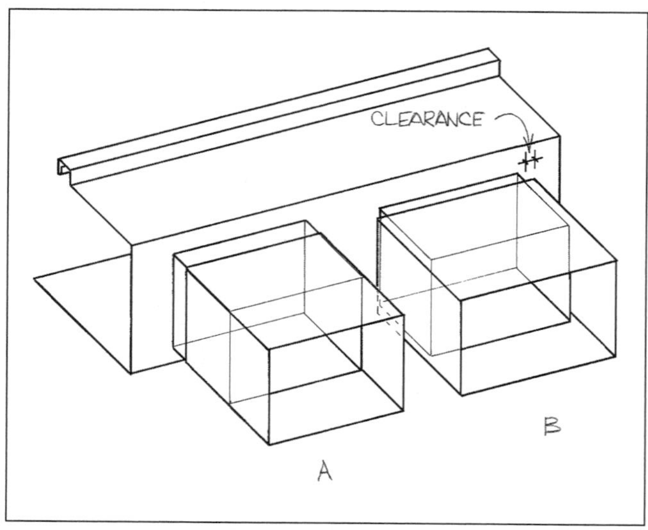

Figure 12.30 Outlet tubes without and with clearance.

One factor is length of downspout. If the downspout length exceeds 40 ft, vacuum can occur which will restrict water flow. This is prevented by designing conductor heads into the downspout system. (See Sec. 12.2.8.)

Another design factor is any turns or bends the downspout must make on the building face. Turns and bends should be avoided if possible. If required, limit the angle of the downspout elbow bend to 45° or less. The more acute the elbow, and the more the elbow bends within a downspout pipe system, the greater the possibility of downspout obstruction from debris.

Where debris can be expected on the rooftop and subsequently in the gutter downspout system, consider debris screens on the gutter or strainers at the downspout opening. Strainers can be easily constructed from stainless steel wire rolled into a ball shape larger than the outlet tube opening. The ball of wire is placed into the top of the gutter outlet opening and formed so it cannot slide into the downspout pipe.

The thickness of the metal from which the downspout is to be made is usually standard. For rectangular downspouts up to 4 in × 6 in and for 6-in round downspouts, use:

- 26-gauge stainless steel
- 26-gauge galvanized or coated steel
- 16-oz copper
- 0.032-in aluminum

Seldom will downspouts exceed this size. In the event that they do, use the next-thicker-weight material.

In high-traffic areas, or where vandalism can occur, cover the bottom of the downspout with a heavy metal guard. The guard covers the downspout face and sides and is bolted to the building wall. Use 10-gauge steel or heavier.

If the downspout system feeds into an underground drainage system, design clean-out drains at the base of the downspout. If the downspout feeds onto the ground, use splash blocks to prevent erosion of the ground at the downspout discharge location. Splash blocks can be of the same metal as the gutter and downspout system or they can be of concrete.

12.2.8 Conductor Heads and Scuppers

CONDUCTOR HEADS

Conductor heads are used to collect water exiting from a roof discharge component and feed the water into a downspout. Conductor heads are shop-fabricated or, for more ornate appearances, they can be supplied from a specialty manufacturer. (See Fig. 12.31.)

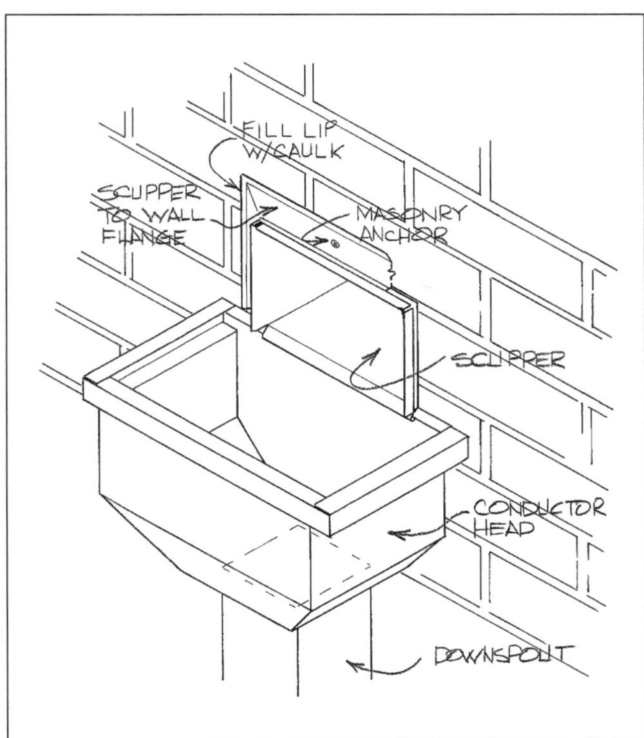

Figure 12.31 Conductor head and scupper.

Design guidelines for conductor heads require an overflow to be included in the conductor (style B from Fig. 12.32) or that the conductor head be recessed 1 in below the bottom of the scupper. In the event that the downspout becomes clogged with leaves, debris, or ice, water will not back up on the roof due to restricted flow. This is important! In Fig. 12.31, the conductor is recessed 1 in below the scupper. This is considered to be the best design practice.

The size of the conductor must be a minimum of 2 in wider than the scupper opening. The side dimension depth is ⅔ of the width.

The conductor head must be firmly attached to the building wall. Noncorrosive fasteners should be used. In addition, the conductor outlet tube should be strapped to the building wall where it enters the downspout.

The conductor head outlet tube should extend into the downspout a minimum of 4 in. If leaves or rooftop debris are a consideration, a screen guard should be placed across the top of the conductor.

The conductor should be of the same metal as the scupper and/or metal edge system. All joints on the conductor head should be soldered. If aluminum is used, the joints can be welded or sealed with caulk. Caulk is used for painted steel.

Conductor heads should be fabricated from 24-gauge galvanized or paint-coated steel, 26-gauge stainless

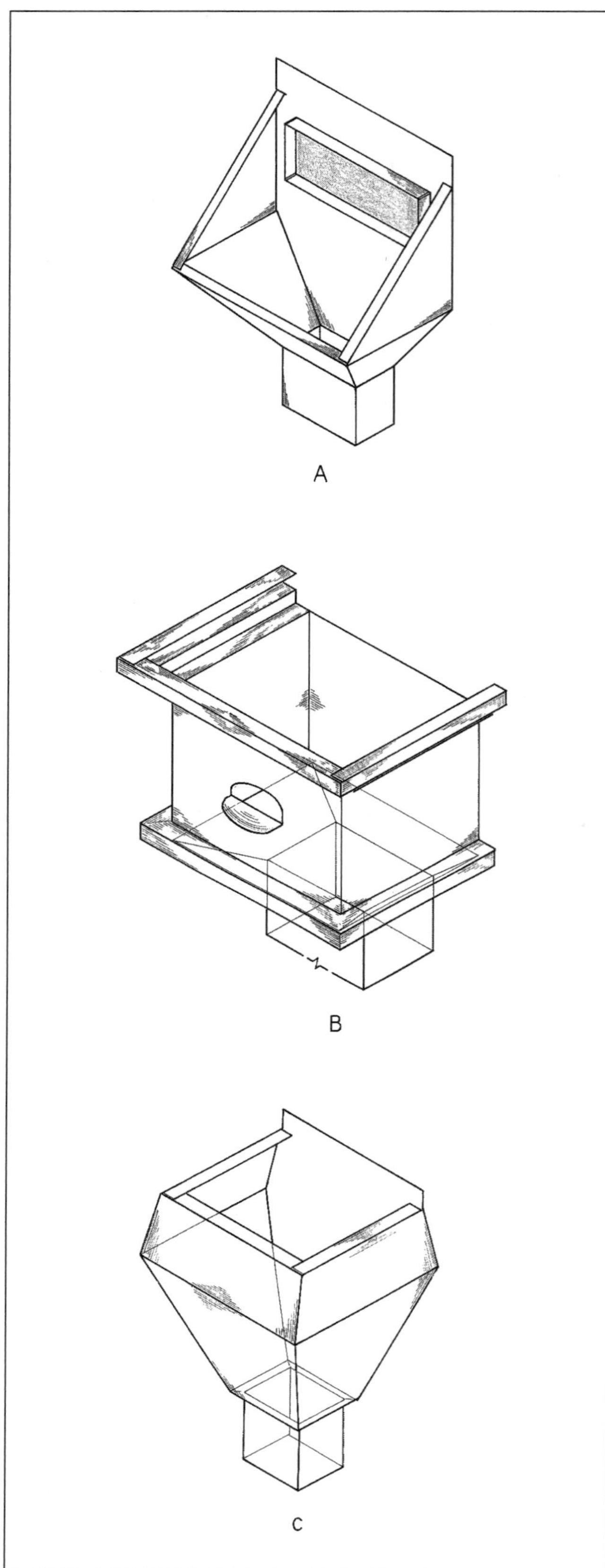

Figure 12.32 Conductor head styles.

steel, 0.032-in aluminum or 16-oz copper. A conductor head's resistance to water or wind load is a function of how well it is fastened to the building, not the thickness of the metal. Numerous breaks are incorporated into the conductor during fabrication, giving the metal maximum stiffness.

The top of the rear flange of the conductor should be hem-locked to the scupper. If face plate is used to seal the scupper opening, this should also hem-lock to top of conductor.

SCUPPERS

Scuppers are required to create a water exit from a roof through a parapet wall, or they are used to allow water to pass through an elevated metal edge system. (See Sec. 12.2.6.)

The roof membrane is installed before the scupper is placed, fastened, and sealed. It is good design practice to require the roof membrane to be watertight at the scupper location before proceeding with scupper installation.

All joints of the scupper should be soldered or welded watertight. In the event that a flame-applied or hot-air-applied roof membrane is being installed, solder joints will do little good. The heat of the flame or air will often melt the solder. In such cases, options are available. As previously stated, welding of the joints will avoid soldering of scupper joints. For welding, the metal must be a minimum of 14-gauge steel or 0.080 aluminum.

However, if open flame is being used, the roof membrane is probably a modified bitumen membrane. Hot air is normally used for single-ply polymeric membranes. Both membrane types can be used to seal the joints of the scupper.

The scupper must be properly primed and prepared. The elastic membranes are carefully fused to all lap joints of the scupper. The flashing plies of the roof membrane are then installed as would be required if the scupper was of welded construction.

Scuppers are fabricated from 26-gauge galvanized or paint-coated steel, 26-gauge stainless steel, 16-oz copper, 0.032- or 0.040-in aluminum. Aluminum and coated steel of such thickness cannot be welded, and since these metal types cannot be soldered, the above options must be considered.

The scupper must be compatible with the conductor head, the metal edge (if present), and the downspout. Stainless steel scuppers are often used. Stainless steel is normally compatible with all types of common roof flashings and can be soldered.

When a scupper extends through a parapet wall, as in Fig. 12.31, some metal thicknesses will vary when compared with a scupper extending through a raised roof edge, as in Fig. 12.19. When encased within a parapet wall, the metal is given support from the wall opening. When installed through a raised roof edge, the metal must be more rigid due to lack of support from other construction. (See Table 12.7.)

Scupper opening size is determined by the amount of roof area the scupper must drain and the rainfall intensity for the geographic location. The larger the scupper, the fewer units required. The smaller the scupper, the more units required, possibly including conductor head and downspout.

Roof crickets are normally required to force the water to scupper openings. Crickets are created from tapered roof insulation, tapered-edge strip (see Figs. 12.17 and 12.18) or formed as part of a wet-slur cementitious roof deck pour. (See Sec. 3.1.5.)

Through-Wall Scuppers. All scuppers should be entirely shop-fabricated and soldered. The metal should extend 2 in past the exterior building face when inserted through the parapet wall. These edges are hem-returned to lock the conductor head and scupper flange in place.

A face-plate flange is required to seal the scupper to the exterior building face. The flange is set in a bed of caulk, hem-locked to the scupper, and sealed watertight to the building face. (See Fig. 12.31.)

The metal roof flange of the scupper should extend past the cant strip and 4 in out onto the roof membrane. This allows enough sheet metal flange for proper sealing into the roof system. (See Fig. 12.33.) When the scupper is an emergency overflow component, the bottom of the roof side flange is not sealed. (See Fig. 12.34.) It is installed after the roof membrane and base flashing but prior to installation of the parapet wall flashing.

Emergency overflow scuppers are always an important design item for roof systems surrounded by parapet walls. In the event that the roof drains, roof scuppers, or underground drainage utilities become obstructed, water can pass from the roof through the emergency overflow scupper outlets.

When the purpose of the scupper is to direct water from the roof surface (see Fig. 12.33), the 4-in flange is sealed with roof flashing felt plies. The parapet wall

Table 12.7 Scupper metal thickness.

	Through-wall	*Raised edge*
Aluminum	0.032-in	0.040-in
Copper	16 oz	16 oz
Galvanized steel	24-gauge	24-gauge
Stainless steel	26-gauge	26-gauge

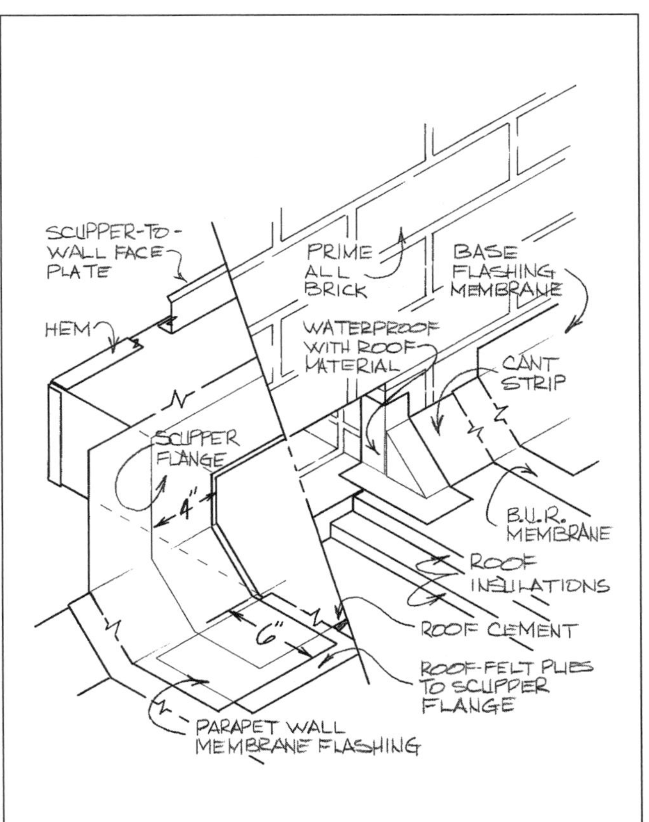

Figure 12.33 Scupper through-wall/interior.

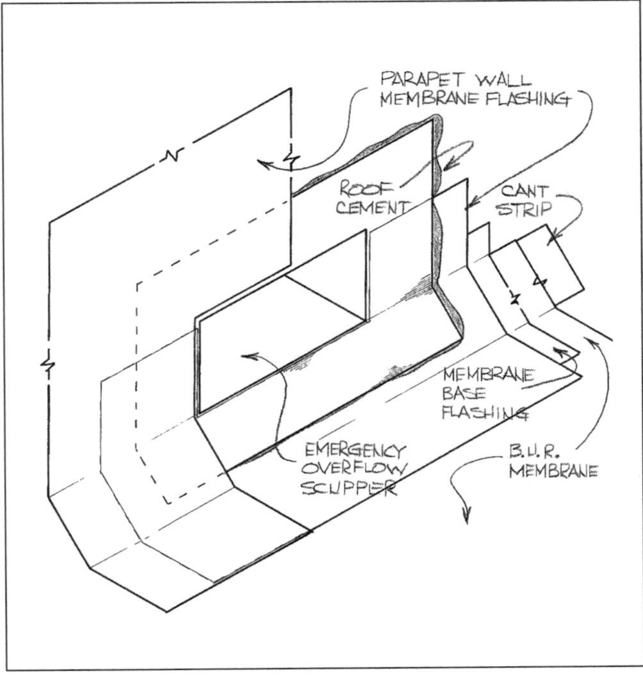

Figure 12.34 Emergency overflow scupper/interior.

flashings are then installed and, in most cases, once again seal the scupper flanges.

Wood cant strips or wood nailer mounted to the roof deck is an option for scupper attachment. However, due to the rigidity of a properly fabricated and sized scupper, as well as the secure attachment provided by the hem-locks on the exterior face, such nailer blocking is seldom required.

ROOF EDGE SCUPPERS

It is recommended that all metal edges be installed on raised blocking. (See Sec. 12.2.6.) If the designed roof slope requires the water to exit over the edge of the roof, scuppers will be required within the raised edge blocking/metal edge system.

The scupper should be sized and located to accommodate the maximum amount of rainfall expected for the geographic location. Water from the roof scupper can be expelled into a gutter and downspout system or allowed to free-fall from the roof scupper.

In a free-fall design, make sure there are no building wall units or penetrations directly under the scupper water cascade which could leak when exposed to the waterfall created by the scupper. Also, erosion of the ground can occur over time if provisions are not taken for such.

The scupper should be entirely shop-fabricated and solder-sealed, if possible. The roof edge flanges should extend 4 in onto the roof in all directions and be set in a complete bed of roof mastic. A backer and cover plate are suggested at the scupper and metal edge joints on either side of the scupper. (See Fig. 12.19.)

The scupper is attached to the roof edge blocking, primed with proper material, and sealed to the roof membrane and roof edge system with roof flashing plies.

Roof edge scuppers can feed water directly into a conductor head or gutter system. Such a design usually requires the conductor or gutter to be hem-locked to the exterior scupper opening. For such a design, fix the gutter to the building at scupper outlets and provide for gutter expansion between scupper locations. The hemmed lock at the scupper and conductor or gutter is then folded over to conceal and waterproof the fastener head, which is used to fix the flashing to the building wall at the scupper location. If a conductor head is used to collect water from the scupper, attach the outlet tube of the conductor head to the building.

Scupper metal should be compatible with all other adjoining metal flashing systems. Since all water from the roof surface will pass through the scuppers, sealing of the lap joints of the scupper is crucial. Aluminum and paint-coated steel scuppers should be avoided if possible due to the inability to solder-seal these metals. Stainless steel is often used to create scuppers since it is noncorrosive, is compatible with most roof flashings, and can be soldered.

12.2.9 Metal Wall Flashings

GENERAL

Metal wall flashings are used to waterproof the top of roof-membrane base flashings which extend up the building or parapet wall. In such cases, the metal flashing, referred to as counterflashing, can extend into the wall (see Fig. 12.35), extend through the wall (see Fig. 12.36), or be surface-mounted to the wall (see Fig. 12.37).

Through-wall flashings also serve the purpose of diverting any interior withe water to the building wall exterior. The through-wall flashings can be of flexible membrane material or metal flashing material.

Roof Maintenance Design. Roof membrane base flashings require maintenance and possible repair at some time during their life. The metal counterflashings which seal the top of the membrane base flashings should always be designed to allow for such roof maintenance and/or repair work.

Through-wall and in-wall flashings usually require a two-piece flashing design to accomplish this requirement. Surface-mounted counterflashings require a two-piece flashing design unless the surface-mounted flashing is a termination bar.

Termination bars are pinned to the building wall and sealed at the top edge with caulk. (See Fig. 12.37.) It is sometimes more effective to mount another termination bar below the existing one than it is to remove the bar to perform roof work and then reinstall or mount a new replacement bar.

IN-WALL FLASHINGS

In-wall flashings are often incorporated within masonry unit joints or installed under the building wall cladding system, such as metal or wood siding. As such, it is not practical to remove the in-wall flashing for roof or flashing service or repair. Instead, a removable flashing should be incorporated into the in-wall flashing. This can be accomplished in numerous ways, all of which are acceptable so long as the joint between the in-wall flashing and removable flashing is waterproof.

In view A of Fig. 12.35, the exposed hem edge of the in-wall flashing can be raised to a horizontal position, which allows the counterflashing to be removed. After service work is complete, the counterflashing is reinstalled into the receiver and the exposed hemmed edge of the in-wall flashing is malleted back down to secure the counterflashing in place.

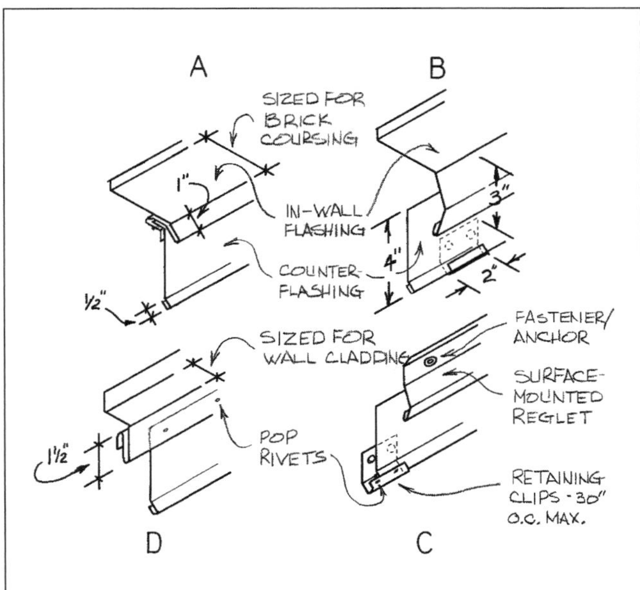

Figure 12.35 Through-wall/in-wall and surface-mounted flashings.

In view B, a 2-in-wide retaining clip is attached over the membrane base flashing approximately 30 in on-center. The counterflashing is then installed under the in-wall flashing and supported by the clip, which is bent up and pop-riveted to the bottom of the counterflashing. If the exposed portion of the in-wall metal flashing is subject to damage and deformation by other crafts and trades, such as that of masons, prior to completion of roof and sheet metal work, surface-mounted flashing per view C may be considered. C is performed only after roof system installation.

View D uses the same principal of design as C, except the top portion of the counterflashing is secured into the receiver, forming the bottom of the in-wall flashing. The receiver provides extra strength and rigidity to the total wall flashing system.

All of the flashing systems shown can incorporate the retaining clip to provide additional resistance to wind stress.

All counterflashing systems should extend a minimum of 3 in over the top of the roof base flashing membrane. Wall flashing systems are water shedders, not water barriers, and as such must allow enough lap at all vertical and horizontal joints to restrict wind-blown rain from entering the flashing system.

Counterflashing girth should not exceed 6 in. The counterflashing and in-wall flashing is fabricated from:

26-gauge stainless steel
26-gauge galvanized or painted steel
16-oz copper
0.032-in aluminum

All end laps should be 4 in. The in-wall flashing, probably being installed by the wall erector, should have a liberal application of elastomeric caulk applied between the lap joints.

THROUGH-WALL FLASHINGS

Refer to Fig. 12.36. The internal lap joints of the through-wall flashing and the weep holes in the exterior wall are crucial for a waterproof wall assembly. Water which passes through the exterior wall will travel down until it reaches the through-wall flashing, where it should be forced to the building exterior through the weep holes.

An angle should always be created on the interior face of the through-wall flashing. This forces water to the weep holes and prevents water back-up on the interior flashing. The laps of the flashing should be sealed by a liberal application of a proper type of elastomeric caulk. Do not use silicone caulk!

The joints should be pop-riveted or screw-fastened together, with the fastener also being sealed by caulk.

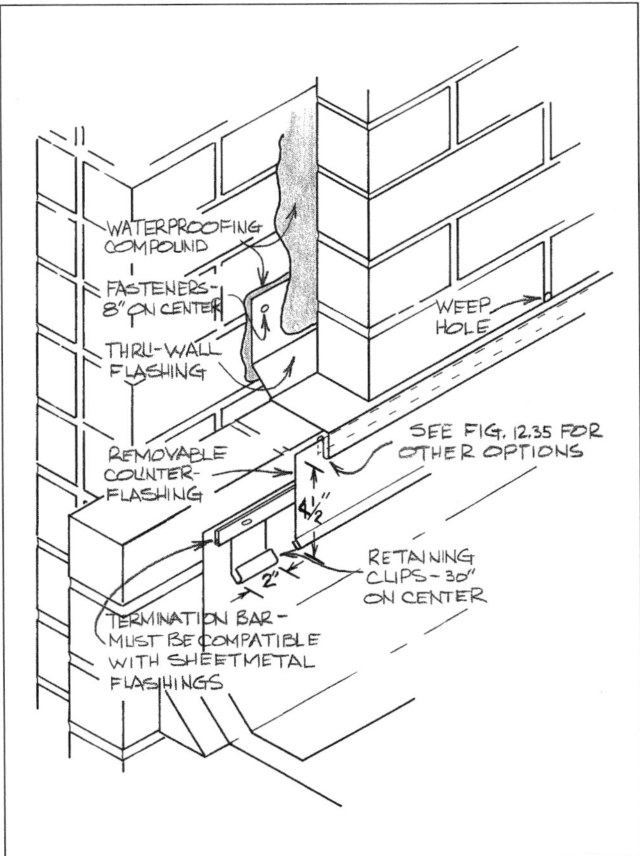

Figure 12.36 Through-wall flashing.

The rear flange of the flashing extending up the interior withe wall should be set in a 1/8-in-thick bed of waterproofing compound. The exterior of the flange and the entire interior withe wall is sealed by the same waterproofing compound or a waterproofing membrane system.

Most of the same design styles and requirements used for in-wall flashings can be used with the through-wall flashings. It is imperative that the counterflashing be removable. Always stagger the lap joint of the counterflashing from the lap joint of the through-wall flashing.

In earthquake-prone areas, through-wall flashing should be avoided. If building wall movement is a concern, other material may be better suited for through-wall applications. Elastomeric, plastic, fabric, and metal to membrane laminate materials are available.

SURFACE-MOUNTED FLASHINGS

Termination bars are a common surface-mounted flashing used in today's construction market. They can be fabricated by some sheet metal shops but are more often supplied or specified by the roof membrane manufacture. (See Fig. 12.37.)

The termination bars are mounted at the top of the roof membrane base flashing. They are pinned or fastened to the building wall, normally on 6- to 8-in centers. The top of the bar normally has a caulk receiver which allows an elastomeric caulk bead to seal the metal flashing to the building wall.

It is good design practice to require the first roof felt or membrane to be sealed directly to the building wall at the top leading edge. After the subsequent roof plies have been installed, the top leading edge of the base flashing should be coated with a compatible sealant. Into the sealant bead, the termination bar is set and fastened through the sealant and membrane layers and into the wall.

The termination bar is usually of aluminum metal. The holes in its face should be elongated to allow for movement. Likewise, the ends of the termination bars should be spaced apart a minimum of 1/16 in and a maximum of 1/8 in.

In the event that the roof membrane base flashing must be replaced, best practice might be to leave the existing termination bar in place. New roof base flashing is installed and terminated directly under the existing termination bar. A new termination bar is then installed and sealed to the building face, exactly as if it were the original construction.

Surface-mounted flashings can also be fabricated from sheet metal. A removable counterflashing should be part of the surface-mounted flashing design. (See view C in Fig. 12.35.) The removable counterflashing is held in place by retaining clips spaced 18 to 30 in on-center. As Fig. 12.38 shows, the top of the removable flashing is hemmed to add strength. The break through the face helps hold the bottom of the flashing tight to the roof base flashing.

The 2-in-wide area of the surface-mounted flashing is set into a bed of proper sealant. The holes through which the fasteners penetrate are elongated. A caulk receiver is fabricated into the top of the flashing, and once completely filled with caulk, seals the flashing to the building wall.

EXPANSION JOINT WALL FLASHING

Some roof decks are not supported by the building wall. Thus, they will move independently of the building

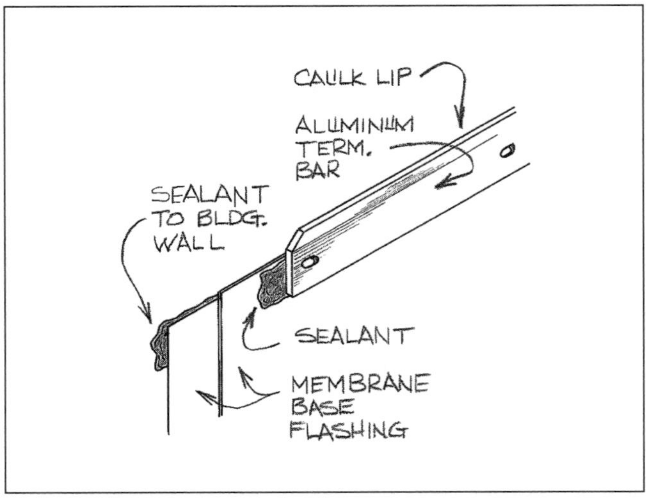

Figure 12.37 Termination bar to base flashing.

Figure 12.38 Surface-mounted two-piece removable counterflashing.

wall. If a parapet wall exists at the roof deck perimeter, and the roof deck is not supported or attached to the parapet wall, a flashing which will allow building movement is required. (See Sec. 3.1.7.)

The same principles of design apply for this type of flashing as for the others previously discussed. In many instances, a flexible, premanufactured expansion joint is used for such design situations.

COPINGS

Metal copings are used to seal and waterproof the top of a parapet or building wall. Considerations for coping design include:

- Thickness of metal required for the girth
- Linear movement
- Types of joint to use to seal the coping pieces together
- Appearance
- Support under the coping
- Rooftop traffic

Because copings are normally mounted to the top of building walls, and since they are normally of large girth, they constantly experience a certain degree of stress. Stress in the form of wind uplift and contraction and expansion must be accommodated by the coping system.

Copings should be designed fully supported by the building wall top surface and it should be secured tightly down over this surface. The coping side face on the building wall exterior is secured by a continuous cleat and hemmed edge of the coping. The hemmed edge of the coping should not exceed 30°.

The roof side of the coping is held to the building wall by screw fasteners 24 in on-center. The screw fasteners have gasketed heads and are installed through elongated holes to allow for linear movement.

Copings should always have a slope on the top surface equaling 1 in per foot slope. The slope should direct water to the roof side of the parapet. Without such slope, water could stand on the large top face of the coping. Standing water can deteriorate some metals as well as leak through the lap joint of the coping pieces.

Blocking is sometimes used to elevate one side of the building wall to achieve the desired slope of the coping top. However, this results in the coping not being fully supported by the building wall top. In such a case, increase the metal flashing thickness to the next-thicker gauge than what is appropriate for that girth of coping flashing. (See Table 12.8.) It may also be advisable to place a crimp break through the center of the coping top to increase the stiffness of the coping. If routine rooftop traffic is expected over the coping, design a solidly supported coping. (See Fig. 12.39.)

Coping side edges should extend down and over the roof membrane flashing a minimum of 2½ in. If possible, extend the roof membrane over the building wall, creating a watertight wall-top area before coping is installed. Building paper or slip sheet may need to be installed to the roof membrane prior to installation of the coping if the coping can get hot enough to fuse to the underlying roof membrane.

Coping should extend a minimum of 1 in below wood blocking on the building wall exterior. The side edge of the coping should not exceed 4 in in face dimension. A larger face dimension than this could be considered a fascia and a two-piece system is recommended. (See Fig. 12.14.)

Joint design between the coping pieces is important. A double-lock standing seam is the most efficient, if the metal is thin enough to allow such bends. For thicker metals, use the cover and backer plate system. (See Fig. 12.40.)

12.3 MEMBRANE BASE FLASHINGS

GENERAL

Membrane base flashings are used to join the primary roof field membrane to a roof penetration, a building wall, an expansion joint, a metal edge system, roof curbs, or other roof structures. Building movement, roof structure movement, expansion and contraction of the roof membrane system, abuse by service workers, and stress due to wind loads often are greatest at base flashing areas.

Therefore, in addition to providing the joining mechanism between the roof membrane and the roof structure being sealed, the membrane base flashing's primary function as a joiner is to add strength at the flashing location. In addition, it must be:

- Waterproof
- Resistant to environmental attack and deterioration
- Serviceable
- Compatible with the roof membrane and conditions

Table 12.8 Metal weight for coping per girth.

Girth, in	*Aluminum*	*Copper*	*Galvanized steel*	*Stainless steel*
<12	0.032	16 oz.	24-gauge	26-gauge
12–18	0.040	20 oz.	22-gauge	24-gauge
18–22	0.052	24 oz.	20-gauge	22-gauge
22–26	0.080	32 oz.	16-gauge	20-gauge

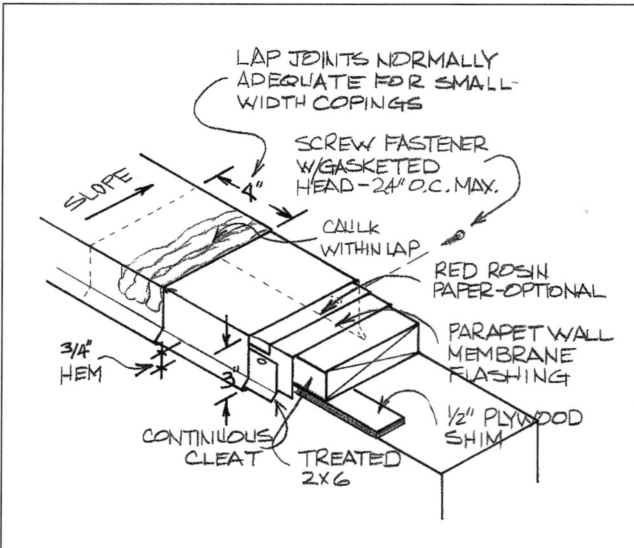

Figure 12.39 Coping system.

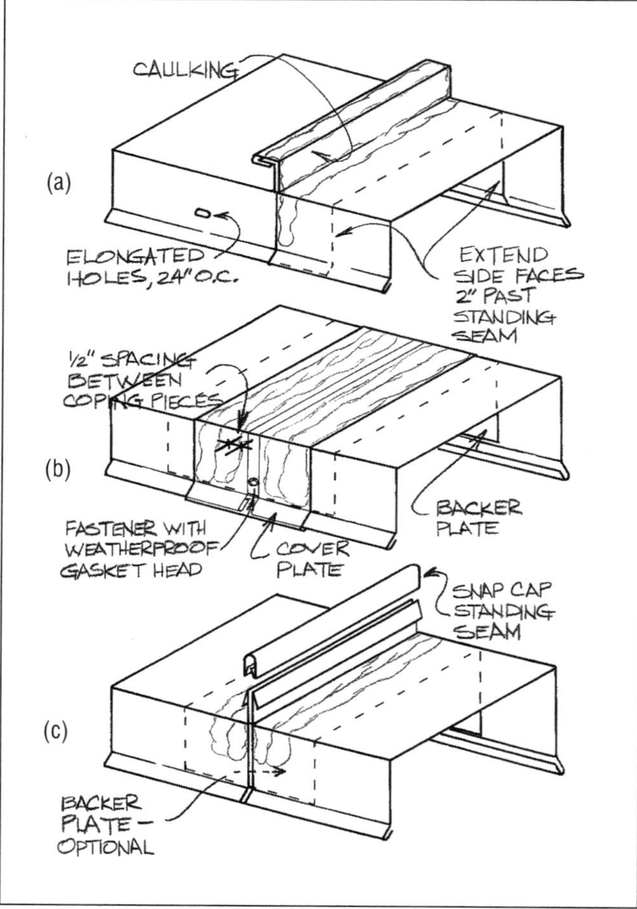

Figure 12.40 (*a*) Double-lock standing seam; (*b*) cover/backer plate; (*c*) snap-cap seam.

- Able to become permanently fused to the roof membrane, at all locations and throughout the flashing membrane

A membrane base flashing can extend up the side of an object penetrating the roof plane, such as a parapet wall or roof curb. (See Fig. 12.1.) It can also be used to seal components or systems which are on the same plane as the roof surface, such as a vent stack flange or metal edge system. (See Fig. 12.5.)

A membrane base flashing is normally of the same material, or from the same material family, as the primary roof felts or roof membrane. The membrane base flashing is created by layering additional roof sheets or membranes over the installed roof membrane system at the base of the component being sealed. This is referred to as *flashing of the component.*

Metal is also used to flash a component. (See Sec. 12.2.) Metal flashing can be a water-shedding system, whereas membrane flashing is a water-barrier system. Also, metal flashing is used to terminate the roof membrane and membrane flashing systems. Membrane flashing is often used to join the roof membrane to or into the metal flashing.

As an example, membrane flashing is used to join the roof *to* a metal edge system by being attached and sealed to both the roof and the metal. (See Fig. 12.20.) However, membrane flashing can also join the roof system *into* the metal flashing system on a parapet wall, but it does not seal to the metal flashing. In such a case the metal flashing sheds the water over the top of the membrane flashing barrier. (See Fig. 12.36.)

It is impossible to reference and completely illustrate every type of membrane flashing system and requirement that will be encountered on a rooftop. Different roof material manufacturers have different requirements for their roof and flashing systems. Also, different and unusual situations, not referenced in any manual, will be encountered in roof design. This especially holds true for reroof design.

Therefore, in the following sections we will discuss design theory of membrane base flashing rather than attempt to reference all the membrane base flashings available. Only bituminous materials are referenced. Polymeric single-ply materials are too manufacturer-specific to be generically discussed within the scope of this manual. However, many of the same design principles and theories will apply.

DESIGN CONSIDERATIONS

Membrane base flashings are used with all types of bituminous roof membrane systems, including:

- Asphalt built-up roof systems, both hot-applied and cold-process
- Coal tar pitch built-up roof systems
- Modified bitumen roof systems

Polymeric single-ply roof systems and polyurethane foam roof systems, not specifically addressed herein, also normally require membrane base flashings.

Membrane base flashings are required on any type of roof system created from roof felts, sheets, or membranes. The membrane base flashing is installed at the roof area where the roof field membrane joins into a roof penetration or roof structure. In general, it is common practice to use a modified bitumen membrane (see Chap. 9) as the base flashing material, whether it is a built-up roof (BUR) system or modified bitumen roof system.

However, some manufacturers of BUR system materials may not specify this procedure. In such cases, especially if a manufacturer's warranty is a requirement, this application is not a design consideration. In these cases, fiberglass cap sheets, cold-process roof mastic and membranes, or simply additional roof ply sheets in bitumen moppings are required. Some manufacturers have required neoprene flashing sheets at base flashing areas.

Today, we normally see manufacturers requiring modified bitumen membranes as the base flashing materials. Modified bitumens offer several advantages over the once-customary roof sheet plies or cap sheets installed in bitumen moppings as the base flashing. Modified bitumen flashings are more flexible, more resistant to environmental attack, and, because they are a factory-produced roof membrane and flashing sheet, can be considered easier and quicker to install.

The modified bitumen membrane base flashing is normally installed to the top of the completed field membrane, be it a BUR or modified bitumen roof system. However, in some situations a flashing sheet is installed prior to application of the field membrane. This subflashing sheet can provide a strong yet flexible base onto which the subsequent roof and flashing sheets are installed.

It is good design practice to include at least two modified bitumen membrane flashing sheets as the base flashing system. This suggestion may supersede the material manufacturers' requirements for some roof systems.

Figure 12.41 shows several configurations of base flashing systems, with and without modified bitumen flashing membranes.

The roof flashing sheets or membranes should extend a minimum of 4 in past the toe of the cant strip out onto the roof field membrane. If multiple membranes are

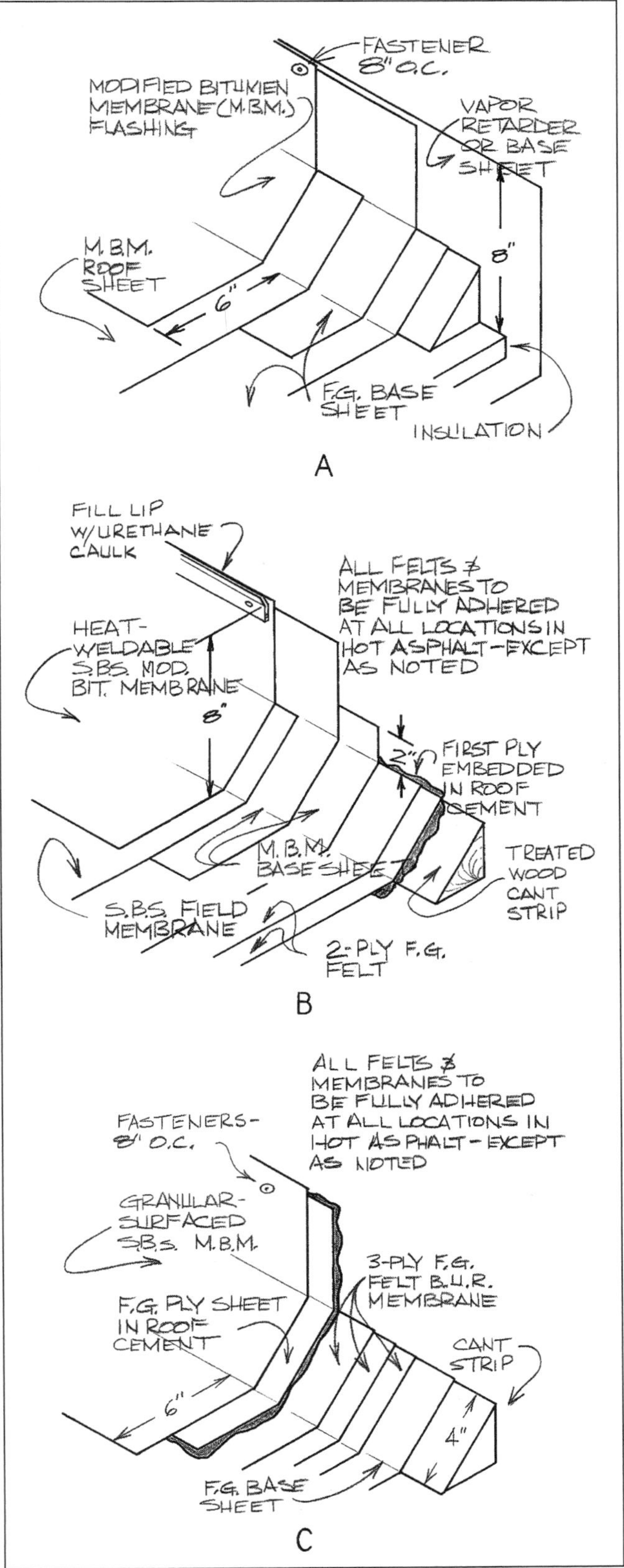

Figure 12.41 Membrane base flashing.

being used to complete the base flashing membrane, the final top surfacing sheet should extend approximately 1 in farther out onto the field membrane than the underlying sheet(s). This requirement reduces exposed edges of membranes to a minimum. Since membrane edges are where water can infiltrate under flashing and roof sheets, covering all edges possible with subsequent sheets or membranes is accepted practice. The same principle of design and installation holds true for the top leading edges of the membrane flashing as it extends up vertical faces.

All membrane flashings should be nailed at the top leading edge. The weight of the membranes, combined with high rooftop temperatures, can cause the membrane flashing to slide from the roof curb or wall. Nailing is usually accomplished with 1-in square-head nails, roof tacks through tin caps, masonry anchors, or screw fasteners through the termination bar. The fasteners should be spaced a minimum of two per curb side or 8 in on-center.

The height requirement of membrane base flashings is also 8 in. The top of the membrane flashing must be a minimum of 8 in measured from the top of the roof membrane surface. This allows enough room for installation of adequately sized cant strip and enough room to allow roof workers to turn and embed roof felts and/or membranes up the roof curb or wall. Additionally, an 8-in minimum height elevates the top of the membrane flashing far enough above the roof surface to eliminate the normal risk of wind-blown rain or melting snow from reaching and infiltrating the top edge of the membrane flashing.

DESIGN THEORY

As stated under the previous heading, most bituminous base flashing membranes today are created from modified bitumen membrane materials. This can consist of as few as one or as many as three flashing sheets. It is good practice to include at least two flashing sheets at the base flashing area. This suggestion may supersede some material manufacturers' requirements.

Since roof leaks often originate at flashing areas, whether they are membrane or metal flashings, the author's flashing design theory requires redundancy. This has been referred to as the "doom-and-gloom" approach. This design theory assumes that the top-surface flashing sheet, exposed to the environment, will leak. In such a case, the sublayer must be waterproof to stop water infiltration. We then assume that the sublayer will leak and we design another water barrier.

If all three barriers leak, it is the result of improper workmanship (performed incorrectly three times in a row), unexpected exceptional building movement (which should be properly assessed before design), damage by rooftop workers, or faulty material. In any of these cases, the roof leak did not occur because of minimal, inadequate, or negligent design.

It is further suggested that the top modified bitumen membrane at the base flashing be either open-flame welded or adhered in an application of cold-process mastic. Again, this is regardless of whether the roof-membrane system is a BUR assembly or a modified bitumen system.

This is not industry standard but in compliance with the doom-and-gloom theory. Detail work is where many flashing systems fall short. Torch-welding or cold-process mastic adhesive application of the flashing sheets or membranes requires more scrutinizing work and process by the roof installer. In theory, this helps eliminate defects due to poor workmanship.

For modified bitumen systems, the membrane type will normally be either APP or SBS. (See Secs. 9.1.2 and 9.1.3.) The flashing membrane sheets for these systems must be of the same material type as the primary roof membrane. APP and SBS modified bitumen may not be compatible, and mixing of the two can lead to roof problems.

APP is only heat-fused, sometimes with hot air, but most often with open flame. SBS is normally installed with hot asphalt moppings, although, as recommended, it can be installed with cold-process cutback mastic or it can also be manufacturer-formulated for open-flame welding.

Either SBS or APP modified bitumen membrane is acceptable for use as base flashing membrane on an asphalt BUR system. However, since APP is not intended for use with asphalt, if the roof surfacing is to be hot asphalt and gravel, the material manufacturer of the modified bitumen should be consulted.

Verify that there is not a problem with the permanent adhesion and penetration of the asphalt to the surface of the APP modified bitumen flashing. In such a case, the asphalt and gravel surfacing may delaminate from the APP modified bitumen membrane.

For membrane base flashings not using modified bitumen membranes, require a minimum of two roof ply sheets followed by a roof cap sheet membrane as the base flashing system. This system can be enhanced by installing the cap sheet in a troweling of plastic roof cement.

12.3.1 Elevated Base Flashings

Base flashings are created in two different manners, either elevated above or level with the roof surface. It is recommended, whenever possible, to design elevated base flashing membrane systems.

At components which create a right angle at their intersection with the roof deck, a cant strip is required. The cant strip is secured in place at the right-angle intersection, creating two 45° angles.

The roof membrane system is applied over the cant strip face. Most material manufacturers recommend the roof sheets to extend above the cant strip and up the vertical face of the roof structure approximately 2 in.

After application of the roof membrane is completed at the roof component, the membrane flashing is installed. As a minimum, the flashing system should consist of two roof sheets or membranes, although this recommendation supersedes some manufacturers' requirements. (See Sec. 12.3.)

CANT STRIPS

Cant strip is required because roof felts and membranes cannot turn 90° without experiencing voids between ply layers and interply adhesives. Additionally, roof felts will split and crack at a 90° bend after a short time.

Some modified bitumen membrane manufacturers state that their material can perform adequately at a 90° bend. However, most prudent people in the roof industry prefer to include the cant strip at a right-angle intersection, and this remains common practice.

The cant strip is either of wood or rigid insulation material such as perlite or wood fibers. Wooden cant strips are the most rigid and are effective in resisting damage at the base flashing caused by foot traffic, hailstones, or other impact forces.

The cant strip is attached:

1. To the roof deck or substrate (roof insulation) and covered with the field membrane, or
2. To the roof deck, covered with the base sheet, which is then covered with roof membrane felts
3. Atop the base sheet which is attached to the roof deck and covered with the roof membrane

BASE SHEET FUNCTION

View A in Fig. 12.42 shows a situation where a base sheet is not used. Instead, the roof plies are adhered directly to the roof deck, such as in a structural concrete system, or directly to the roof insulation as well as to the cant strip face.

Any tensile strength derived from a base sheet adhered with the roof-ply system is not available with such design. Lateral movements of the building or construction at the cant strip flashing location will be transferred directly to the roof felt at the cant strip face with such design.

An unadhered base sheet to cant strip face, as in view B, allows for minor lateral movement without stress to the roof ply and base flashing system. This design creates a slip sheet at the cant strip, which can aid in movement accommodation at the base flashing.

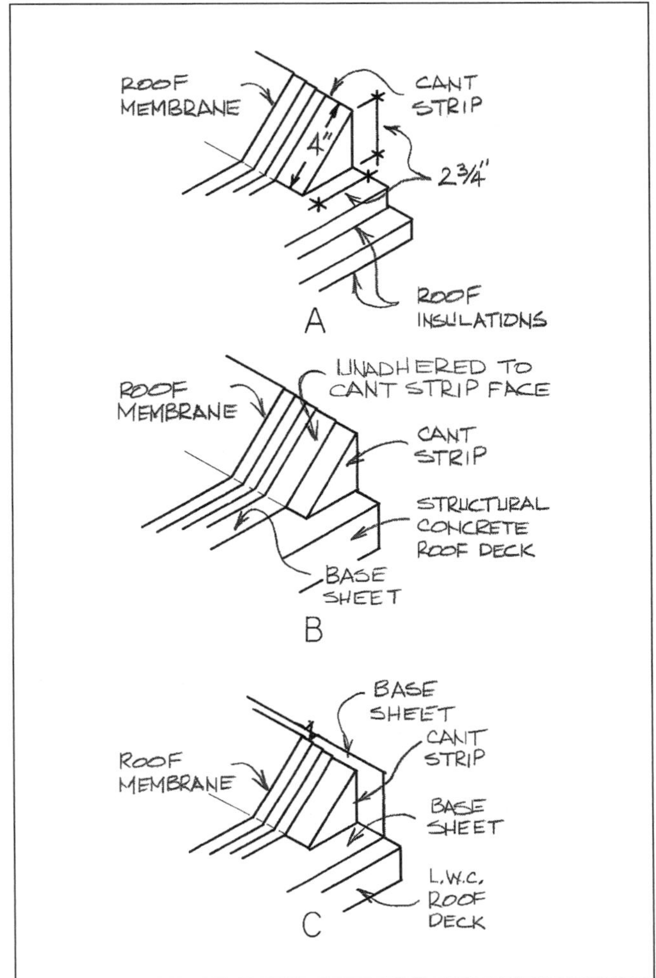

Figure 12.42 Elevated base flashing.

View C shows a lightweight concrete roof deck. In order to eliminate the possibility of moisture transfer from the deck into the cant strip, and to provide for deck ventilation, the base sheet is designed as a vapor retarder. Any moisture gases can pass out the top leading edge of the base sheet which extends to the top of the roof curb (not shown). Also, since the base sheet is not fully adhered to the side of the roof curb, it can, to a lesser extent than in B, act as a slip sheet.

At mechanical equipment curbs and at parapet walls, or at any roof structure where slight movement might occur, it is good design practice to include an unattached roof sheet. Many roof-material manufacturers include such a design detail in their systems manuals, and although it can vary, the principle remains the same. (See Fig. 12.43.)

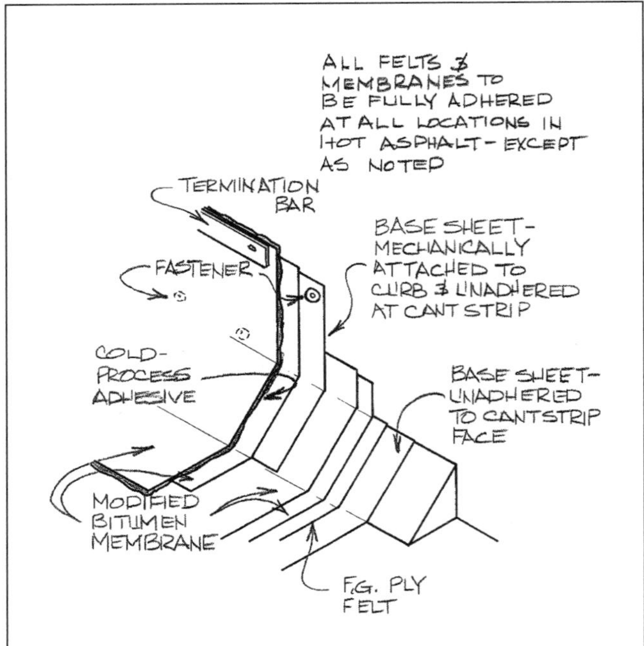

Figure 12.43 Elevated base flashing with slip sheets.

Although not always required, this design for movement is good practice at most base flashing areas. With roof design, and especially with flashing systems, it is better to be safe than sorry. Overdesign seldom causes problems; underdesign almost always does.

This allowance for movement should not be construed as taking the place of special design considerations and systems where excessive movement can be expected. It will only help compensate for slight movement, due to thermal loading of the roof membrane, vibration of small equipment, deck movement due to live loads, etc. For design requiring expansion joint provisions, see Sec. 3.1.7.

A system disadvantage to such slip-sheet movement design is the total strength of the flashing system. Everywhere a slip sheet is incorporated into the system, it effectively separates the roof materials above from the roof materials below. A monolithic reinforced system extending completely through the membrane flashing is eliminated by such design.

Also to be considered is the stress transfer, if any, which will occur to partially adhered base flashing systems. Any stress which does occur will be transferred and absorbed at the line where the slip-sheet system ends and the adhered portion of the flashing begins. With fully adhered flashing systems not incorporating a slip sheet, the stress is dispersed more evenly throughout the flashing system.

ROOF MEMBRANE

The roof membrane is generally required to be installed up the cant strip face in the same configuration and manner in which it is applied in the roof field. In the past, roof felts were cut at the top of the cant strip. Today, most material manufacturers require the roof membrane to extend a nominal 2 in above the top of the cant strip.

In situations where abnormal, but not excessive, stress can be expected at the base flashing area, some designers include roof mastic at some location within the roof ply system. This is not a standard practice; however, the roof mastic remains pliable and allows the base flashing to move due to the imparted elastoplastic characteristics provided by the roof mastic.

The procedure shown in Fig. 12.44 will not be found in any material manufacturer's manual. It is shown to demonstrate the design versatility available and sometimes needed in special situations.

Another option would be to use the roof mastic under the first roof ply installed to the cant strip face, with all other roof plies being installed as normal. This option is not as radical as mastic between all plies, while still providing a movable interface between the cant strip and roof curb and the subsequent applied base flashing.

If this process is used, verify the compatibility of the roof membrane with the cold-process adhesive. Many modified bitumen membranes will be damaged by the excessive and encapsulated mastic adhesive.

Some manufacturers' flashing details show the top edge of the base flashing sealed watertight by roof mastic and reinforcing membrane. This is also a standard detail requirement within the National Roof Contractors Association (NRCA) *Roofing and Waterproofing Man-*

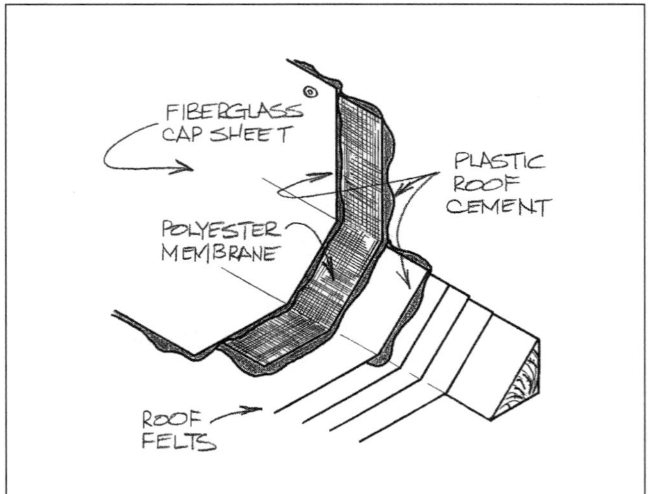

Figure 12.44 Roof cement in base flashing.

ual. However, most material manufacturers do not require this entire waterproofing process.

In a case where the roof ply felts or base flashing will remain exposed for a period of time and could be subjected to rain, the top must be sealed watertight. Moisture cannot be allowed to infiltrate the roof felts or flashing membrane. This is most often accomplished by a troweling of roof mastic cement to the top of the flashing or felt membrane. Subsequent work and sheet metal flashing or equipment base should be set to the top of the curb as soon as possible to prevent water infiltration and to permanently waterproof the base flashing system.

BASE FLASHING MEMBRANES

Modified Bitumen Membranes. Base flashing membranes are normally installed to the top of the applied roof membrane. "Normally" is the term used because, in some cases with modified bitumen membrane (MBM) roof systems, a roof flashing membrane starter sheet is installed to the cant strip face prior to application of the field membrane.

Not a standard requirement throughout the roof industry, this starter sheet can provide an MBM base for the field membrane at the crucial base flashing area. A modified bitumen membrane can also be used with BUR systems. (See Fig. 12.45.) Attachment of the MBM roof field membrane at the cant strip to an MBM flashing sheet can provide more positive and flexible attachment than if the field MBM sheet were attached to a fiberglass or organic base sheet.

The MBM starter flashing sheet helps eliminate voids at the base flashing within modified bitumen roof membrane sheets. Not required by all roof system material manufacturers, this process is herein recommended for consideration in some design situations.

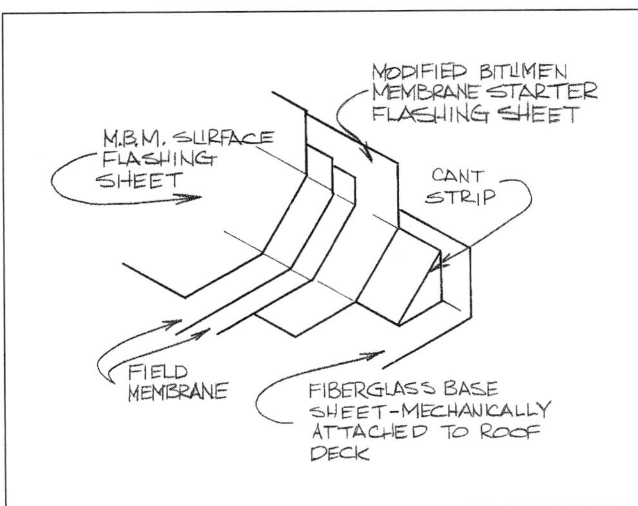

Figure 12.45 Modified bitumen starter sheet within base flashing.

Often only the top edge of this flashing membrane is attached to the roof curb or wall. This allows the remaining and unattached portion of the flashing sheet above the cant strip to help compensate for any future minor movements at the base flashing area. (See Sec. 12.3.)

The modified bitumen flashing membranes installed to the top of the roof membrane at the base flashing area can be as few as one or as many as three. A three-ply system usually consists of a base sheet, followed by a smooth-surfaced MBM sheet, followed by a mineral-surfaced MBM sheet.

This three-ply system is used mostly where the base sheet is attached only to the roof curb or wall, being left unattached over the cant strip face and roof surface. Therefore, the following two modified bitumen flashing sheets provide the waterproofing integrity, with the base sheet acting as a slip-sheet mechanism.

Not always in accordance with material manufacturers' requirements, if possible, install the final surface sheet either with open flame or with cold-process mastic. This installation process can eliminate application errors. Most material manufacturers will assist with alternate design and materials for this application.

Built-up Roof Membranes. Roof ply and cap sheets as used in built-up roofing are now the exception instead of the rule when constructing membrane base flashings. At one time the accepted materials, they have now been replaced by MBMs. If required by a material manufacturer, the types and amounts of material must be strictly followed.

As a general rule, a minimum of two ply sheets should be installed to the top of the field membrane at the base flashing area. These two sheets are then covered with a final surface sheet, normally a fiberglass cap sheet. (See Sec. 7.1.2.) In some cases, the fiberglass cap sheet is replaced with an MBM sheet.

BUR base flashings are normally installed with hot asphalt mopping, although cold-process mastic can also be used. The items of concern are voids and bridging of the felts at the cant strip location, and asphalt too cold to be properly applied.

12.3.2 Level-Surface Base Flashings

These types of base flashings are used to seal metal edge systems into the primary roof field membrane and to seal scuppers and roof drain flashings, or they can occur at details such as pitch pans. Level-surface base flashings are also referred to as *stripping plies*. (See Fig. 12.46.)

The stripping plies can be either of modified bitumen materials or roof-felt plies. With BUR systems, the stripping plies are of the same roof-ply materials as the roof membrane. With modified bitumen systems the stripping ply or plies are also of the same membrane type as the roof system.

Since level-surface base flashing stripping plies are used mostly to seal metal flashing components, care in the design and installation of metal flashing systems must be used. Optimum design requires that the metal flashing to be set into a complete bed of plastic roof cement, nailed or otherwise attached to the building, and then sealed watertight with the stripping plies. This optimum design becomes required design if the metal flashing is not elevated on wood blocking. (See Fig. 12.5.)

Whether a BUR assembly or a modified bitumen system, it is good design practice, if possible, to require a 9-in-wide modified bitumen sheet to be installed under the metal flashing. In the event that the stripping plies and metal flashing leak, the modified bitumen sheet can act as a water barrier. (See Fig. 12.47.)

It is crucial for the metal flashing to be completely and heavily coated with asphalt primer prior to installation of any stripping plies. The primer must completely dry before work proceeds.

If hot bitumen, either asphalt or coal tar, is used for installation of the stripping plies, care must be taken by the roof workers not to allow the bitumen to cool. Stripping-ply installation is tedious and time consuming, which often allows the bitumen to cool before it is used.

In addition to bitumen of the correct temperature, it is extremely crucial for the stripping plies to be positively

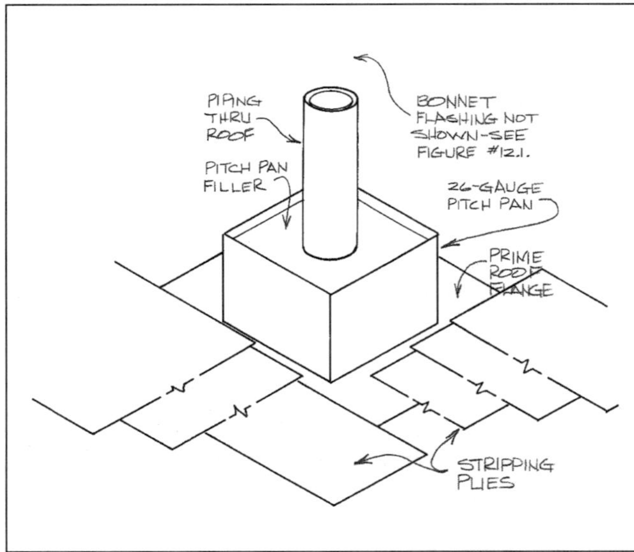

Figure 12.46 Flashing at pitch pan.

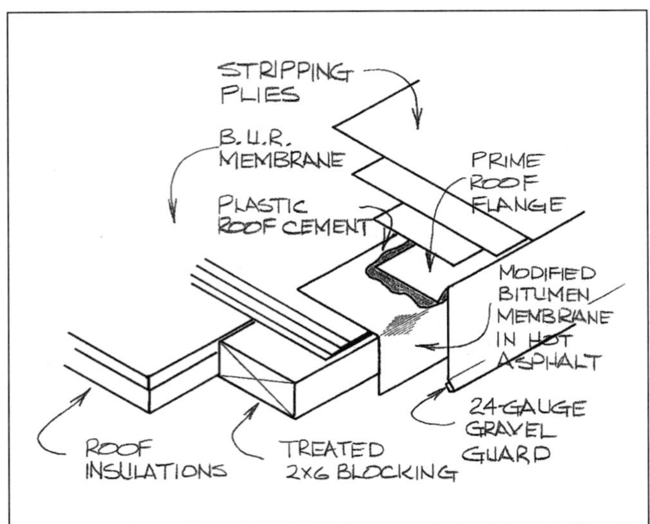

Figure 12.47 Level base flashing with MBM and cement.

embedded into the bitumen applied or completely adhered to the metal surface of the flashing. This is accomplished by brooming-in of roof felt plies into the bitumen mopping or rolling of modified bitumen flashing plies if they are torch-applied. (See Sec. 9.1.2.)

Since these types of membrane flashings exist at roof areas most subjected to stresses and adverse conditions, it is recommended that the roof system be sealed watertight before installation of these flashing plies. Expect the roof flashing plies or membranes to leak at some time during their life cycle. The roof membrane and system under the flashing component and flashing plies then becomes the water barrier.

MODIFIED BITUMEN MATERIALS

Torch Grade. Torch-applying modified bitumen flashing membranes to a primed metal surface should be avoided. Premature failure of the waterproofing seal is often seen with such installation.

When the metal flashing expands and contracts during temperature changes, stress is created at the metal and modified bitumen stripping-ply interface. As the system ages, the modified bitumen membranes become stiffer than when new. Also, the primer on the metal will deteriorate with time.

As the membrane decreases in elongation properties and the primer loses adhesion to the metal surface, the weak bond areas of the metal and modified bitumen interface release during thermal movement cycles. The membrane begins to release from the metal, normally seen first at lap joints of the metal flashing system and at the leading edge of the membrane where it is joined to the metal flashing. As water and rooftop dirt enter the void, the release process is accelerated. Roof leaks are often the result.

If an APP modified bitumen roof system has been designed, the stripping-ply procedure to metal flashing is often unavoidable. In such design, specify high-quality asphalt primer for use. Require the primer to be applied thick enough so that none of the metal can be seen through the finished primer coat. Require the primer to completely dry before stripping-ply work proceeds.

It is also advisable to include cover and backer plates at all metal edge lap joints to reduce stress caused by metal movement. (See Fig. 12.11.) The 9-in-wide MBM strip installed under the metal edge is also good design practice. (See Fig. 12.47.) A weighted roller manufactured for use with heat-fused MBMs should also be used at the crucial flashing locations.

Another option is to specify for use special metal flashing with modified bitumen flashing membrane factory-laminated to the metal edge flashing. This specialty system is available from a limited number of material manufacturers.

APP modified membrane can be applied only with open flame or with hot air. Therefore, the use of solder joints within the metal flashing system will often be negated. The heat of the installation process will melt solder. The heat will also often damage and destroy the properties of caulking. Take care when designing metal flashing which is to be sealed and waterproofed with a heat-fused MBM.

Mop Grade. The other common type of modified bitumen membrane is SBS. It can be applied with either hot-mopping or cold-process asphalt materials. It is not compatible with APP material.

Metal flashing is often designed to be sealed with a minimum of one layer of modified flashing sheet. However, it is better practice to require two and sometimes three flashing sheets at metal flanges which are to be sealed into the roof system.

It is again recommended that cover and backer plates be used at all metal edge lap joints, that the metal be correctly and fully primed, that a starter sheet be installed under the metal edge, and that all flashing sheets be fully broomed into the mopping bitumen.

For optimum design, the first ply to the metal flange can be a fiberglass roof sheet. The next ply is a modified bitumen base sheet, which in turn is covered with an SBS membrane. All sheets are normally set into hot asphalt mopping, although cold-process mastic is sometimes acceptable as the inner-ply adhesive.

The most economical optimum design is requiring mastic under the top surface sheet only. If only a single ply of SBS is being used to seal a metal edge flange, requiring trowel-grade cold-process mastic is strongly suggested. Verify the acceptability of the cold-process mastic with the modified bitumen manufacturer.

BUILT-UP ROOF MATERIALS

Level-surface base flashing stripping plies, as used on a BUR assembly, are normally of the same ply felts as used to create the roof membrane. The number of stripping plies, at a minimum, should be two.

The metal flange to which the stripping plies are normally applied should be completely and thoroughly primed. Primer must dry before proceeding with roof work. The plies must be completely adhered into the mopping bitumen by use of a broom or other instrument. The bitumen must be hot enough to fuse all the ply sheets together.

It is good design practice to incorporate a modified bitumen roof sheet under the metal to act as a future water barrier. If this is not acceptable, the metal flashing should be set in a bed of plastic roof cement. In critical design situations, both procedures can be used.

To help accommodate expansion and contraction of the metal flashing being sealed by the stripping plies, a layer of plastic roof cement can be applied to the metal surface and the first flashing ply installed into this cold-process adhesive. The pliability of the mastic will help prevent stress failure at the felt and metal interface. Verify the acceptability of this procedure with the roof material manufacturer.

Solder joints are acceptable with built-up flashing systems since hot bitumen temperatures will not melt the solder. However, bitumen will not adhere to areas where some types of fluxes have not been completely removed from the solder area.

CHAPTER 13

Systems Evaluation

13.1 GENERAL REQUIREMENTS OF SURVEYS

GENERAL

A roof survey can be commissioned by a building owner for several different reasons. The most common reason is roof leaks. However, a survey might be necessary to gather data and information concerning:

- Insurance claims (e.g., fire or wind damage assessment)
- Ongoing roof maintenance and repair program (e.g., a semiannual roof inspection is recommended for roof systems in order to assess any needs of maintenance or repair)
- Condition prior to building purchase (e.g., major capitol expenditures required after the purchase may need to be factored into present lending negotiations)
- Maintenance/repair cost budgeting for the upcoming fiscal year(s) (e.g., municipal and industrial facilities often operate on budgets prepared and allocated months in advance)

For our purposes, a site survey can be defined as a detailed study by which the information and data on existing conditions are gathered. The data can be analyzed and analysis can result in a plan of action or a recommended course of practice. The roof site survey is normally performed by a member of the design team.

We most often are required first to perform an initial cursory site investigation in order to determine the needs, responsibilities, and scope of the survey desired by the owner. After the initial survey and interview with the owner, agreement is made as to the requirements of the survey.

The agreement should define:

- Responsibility of the surveyor and owner
- Special equipment, data, and outside sources, if any, required by the surveyor and who is responsible for producing or obtaining such
- Scope, magnitude, and extent of the survey
- Information and data to be furnished as a result of the survey
- Form in which the information should be presented

A survey is a means to an end. The end result can be a budget for the construction being considered, a set of Construction Documents, an insurance settlement, budgets for the upcoming year, etc. There are times when all that is required is a report of existing conditions, with no opinions, recommendations, or budgets.

RESPONSIBILITIES

It is important for the surveyor to understand the needs and desires of the owner. The surveyor has the responsibility to produce a product (data and information) to meet these needs and desires.

The agreement should state:

- What the produced material will be (a report of data findings and evaluation of the existing condition of the systems, often listed specifically—roof membrane, base flashings, sheet metal flashings, roof deck, structural roof framing, etc.)

- What the data, information, and evaluation will accomplish (dollar amounts to repair or replace; if repair is an option in lieu of replacement, time required for construction, materials salvageable at present, reasons for persistent problems, etc.)
- How the needed information will be obtained (nondestructive analysis of the system, destructive core sampling, testing of materials at independent laboratories, outside specialists, etc.)

To further define the responsibilities of the parties, it should be determined if the owner can and will produce records of original and subsequent construction and any previous reports on the condition of systems. Sometimes testing of existing materials and systems is required to make value judgments, and it should be determined who is responsible for providing and purchasing such testing, if and when required.

SCOPE OF SURVEY

It is important to define exactly what building, building area, or system will be evaluated under the scope of the survey. Sometimes adjacent buildings or systems interact or adjoin the building or system which you are evaluating. In this case, the adjoining or interacting assembly will have to be considered in relation to the system under survey. However, it should be made clear that evaluation of the adjoining system is to be contemplated in a limited manner under the survey.

It may not be feasible to examine all conditions of the system due to access problems. For example, it is not possible to view the top of the roof deck assembly without total removal of the roof covering. Other areas of the site may not be able to be evaluated because of inaccessibility. These areas should be noted within the agreement.

Sometimes other areas of the building are discovered to be in distress when surveying and evaluating the roof system. It may not have been possible or practical to find or observe these conditions during the initial cursory survey of the building site—for example, a clogged roof drain piping which becomes evident after a rain or a cracked beam concealed between the ceiling and roof deck in the plenum. However, since these component systems have a direct and important relationship with the assembly you are engaged to survey, evaluation and recommendation for repair procedures would be in order.

If you are to be producing a set of construction documents for the system being surveyed, complete and accurate evaluation can be postponed until the design phase begins. At that time it may be necessary to involve other parties with expertise in these fields in order to comply with building codes, etc. However, it may be required that complete analysis be performed and recorded in the survey findings. The scope of the survey should allow addition of these services at no penalty to the surveyor.

DATA TO BE FURNISHED

The information and data to be gathered under the survey should be defined. Assumptions, opinions, budgets, and recommendations may be required of the designer after the survey is complete. The data and information gathered during the survey are the basis for such.

For example, if energy conservation is an issue with the owner, analysis of energy loss through the roof and roof insulation system should take place during the survey. This can be followed by a recommendation for increased R-value roof insulation in a new roof system, or it may be determined that the existing insulation functioned fine, up to the point where it was contaminated with water from roof leaks.

To determine if water infiltration is responsible for lessened insulation efficiency, a moisture survey will be required. A moisture survey can be performed by nondestructive means, such as a scan by an infrared thermography camera, a nuclear scan meter, or an electronic capacitance meter. Core samples of the roof and insulations will also be required, as well as repairs to the system where the samples were taken.

In addition, energy conservation upgrade will probably require analysis and evaluation of the rooftop mechanical HVAC equipment. If it needs major servicing, overhaul, or replacement, the time to perform such operations is at the time of reroofing or roof repairs. Historical data concerning service of the equipment will need to be gathered.

As already mentioned, the data and information needed may be more than can be easily discerned from visual examination. Structural analysis, mechanical analysis, moisture contamination, corrosion control, as well as other disciplines may be assumed to be involved in the survey by the owner, or they may need to be included in survey to fulfill all of the owner's needs.

A list of components, assemblies, or systems to be evaluated during the survey should be included in the agreement with the owner. The expected results of such evaluation may also need to be listed in order to keep the agreement clear. For example, if the roof insulation system is to be evaluated as described earlier, then the expected results will be a determination of the extent of insulation failure due to moisture contamination. Possibly the roof membrane only is to be evaluated for a repair and maintenance program, in which case the condition of the base flashings will be a key item of evaluation in the survey.

REPORT OF SURVEY

The information gathered in the survey must be recorded in some form, which usually culminates in a written report to the owner. However, other forms of data recording are usually required, depending on the extent of the survey and the size of the building or system surveyed. For example, if a moisture survey was included, a grid overlay on a roof plan is required. The grid and plan should show the extent and levels of water infiltration. If water infiltration is excessive, roof deck repair may need to be allowed for during the construction phase. (See Fig. 13.1.)

If mechanical HVAC systems were tested and analyzed, a report of the findings will be included within the main report, usually on the mechanical engineer's (if used) letterhead. Graphs showing initial cost outlay versus return on investment are useful in demonstrating life-cycle cost. (See Sec. 2.1.4.)

Photographs with a day/date stamp are very useful, not only in showing the extent of the damage or work required, but also as a future reference. The photographed component and location can be referenced on the building site plan by use of numbers on photographs which correspond to labeling on the drawing. However, because of very poor reproduction quality, it is not recommended to use photographs for reference within the plan and detail drawings of the ConDocs.

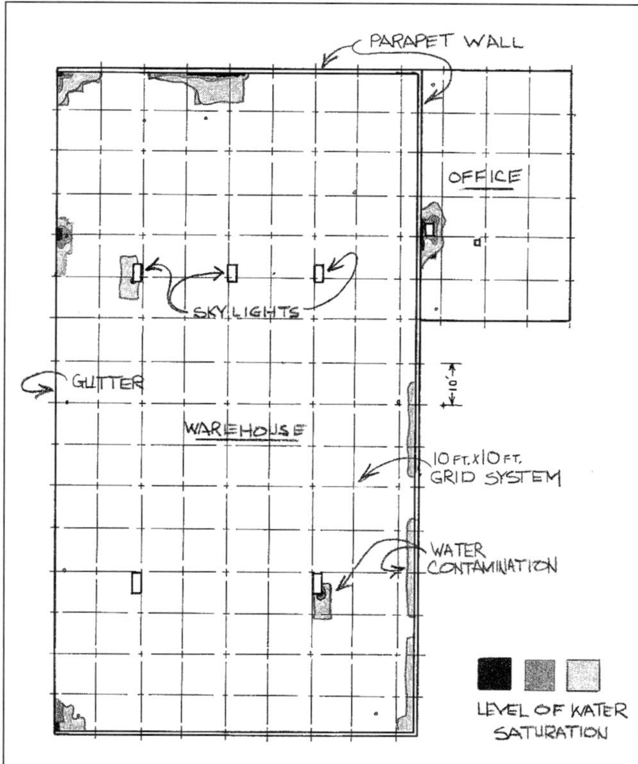

Figure 13.1 Moisture survey findings.

Additionally, if construction design is to follow the report and approval by the owner, detailed information needs to be on file in the design office. One of the best ways to access information and situations of the building site is by use of a videotape produced with a handheld camcorder. The camcorder records audio as well as video, allowing notes to be recorded along with the view. This tape is sometimes useful in showing actual situations to the owner.

Drawings for office use can be produced during the survey which accurately locate and depict building systems and components. In repair and reroof design, accurate measurement of details becomes important when you are in the office trying to fit new components and flashings to existing structures.

In regard to deciding whether to reroof or merely repair, computer programs are available for analyzing the condition of roof systems. Using a numerical scale rating system which is inputted by the surveyor, the program assists with decision making regarding proper procedures for repair, maintenance, or replacement.

13.1.1 Surveyors, Inspectors, Managers

GENERAL

Although survey procedures could be used to some extent to analyze new construction design, this is usually left to other procedures more suited for new construction. (See Chap. 15.) A site survey is normally conducted at an existing building site where components, systems, and materials are measured, analyzed, and evaluated. This is usually to accomplish an end result, which will be based upon accurate and complete knowledge of the existing components and systems. The accuracy and completeness of the data and information is crucial in order to achieve proper end results.

The end result can be varied, from a report of existing conditions only, to a budget report for cost to correct current damage, etc. However, the survey information normally results in a recommended plan of action to the owner from the designer.

Upon acceptance of the recommendations by the owner, the designer often produces a set of construction documents, using information and data gathered from the site survey.

SURVEYOR

The information gathered from the site is very important. It has to be complete and accurate. It has to encompass many items, some of them obvious, many of them less obvious, unless it is known where and how to look and investigate.

The information gathered determines the end result. It is what the client bases a plan of action and often large capital outlays upon. The person gathering this data and information is very important.

A surveyor needs to be:

- Analytical, weighing one option against the other, thereby determining which is the best course of action
- Experienced with existing roof systems
- Observant and accurate
- Familiar with design requirements
- Familiar with construction processes and techniques

In most cases, a survey is conducted in order to initiate and complete a design for roof replacement. Reroof design is more complicated than new construction design and the surveyor must take note of special situations that will exist during the reroof process.

Unfortunately, the original roof system might not have been designed or installed correctly. The surveyor must recognize these situations and formulate a tentative plan of action for correction while doing the survey. In reroof design, these situations must be corrected, which often involves redesign of components and flashings, which in many cases do not readily adapt themselves to the existing building structure.

INSPECTORS

A survey involving roof systems can be as previously defined, or it can also be a survey of the construction process of the roof system. We term this surveying of construction processes *roofing inspection* or *roofing observation*. It is often performed by a third party under contract to the building owner. (See Sec. 13.1.3.)

Roof inspection/observation personnel evaluate roof construction procedures, materials, and means during the installation process. Verifying the quality of materials and workmanship used in the construction is the main purpose of the roofing inspector. Many in the roofing industry consider roofing inspection to be a key ingredient in assuring the owner a quality roof system.

Inspectors perform an important and key function. They need to be competent and experienced with both the practical and technical sides of roofing. Roof inspectors/observers can be qualified and certified through organizations such as the Roof Consultants Institute.

This person must:

- Understand the requirements of the design and intentions of the designer
- Understand the accepted practices and standards of roof application
- Be a good record keeper
- Be a compotent photographer
- Be a good communicator
- Be a good observer
- Be diplomatic

A roof observer/inspector is at the center of the roof project. Normally under contract to the owner, the inspector's main responsibility is to see that the roof system is installed to plans and specification, the hypothesis being if the system is installed as designed, it will function correctly for the expected life span required. The owner, having faith and confidence in the designer, has every reason to believe this will be the end result.

The inspector must work closely with the designer. Communication is important, especially in reroof construction where unexpected items and situations sometimes occur. If a change in the construction occurs without the designer's knowledge or approval, and that area or system prematurely fails due to the unauthorized change, the inspector could be liable to some extent due to negligence of duties.

The inspector should work closely with the contractor. Quality control is the overall purpose of the inspector, but "control" of the application is generally the responsibility of the contractor. The inspector merely verifies conformance or nonconformance. An inspector/observer typically has no contractual responsibility to direct the contractor, his or her agents, subcontractors, employees, or suppliers in performance of the duties.

However, the inspector must report and make note of all items that are not in compliance with:

- Specifications and drawings
- Industry standards
- Material manufacturers' requirements
- Accepted roofing practices

In the event that such noncompliance is observed by the inspector, there are three choices.

One choice is to ignore such noncompliance. The second choice is to report noncompliance to the designer, who may then require the contractor to remove all materials installed in order to rid the system of the material that was worked and installed to below standards. This can cause serious problems such as delays, a weakened roof system as the result of numerous patches, or additional drawings and specifications from the designer detailing how the contractor is to remove and replace sections of the completed roof system. Such corrective procedures could possibly lead to later problems if roof warranty claims become necessary.

The third and best choice the inspector can make is to communicate in a diplomatic manner with the contractor and roof workers. Again, the inspector cannot direct or supervise workers but can point out procedures, work, or materials being used which are not in compliance with the Construction Documents. If at that point the contractor thinks that fully complying with the design is causing undue and unexpected hardship, there are again choices to be made.

The best solution is to contact the designer and inform him or her of the situation and problem. With the inspector perhaps taking a mediator role, a solution that is satisfactory to both the designer and contractor might be found. Then everyone goes back to work.

The alternative is that the contractor refuses to heed the warnings of the inspector and installs the systems as he or she pleases. In this event, the inspector must make a complete record of all such noncompliance and pass this information, the records, and the data on to the owner or the designer. It is then the owner's or designer's responsibility to make a decision as to the course of action necessary.

MANAGERS

Within the same area of responsibility as inspection and observation, another scope of responsibility exists: construction management. Roofing contractors continually perform construction management, wherein they have to organize and schedule equipment, material, and workers. At times, the designer may be called on to perform or assist with construction management—as part of a design/build team, a cost-plus project, or a complicated project requiring special guidance and expertise.

The designer should understand the complexities of construction management in order to design the most efficient roof system. The contractor and inspector should understand the complexities of design in order to most efficiently provide the required system. Unfortunately, in the real world, designers are not roofers or contractors, inspectors are not designers or contractors, and contractors are not designers. Conflicts often occur, resulting in addenda, change orders, revised drawings, construction schedule extensions, meetings, and sometimes lawyers and court. It is hoped that all parties will become more enlightened to the responsibility and duties of each of the other parties, and everyone can play nice with each other.

13.1.2 Building Site Survey

SITE EVALUATION

Before evaluation of the roof system can begin, the total building and building site must be considered. There are certain requirements of the building and building site which govern what type of roof can or cannot be used on the facility. (See Secs. 2.1 and 15.1.)

Some of the items listed below can "raise a red flag." As the survey progresses, items must be researched and investigated to determine if problems stem from any of the following items.

This list is indicative merely of the analytical attitude and building knowledge that must be used for a building/roof/site survey. Other items not listed could become factors. Some items to be considered before proceeding to the roof survey are as follows.

Geographic Location. Cold climates, hot climates, wet climates, high-wind areas, storm areas, city or rural area, etc., will have a bearing on what type of roof and roof components can be used successfully. Insulation (Chap. 8) as well as ventilation (Sec. 10.2.2) are prime considerations in hot climates and cold climates. Wet climates require low-slope roof membrane systems to have proper slope to shed possible excessive and torrential rains, and to keep the roof free of ponding water areas even during periods when drizzle and overcast skies remain for extended periods of time. High-wind areas require wind-resistance design (Secs. 2.2.2 and 14.3.1) at the roof perimeter, for insulation for the roof deck and metal flashing areas. Buildings in storm areas, such as areas where hailstorms are common, will need a roof membrane, roof flashings, and roof surfacing which can resist hailstones and/or be easily inspected for damage. (See Secs. 2.2.1 and 6.1.2.) City and industrial settings often require pollutant consideration and green design, which can include rooftop gardens. Rural settings may limit the number of locally qualified roof applicators and may also affect the construction budget as a result of the cost of transporting materials.

Environment. In a direct function of geographic location, some areas are subjected to pollutant fallout, such as (but not limited to) that of airports, paper mills, and petrochemical plants. Other areas naturally have a corrosive environment such as coastal regions where salt air is normal. In such situations, the roof system must be able to resist these types of environmental pollutants and corrosives.

Building Use. High-humidity interior conditions (laundries), corrosive interior conditions (some textile plants), restaurants with rooftop cooking exhaust, temporary structures (emergency or intermediate housing or offices), permanent structures (registered historic sites), or emergency shelters and disaster centers will all, from a practical viewpoint, require different types and quality of roof systems.

Age. If the building is relatively new and serious roof problems have developed, you must first determine *why* failure has occurred before you can determine *how* to fix it.

If a building is an old wood-frame structure, fatigue of the roof deck and structural supports must be closely evaluated, as well as any required fire-rated assemblies. Older structures may require more structural rehabilitation than would a newer building.

Also, older buildings with flat roofs were often designed with a minimal roof slope. After time and fatigue have taken their toll, the positive slope of the roof deck may no longer exist.

Architectural Style. If the building is composed of numerous roof levels with a multitude of inside and outside angles, metal flashings at eaves and building walls, etc., an installer-friendly roof membrane is preferred to accommodate all the flashing detail required. For steep-sloped structures, metal roofing can be used, as well as tile and slate and, for some of these more exotic steep-sloped systems, architectural expression as compared to budget allocations must be accurately considered before proceeding with design.

Historical. Locate and review as many of the existing records of construction as possible. Perhaps prior surveys have been conducted, past repairs, roof replacement, original drawings, as-built drawings, names of contractors who can be interviewed, etc.

Talking with occupants of the building is sometimes very helpful in determining past problems experienced with the roof. The time of occurrence and duration of problems are indications of damage to be expected to insulation, decking, and wood nailers. The amount and extent of past repair procedures may also be obtained from informal interviews with occupants. A good source of information are the maintenance or custodial personnel.

Also, looking closely at the structure should reveal if building additions have been performed. Building additions often require expansion joints to allow movement between the old and new roof deck. New additions may not have duplicated existing structural systems, such as change from wall-supported roof deck to non-wall-supported roof deck. (See Sec. 3.1.7.)

Determine if the historic use of the building has changed in the recent past. Roof problems could be related to changes in the interior building environment, suspended loads placed to the roof structure, etc.

BUILDING ENVELOPE

A visual examination of the exterior building facades must be performed. During this survey, the condition of the building envelope is evaluated for cracks or splits in the walls which indicate excessive building settlement or movement. If such is discovered, additional investigation of the support and foundation structure will be required.

Integrity of the wall waterproofing elements should be investigated. Many problems are reported in which the building envelope allows water to penetrate its surface. A wall leak can be misconstrued as a roof leak.

STRUCTURAL COMPONENTS

Location and style of the roof support structure needs to be examined and visually evaluated for adequacy. Examination should be performed at several different locations, verifying that the same system and style was used throughout the roof structure.

The roof structural support system should be located and plotted, if not on paper, within your head. Once on the rooftop, look for signs of structural deficiencies. In many cases, structural failure will telegraph itself through the roof membrane.

If adding additional weight to the roof is being considered under the design, the manner in which the weight load is dispersed and transferred throughout the structure is important. Check interior finishes and confirm that additional loading will not be reflected at these areas.

Roof Deck. Examine the bottom of the roof deck while investigating the structural support system. The bottom of the deck gives an indication of water infiltration as rust areas, water stains, etc.

If it is a metal roof deck, determine if roof insulation panels are attached with the proper amount of screws or fasteners. Fastener types and patterns can be viewed from below the roof deck. The amount of fasteners will be a cost factor if roof tear-off is required.

If it is a lightweight concrete or gypsum roof deck, excessive leaking for extended periods of time may have caused damage to the lightweight deck materials. Excessive and extended leaking is visually evidenced on the underside of the deck by residual lightweight material in exceptional amounts at the laps of the form decking in leak areas. In such a case, allowances for deck repair and replacement must be made in budgets and specification.

Building Design. In reroof design, the building appearance can be accommodated or changed by a new roof system. A low-sloped conventional built-up roof (BUR) system can be retrofitted with a new metal roof covering, which, if visible, will change the appearance of the building.

The building roof design can be an open and flat plane, with little slope, roof penetrations, equipment, etc. In such situations, most types of low-sloped roof systems will function well. These types of roof areas are low-maintenance by design.

The building roof design can include numerous hard-to-access areas, with slopes varying from steep to low pitch, numerous roof vents and roof penetrations, etc. In such situations, the best selections for roof replacement may be somewhat limited. The roof system must be visually pleasing because of steep slopes, and because of the roof flashings and penetrations, it must have low maintenance requirements or be easy to maintain. The roof system materials must be acceptable for both steep and low slopes, or different materials and systems must be selected for different roof slopes and areas.

In surveys which culminate in a reroof design, consider the type of roof system which was originally designed for the building. This is often the path of least resistance to an effective roof system. (See Sec. 15.1.)

In new construction design, consider difficult access areas, such as tall buildings, numerous roof levels, and roof areas or buildings with a complex roof design. Again, an installer-friendly roof is best suited for complex roof shapes. Difficult access areas are often best suited for premanufactured roof membranes, such as modified bitumen, metal panels, or polymeric single-ply.

Roof surfacings can have an effect on new construction design, in that white or reflective roof surfacings will lower cooling costs as compared with darker or nonreflective surfacings. However, be aware that if such a coating dissipates and the HVAC equipment is not designed to compensate for the increased heat absorption, the unbalanced HVAC system will not operate efficiently. Proper ventilation of the attic/plenum cavity is usually a much better design practice to lower cooling costs and is best incorporated into the original roof system design. (See Sec. 10.2.2.)

13.1.3 Roof Survey

OBJECTIVES

A roof survey usually involves the appraisal of an existing roof system. The survey is necessary so that the best course of action can be implemented, be it repairs to the system, maintenance of the system, a combination of both, or reroofing of the building.

A complete roof site survey should determine:

- Roof areas and dimensions
- Amount and type of roof-mounted equipment
- Parapet wall and coping size, height, and type
- Number of roof felt plies or membranes existing
- Type of bitumen used as interply mopping
- Type of membrane used as roof covering
- Type of surfacing used for roof protection
- Materials and procedures used at base flashings
- Approximate age of existing roof system
- Repair procedures used in the past
- Roof deck type, thickness, and support design
- Attachment
- Extent and location of water leakage

INITIAL PROCEDURES

A survey is a means to an end. If the end result is recommendations for repair or replacement, maintenance procedures, facts and data regarding replacement design, etc., the survey should concentrate on providing data that will lead to the correct answers. The correct answers are included in a report to the owner, the new roof design, a successful maintenance program, successful repairs, etc.

Looking at an existing roof that has experienced failure or is experiencing problems can tell a cognizant and qualified observer many things. If a system or component has failed prematurely, it is important to determine why it failed so that the same mistake will not be made by your design or recommendations. Likewise, if the system or component has functioned effectively for its expected life cycle, should you try and improve on the wheel?

If determinations are inconclusive, further investigation is required. Assumptions from the visual survey can be made which will direct special efforts and attention during the remaining course and means of the roof survey. Examination of existing conditions can lead to assumptions on:

- Age of the existing roof system
- Past repairs and maintenance performed thereon
- Success or failure of the past repairs
- Ability of the roof to function to date as designed and installed
- Damage to underlying components
- Cause of failure areas
- Original design and/or installation mistakes

These initial observations are to be combined with data gathered in accordance with Sec. 13.1.2. With this information, a great deal has already been learned about the roof system. Sampling (and testing if required) now will complete the analytical portion of the survey.

MEASUREMENTS

Measurement of the roof is usually a good way to begin the data-gathering procedure. It allows for an overall view of the different areas of the rooftop. Using grid paper for the field drawing helps keep distances in proper scale perspective.

Measurements should enable you to locate on the drawing all rooftop vents and equipment at their precise locations. Accurate drawing of the dimension, height, and size of existing equipment often proves helpful when in the office designing new flashings for these components.

Measurements and drawings should be made of all existing roof edge details, base flashing details existing at building walls, equipment flashings, parapet walls, roof drains, and sheet metal flashings. These should all be redimensioned accurately. Reference each item to its location on the roof plan.

Using a camera or a camcorder, photograph overall views of the roof as well as detail areas where problems are occurring on the roof. These pictures of base flashing details are helpful as references. Any object or situation which you think will be difficult to draw should be photographed. Any situation that is better explained with a photograph should be included.

TESTING AND SURVEYS

Testing may be required. This can include many different types of tests, depending on the end result desired of the survey.

- Wind-uplift resistance tests can be performed on the in-place roof membrane.
- Samples can be taken for chemical and component analysis at testing laboratories.
- Moisture scans can be performed to test for wet insulation or roof decking.
- A topographical survey can determine the slope of the roof deck.

Some of these test and survey procedures will require puncturing the roof membrane or removing sections of the roof. A survey usually requires examination of the roof deck and verification of the roof insulation type and thickness (if any). If testing is to be destructive, you can examine the underlying components at the same time as testing.

Also, some testing, such as moisture survey, uses nondestructive equipment which scans through the surface of the roof and gives an indication of wet or dry areas. However, destructive analysis measures are normally also required. Nondestructive moisture scan equipment is usually categorized as

- Capacitance
- Nuclear backscatter
- Infrared thermography

Wet and dry roof areas are indicated by this equipment. These indications must be confirmed by removing an area of the roof and testing it with a hand-held moisture meter. The moisture meter reading is compared to the reading of the nondestructive moisture scan equipment. From these two comparisons the operator is able to confirm wet and dry areas of the roof that are detected by the nondestructive scan equipment.

Topographic surveys are often conducted on a roof system. This survey will indicate depressions in the roof deck. Such depressions pond water and must be corrected in the design that is forthcoming.

Topographic surveys are sometimes destructive, since the transit may have to be rested to the roof deck top surface. All holes caused by such must be immediately repaired.

ROOF SAMPLING

Surveys of low-sloped roof systems normally require, at some point, roof sampling. It is important to know what exists within the roof assembly. This cannot be known without cutting a piece from the roof and examining it.

For example, the thickness of the existing roof insulation is important in reroof design. It is usually not practical to remove metal flashings to examine wood nailers for thickness. However, the thickness of the roof insulation normally equals the thickness of the wood nailers at roof curbs and roof edges.

If the insulation is 1 in thick, it can be assumed that the wood nailer is 1 in thick, which is pretty unusual since 2x material is 1½ in thick. In this case, further examination at the roof edge is demanded. See Fig. 13.2.

Cutting the roof at a location where the edge of a wood nailer should exist may reveal a 1-in-thick wood nailer ripped from 2x material, layered plywood ripped to width, or no wood nailer at all. Having no wood nailer might cause substantial change orders if unknown and unaddressed in the construction documents.

Sampling of the roof membrane will allow examination of the plies or membranes. If problems have been experienced in the field of the roof, choose this area as a sampling location. Examining the sample will help confirm or deny membrane failure as the cause for roof leaks.

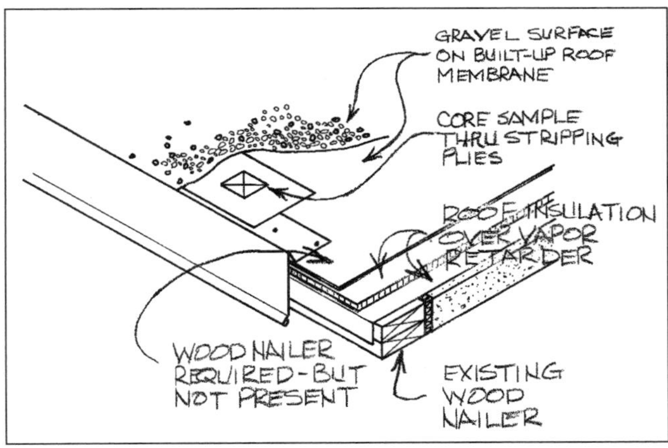

Figure 13.2 Roof edge, blocking, and insulation.

For built-up roofing examine the inner-ply moppings to determine if they are continuous and of correct thickness. Examine the roof felts for adhesion in the moppings and for rot. (See Sec. 7.1.)

For single-ply roofing, examine the membrane sheet for elasticity, for complete bonding of the sheets at seam locations, for puncture by mechanical fasteners, and for rot or delamination of the inner scrim from the elastomeric material.

Again, finding the reason that failure occurred is relevant, if for nothing else than your own knowledge. For example, if the built-up roof sample showed felt rot, it was because that area of roof was covered a majority of the time by a pond of water, or the interply moppings were insufficient and allowed water to infiltrate between the plies and remain, or . . . whatever the reason, find out why, so that you do not make the same mistake with your future designs.

Samples should also be taken of the membrane at the base flashing areas. The strip-in plies on the metal flashings should be examined via a sample.

Sometimes water is found entrapped between plies of the membrane at base flashing areas. Could the roof leaks be at this location? If so, how is it occurring? It may be a wall leak that is infiltrating the base flashing, making it appear as a roof leak.

Entire buildings have been reroofed, at great expense, only to continue to experience roof leaks. The leaks were found to be the result of plugged weep holes. Once the weep holes at the base flashings were cleared, at minimal expense, the building became watertight.

Find the roof leak. Verify it through sampling and examination of the sample. Plug and seal the sample area.

Plugging and sealing the sample area may not be simple for those who are inexperienced at roof repair. Also, evaluation of existing, in-place systems as described above may sometimes be difficult. One solution is to solicit the help of a material manufacturer's representative or ask for assistance from a local roof contractor. Both will help with rooftop advice and opinions of samples, conditions, and remedies. They have been trained and have experience (it is hoped) with roof repair. Certified roof consultants can also be very helpful at this stage.

13.1.4 Maintenance and Repair Surveys

OBJECTIVES

Many of the same procedures as required for a site/building/roof survey are required for a roof repair and maintenance survey. The objectives, being repair and maintenance of the existing system, can change from a repair and maintenance survey to a reroof survey, and vice versa, depending on the condition of the roof as discovered during the survey.

When performing a roof survey with the end result being roof repair and maintenance, the observation and evaluations used are even more specialized than those used during reroof survey. With a survey where roof replacement is the end result, the existing materials are considered from a point of view of usually being completely removed and replaced with new materials. In reroof survey, more attention is paid to the structure, geometry, location, and size of the roof components than to the existing waterproofing materials.

With a repair and maintenance survey, the objective is to utilize the existing, in-place roof materials and components as much as possible. The survey determines the roof area, system, component, or material in need of:

- Replacement (beyond the practical scope of repair or maintenance to restore watertight integrity)
- Repair (removal of limited amounts of deteriorated materials, leaving the majority of materials, systems, and/or components in place, and applying new materials in quantities to equal or exceed the original)
- Maintenance (application of material(s) to an existing component or system which has not been reworked as in repair, in order to allow it to continue to provide watertight service without rework)

The extent of the failure, as determined by the survey, establishes which of the three procedures is required.

A roof being surveyed and analyzed for necessary repair and maintenance procedures will usually be a roof which has proven it can function effectively. This can be a relatively new roof system (less than 5 years old) that is not leaking but the owner wants to maintain the initial investment. However, it is usually a roof in the 10-year range that is starting to experience some minor leaking. It can also be a roof in the later years of its life cycle that the client wants to repair and maintain in lieu of replacing. In such a case, the procedures may be ineffective, and wasted money and a dissatisfied client are the only results.

Upon completion of the survey, a roof repair and maintenance program is developed. If you are working within the parameters of an already established program, the end result of the survey will be specification and the extent of repairs and maintenance needed at present.

Life-cycle cost is an important consideration within a maintenance/repair program. Maintenance and repair work can become expensive. At a certain point, it is no longer cost-effective to repair and attempt maintenance. Most people consider the cutoff point to be in the 15 to 20 percent range of the total current roof replacement cost. This percentage is usually the total amount spent to date to keep the system effective. (See Sec. 2.1.4.)

INITIAL PROCEDURES

The same overall procedures of site, building, and roof survey, as described in Secs. 13.1 through 13.1.3, are required for maintenance survey. However, some items change.

Historical data gathering should be concentrated on, often requiring more time than a survey for reroofing. Any past reports, survey findings, and test results become very helpful in evaluating the rate of deterioration of the existing systems.

The success or failure of past repairs and maintenance, and the time span without problems after said work, are important and can usually be determined from interviews with building occupants, maintenance personnel, custodial staff, etc. The age of the roof and building as well as roof additions, structural additions, or modifications to the original design are important.

Another area where special interest should be shown is evaluation of the entire building envelope. As mentioned, wall leaks are common and sometimes can be mistaken for a roof leak.

The structural integrity of the system should be closely evaluated. It does no good to repair and maintain roof materials when the overall structure is defective and will need rework or adjustment. Structural capability inadequacies can destroy proper maintenance and repair work, making it appear that the work was ineffective.

MAINTENANCE AND REPAIR SURVEY PROCEDURES

The initial procedures as previously described should indicate whether the roof system is suitable for repair and maintenance work. The survey procedures described in the following will confirm the initial assumptions and define the scope of work to be performed.

Roof Leak Detection. Look inside the building to determine the area and location where water is coming through the roof decking. This is but an indication of where to start looking on the top side of the roof. Roof leaks can be many feet away from interior leak locations.

Roof leaks are normally found in the base flashing system around rooftop equipment or at the sheet metal flashing areas. Roof leaks can also be in the field of the roof membrane covering, especially in the case of roof blisters or roof rot.

Visual examination of leaking flashing areas usually reveals roof ply delamination, splits in the flashing membrane at underlying sheet metal joints, delamination of the membrane flashing from the structure to which it was once adhered, delamination of the flashing membrane joints, etc. Further verification of the roof leak area can be obtained by removal of a roof sample at the suspected leak location.

The location and extent of roof leaks can also be discovered and pinpointed by testing procedures. A moisture survey with capacitance, nuclear, or infrared thermography equipment will show areas of the roof that are most saturated with water from roof leaks. These tests are most effective when roof insulation is present under the roof membrane covering.

Another way to detect roof leak locations is by use of a moisture meter, such as the type commonly used to evaluate the moisture content of lumber, plaster, concrete, etc. This involves probing through the roof membrane to the level where roof leak moisture is residing. This underlying water can then be traced back to the source. This testing method will require roof repairs at the probe locations.

In repairs and maintenance, you must find the fault with the roof membrane covering, determine why it failed, and design proper and permanent procedures to correct the problem, not the event. For example, correcting the event may involve covering the hole or split in the membrane with plastic roof cement. Correcting the problem may mean replacing underlying components that caused the split or hole in the roof covering.

After the roof leak is found and the cause of failure is determined, the design of roof repairs can be correctly accomplished.

Roof Component Investigation. The entire roof surface must be examined. Special attention needs to be directed at flashing areas, such as the roof edge, roof and building wall intersection areas, base flashing at rooftop equipment, roof drains, and doorway and roof hatch access locations. Any place where the roof system is required to stop, abut, or terminate at or to another component is suspect.

If roof leaks are not occurring at these areas, it will probably be where they will start. The surveyor's job is to evaluate the extent of wear or extent of failure at these locations. The surveyor must then determine if roof repairs or roof maintenance are in order.

The surveyor needs to use other senses besides the eyes. As you walk across the roof surface, it is possible to detect wet underlying roof insulation by feel. Wet and soggy insulation will be softer than other roof areas. Good roof surveyors must see through the bottoms of their feet as well as through their eyes.

Evaluate any past repair areas. Try to determine what the intent of the repair was, if it was successful, and how long ago it was performed (another indication of success).

It should be assumed that the roof system, being installed at the same time by the same workers with the same materials, will probably be experiencing problems in the same type of locations as where past repairs have been performed. These areas should be closely examined by the surveyor for indications of problems, either present or future. Indicated past problems may not relate to future problems in building addition areas, equipment addition areas, or in the field of the roof.

If problems are occurring in the field of the roof, be especially observant. Evaluate material condition and composition closely. It is unusual for roof systems to experience problems in the field of the roof, away from problem areas such as flashings.

Problems isolated to the roof field area can indicate a problem during construction that may be restricted only to a specific area of the total roof system or a problem that will spread like a cancer, destroying the entire roof membrane. Problems such as improper roof membrane application in the field of the roof are often correctable only by roof replacement.

Associated Systems Investigation. Roof component investigation is not limited only to waterproofing materials, but must encompass all items on the roof. The waterproof integrity and water-shedding ability of items such as penthouse walls and equipment cowling covers are crucial to a dry building interior. Failure of an associated system to keep water from restricted areas can lead to roof damage and subsequent failure.

Also, as a service to your client, evaluate the surface maintenance needs of rooftop equipment. This is usually in the form of corrosion control of steel and metal components. Often mechanical rooftop equipment also needs replacement of deteriorated or missing bolts and screws, waterproofing gaskets, etc.

Sampling. Past survey reports are nice. So are original construction documents and shop drawings. As-built drawings are even nicer. However, too much is at stake for you to assume that the information and data provided to you are complete and accurate.

Confirm all assumptions made and all data presented by physical examination of roof components, materials, and systems. This requires core sampling of the roof system. The same cautions and procedures as described in Sec. 13.1.3 should be used.

13.1.5 Construction Site Inspection

INSPECTOR'S DUTIES

The main duty of the construction site inspector is to observe the construction process. This observation should result in roof system installation which conforms to:

- Architect's specification and drawings
- Industry standards
- Material manufacturer's requirements
- Accepted roofing practices

As discussed in Sec. 13.1.1, an inspector's duties are often more numerous than mere observation. An inspector must also be a good

- Communicator
- Record keeper
- Photographer
- Diplomat
- Mediator
- Systems tester

The inspector is normally retained by the owner. From a liability position, it is better for the designer if the owner employs the inspector. Therefore, the inspector's first responsibility is to the owner. It becomes the inspector's duty to work closely with the designer and the contractor.

An inspector's duties begin with review of the construction documents (ConDocs), submittals, and shop drawings. The designer should review all relevant aspects of the job with the inspector. It is important for a good line of communication to be established between the designer and the inspector.

The inspector should be present at the prejob conference. At the conference, the duties and responsibilities of the inspector should be made clear. If not included in the ConDocs, these duties and responsibilities should be put in writing and distributed to all parties.

The inspector typically does not have the authority to change specifications, drawings, or the requirements of the job. The inspector does not usually have the authority to issue change orders. The inspector normally does not have the authority to direct the manner in which the work is performed. If an inspector ever assumes, or attempts to assume, any of these duties or authority, without specific agreement and instruction from the designer and/or owner, it is probably best to immediately dismiss the inspector from service.

An inspector must fully comprehend the duties required of site inspection. The main purpose is quality control. In order to ensure quality control, the inspector should be at the job site at the same time as crew arrival and remain for the entire workday.

Documentation of the activities of the crew should be recorded by the inspector. The documentation should include:

- Number of workers
- Classification of workers
- Type of equipment used that day for construction or demolition
- Work performed
- Area of building worked on
- Weather conditions throughout the workday
- Problems encountered and their solutions
- Measurements, testing, and sampling performed and results thereof
- Any visits, comments, instructions, or changes from the owner, designer, or other interested parties. See Fig. 15.2 for an example of the form used as a *daily report*.

If change orders are required, the inspector can verify to the designer the scope of the change needed. The inspector verifies the amount of work and/or materials installed if there is a unit price cost involved in the job, such as deteriorated roof deck replacement.

The inspector verifies that the proper materials have been delivered to the job site. If improper, they should be marked and not brought up on the roof. The inspector verifies that the proper amount of materials are used in the construction, at locations and areas specified by the designer. Preparation of roof deck, metal flashings, parapet walls, wood nailers, and curbs, etc., are verified and approved by the inspector. Nothing should be installed to the roof system without the knowledge of and acceptance by the inspector.

If the inspector does not approve of the materials, components, or manner of installation, a problem exists which must be resolved. (See Sec. 13.1.1.) The first point of contact for the inspector is naturally the supervisor of the construction crew. However, the supervisor is under the direction of the contractor and the inspector cannot countermand any directions or instructions of the contractor to the supervisor.

If the inspector is unable to resolve the problems with the supervisor, the inspector communicates directly with the contractor. Hopefully the contractor will redirect the supervisor and the problem will be resolved. Notes on the problem and resolution are entered into the daily report of the inspector.

If the problem is not resolved between the inspector and the contractor, the inspector should immediately notify the designer. Photographs and documentation of unsatisfactory work and/or materials are recorded by the inspector. At this point, the inspector should take direction from the architect of record as to the course of action to be pursued.

The inspector, if employed by the owner, may also wish to notify the owner of problems, if problems have become of such magnitude as to possibly cause the involvement of the owner at a later date. However, the designer should have the best interests of the owner at heart, and problems should first be brought to the attention of the owner by the designer.

The inspector performs his or her duty when unsatisfactory conditions of construction are reported. It is the designer's duty to determine the means and manner of corrective measures required.

INSPECTOR QUALIFICATIONS

An inspector must be competent in many areas of construction. He or she must understand construction design, from the drawings and specifications, to the general requirements and legalities of such, to change orders, to submittals, to standards and codes.

Additionally, material manufacturers' requirements of product installation, accepted roofing practices, and industry standards must be fully understood by the inspector. The inspector should also be familiar with roof installation crafts, such as the mop, torch, kettle, sheet metal, single-ply, and roll personnel.

A perfect inspector would be an engineer or architect with several years of commercial building design experience who also has been a full-time commercial roofer for seven or more years, with a degree and experience in construction law, also having good people management skills. (If you know where this person is, let me know.) All of these qualifications will probably not be found in an inspector. However, a good inspector has knowledge and experience in all categories.

A qualified inspector is one of the best investments a building owner can make during roof construction. An unqualified inspector can be a detriment to an otherwise good job.

There are several good sources for qualified inspector referrals—and no, this does not mean the Yellow Pages. One good source is the Roof Consultants Institute in Raleigh, North Carolina. It has a directory of certified roof inspectors from across the United States. These people have attended classes and are trained in the duties, responsibilities, and means of performing roof construction inspection.

Another possible source is the local material manufacturer's representative. The manufacturer who is supplying roof materials to your project normally has a local representative in your area. This person will probably know of anyone locally who is qualified to perform roof inspection.

CONTRACTOR PERFORMING SITE INSPECTION

(See Sec. 15.3.2.) Construction contractors continually perform site inspection and use quality control procedures. However, some of the inspection and quality control are not to the standards sometimes wished by the designer or owner. When a construction system fails, the owner contacts the designer. The designer then usually investigates to determine the cause.

Fingers are pointed, accusations made. The designer blames failure on the contractor's workmanship because the design is proper, therefore failure must be the result of improper workmanship. The contractor states that it was installed correctly, according to the designer's specification. It must be the design that is incorrect.

It most often is a lack of proper workmanship that causes roof problems. A knowledgeable and professional roof contractor will not install a system that is improperly designed and which he or she knows will fail. In the event that an unexpected situation is encountered during construction, for which the design does not allow in enough detail to give full direction to the applicator, problems can arise, even if a professional contractor is doing the construction.

The author wishes to provide the theory and procedure which he believes may avert problems due to construction procedures, or which may reduce the liability exposure of the designer. Be forewarned that this procedure creates more work for the designer, and if not performed completely, may not reduce liability exposure and could increase it.

Negligence is a big word in the legal arena. If the designer is found to be negligent, even current omissions and errors (O&E) insurance may be insufficient to allay disaster. The best way to stay out of trouble is to avoid it. If a competent designer is aware of a problem at the job site involving the application of materials and systems, it must be assumed that the designer can rectify it. The big surprises come when you investigate a failed system and find materials that were installed incorrectly, in a situation which you were not aware existed. No one ever told you! Are you negligent because you did not monitor the job closely enough? Are you negligent because you did not see the situation before you issued a certificate of completion? Many other questions can be asked.

Of course, if a qualified site inspector had been present on the job site, you would have been made aware of the situation. You then could have figured out a solution, issued direction to the contractor, and everything would be fine. A site inspector was not on the project because of budget constraints. Now money and time are being spent on depositions, attorneys, consultants, etc.

However, we can make the contractor the site inspector. Using the form as shown in Fig. 15.2, or something similar, the designer can be made aware of the construction activities on a daily basis. On the form is the statement: "Jobsite Foreman or Superintendent must complete form daily. Misrepresentations will be grounds for barring same from Job site." Instructions within the ConDocs should require photographs with a day/date stamp to be taken during the course of the workday, showing the materials and systems being installed. Any unusual situation should be photographed.

If a problem arises or an unusual situation is uncovered, it must be noted on the form. In reviewing the form, the designer is made aware of any problems encountered during the workday. The form should be submitted daily to the designer. If no problems are reported, then the designer has every right to assume that all things are fine, and the finished product will be as expected.

If problems are encountered by the contractor and not reported on the form or with photographs, then the contractor is intentionally concealing situations of which the ConDocs require him or her to make the designer aware. How can the designer be negligent in duty and responsibility if the contractor took extra means and methods to conceal problem situations?

This process tends to shift some liability to the contractor and is a form of risk management partnering. Most competent contractors figure this out on about the second day into the job. They become much more communicative. They inform you of any unusual situations. They do not want any problems, and if there are problems, they may want you in the middle of it with them.

As stated earlier, this process often creates more project administration and change-order work for the designer. However, when the job is done, you are much more aware of what was installed and how it was applied.

If a roof warranty is required from the roof material manufacturer, send copies of daily reports along with duplicate copies of all photographs to the warranty department of the manufacturer. Send the information by registered mail and file the return receipt.

If a problem arises later, the manufacturer cannot state that it was unaware of such a situation and that warranty coverage does not apply to such. In such cases, you can reply with a smile on your face, "If you will kindly refer to daily report of (*date*) and subsequent photo #3, you can clearly see . . ." It must be assumed that the manufacturer was aware of such a situation since the documentation was sent to it before the warranty was issued.

The designer should customize the daily report for the type of roof system being installed. For example, a report form for the construction of a built-up roof, with hot asphalt mopping and equipment, will be different from a report form for a single-ply membrane with lap sealants and caulk.

Also, include a miniature roof plan drawing on the reverse side of the daily report form. The superintendent can use the roof plan to show where work was performed on that day. Include the form along with instructions and requirement within the ConDocs. Format the page so it is easily reproduced on an office copier.

Accurate and truthful information is important for this process to work. Make it clear to the contractor that if inaccuracies are discovered by you when on a site visit, you will bar the superintendent from the project site. This can cause problems for the contractor, who may have to put a person of less talent and ability on the job or move a better person from another job site.

Remember, all the designer wants to accomplish is an awareness of a problem before it gets covered up. By being aware of it, you can work with the contractor to fix it. This is in the best interest of the contractor, the owner, and the designer.

CHAPTER 14

Standards

14.1 GENERAL

ASTM

The American Society for Testing and Materials (ASTM) was established in 1898. It is one of the largest voluntary standards development organizations in the world. An annual membership fee is required by this nonprofit organization.

As a member of ASTM, a person is allowed to sit on any of the 131 standards-writing committees and have a voice and a vote in standards development and revision. Members normally include manufacturers, specifiers, consumers, and representatives of government agencies and academia.

ASTM is responsible for the annual publication of more than 9000 standards, published in 70 volumes (at time of this publication) divided into 16 sections. Each volume is titled *Annual Book of ASTM Standards*.

ASTM Headquarters is located at:

1916 Race Street
Philadelphia, Pennsylvania 19103
(215) 299-5454

ASTM has no research or testing facilities. Instead, many of the 35,000 technically qualified members voluntarily perform such duties.

There are three basic categories used by ASTM:

Standards. A document that has been developed and established within the consensus principles of the Society and that meets the approved requirements of ASTM procedures and regulations. The term *standard* serves as an adjective in the title of documents, such as "*standard* test method for" or "*standard* specifications for," to indicate specified consensus and approval. The various types of standard documents are based on the needs and usages as prescribed by the technical committees of the Society.

Proposal. A document that has been approved by the sponsoring committee for publication and comment prior to its consideration for adoption as a standard. Complete balloting procedures are not required to create a proposal.

Emergency standard. A document published by the Society to meet a demand for more rapid issuance of a specific standard document. The Executive Subcommittee of the sponsoring committee must recommend the publication of an emergency standard, and the Committee on Standards must concur in the recommendation. Emergency standards are not full consensus documents, because they are not submitted to Society ballot.

Under the three categories, there are six types of ASTM documents. The type of ASTM document which is developed and titled is based upon the technical content and intended use. ASTM documents will be one of the following types:

Classification. A systematic arrangement or division of materials, products, systems, or services into groups based upon similar characteristics such as origin, composition, properties, or use.

Guide. A series of options or instructions which do not recommend a specific course of action.

Practice. A definitive procedure for performing one or more specific operations or functions that does not produce a test result. (See *test method*.) A *practice* includes such things as procedures for conducting interlaboratory testing programs; procedures for writing statements on precision and bias; and procedures for selection, preparation, inspection, application, and necessary precautions for use or disposal, installation, maintenance, and operation of testing equipment.

Specification. A precise statement of a set of requirements to be satisfied by a material, product, system, or service which indicates the procedures for determining whether each of the requirements is satisfied.

Terminology. A document comprising definitions of terms, descriptions of terms, and explanations of symbols, abbreviations, and acronyms.

Test method. A definitive procedure for the identification, measurement, and evaluation of one or more qualities, characteristics, or properties of a material, product, system, or service that produces a test result. (See *practice*.)

In general, ASTM *specification* only defines the minimum and maximum tolerances of a material. The best quality material available cannot be determined by its conformance with this specification. Conformance with an ASTM specification only insures that minimum quality standards are met by the material.

Be aware of distinctions made between ASTM *specifications, test methods* and *practices*. For example, specifying a material to be in conformance with a test method, and not specifying the results required of the test method, negates quality control intentions.

FACTORY MUTUAL (FM)

Factory Mutual (FM) is most often referenced as a wind resistance standard within the roof industry. However, FM also issues standards for fire resistance and corrosion resistance, among many others, which are also sometimes referenced within specifications.

In Sec. 14.3.1 we review the main data sheet standards normally used within the roof industry. Fire ratings are only briefly referenced, since building code bodies normally set construction parameters for the general design community.

The Factory Mutual System is made up of several organizations, namely the FM Research Corporation, the FM Engineering Corporation, and the FM Engineering Association.

Factory Mutual's main purpose is property conservation. It prevents property losses by having strict standards by which buildings should be constructed, maintained, renovated, or repaired. In this regard FM is unique among other organizations. If the building is insured by FM, any construction design must be in compliance with all FM requirements.

We often make the mistake of referencing FM requirements within the specifications, such as *FM 1-90*. Merely stating that the roof system is to be constructed in compliance with FM 1-90 wind uplift resistance requirements is incorrect, and often impossible.

Most FM approval standards are based upon *total system* compliance. If all the components of the roof system have not been tested and approved by FM as a system, then the roof system cannot be constructed in compliance with FM 1-90 rating.

In order for a material or component to be approved for use by FM, the manufacturer normally has to pay a fee for testing by the Factory Mutual Research Corporation. The material is normally part of a roof system, and as such, the material can only be approved for use within that specific system. If the material is tested in another system, and that system passes FM testing, then that system can also be approved. Combining materials into a system not tested and approved by FM will void FM approval.

If the total roof system, including the roof deck, roof insulations (if any), fasteners, roof ply membrane, and surfacing have not been tested and approved as a roof system, then FM acceptance is not possible. Therefore, specifying the roof system to be in compliance with FM standards may not be possible if the exact same system as designed has not been tested and approved by FM.

14.2 ASTM SECTION OUTLINE

For ease of reference, this section outlines the most commonly referenced ASTM specifications, test methods, and practices as used for roof systems. Be aware of ASTM distinctions made between specifications, test methods, and practices. (See Sec. 14.1.1.)

14.2.1 ASPHALT PRODUCTS—MOPPING, COATING, AND SEALING

MOPPING ASPHALTS—HOT PROCESS

D 312-95a Standard Specification for Asphalt Used in Roofing

MOPPING ASPHALTS—COLD PROCESS

D 3019-94 Standard Specification for Lap Cement Used with Asphalt Roll Roofing

CUTBACK ASPHALT PRODUCTS

D 2822-91 Standard Specification for Asphalt Roof Cement

D 4586-93 Standard Specification for Asphalt Roof Cement—Asbestos Free

D 2824-94 Standard Specification for Aluminum-Pigmented Asphalt Roof Coatings

D 2823-90 Standard Specification for Asphalt Roof Coatings
D 4479-93 Standard Specification for Asphalt Roof Coatings—Asbestos Free
D 41-94 Standard Specification for Asphalt Primer Used in Roofing, Dampproofing, and Waterproofing

ASPHALT EMULSIONS

D 1187-97 Standard Specification for Asphalt-Base Emulsions for Use as Protective Coatings for Metal
D 1227-95 Standard Specification for Emulsified Asphalt Used as a Protective Coating for Roofing

14.2.2 ROOF FELTS, BASE AND CAP SHEETS, AND FABRIC MEMBRANES

ROOF FELTS—FIBERGLASS FELTS

D 2178-96 Standard Specification for Asphalt Glass Felt Used in Roofing and Waterproofing

ROOF FELTS—ORGANIC

D 4869-88 (1993)e1 Standard Specification for Asphalt-Saturated Organic Felt Shingle Underlayment Used in Roofing
D 226-95 Standard Specification for Asphalt-Saturated Organic Felt Used in Roofing and Waterproofing

BASE SHEETS

D 4601-97 Standard Specification for Asphalt-Coated Glass Fiber Base Sheet Used in Roofing
D 4897-97 Standard Specification for Asphalt-Coated Glass Fiber Venting Base Sheet Used in Roofing
D 2626-97 Standard Specification for Asphalt-Saturated and Coated Organic Felt Base Sheet Used in Roofing

CAP SHEETS/ROLL ROOFING

D 3909-97 Standard Specification for Asphalt Roll Roofing (Glass Felt) Surfaced with Mineral Granules
D 249-89 Standard Specification for Asphalt Roll Roofing (Organic Felt) Surfaced with Mineral Granules

MEMBRANES

D 4830-95 Standard Test Methods for Characterizing Thermoplastic Fabrics Used in Roofing and Waterproofing (Polyester)
D 1668-95 Standard Specification for Glass Fabrics (Woven and Treated) for Roofing and Waterproofing

14.2.3 COAL TAR PITCH ROOF PRODUCTS

D 4990-97 Standard Specification for Coal Tar Glass Felt Used in Roofing and Waterproofing
D 227-95 Standard Specification for Coal Tar-Saturated Organic Felt Used in Roofing and Waterproofing
D 450-96 Standard Specification for Coal Tar Pitch Used in Roofing, Dampproofing, and Waterproofing
D 4022-94 Standard Specification for Coal Tar Roof Cement, Asbestos-Containing
D 43-94 Standard Specification for Coal Tar Primer Used in Roofing, Dampproofing, and Waterproofing

14.2.4 MODIFIED BITUMEN MEMBRANES

D 1970-97 Standard Specification for Self-Adhering Polymer Modified Bituminous Sheet Materials Used as Steep Roofing Underlayment for Ice Dam Protection
D 5147-95 Standard Test Method for Sampling and Testing Modified Bituminous Sheet Material

14.2.5 ROOF MEMBRANE SURFACINGS

D 2824-94 Standard Specification for Aluminum-Pigmented Asphalt Roof Coatings
D 2823-90 Standard Specification for Asphalt Roof Coatings
D 4479-93 Standard Specification for Asphalt Roof Coatings—Asbestos Free
D 1863-93 Standard Specification for Mineral Aggregate Used on Built-up Roofs

14.2.6 QUALITY CONTROL REFERENCES

D 3617-83 (1994)e1 Standard Practice for Sampling and Analysis of New Built-up Roof Membranes
D 5295-92 Standard Guide for Preparation of Concrete Surfaces for Adhered (Bonded) Membrane Waterproofing Systems

14.2.7 SHEET METAL PRODUCTS

A 792/A792M-96 Standard Specification for Steel Sheet, 55% Aluminum-Zinc Alloy-Coated by the Hot-Dip Process
B 209-96 Standard Specification for Aluminum and Aluminum-Alloy Sheet and Plate
A 167-96 Standard Specification for Stainless and Heat-Resisting Chromium-Nickel Steel Plate, Sheet, and Strip
A 525-A361 Standard Specification for Sheet Steel Hot-Dipped Galvanized Coated
B 370-92e1 Standard Specification for Copper Sheet and Strip for Building Construction
B 101-96 Standard Specification for Lead-Coated Copper Sheet and Strip for Building Construction

14.2.8 METAL ROOFING PRODUCTS

ROOF SYSTEM TEST METHOD STANDARDS

E 1592-95 Standard Test Method for Structural Performance of Sheet Metal Roof and Siding Systems by Uniform Static Air Pressure Difference
E 1646-95 Standard Test Method for Water Penetration of Exterior Metal Roof Panel Systems by Uniform Static Air Pressure Difference
E 331-96 Standard Test Method for Water Penetration of Exterior Windows, Curtain Walls, and Doors by Uniform Static Air Pressure Difference
E 1680-95 Standard Test Method for Rate of Air Leakage Through Exterior Metal Roof Panel Systems
E 283-91 Standard Test Method for Determining the Rate of Air Leakage Through Exterior Windows, Curtain Walls, and Doors under Specified Pressure Differences across the Specimen

METAL PANEL COATING FINISH—PHYSICAL PROPERTIES

D 523-89 (1994)e1 Standard Test Method for Specular Gloss
D 3359-95a Standard Test Method for Measuring Adhesion by Tape
D 2794-93 Standard Test Method for Resistance of Organic Coatings to the Effects of Rapid Deformation (Impact)

ABUSE TOLERANCE

D 968-93 Standard Test Method for Abrasion Resistance of Organic Coatings by Falling Abrasive

CORROSION, CHEMICAL, AND POLLUTION RESISTANCE

D 1308-87 (1993)e1 Standard Test Method for Effect of Household Chemicals on Clear and Pigmented Organic Finishes

D 2247-94 Standard Practice for Testing Water Resistance of Coatings in 100 Percent Relative Humidity

WEATHERING PROPERTIES

D 822-89 Standard Practice for Conducting Tests on Paint and Related Coatings and Materials Using Filtered Open-Flame Carbon-Arc Exposure Apparatus

D 4214-89 Standard Test Method for Evaluating the Degree of Chalking of Exterior Paint Films

14.2.9 ROOF INSULATIONS

REFERENCES FOR ROOF INSULATION PROPERTIES

C 165-95 Standard Test Method for Measuring Compressive Properties of Thermal Insulation

D 1621-94 Standard Test Method for Compressive Properties of Rigid Cellular Plastics

D 2126-94 Standard Test Method for Response of Rigid Cellular Plastics to Thermal and Humid Aging

C 177-85 (1993)e1 Standard Test Method for Steady-State Heat Flux Measurement and Thermal Transmission Properties by Means of the Guarded-Hot-Plate Apparatus

C 203-92 Standard Test Methods for Breaking Load and Flexural Properties of Block-Type Thermal Insulation

C 209-92 Standard Test Methods for Cellulosic Fiber Insulating Board

E 96-95 Standard Test Method for Water Vapor Transmission of Materials

E 84-96a Standard Test Method for Surface Burning Characteristics of Building Materials

ROOF INSULATION STANDARDS

C 208-95 Standard Specification for Cellulosic Fiber Insulating Board

C 552-91 Standard Specification for Cellular Glass Thermal Insulation

C 578-95 Standard Specification for Rigid Cellular Polystyrene Thermal Insulation

C 591-94 Standard Specification for Unfaced Preformed Rigid Cellular Polyurethane Thermal Insulation (Polyiso)

C 289-95 Standard Specification for Membrane-Faced Rigid Cellular Polyisocyanurate Thermal Insulation Board (Polyiso)

C 726-93 Standard Specification for Mineral Fiber Roof Insulation Board

C 728-91 Standard Specification for Perlite Thermal Insulation

C 1289-95 Standard Specification for Perlite Board and Rigid Cellular Polyurethane Roof Insulation

C 1050-91 Standard Specification for Rigid Cellular Polystyrene-Cellulosic Fiber Composite Roof Insulation

C 1126-89 Standard Specification for Faced or Unfaced Rigid Cellular Phenolic Thermal Insulation

14.2.1 Asphalt Products—Mopping, Coating, and Sealing

MOPPING ASPHALTS—HOT PROCESS

ASTM D 312-95a Standard Specification for Asphalt Used in Roofing. Asphalt used as the interply mopping bitumen between roof felts and roof membranes and as the top pour coating for built-up roof assemblies should conform to the requirements of ASTM D 312.

Type I, Type II, Type III, and Type IV asphalts (see Sec. 4.1.4) should comply with the requirements of this ASTM specification. The requirements of the specification are further defined by the following ASTM standards:

D 5 Test Method for Penetration of Bituminous Materials

D 36 Test Method for Softening Point of Bitumen

D 92 Test Method for Fire and Flash Points by Cleveland Open Cup Method

D 113 Test Method for Ductility of Bituminous Materials

D 140 Practice for Sampling Bituminous Materials

D 2024 Test Method for Solubility of Asphalt Materials in Trichloroethylene

Characteristics. The different types of asphalt are suited for different roof slopes, based upon softening point ranges of the asphalt type:

Type I. Roof slopes up to ½:12 in.

Type II. Roof slopes up to 1½:12 in.

Type III. Roof slopes up to 3:12 in.

Type IV. Roof slopes up to 6:12 in.

Use of these slope guideline requirements must be evaluated against high temperature extremes which will exist at the installed roof surface. Such temperature extremes are influenced by, but not limited to, roof insulations, building interior uses, orientation of the roof plane surface, type and color of roof surfacing material used, and so on. Follow local practices in selecting the type of asphalt bitumen to use. (See Sec. 4.1.4.) Some types may have a longer working life than other types, based upon the conditions within which the installed product exists.

MOPPING ASPHALTS—COLD PROCESS

ASTM D 3019-94 Standard Specification for Lap Cement Used with Asphalt Roll Roofing. Asphalt used as the interply adhesive bitumen, normally brush-applied or sprayed, between roof felts and roof membranes and sometimes as the top pour coating for cold-process built-up roof assemblies should conform to the requirements of ASTM D 3019-94.

Type I, Grades 1 and 2, Type II, and Type III cold-process adhesive asphalts should comply with the requirements of this ASTM specification. The requirements of the specification are further defined by the following ASTM standards:

D 4 Test Method for Bitumen Content

D 36 Test Method for Softening Point of Bitumen

D 95 Test Method for Water in Petroleum Products and Bituminous Materials by Distillation

D 140 Practice for Sampling Bituminous Materials

D 146 Test Methods for Sampling and Testing Bitumen-Saturated Felts and Woven Fabrics for Roofing and Waterproofing

D 249 Specification for Asphalt Roll Roofing (Organic) Surfaced with Mineral Granules; Wide Selvedge

D 402 Test Method for Distillation of CutBack Asphaltic (Bituminous) Products

Characteristics. *Type I* cutback asphalt (see Sec. 4.6) is nonfibered, and as such is more suited to be used as a coating than as an interply adhesive.

Type I, Grade 1 cutback asphalt is made from air blown asphalt, whereas *Type I, Grade 2* is made from the less common steam-refined or vacuum-reduced asphalt bitumen material.

Type II cutback asphalt adhesive *contains asbestos fibers.*

Type III cutback asphalt adhesive does not contain asbestos, and is the most common type of asphalt cold-process adhesive used.

Some cutback adhesives contain polymers and are specified for use with polymer modified bitumen roof membrane systems, such as SBS modified bitumen membranes.

CUTBACK ASPHALT PRODUCTS

ASTM D 2822-91 Standard Specification for Asphalt Roof Cement. Sometimes referred to as *plastic roof cement* or *trowel grade roof cement,* this material is used at roof flashings and other areas of the roof where extra stress and strain can be expected. (See Sec. 4.1.5.) Roof cement must contain mineral stabilizers and sometimes fibers, and the material produced under this specification often contains asbestos.

Type I (Class I and Class II) and Type II (Class I and Class II) asphalt roof cement should comply with the requirements of this ASTM specification. The requirements of the specification are further defined by the following ASTM standards:

D 4 Test Method for Bitumen Content

D 95 Test Method for Water in Petroleum Products and Bituminous Materials by Distillation

D 140 Practice for Sampling Bituminous Materials

D 312 Specification for Asphalt Used in Roofing

D 449 Specification for Asphalt Used in Dampproofing and Waterproofing

D 946 Specification for Penetration-Grade Asphalt Cement for Use in Pavement Construction

D 3409 Test Method for Adhesion of Asphalt Roof Cement to Damp, Wet, or Underwater Surfaces

Characteristics. *Type I* roof cement is made from more ductile roof asphalt bitumen than is Type II.

Type II roof cement is made from asphalt bitumen with a higher temperature softening point, and as such is more often used as a *flashing* cement where vertical walls are coated with the cement material. However, both types are tested in an oven on a vertical surface for five hours and must not sluff or slide from the vertical surface to detrimental extents, for example:

ASTM D 2822-91

7 Physical Requirements

7.3 *Behavior at 140°F* The cement shall show no evidence of blistering, and sag or slide shall be no greater than 6 mm (¼ in).

Under both Type I and Type II there is Class I and Class II. *Class I* is used for application to essentially dry surfaces, and *Class II* is used for application to damp, wet, or underwater surfaces.

This material *may or may not contain asbestos.*

ASTM D 4586-93 Standard Specification for Asphalt Roof Cement—Asbestos Free. Virtually the same material, used for the same purposes, as roof cement containing asbestos (see preceding), with the exception that the material is not tested for or required to adhere to wet, damp, or underwater surfaces. The requirements of this ASTM specification are defined by the same ASTM standards listed under ASTM 2822-91, with exception that Test Method D 3409 is not used.

Type I and Type II are defined by the ductility of the asphalt from which the cement product is made (as with 2822-91), but Class I and Class II do not exist since this material is not for use on damp, wet, or underwater surfaces. Another difference is that asbestos-free roof cement may contain less asphalt (approximately 5 percent) than roof cement containing asbestos. However, this difference is at the discretion of the manufacturer; the ASTM specification only defines minimum and/or maximum tolerances.

ASTM D 2824-94 Standard Specification for Aluminum-Pigmented Asphalt Roof Coatings. Normally referred to as *aluminum roof coating,* this material is often used on smooth-surfaced roof systems as the protective surfacing.

Type I, Type II, and Type III aluminum roof coating should comply with the requirements of this ASTM specification. The requirements of the specification are further defined by the following ASTM standards:

- D 4 Test Method for Bitumen Content
- D 95 Test Method for Water in Petroleum Products and Bituminous Materials by Distillation
- D 140 Practice for Sampling Bituminous Materials
- D 562 Test Method for Consistency of Paints Using the Stormer Viscometer
- D 962 Specification for Aluminum Pigments, Powder and Paste, for Paints
- D 2823 Specification for Asphalt Roof Coatings
- D 3279 Test Method for *n*-Heptane Insolubles
- E 200 Practice for Preparation, Standardization, and Storage of Standard Solutions for Chemical Analysis

Characteristics. The reflective ability of aluminum roof coating is greatly influenced by the type and the amount of aluminum leaf pigments within the material. Under this specification, *Type I* is required to contain a minimum of 11 percent aluminum, and *Type II* and *Type III* are required to contain a minimum of 9 percent aluminum. However, Type I may be nonfibered, which often indicates a material of less durable nature. Like all roof coatings, aluminum roof coating is sacrificial, and will need to be reapplied periodically.

Type I. Nonfibered, containing no asbestos.

Type II. Fibered, *containing asbestos fiber.*

Type III. Fibered, containing no asbestos fiber.

ASTM D 2823-90 Standard Specification for Asphalt Roof Coatings. Roof coatings are a cutback asphalt product (see Sec. 6.1.3) but are not intended as an adhesive material, as are roof cements or lap cements. Roof coatings are sometimes used by maintenance personnel to attempt temporary roof repairs or as a maintenance coating applied to the top of asphalt roof systems.

Type I and Type II asphalt roof coating should comply with the requirements of this ASTM specification. The requirements of the specification are further defined by the following ASTM standards:

- D 4 Test Method for Bitumen Content
- D 95 Test Method for Water in Petroleum Products and Bituminous Materials by Distillation
- D 140 Practice for Sampling Bituminous Materials
- D 224 Specification for Smooth-Surfaced Asphalt Roll Roofing (Organic Felt)
- D 312 Specification for Asphalt Used in Roofing
- D 449 Specification for Asphalt Used in Dampproofing and Waterproofing
- D 562 Test Method for Consistency of Paints Using the Stormer Viscometer
- D 946 Specification for Penetration-Grade Asphalt Cement for Use in Pavement Construction
- E 1 Specification for ASTM Thermometers

Characteristics. *Type I* asphalt roof coatings are made from asphalt with low softening points, such as Type I mopping asphalt per ASTM D 312.

Type II asphalt roof coatings are made from asphalt with higher softening points than those used for Type I coatings. Type II asphalt roof coatings may be more suited to inclined roof surfaces. Under this specification, fibrous material within the material *may be asbestos.* The coating is suitable for application by brush, mop, or spray equipment.

ASTM D 4479-93 Standard Specification for Asphalt Roof Coatings—Asbestos Free. The material produced in conformance with this ASTM specification is the same as the asphalt roof coating produced under ASTM 2823-90, with the exception that no asbestos fillers or fibers are contained within the finished product.

ASTM D 41-94 Standard Specification for Asphalt Primer Used in Roofing, Dampproofing, and Waterproofing. A cutback asphalt, this material is essential in coating and preparation of surfaces prior to application of asphalt roofing bitumens. Primer is also sometimes used to separate dissimilar metals. Asphalt primer should comply with the requirements of this ASTM specification. The requirements of the specification are further defined by the following ASTM standards:

- D 5 Test Method for Penetration of Bituminous Materials
- D 88 Test Method for Saybolt Viscosity
- D 95 Test Method for Water in Petroleum Products and Bituminous Materials by Distillation
- D 402 Test Method for Distillation of Cutback Asphaltic (Bituminous) Products
- D 2042 Test Method for Solubility of Asphalt in Trichloroethylene

Characteristics. Some primers are more quick-drying than others. For reroof situations, where the removed roof must be reinstalled the same day, specifying a quick-dry primer conforming to this specification will help to provide that proper roof practices are followed by the roof installer.

ASPHALT EMULSIONS

ASTM D 1187-97 Standard Specification for Asphalt-Base Emulsions for Use as Protective Coatings for Metal. Asphalt emulsion is a good and durable protector of metal roof panels, often applied as a maintenance finish after the original coating has deteriorated or as the base coat of a dual-coating maintenance finish. Emulsion coatings dry dull black.

Emulsions suitable for coating of metal roof panels should comply with the requirements of this ASTM specification. The requirements of the specification are further defined by the following ASTM standards:

C 150 Specification for Portland Cement

D 2939 Test Methods for Emulsified Bitumen Used as Protective Coatings

Characteristics. Asphalt emulsion is noted for failure occurrences due to ponding water, which often causes the emulsion material to dissolve and, therefore, dissipate. Emulsion is also noted for its excellent adhesion to many types of surfaces and its excellent durability characteristics when installed in proper situations. Type I and Type II emulsion coatings are available.

Type I is suitable for continuous exposure to *water* within a few days after application and drying.

Type II is suitable for continuous exposure to the *weather* only after application and drying.

Note that Type I is suitable for *continuous* exposure to water. Ponding-water situations on a roof do not provide continuous exposure, but instead cause cyclic exposure, which will probably dissipate this material type. Also, ponding-water situations should never occur on a metal roof panel.

ASTM D 1227-95 Standard Specification for Emulsified Asphalt Used as a Protective Coating for Roofing. Asphalt emulsion is often used for a surface coating base on asphalt built-up roof systems, as well as on modified bitumen roof membrane systems. Because it dries dull black, the emulsion is often coated with aluminum roof coating. Some asphalt emulsions are manufactured with aluminum flake pigments, allowing a one-step reflective coating process. (See Sec. 6.1.3.)

Type I through Type IV asphalt emulsion should comply with the requirements of this ASTM specification. The requirements of the specification are further defined by the following ASTM standard:

D 2939 Test methods for Emulsified Bitumen Used as Protective Coatings

Characteristics. Asphalt emulsion as normally used in roof construction is available in four types, Type I through Type IV. Being water soluble, the material must dry completely before exposure to rain. Temperature, humidity, and application rates affect drying time.

Ponding water can cause the emulsion coating to dissipate. Not recommended for water-covered roof systems.

Very resistant to ultraviolet attack from sunlight and also effectively resists many airborne chemical and corrosive elements. Adheres well to many roof materials, including aged membranes.

Type I may contain asbestos fibers. It is suitable for application by brush, spray equipment, or mop, and can be applied to all roof slopes, including vertical.

Type II does not contain asbestos fibers. Instead, it normally contains mineral fillers and fibers, and is different from the other types in that the emulsifier is chemical instead of a mineral colloid. Type II can be applied with spray equipment and is suitable for roof slopes up to 6:12 in.

Type III does not contain any fibrous reinforcement. As such, it requires an open-mesh fabric when installed on steep or vertical surfaces. It is suitable for application by brush or spray equipment.

Type IV is the most commonly specified asphalt emulsion used for roof construction. This material contains mineral fillers and fibrous reinforcement, is applied by brush, spray equipment, or mop, and is suitable for all roof slopes, including vertical.

14.2.2 Roof Felts, Base and Cap Sheets, and Fabric Membranes

ROOF FELTS—FIBERGLASS FELTS

ASTM D 2178-96 Standard Specification for Asphalt Glass Felt Used in Roofing and Waterproofing. Fiberglass roof felts are the most common roof ply materials used in built-up roof systems. (See Sec. 7.1.2.) Type III, Type IV, and Type VI fiberglass roof felts should comply with the requirements of this ASTM specification. The requirements of the specification are further defined by the following ASTM standards:

D 146 Test Methods for Sampling and Testing Bitumen-Saturated Felts and Woven Fabrics for Roofing and Waterproofing

D 312 Specification for Asphalt Used in Roofing

D 449 Specification for Asphalt Used in Waterproofing

Characteristics

PHYSICAL PROPERTIES

	Type III	*Type IV*	*Type VI*
Breaking strength (minimum), lbf/in			
Longitudinal	22	44	60
Transverse	22	44	60
Pliability		No failures	

ROOF FELTS—ORGANIC

ASTM D 4869-88 (1993)e1 Standard Specification for Asphalt-Saturated Organic Felt Shingle Underlayment Used in Roofing. Referred to as *organic felt,* this material is to be used only as a separator sheet between the roof deck and the roof shingles. Thin and lightweight, this felt is not durable as a *dry-in* material. For more durable and waterproof organic felt, see ASTM 226-95.

ASTM defines the two types of organic felt available under this specification as Type I and Type II; however, they are more commonly referred to (incorrectly) as #15 and #30 organic felt. Be aware that they are to be considered utility-grade felts, suitable only as underlayment. (See Sec. 7.1.1.) Type I and Type II organic shingle roof felts should comply with the requirements of this ASTM specification. The requirements of the specification are further defined by the following ASTM standards:

- D 146 Test Methods for Sampling and Testing Bitumen-Saturated Felts and Woven Fabrics for Roofing and Waterproofing
- D 1922 Test Method for Propagation Tear Resistance of Plastic Film and Thin Sheeting by Pendulum Method
- E 96 Test Methods for Water Vapor Transmission of Materials

Characteristics. *Type I* is a thin organic felt. It should only be used on a wood roof deck where composition shingle installation is soon to follow and where keeping contents of the building interior dry before shingle application is not a major concern.

Type II is twice as heavy as Type I. As such it will perform better in resisting wind forces and roof traffic. However, it may be better design practice to specify #30 organic felt per ASTM 226 if keeping the building interior dry during construction is important.

PHYSICAL PROPERTIES

	Type I	*Type II*
Tear strength (minimum), lbf/in	0.44	0.88
Net mass of felt (minimum), lb/100 ft^2	8.0	20.0

ASTM D 226-95 Standard Specification for Asphalt-Saturated Organic Felt Used in Roofing and Waterproofing. Before the advent of fiberglass felts, #15 perforated organic felt was the type of roof ply used in built-up roof membranes. Today we use organic felts as *dry-in* sheets, with the materials under this specification being used when heavy-duty organic felt plies are needed.

Type I (#15) felt is available in both nonperforated (plain) and perforated. Perforated should be used when installing the felt into hot moppings of asphalt, although fiberglass felt (see Sec. 7.1.2) is more suited to this application.

Type II (#30) felt is often used as the underlayment for tile, slate, or wood shake roof systems. It is sometimes used in a double layer system for a tile roof system where a durable water-shedding underlayment system is required. (Also used are organic base sheets per ASTM 2626-97; see Sec. 11.2.)

Type I, usually referred to as #15, and Type II, usually referred to as #30, organic roof felts should comply with the requirements of this ASTM specification. The requirements of the specification are further defined by the following ASTM standards:

- D 70 Test Method for Specific Gravity and Density of Semi-Solid Bituminous Materials
- D 146 Test Methods for Sampling and Testing Bitumen-Saturated Felts and Woven Fabrics for Roofing and Waterproofing
- D 312 Specification for Asphalt Used in Roofing
- D 449 Specification for Asphalt Used in Dampproofing and Waterproofing
- D 727 Test Method for Kerosene Number of Roofing and Flooring Felt by the Vacuum Method

Characteristics. Type I (#15) felt does not remain waterproof as long as Type II (#30) felt when used as a dry-in sheet on a sloped wood roof deck. #30 felt, being thicker, also resists roof top traffic and wind blow-off better. (See Sec. 8.1.1.)

PHYSICAL PROPERTIES

	Type I	*Type II*
Average breaking strength (minimum), lbf/in		
With fiber grain	30	40
Across fiber grain	15	20
Net mass of felt (minimum), lb/100 ft^2	11.5	26
Mass of saturant	6.2	15.0
Mass of desaturated felt	5.2	10.0

BASE SHEETS

ASTM D 4601-97 Standard Specification for Asphalt-Coated Glass Fiber Base Sheet Used in Roofing. Base sheets are used as the bottom ply in a roof system, normally being installed in a single layer with subsequent roof plies or membranes installed on their surface. Fiberglass base sheets may or may not be required, depending upon the substrate over which the roof membrane is being installed, the number of roof felt plies being specified, and other job-specific conditions. (See Sec. 7.1.2.)

Type I and Type II fiberglass base sheets should comply with the requirements of this ASTM specification. The requirements of the specification are further defined by the following ASTM standards:

D 146 Test Methods for Sampling and Testing Bitumen-Saturated Felts and Woven Fabrics for Roofing and Waterproofing

D 228 Test Methods for Asphalt Roll Roofing, Cap Sheets, and Shingles

Characteristics

PHYSICAL PROPERTIES

	Type I	*Type II*
Breaking strength (minimum), lbf/in		
Longitudinal	22	44
Transverse	22	44
Pliability, ½-in radius	No failures	
Net dry mass (minimum), lb/100 ft^2	13.4	15.5
Asphalt (minimum), lb/100 ft^2	5.6	7.0

ASTM D 4897-97 Standard Specification for Asphalt-Coated Glass Fiber Venting Base Sheet Used in Roofing. Venting base sheets are used to cover a roof deck where moisture vapor pressure can be expected within the roof deck assembly; for example, a lightweight concrete roof deck or a roof deck that has experienced roof leaks and subsequent water absorption. In theory, when the moisture vapor permeates from the roof deck, it will be directed to the roof perimeter by the venting base sheet, causing no harm to the roof membrane and insulation system. Venting base sheets are manufactured as Type I and Type II. Both types should comply with the requirements of this ASTM specification. The requirements of the specification are further defined by the following ASTM standards:

D 146 Test Methods for Sampling and Testing Bitumen-Saturated Felts and Woven Fabrics for Roofing and Waterproofing

D 228 Test Methods for Asphalt Roll Roofing, Cap Sheets, and Shingles

Characteristics

PHYSICAL PROPERTIES

	Type I	*Type II*
Breaking strength (minimum), lbf/in		
Longitudinal	22	44
Transverse	22	44
Net dry mass (minimum), lb/100 ft^2	13.4	15.5
Asphalt (minimum), lb/100 ft^2	10	12
Any roofing in shipment (minimum), lb/100 ft^2	50	55

Venting base sheet is not fully adhered to the roof deck or deck substrate, since this would prevent gas venting along the underside of the sheet. This is a specialized material, and consideration must be given to job-specific requirements, such as—but not limited to—the wind blow-off resistance of the roof membrane system applied to this partially attached sheet.

ASTM D 2626-97 Standard Specification for Asphalt-Saturated and Coated Organic Felt Base Sheet Used in Roofing. Organic base sheets are sometimes used as the first base ply in a built-up roof system and are sometimes fully adhered in asphalt mopping to create a vapor barrier under roof insulation systems. They are also sometimes used as the waterproofing underlayment of tile and slate roof systems.

Organic base sheet material should comply with the requirements of this ASTM specification. The requirements of the specification are further defined by the following ASTM standards:

D 146 Test Methods for Sampling and Testing Bitumen-Saturated Felts and Woven Fabrics for Roofing and Waterproofing

D 228 Test Methods for Asphalt Roll Roofing, Cap Sheets, and Shingles

E 96 Test Methods for Water Vapor Transmission of Materials

Characteristics. Organic base sheet is a waterproof roofing sheet, unlike a fiberglass base sheet which sometimes (although not always) has pinholes in the sheet where the asphalt coating is not complete. Organic base sheets often fall within a 40-lb weight category, with a common type of organic base sheet referred to as *#43 base sheet* within the roof industry.

The minimum weight requirements for the roof sheet, per this ASTM Specification, is 37 lb/100 ft^2. Organic base sheets are thicker than fiberglass base sheets, but are not as strong with regard to tensile strength. They can be obtained with perforations to aid in the release of gases created by hot asphalt mopping installation.

CAP SHEETS/ROLL ROOFING

ASTM D 3909-97 Standard Specification for Asphalt Roll Roofing (Glass Felt) Surfaced with Mineral Granules. Fiberglass cap sheets are used to surface a completed roof system, normally an asphalt built-up roof system. They can also be used as the top surface ply layer of base and wall flashings of asphalt built-up roof systems. The mineral surfacing applied at the factory is provided in colors ranging from white to black.

There are no different types or classes of cap sheets. The mineral-surfaced roll roofing cap sheet should conform to the requirements of this specification. The requirements of the specification are further defined by the following ASTM standard:

D 228 Test Methods for Asphalt Roll Roofing, Cap Sheets, and Shingles

Characteristics. Keeping the rolls stored on end prior to application is important in avoiding transverse splitting or cracking of the cap sheet. Fully adhering the roll in a complete mopping of either hot or cold process is important. Roof inspection and maintenance and repair is made easy with a cap sheet surfacing. (See Sec. 7.1.2.)

ASTM D 249-89 Standard Specification for Asphalt Roll Roofing (Organic Felt) Surfaced with Mineral Granules. This material is usually referred to as *roll roofing* instead of cap sheet, because the roof sheet is often the total waterproofing membrane of the roof and not the cap sheet of a roof membrane system. The roof sheet material is often installed on utility structures, such as sheds, being placed directly on top of an organic roof felt sheet such as is used under composition shingle roofing. The top and bottom edge of the cap sheet is nailed to the roof with tacks, and the seams of the cap sheet may or may not be sealed with roof cement.

There are two types of organic mineral-surfaced roll roofing available. The roll roofing sheet should conform to the requirements of this specification. The requirements of the specification are further defined by the following ASTM standard:

D 146 Test Methods for Sampling and Testing Bitumen-Saturated Felts and Woven Fabrics for Roofing and Waterproofing

D 228 Test Methods for Asphalt Roll Roofing, Cap Sheets, and Shingles

D 3019 Specification for Lap Cement Used with Asphalt Roll Roofing

Characteristics. *Type I* organic felt asphalt roll roofing with mineral granules must weigh a minimum of 74.0 lb/100 ft^2, weighing only the area covered by the granules.

Type II organic felt asphalt roll roofing with mineral granules must weigh a minimum of 71.5 lb/100 ft^2, weighing only the area covered by the granules.

MEMBRANES

ASTM D 4830-95 Standard Test Methods for Characterizing Thermoplastic Fabrics Used in Roofing and Waterproofing (Polyester). This ASTM reference governs polyester membranes sometimes used in roof systems. Polyester membranes can be used as the roof felt membrane in cold-process asphalt built-up roof systems, as well as for the membrane plies in base flashing details. (See Sec. 7.1.3.) Polyester membranes are often specified as part of a specialty roof system as provided by a specific manufacturer.

The characteristics of a polyester membrane, being a thermoplastic material, are defined by use of this test method. No minimum or maximum tolerances are prescribed as with an ASTM specification. Therefore, merely referencing this method will not define the quality desired of a polyester membrane.

This method tests seven characteristics of thermoplastic membranes:

1. Unit mass
2. Breaking load, elongation, and work-to-break
3. Trapezoid tearing strength
4. Simulated asphalt retention
5. Puncture strength
6. Static heat stability
7. Dynamic heat stability

This method uses the following ASTM standards to further define the characteristics being tested:

D 76 Specification for Tensile Testing Machines for Textiles

D 629 Test Methods for Quantitative Analysis of Textiles

D 751 Method of Testing Coated Fabrics D 885—Methods of Testing Tire Cords, Tire Cord Fabrics, and Industrial Filament Yarns Made from Man-Made Organic-Base Fibers

D 1117 Methods of Testing Non-Woven Fabrics

D 1682 Test Methods for Breaking Load and Elongation of Textile Fabrics

D 1776 Practice for Conditioning Textiles for Testing

D 4354 Practice for Sampling of Geosynthetics for Testing

Characteristics. Polyester membranes have excellent elongation and tear resistance. They work extremely well with cold-process roof products.

ASTM D 1668-95 Standard Specification for Glass Fabrics (Woven and Treated) for Roofing and Waterproofing. Often referred to as *fiberglass membrane,* this material is often used in conjunction with plastic roof cement. It is used as a reinforcing mesh within troweled layers of the roof cement. In the past, it was common practice to seal parapet wall interiors with two layers of plastic roof cement with corresponding layer applications of fiberglass membrane.

There are three types of woven and treated fiberglass fabric governed by this specification:

Type I. Asphalt treated.

Type II. Coal tar pitch treated.

Type III. Organic-resin treated.

14.2.3 Coal Tar Pitch Roof Products

ASTM D 4990-97 Standard Specification for Coal Tar Glass Felt Used in Roofing and Waterproofing. Tarred fiberglass felts are the predominant type of roof felt used in a coal tar pitch built-up roof system. There is only one type.

Type I fiberglass tarred felt should comply with the requirements of this ASTM specification. The requirements of the specification are further defined by the following ASTM standards:

D 146 Test Methods for Sampling and Testing Bitumen-Saturated Felts and Woven Fabrics for Roofing and Waterproofing

D 450 Specification for Coal Tar Pitch Used in Roofing, Dampproofing, and Waterproofing

Characteristics

PHYSICAL PROPERTIES

Breaking strength (minimum), lbf/in	*Type I*
Longitudinal	44
Transverse	44
Pliability	No failures

ASTM D 227-95 Standard Specification for Coal Tar-Saturated Organic Felt Used in Roofing and Waterproofing. Until the advent of fiberglass felts, this was the predominant type of roof felt used in a coal tar pitch built-up roof system. Resaturation of a coal tar pitch built-up roof system is best accomplished if organic roof felts are present instead of fiberglass felts.

Commonly referred to as *tarred organic felt,* the material under this specification is further defined by the following ASTM standards:

D 146 Test Methods for Sampling and Testing Bitumen-Saturated Felts and Woven Fabrics for Roofing and Waterproofing

D 450 Specification for Coal Tar Pitch Used in Roofing, Dampproofing, and Waterproofing

Characteristics. This felt is only available in what is commonly referred to as *#15 felt,* although this specification requires the felt to have a minimum weight of 13 lb/100 ft^2. Normally the felt is nonperforated, so immediately brooming the felt into the hot bitumen during roof application is essential. Brooming helps limit any blistering of the felt caused by gases released from the felt when it is placed into hot bitumen.

ASTM D 450-96 Standard Specification for Coal Tar Pitch Used in Roofing, Dampproofing, and Waterproofing. This material is used for interply mopping between the roof felts of the built-up roof system and as the top pour material into which aggregate surfacing material is embedded. For roof applications this material is available in two types, *Type I* and *Type III.* The materials should comply with this specification, which is further defined by the following ASTM standards:

D 4 Test Method for Bitumen Content

D 20 Test Method for Distillation of Road Tars

D 36 Test Method for Softening Point of Bitumen

D 70 Test Method for Specific Gravity and Density of Semi-Solid Bituminous Materials

D 92 Test Method for Fire and Flash Points by Cleveland Open Cup Method

D 95 Test Method for Water in Petroleum Products and Bituminous Materials by Distillation

D 140 Practice for Sampling Bituminous Materials

D 173 Specification for Bitumen-Saturated Cotton Fabrics Used in Roofing and Waterproofing

D 227 Specification for Coal Tar Saturated Organic Felt Used in Roofing and Waterproofing

D 1327 Specification for Bitumen-Saturated Woven Burlap Fabrics Used in Roofing and Waterproofing

D 1668 Specification for Glass Fabrics (Woven and Treated) for Roofing and Waterproofing

D 2398 Test Method for Softening Point of Bitumen in Ethylene Glycol

D 2415 Test Method for Ash in Coal Tars and Pitch

Characteristics. This material has a low softening point and as such can only be installed on roof slopes not to exceed ½:12 in. However, even this low slope can cause pitch runoff or sluffing if high temperature extremes will exist on the roof surface. (See Sec. 5.1.)

Type I pitch was the only type of coal tar bitumen available for roof use until the 1970s, when Type III was introduced.

Type III has a slightly higher softening point than Type I and contains less-volatile components, making for easier working conditions.

ASTM D 4022-94 Standard Specification for Coal Tar Roof Cement, Asbestos-Containing. This material is used for the same purposes as is asphalt roof cement, except that tar cement is for use only within coal tar pitch roof material systems. Tar roof cement should adhere to the requirements of this specification. The requirements of the specification are further defined by the following ASTM Standards:

D 4 Test Method for Bitumen Content

D 95 Test Method for Water in Petroleum Products and Bituminous Materials by Distillation

D 140 Practice for Sampling Bituminous Materials

D 2822 Specification for Asphalt Roof Cement

D 3143 Test Method for Flash Point of Cutback Asphalt with Tag Open-Cut Apparatus

D 3409 Test Method for Adhesion of Asphalt-Roof Cement to Damp, Wet, or Underwater Surfaces

Characteristics. Tar roof cement *may contain asbestos fibers.* It will adhere to damp and wet surfaces. If installing on steep or vertical surfaces, we recommend reinforcing the cement with a roof felt or mesh fabric.

ASTM D 43-94 Standard Specification for Coal Tar Primer Used in Roofing, Dampproofing, and Waterproofing. This primer is for use with coal tar pitch roofing, waterproofing, and dampproofing systems. It is to be used to treat concrete, masonry, and metal surfaces prior to application of roofing bitumen. Often referred to as *pitch primer,* the material should conform to the requirements of this specification. The requirements of the specification are further defined by the following ASTM standards:

D 38 Test Methods for Sampling Wood Preservatives Prior to Testing

D 168 Test Methods for Coke Residue of Creosote

D 246 Method for Distillation of Creosote and Creosote–Coal Tar Solutions

D 347 Test Method for Volume and Specific Gravity Correction Tables for Creosote and Coal Tar

D 367 Test Method for Xylene-Insoluble Matter in Creosote

D 368 Test Method for Specific Gravity of Creosote and Oil-Type Preservatives

D 370 Test Method for Dehydration of Oil-Type Preservatives

Characteristics. EPA and VOC requirements and restrictions for shipping, handling, and disposing of this material often apply. It is hazardous in contact with skin.

14.2.4 Modified Bitumen Membranes

ASTM 1970-97 Standard Specification for Self-Adhering Polymer Modified Bituminous Sheet Materials Used as Steep Roofing Underlayment for Ice Dam Protection. This modified bitumen material is installed at roof eaves, valleys, crickets, or other areas on the roof where water backup can occur under the roof shingle/tile/slate system due to ice damming. (See Sec. 2.2.1.) Normally referred to as *ice and water shield,* the material should conform to this specification. The quality of the material is further defined by the following ASTM standards which are referenced as part of this specification:

D 95 Test Method for Water in Petroleum Products and Bituminous Materials by Distillation

D 228 Test Methods for Asphalt Roll Roofing, Cap Sheets, and Shingles

D 751 Method of Testing Coated Fibers

D 903 Test Method for Peel or Stripping Strength of Adhesive Bonds

D 1204 Test Method for Linear Dimensional Changes of Nonrigid Thermoplastic Sheeting or Film at Elevated Temperature

D 2523 Practice for Testing Load Strain Properties of Roofing Membranes

D 4073 Test Method for Tensile-Tear Strength of Bituminous Roofing Membranes

E 96 Test Methods for Water Vapor Transmission of Materials

Characteristics. The material is flexible, even at low temperatures. Fasteners penetrating the ice dam sheet should be sealed by the sheet membrane. The material is often installed directly on the roof deck and then covered by the roof felt underlayments.

ASTM 5147-95 Standard Test Method for Sampling and Testing Modified Bituminous Sheet Material. *This is not a specification standard!* This is a test method standard describing the procedures to be used to test a modified bitumen membrane. Modified bitumen membranes are a popular form of roof membrane within the roofing industry today. The membrane sheet can be installed in a single layer over a base sheet of felt or approved roof insulation surface, or can be installed as multiple layers of modified bitumen membranes.

The membrane material type is determined by the polymer type used to modify the bitumen, that is, APP or SBS. The membrane is installed by numerous means, such as hot-air welding, open-flame welding, hot bitumen mopping, self-adhering bottom surfaces to a prepared roof substrate, and so on. (See Chap. 9.)

ASTM Test Method 5147-95 evaluates 12 characteristics of the modified bitumen membrane using the following test methods:

- Conditioning
- Thickness
- Load strain properties
- Tear resistance
- Moisture content
- Water absorption
- Dimensional stability
- Low temperature flexibility
- Heat conditioning
- Accelerated weathering
- Granule embedment
- Compound stability

This test method, by using the preceding test procedures, can evaluate what has been defined by the ASTM Committee as important characteristics of a modified bitumen membrane roof sheet. *However, no values under this method are reported; therefore, this cannot be a reference in specification to define the quality desired of a modified membrane roof sheet.*

If values under this method were reported, it could be an ASTM specification. For over a decade, agreement on how to test a modified bitumen membrane has not been reached. Many of the manufacturers today do not test their material in accordance with this method. Some may only use some of the test procedures described under this method, while others modify the test procedures to better reflect the characteristics of their membranes.

14.2.5 Roof Membrane Surfacings

ASTM D 2824-94 Standard Specification for Aluminum-Pigmented Asphalt Roof Coatings. Normally referred to as *aluminum roof coating,* this material is often used on smooth-surfaced roof systems as the protective surfacing.

Type I, Type II, and Type III aluminum roof coating should comply with the requirements of this ASTM specification. This specification is further defined by inclusion therein of the following ASTM standards:

- D 4 Test Method for Bitumen Content
- D 95 Test Method for Water in Petroleum Products and Bituminous Materials by Distillation
- D 140 Practice for Sampling Bituminous Materials
- D 562 Test Method for Consistency of Paints Using the Stormer Viscometer
- D 962 Specification for Aluminum Pigments, Powder, and Paste, for Paints
- D 2823 Specification for Asphalt Roof Coatings
- D 3279 Test Method for *n*-Heptane Insolubles
- E 200 Practice for Preparation, Standardization, and Storage of Standard Solutions for Chemical Analysis

Characteristics. The reflective ability of the aluminum roof coating is greatly influenced by the type and the amount of aluminum leaf pigments within the material. Under this specification, *Type I* is required to contain a minimum of 11 percent aluminum, and *Type II* and *Type III* are required to contain a minimum of 9 percent aluminum. However, Type I may be nonfibered, which often indicates a material of less durable nature. Like all roof coatings, aluminum roof coating is sacrificial, and will need to be reapplied periodically.

Type I. Nonfibered, containing no asbestos.

Type II. Fibered, *containing asbestos fiber.*

Type III. Fibered, containing no asbestos fiber.

ASTM D 2823-90 Standard Specification for Asphalt Roof Coatings. Roof coatings are sometimes used by maintenance personnel to attempt temporary roof repairs or as a maintenance coating applied to the top of asphalt roof systems. (See Sec. 6.1.3.) When ceramic mineral granules are to be field-applied to a roof membrane surface, roof coating is sometimes use as the top pour into which the granules are installed.

Type I and Type II asphalt roof coating should comply with the requirements of this ASTM specification. This specification is further defined by inclusion therein of the following ASTM standards:

- D 4 Test Method for Bitumen Content
- D 95 Test Method for Water in Petroleum Products and Bituminous Materials by Distillation
- D 140 Practice for Sampling Bituminous Materials
- D 224 Specification for Smooth-Surfaced Asphalt Roll Roofing (Organic Felt)
- D 312 Specification for Asphalt Used in Roofing
- D 449 Specification for Asphalt Used in Dampproofing and Waterproofing
- D 562 Test Method for Consistency of Paints Using the Stormer Viscometer
- D 946 Specification for Penetration-Grade Asphalt Cement for Use in Pavement Construction
- E 1 Specification for ASTM Thermometers

Characteristics. Type I asphalt roof coatings are made from asphalt with low softening points, such as Type I mopping asphalt per ASTM D 312.

Type II asphalt roof coatings are made from asphalt with higher softening points than those used for Type I coatings. Type II asphalt roof coatings may be more suited to inclined roof surfaces.

Under this specification, fibrous material within the material *may be asbestos*. The coating is suitable for application by brush, mop, or spray equipment.

ASTM D 4479-93 Standard Specification for Asphalt Roof Coatings—Asbestos Free. The material produced in conformance with this ASTM specification is the same as the asphalt roof coating produced under ASTM 2823-90, with the exception that no asbestos fillers or fibers are contained within the finished product.

ASTM D 1863-93 Standard Specification for Mineral Aggregate Used on Built-up Roofs. Aggregate (crushed stone and crushed slag, but mainly river gravel) is often used as the protective surfacing for a built-up roof system. Without proper specification, the aggregate surfacing material can be of the wrong size or be too wet or too dirty to properly adhere and protect the membrane.

Aggregate roof surfacing is extremely durable, and does not need maintenance or repair when specified and installed correctly. In comparison with a smooth-surfaced roof system, aggregates can help protect the roof from foot traffic and hailstone damage. However, aggregates are restrictive during roof inspection, repair, and reroofing.

Crushed stone, crushed slag, and gravel roof-surfacing aggregates should comply with the requirements of this ASTM specification. This specification is further defined by inclusion therein of the following ASTM standards:

- C 29/C 29M Test Methods for Unit Weight and Voids in Aggregate
- C 33 Specification for Concrete Aggregates
- C 117 Test Method for Materials Finer Than 75 μm (No. 200) Sieve in Mineral Aggregates by Washing
- C 136 Test Method for Sieve Analysis of Fine and Course Aggregates
- D 75 Practice for Sampling Aggregates
- D 448 Classification for Sizes of Aggregate for Road and Bridge Construction
- D 1864 Test Method for Moisture in Mineral Aggregate Used on Built-Up Roofs
- D 1865 Test Method for Hardness of Mineral Aggregate Used on Built-Up Roofs
- E 11 Specification for Wire-Cloth Sieves for Testing Purposes

14.2.6 Quality Control References

ASTM D 3617-83 (1994)e1 Standard Practice for Sampling and Analysis of New Built-up Roof Membranes. In the event a dispute arises between the designer and the applicator as to the acceptability and conformance of the built-up roof membrane with accepted practices and industry standards, this practice details how to remove a roof sample and evaluate it. This practice requires a 12 × 12- and a 4 × 40-in template to be used to remove roofing samples. The practice then directs the user to calculation tables and formulas to determine compliance.

ASTM D 5295-92 Standard Guide for Preparation of Concrete Surfaces for Adhered (Bonded) Membrane Waterproofing Systems. Structural poured-in-place concrete roof decks often have roof insulation or roof membranes applied directly to their surface. This ASTM guide provides recommendations for concrete that will have adhered roofing systems applied to its surface.

The guide discusses adhesion inhibitors, that is: form-release agents such as oil, grease, or wax; concrete curing compounds which may contain wax, grease, or film formers; admixtures such as water-immiscible chemical curing agents; and laitance, dust, and dirt which can restrict or prevent adhesion of the roof materials to the concrete surface. The guide discusses how to evaluate surface defects, and the repair of such. Preparation of concrete surfaces is described, as well as how to evaluate the surface conditions for acceptability of application of roofing materials.

14.2.7 Sheet Metal Products

ASTM A 792/A792M-96 Standard Specification for Steel Sheet, 55% Aluminum–Zinc Alloy–Coated by the Hot-Dip Process

ASTM B 209-96 Standard Specification for Aluminum and Aluminum-Alloy Sheet and Plate. H1 series is most often used for roofing sheet metal work, that is, H14, alloy 3003 or 3004.

ASTM A 167-96 Standard Specification for Stainless and Heat-Resisting Chromium-Nickel Steel Plate, Sheet, and Strip. Type 302 or Type 304 is most often used, with 304 being slightly more resistant to severe corrosive conditions. 2D finish provides a nonreflective, nondirectional matte finish. 2B finish provides a bright, nonmirror, slightly smoky finish.

ASTM A 525-A361 Standard Specification for Sheet Steel Hot-Dipped Galvanized Coated. G90 coating is normally required.

ASTM B 370-92e1 Standard Specification for Copper Sheet and Strip for Building Construction

ASTM B 101-96 Standard Specification for Lead-Coated Copper Sheet and Strip for Building Construction

14.2.8 Metal Roofing Products

ROOF SYSTEM TEST METHOD STANDARDS

ASTM E 1592-95 Standard Test Method for Structural Performance of Sheet Metal Roof and Siding Systems by Uniform Static Air Pressure Difference. This test method evaluates the strength of the connection of a metal roof system to the structural roof purlin system, referred to as *anchor to panel*. The test method seals a metal roof system section into or against one face of a test chamber. As a minimum the system section must be made up of at least three full panel sections and five structural elements, with normal rake or gable supports at each end. Air is supplied into or exhausted from the chamber to create either bottom-side positive pressure and/or top-side negative pressure across the roof system specimen. Deflection, deformations, or failure of principal or critical elements of the metal roof panel system are measured. Loading is performed as required to obtain a sufficient number of readings to determine the load deformation curve of the system.

This test method best simulates actual installed conditions under which a metal roof system functions during a negative pressure uplift situation. When the uplift resistance required of the metal roof system has been determined, often by use of ASCE 7-88, the values required should be verified by use of this test method.

However, ASTM warns that this test method is not to be considered as a wind design standard. Wind and resulting pressure loads are not consistent or uniform as generated by this test procedure, but are fluid and dynamic. This test method will provide the designer with the anchor-to-panel strength of the overall metal roof cover system. Proper wind design providing additional fastening considerations and/or allowances must be made at critical areas of the roof system.

This test method is very reliable and accurate in predicating the uplift resistance of the main roof system. For example, if the metal roof system, in general, must resist 90 lb/ft^2 negative pressure, require the metal panel roof system to be tested in accordance with this test method. The values obtained from the test will confirm the roof system's ability to resist wind uplift forces as required.

ASTM E 1646-95 Standard Test Method for Water Penetration of Exterior Metal Roof Panel Systems by Uniform Static Air Pressure Difference. This test method submerges a metal roof panel system section with a ½-in minimum to ¾-in maximum flood of water from nozzle spray. The water spray is specifically directed at the standing seams of the metal panels.

Positive pressure equaling 20 percent of the positive wind pressure design is applied to the top of the water-covered roof section specimen. The bottom of the test specimen is also exposed at the same time to a negative pressure, with the pressure differential being 2.86 lbf/ft^2. The flooding and pressure differentials last for 15 minutes. Upon completion of the test cycle, any water leakage is observed and documented. In addition, prior to flooding with water, the specimen is subjected to both positive and negative pressure loading cycles.

This test method is similar to ASTM Test Method E 331. However, E 331 is used for panels installed on *steep slopes*. Test Method E 1646 is used to evaluate the watertight integrity of metal roof panels installed on *slopes of 30° or less*.

Passing or failure of the panel system subjected to this test can be as required by the specifier. Normally, any water passing through the panel system results in failure.

ASTM E 331-96 Standard Test Method for Water Penetration of Exterior Windows, Curtain Walls, and Doors by Uniform Static Air Pressure Difference. As previously stated, this test method is similar to Test Method E 1646, in that both are used to evaluate potential water infiltration through metal roof panel systems. Test Method E 331 is used as an industry standard to evaluate water leakage potential through metal roof panel systems installed on steep slopes. E 1646-95 (preceding) is used to evaluate metal roof panel systems normally installed on low slopes. Steep-sloped panels, often water shedders instead of water barriers (see Sec. 10.3.1) have different mechanical and physical qualities than do most structural water-barrier panels.

However, there are major differences between the two test methods. Whereas E 1646 tests a panel system in the horizontal position, covered to a depth of ½ to ¾ in with water, E 331 tests a panel in a vertical or sloped position exposed to a water spray; therefore, with no ponded water covering. Both tests utilize pressure differentials between the bottom and the top side of the specimen, but E 331 normally uses a pressure differential of 6.24 lbf/ft^2, whereas E 1646 normally utilizes a 2.86-lbf/ft^2 pressure differential. Both tests apply 5 gal/ft^2/hr to the panel system for a 15-minute period.

E 331 is an adequate mechanism to evaluate the waterproof integrity of a joined metal roof panel system. However, there can be great and misleading discrepancies in the report of findings from one manufacturer to another.

First, this method is a pass/fail test, but in actuality the pass/fail standards are determined by the specifier, normally the manufacturer which is testing its panel system. In such a case they can pass with a 20 percent leakage rate, if such a rate is considered acceptable by the specifier.

In addition, and of importance to the roof designer requiring this test method for the comparison and evaluation of different manufacturers panels, the position of the panel during testing can and will differ from manufacturer to manufacturer. Since E 331 is for testing curtain walls, windows, and doors, the test method describes how to mount and seal the specimen into the test chamber in a vertical position. In a vertical position water will not infiltrate as readily as it will when being applied to a specimen in a sloped position.

Some manufacturers test the roof panel system in a 20° to 30° sloped position. This best simulates actual installed conditions. On the other hand, some manufacturers test their panel system in the vertical position, in strict accordance with the procedures as described in E 331. Even though the panel system shows no water leakage in a vertical position during the test, once installed to the roof in a sloped position, leakage can well occur.

Designers should require the panel system to be tested using the same approximate slope as that which exists at the building site. Also bear in mind that this test method does not evaluate the waterproof integrity of such items as flashings which may exist throughout the roof system.

ASTM E 1680-95 Standard Test Method for Rate of Air Leakage Through Exterior Metal Roof Panel Systems. This test method determines the amount of air leakage through a metal roof panel system. It is the designer's responsibility to determine the amount of permissible air leakage through the roof assembly. This is important to the HVAC balance and calculations, and the values for such are usually provided by the mechanical engineer.

Roof configuration can create and influence both positive and negative pressure areas. (See Sec. 10.2.2.)

This test method is for analysis of low-sloped roof systems. ASTM E 283 is for use when analyzing steep-sloped roof systems where pressure areas can be more extensive and of greater pressure.

Roof penetrations, eaves, ridges, hips, rakes, and any other avenues for air egress or exfiltration will affect the amount of air passing through the roof system proper. Any results obtained from this test must be balanced with common sense in regard to the overall roof design.

As an example, some metal roof panel systems allow air passage of only .06 $ft^3/(min \cdot ft^2)$ of roof area when tested per this method. If the entire building envelope was this airtight, serious problems with the interior building environment could result.

However, if there are numerous areas for air infiltration through the roof system, such as roof penetrations, this strict value is required in order to balance the overall air exchange which will occur through the roof system.

This test method analyzes a metal roof system specimen in a sealed chamber. Air is supplied to or exhausted from the chamber at the rate required to maintain the specified test pressure differentials across the test specimen. The air flow through the specimen is measured and recorded.

E 1680-95 tests specimens in a horizontal position. The pressure differential is -1.57 lbf/ft^2. The test specimen is loaded prior to the test with three positive and negative pressure differential cycles, each lasting 10 seconds. The pressure differentials used for the preload stress are determined by the building design wind uplift pressure and the building design positive wind pressure.

ASTM E 283-91 Standard Test Method for Determining the Rate of Air Leakage Through Exterior Windows, Curtain Walls, and Doors under Specified Pressure Differences across the Specimen. E 1680-95 (preceding) is a variation of this test method. This method does not require pressure loading cycles prior to testing, as does E 1680-95. A pressure differential of 1.57 lbf/ft^2 is applied across the test specimen and air leakage through the specimen is recorded. The specimen is tested in a vertical position.

METAL PANEL COATING FINISH—PHYSICAL PROPERTIES

ASTM D 523-89 (1994)e1 Standard Test Method for Specular Gloss. Testing and establishing a paint coat finish with regard to specular gloss is a very complex process. If the author could properly explain all parameters, considerations, means, and methods used to establish numerical ratings for specular gloss of different paint coat finishes (doubtful), it is as unlikely that most building designers could understand the described processes.

However, in general, an incandescent light is used to create an *incident beam*. The beam travels through a *condenser lens* to a *source field aperture* and then travels through a *source lens*. From the source lens the incident beam strikes the *test panel specimen* and is refracted to a *receptor lens*. The light image passes from the receptor lens through a *receptor field aperture* to a *collector lens*. The image continues on to a *spectral correction filter,* where it passes to the final destination, the *photodetector.*

The incident light and recording instrument is placed at either a 20°, 60°, or 85° angle. The different angles are used for different specular glosses; for example, the 20° angle is used for comparing specimens having 60° angle gloss value ratings higher than 70. Different numbers of readings are taken per angle, depending upon the size and gloss of the test specimen. A black glass is used a standard.

ASTM D 3359-95a Standard Test Method for Measuring Adhesion by Tape. This test method uses a simple but effective process to determine if the finish, normally paint, on the metal panel is adhered to the metal substrate in a durable fashion. Using a razor blade or other such sharp object, the finish is cut through to the metal substrate. The cut can be either an X-cut (method *A*) or a series of cuts in a lattice pattern (method *B*). Pressure-sensitive tape is placed on the cut area and then removed. Method *A* is normally used for field testing and method *B* is used for laboratory analysis.

A rating of 0 to 5 is used to evaluate the coating adhesion. 0 is failure, indicating unacceptable adhesion of coating finish, and 5 indicates no coating finish removal by the tape.

ASTM D 2794-93 Standard Test Method for Resistance of Organic Coatings to the Effects of Rapid Deformation (Impact). This method tests the ability of the finish coating of a metal roof panel to resist impact. Coatings applied to metal roof panels will exhibit cracking when subjected to rapid deformation, such as is caused by impact. This test method determines when that point of failure occurs and allows for comparison of different coating finishes.

Severe impact can occur to metal panels during either the manufacturing process or the construction process, or during building service operations. Impact, if severe enough, can deform the metal substrate and cause the coating finish to crack and/or delaminate from the metal substrate.

This test uses a steel punch with a head approximately ½-in in size. The punch rests against either the top or bottom surface of the metal panel. A weight encased within a guide tube is dropped onto the punch. The drop distance is increased until cracking of the coating is achieved. Upon failure the in · lb value at the impact failure point is determined.

ABUSE TOLERANCE

ASTM D 968-93 Standard Test Method For Abrasion Resistance of Organic Coatings by Falling Abrasive. The longevity of a steel roof panel is strongly influenced by the ability of the coating to be durable. Metal roof panels will be exposed to abrasion at some time during their life cycle, mainly by foot traffic during construction and later during roof and building service operations. The extent of expected foot traffic determines the abrasion resistance required of the coatings on the metal roof panel.

This test method uses either sand or silicon carbide as the abrasive. Metal roof panels are normally tested using sand. The abrasive is directed down a guide tube approximately ¾-in in diameter and 36 in long. The sands falls approximately 1 in from the tube to the surface of the panel being tested. The abrasive impacts the test panel until an area of the metal substrate 5⁄32-in in diameter has been exposed.

When exposure occurs, the amount of abrasive required is measured. The amount required is reported, normally as L/mil of coating abraded or as kg/mil.

CORROSION, CHEMICAL, AND POLLUTION RESISTANCE

ASTM D 1308-87 (1993)e1 Standard Test Method for Effect of Household Chemicals on Clear and Pigmented Organic Finishes. This test method is often referenced and used by metal panel manufacturers to evaluate a coating's finish in the presence of acids and alkali. This method lists a number of reagents suggested as suitable or allows for other reagents to be used.

Test procedures range from applying the reagent to the panel surface and covering with a watch glass, to applying the reagent without covering, to immersion of the panel in a reagent solution. The testing period is as agreed between the purchaser and the seller, and is often for 15-minute, 1-hour, or 16-hour periods.

After the specified time of testing has elapsed, the coating of the test specimen is examined immediately or after a specified time for discoloration, change in gloss, blistering, softening, swelling, loss of adhesion, or special phenomena.

ASTM D 2247-94 Standard Practice for Testing Water Resistance of Coatings in 100 Percent Relative Humidity. This test method places a metal roof panel specimen in a 100 percent relative humidity chamber. The chamber is normally operated at 100°F. Moisture condenses on the surface of the specimen and any defects caused to the coating by the continuous condensate is observed and noted.

Defects of the coating such as blistering, cracking, loss of adhesion, softening, or embrittlement are observed and noted. This is a pass/fail test, and the duration of the test should always be stated.

WEATHERING PROPERTIES

ASTM D 822-89 Standard Practice for Conducting Tests on Paint and Related Coatings and Materials Using Filtered Open-Flame Carbon-Arc Exposure Apparatus. This practice evaluates coatings for stability when exposed to ultraviolet (UV) light and moisture. An open-flame carbon-arc light is sent through a special glass filter. The filtered light strikes the test specimen for a specified amount of time. In addition, water spray is often applied to the specimen for a specific time cycle while being exposed to the carbon-arc light.

The cycle time varies, depending upon the type of coating being tested, that is, general coatings, marine enamels, exterior wood stains, and so on. Color retention of paint coatings on metal roof panels can be compared when evaluated per this practice.

ASTM D 4214-89 Standard Test Method for Evaluating the Degree of Chalking of Exterior Paint Films. This test method is used to evaluate the amount of friable residue powder (chalking) evolved from the paint coat film at or just beneath the surface. The test specimen is normally conditioned in a laboratory or in the field environment for a time agreeable to all interested parties.

Several different procedures can be used to evaluate chalking per this test method, including using a wet finger, rubbed for 2 to 2½ in along the specimen surface, which is then evaluated for chalk-film transfer. For more scientific evaluation of metal roofing, a *tape test procedure* is most common.

When tape transfer is used, 10 pieces of transparent tape are applied to the test specimen. They are removed and compared using a *reflectometer.* Using white, black, and clear reflectance fields, a value is established for each tape and the overall degree of chalking is established.

Another popular method also uses tape to transfer chalking from the test specimen. The tape is then compared with a series of photographs progressing from light to dark shades. The photographs are numerically rated, and the tape specimen is assigned a numerical rating equivalent to the matching photograph.

14.2.9 Roof Insulations

REFERENCES FOR ROOF INSULATION PROPERTIES

Roof insulation manufacturers use many of the following test methods to evaluate their products. We list the most common test methods.

ASTM C 165-95 Standard Test Method for Measuring Compressive Properties of Thermal Insulation. This test method is used to determine the compressive values (see Sec. 8.1) of both rigid roof insulations as used in commercial roof systems and batt- and blanket-type fibrous insulations. The insulation test specimen is compressed at a specified rate in an apparatus until a specific consolidation of the material is achieved. Consolidation is normally 5, 10, or 25 percent. During the compression cycle load and deformation readings are taken, from which a load-deformation curve is mathematically created.

Compressive values of different roof insulations can range from 12 to 115 lb/in^2. Single-ply or thin roof membranes usually need insulations with compressive strength approaching or exceeding 40 lb/in^2.

Of possible interest to designers when evaluating unfamiliar roof insulations and the manufacturer-reported compressive strength is Note 3 from this standard:

> The speed of crosshead travel can have considerable effect on the compressive resistance value. In general, higher crosshead speeds usually result in higher compressive resistance values. Take this into account in selecting crosshead speed other than standard when comparing different types of thermal insulation.

In addition to compressive values, a roof insulation's ability to resist foot and equipment traffic is also determined by its *flexural properties* and its *fatigue-, impact-, and creep-resistance properties.*

ASTM D 1621-94 Standard Test Method for Compressive Properties of Rigid Cellular Plastics. Similar to Test Method C 165-95, this method is used for plastic foam insulations, such as ISO.

ASTM D 2126-94 Standard Test Method for Response of Rigid Cellular Plastics to Thermal and Humid Aging

ASTM C 177-85 (1993)e1 Standard Test Method for Steady-State Heat Flux Measurement and Thermal Transmission Properties by Means of the Guarded-Hot-Plate Apparatus. This method is often used to obtain the C-value of insulation. (See Sec. 8.1.1.)

ASTM C 203-92 Standard Test Methods for Breaking Load and Flexural Properties of Block-Type Thermal Insulation. This test method determines the breaking load and flexural strength of rigid insulation panel material. The test specimen is analyzed as a simple beam, supported at both ends, with a specified load placed midspan or placed in two locations across the specimen span.

ASTM C 209-92 Standard Test Methods for Cellulosic Fiber Insulating Board. Although the title of the test method refers to cellulosic fiber (wood fiber) insulation, many of the test methods within the standard are used to evaluate certain characteristics of other types of insulation products.

Relevant test procedures under this method, which are often used to test other types of insulations include:

Water absorption, percent by volume
Transverse strength
Deflection
Tensile strength parallel to surface
Tensile strength perpendicular to surface (laminar tensile strength)

ASTM E 96-95 Standard Test Method for Water Vapor Transmission of Materials. Water vapor permeability, permeance, and transmission rate are determined under this test method. Two similar procedures can be used, one with distilled water and the other using a desiccant of anhydrous calcium chloride. A dish is most often used, to which the test specimen is sealed. The dish and test specimen are placed in a sealed chamber with a controlled atmosphere. Exacting measurements are taken to determine material loss from the dish, through or into the test specimen, and into the controlled atmosphere within the chamber. High or low humidity within the chamber can influence vapor transmission through the test specimen; however, resulting values should be the same. The results are usually expressed as the *perm rating* of a material.

ASTM E 84-96a Standard Test Method for Surface Burning Characteristics of Building Materials. This test method has a long history, its origins beginning with Underwriters Laboratories. A 25-ft-long tunnel, 18 in wide by 12 in deep, referred to as a *Steiner tunnel,* is used. At one end of the tunnel a gas flame from two nozzles is used for the ignition source. The test specimen forms the ceiling of the tunnel. Opposite the fire end of the tunnel a pipe flue is connected, to provide draft and allow venting. Thermocouples are incorporated into the tunnel to measure heat, and a photometer system is used to measure smoke developed during burning.

Red oak lumber is used as the standard to express maximum burning, rated 100. Inorganic reinforced-cement board is used to express minimum burning characteristics, rated 0.

The material to be tested is secured in place at the ceiling level of the tunnel. The gas burners are ignited and the time and distance required for maximum flame travel during a 10-minute test period are recorded. At the same time, the photocell allows recording of the amount of smoke developed during the test.

Burning and smoke-release rates of roof insulations are often compared by this test. However, it must be understood that this standard should be used to measure and describe the response of materials, products, or assemblies to heat and flame under controlled conditions. ASTM warns that the results obtained from this test should not be used to describe or appraise the fire hazard or fire risk of materials, products, or assemblies under actual fire conditions.

ROOF INSULATION STANDARDS

ASTM C 208-95 Standard Specification for Cellulosic Fiber Insulating Board. Cellulosic fiber insulating board is defined by ASTM as a fibrous-felted, homogenous panel made from lignocellulosic fibers (usually wood or cane) and having a density of less than 31 lb/ft^3 but more than 10 lb/ft^3. We normally refer to this type of insulation board as *wood fiber.* (See Sec. 8.1.8.)

This standard includes six types of wood fiber insulation products which can be used for applications from acoustic control, to wall sheathing, to roof decking. We are concerned with *Type II,* which is designated for use as roof insulation board. Type II is further categorized into Grade 1 and Grade 2.

Grade 1 is for use under built-up roof assemblies.

Grade 2 is for use under single-ply roofing systems.

Although the standard does not reference density requirements for either Grade 1 or 2, high-density board is Grade 2. High-density insulation board can create problems if installed into hot moppings of asphalt as used in built-up roofing. (See Sec. 8.1.8.)

ASTM C 552-91 Standard Specification for Cellular Glass Thermal Insulation. This standard includes Type I through Type IV, with Grade 1 and 2 under Type II. Cellular glass insulation is often used in high heat, high impact applications such as pipe and vessel insulant and other specialized industrial applications. Type IV is used for roof insulation. (See Sec. 8.1.5.)

ASTM C 578-95 Standard Specification for Rigid Cellular Polystyrene Thermal Insulation. Expanded polystyrene and extruded polystyrene roof insulations are included under this standard. The standard addresses 10 types in all. (See Sec. 8.1.6.)

ASTM C 591-94 Standard Specification for Unfaced Preformed Rigid Cellular Polyurethane Thermal Insulation (Polyiso). Even though the standard refers to polyurethane, the insulation is normally referred to within the roof industry as *polyisocyanurate, isocyanurate,* or *ISO.* (See Sec. 8.1.7.) The standard references three types of ISO insulation: Type I, Type II and Type III.

PHYSICAL PROPERTY REQUIREMENTS

PROPERTY	*Type I*	*Type II*	*Type III*
Compressive resistance at 10% deformation or at yield	16	35	50
Water vapor permeability, maximum	4.0	3.0	2.5
Response to thermal and humid aging, dimension change (maximum), %	4	4	4
Closed cell content % (minimum),	90	90	90
Minimum R-value, 75°F	6.2	6.2	6.2

As shown in the preceding table, the main difference with the different types of ISO per this standard is the compressive values.

This standard also refers only to *unfaced* ISO, which may be acceptable for applications under single-ply membranes, but is *normally unacceptable for built-up* and other systems where the board must be adhered in hot bitumen moppings. (See Sec. 8.1.7.) This type of insulation board is also used at other building locations beside the roof.

ASTM C 289-95 Standard Specification for Membrane-Faced Rigid Cellular Polyisocyanurate Thermal Insulation Board (Polyiso). Even though the standard refers to polyurethane, the insulation is normally referred to within the roof industry as *polyisocyanurate, isocyanurate,* or *ISO.* (See Sec. 8.1.7.) The insulation governed by this standard is manufactured with a felt-type membrane covering, making it suitable for receiving hot mopping bitumen applications.

PHYSICAL PROPERTIES

Property	*Minimum*	*Maximum*
Dimensional stability, % (ASTM 2126)	4	
Breaking load, lbf (ASTM C 203)	17	
Compressive strength, lb/in^2 (ASTM C165)	16	
Tensile strength perpendicular, lb/ft^2 (ASTM C 209)	500	
Water absorption, 2 h., % volume (ASTM C 209)	1.5	
Thermal resistance, R-value at 75F° (ASTM C 177)	6.2	

ASTM C 726-93 Standard Specification for Mineral Fiber Roof Insulation Board. This material is normally referred to as *fiberglass roof insulation*.

PHYSICAL PROPERTIES

Property	*Requirement*
Compressive resistance at 25% (minimum), lb/in^2	12
Tensile strength perpendicular (minimum), lbf/ft^2	100
Breaking load (minimum), lbf	20
Water absorption (maximum), % volume	10
Thermal and humid aging, linear dimension change (maximum), %	
Length and width	5
Thickness	7

ASTM C 728-91 Standard Specification for Perlite Thermal Insulation. Perlite roof insulation is commonly used within the roofing industry. This standard addresses both regular and high-density product. High-density insulation, normally ½-in thick, can create concern when adhered and coated on both sides with hot asphalt while being encapsulated within the roof system. (See Sec. 8.1.3.)

STANDARD INSULATION PHYSICAL PROPERTIES

Property	*Requirement*
Compressive strength at 5% consolidation (minimum), lb/in^2	20
Tensile strength perpendicular (minimum), lbf/ft^2	575
Flexural strength (minimum), lb/in^2	40
Water absorption (maximum), % volume	1.5
Density (minimum), lb/ft^3	8

HIGH-DENSITY PHYSICAL PROPERTIES

Property	*Requirement*
Compressive strength at 5% consolidation (minimum), lb/in^2	20
Tensile strength perpendicular (minimum), lbf/ft^2	700
Flexural strength (minimum), lb/in^2	60
Water absorption (maximum), % volume	3.5
Density (minimum), lb/ft^3	10

ASTM C 1289-95 Standard Specification for Perlite Board and Rigid Cellular Polyurethane Roof Insulation. This standard refers to ISO/perlite composite roof insulation boards. (See Sec. 8.2.) The perlite layer is usually the thinner and top layer of the composite.

ASTM C 1050-91 Standard Specification for Rigid Cellular Polystyrene-Cellulosic Fiber Composite Roof Insulation. A more unique than normal roof insulation material, the polystyrene can be either expanded or extruded. (See Sec. 8.1.6.) The wood fiber insulation product is normally the thinner top layer. The materials are classified into three types, three grades, and four classes.

ASTM C 1126-89 Standard Specification for Faced or Unfaced Rigid Cellular Phenolic Thermal Insulation. At the time of publication of this volume, phenolic foam roof insulation is not being marketed by any major producer within the United States. However, for several years during the 1980s and 1990s phenolic foam was extensively used, but it waned in popularity when deterious reactions between wet steel roof decks and the insulation sometimes occurred. (See Sec. 8.1.9.)

14.3 FACTORY MUTUAL SECTION OUTLINE

14.3.1 DATA SHEET 1-7: WIND FORCES

14.3.2 DATA SHEET 1-28: WIND LOADS TO ROOF SYSTEMS AND ROOF DECK SECUREMENT

14.3.3 DATA SHEET 1-29: ABOVE-DECK ROOF COMPONENTS

14.3.4 SUMMATION OF FM REQUIREMENTS

14.3.1 Data Sheets 1-7: Wind Forces

This data sheet addresses wind forces on building structures. The first part of the data sheet discusses wind forces on buildings under construction and how to prevent wind damage to such items as structural steel frame, building walls, and roof coverings under construction and not complete. Temporary bracing and securement methods are discussed and illustrated.

The rest of the data sheet is concerned with wind forces and how they interact with completed building structures. The data sheet explains wind maps and ground roughness factors, and has tables which are used to determine wind velocity pressures. It continues by explaining pressure coefficients, which leads to building design considerations regarding wind forces.

This data sheet standard basically explains how the designer can limit wind losses by providing appropriate wind design pressures on the building components and other structures. Many of the other data sheet standards are referred to for specific information.

The data sheet standard refers to American National Standards Institute (ANSI) Standard A 58 for ground roughness determinations. ANSI A 58 is also often used by designers to determine wind forces on building structures.

Wind force pressures which can be experienced by roof corners and roof perimeters, as well as by objects such as billboards, antennas, and chimneys, are discussed. Tables are included for determining the force on such objects.

Special fastening areas are often referred to in the data sheets. These special areas are the roof corners and roof perimeter. Wind uplift forces are the greatest at roof corners, followed by the roof perimeter and are least within the field of the roof.

Designers must also be aware that parapet walls can create special fastening areas. If the parapet wall is less than 3 ft high, uplift forces can be as extreme as in the roof perimeter area. If the wall is over 3 ft high, FM treats the adjoining roof area(s) the same as the roof field.

14.3.2 Data Sheet 1-28: Wind Loads to Roof Systems and Roof Deck Securement

This data sheet standard provides guidelines for:

- Determining wind uplift pressures
- Installation of structural steel decking (insulated) to steel supports
- Installation of lightweight insulating concrete roof decks
- Design recommendations of cementitious wood fiber roof decks
- Design recommendations of lumber and plywood decks
- Design recommendations of structural concrete roof decks

WIND UPLIFT PRESSURES

Wind uplift pressures which can be experienced in the field of the roof are determined using several factors: ground roughness coefficient, building height, and the expected wind velocities for the geographic location where the building exists. Perimeters, corners, and ridge areas are not specifically addressed in this data sheet. Once the field of roof uplift pressures is determined, additional fastening may be required of the roof deck assembly. This is dependent upon the fastening requirements of an approved system as listed in the *Factory Mutual Approval Guide,* or additional fastening of a roof deck is required if the type of deck and/or specific method is not outlined in this data sheet.

Ground roughness is listed as three categories, or coefficients: B, C, or D. Coefficient B is for urban and suburban areas which are well wooded and/or terrain with numerous closely spaced obstructions equal to or larger than single-family dwellings. Buildings within large cities normally fall within this category/coefficient. Coefficient C designates structures in open terrain with scattered obstructions (trees, buildings) of heights generally less than 30 ft. Open country, flatlands, and airports are examples where coefficient C would be used. Coefficient D is used for buildings next to large bodies of water where wind speeds are usually the greatest.

Using wind-speed maps included within this data sheet, the wind speed for the geographic location of the building is determined; i.e., Houston, Texas, exists in a 90-mi/h wind-speed area; Miami, Florida, exists in a 125-mi/h wind-speed area. Using a chart within the data sheet, the height of the building is interpolated with the wind speed (determined from the wind-speed maps) and uplift pressure in either lb/ft^2 or kPa is determined. The height of the building is important, in that the higher the roof above ground level, the fewer obstructions there are to restrict the wind stream, thereby resulting in greater wind uplift pressures to the roof system.

In addition to providing the force of uplift pressures, the chart also determines if the roof system is in wind exposure 1 through wind exposure 5, with 5 being the extreme. Using another chart, the FM recommended approval rating is determined, being either Class 1-60, Class 1-90, Class 1-120, Class 1-150, or Class 1-180, which is a direct function of the wind exposure, being either 1 through 5.

The last factor to be considered in determining uplift pressures on the field of the roof is wall openings. Wall openings, such as windows and doors, can be compromised during high winds, and the breached openings will allow wind to enter the building interior, possibly increasing positive pressures within the building interior. These positive pressures, when combined with the negative pressures being experienced to the exterior roof system, make additional fastening a requirement.

Pressure values may increase by as much as 50 percent due to the number of wall openings.

FASTENING FOR STRUCTURAL STEEL DECKING

Structural steel decking must be covered with roof insulation. The decking can be attached to steel support members either by use of welds or with screw fasteners. (See Sec. 3.1.1 and Fig. 3.3.)

For wind exposures 1 or 2, welds must be a maximum of 12 in on center at all supports in the field of roof. At corners and perimeters, welds are spaced a maximum of 6 in on center at all supports. For wind exposure 1, welds must be a minimum of ½-in diameter; for wind exposure 2, welds must be a minimum of ⅝ in. Each side lap must be welded to the underlying steel support member, regardless of spacing occurrence. If using screw fasteners for attachment of steel deck in wind exposures 1 or 2, the spacing is the same as that for welds.

LIGHTWEIGHT INSULATING CONCRETE DECKS

The attachment method for 1½-in-deep corrugated or fluted steel form decking is basically the same as that for structural steel decking, with the exception that, since lighter-grade metal is often used, on decking less than 22 gauge, ⅜-in weld washers are required. (See Sec. 3.1.5.) In addition, all form decking must be galvanized coated only.

For form decking which is not of 1½-in-deep flute profile, the decking must be secured in accordance with the current *FM Approval Guide*. Fastener density in the corners and perimeters may vary.

CEMENTITIOUS WOOD FIBER ROOF DECKS

(See Sec. 3.1.2.) These types of deck panels are attached in the field of roof per the current *FM Approval Guide*. For panels that are through-fastened, the roof perimeter and corner areas may have fastener density increased by 70 percent and 160 percent, respectively. Clips can also be used to secure the panels to the roof, and at the perimeter and corner areas the clips are normally increased, or through-fasteners can be substituted for clips if required.

LUMBER AND PLYWOOD DECK

FM requires all new wood deck materials to be fire-retardant treated. Wood plank should be 2 in nominal thickness and plywood deck panels should be ¾ in nominal thickness. For decking thinner than the FM requirement, pull-out tests are required, per Data Sheet 1-29. Plywood thinner than ⅝ in nominal is not approved. Roof systems on wood decks are approved only for 1-60 and 1-90 rating; therefore, deck fastening recommendations are for wind exposures 1 and 2 only.

8d smooth-shank nails are acceptable for fastening of ⅝-in nominal plywood, with thicker plywood requiring 10d nails. In wind exposure 2, ring-shank nails are required in the corner areas.

Two-inch nominal thick wood plank should be attached with 12d minimum nail. The fastening pattern requirements vary, according to nail size and penetration into the deck support member. Fasteners are increased at the roof perimeter and corner areas per the same calculations used to determine additional fastener requirements for other types of roof decks.

STRUCTURAL CONCRETE ROOF DECKS

Structural concrete roof decks are approved for use in all wind exposures. FM suggests that securement design of precast panel be performed by a civil or structural engineer.

14.3.3 Data Sheet 1-29: Above-Deck Roof Components

This data sheet is the foundation upon which wind-resistant roofing specification and design is built. This data sheet describes the calculation methods and provides the charts and tables whereby the amount of fastener per each insulation board is determined and the amount and spacing for fasteners through base sheets is determined, and, although not approved, describes the weight required of either ballasted or paver-secured roof systems. This data sheet also refers the user to Data Sheet 1-28 for needed information, such as the field of roof wind uplift pressures, corresponding wind exposure, recommended FMRC wind uplift rating, as well as the amount of fasteners needed in the roof corner and perimeter areas for special designs. Data Sheet 1-49, for perimeter flashing attachment, is referred to.

WIND UPLIFT RESISTANCE—DESIGN RECOMMENDATIONS

Using Data Sheet 1-28, the wind uplift pressure which will be experienced in the field of the roof is determined, as well as the wind exposure (1 through 5) and the required wind uplift rating (1-60 through 1-180). Data Sheet 1-28 also is used to determine size of roof corner and perimeter areas which require extra fastening. (See Figs. 2.6 and 2.11.) The perimeters areas require 50 percent more fasteners and the corner areas require 75 percent more fasteners over those which are used to secure the field of the roof. The designer/installer is instructed to treat each insulation panel or base sheet which extends even partially into the perimeter or corner areas as if the entire component was fully within the special fastening area.

Data Sheet 1-29 illustrates 25 different fastener patterns for different-sized insulation panels, which will exist within different wind exposures, which in turn create the different wind uplift ratings. The current *FM Approval Guide* must be consulted to determine which fastening pattern is appropriate for the specific type and brand of roof insulation, roof deck, and roof membrane cover being specified.

A word of caution: Many times designers refer to the attachment pattern for roof insulation as found in the material manufacturer's catalog and specify this fastener pattern. This often is not correct. Wind exposure on the roof system is usually different for each building, being a function of height, slope, parapet walls (if any), and surrounding terrain. Two buildings within a mile of each other can very easily exist within different wind exposures, thereby requiring different fastening patterns of the roof insulation to achieve compliance with FM wind uplift ratings.

The FM-recommended fastener length used to secure components to a structural concrete deck is 1 to 1½ in. It should be noted that mechanically attaching components to a structural concrete deck is far more time-consuming than adhering components in a full mopping of asphalt or adhesive, which is also approved by FM.

On wood roof decks, screw fastener length is to be a minimum of 1 in long. Wood roof decks are rated for wind exposures 1 and 2 only, being 1-60 and 1-90, respectively.

On structural steel roof decks, the screw fastener is to be the shortest length possible, defined as being approximately ¾ in longer than the components being attached to the roof deck. This will prevent the fastener from being installed into the flute of the steel deck instead of the top pan, as is required to achieve proper wind resistance. (See Sec. 3.1.1.)

Recover of an existing roof system can be approved by FM, if testing reveals no wet insulation or moisture-contaminated underlying components. The new roof system can be attached with approved fasteners through the existing roof system, or in some cases the new system can be adhered with hot asphalt moppings or FM-approved adhesives directly to the surface of the existing roof membrane. If adhering to the surface of an existing membrane which may not be properly attached to the roof deck, FM requires fastening of the existing roof system to the deck before installation of the new roof covering. Fastener application rate for existing BUR securement is defined within Data Sheet 1-29.

When reroofing (complete removal) or recovering (retrofitting) over gypsum, lightweight insulating concrete, or cementitious wood fiber roof decks, field-testing of fastener pull-out resistance is required. Ten pull-out tests per 50,000 ft^2, with a minimum of 10 tests is recommended by FM. Based upon the pull-out resistance, fastener requirements are then determined using tables and calculation per this data sheet (1-29). For structural steel, structural concrete, and wood roof decks, pull-out tests are required only if the condition of the roof deck is in question. Data Sheet 1-52 describes means and methods for field-performed pull-out tests.

When a base sheet is to be mechanically fastened to the roof deck, usually lightweight concrete or wood, the *F.M. Approval Guide* should be consulted for proper fastener type and pattern density. Wood decking covered with a mechanically attached base sheet and roofed with a BUR or modified bitumen system is not included within the *F.M. Approval Guide*. However, Data Sheet 1-29 provides tables wherein a wind-resistance design can be obtained for base sheets to a wood or other nailable types of roof decks.

The number of fasteners securing the base sheet should be increased over the FM-approved roof field spacing by 70 percent in the perimeter areas and 160 percent in the corner areas. Fasteners in lightweight concrete decking should not be closer than 4 in on center to avoid cracking the deck.

14.3.4 Summation of FM Requirements

The preceding sections on FM cannot be used as design documents for roof systems. It is hoped they can be used to strengthen and clarify specification requirements in regard to FM. The sections merely attempt to explain the key items within data sheets concerned with roof systems. Some standards, such as 4470, have been omitted from the sections due to complexity and space constraints.

To design a roof system to FM requirements, the data sheets must be used in conjunction with the current *Factory Mutual Approval Guide* (FMAG) It is impossible, and inappropriate, to include the 600+ page FMAG within this manual. However, it is hoped that designers can now understand why specifying a roof system to be installed to FM 1-90 requirements, without the proper consideration and design, is impossible.

In example, the FMAG tells the designer the amount of and type of fastening and fasteners needed for the components of the roof. (The *Approval Guide* must be purchased annually from FM.) If the roof zone (1-3) requires 16 mechanical fasteners for a 4-ft × 8-ft × 1½-in isocyanurate insulation panel, approved within a roof system assembly listed within the FMAG, the designer refers to Data Sheet 1-28, which shows the fastener pattern to be used in the 4 × 8 panel when 16 fasteners are required.

Always remember that the total and specific system must have been tested and approved by FMRC or the system cannot be installed to FM standards. As an example, different types of isocyanurate roof insulations will have different densities, flexural characteristics, and so on. Substituting one manufacturer's ISO insulation product into the roof system as opposed to the brand approved by FM will void the system's conformance to FM standards. This holds true of all components of the roof system, from the roof deck to the roof surfacing.

Designers must realize that many roof systems are not tested and approved by FM. Material manufacturers have to pay the testing and certification fee required by the FMRC. Changing the brand of the top layer of roof insulation in a two-layered insulation assembly, even if it is the same material, will require testing and certification from FM. As another example, only metal deck manufacturers who have their steel deck tested as part of a specific roof system will be approved by FM, and so on.

Within the data sheets, FM does sometimes refer to roof systems which are "nonapproved but acceptable." However, they do not specifically tell the user how to configure or design such systems. In such case, the designer must consult with an FM field office and the engineer within that office. FM cannot provide design assistance or consultation to a designer unless the designer is working for an FM-insured entity. If the building is not insured by the FM system, no assistance or guidance can be provided by FM.

FM addresses other roof issues besides wind loss prevention. Of major concern to FM, and probably their best-known field, is fire prevention. Additionally, FM addresses durability of roof membranes including, but not limited to, ultraviolet resistance, hailstone resistance, foot and equipment resistance, leak resistance, and corrosion resistance of associated roof components.

CHAPTER 15

Definition, Selection, Design, and Specification

15.1 DEFINING THE SYSTEM

Premature roof-system failure and ongoing roof problems can be the result of improper system selection. Many factors must be considered before the final decisions are made. There are more than 300 different roof systems which can be created by the designer to accommodate any situation.

The roof system must blend with the total building structure and should complement the structure, design, and overall building envelope requirements. Information and considerations essential to the design selection process are referenced in Secs. 2.1 through 2.1.6.

In the roof material and system selection phase of the design, factors to be considered include:

Components of the building which will interact with the roof system, including, but not limited to:

- Extent and type of rooftop equipment and equipment penetrations through the roof
- Roof deck supports
- Parapet walls

Systems of the building which will interact, could cause *interaction* or *cannot* be allowed to *interact with the roof system,* including:

- Heating, which can create high humidity levels and vapor drive to the roof deck location
- Systems such as window walls or HVAC equipment, which will also make the roof covering a work platform
- Structural support system, which may require expansion joints or area dividers that can influence drainage and slope direction

Overall *building structure objectives,* including:

- Thermal resistance performance
- Acoustic control
- Wind resistance
- Fire resistance
- Appearance
- Durability
- Maintainability

Project limitations, possibly including:

- Budget
- Climate
- Internal building environment
- Construction personnel available
- Work site
- Health and safety
- Local pollutants
- Other crafts and trades required to access the roof during and after roof construction

Design parameters and building configurations established and/or required, such as:

- The required area of the roof which can dictate slope and drainage requirements
- Height of the roof structure and wind-load resistances required by code, building insurer, or designer
- Support of roof deck at building walls

- Finish of the roof system due to visibility from the ground, from within the building, or by others in adjacent taller buildings
- Discharge from any roof vents which penetrate the roof system
- Roof traffic expected for the service and maintenance of building equipment or systems

DESIGN PARAMETERS

- *Design parameters must be fully determined.*
- *Design parameter considerations are more easily defined in rework than in new construction design.*

Design parameters are boundaries within which the design must conform or function when complete, such as budget, or they can be limitations within which the design must function, such as restricted site access or airborne pollutants. Parameters can also be categorized as objectives and limitations.

If there were no parameters in roof design, one roof-system design would be acceptable for all conditions and situations. However, parameters exist for all building designs and structures.

Some roof design parameters are established early on in preliminary planning, such as environmental forces that the roof system must resist. These types of design considerations are mandatory, and the factors cannot be changed.

Other design parameters are established either early on or can be established and later changed or modified, such as structural support and, hence, roof deck and load limitations thereof. However, after a certain point, some modifications to the selection or design are not practical. For example, to start adding unanticipated loads to the roof structure in the final plan stage may require additional supports or an increase in the size of structural supports throughout the building structure.

Some parameters are established early on but must remain flexible to accommodate changes which can occur with the building design. Such changes will require adaptation or change of the roof system, such as addition or reduction of roof insulation layers to allow for maximum efficiency of the HVAC system.

Design parameters are more fully established by existing conditions in roof repair and maintenance design than they are in reroof design. In reroof design, parameters are more established than they are in new construction design. The more defined the parameters within which the completed roof design must fit, the more knowledgeable the designer must be of material types, functions, and limitations.

OBJECTIVES AND LIMITATIONS—REWORK

In roof repair and maintenance design or roof replacement design, the parameters normally include, but are not necessarily limited to:

- *Appearance* Should existing components, which are removed to perform work, be reinstalled or should new components be furnished (i.e., gravel surfacing or sheet metal vents)?
- *Budget* Funds allotted often define parameters of design.
- *Durability requirements* Repair and maintenance procedures should consider the life-cycle cost of the roof system in relation to the effectiveness of roof work procedures, thereby defining durability requirements.
- *Environment* The external environment or the internal building environment may have changed since original construction and consequently be affecting the roof system, or perhaps the environments were not properly considered in the original design. Roof replacement can correct the situation, but roof repair or maintenance can only postpone replacement. Cost of repair must be closely watched in relation to life-cycle cost.
- *Existing roof system* Repair and maintenance work must be acceptable and compatible with the existing material types and design.
- *Existing site conditions* These can determine accessibility to the work areas and influence the materials used, such as restriction of hot asphalt, which requires kettles, pumps, and pipes and transporting to the work area. Sometimes this is not feasible or practical for limited amounts of work, and different materials are required.
- *Existing structure* Decay and rot of the structure may prohibit cost-effective repairs, or planned additions, considered demolition, or sale of the building may require only limited roof work due to the uncertain future of the building structure.
- *Safety and health* Building occupants, pedestrians, building contents, and vehicles influence the type of materials used and methods of construction—for example, relationships between schools and injury to curious children, hospitals and fumes from materials, downtown areas and protection of pedestrians below and adjacent to buildings, computer rooms and prevention of moisture and dust entry during roof demolition work.

OBJECTIVES AND LIMITATIONS—NEW CONSTRUCTION

The design parameters considered in new construction are more numerous and less defined at the beginning than are the design parameter considerations for rework. In new construction design, the parameters are expanded and more generalized than those just mentioned.

It is more difficult to establish the correct and complete objectives and limitations, since many of these factors evolve with the building design. If parameters are not properly considered and defined, the building structure design may be finalized and the total building objectives not met, often due to the roof design, which can become surprisingly evident.

Objectives and limitations of roof design that need to be considered during the new construction design process include, but are not limited to:

Appearance	Environment
Budget	Function
Building codes	Health and safety
Configuration	Roof support
Conservation	Security
Contractors	Site
Durability	Standards

Many of these factors are both objectives and limitations—i.e., budgets and building codes. It is best if the design parameter factors can be established early in the building design process; however, we are often forced to define the parameters as the design proceeds. Defining the parameter design factors leads to the type of roof-membrane system best suited for the building. The result is a specification describing the method of construction.

Appearance. The final appearance of the overall building structure is influenced, sometimes slightly and sometimes greatly, by the roof or roofline. Appearance of the completed roof is influenced by:

Surfacing One of the most influential elements of roof appearance, roof surfacings are sometimes inherent to the roof membrane sheet, such as mineral-granule-surfaced cap sheets or paint-coat finish on metal roof panels. Often a surfacing is required to the membrane, such as aluminum-pigmented roof coating or gravel to a built-up roof (BUR) membrane.

Some surfacing will change with time. Aluminum-pigmented roof coating will begin to dissipate from the day it is installed. Green patina will form on copper roofing. If surface appearance is elemental in the continued appearance of the building, take into account changes which will occur.

Gravel, pavers, or ballast as a finished surfacing can add considerable dead load to a low-slope roof structure. Using surfacings lighter in weight can reduce budgets by reducing structural support requirements and can increase free-span capabilities of roof support beams. This should be considered during the preliminary design phase for new construction.

Membrane types Obviously, different membranes have different appearances—for example, metal roof panels as compared with gravel over a bituminous membrane. The slope requirements of these two systems are also far different and must be considered early in the building design.

Different membrane types have different methods of attachment and seaming. A single-ply membrane will normally have more discreet lap seams than will other types of low-sloped exposed membrane roof systems.

Roof penetrations The amount and the size of roof penetrations, such as fan curbs, mechanical units, and plumbing soil stacks, will affect the overall appearance of the roof. At additional expense, we can sometimes group rooftop equipment together into one location and surround the equipment yard with screens.

Sheet metal flashing The type of metal used to create the roof flashings, the finish of the metal, and the size of the flashing will affect roof appearance. Metals can be specified with numerous paint-coat color finishes, they can be specified to have mill finish of either dull or bright, or they can be specified to have a paint-grip finish allowing for field-painting, although this will require maintenance by the owner.

Some flashing components' sizes are dictated by roof structure. Sheet metal copings atop parapet walls are dictated by the width of the parapet wall. Gutters and downspouts are sized according to the amount of roof area they must service. Internal roof drains can eliminate gutter and downspouts, but require roof slope to all internal roof drains. The expense of roof drains versus gutter versus the expense to slope the roof system in numerous directions for roof drains should be considered early in the design.

Budget. All experienced building designers have at one time or another received construction pricing which exceeded the funds budgeted. In some cases the project is modified and rebid, and in other cases negotiations are initiated with the contractor to modify the design in order to reduce cost.

If the roof system is modified to reduce cost, normally something is taken away, not added. The reduction often relates to durability. Therefore, proper budgeting of the roof system is important. Properly budgeting the roof system cost is often as easy as making a few phone calls to local contractors or experienced local designers. Sheet metal contractors are also important since sheet metal flashings often account for 10 to 20 percent of roof-system cost.

If the roof-system cost is budgeted as a percentage of total construction cost, the cost overrun may be due to items other than the roof system. In such a case, compare the life-cycle cost of the designed roof as compared with the life-cycle cost of modified roof design, being sure to take into account maintenance and repair costs. (See Sec. 2.1.4.) This can then be expressed as a percentage per annum for required service life as compared with expectations for other systems of the building. Avoid budgeting roofs as a proportion of the total building costs.

Budgets often limit the design options available for the roof system. Roof systems are often selected and designed mainly from and by budget constraints, with little consideration given to life-cycle cost, compatibility with the environment, annual energy costs, etc.

Building Codes

- *Building code compliance of the roof system can be achieved in many ways and is dependent upon materials used and the configuration of the materials in the roof assembly.*

Different geographic areas have different code requirements. Code requirements vary for different types of buildings, such as residential housing versus hospitals. Code requirements of the roof system must be considered early in the design stage.

Rigid insulations under the roof membrane, coatings applied to the roof surface, or special combinations of materials within the roof membrane can sometimes achieve the ratings required to comply with code requirements. A quick phone call to the technical department of a roof-material manufacturer can sometimes reveal cost-efficient and durable systems which comply with code.

Configuration

- *Intricate roof-system configuration can create unique architectural expression as well as roof problems if all objectives and limitations are not considered.*

The roof can be a strong aesthetic component or can be completely hidden from view by the configuration of the roof structure. This decision is made during the early stages of design.

The roof shape and size is usually dictated by the other design decision processes—mainly by the foundation area—but considerations also include any building restrictions such as building height and air rights. Sometimes the owner has requirements such as a corporate image the building should project, thereby dictating the configuration of the roof, or sometimes there are requirements of the building to blend with other adjacent buildings on the same property.

The configuration of the roof can be of such size that economical sheet metal flashing design can save budget funds. For example, use of internal roof drains with a sloped roof deck is more economical on large roof areas than are gutters and downspouts around the roof perimeter. However, intricate roof configurations, with numerous roof areas, often require the reverse, as well as possibly roof dividers, expansion joints, and associated flashing work.

Wintertime condensation and summertime heat buildup within attic/plenum cavities can be prevented in some cases by ventilation. (See Sec. 10.2.2.) If the roof is configured properly to allow adequate and complete ventilation, the roof insulation can be decreased, initially saving building funds and continuing to save on energy costs.

Design style is accentuated by configuring roofs to be visible, using architectural roof membrane—often metal panels. Roof configuration expressing architectural style is interesting and can be accomplished by creating fluid, open design. However, such expression must not be allowed to overshadow limitations that come with a singular objective.

Roof gardens and roof terraces will become more popular forms of architectural expression as time passes. They are already popular in Europe. Roof configuration allowing for these terraces should provide overhang protection, sunlight consideration, etc.

Skylights, clerestory windows, walls, as well as roof terraces and gardens can be avenues for unauthorized entry. Security should be a consideration in the design configuration of the roof structure(s).

Conservation

- *'Green design' is a term we are beginning to hear more often. The environment of the building occupants can be enhanced by roof terraces and gardens, and the ecological environment can be enhanced by use of recyclable and durable roof materials.*

Resource conservation is discussed in Sec. 2.1.5. Landfills are being overused and closed. Disposal of construction debris will become a large expense of construction in the future.

An objective of the design is to use materials that are recyclable, either by process remanufacturing or more preferably by recycling into the next roof installed to the building. (Try not to make the recycled material a limitation of design for the next designer.)

Contractors. Availability of local craftsmen who are capable of installing the type of roof system designed is important. The roof system best suited for the building may not be the best selection if local contractors are not capable of installing it correctly and in an economically efficient manner.

If in doubt as to the availability of local craftsmen, a telephone call around town will confirm the local familiarity of the roof system under consideration. Another option is to contact the local material-manufacturer representative of the considered roof material and inquire as to the number of certified or approved contractors in the area.

Environment

- *The natural environment is probably the main design parameter considered in roof design. The proper consideration and analyzation of environmental forces creates a durable roof system.*
- *Roof function is closely tied to environmental resistances and durability requirements, and is also one of the main considerations of roof design.*
- *Corrosive and polluted environments are more common than many would realize, and can lead to serious roof problems if not included as design factors.*

Some roof-membrane materials resist certain caustic environments and chemical pollutants better than others.

Be aware of local industries, even if they are several miles from the building site. A phone call to such an industrial facility may provide information as to type of airborne chemical to be aware of. This may be important for all building finishes, not just the roof system. Be aware that the roof system will take the brunt of the pollutant fallout.

Metal roof systems must be closely considered in relation to caustic environments, as must sheet metal flashings. The finish on the metal may be adequate in resisting damaging environments, but the cut edges, wherein the bare steel is exposed, are not resistant. Even though many of the cut edges are concealed, the airborne corrosives can attack the concealed edges.

Coastal regions can be especially hazardous to steel roof materials. Rust and deterioration will spread from under laps and seams and consume the metal. The problem can often be avoided with selection of proper nonferrous metals.

Vegetation surrounding the roof must be a consideration. Leaves can clog gutter systems, create water backup at crickets and roof drains, and/or cause roof rot when covering certain roof membranes. Sheet metal flashing systems are especially vulnerable, as are any type of water-shedding system, as opposed to water-barrier systems.

Strainer pans at roof drains, often 36 in × 36 in, are useful in keeping vegetation from the roof-drain strainer basket. Wire strainers can be included at downspout openings in the gutter. Gutters can be covered with wire screen to keep debris from entering.

Cold environments lead to special concerns: ice damming at cold eaves, moisture condensation within attic/plenum cavities, loading of the structure, deck deflection and membrane movement due to snow loads, and additional insulation layers, which in turn can cause elevated thermal loading of the roof membrane. Many roof materials cannot be installed in cold conditions, often 45° or less.

Hot environments lead to thermal shock of the membrane during summer rain showers, excessive annual thermal movements of metal flashings, and accelerated aging of the roof membrane. If the roof is being installed in hot summer months, detail areas are sometimes lacking due to worker fatigue and heat stress.

Some environments have extraordinary rainfall amounts, winds, hail, and snow. Thus, local building codes more closely address these geographic concerns than do national or standard building codes. However, be aware that special considerations, often exceeding local codes, may be required for roof systems in such environments, such as FM attachment methods for wind loads.

Interior building environments can influence the durability of the roof system. High-humidity interiors, cold storage rooms, high-occupancy buildings, high-rise structures, as well as the interior environment of the attic/plenum cavity will influence the roof system. The concerns are mainly vapor drive and condensation.

However, the roof system can also influence the building interior instead of being influenced by the interior. The roof system can have a substantial effect on interior noise decibel level, flame-spread rate through the structure, and heating and cooling costs.

Durability. As an objective, the most durable roof system should be designed, requiring the least amount of maintenance, and for the least amount of funds. (See Sec. 2.3.5.)

Loss of durability to a roof system can be influenced by three items:

- Material
- Application
- Design

An objective of the design is to consider all elements that probably will or possibly could interact with the system. Design, if proper and complete, will prevent the loss of durability unless materials are not properly supplied or work is not performed to design requirements.

Function. An objective of the roof design is to create a system that does more than keep water from the building interior. It must conserve energy by controlling heat loss and gain; it must restrict fire, noise, intruders, and both normal and extraordinary acts of nature; it should be as maintenance-free as design for the type of system will allow, in order to conserve owner funds, as well as to accomplish all other objectives as listed in this section.

Roofs must function as work areas for equipment and systems-maintenance personnel, viewing platforms during festivals, and sometimes as emergency escape routes for building occupants. Inevitably, the roof becomes an area of the building which must undergo major reconstruction, which is another factor under which it must function, in regard to reworking, loading, and buildability.

Health and Safety

- *The health of construction workers and later building occupants is influenced by the design.*
- *Security of the building structure is influenced by the roof system, not only in preventing unauthorized entrance, but by allowing the building to remain secure and operational during times of natural disaster.*

OSHA, EPA, NESHAPS, and others are acronyms that suggest ill feelings for many, but these are agencies essential to protecting our health. Health and safety concerns can involve limitations due to existing materials or conditions, or objectives to achieve by design which limits or eliminates harmful materials or procedures.

Regarding health, different aspects must be considered depending upon the type of design. Under new construction, designers have often required certification from suppliers that materials contain no carcinogens—for example, asbestos.

With reroof design, it is often required to initiate a survey and testing of existing materials to determine the content and extent of any harmful materials. Both procedures are necessary design objectives to protect the health of construction workers and, later, occupants or users of the building.

Health of building occupants must also be considered as a design objective which can be addressed under roof design. Noise levels within the building can be reduced by proper or complete acoustic consideration and design. (See Sec. 2.3.2.) Arrangement of natural lighting through the roof structure, as well as roof views or access to roof gardens and terraces, can aid in the mental health of building occupants.

Safety is tied to health in that unhealthy materials can create unsafe conditions. However, more specifically, safety should be considered in the design as it relates to the accomplishment of the work.

For a designer unversed in the actual field applications of roof systems, addressing safety concerns in all but a general manner will not be possible. Be aware that an unsafe design will restrict the competitive bid process and increase bid pricing.

A designer must not get too deeply involved in safety design. If the line between safety caution and safety guidance is crossed, the designer might be liable for accidents which occur regardless of the safety design.

Security. Security of the building structure is normally an objective of the design. Unauthorized entry through the roof is a special concern on structures such as pharmacies, banks, and stores and is usually best addressed with alarm systems. However, simple procedures, such as mounting a ladder on the interior of the building leading to a roof hatch instead of a ladder up the side of a building wall, should be followed.

Security of the community is something seldom considered in regard to roof design on emergency and/or critical structures. Hospitals, police stations, fire departments, government agency buildings, and the like can be critical to organizing and controlling the response to emergency situations. Such situations are often the results of acts of nature, and the roof systems on these critical buildings must be designed to resist such acts of nature.

Earthquake, wind, fire, and rain can devastate a community and require emergency response. An objective of roof design on critical buildings is to supersede established design parameters to ensure that the roof structure remains secure and operational in such disasters.

Sheet metal flashing accessories are becoming more vulnerable to theft. Copper and aluminum downspouts are often removed from buildings and sold for scrap value. If a building is in an area where such theft is likely to occur, this must be figured as a limitation of the design.

Site

- *Difficult access to a work site is a limitation, but can be cost compensated for with thoughtful design.*

The physical condition of the site can be a limitation on the roof design. Large roof areas may require movement of the construction equipment in order to maintain proper application tolerances of the materials (see Sec. 4.1.3), the roof height might be too great for efficient roof-application methods, or access to the site might be restricted due to density of buildings, public parking, etc.

Consider cost and end-product quality. Contractors can perform work in adverse conditions, to requirements not best suited for existing site conditions. Cost can escalate, but not necessarily in proportion to the quality of the end product.

If site limitations exist, an objective must be to reduce obstructions to the contractor in order to reduce construction expense or enhance safety. If transporting materials from the storage site to the work area causes excessive expense or safety risk, reduce the amount of materials required for roof installation.

This can be accomplished by numerous design methods, such as higher-R-value insulation, reducing the total number of insulation panels required, and/or specifying a roof system with fewer roof membrane layers but equal in durability. Even if the material cost is higher, the labor and equipment cost is reduced due to the need to handle less material.

Also it is important to realize that access to the construction site is not likely to become easier as time goes on. Therefore, roof maintenance and repair costs will be greater than normal. In the owner's best interest, a durable, low-maintenance roof system will be the best design option, even though the front-end cost may be greater than normal.

Standards

- *Standards governing the design may limit the materials or systems available for use.*

An objective of the design must be adherence to industry standards. Not the same as building code requirements, standards are practices generally accepted by the roofing industry, metal building industry, etc.

On the other hand, it may be a requirement for the structure or system to be built according to standard as specified by a particular organization. This can apply to a specific area, such as roof membrane fire resistance per Underwriters Laboratories (UL) requirements, or it can apply to the total system, such as wind-uplift resistance of the roof system per Factory Mutual requirements.

Often, specific standard compliance of a total system can be a limitation on the design. Manufacturers sometimes have not provided for testing of all materials in all acceptable combinations. Without such testing, systems cannot achieve certification.

Therefore, in order to ensure that a system is in compliance with a standard, only materials assembled and tested as a system can be specified. Substitution of materials into the system, which have not been tested as part of the total system, will violate the design requirement.

Roof Support. An objective of the design is to create a roof support system which can withstand live loads and dead loads without permanent deformation, transfer load movements evenly throughout the structural roof support system, provide a base for securement of the roof membrane system, and be resistant to moisture.

The structural roof deck and deck support system are usually designed by engineers. Architectural designers must select the roof insulation, which is the structural substrata base for flexible roof membranes.

Thus, the insulation substrate must be selected to withstand roof traffic loads, normally evaluated in relation to the roof insulation's compressive strength. (See Sec. 8.1.) The structural characteristics of the insulation must make it dimensionally stable and the chemical characteristics must make it compatible with both the structure and membrane system.

The roof support system can be a limitation on the design, particularly the structural roof support system in a reroof design situation. The loading capability of an existing structural roof support system must be analyzed and not exceeded by the replacement roof-membrane system.

SUMMARY

The preceding is a brief synopsis of considerations about limitations and objectives, defined herein as design parameters. These can, and should, be expounded upon as the designer considers each new roof design situation.

Figure 15.1 is a flowchart indicating the design processes and decisions required.

15.1.1 Defining the System—Outline

The following outline presents items, factors, and design parameters representing both limitations imposed and objectives desired. There can and will be variables to the outline, but in general it represents most of the major factors to be considered when roof design is initiated.

The categories and items listed are factors which must be considered and/or determined early on in the design. These factors are either limitations or objectives of the design which normally are predetermined by other forces, elements, influences, or requirements, and are normally beyond the control of the designer. Therefore, they must be accounted for early in the process since they are not changeable. Later considerations, in

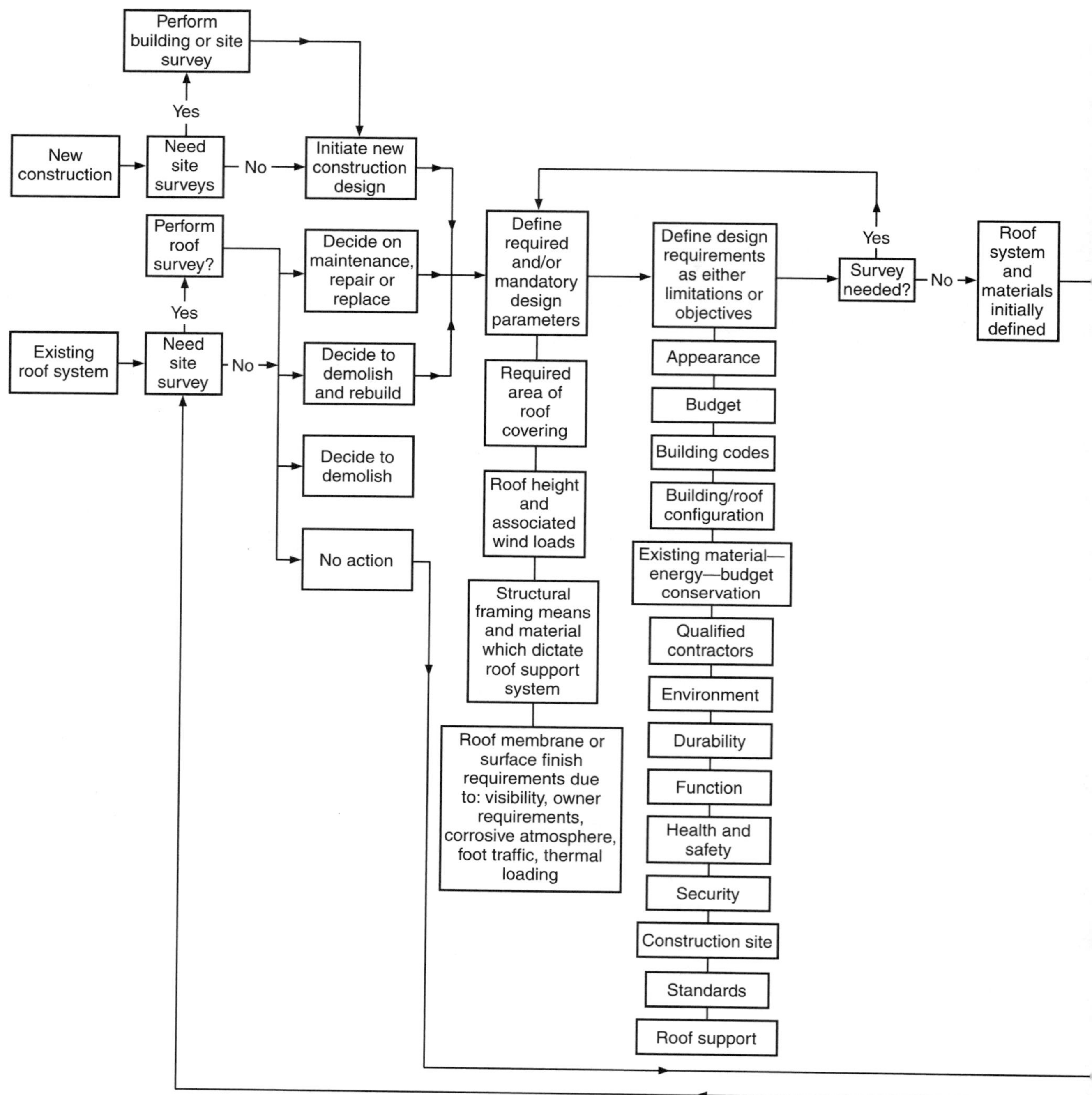
Perform building or site survey
Yes
New construction
Need site surveys
No
Initiate new construction design
Perform roof survey?
Yes
Existing roof system
Need site survey
No
Decide on maintenance, repair or replace
Decide to demolish and rebuild
Decide to demolish
No action
Define required and/or mandatory design parameters
Required area of roof covering
Roof height and associated wind loads
Structural framing means and material which dictate roof support system
Roof membrane or surface finish requirements due to: visibility, owner requirements, corrosive atmosphere, foot traffic, thermal loading
Define design requirements as either limitations or objectives
Appearance
Budget
Building codes
Building/roof configuration
Existing material—energy—budget conservation
Qualified contractors
Environment
Durability
Function
Health and safety
Security
Construction site
Standards
Roof support
Yes
Survey needed?
No
Roof system and materials initially defined

Figure 15.1

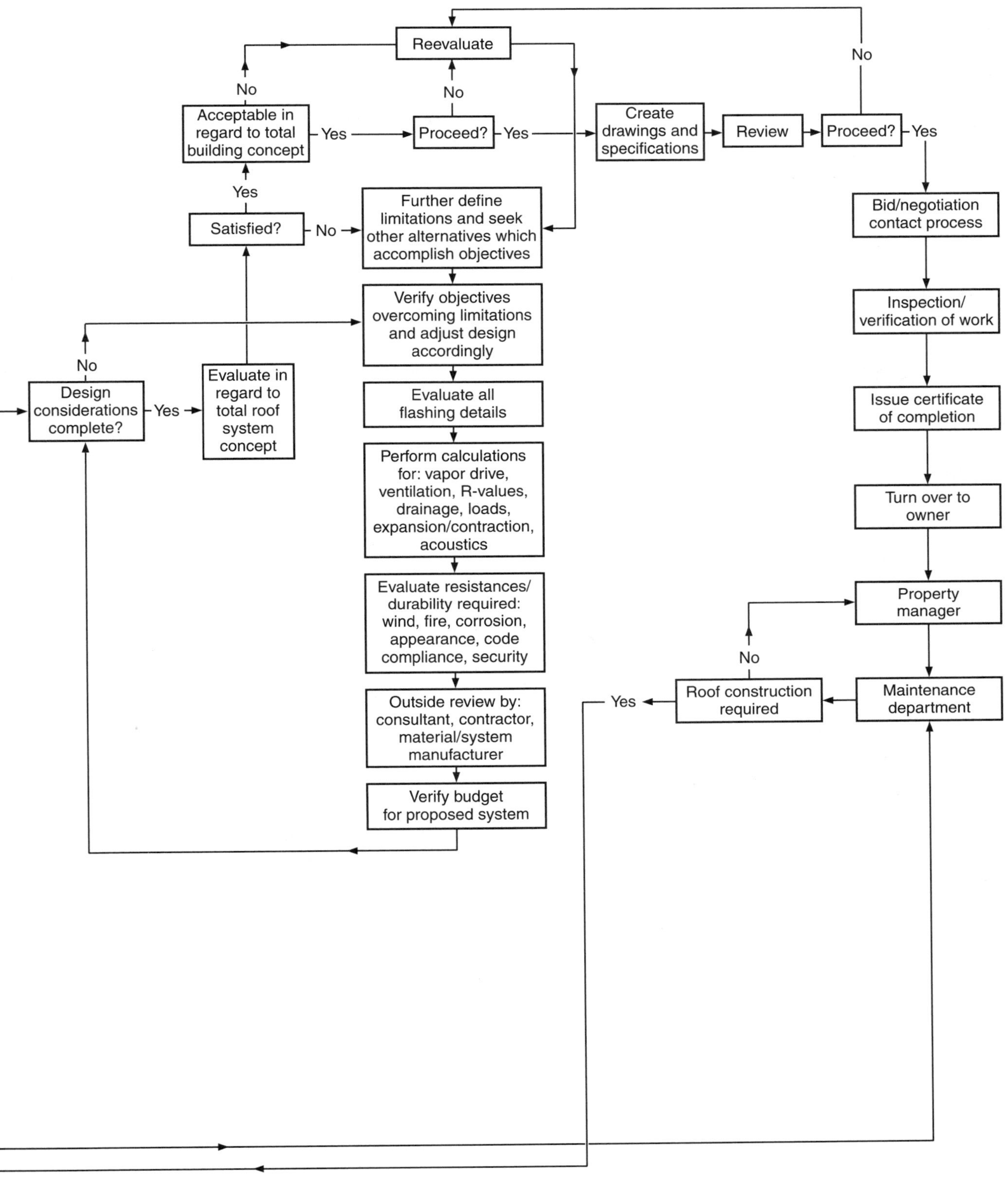
Reevaluate
No
No
No
Acceptable in regard to total building concept
Yes
Proceed?
Yes
Create drawings and specifications
Review
Proceed?
Yes
Yes
Satisfied?
No
Further define limitations and seek other alternatives which accomplish objectives
Bid/negotiation contact process
Verify objectives overcoming limitations and adjust design accordingly
Inspection/ verification of work
No
Design considerations complete?
Yes
Evaluate in regard to total roof system concept
Evaluate all flashing details
Issue certificate of completion
Perform calculations for: vapor drive, ventilation, R-values, drainage, loads, expansion/contraction, acoustics
Turn over to owner
Evaluate resistances/ durability required: wind, fire, corrosion, appearance, code compliance, security
Property manager
No
Yes
Roof construction required
Maintenance department
Outside review by: consultant, contractor, material/system manufacturer
Verify budget for proposed system

conjunction with factors determined herein, provide conclusions on the types and amounts of roof-system materials and components which have to be used in a proper roof design.

The outline is presented in a logical fashion. As one determination is made, it in turn leads to other considerations, eventually resulting in preliminary selection of roof-system type. Some designers do this process in their minds; others do it in a different manner and/or sequence. However, at some time during the design process, the elements listed in the outline must be considered, if only for a brief instant—or for an extended period of time when trouble arises.

OUTLINE OVERVIEW

Roof Function Requirements

- Aesthetics
- Energy conservation
- Work platform
- Viewing platform
- Essential equipment protection
- Interior environment control

Environmental Considerations

- Cold
- Hot
- Wet
- Hazards
- Materials impact
- Local environment
- Pollutants or corrosive atmosphere
- Building interior environment

Durability Design Parameters

- Owner requirements
- Roof material manufacturer's warranty
- Code and standards compliance
- Geographic location
- Building structure considerations
- Maintenance

Roof Size

- Budget
- Drainage

Roof Configuration Design Required

- Numerous areas/different levels
- Extreme height
- Extreme slope

Budget

- Preliminary considerations
- Mandatory roof functions and factors
- Roof membrane

The following outline is meant as a checklist, and as such, can be copied and used for making notes as the design parameters are defined and decisions made. Numbers refer to sections in this book.

Roof Function Requirements

Aesthetics

- *Appearance*
  - Visible?—*consider*
    - Durability of surfacing finish (6.1)
    - Environment (2.1.6)
    - Foot traffic (2.2.6)
    - Requirements to maintain appearance (2.1.2)

***Energy conservation**—requires*

- *Insulations* (8.1)
- *Reflective surfacings* (6.1.3)
- *Ventilation of attic/plenum cavity* (10.2.2)

Work platform

- *Extent and type of rooftop equipment*
  - Equipment maintenance requirements/schedules
    - Roof protection
      - Walkways or traffic pads (6.1.2)
- *Worker access?*
  - Window washers—*consider*
    - Parapet wall protection
    - Movement of roof anchors used to secure work platform
  - Weather information gathering
    - Roof protection
      - Walkways or traffic pads
      - Pavers

Viewing platform

- *Roof protection*
  - Walkways or traffic pads
  - Concrete roof pavers (6.1.2)
- *Safety*
  - Parapet wall
  - Banister

Essential equipment protection

- *Mainframe computers*
- *Disaster response centers*
  - Resistance to
    - Hail impact resistance (2.2.1)
    - Wind-uplift resistance (2.2.2)
    - Earthquake seismic loading (2.2.4)
    - Snow/dead load (2.2.1)
  - Exceptionally durable roof system required (2.3.5)
  - Evaluate owner's maintenance program (2.1.2)

Interior environment control
- *Acoustics* (2.3.2)
  - Noise control required—*for*
    - Airports
    - Funeral homes
    - Industrial areas—*consider*
      - Roof insulations (8.1)
      - Separation of roof deck link to structure
- *Attic cavity moisture condensation control required*
  - Cavity venting (10.2.2)
    - Soffit and ridge vents
  - Vapor barrier within roof insulation layers
- *Flame-spread control required* (2.2.3)
  - Fire rating of roof deck and roof insulation assembly

Environmental Considerations

Cold *(0°F or less)—consider*
- *Low-temperature flexibility of roof membrane*
- *Vapor-retardant requirements* (2.3.3)
- *Insulation requirements* (2.3.1)
- *Snow loading of the roof structure* (2.2.1)
- *Ice damming at eaves* (2.2.1)

Hot *(100°F or more)—consider*
- *Insulation requirements*
- *Ventilation requirements* (10.2.1)
- *Reflective roof surfacing* (6.1.3)
  - Maintenance costs
- *Bitumens softening points and roof slope* (4.1.4)
- *Metal flashing expansion and contraction extremes*

Wet *(tropical)—remember*
- *Adequate roof slope to remove excessive water*
- *Adequate size and amounts of roof drainage components*
- *Proper height of base flashing components, 8 in standard*
- *Noncorrosive sheet metal flashing material*

Hazards
- *Asbestos-containing materials*
  - Existing systems may require testing (13.1.3)
  - Restrict from use in specifications
- *Volatile organic contaminants*
- *Regulations governing design*

Materials impact*—consider*
- *Energy used to manufacture* (2.1.5)
- *Durability (life cycle) before failure (remove to landfill)* (2.3.5)
- *Recyclability* (2.1.5)
- *Retrofit possibilities* (2.1.5)

Local environment*—consider* (2.1.6)
- *Annual temperature extremes*
  - Expansion and contraction movements of metal (11.3.1)
  - Insulation requirements (8.1)
  - Freeze-thaw cycles (11.2.1)
- *Winds* (2.2.2)
  - Codes and standards requirements for attachment of roof system to the building structure
  - Wind-blown water and height of base flashings (12.3.1)
  - Wind-blown water and water-shedding membranes (11.1)
  - Large building-wall openings, i.e., open bay doors create positive pressures within building during strong winds, adding to roof blow-off concern (2.2.2)
  - Terrain and structures surrounding building
  - Roof height

Pollutants or corrosive atmosphere
- *Verify membrane material resistances*
- *Verify sheet metal resistances*
  - Concealed raw lap edges and nail heads are susceptible to corrosion.

Building interior environment*—consider*
- *Extreme humidity generated by* (2.3.3)
  - "Hot" rooms
  - High-occupancy buildings
  - Textile facilities
- *Requires?*
  - Vapor retardant
  - Ventilation of attic/plenum (10.2.2)
- *Vapor drive due to regular anticipated interior humidity or temperature extremes within attic cavity and building exterior—consider* (2.3.3)
  - Dew-point calculations
    - Vapor retardant as required
- *Code requirements*
  - Building interior ventilation
    - May require additional roof vents (10.2.3)
  - Fire (2.2.3)
    - Flame spread of roof deck assembly
    - Smoke development rating of roof deck assembly
    - Escape routes required across roof surface
- *Acoustic control—consider* (2.3.2)
  - Additional or special insulations
  - Isolation of rooftop equipment
    - Equipment yards surrounded by expansion joints
    - Isolation pads or isolation components under equipment

Durability Design Parameters

***Owner Requirements**—for*
- *Emergency response buildings*
  - Fire stations
  - City hall
  - Hospitals
  - Police stations
  - Emergency shelters
    - Must survive natural disasters, as best as possible
    - Design for durability against (2.3.5)
      - Fire
      - Wind
      - Hail
      - Earthquake
- *Economy/budget—design liability due to*
  - Possible reduction of
    - Roof insulation (8.1)
    - Membrane layers
    - Sheet metal (12.1.1)
      - Corrosion resistance
      - Gauge (12.2)
      - Gutter system (12.2.2)
      - Movement design (12.2.1)
    - Roof surface finish (6.1)

Roof material manufacturer's warranty (15.3.3)*—consider*
- *Design conformance to requirements of manufacturer*
  - Roof deck type (3.1)
  - Deck deflection under load
  - No ponding water after short period of time 24–72 h
  - Roof insulation types, amounts, and installation procedures (8.1)
  - Roof membrane and adhesive types, amounts, and installation procedures
  - Flashing material types, amounts, and installation procedures (12.1)
  - Roof surfacing types, amounts, and installation procedures (6.1)
- *Review omissions, disclaimers, and exclusions of warranty—i.e.* (15.3.3)
  - Maintenance requirements
  - Ponding water
  - Improper installation of materials by contractor
  - Fastener back-out due to thermal bridging (Fig. 2.2)
  - Prorating
  - Flashing integrity
  - Warranty transfer to other owners
  - Materials not produced or marketed by warranty issuer

Code and standards compliance (14.1)
- *Wind resistance*
  - Factory Mutual (14.2)
  - Underwriters Laboratories
- *Fire resistance*
  - Underwriters Laboratories
  - ASTM (14.2.9)
- *Hail resistance*
  - ASTM (14.2.8)
  - Factory Mutual (14.3.4)
- *Seismic resistance* (2.2.4)

Geographic location (2.1.6)
- *Environment—consider*
  - Thermal shock (2.3.4)
  - Pollutants
  - Corrosives (13.1.2)
  - Thermal loading (2.3.4)
  - Winds (2.2.2)
  - Rains (2.2.1)
- *Qualified contractor availability*

Building structure considerations
- *Use—consider*
  - Interior environment controls (2.2.5)
  - Roof traffic (2.2.6)
  - Planned additions and possible alterations
- *Structure*
  - Movements*—such as* (2.2.4)
    - Structural
    - Noise/vibration
    - Air (10.2.2)
      - Tight or loose construction
- *Roof configuration* (2.1)
  - Complex/intricate
    - Maintenance requirements
    - Roof penetrations (12.1.1)
    - Metal flashings (12.2.1)
    - Life-cycle cost (2.1.4)
      - Design for durability
  - Simple
    - Low installation cost
    - Low maintenance cost
    - Low design costs

Maintenance
- *Owner maintenance program* (2.1.3)
  - Conference with client
    - Roof maintenance is a requirement for durability (2.1.2)
- *Systems maintenance requirements*
  - Manufacturer's requirements (15.3.3)
  - Amount of flashings (12.1)
  - Environment (2.1.6)
  - Rooftop traffic (2.2.6)
  - Roof surface finish (6.1)

Roof Size

***Budget**—savings*

Roof deck support system

Gravel, aggregate, and roof pavers place far more load on a structure than do smooth-surface roof systems. (6.1)

Lightweight roof systems can reduce structural support costs. (9.1)

Roof insulations (8.1)

Compare ceiling insulation costs versus roof insulation cost in relation to U-value requirements.

Evaluate attic/plenum cavity ventilation possibilities. (10.2.3)

Net free vent area and air wash across entire underside of roof deck critical, and often not obtainable

Evaluate cost per inch thickness per R-value obtained.

Less handling of less material often achieves cost savings due to reduced labor costs.

Roof membrane—consider

Local contractor base (2.1.6)

Type of membrane most often installed locally

Manufacturer-approved applicators

Roof warranty required

Other roof systems, of same type and configuration, installed locally

Applicator familiarity often results in labor cost savings

Amount of roof flashing(s) (12.1)

Ease of roof flashing application

Standardize roof flashing details

Initial cost of roof membrane system (budget) versus life expectancy and maintenance costs (LCC) (2.1.4)

Client conference for deciding

Front-end savings versus long-term expenditure

Time required for installation

Estimate from local contractors

Work site (13.1.2)

Less material handling results in savings for difficult access areas and complex roof configuration areas.

Season

Hot or cold season limits worker efficiency.

Wet season limits workdays.

Other trades performing work before roof work can be completed

Contractors consider this a cost factor.

Drainage

Low-sloped water-barrier systems—remember

Positive slopes to drains required in all areas

Roof-material manufacturer or code requirements for slope

Taper insulation required (8.1.4)

Expense

Sloping roof deck structure to eliminate dead flat areas may cost less than tapered-ins

May be expensive or impractical on complex configurations

Lightweight concrete slur as roof deck substrate (3.1.5)

Provides field-formed slopes to unusual or difficult drainage areas

Provides insulation

Roof drains are usually less costly than gutter systems. (12.2.7)

Steep-slope water-shedding systems—remember (10.3.1)

Roof material manufacturer's minimum slope requirements may have to be exceeded for large roof areas.

Water-shedding design of flashing components essential.

Expansion and contraction of sheet metal flashings must not be restricted. (12.2.1)

Carefully analyze valleys, crickets, roof penetrations, and gutters

Wind-blown rain can travel upslope and therefore under roof penetrations.

Long valley runs can flood at valley ends during heavy rains. (11.1)

Consider water-barrier design at possible flood areas.

If possible, avoid built-in gutters.

More roof area to drain in comparison with low-sloped systems

Roof Configuration Design Required

Numerous areas/different levels

Extensive flashing details

Additional expense and time

Relocation of roof construction equipment as required

Additional expense and time

Extreme height

Hot bitumen–applied systems often impractical

Cold-process asphalt (4.1.5)

Modified bitumens (9.1)

Single-ply membranes (*not referenced*)

Metal roof panels (10.1 and 11.3)

Wind loads
Factory Mutual standards (14.3)
Difficult-access work area
Limit amount of roof materials required.
Replacement costly
Design for durability (2.3.5)

Extreme slope
Defects in workmanship visible
Defects in finish visible
Aging of surface finish visible
Design for durability
Repairs and maintenance costly
Replacement costly

Budget

Preliminary considerations*—of*
Local area (2.1.6)
Completed costs of similar systems
Contractor workload at time of bidding
Pricing often influenced by supply and demand
Difficulties due to season at time of construction
Hot
Cold
Wet
Requirements of contractor which can increase costs (15.3.3)
Bonds
Warranties
Paperwork
Submittals
Shop drawings
Construction log
Site inspector (13.1.5)

Mandatory roof functions and factors
Roof size
Square-foot pricing on complex or unusual roof systems not practical
Insulation requirements—remember
Dual layers of roof insulation normally recommended (8.1)
Batt-type or blown-in loose fill insulation above ceiling system often more economical
Heat loads to building economically controlled with attic/plenum ventilation (10.2.1)
Not always possible or practical (10.2.2)
Complexity and intricacy of roof structure
Height
50 feet or more can increase roof costs
Slope
Extreme slopes increase labor costs
Levels
Numerous levels often require more flashing details
More movement of roof construction equipment penetrations and structures
Increased flashing details and costs
Codes and standards compliance required of the design (14.1)
Wind resistance
Approved materials and systems
Fire resistance
Approved materials and systems
Thermal resistances
Amount and type of roof insulation
Wood nailer and curb design considerations relevant to insulation thickness (12.1.1)
Environmental hazards—consider
Temperature extremes
Metal flashing system's design and installation requirements due to movements (12.2.2)
Roof covering's ability to resist extremes
Freeze/thaw cycles (Fig. 11.5)
Cold flexural abilities
Movement, oxidation, and/or deterioration in superheat (2.3.4)
Corrosive atmospheres
Materials' resistances
Winds
Securement requirements from the roof deck system to the roof surfacing materials
Building location and height (2.2.2)
Tested and approved systems (14.1)
Long-term durability—consider
Manufacturer's warranty (15.3.3)
Verify roof insulation type and amounts
Flashing detail requirements
Limited bidders may increase costs
Limitations and exclusions of warranty
Low maintenance required
Metal flashings required
Corrosion resistance (12.2.3)
Careful design
Accurate installation
Surfacings to prevent roof damage from either manmade or natural causes (6.1)
Full-time site inspection (13.1.5)
An additional cost well worth funding

Roof membrane*—consider type required*
Built-up asphalt roofing (4.1)
Surfacing selected influences weight of roof system (1–5 lb/ft^2), cost of system and durability—*i.e.*

- Gravel surfaced (6.1.1)
  - Low in cost
  - Extremely durable
  - 3.5–4.5. lb/ft^2
- Insulated roof pavers (6.1.2)
  - Costly
- Provides excellent roof protection—*from*
  - Solar radiation
  - Thermal shock
  - UV exposure
  - Foot and equipment traffic
  - 1.5–2.0 lb/ft^2

Cap sheet—*of*
- Fiberglass/asphalt (7.1.2)
  - Often same cost as gravel surfacing
  - Less than 1 lb/ft^2
    - Sacrificial and requires maintenance
- Modified bitumen membrane (9.1.3)
  - More durable than fiberglass/asphalt cap sheet
  - *Creates—*
    - Very durable BUR
  - Above-average roof costs
  - Approximately 1.0 lb/in^2
- Coatings (6.1.3)
  - Reflective types can decrease heat loading
  - Maintenance and replacement required
  - Quality and cost can vary greatly

Materials used and manner of installation of BUR influences resistance, application efficiency, and costs—*via*
- Cold process (4.1.5)
  - Difficult in cold weather
  - Requires more application diligence than hot process
  - Often more expensive than hot process
  - Good resistance to rooftop traffic
  - Creates durable base flashings
- Hot process
  - EVT critical—*consider* (4.1.3)
    - Distance hot asphalt must be transported to work area
      - Cold weather
  - Many contractors and crews experienced with application techniques

Coal tar pitch built-up roofing (5.1)
- EVT critical—consider (5.1.4)
  - Distance hot bitumen must be transported
  - Cold weather
- Surfacing weight and dead-load weight capability of roof support structure—*system requires*
  - Gravel (6.1.1)
  - Pavers (6.1.2)
    - Exceptional proven durability
- Usually more costly than asphalt BUR
- Cold-flow characteristics reduce maintenance requirements. (5.1.3)
- Roof penetrations and flashing details require special design and installation consideration. (5.1.3)

Modified bitumen membrane system (9.1)
- Can be very economical
  - One-ply systems acceptable but can be considered a utility roof design (9.1.1)
- Surfacing
  - Factory-applied ceramic mineral granules (6.1.1)
  - Field-applied coating (6.1.3)
    - Light in weight
- Flame- or heat-applied—*consider* (9.1.2)
  - Combustible components of roof structure—*i.e.*
    - Wood roof deck
    - Combustible roof insulation
    - Wood roof curb and flashing areas
- Hot asphalt applied—*remember* (9.1.3)
  - High-temperature asphalt required at point of application—*consider* (4.1.3)
    - Distance hot asphalt must be transported
    - Cold weather
- Cold-process asphalt applied (4.1.5 and 9.1.3)
  - Often more costly than hot-process application
  - Difficult in cold weather
  - Only manufacturer-approved adhesives can be used.
  - Often specified for roofs with numerous detail areas and difficult access
- Self-adhering membrane is often more costly than other modified bitumen membrane types. (9.1.1)
  - Equipment and labor costs are reduced.
  - Often specified for difficult access areas.
  - Surface preparation and lap seaming are crucial.

Single-ply membrane (not referenced herein)

Metal roof systems (10.1)
- *Retrofit design—consider*
- Moisture survey of existing roof is recommended. (13.1.3)
- All wet roofing and roof insulation must be removed.
- Is water damage to building interior during construction a possibility?
  - Ventilation of attic cavity required
  - To eliminate moisture condensation on panel bottom side (10.2)

To remove moisture-laden air caused by any remaining wet materials from original roof system
Must be of proper and adequate design (10.2.2)
Sometimes not possible or practical
Roof structure support survey required prior to new roof design
Locate roof deck supports
Determine load capability of support system
Engineer report
Retrofit design feasible
Standing-seam water-barrier design as required for low-slopes—*consider* (10.3.1)
Roof deck required
Dependent upon gauge of metal roof panels and configuration style of metal roof panel
Concealed clip fastening required
Minimum roof slope considerations
Material manufacturers' requirements
Panel run lengths and rainfall intensity expected
Complexity of roof configuration—*consider*
Cost evaluation of panel seaming and flashing requirements—*regarding*
Shop fabrication of special panels and flashing components (10.4)
Amount and complexity of roof penetrations and structures requires additional design and installation cost
Drainage
Built-in gutters should be avoided if possible. (Fig. 11.11)
Size and extent of gutter systems (12.2.7)
Attic/plenum cavity ventilation—*investigate* (10.2.2)
Building code requirements
Standards
Based upon humidity levels and temperature extremes within building, exterior environment, and cavity space
Practicality of proper ventilation design
Costs of proper ventilation system
Availability of qualified bidders
Insulation requirements
Unfaced batt insulation at ceiling level
Vinyl-faced batt insulation under roof panels
Normally specified for exposed roof areas
Warehouses
Gymnasiums
Solder-seam water-barrier design as required for low-slopes—*consider* (11.3.5)
Acceptable materials
Copper
Extremely durable
Water wash can stain building faces below
Terne-coated carbon steel
Durable as long as lead surface coating remains on panels
Maintenance painting acceptable
Terne-coated stainless steel
Lead coating facilitates solder joints
Not as malleable as copper or carbon steel
Extremely durable
Galvanized coated steel
Requires paint coating to provide durability
Maintenance costs
Minimum roof slope—*consider*
Ponding water prohibited due to different surface temperatures at various locations resulting in nonuniform expansion and contraction rates
Can be completely water covered (Fig. 11.26)
Complexity of roof configuration—*consider*
Cost evaluation of panel seaming and flashing requirements—*regarding*
Shop fabrication of special panels and flashing components
Amount and complexity of roof penetrations and structures
Requires additional design and installation cost
Drainage
Built-in gutters and internal roof drains standard to these systems
Condensation on bottom side of roof panels—*investigate*
Building code requirements for roof cavity ventilation
Accepted practices in local areas and standards for condensation prevention
Resistances of roof deck to moisture
These systems can last for 50 or more years.
Complexity of design and installation—*consider*
Designer experience with these types of systems
Applicator availability and qualifications
Budget
Extremely costly
Excellent LCC

Standing-seam water-shedding design as required for steep-sloped roofs (10.3.1)
- Aesthetic requirements
  - Color—*consider* (10.3.2)
    - Custom paint coating colors require additional lead time and costs.
  - Durability of paint coating in regard to environment in which it will exist.
- Concealed clip fastening required (10.1)
  - Exposed fasteners must be noncorrosive, are unsightly, and provide little cost savings.
- Roof panel properties
  - Structural or nonstructural (10.3.1)
    - Structural panels sometimes cost more but roof decking costs are saved.
- Ability of the panel and accessories to conform to water-barrier design at roof areas if required
- Roof panel style
  - Some styles are more labor-intensive to erect than others.
  - Some styles require mechanized and specialized equipment for panel attachment and seaming.
    - Bidders will often be only those experienced with that particular type of roof system.
      - Limited bidder pool
  - Minimum roof slope considerations
    - Material manufacturers' requirements
      - Panel run lengths and rainfall intensity expected (10.3.1)
      - Slope may have to exceed minimum requirements.
  - Complexity of roof configuration—*consider*
    - Cost evaluation of panel seaming and flashing requirements—*regarding*
      - Shop fabrication of special panels and flashing components (10.4)
      - Valleys, ridge and hips, eaves, rakes, and built-in gutters
  - Amount and complexity of roof penetrations and structures
    - Requires additional design and installation cost
- Drainage
  - Built-in gutters should be avoided if possible. (Fig. 11.11)
    - Requires additional and specialized design
    - Requires careful and correct installation
    - Extremely costly and difficult to repair in the event of leakage
  - Consider roof areas which could possibly flood during torrential rains or ice-damming conditions. (2.2.1)
    - Require water-barrier design and installation.
    - Additional costs (10.3.1)
  - Size and extent of gutter systems per linear foot pricing, based upon size and material type
- Attic/plenum cavity ventilation—*investigate*
  - Building code requirements
  - Standards (10.2.1)
    - Based upon humidity levels and temperature extremes within building, exterior environment, and attic cavity space.
  - Practicality of proper ventilation design (10.2.2)
  - Costs of proper ventilation system
- All metal roof panels finishes will change with aging—*consider* (10.3.2)
  - Paint coat finishes in regard to (14.2.8)
    - Durability
    - Environment
    - Maintenance requirements

COMMENTS: ____________________

The preceding section should more clearly define roof-material and system requirements as they relate to objectives of the roof design and the total building design. Limitations of the design also have an influence on roof selection and should be more clearly defined after reviewing the preceding section.

15.2 SELECTING THE SYSTEM

- *Design parameter requirements, after being initially defined, must be further examined and defined to blend with the total building system requirements.*

As stated in Sec. 15.1, there are many general considerations and evaluations needed in roof-system design. The roof system must complement and work with the total building structure, climate, and environment, and could be further defined in terms of its durability as it relates to life-cycle cost. The roof system must be buildable in a cost-effective manner and should be maintainable at expected expense levels for the required life of the system.

System is a key word. The system includes the roof support structure, roof insulation, roof membrane, metal flashings, flexible flashings, and roof surface finishes. These items of the roof system must be selected based upon the design parameter requirements of the roof and building system.

Parameters were discussed, as they generally apply to roof system design, in Sec. 15.1. Parameters define goals to be obtained by the design or impose restrictions on the system which the design must compensate for. All parameters which will or can be encountered during roof design are not included in this manual, simply because too many variables exist which can negate some parameter requirements or accentuate others.

In Sec. 15.1.1, we reviewed some of the most common considerations involved in preliminary roof-system selection. Many of the items therein are dictated by conditions, situations, influences, or objectives beyond the control of the designer. These design parameters lead to preliminary system selection or rejection, whereby roof support structure requirements should have been better defined, along with insulation types and amounts, roof membrane type, and roof surfacing, as well as flashing components.

In this section we will examine some of the most common parameter requirements over which the designer has control, although in some cases these parameters may be limited and subservient to other systems of the building structure. As an example, the roof support structure requirements should have been somewhat defined by the previous outline, based upon the requirements of what appears to be the best roof-system selection. However, the support structure of the entire building dictates to a great extent the type of roof support structure which will be available for use. If excessive costs are required to adapt the building support structure to accommodate the roof system, another roof system selection should be considered.

Another example of other building systems and requirements which have dominance over the roof system, but are also essential elements of the roof system, are roof configuration, which is dictated by the shape of the building, and roof materials and systems, which must comply with code or standards requirements.

There are many ways of designing building systems, including the roof. More experienced designers have their own means and methods. The following is but an example of the process required to generally arrive at a suitable system, designed for a specific building situation.

The first order of roof design should be defining what conditions exist and cannot be changed, as was determined in Sec. 15.1.1. After the factors within these parameters are established, the remaining design parameters are considered. These possible factors normally do not have as rigid an effect on selection and design as do the parameter factors first established. However, they must blend with the determinate factors of the design and can be used to fine-tune the design.

15.2.1 Selecting the System—Outline

The following outline presents items, factors, and design parameters representing both limitations imposed and objectives desired. There can and will be variables to this outline, but in general it represents most of the major factors to be considered when roof design is initiated.

The categories and items listed are factors which usually can be considered after initial roof design parameters have been established. These factors are either limitations or objectives of the design. They are sometimes subservient to other elements of the building structure design and, as such, must function not only within the established design factors of the roof system, but they must also blend with other building design parameters.

The factors listed in the following outline are considerations required of the roof design and are sometimes also influenced by other forces, elements, or requirements that are beyond the control of the designer. However, many of the factors listed here are not predetermined by stringent and unchangeable requirements, therefore they can be customized to the many building-structure, environmental, and roof-system requirements. These design parameters must be established and then can be used to blend all forces, both artificial and natural, into a complete and durable system. They are not accounted for early on since many of the factors are changeable.

As was the previous outline, this outline is presented in a logical fashion and lists elements that must be considered, if only briefly, or in greater depth when trouble arises.

In the outline in Sec. 15.1.1 preliminary determination and selection of roof-system materials, systems, and requirements were made. These selections are now to be compared against and blended with the design parameters which follow. Copy the following outline and use it as a checklist, making notes and annotations as the design process evolves.

OUTLINE OVERVIEW

Roof Membrane System
- Budget allotments
- Characteristics required
- Appearance considerations

Roof Support System
- Load capabilities required
- Roof deck type
- Movement control required
- Roof slope

Roof Thermal Resistance System
- Thermal resistance required
- Roof insulation

Roof Penetrations and Structures
- Roof penetrations
- Roof structures

Roof Configuration
- Slopes
- Drainage
- Visual effect
- Architectural structures

Code Requirements
- Wind resistance
- Fire resistance
- Local code requirements

Contractors
- Means of procurement
- Availability of contractors

Health and Safety
- Building occupants
- Worker safety
- Environmental concerns

Security
- Building contents
- Roof drainage components

Roof Membrane System

Type preliminary selected (per Sec. 15.1.1)—compared against:

Budget allotments
- *Apportionments*
  - Roof insulation (8.1)
  - Roof membrane
  - Flashings
    - Sheet metal (12.2)
    - Bituminous (12.3)
  - Surfacing (6.1)

Characteristics required*—performance and physical*
- *Durability* (2.3.5)
  - Life-cycle cost (2.1.4)
    - Maintenance
    - Repair
- *Resistances*
  - Fire (2.2.3)
    - Membrane
      - Class A, B, or C
    - Total roof system
      - Class I, II, or III
  - Equipment and foot traffic
    - Roof surfacing (6.1)
      - Excellent, average, or poor (2.2.6)
      - Roof substrate/insulation
        - Compressive strength (8.1)
  - Corrosives and pollutants—*consider* (2.1.6)
    - Coastal regions' air containing salts
    - Local industry
    - Venting of corrosives onto rooftop
  - Winds—*consider* (2.2.2)
    - Attachment methods
    - Standards governing the design
      - Factory Mutual
      - Underwriters Laboratories
    - Total roof assembly wind-resistance ratings
  - Hail—*consider* (2.2.1)
    - Roof surfacing selection
    - Impact resistance of the roof membrane
  - Seismic loads—*consider* (2.2.4)
    - Membrane flexibility
    - Cold-weather extremes
    - Attachment method at parapet walls—especially
      - Non-wall-supported roof decks (Figs. 3.1 and 3.2)
  - Temperature extremes
    - Cold climates—*consider*
      - Membrane flexibility
      - Freeze/thaw cycles
      - Thermal shock (2.3.1)

Laminate surfacings
Ceramic glaze to roof tiles (11.2.1)
Hot climates—*consider*
Roof bitumen softening points
Roof slope and bitumen type (4.1.4)
Roof membrane temperatures can be increased by roof insulations.
Application temperature tolerances
Anticipated temperatures at time of construction
Weight
Roof surfacing
Reflective ability
Coatings
Will dissipate
Reflective ability will change.
Heat loading (Fig. 2.17)
Dark membranes/surfacings
Blackbody radiator (2.3.4)
White/reflective membranes/surfacings
Emissivity (2.3.4)
Lowers membrane temperature
Vapor retarder required
Maintenance requirements

Appearance considerations
Visibility—due to
Roof slope
Surrounding and taller buildings
Owner requirements—i.e.
Red Roof Inns, Inc.
Building addition
Durability of roof finish
Maintenance requirements
Manufacturer's warranty (15.3.3)
Review disclaimers

Roof Support System

Load capabilities required—*consider*
Live- and dead-load limits required (3.1)
Rooftop equipment weight and movements
Foot and equipment traffic (2.2.6)
Snow loads (2.2.1)
Wind loads (2.2.2)
Seismic (2.2.4)

Roof deck type—*consider*
Fire codes
Free-span capabilities under anticipated loads
Deflection (per above)
Fastener assembly to be used to secure roof system and compatibility of all items, per ratings and codes required

Movement control required—*consider*
Expansion joints—due to
Non-wall-supported roof deck (3.1)
Factory-formed deck, i.e., steel (3.1.7)
Turning direction and, if so, any movement at joint location
Differential movements of deck areas due to
Excessive vibration (rooftop equipment) or different temperature extremes due to building interior conditions (hot rooms, cold rooms) or different deck types (different coefficients of expansion) (3.1.7)

Roof slope—*consider*
Limitations (if any)—due to
Architectural style of building
Minimum clearance requirements for equipment within plenum/attic cavity (if any)
Minimum slope requirements for type of roof membrane being preliminary considered (therefore also an objective)
Low-sloped systems are difficult to properly ventilate. (10.2.2)
Objectives
Facilitate proper drainage.
Crickets and saddles used to direct water to drainage outlets are often more economically created by roof deck than with tapered insulation. (8.1.4)
Equalize water run-off—*consider*
Collection locations and amounts of run-off at any location
Excessive amounts, requiring oversized gutters or other collection components
May require slope direction change
Consistent roof slope

Roof Thermal Resistance System

Thermal resistance required—*consider*
HVAC capacity
Attic/plenum cavity ventilation (10.2.1)
Intake and exhaust vent amount and location is critical.
Slope of roof deck
Configuration of roof structure
Code requirements and regulations
Winter temperature extremes—consider
Dew-point calculations (2.3.3)
Vapor retardant
Locate at ceiling or at roof deck
Ease of application
Expense
Efficiency
Penetrations
Summer temperature extremes—consider
Temperature at roof membrane (2.3.4)
Quicker oxidation of some roof materials (4.1.4)

Softening-point range of roof bitumens
Slope of roof deck
Ability to properly ventilate attic/plenum cavity (10.2.2)

Roof insulation *(if required)—consider*
Configuration
Single or dual layer (8.1)
Vapor retarder requirements?
Temperature
Location
Thickness required to achieve required R-value or U-value—remember (8.1)
Roof-access door threshold heights (12.3)
Base flashing height of rooftop equipment
Attachment method to roof deck
Mechanical (8.1)
Fastener compatibility with roof deck
Corrosion
Codes compliance and approvals
Spacing requirements
50% more at corners and perimeters
Adhering with hot bitumen
Must be structural concrete (3.1.3)
Off-gassing of roof deck or insulation when hot-mopped (8.1)
Compressive strength—required for
Equipment traffic
Material loading
Compatible/acceptable—with
Adhesives or mopping
Polystyrene and some cutback asphalt adhesive incompatible
Off-gassing of vapors from hot mopping should be absorbed by other insulation layers or vented by roof base sheet type or by roof system design. (8.1)
Roof deck
Phenolic foam corrodes steel deck in presence of moisture. (8.1.9)
Fasteners
To be manufactured, tested, and approved for attachment of insulation to specific roof deck being used
Moisture levels to be expected *within* insulation system (8.1)
Self-drying roofs (2.3.3)
High humidity levels below vapor retarder
Roof leaks which will probably go unaddressed for extended periods of time
Undetected because of structural concrete roof deck, vapor retardant below insulation, or because owner has no maintenance/repair/inspection program/budget

Environmental impact—is it (2.1.5)
Recyclable
High R-value per inch thickness
Less mass in landfill when replaced
Green design approved

Roof Penetrations and Structures

Roof penetrations*—consider*
Independent movement between roof deck and penetration component (12.3)
Vent fan or A/C curb vibration
Require flexible or moving base flashing to accommodate independent movement.
Consolidating pipe and ducts into fewer but larger penetrations
Codes
Cost
Plenum/attic cavity access
Side-wall venting
Type of penetration—consider
Steel, such as metal duct, often is supplied with standard curb flashing requiring insulation by roofer before flashing into bituminous roof system. (Fig. 2.8)
Are required materials standard to roof project?
Primer, hot asphalt, or adhesive insulation type required for proper R-value at side of steel curb.
Metal cant at curb base should be prohibited.
Wooden curb frames substituted for, or in place of, steel curbs
Fire risk with torch-applied systems (9.1.2)
How to secure to roof deck
How to seal off at top with roofing material
Maintenance
Attachment
Roof manufacturers requirements
Expense
Metal roof systems will require curb base flashing to be of same metal as roof membrane, for appearance and possibly compatibility. (10.4.1)
How to seal laps and joints of curb flashing
Caulk
Solder (12.2.4)
Compatibility of metal curb flashing with metal penetration object, such as the ductwork (10.4.1)
Cost per curb flashing × amount of curbs
Often custom-made by contractor
Special design and installation procedures, requiring extra time

Pipe penetrations
Elevated base flashing (12.3.1)
Requires roof curb, cant strip, and membrane flashings
Level-surface base flashing (12.3.2)
Less cost than elevated base flashings
Places metal flashing at roof level, and should be avoided if possible
Roof material manufacturer's warranty (15.3.3)
Flashing system requirements
Coverage exclusions
Costs

Roof structures: *penthouse walls, parapet walls, columns, equipment screens, etc.—consider*
Movements (12.3.1)
Independent movement between structure and roof
Requires flexible membrane flashing or movable metal flashing
May require expansion joint (Fig. 3.16)
Method of flashing the considered roof membrane to the structure—consider
Warranty requirements
Surface-mounted (12.2.9)
Through-wall (12.2.9)
In-wall (12.2.9)
Costs
Anticipated maintenance costs (12.2.9)
Waterproof integrity of the structure above roofline
In-wall and through-wall flashings or interior wall dampproofing must be adequate to prevent what can appear as roof leaks. (12.2.9)
Coordination of different trades
Crafts, trades, foot, and equipment traffic required to build structure above roofline
Resistance of the roof membrane to damage
Complete before roof is installed
In-wall or through-wall flashing placement may prevent proper roof installation at flashing area.
Complete after roof is installed
Damage to roof surface by other crafts and trades
Use protection overlay board
Often not effective

Roof Configuration

Slopes

Low-slope
Visible by occupants of building or of other buildings
Consider final appearance
Emergency overflow scuppers if surrounded by parapet wall (12.2.8)
Flexible membrane flashing details (12.3)
Elevate per manufacturer's and NRCA requirements (12.3.1)
Sheet metal flashing details (12.2)
Allow for expansion and contraction (12.2.1)
Elevate per SMACNA requirements (12.2.6)
Specify proper gauge for design dimensions (12.2.5)
Steep-slope
Roof finish is important for visible roof systems.
Durability
Environment
Foot traffic
Maintenance requirements
Manufacturer's warranty
Disclaimers
Flashing details—visible?
Valleys
Hips
Ridges
Additional design and construction costs
May require water-barrier design at roof areas prone to water flooding or ice damming (10.3.1 and 11.1)

Drainage

Internal roof drain assemblies
Insulated leader pipe required under deck, sloped for drainage
On large buildings usually less costly than gutter and downspout systems
On metal roofing systems, avoid internal gutter drains if at all possible.
Taper insulation crickets often required between roof drains (8.1.4)
Gutter and downspout—consider (12.2.7)
Cost
Eliminate in entirety
Water washing over building face
No windows or doors on that face
Stain and mildew possible
Moisture entry through wall possible
Overhang or eave design
Keeps water and water damage from building wall face
Allows for attic/plenum ventilation design consideration
Possible erosion to landscaping
Scuppers can limit problem. (12.2.8)
Sheet metal type
Compatibility with adjacent sheet metal (12.2.3)
Appearance
Present and future

Corrosion resistant
Aluminum
Copper
Stainless steel
Terne (lead coated)
Joint and lap seaming
Caulk or solder
Cost of various metal types being considered
Material cost
Forming costs
Installation costs
Expansion design for gutter (12.2.7 and 12.2.1)
Mounting to building structure
Expansion joint every 50 ft
Movement at outlet tubes
Water discharge areas
Landscaping damage
Pedestrian-area flooding and subsequent icing

Visual effect

Parabolic, barreled, hyperbolic
Metal roof panels (10.1)
Custom manufactured at factory
Allow sufficient lead time
Provide accurate roof dimension drawings
Properly budget
Qualified contractor availability
Flexible roof membrane
Often polymeric single-ply (*not referenced herein*)
Modified bitumen membrane (9.1)
Heat-welded
Metallic laminate surfacing
Manufacturer's warranty (15.3.3)
Polyurethane foam (*not referenced herein*)
Cold-process asphalt built-up roof system (4.1.5)
Roof finish maintenance requirements (6.1)
Roof structure movements
Parabolic and hyperbolic structures sometimes experience extraordinary movements.
Isolate movements to ridge and valleys, if any, and allow for roof movement at those areas.
Prevent any structure movement with proper engineering.

Architectural structures

Roof gardens and terraces
Root barrier over waterproofing membrane
Direct water discharge from other areas of the roof away from garden/terrace.
Provide overhang at doorways for sun and rain protection.

Clerestory windows and skylights
Provides economical lighting to building interior
Interior window wall flashings critical to long-term waterproofing
Elevate skylight curbs a minimum 8 in above roof surface level.

Code Requirements

Wind resistance*—consider* (2.2.2)
Deck attachment
Insulation attachment
Wood-nailer attachment
Membrane attachment
Aggregate or ballast type, size, and attachment

Fire resistance*—consider* (2.2.3)
Deck type
Insulation type
Requirements vary with type of roof deck and type of roof-membrane system.
Membrane type
Can vary with type of surfacing and type of insulation or roof deck
Verify compliance of total roof system with roof-material manufacturer.
Send to technical department

Local code requirements
Seismic (2.2.4)
Surfacings (6.1)
Insulation (8.1)

Contractors

Means of procurement

Competitive bid
Specification requirements and design must be complete, nonambiguous, and enforceable, clearly stating all requirements of end products.
Limiting bidder pool
Manufacturer-approved applicator
Prebid approval by designer
Performance bond requirements
Increased cost
Often less project administration and site inspection
Owner required contractor
Clearly define the designer's scope of responsibility.
Site inspection
Rejection of work
Contractor experience with roof system being designed and specified

Negotiated
Often lower cost than competitive bid pricing
Selected contractor available to assist with preconstruction detail drawings
Manufacturer data and approvals
Fast-track scheduling and compliance often more feasible
Intricate and complex systems often best negotiated with qualified contractor

Availability of contractors
Seasonal workload at time of construction
Costs often related to supply and demand
Contractors familiar with type of system designed
New or unfamiliar types of systems often lead to excessive bid pricing or inadequate bid pricing and poor performance.
Local contractor advantage if
The system is standard to local area.
Contractors are comfortable with general contractor, if any.
Workload is not excessive.

Health and Safety

Building occupants
Noise levels (2.3.2)
Acoustic control design
Light entry
Skylights
Clerestory window wall
Roof overhangs to limit radiant sunlight energy
Temperature comfort in relation to energy consumption
Roof insulations (8.1)
Attic/plenum ventilation (10.2.2)
Roof loads and collapse (2.2.1)
Adequate roof drainage
Emergency overflows (12.2.8)
Snow loads
Roof configuration

Worker safety
Hazardous material survey (13.1.3)
Asbestos-containing materials
OSHA compliance
Designer's responsibility limits

Environmental concerns
VOC requirements
Caulks and liquids
EPA
Hazardous materials
Recyclability (2.1.5)
Roof insulations
Roof pavers
Sheet metal

Security

***Building contents**—consider*
Roof access—via—
Exterior wall-mounted ladders
Access from adjacent rooftops
Access via building-wall structures
Fire escape routes
Roof deck type (3.1)
Structural concrete versus light-gauge steel insulated roof deck
Skylights
Roof hatches
Roof-mounted equipment
Vent fan assemblies

Roof drainage components
Gutter and/or downspouts (12.2.7)
Copper and aluminum
Theft for scrap value

COMMENTS: ____________________

15.3 GENERAL REQUIREMENTS OF DESIGN AND SPECIFICATION

GENERAL DESIGN CONSIDERATIONS

There are numerous styles, means, and manners by which designers create the roof drawings apportionment of the contract documents. All designs include the roof plan, but the manner in which the roof details are addressed varies. One variable is whether the design is for new construction or for reroof construction.

In new construction, standard details are often copied from industry manuals, such as the *NRCA Roofing and Waterproofing Manual, SMACNA Architectural Sheet Metal Manual,* or from the roof material manufacturer's specification manual. This normally suffices, so long as the roof curbs, wood nailers, and other associated flashing structures are built to allow for the shown construction.

For this design process to work correctly, other craft and trade personnel must be fully aware of all requirements of the flashing structure, such as minimum or maximum height or thickness of wood curbs and blocking. Standard roof flashing details from manuals do not always completely address these items since it is not within the scope of work required by roofing personnel.

If standard details are copied from a reference source, additional dimension requirements may be necessary to the drawing. In order to accomplish this, additional steps may first be necessary to determine accurate size and dimension requirements. For example, scuppers through a roof edge may be a generic detail within a reference manual. A tapered cricket system is normally required between the two scuppers. Seldom are the tapered insulation and subsequently applied roof edge blocking shown in entirety within the manual reference. This complete layout must be considered to create a proper flashing detail of the scupper. (See Fig. 12.17.)

The use of unedited standard details for roof design often requires interpretation and understanding of all design requirements by the contractors. The design requirements are implied instead of expressed.

Clarity of all design requirements is often achieved from shop drawings submitted by the roof contractor. Copies of these approved drawings are forwarded to the general contractor, who then has the responsibility to build or install the required wood blocking and other components which will allow for proper roof installation.

In theory this design process should work. However, if the designer is not aware of all unusual or critical situations which will occur with the roof construction, they cannot be sure that all required shop drawings are produced correctly and completely.

In reroof design there are often roof problems and failure at detail areas which were not properly built during original construction. Such deficiencies may be covered over by roof construction and are not easily discerned during the original construction inspection prior to reroofing.

In theory, once again, we assume that the roof applicator would not proceed with work which will produce unsatisfactory results. However, in the real world this often happens. The roof applicator has production deadlines to meet and stopping the roof work to get the designer involved in a problem, possibly requiring work stoppage by other parties to once again build a roof component, is sometimes difficult for the roof applicator/contractor. In addition to lost production, any discontent that is created can possibly affect payments to the roof contractor.

GENERAL SPECIFICATION CONSIDERATIONS

Specifications describing the work or the system required is a key element of the construction documents. The format used for specification is normally MasterSpec by the American Institute of Architects or SpecText by the Construction Specifiers Institute.

This is usually where similarities end, especially for roofing specifications. Some specification documents are extremely general, relying on the referencing of standards or codes to describe the materials and work required. Thus, the designer states what is expected of the completed construction, creating what is referred to as *performance specification*. The contractor determines what materials, means, and methods are necessary to create such a system. Preconstruction shop drawings, material data, and other submittals are usually essential.

Performance specification could probably be created in several sentences, and we have often seen such, usually created by building owners or managers. For example:

> Provide and install roof insulations acceptable to roof material manufacturer, providing required U-value of __________ .
>
> Provide and install gravel-surfaced asphalt bituminous built-up roof system in accordance with material manufacturer's published specifications and general requirements for a twenty-year bondable-type roof system. Adhere to industry standards and accepted practices, both local and industrywide.
>
> Provide and install sheet metal flashings of (*material type*) to proper size and thickness, in proper amounts, at proper location, to provide adequate drainage and per-

manent waterproofing in full accordance with SMACNA requirements, industry standards, and accepted practices, both local and industrywide.

Performance specifications work fine, often saving design time by transferring system research to the contractor. However, if the contractor is not accurate or complete in research or understanding of governing standards or code, the results can be rework, dispute, and construction delay.

The other type of specification, which is the most common to the industry, is *prescriptive specification*. This means that a complete and comprehensive specification is required. However, omission of a particular duty or material description can imply that such is not required, and disputes can arise. It is therefore standard practice to state within the contract documents that, in the event of a dispute, discrepancy, or omission, the drawings will take precedence. Specifications are tied closely to the drawings.

On projects involving public funds, the contractor and material manufacturers cannot be discriminated against, and a more open and general prescriptive specification is used. This is sometimes the most difficult type of specification to create. In such cases, the designer can only specify the *type* of material to use, relying on code or standards reference to define specific products required, or sometimes more importantly, products not acceptable.

An example is roof insulation. The designer might specify polyisocyanurate, but might not limit selection to a particular manufacturer. The designer must accept all products equal to the specification requirements. It is therefore essential for the specifier to include all characteristics required of the roof insulation, or to include in the specification any properties or proven characteristics not allowed of the roof insulation.

This can be accomplished by referencing ASTM standards for such items as dimensional stability or compressive strength requirements. (See Sec. 8.1.) Any material not meeting the requirements can be rejected by the designer.

Therefore, a mingling of performance specification and prescriptive specification is used, which is the most common specification means used in the United States. The outlines in Secs. 15.1.1 and 15.2.1 help define the standards that are essential to the design. The most commonly used standards and references can be found in Chap. 14.

In Sec. 15.3.3, specification cautions, clauses, and examples are used to help define and assist with roof specification requirements. They are used mainly to illustrate how quality of the application can be further defined, and they are not all-inclusive.

In Sec. 15.3.2, design liability and how it can be reduced through specification requirements is discussed. This is achieved mainly through a submittal process.

15.3.1 Roof Design

ROOF PLAN

Several good design practices should be observed when designing the roof system. A complete roof plan should be created, showing both the roof area in its entirety and the roofline elevations. Even little areas—perhaps extending 6 in in and/or 6 in wide (though difficult to show)—should be included, as much for the designer's consideration as for the bidders.

Including notes on the roof plan is often helpful. Notes can reference the bidder/contractor to special situations or considerations. For reroof design, we sometimes see black-and-white photographs of existing conditions reproduced on a roof plan.

Looking at the completed roof plan should show where all roof flashing detail areas will occur. *All* detail flashing areas should be addressed by the design. Upon completing a flashing detail design, the roof plan is referred to, verifying that the height and dimension of the detail will fit appropriately within the roof plan and building-structure dimensions and requirements.

All rooftop equipment should be shown on the roof plan. This includes power ventilators, gravity ventilators, HVAC equipment, conduit lines, drainage systems, roof hatches and doors, walkways and traffic pads, and plumbing vents. The exact location and size of the rooftop equipment should be shown.

Many of these items are coordinated with the mechanical and electrical apportionment of the contract documents. Do not reproduce roof flashing details as provided by these engineers without verifying that such details are appropriate for the flashing situation and the roof system being designed.

Any equipment supports, roof penetrations, and roof drains will require a roof flashing detail. Often such details are not standard with other flashings on the roof and require special attention.

Special consideration must be given to the location of the flashing penetrations. Do not allow flashing penetrations or structures to be within 24 in of another.

All areas where the roof will be accessed by service personnel or inspectors should have roof pads or walkways installed. This will protect the roof during equipment loading (of tool boxes, freon bottles, etc.) at the access area and from the concentrated amount of foot and equipment traffic to be expected at the access/egress area.

Pads are especially important at doorways, roof hatches, and ladders. They may also be required across the roof from the access point to rooftop equipment that will need regular inspection and servicing.

General Drainage Requirements. Roof drain size and amounts should comply with code requirements, such as the Standard Plumbing Code, or conform to requirements from sources such as the SMACNA drainage tables. However, as a general rule of good design, a minimum of two roof drains should be included per roof area, with drains no further than 50 ft apart. Irregularly shaped roofs or roofs with penthouses and other structures often require additional roof drains for adequate drainage.

Many roof-material manufacturers require all water to be removed from the roof surface within a 48-hr period. This time frame indicates that evaporation is also an element of roof drainage, but is not necessarily good design practice or consideration. Instead, proper design should create a positive slope at all locations on the roof surface, which may require saddles and crickets between roof drains.

If peripheral drainage is designed, require all water to flow from the interior of the roof plan to the building wall exterior, where it is further directed to gutters or scuppers. In proper roof design, the roof edge flashing is elevated with scuppers, allowing for water discharge. (See Fig. 12.19.)

Again, saddles or crickets are often required to direct the water flow at the roof edge into scuppers. Such saddles or crickets are created by tapered roof insulation or wet-slur cementitious fill. In such design, consideration must be given to the wood nailer at the roof edge. (See Table 12.4.)

On steep-sloped roof systems, such as metal, tile, or slate, water may be drained into a gutter system where saddles or crickets are not required. Avoid built-in or internal gutters if possible.

However, on steep-sloped as well as low-sloped roof systems, it is often required to include crickets behind roof structures in order to prevent water accumulation and ponding behind such structures. (See Fig. 11.4.) On low-sloped roof systems this can require special base flashing design at the cricket, since roof-surface elevation changes with the increasing and decreasing thickness of the tapered insulation. The standard base flashing detail, as used elsewhere on the roof, may not work.

Roof Slope. As a general rule of good design practice, it is recommended that roof slope for bituminous membranes be a minimum of ¼ in:12 in. We also find it good practice to indicate roof slope direction and changes on the roof plan. Include any tapered insulation layout schematic, showing where tapered insulation panels are to start and end. This allows the designer to consider the thickness of roof insulation at any location, which in turn determines roof-surface elevation, which in turn can affect flashing details.

For example, doorway thresholds leading out onto the roof surface may not be high enough after installation of tapered roof panels. The same can be true for roof penetrations or structures. In such cases, additional design consideration must be given to these items to allow for the required height of the roof base flashing system, normally being 8 in. (See Sec. 12.3.1.)

GENERAL DETAILS

It may be appropriate to include sectional drawings of the roof system for generally occurring situations. This includes such items as the total roof assembly, including the roof deck, roof insulation layer(s), roof membrane, and surfacing. Such sectional drawings allow the designer to show how the roof insulation is to be (and not to be) attached to the deck, the minimum joint offset required of dual insulation layers, roof ply/membrane amounts and locations, and any special requirements of the basic roof system.

The roof insulation fastening pattern layout is often appropriate. This defines the amount of fasteners required per insulation panel and the placement location of the fasteners. Merely referring in the specification to manufacturers' requirements for fastening often results in a standard pattern of fastener placement. This standard pattern may not correctly address wind loads to be expected on a particular building. (See Sec. 14.3.) Also, since roof corners and edges require 50 to 100 percent more fasteners than the roof field, the placement pattern changes dramatically and needs to be shown to the roof applicator.

FLASHING DETAILS

Correct, complete, and proper flashing details are extremely important for a durable roof system.

- The detail area must be analyzed in relation to independent movement between the roof structure or roof penetration and the roof membrane system. (See Sec. 12.1.)
- A hot stack penetration must be flashed differently from a cold stack. (See Fig. 12.1.)
- If foot traffic is expected around the rooftop equipment for servicing and repair work, extra-durable base flashing is required. (See Fig. 2.13.)
- How the top of the base flashing can be attached to the roof structure/penetration is often an important consideration. Sometimes additional components or nailers must be installed to the roof structure/penetration. (See Fig. 3.17.)

- Sheet metal flashings must be analyzed in relation to: their expected movements during an annual thermal cycle, expansion joints incorporated into the flashing system, and the ability of the roof membrane to accommodate such movements for extended periods of time. (See Sec. 12.2.1.)
- Maintainability of the flashing systems is a consideration, especially in life cycle costs analysis. (See Secs. 2.1.2 and 2.1.4.)

Every flashing detail situation should be shown in the drawings. Isometric layout best reveals all intricacies and requirements, not only to the bidder/contractor, but to the designer as well. There are numerous times when a detail drawn to accurate dimension is discovered to be inappropriate.

For example, the 8-in required height of the completed elevated and cant-stripped base flashing may not be possible because other components of the roof penetration or structure are flashed, or because components of the flashing structure might be too large or too small as designed and need alterations. It is far easier to correct problems on the drawing board than in the field.

The use of standard details is one of the biggest design problems in the roof industry. The worst case is when a detail is copied from a manual and inserted directly into the drawings. Other times, a flashing detail is created and used throughout the drawings, even though it is not correct for all situations.

Many designers state that the detail drawing is meant merely to show the scope of the work required and the intention of the design. It is up to the roof installer to build the detail as required to meet the construction situation. To some degree, a conflict is created between what is shown and what is required.

Soapbox time: Contract documents, and particularly specifications and drawings, are meant to communicate requirements to the contractor. However, if communication were a simple task, then a meeting could be arranged and the designer could verbally explain what was needed by the contractor. No drawing or specification would be required. We all know this is not practical, prudent, or possible. Written and illustrated documents are required to convey the entire meaning and requirements to all parties involved in the construction.

Yet we see documents created that do not communicate well, and it must be said that this ability to communicate is one of the key elements which separate good designers from the average and below-average designers.

State and draw what you mean. If you use a standard detail and expect it to be adapted as required for the construction, state such on the drawing as well as in the specification. In such case, require a shop drawing from the contractor which accurately shows all dimensions and layouts.

However, this may not work either. Designers use standard details for three reasons: they are too ignorant of roof design requirements to create correct drawings, they are too lazy to take the time and effort to research and produce correct drawings for different detail areas, or they are too busy to custom-draw details. Because of this, it is doubtful if proper review and consideration can or will be given to shop drawings.

Another consideration in using standard detail drawings and expecting roofers to build them as required concerns the fact that there are different levels of knowledge, expertise, and management ability within a roof construction company. Many commercial roofing companies have estimators, project managers, superintendents, foremen, and lead employees. Designers are most accustomed to dealing with owners, estimators, managers, and superintendents. However, these are not the people installing our roof systems.

Foremen or lead employees are usually the people with their hands on the equipment and materials, and they are the ones who will produce roof systems as required. They have had instructions at prejob and job conferences. They supposedly have reviewed the specifications and drawings. They supposedly are professional craftsmen—but this may not always be the case. Especially since roof failure is a major reason for litigation, often traced directly to misapplication of materials or intent of the design in regard to application of materials, real-world realities should be considered.

It may well be proper to assume that the estimator, or project manager (if there is one), can interpret your meaning in the drawings. It may be proper to assume that such understanding will be conveyed to the roof applicators. It may not be proper to assume that these people will always be around to support and guide the applicators.

The link between contractor personnel from the time of bidding (estimator) to time of material purchase (project manager or superintendent) to time of crew organization and prejob conference (foreman) to time of material application (lead employee) is not always efficient or complete. In such a case, the applicator must rely on what is shown in the drawings. (Drawings are referred to much more often by the field personnel than are the specifications.) The general contractor often checks on produced product to determine acceptability but is guided not by his or her knowledge of roof systems (since this is not his or her area of expertise) but by the contract document drawings and specifications.

Also understand that roof contractors are not all equal. Some have far better management structures, quality control procedures, and qualified personnel than do others. This is evident across the entire country. If you designed the roof and the contractor applying your roof is not as professional as you expected, you are going to have problems with project administration, quality control, and end-result requirements. As a matter of fact, even the best contractor sometimes has major problems.

We believe that determination of what is needed for the roof system should not be left up to the roof contractor or even a material manufacturer. Please remember that standard details, like standard specifications, are to be used as a guide.

Each situation must be considered upon its own requirements and merits. A standard detail shows the basic requirements of the design for a particular situation, but the designer must adapt the standard detail to blend with the overall requirements and objectives of the roof system.

People who are recognized as leaders often attribute their success to paying close attention to the details.

15.3.2 Design Liability and Quality Control

GENERAL

Many designers think that roofing specifications and design are not the most interesting aspects of the construction documents. Combine this often-inherent lack of enthusiasm with the fact that roof systems are multifaceted, labor-intensive, and complicated, and the result may be premature roof failure.

The following reviews some procedures developed over the years that can help protect the designer's liability position. This is accomplished by obtaining statements of compliance along with data compilation from others, which can transfer much of the responsibility for roof performance to them.

Also included are procedures to use for help in obtaining guidance and expert review of the roof design documents, wording to include within the specifications to aid in quality control, and forms to use which allow the contractor to perform site inspection and quality control of the work. Section 15.3.3 addresses specification requirements more specifically in regard to key items to be considered.

SCENARIO

No matter if the roof designer is experienced with roof systems or is relatively inexperienced at the evaluation and design process, there are sometimes problems which can occur. A fictitious example of a problem scenario which can be avoided is as follows:

A roof designed by you five years ago begins to leak. Your client calls your office to inform you that his "20-year bonded roof" leaked last night directly over his new mainframe computer terminal. He is upset, but you assure him that warranties will fix all problems.

Upon examining the roof later (a built-up roof assembly in this case) you discover what appears to be ridges and cracks in the roof membrane. In addition some of the roof at the parapet walls is coming away from the wall and the roof drains are starting to be filled by the asphalt and gravel surfacing.

Upon checking your project file it is discovered that the roof contractor who installed the system is no longer in business. The general contractor is unresponsive, explaining that he is sympathetic to the situation but manufacturers' inspections were performed and warranties were issued, and the matter is out of his hands.

You may not be aware of all things at this point, but your client makes you very aware that he just incurred a $25,000 loss in one night and you are afraid he is about to incur a $250,000 massive roof loss. Lawyers names have been mentioned.

Not to worry, the material manufacturer's warranty bond will cover any problems. However, after days of correspondence, photographs, and site investigation by manufacturers' representatives, several things can happen here:

1. The manufacturer says yes, the problems may well be covered under a warranty claim, if that corporation were still a viable entity. However, after bankruptcy and reorganization several years ago, the company no longer exists such that it can respond to situations like this. The newly organized company merely acquired the material production equipment and other physical assets, and did not legally assume any of the liabilities. In good faith, the current corporation will donate some material to help with replacement costs, but does not by this offer imply or assume any responsibility or liability toward any future costs, etc., etc.
2. The manufacturer agrees that you and your client seem to have a serious problem, but the problem does not stem from products they supplied to the project. In the manufacturer's opinion, roof insulation is bridging under the roof membrane, thereby causing excessive movement that their roof membrane materials were never intended to withstand. Since they did not manufacture or supply the roof insulation materials, their warranty obligations are only for the bituminous waterproofing material system installed to top of the roof insulation. They are sympathetic to your situation and will do whatever they

can to provide assistance in the matter, so long as it does not expose them to loss or potential liability.

You retain the services of a roof expert to evaluate the existing system. The problems of roof membrane bridging and cracks, delaminating wall base flashing, and bitumen sluffing into roof drains are explained as follows.

Roof Membrane Bridging and Cracks. The type of roof insulation used proved to be dimensionally unstable. It was reformulated and different facers placed upon it. Since that time it has worked effectively within the roof industry.

Further investigation reveals that the panels were not attached properly to the metal roof deck. Additional fasteners were required in some locations and in other locations the screw fastener penetrated the lower flute of the metal deck pan instead of the upper pan portion as required. The screw fasteners as applied allowed too much movement of the panels. Combine this with areas of inadequate fastener amounts and a dimensionally unstable panel, and excessive movement is the result. (There goes any solid legal claim against the roof insulation manufacturer, since the panels were not installed as required.) It was also pointed out, much to your chagrin, that dual-layered insulation assemblies are industry standard, and not single-layer as that which is existing.

Delaminating Wall Base Flashing. It is determined by the roof consultant that several factors are contributing to the delamination of the base flashing from the parapet building wall. One item is the lack of asphalt primer, per material manufacturers' requirements and industry standards, which must be applied to a masonry wall before application of roofing materials. Somehow this was overlooked in the specifications and drawings and was not installed by the roofing applicators. Therefore, adhesion of the mopped asphalt to the masonry-covered parapet wall is inadequate.

Another item is the termination bar installed to the top of the base flashing system. The pin grip anchors are not holding in the masonry-clad wood wall frame structure. Longer and larger anchors may have sufficed, or a screw fastener would have been more appropriate. Also, the movements of the roof insulation layer are probably aiding in delamination of the flashing from the parapet.

Asphalt Bitumen and Gravel-Surface Sluffing. This problem is determined to be twofold. One factor is the 3-in-thick plastic foam roof insulation with an R-value of 16.8. In the hot climate in which the roof exists, the insulation holds the heat directly under the roof membrane, accelerating roof-membrane temperatures into the 150 to 170° range during summer months.

Type I asphalt was used as the top pour into which 400 lb per square of gravel surfacing were embedded. Type I asphalt is only used on low slopes because of its cold-flow abilities, being acceptable on slopes up to ½ in. The cold-flow characteristics should help lend durability to the roof system. The roof slope is ¼ in to prevent the possibility of any ponding water. However, the slope and the temperature extremes are causing the asphalt to flow in the hot summer months.

Compounding this phenomenon is the gravel surfacing. It is acting as a heat sink, and retains and extends the daytime heating period. The gravel prevents the heat repelled by the high-performance insulation from readily escaping.

Even with all these factors considered, the movement is still unusual. It is further rationalized that perhaps the asphalt was improperly heated by the roof applicators. (Sec. 4.1.3.) This, combined with the other factors, is causing the asphalt and gravel to sluff into the roof drains.

The preceding fictitious account is not intended to single out roof insulation as a major cause for roof failure. It is an exaggerated version of events remotely possible, and other scenarios not directly involving roof insulation, but just as serious, could be envisioned.

DESIGN QUALITY CONTROL AND PREVENTATIVE PROCEDURES

The scenario described in the preceding section, or others like it, can be avoided, while at the same time reducing design liability exposure. To avoid such scenarios, the specifications and drawings can be reviewed by the technical department of the material manufacturer's organization. Such review by recognized experts on roof materials and systems reduces design mistakes and, therefore, liability.

Clearly understand that review of design documents is not a standard practice of manufacturers, nor are they required to perform such a service. However, if their products are going to be used and a warranty bond will be required from them covering the completed system, then it is usually possible to get assistance from the warranty or technical department of the material manufacturer.

In some cases, an extensive review, certification, and submittal process is required, which is the responsibility of the contractor to produce for the designer. The process, as described below, is extraordinary within the roof industry. Contractors do not like providing all the paperwork, and it is often difficult to get a complete package from the contractor on the first submittal attempt.

However, the process supplies the designer with layers of liability protection. Although this process has never been tested with litigation, we believe the biggest harm can come to a designer through negligence.

If a designer can prove he or she has not been negligent, but has been diligent and performed all tasks required to ensure that a correct and durable system was designed, then liability risk should be reduced. Additionally, manufacturer review of the design should bring inadequacies or deficiencies to the designer's attention.

Following is an overview of a submittal process which can be used for design quality control. We recommend that, upon completion of the design but before it is released for bid, all specifications and drawings be sent to the material manufacturer. Any necessary corrections can be made before bid release instead of later as addenda or change orders.

Specification Submittal Requirements. After a successful bidder has been selected, but before Notice To Proceed is issued, require the contractor to provide submittals as follows:

Roof insulations. The primary roof-material manufacturer shall approve in writing of all roof insulations, fasteners, and plate assemblies to be used on the project, and provide a written statement that all of the insulation systems shall be covered and included in their (10-, 12-, 15-, 20-year) warranty.

Manufacturer's data shall be submitted verifying that all materials meet the minimum requirements as outlined in section *(include specification section number for material requirements—normally ASTM standards. Each requirement, e.g., a density requirement of 25 lb/ft^3, must be verified by a technical data sheet for the insulation material).*

Roof felts or membrane roofing. The primary roof-material manufacturer shall provide written certification that:

- They have reviewed all construction documents pertaining to the roof design, and all materials/systems/components specified for the project are physically and chemically compatible, one with the others.
- Materials conform to and comply with requirements of this specification.
- Each material and the system is acceptable and suitable for the intended purposes and guarantees.

Requirements of Section (number) shall be specifically included and referenced in this submittal.

Under the warranty requirement section of the specification, the length and type of warranty will be described. Also include the following as a warranty requirement submittal under that section:

- The primary roof material manufacturer shall, as a standard practice of doing everyday business, offer a *(10- to 20-year guarantee)* with *(include limits, e.g., no dollar limit)* on labor and materials.
- The guarantee/warranty shall include all roofing components/materials/systems from the roof deck and wood blocking up, with the exception of only the lead and sheet metal flashings, but shall include the flashing materials and plies which seal these flashings into the roof system.
- Supply materials data sheets or catalog cuts which list the following materials' ASTM compliance, federal specification numbers, Factory Mutual certifications, and/or Underwriters Laboratories certifications, verifying that the following materials meet requirements as listed in Section *(whatever section number was used to list references—ASTM, FM, NRCA, SMACNA, etc.)* of this specification.

  (List all of the main materials to be used in the roof construction, i.e.:)
- Metal screw fastener assemblies as per FM Approval Standard #4470

  (You probably will not be specifying an FM-rated system, but the #4470 Standard addresses corrosion and wind blow-off resistance of a fastener assembly. Therefore, you should require the fastener assembly (screw and metal stress plate) to have been tested and certified as complying with this standard.)
  - Asphalt primer
  - Roof cement
  - Fiberglass ply sheets
  - Gravel surfacing
  - Metal roof panel
    - Finish
    - Wind resistance

Show evidence that the primary roofing components and materials incorporated into the system are manufactured by a company producing and manufacturing such materials for commercial roof applications for at least five years within the United States.

Submit roof warranty/guarantee for review, including any and all exclusions, riders, and addenda.

Submit complete shop drawings showing roof configuration, sheet layout, seam locations, details at perimeters, and any special conditions. *(These drawings should already be in your documents.)*

The warranty/guarantee department which will be issuing the roof warranty shall provide written approval of the roof contractor for the project, and shall reference the project name and address.

(If asphalt or coal tar pitch is being used, require-)
Submit from the *(asphalt, coal tar pitch)* manufacturer, for all mopping bitumen to be used:

- Flash point
- Finished blowing temperature (for asphalt)
- Equiviscous temperature range (EVT)

Sheet metal flashing. The primary roofing contractor shall submit a certification statement, on the metal supplier's letterhead, stating that all metals supplied to the roof project conform to all requirements under Section *(number)*.

Submit complete shop drawings showing any special consideration concerning metal flashing styles, joints, and/or layout. *(These drawings should already exist within your documents.)*

This submittal process brings two other groups indirectly into your design team. These other parties, the roof contractor and the roof-material supplier, must review and approve of the design as complying with roof industry standards and proper roof design practices. Such review by these experts of roofing systems and materials will help assure the designer that the roof system is designed properly.

However, clearly understand that it is not the function or responsibility of either of these outside parties to design the system. As a matter of fact, they cannot be linked to decision-making processes. That is the designer's responsibility.

As stated previously, most contractors do not like performing this extensive submittal process. Additionally, we have found that sometimes the material manufacturer does not or cannot provide all the certification statements required within the submittal process.

If used, the submittal requirements should be fine-tuned to your particular practice and to the specific project. Most important, remember that the material manufacturer should be your friend and ally, but cannot be your designer—and can be, on a limited basis, your consultant.

A material manufacturer has two primary goals. One is to sell materials. The other is for roof systems using their materials to function trouble-free.

A contractor's primary goal can be defined as being profit-motivated. How to best accomplish this is the business decision of the contractor, and is what creates so many differently managed and structured companies. The submittal process previously described will cost the contractor time and, therefore, money. You can expect higher bid prices when including these requirements.

However, most professionally managed contracting companies realize that by installing quality roof systems, which are durable and functional, their bottom-line profit is increased. The submittal process further defines all areas of responsibilities and requirements of the contractor. It protects the contractor as well as the designer.

Job-Site Documentation Control. No matter how well and complete the roof system is designed, if it is not installed correctly, it will fail. In this event, the designer once again is in the middle of possible litigation, defending the design.

The best money a building owner can spend is on full-time, third-party site inspection. This is also to the advantage of the designer. (See Sec. 13.1.3.) However, most roof systems are installed without the quality control benefits of a full-time inspector. Following is a means by which the roof applicator becomes the roof inspector. This process again will increase the cost of the roof system, and once again, it is difficult to get contractors to follow the requirements accurately and diligently.

The program consists of a Daily Report Form to be filled out every day by the superintendent or foreman. Included must be photographs of all major items of work for that day, as well as photos showing key components being installed. A Roof Plan on the back of the form shows where work was performed that day. Also included are sections listing workers and their classification, weather conditions, and, if required, temperatures of mopping bitumen. Other pertinent information is also to be included on the Daily Report Form. (See Fig. 15.2.)

The program has procedures built into it which limit and discourage false information and statements. Another key reason for use of the form is to limit the liability exposure of the designer, although, if used incorrectly, the form could increase designer liability.

The designer usually makes rooftop inspection of the work in progress and of the completed system. However, such inspection cannot confirm correct installation of roof components and materials that are hidden from view. These hidden materials, such as type and amount of roof plies at base flashing areas, attachment of the roof insulation layers, mopping bitumen amounts, and uniformity between the plies, are key ingredients of a durable roof system.

If a roof warranty is being specified for the job, and roof problems develop due to improper application of materials, most warranties have exclusion of coverage for such problems. (See Sec. 15.3.3.) The Daily Report Forms can be sent to the material manufacturer, along with photos, showing and describing the system application as it progresses. Theoretically, in the event that warranty problems develop due to misapplication of

DAILY REPORT FORM

ROOFING OF:

ROOFING BY:

(Include project name and address) ______________________________

(Include contractor name and address) ______________________________

WORKERS:

Classification	*#*	*Hours*	*Location*	*Duties Performed*
Journeymen	______	______	______	______
	______	______	______	______
Helpers	______	______	______	______
	______	______	______	______
Laborers	______	______	______	______
	______	______	______	______

INSPECTION:

Was the roof deck inspected before application of roofing? ______________________________

Was it acceptable? ______________________________

Were fastening patterns inspected and acceptable before further application of roof material? ______________

Insulation? ______________________________

Base sheet? ______________________________

Metal flashings? ______________________________

Was metal primed? ______________________________

WEATHER CONDITIONS: **Sky** ______ **Wind** ______ **% Chance of Rain** ______ **Temperature** ______

(i.e.—clear——N.—gusting——10%——55°)

A.M. ______________________________

____

P.M. ______________________________

____

E.V.T. TEMPERATURE READINS AT MOP CART: (Take readings hourly)

Temp @ Time	Temp @ Time	Temp @ Time	Temp @ Time	Temp @ Time	Temp @ Time
____ @ ____	____ @ ____	____ @ ____	____ @ ____	____ @ ____	____ @ ____
____ @ ____	____ @ ____	____ @ ____	____ @ ____	____ @ ____	____ @ ____

ADDITIONAL COMMENTS: (Instructions from designer/consultant/engineer; instructions from general contractor; unusual situations or demands encountered today)

____

____

____

NAME ______________________ **Day and Date** ______________________

FALSIFYING OR MISREPRESENTATION OF INFORMATION WILL BE GROUNDS FOR RESTRICTING THE FOREMAN/SUPERINTENDENT PERMANENTLY FROM THE PROJECT SITE.

Figure 15.2

materials, the Daily Report Form with photos should strengthen your, or your client's, position.

If a warranty is not required, the designer still needs to be informed of the quality of the roof-system application. The Daily Report Form provides this and, as stated earlier, can reduce the designer's liability exposure in the event that problems with the roof develop due to poor workmanship. If the photos in the report do not show problems with the installation or if the form does not indicate any problems with the installation, then the designer had no reason to expect or anticipate any problems. The designer was not negligent, and due to misrepresentation on the part of the contractor, had no reason to assume that any potential problems existed within the system.

The downside to this process is that if something *is* wrong and is shown in the photos or listed on the report, and the designer does not respond with corrective requirements, then he or she can be considered negligent.

15.3.3 Roof Warranties

GENERAL

Roofing warranties may provide a false sense of security for the designer and the building owner. Manufacturers' warranties often contain exclusions and limits to coverage not explicitly stated. Different types of warranties are appropriate for different kinds of coverage. The owner has certain responsibilities to maintain the roof under warranty. Architects can limit liability with proper roof system design and field inspection.

Roof leaks and liability exposure are facts of life that designers and others in the building trade dread. If a roof leaks, the client often expects the designer to accept liability. Many design professionals use the roof warranty as an instrument to get a leak-free roof and, in the event of a problem, to transfer liability to another party—the material manufacturer that issued the warranty.

But the designer's liability exposure may be increased when specifying a warranty. A warranty does not always guarantee a leak-free roof nor does it always give the building owner relief from roof leaks. We have inspected scores of roofs that have failed while still under warranty. Most often, the building owner (the warrantee) gets no relief from the material manufacturer (the warrantor).

The owner is often confused, then angry. A warranted roof usually costs more than a nonwarranted system, but the owner may have been told by the designer that a warranty would provide protection in the event of roof leaks, so why must the owner now pay for another new roof?

THE MANUFACTURER'S VIEWPOINT

Manufacturers of roofing materials are not in the design business—a fact they will quickly point out. They only make roofing products which must then be cut, shaped, and placed by roofing applicators to rooftop and roof deck equipment. Nor do they design, manufacture, or install rooftop or roof deck components. Therefore, if a roof leaks or fails around a rooftop component, such as a ventilator which is not installed properly, the warranty probably will not cover it. If the water that intrudes around that component spreads to other areas of the roof, the subsequently affected area and the resulting roof damage will not be covered under the warranty either.

The argument presented to the manufacturer by the designer or owner is: "Your representative looked at the roof and you accepted it as warrantable!" "Yes," the manufacturer will admit, "but we are not hired to provide, nor do we engage in, the design of roof systems. If you will look closely at our warranty, you'll see that we state clearly it does not cover the roofing material or system when applied to or over items that are not designed or installed to manufacturer and industry standards. We know you are aware of this because you were given a warranty, and this statement is in paragraph D, clause 4, line number 7." The designer then gets out the magnifying glass and reads the fine print.

WHY YOU'RE NOT COVERED

To further understand this, a few examples are in order. A rooftop power ventilating fan may come from the factory mounted to a metal base and flange. The base is normally 4 to 6 in high. Roof industry standards and material manufacturers' specification manuals require that all roofing at such penetrations terminate a minimum of 8 in above the roof surface.

For roofing to be installed properly around the power fan assembly, it must be raised to the required height by a wooden curb, to which cant strips and roofing are applied. All roofing is then attached at the top to the curb with fasteners 8 in on center. If this is not done (and normally it isn't), then any leakage around the power fan is not covered by the warranty.

Another example is failure caused by roof insulation that is not firmly attached to the roof deck. The unattached roof insulation moves and warps, causing the roof system to split and crack. When confronted with this, the material manufacturer may deny coverage under warranty because the manufacturer's specification manual and industry standards state that all roof insulation must be firmly attached to the roof deck or substrate. Their inspector has no way of knowing that the insulation is not attached when the warranty inspection of the completed roof is performed.

Any damage caused by traffic across the rooftop (window washers, HVAC mechanics, etc.) is not covered under a warranty. Also normally excluded are damage caused by ice and snow, and acts of God. Roof loss or damage caused by ponding water, damage or loss because of deck deflection or movement, sheet metal flashings, and damage caused by expansion and contraction of such is normally excluded under warranty exclusions.

Some warranties don't cover any of the base flashings, even though they are bituminous materials produced the manufacturer. In order to get a warranty for these items, a *flashing endorsement* may be required.

THE EXCLUSION GAME

Often there is not enough money in the budget to install a superior roof system including dual layers of roof insulation, wood curbs for power fan motors, and raised blocking at roof edge. If a manufacturer will not issue a warranty because the roof, as designed, doesn't have all the bells and whistles required by stringent roof industry standards, the designer's natural response might be to find a manufacturer that will. In order not to lose the job, the sales representative will issue a warranty with the normal exclusions.

One exclusion can be for materials that warrantors do not manufacture. Most warranties cover only items produced by that manufacturer, unless specifically stated otherwise. When a roof fails, the failure is often claimed to be directly related to the components not manufactured by the warrantor. And the building owner is out of luck.

This hazard can be avoided by designing and specifying a roof that has a *full-system warranty*. All materials used in the roof should then be included in the warranty. A full-system warranty fee (either a lump sum or one related to the roof area) is normally required. In many cases, the most expensive components the manufacturer produces are then required to be incorporated into the roof system, sometimes in generous amounts.

A NECESSARY EVIL

Many manufacturers hope that, eventually, labor and material warranties will be a thing of the past. Trouble and problems arise due to misunderstandings between parties about responsibility and remedies offered under warranties, as well as the manufacturer's cost of warranty administration and legal expenses.

Manufacturers are in the business to produce and sell products. Without sales, they cease to exist. Sales representatives use the warranty to sell materials.

If a manufacturer initiates a warranty program that no other manufacturer offers, that manufacturer will start to take product sales from the others. Designers want the most comprehensive and long-lasting warranty they can get for the least cost. A vicious circle is set up, whereby manufacturers cannot allow one particular product line to offer a warranty program that is superior to all others.

Warranty claims and the related expenses have caused major manufacturers to abandon, sell, or bankrupt entire product lines. As roofing becomes more expensive, lawyers become more aggressive. To boost sales and marketing, warranties also become more aggressive. Manufacturers have no choice but to play the warranty game. If they abandon or curtail their warranty programs when others do not, their sales can be drastically affected.

WARRANTY TYPES AND CONDITIONS

Roof warranties fall into four common categories:

- Warranties that encompass material performance only.
- Labor and material warranties, which are prorated and decrease in value as the roof ages.
- Warranties that will pay to only a specific dollar limit, which usually does not exceed the cost of the original installation.
- No-dollar-limit (NDL) warranties that pay all material and labor costs, no matter what the amount. An NDL warranty is usually provided for only a full-system warranty design. If your client requires a roof warranty, a full-system NDL warranty is the best, but be prepared to pay top dollar for it!

Some manufacturers offer dual-term warranties, such as 5-year/5-year or 10-year/10-year. At the end of the first term, the manufacturer and the contractor examine the roof. Any additional work required to renovate and restore the roof is performed at a cost to the building owner. The second term of the warranty is then initiated. Additional exclusions may be added for the second term.

OWNER RESPONSIBILITIES

An important but often overlooked item is owner responsibility under the warranty. The owner cannot directly engage a contractor to do work on the warranted roof system. Instead, the owner must notify the material manufacturer of any roof performance problems or any additions or renovations planned for the roof system. The manufacturer then provides written approval of the proposed work and may also provide a list of the contractors approved to perform the work. If this process is not followed, a warranty may be voided. A complete paper trail is important.

Periodic inspection of the roof system, although not a specific requirement of some warranties, is strongly urged by material manufacturers. Most warranties require proper maintenance to be performed to the roof system. If large areas of the roof system deteriorate or fail because of lack of inspection and care by the owner, it is possible that the warranty will exclude coverage for such losses.

Although warranties may cover both labor and materials, coverage may be denied if the materials are not installed to the manufacturer's specifications and requirements. Only manufacturer-certified and -approved applicators can install warranted roof systems. Manufacturers screen contractors before certifying them and often have training programs for applicators.

Usually a legal agreement between the contractor and the manufacturer states that any problems experienced on the warranted roof shall be repaired at no labor cost to the manufacturer. In such cases, if leaks develop because of improper application of materials, the original roofing contractor is legally bound to repair the affected area at no cost to the manufacturer.

In the event that the roof leaks because of improper application of materials and the original contractor is no longer in business, the manufacturer may not be legally bound to the owner to correct such deficiencies. This is because many warranties state in the exclusion section that all materials not installed to all of the manufacturer's current published specifications and requirements are excluded from coverage. This means that all requirements in the manufacturer's specification manual may apply to the construction—these specification manuals are several inches thick!

A cursory inspection of the completed roof by a manufacturer's representative cannot determine the adequacy and correctness of many items such as inner-ply bitumen moppings, temperature of the bitumen during construction, placement and installation of roof insulation, and flashing plies at roof penetrations.

HOW TO COVER YOUR ASSETS

There are ways by which designers can protect themselves and the building owner. The best way is to design a complete roof system. All roof penetrations and details must be accurately and completely drawn, noting all roofing and flashing components to be used. Often designers use the National Roofing Contractors Association (NCRA) *Roofing and Waterproofing Manual,* the Sheet Metal and Air-Conditioning Contractors National Association (SMACNA) *Architectural Sheet Metal Manual,* or material manufacturers' manuals and copy the standard details therein. But the actual roof penetration, equipment, or component is usually not the exact design, shape, height, or configuration illustrated in the standard details. The detail must be tailored to existing conditions.

During the design stage, one should consult a technical representative in the roofing manufacturer's warranty department. Sales representatives are usually very competent at sales and service, but for technical assistance and guidance it is best to go directly to the manufacturer.

Fax your preliminary drawings and design information to the technical consultant. If it is a reroofing project, send photographs, core sample analysis, and any other survey information that could be helpful. We find that most reputable manufacturers are very willing to work with the designer at this stage—and it's free!

However, manufacturers will not (and should not) design the roof for you. This will put them in a position of liability which they will not assume. When a design is completed, send the entire set of contract documents to the warranty department for review.

WORKING WITH THE CONTRACTOR

During the contractor submittal process, require (see Sec. 15.3.2):

- A letter from the manufacturer's warranty department stating that all contract documents relating to the roof system have been reviewed, that all materials are physically and chemically compatible with each other, and that the system, as designed, is suitable for the specified warranty
- For a full-system warranty, a statement verifying that all materials, from the roof deck up, excluding metal flashings but including the roof materials used to seal the metal flashing, are included under the warranty
- A statement from the manufacturer that the roof contractor is an approved applicator of the material manufacturer and is in good standing
- Address and location of the building to be included in the written statement from the manufacturer

Submittals from the contractor should also include every item that is to be used in roof construction. Submittals must verify that all materials conform to references within the specifications as they relate to, but are not limited to: the American Society for Testing Materials (ASTM); Factory Mutual (FM); and/or Underwriters Laboratories (UL) standards. Since contractors often select materials that are equal to what is specified, send the entire submittal package to the material manufacturer for review and approval.

This may seem like a lot of trouble, and some manufacturers will not want to provide the statements listed above. By the time you get to the contractor submittal process, the bidder will usually have found a manufacturer who will work with you on the project—hopefully, the one who reviewed the design before the bid process.

It is to the manufacturer's advantage to work with you. If the roof system is designed and specified completely and installed accurately, the roof should last the intended life span.

FIELD INSPECTION

One other problem remains. Even with a proper and complete roof design, how do we know that the roofing crew is going to install the system as it was designed and specified? A full-time, qualified inspector is the best investment of the client's roofing money.

From a liability position, it is ideal if the owner hires the inspector. Many manufacturers can suggest a qualified roof inspector. The key word here is *qualified*. The roofing manufacturer's sales representative can usually provide the names of local people who are qualified inspectors.

Since full-time inspection normally costs from 5 to 8 percent of the total roof cost, it is often not provided. In that case, the roofing foreman should be required to complete and submit a daily report. (See Fig. 15.2.) The report should list the major items of concern during roof construction, such as acceptability of roof deck, proper layout and attachment of roof insulation, ambient temperatures, weather conditions, size of crew, and type of equipment used that day. If a built-up roof is being installed, list the temperature of mopping bitumen (at the mop cart). These readings should, at a minimum, be taken hourly.

You can include a Daily Report Form in your contract documents (the best way), or you can require the contractor to submit a report form to you for approval prior to beginning work. Include a roof plan, usually on the back of the form, and have the work area for that day shown on the drawing. In addition, require the contractor to take photographs daily during the roof construction process.

CONCLUSION

It should be understood that this discussion of warranties has been in the broadest terms. Since a warranty is a legal instrument, lawyers are the people best qualified to determine how the wording is to be interpreted, what is the manufacturer's intent, and how relief is provided under the terms of the warranty. Each manufacturer's warranty program is different, and each warranty claim must be evaluated on a case-by-case basis. But keep in mind that an unenforceable warranty may increase a designer's liability, not diminish it, since the design or practice did not provide that which was promised, paid for, or intended.

15.3.4 Specification Requirements

GENERAL

Since roofing is a complicated construction system, we believe that being as explicit as possible about requirements or restrictions placed upon materials or workers is the best course of design. Following are examples of some of the dos and don'ts to use within roofing specification documents.

WOOD NAILERS AND BLOCKING

Moisture Content. It is preferable if lumber incorporated into a roof system has a moisture content of 19 percent or less. This requirement does little good for lumber installed and then left exposed to the elements of rain or snow. Wood nailers, wood blocking, and equipment curbs of wood are often installed to a roof deck in advance of roofing operations.

However, the moisture content of 19 percent or less means the material was kiln-dried to an acceptable level, and later exposure to water or moisture. This should not have an adverse effect. Adverse effects happen when the lumber contains excessive amounts of moisture which make it curl and warp after being installed and encapsulated within the sometimes superheated roof system.

Decay-Resistant Lumber. Lumber treated to resist rot or decay should be used at all roof flashing areas, such as the wood nailer or blocking onto which subsequent roof flashing materials will be mounted. This is because roof flashings are often known to leak for extended periods of time before roof repair is initiated. The treated lumber will resist water for the extended periods of time that may be required. Treated lumber is not required for the roof deck system.

The chemical used to treat the lumber for decay resistance is normally chromated copper arsenate (CCA). CCA-treated lumber is provided in two categories in compliance with the American Wood Preservers Association (AWPA) standard C-2—95, which refers to the amount of preservative within the lumber.

For aboveground use, specify treatment as .25 CCA, and for ground contact require .40 CCA treatment. The percentages refer to the pounds per cubic foot of the preservative within the lumber. A treatment of .25 is normally sufficient for a roof application.

Other forms of chemical combinations used to preserve lumber are ammoniacal copper zinc arsenate (ACZA), normally used for treating Douglas fir, and newer formulations on the market, such as ammoniacal copper quat, Type B (ACQ) and copper citrate. ACQ and copper citrate do not contain arsenate or chromium and are favored for "green design."

At one time, some wood preservatives were made from a salt-base formulation, and as such, corrosion was possible with some fasteners and sheet metal. Today the salt-base chemical formulation is not used; however, compatibility can still be a concern. For example, aluminum sheet metal flashing, as would be used as the metal edge flashing on a roof, is not compatible with ACQ.

As a rule, carbon steel nails should never be used with any preservative-treated lumber. As a minimum, specify hot-dip galvanize-coated fasteners, and in conditions where moisture will be present, stainless steel nails should be used.

Attachment Requirements. Wind-load resistance of a roof system is highly dependent upon the manner of attachment of the wood nailer to the roof structure, especially the wood nailers around the roof perimeter. Spacing requirements of the fasteners may vary, as well as the specific types of fasteners required, all of which are dependent upon the wind-load stresses which can occur to a specific building and roof structure.

Model building codes have standards or references for attachment procedures and means of wood blocking and nailers to the roof and building structure. Also consider Factory Mutual (FM) Standard 1-49, which is a very comprehensive requirement standard. It addresses not only how the nailer/blocking should be secured to the building and roof structure, but also how the sheet metal roof flashings should be attached to the wood nailer.

It is good design practice to routinely require all lumber to bear the stamp of a recognized grading bureau, such as the Southern Pine Inspection Bureau (SPIB), and be graded at least as number 2 or better. Pine is the material normally required for wood blocking, nailers, and curbs on a roof system.

Specifications should require all lumber to be installed in straight, accurate and true, plumb and level lines. All adjacent end joints of lumber (if any) should be offset, one from the other, a minimum of 24 in. All lumber should be fitted tightly and consistently to the structure upon which they are mounted.

Fasteners, if nails or screws, should be of such size that the fastener penetrates a minimum of 1 in into the structure or component to which it is being attached. For example, a 2 × 4 being attached to an installed wood nailer must be attached with fasteners a minimum of 2½ in long. Also realize that the underlying component must be, at a minimum, 1 in thick.

Only hot-dip galvanized fasteners or other fasteners meeting corrosion-resistance ratings per ASTM should be specified for use.

Roof Decking. When wood materials are used as the roof decking it is important that they are completely cured—especially wood plank. Again, a stamp certification of a major grading bureau or lumber association, such as the SPIB, the West Coast Lumber Bureau (WCLB), or the American Plywood Association (APA), is visible on each piece of wood material delivered to the job site. This indicates that the lumber has been properly dried and cured and graded for acceptable uses. Treated lumber is not required of roof decking materials.

Make sure that attachment means and methods are referenced. The APA has a reference guide to be used for attachment patterns of plywood to a roof structure. Additionally, consider local and regional building codes. Normally, additional fasteners are required at eaves, rakes, gables, and hips.

Always leave a space at the end and side joints of wood roof decking. Superheating and cooling is extreme under a roof system, and allowances for expansion and contraction must be made. Also remember that ring-shank nails have far better back-out resistances than do smooth-shank nails or screws. (See Sec. 2.1.1.)

More information on wood roof decks can be found in Sec. 3.1.4.

ROOF INSULATIONS

We are not concerned with the type of roof insulation selected for the design, the determination of which is discussed in previous sections. The characteristics required of the insulation(s) can be defined by the use of reference standards as found in Chap. 14. In this section we are concerned with how the materials are installed into the roof system. For general design practices and consideration to be used when specifying roof insulation, see Chap. 8.

Mechanical Attachment. Roof insulation is often installed to a metal roof deck. In such cases, there should be two layers of roof insulation specified. The bottom layer is mechanically attached to the steel roof deck panels using self-tapping screws with metal stress plates. (See Fig. 3.4.)

The attachment location of the screw fastener is important. It should only penetrate the pan of the metal roof deck and not the flute. (See Fig. 2.5.) Wind-load resistance is severely compromised if the fastener is rotated due to penetration of the flute instead of the pan. Fastener rotation can also occur if the insulation layer is too thick.

To avoid this possibility, specify the screw length. For example, if the roof insulation is 1 in thick, specify the screw length to be 1¾ or 2 in long. If the roof installers place the fastener over the flute instead of the pan, the fastener will not be able to engage the deck because the flute is normally 1½ to 2½ in deep. The short fastener will not reach to the bottom of the flute.

Also remember to specify the accuracy of installation of the metal roof deck. If the roof deck deviates, the side edges of the roof insulation will not rest upon the metal deck pan at all locations. The side edges of insulation panels cannot occur over a deck flute. (See Fig. 8.2.)

To avoid this occurrence, require no more than ¼ in deviation in a straight line per 100-ft run of metal roof decking. Sometimes deviations greater than this occur, and they may still be acceptable so long as at least 1½ in of the roof insulation panel rests upon the pan of the metal roof deck. (See Sec. 8.1.)

Require all fasteners to be tested and approved per Factory Mutual Standard #4470. This standard addresses corrosion.

Attachment patterns of fasteners should not be specified to conform with material manufacturers' recommendations. These recommendations normally do not address job-specific conditions. Instead, require the fastener patterns to be in accordance with Factory Mutual requirements for either 1-60, 1-90, or 1-120 system standards.

Remember that to achieve such certified rating, not only the fastener and the pattern of fastening, but the roof insulation type as manufactured and the roof deck assembly type must have been tested and certified under FM requirements. Also remember that, per FM requirements, fasteners must be increased by 50 to 100 percent in the corner and edge areas of the roof.

Adhesive Attachment. To the top of the mechanically attached roof insulation layer, an additional layer or layers of roof insulations are normally installed. These layers are installed with adhesives—normally hot-asphalt bitumen.

There are certain requirements that should be followed by the roof installers. One requirement is the full adhesion of the insulation panel into the hot-mopping layer. This is emphasized by requiring the roof installers to fully "walk in" the panel immediately upon laying into the adhesive moppings.

Also, all end joints of the insulation panels should be offset from each other. The spacing may be a specific requirement of the insulation or roof-material manufacturer, but as a general rule the minimum distance should be 12 in.

This spacing requirement can become difficult in a dual-layered system, since not only are we concerned with the end joints of the top layer, but we are also concerned with the end joints of the bottom layer and their distance from the top-layer joints. If care is not taken, the end joints of the top and bottom layers will position one over the other. (See Fig. 3.5.)

General Requirements. No joints between insulation panels larger than ¼ in should be allowed. In the event that such are created during construction, as often happens even with competent installation crews, the gaps should be filled with roof insulation materials or flooded level with hot asphalt.

Panel pieces smaller than 24 in × 24 in should be avoided within the roof areas requiring additional attachment, which are mainly the roof edge and roof corner areas where mechanical fasteners must be increased by 50 to 100 percent. Small pieces do not have the wind-uplift resistance that larger insulation panels do. (See Fig. 2.6.)

Roof insulation, when stored outdoors at the job site, must be elevated a minimum of 4 in off ground or roof deck, normally on pallets. The material must be covered securely with a tarp, and in the event that a plastic tarp is used, air ventilation must be allowed between the tarp and roof insulation.

All insulation installed must be covered to a watertight condition before the end of the workday. In the event that any insulation becomes contaminated with moisture, it must be removed in its entirety and replaced with dry material. The concept of contamination is often a matter of debate between the designer/inspector and the roof applicator/contractor.

Sometimes excessive dust and small debris are created when cutting and fitting roof insulation panels. Excessive dust and debris can hinder attachment of subsequently applied insulation panels that use adhesive, such as hot-asphalt moppings. Require excessive dust to be swept clear of application areas after forming and fitting is complete.

Inspection. The roof applicator should verify the acceptability of the roof deck system. However, the roof applicator cannot verify the slope of the roof deck system, although this requirement often appears in specifications, either expressed or implied.

If you are relying on the roof applicator to determine if the structural roof deck system is erected to the proper slope in order to prevent ponding-water areas, you are misguided. This quality control requirement should be the responsibility of others. The roof applicator does not have the equipment or training to provide such certification.

However, before application of roof materials to the roof deck, the applicator should verify that roof surface is:

- Completely dry
- Free of loose demolition debris
- Level and smooth, being free of excessive depressions, waves, and buckles
- Secured to building structure

Beginning the roof work means that the contractor accepts the surface and condition of the roof deck.

ROOF FELTS/MEMBRANES

Mop-down Systems. Mop-down systems include roof felts and/or roof membranes which are installed with hot moppings of either asphalt or coal tar pitch. Some essential requirements to use within the specifications, which aid in quality control, are listed in Sec. 15.3.2 and should be inserted within the specification text where and as needed. Other examples to be considered on a job-specific basis are as follows.

Quality Assurance. The (*owner, architect, engineer, consultant, inspector*) reserves the right to remove coupons from the roof system, at any point or time during the construction, in order to verify that proper materials per specification are being installed, and to further verify that workmanship of application is to manufacturers' requirements, industry standards, and accepted practices.

ASTM sampling procedures shall be used and evaluation performed in accordance with NRCA recommendations.

The contractor shall repair the area from which the sample is taken, at no additional cost, and make that area(s) of the roof equivalent to the primary roof membrane.

Application Requirements. Equiviscous temperature (EVT) ranges shall be monitored and adhered to at all times during application. (Consider the Daily Report Form in Fig. 15.2.)

The flash point, finished blowing temperature (for asphalt), and EVT shall be clearly printed on each container of (*asphalt or coal tar pitch*), or shall be included on each bill of lading from the supplier.

The contractor shall provide, and have present on the roof at all times, two undamaged and accurate bitumen thermometers.

The EVT at the mop shall be a minimum of (_F°) at all times during roof felt/membrane application.

Luggers shall not be overfilled so that the bitumen cools while being held for use.

Bitumen within lugger that is within 25°F of the minimum temperature of the required EVT shall be returned to the kettle and fresh hot bitumen substituted in its place.

Transporting hot bitumen in open buckets is prohibited.

(*Asphalt/coal tar pitch*) shall be melted and handled in accordance with ARMA and/or NRCA guidelines.

NRCA safety guidelines shall be strictly adhered to at all times during the course of construction activities.

Roof felts/roof membranes shall be installed in a complete mopping of (*asphalt/coal tar pitch*), being rolled out directly behind the mop.

All felts/membranes shall be embedded into the hot mopping by use of a broom, squeegee, or follow tool, which is to be used immediately behind the roll as it is applied to the roof surface. Such brooming shall eliminate air pockets under the roof sheet.

All roof felts, sheets, and membranes shall be installed to NRCA guidelines, industry standards, and accepted practices, including:

All felts/membranes shall be installed from the lowest elevation area on the roof surface and proceed in manufacturer-required and proper lap fashion upslope to the highest elevation point on the roof surface.

After installation, no edge of felt/membrane shall be opposed to the flow of water across the roof surface.

All felts/membranes shall be laid in straight and accurate fashion, with no deviation in the straight run of felt/membrane of more than 1 in per 100-ft run.

A puddle of hot bitumen will be present in front of the roll at all times during the roll-out application of the roof felt or membrane.

Walking on the roof felt surface is prohibited, as is practical, until the mopped bitumen has cooled to ambient temperatures.

All fishmouths shall be immediately cut and felt membrane set back into the still-hot bitumen.

After application, no felt/membrane shall touch felt/membrane.

Heat-Welded/Torch-Applied Systems. This category encompasses modified bitumen membranes which use an open flame or hot air for melting and attaching the membrane to the roofing surfaces. (See Chap. 9.) The best indication of a properly installed modified bitumen membrane which uses heat for adhesion is the flow-out bead of bitumen at the lap edges of the sheet.

Normally, a flow-out of the bitumen compound is specified to be present at all locations of membrane sheet edges. However, the flow-out should not exceed 1 in in width, and should be a minimum of ¼ in. Additionally, the sheet must be heated completely across the face of the roll in order for it to be adhered properly to the roof surface. If in doubt as to the adhesion of the membrane to the roof surface, remove a 50-in-long by 12-in-wide coupon from the installed roof. The coupon should be transverse to the roll direction and include one entire membrane sheet cross section.

Adhering a modified bitumen membrane with an open flame to wooden flashing structures or roof penetrations which are deteriorated, such as is encountered in reroof design, is hazardous. Require, and make sure, that fire extinguishers are in close proximity to the roof worker and torch. Also be aware that some roof insulations are flammable.

We often find premature failure of the adhesion bond between the sheet metal flashings and torch-applied modified bitumen, such as occurs at the metal edge flashings and the modified bitumen flashing ply. This is best avoided by requiring a roof felt, such as a fiberglass felt, to be installed in hot-asphalt mopping to the metal edge flashing before proceeding with the torch-applied modified bitumen flashing.

However, heat-welded modified bitumen membranes are often specified to eliminate the need for hot-asphalt built-up equipment and crews. As such, requiring hot-process asphalt work may be prohibitive, either from a cost or work-access perspective.

In all cases, require primer to be applied to any sheet metal flashing being sealed by roofing materials; however, for heat-welded modified bitumens, it is essential for a complete, heavy, and continuous coat of asphalt primer to be applied to the flashing. Require primer to be applied in a coating sufficient to completely cover all appearance of the metal flashing through the dried primer. Reprime as required.

Additionally, prohibit the open flame from contacting or being directed at the metal flashing as the modified bitumen flashing sheet is being installed. This normally requires the roof applicator to heat only the top portion of the modified bitumen roll.

As a final procedure, require all of the installed flashing sheet to be immediately "rolled" as it is being applied to the metal flashing. Rounded, weighted rollers are supplied for such applications.

Modified bitumen manufacturers have various requirements for flashing applications. Consult with the manufacturer and review the specification manual carefully.

General Requirements. These requirements are to be expanded upon or deleted as required for each application process and project, and are to be placed within the specification text where required for the format used.

Storage of roof felts and membranes should be on pallets a minimum of 4 in above the ground or roof deck. The rolls should be covered with a tarp, and if plastic material is used, air ventilation should be provided between the tarp and the rolls. Any material that becomes wet should be permanently removed from the work site.

Require the contractor to become familiar with the load limits of the roof structure and prevent overloading of the roof deck structure. Overloading is a concern during material loading onto the roof and debris removal from the roof.

The specifications should prohibit "phase application." This requires all of the roof felts/membranes to be installed the same workday; however, it usually does not require the application of the surfacing material, such as gravel or coatings. Sometimes, it is acceptable and advantageous to have the cap-sheet surface installed after the roof-felt plies are complete. Consult with the material manufacturer on phase-application requirements and restrictions.

In the event that water infiltrates into or between any roof-felt or membrane plies, that area of the roof should be removed in its entirety. If organic felts are being used in a coal tar pitch system, they must be sealed by a thin glaze coating of hot bitumen at the end of each workday. Allow no roofing to be installed to wet, damp, dusty, or dirty surfaces.

Consider any roof flashings or structures which require priming before felt/membrane application. Consider base flashing details and any movements which will occur between the roof membrane system and the flashing structure or penetration. Completely specify procedures to be used at such locations.

Large or significant flashing structures, such as parapet walls, expansion joints, and roof drains, should be separately addressed within the specifications. Describe, step by step, the application procedures required or, perhaps equally as important, the procedures that are prohibited.

SHEET METAL FLASHINGS

Quality Control. For example, only technicians skilled, trained, and experienced in the fabrication and erection of roofing sheet metal components shall install items specified in this section.

All work shall conform to requirements of SMACNA *Architectural Sheet Metal Manual,* NRCA *Roofing and Waterproofing Manual,* industry standards, and accepted practices.

All components to be soldered shall first be pretinned.

Field-forming and soldering shall be held to a minimum with shop-fabrication and soldering preferred and required where possible.

All components to be soldered shall be tightly attached to one another, with pop rivets of the same material as the item being soldered.

Solder shall be slowly and completely sweated between each joint in accordance with accepted practices.

Acid/flux shall be washed completely from the solder joint immediately upon completion.

All joints and cuts in corner and termination pieces are to be soldered permanently watertight.

Dissimilar materials are not to be attached to one another.

All exposed edges are to be hemmed back from view a minimum of ½ in.

Fabricate and install all items with lines, angles, and rises sharp, true, and consistent.

Fabricate all items in 10-ft lengths where possible.

Inspection. Require the contractor to:

- Verify that all surfaces which are to receive metal flashing components are plumb, true, clean, even, smooth, dry, and free of defects and projections which might affect the application.
- Verify that all building components onto or into which metal is to be attached are solid and secured permanently to the building structure and are free of defects.

Installation. The drawings should show examples of fastening patterns, including cleats and the length of nails or screws. Specification further describes the fastening requirements, for example, "Attach gravel guard with 8d galvanized ring shank nails in two rows, 6 in on center per row, with one row ½ in from rear edge of flashing flange and other row 2½ in from rear edge of flashing flange."

Describe material and application rates for all roof cement and caulking required, for example, "All metal flashings shall be set into a complete bed of plastic roof cement, ⅛ in thick, extending past all exposed edges of subsequently installed sheet metal a minimum of 1 in."

The installation procedures to be used at the laps and end joints of the metal flashings should be described. If cover and backer plates are used at the joints, describe their location in regard to the flashing component, as well as how they are to be attached and how they are to be sealed.

Index

About the Author

James Stephen "Steve" Hardy is a roofing consultant and contractor with more than 20 years of experience in the roofing industry. He has written numerous articles on roof design and specification for such noted publications as *Architecture, Progressive Architecture, Architectural Record,* and *The Construction Specifier.* Mr. Hardy also lectures and holds seminars on roofing for professional and licensing groups, such as the U.S. Department of Energy and the American Institute of Architects.